TABLE OF CONTENTS

INTRODUCTION

Welcome to sociology and welcome to this book. Sociology is about you and the society you live in. As such it is important and exciting. And it can also be fun. This book is full of entertaining and amusing cartoons illustrating key points. It is also full of interesting photographs and case studies reflecting issues of the day – online grooming, the growing use of foodbanks, the spike in hate crime following the EU referendum, and how and why young people are being recruited to ISIS.

The book has been specially written for AQA sociology and contains a chapter on how to do well in the exam. But there's a lot more to sociology than passing exams. If we've done our job properly, sociology will open your eyes to all sorts of new ideas. It will help you to see the world and yourself from a variety of different perspectives. It will encourage you to question everything you're told and to criticise politicians of every political party. We hope you'll enjoy the book and do well in the exam.

How to use this book

The book contains a number of features to help you to understand and enjoy sociology and to develop your skills for examination success. They include the following.

Key terms and summary boxes

Each chapter is divided into parts and units. Each unit ends with a key terms box which defines the key terms used in the unit, and a summary box which recaps the main points covered in the unit. The summary boxes provide short and straightforward outlines. They are ideal for revision.

Key terms

Structural theories Theories that see the structure of society as directing behaviour.

Social action theories Theories that see the meanings people construct as directing their action.

Function The contribution made by the parts of society to the maintenance of society as a whole.

Functional prerequisites The requirements that must be met if society is to operate effectively.

Socialisation The passing on of society's norms and values.

Summary

1. Functionalism sees society as a system in which the parts – the structure – direct the behaviour of its members.

2. The function of the parts is the contribution that they make to the maintenance of the social system.

3. Society has functional prerequisites which must be met in order for the system to operate effectively.

Cartoons, photographs and activities

The book contains many specially drawn cartoons. Cartoons are fun. They are also important. They provide entertaining and memorable snapshots of key ideas. They can add clarity and understanding at a glance.

There are lots of carefully selected photographs in the book. Photographs bring the real world into sociology. They show the relevance of sociology to today's society.

Each cartoon and photograph is accompanied by an activity – one or more questions which ask you to think about and comment on the picture with reference to the preceding text. These activities give you the opportunity to apply what you've just learned.

Contemporary issues

Contemporary issues are another type of activity. They ask you to apply sociological ideas to issues of the day. This shows the relevance of sociology to you and the society you live in. For example, do we live in a fair and just society? Is there equality of opportunity? Does everybody have an equal chance to succeed in the education system? These are fundamental questions which we hope will stay with you long after your A-level exams.

Contemporary issues: The Trussell Trust

A Trussell Trust foodbank.

The Trussell Trust is the largest foodbank provider in the UK. In the year ending 31 March 2017, it provided nearly 2 million three-day emergency food supplies to 'people in crisis' with nearly 444 000 going to children,

numbers that have grown rapidly since 2010 (Trussell Trust, 25.04.2017). A study commissioned by the Trussell Trust looked at over 400 households using its foodbanks. Lone parents with children made up the largest number of users. All users faced extreme financial insecurity. Over 78 per cent of households were 'severely food insecure, meaning that they had skipped meals, gone without eating, or even gone days without eating in the past 12 months. For a majority of households, this was a chronic experience, happening every month or almost every month over the past 12 months' (Loopstra and Lalor, 2017).

Question

What does the information in this activity suggest about the social policy priorities of the Conservatives and the influence of sociology on their policy?

Then and now

This is a feature which revisits ground-breaking sociological studies from the last fifty years. Usually written by the original authors, Then and now features assess the significance of these classic studies to today's society. They also give you an insight into how sociologists think and carry out their research.

Then and now: Chas Critcher, *Policing the Crisis: Mugging, the State, and Law and Order* (1978)

"*Policing the Crisis* is a sprawling, multi-faceted book. While we are here concerned with its relevance to the sociology of crime and deviance, it has elsewhere been examined for its contribution to other sociologies: of the media, of Black culture, of policing and even of modern conservative politics. 'Mugging', a term unknown in Britain before being imported from the USA in the early 1970s, was never legally defined. However, it implied the gratuitous use of violence during street robberies. As the book title implies, the argument was designed to explain how the advent of this apparently new type of crime resonated throughout the main institutions of society. We claimed to identify what kind of a crisis this was, as well as how and why 'mugging' came to

symbolise what had been going wrong with British society in the early to mid-1970s.

That period is now over 40 years ago. Much has happened in the meantime to many aspects of British society, which were the focus of the book. The media, crime, policing, race relations, political issues – all these have changed, perhaps beyond recognition. This was before the digital media revolution: no internet, much less social media, no mobile phones, not even satellite TV. Immigration as an issue had a different resonance. Migrants had arrived from the West Indies, India and Pakistan and a few from Africa, but migrants from Europe, East or West, were few and far between. Consequently, 'immigrant' usually referred to somebody who was not White. By

Exam practice

Each chapter ends with exam-practice questions for AS and A-level. In the final chapter, these questions are explored in detail with examiner guidance and sample answers at Grade A and Grade C.

ACKNOWLEDGEMENTS

With many thanks to the following sociologists for contributing a 'Then and now' feature:
- Professor Simon Winlow, Northumbria University
- Professor Chas Critcher, Swansea University; Sheffield Hallam University

Special thanks also to Matt Timson for the excellent cartoons.

With many thanks to the following sociology teachers for reviewing chapters of the book:
Wilhelmenia Etoga Ngono, Brighton, Hove and Sussex Sixth Form College, Brighton; Emily Painter, Cadbury Sixth Form College, Birmingham; Matthew Wilkin, Bellerby's College, Brighton; Zoe Parkinson, Preston College, Preston; Amy Scott, Newcastle Sixth Form College, Newcastle; Heather Green, Batley Girls' High School, Batley; Judith Copeland, Derby College, Derby; Sumita Gupta, The Barclay School, Stevenage; Chris Deakin, Banbury Academy, Banbury; Paul Sullivan, British School of Brussels, Belgium; Charlotte Belmore, Saint Benedict Catholic Voluntary Academy, Derby.

1 THEORY AND METHODS

Chapter contents

This chapter begins with an examination of some of the main sociological theories, from the early theories of Karl Marx, Émile Durkheim and Max Weber to the more recent theories of Ulrich Beck, Manuel Castells, Zygmunt Bauman and Anthony Elliott. The chapter looks at their views of society and explanations of human behaviour. It shows why the early theories stood the test of time and how they developed. It looks at more recent theories and their relevance to today's society.

The chapter then looks at methodology – the study of research methods. Book 1 examined particular research methods, from participant observation to questionnaire surveys, and assessed their strengths and weaknesses. This chapter takes a broader view. It looks at the ideas and assumptions on which sociological methods are based. It asks to what extent research findings are influenced by the methods used. It raises the question of objectivity. Can the findings of sociological research be objective – free from the values, political views, ethnicity, social class, gender and culture of the researcher?

The chapter closes with an examination of the relationship between sociology and social policy. It looks at the influence of sociology on government policy. It asks whether sociologists should be consulted by government. It also asks whether politicians should study sociology before setting out to change society.

PART 1 STRUCTURAL THEORIES

Contents

A theory is a set of ideas that claim to explain something. Sociology has been defined as the study of people in groups. A sociological theory is therefore an explanation of how people behave in groups and why.

Sociological theories can be divided into two types – **structural theories** and **social action theories**. This is a rough and ready division but can help to identify some of the distinguishing features of different theories. Structural theories tend to see society as a system made up of various parts – the social structure – which shape the behaviour of members of society. Social action theory focuses on people constructing meanings that are seen to direct their actions.

Unit 1.1.1 Functionalism

Functionalism, also known as structural functionalism, sees the structure of society as directing the behaviour of its members. This structure consists of institutions such as the family, religion and the judicial and political systems.

Society is seen as a system, as a set of interconnected parts which form a whole. The parts have a **function**, that is the contribution they make to maintain the whole. Society is seen to have basic needs or **functional prerequisites** that must be met in order to maintain the system. For example, social order is often seen as a functional prerequisite. It can be met by shared norms and values. This means that members of society agree on how they should behave and what is right and wrong. As a result, they are not pulling in different directions, conflict is avoided, and order is maintained.

When functionalists examine a part of society, they ask: What is its function? For example, the main function of the family is seen as **socialisation** – the passing on of society's norms and values to the next generation. This contributes to the maintenance of order in the social system.

Functionalists sometimes compare society to an organism in which the various parts, such as the heart and lungs, work together for the benefit of the organism as a whole. Similarly, many functionalists argue that in a well-balanced society, the various parts, for example families, schools and religion, work together for the benefit of society as a whole.

Émile Durkheim

The French sociologist Émile Durkheim (1858–1917) is sometimes seen as the first functionalist. Durkheim

(1938) assumes that society has certain basic requirements which must be met in order to function effectively. The most important of these is **social order**. Durkheim starts with the question of how a collection of individuals can be brought together to form an ordered society. He sees the answer as establishing 'the essential similarities which collective life demands'. These similarities include shared moral beliefs which provide the basis for a **collective conscience** – a shared morality. This binds members of society together and creates **social solidarity** or social unity which, in turn, provides social order.

According to Durkheim, sociology is the study of **social facts**. Social facts are shared aspects of society such as religious beliefs and moral obligations. They are external to individuals in that they are 'general throughout a given society' and they shape and constrain the behaviour of members of society. In Durkheim's words, social facts are 'ways of acting, thinking and feeling, external to individuals and endowed with the power of coercion by reason of which they control him'. Social facts are also part of an individual's consciousness – they form part of their personal beliefs. Durkheim argues that this is essential for society to operate effectively. In his words, 'society has to be present in the individual'.

Durkheim states that sociologists need to explain both the causes and continuance of social facts. He gives the example of Christianity. Its origin and causes lie in the specific circumstances of a group of Jews under Roman rule over 2000 years ago. Its continued existence can be explained by the contribution it makes to the maintenance of society. Social facts such as religion continue to exist because they serve 'some social end', in other words because of the social functions they perform.

Durkheim's theory may be illustrated by his analysis of the functions of religion. He sees religion as expressing and reinforcing the shared morality

Activity

How might families, schools and religion work together for the benefit of society?

which forms the collective conscience. For example, the Christian commandment 'thou shalt not kill' reinforces the value placed on human life. Religion can strengthen social obligations by representing them in sacred terms, which transforms them into religious duties. For example, marriage becomes a religious duty when it receives a Christian blessing. Religion can bind a society together because those who share religious beliefs 'feel themselves united to each other by the simple fact that they have a common faith'. The highly charged atmosphere of religious rituals serves to dramatise this unity and in doing so promotes social solidarity. In the above ways, religion functions to meet the essential requirements of social life.

Talcott Parsons

During the 1940s and 1950s, Talcott Parsons (1902–1979) was the dominant figure in American sociology.

Like Durkheim, Parsons (1951) begins with the question of how social order is possible. His answer is **value consensus** – an agreement about values. If members of society are committed to the same values, they will tend to share a common identity which provides a basis for unity and cooperation. Also, from shared values develop common goals, which provide direction for behaviour.

For Parsons, the main task of sociology is to analyse 'patterns of value orientation in the social system' and

how they become an integral part of society. Value consensus leads to a state of **social equilibrium** in which the various parts of society are in balance. There are two main ways in which social equilibrium is maintained. The first is by socialisation – the transmission of society's values. This is the primary function of the family and to a lesser extent of the education system. The second is by the various mechanisms of social control from the police through to the approval and disapproval of family and friends. Socialisation and social control are essential for social equilibrium and therefore for the maintenance of order in society.

Parsons sees society as a system. He argues that every social system has four basic functional prerequisites – **adaptation**, **goal attainment**, **integration** and **pattern maintenance**.

Adaptation refers to the relationship between the system and its environment. In order to survive, social systems must have some degree of control over their environment. At a minimum, food and shelter must be provided to meet the physical needs of their members. The economy is the institution primarily concerned with this function.

Goal attainment refers to the need for all societies to set goals towards which social activity is directed. Procedures for establishing goals and deciding on priorities between goals are institutionalised in the

3

form of political systems. Governments not only set goals but allocate resources to achieve them.

Integration refers to the 'adjustment of conflict'. The law is the main institution which meets this need. Legal norms define and standardise relations between individuals and between institutions and so reduce the potential for conflict. When conflict does arise it is settled by the judicial system and does not therefore lead to the disintegration of the social system.

Pattern maintenance refers to 'the maintenance of the basic pattern of values, institutionalised in the society'. Institutions that perform this function include the family, the educational system and religion. In Parson's view, 'the values of society are rooted in religion'. Religious beliefs provide the ultimate justification for the values of the social system.

Parsons maintains that any social system can be analysed in terms of the functional prerequisites he identifies. Thus, all parts of society can be understood with reference to functions they perform in meeting the functional prerequisites of adaptation, goal attainment, integration and pattern maintenance.

Social change

Functionalism has often been criticised for failing to provide an adequate explanation for social change. If the system is in equilibrium, with its various parts contributing towards order and stability, it is difficult to see how it changes. Parsons approaches this problem in the following way. In practice no social system is in a perfect state of equilibrium, although a certain degree of equilibrium is essential for the survival of societies. The process of social change can therefore be seen as a 'moving equilibrium'.

Because the various parts of society are connected, a change in one part will result in changes in other parts. For example, a change in the adaptation system will result in a disturbance in the social system as a whole. The other parts of the system will operate to return society to a state of equilibrium. This will lead to some degree of change, however small, in the system as a whole. Though social systems never attain complete equilibrium, they tend towards this state. Social change can therefore be seen as a 'moving equilibrium'.

Robert K. Merton

A student of Talcott Parsons, Robert K. Merton (1949) questions some of the ideas of functionalism.

Universal functionalism

Merton questions the idea that all parts of the social system are functional for the entire system – a view he calls **universal functionalism**. Merton argues that particularly in complex modern societies, this is doubtful. For example, in a society with various faiths, religion may divide rather than unite, as in the case of Protestants and Catholics in Northern Ireland and Sunnis and Shias in Iraq.

Merton argues that a part of society may be **functional** – beneficial to society, or **dysfunctional** – harmful to society, or **non-functional** – it may have no effect on the rest of society.

Indispensability

This idea states that certain institutions or social arrangements are **indispensable** to society – that society cannot operate without them. Functionalists have often seen religion in this light. For example, Davis and Moore (1967) claim that religion 'plays a unique and indispensable part in human society'. Merton questions this assumption, arguing that a functional prerequisite may be met by a range of alternative institutions. To replace the idea of indispensability, Merton suggests the concept of 'functional alternatives' or 'functional equivalents'. From this point of view, a political ideology such as communism can provide a functional alternative to religion – it can meet the same functional prerequisites as religion.

Merton argues that the assumptions of universal functionalism and indispensability should not be taken for granted. They are matters for investigation and should not be assumed. Merton states that the parts of society should be analysed in terms of their 'effects' on or 'consequences' for society as a whole and for individuals and groups within society. This will indicate whether the effects are functional, dysfunctional or non-functional.

Manifest and latent functions

Merton (1949) introduced the idea of manifest and latent functions. **Manifest functions** are the positive functions 'intended and recognised by participants in the system'. **Latent functions** are neither 'intended nor recognised'. For example, the manifest function of sending a person to prison is to punish them for their crime. The latent function is to affirm and reinforce norms of appropriate behaviour. This example indicates how a part of society can function in various ways and link parts of society – in this case, the judicial system and the system of behavioural norms.

Activity

A Hopi rain dance.

The Hopi are a Native American tribe who live in Arizona. Traditionally they were farmers growing corn, beans and squash. They held a rain dance each year to bring rain to water their crops. Merton uses the rain dance to illustrate his idea of latent and manifest functions.

Suggest a manifest and a latent function of the rain dance.

Evaluation of functionalism

Robert K. Merton has answered some of the criticisms of functionalism. However, a number of criticisms remain.

Teleology It has been argued that the type of explanation used by some functionalists is **teleological**. A teleological explanation explains a cause in terms of its effects. For example, to argue that the cause of Christianity is the beneficial effect it has on society is to explain its cause in terms of its effect. This is a teleological argument. As Durkheim states, the cause of Christianity lies in its origins. The objection to teleological reasoning is that it treats an effect as a cause. However, an effect cannot explain a cause because causes must always come before effects.

Continued existence Functionalism is on stronger logical ground when it argues that the continued existence of an institution may be explained in terms of its effects. Thus once an institution has originated, it continues to exist if it has, on balance, beneficial effects on the system. However, there are problems with this type of explanation. It is extremely difficult to establish whether or not the net effect of any institution is beneficial to society. A knowledge of all an institution's effects would be required in order to identify and to weigh the balance of functions, dysfunctions and non-functions.

Questioning value consensus Functionalists such as Parsons who see the solution to the problem of social order in terms of value consensus have been strongly criticised. First, their critics argue that consensus is assumed rather than shown to definitely exist. Second, the stability of society may owe more to the absence rather than the presence of value consensus. For example, a lack of commitment to the value of achievement by those at the bottom of stratification systems may serve to stabilise society. If all members of society were strongly committed to the value of achievement, then the failure of those at the base of the stratification system to achieve well-paid, high status jobs could result in despair and a sense of unfairness which may well produce discord and disorder and destabilise society.

Determinism Functionalism has been criticised for what many see as its **deterministic** view of human behaviour. Its critics have argued that functionalism pictures human behaviour as determined by the system. In particular, the social system has needs, and the behaviour of its members is shaped to meet those needs. Rather than creating the social world in which they live, people are seen as a creation of the system, as directed by forces which are external to them. By means of socialisation, they are programmed in terms of the norms and values of the social system. They are kept on the straight and narrow by mechanisms of social control which exist to fulfil the requirements of the system. Their actions are structured in terms of social roles that are designed to meet the functional prerequisites of society. Members of society are pictured as automatons – programmed, directed and controlled by the system.

Conflict and coercion Critics of functionalism have argued that it tends to ignore conflict and coercion. For example, Alvin Gouldner (1971) states, 'While stressing the importance of the ends and values that men pursue, Parsons never asks *whose* ends and values they are. Are they pursuing their own ends or those imposed upon them by others?' Few functionalists give serious consideration to the possibility that some groups in society, acting in terms of their own particular interests, dominate and exploit others. From this point of view, social order is imposed by the powerful and value consensus is merely a justification and legitimation of the position of the dominant group. As the following unit on Marxism argues, conflict and coercion are not simply minor strains in the system contained by value consensus. Instead, they are a central and integral part of the system itself.

Key terms

Structural theories Theories that see the structure of society as directing behaviour.

Social action theories Theories that see the meanings people construct as directing their action.

Function The contribution made by the parts of society to the maintenance of society as a whole.

Functional prerequisites The requirements that must be met if society is to operate effectively.

Socialisation The passing on of society's norms and values.

Social order A society that runs smoothly without disruption and conflict.

Collective conscience The shared morality of members of society.

Social solidarity Social unity.

Social facts The institutions, norms and values of society that are external to individuals and that shape their behaviour.

Value consensus An agreement about the values of society.

Social equilibrium The parts of society in balance.

Adaptation The need for society to set goals for its members.

Goal attainment Shared goals in society that direct behaviour.

Integration The need for order and stability in society.

Pattern maintenance The need for value consensus.

Universal functionalism The view that all parts of the social system make positive contributions to society as a whole.

Dysfunctional Parts of society that are harmful to society as a whole.

Non-functional Parts of society that have no effect on the rest of society.

Indispensability Institutions or social arrangements that are seen as essential for the operation of society.

Manifest functions Functions that are intended and recognised as such by members of society.

Latent functions Functions that are not intended and recognised by members of society.

Teleology Explaining the cause of something by its effects.

Determinism The idea that all actions, decisions and events are determined by previously existing causes. In particular, the idea that behaviour is shaped by causes that are external to human beings, who are like puppets with society pulling the strings.

Summary

1. Functionalism sees society as a system in which the parts – the structure – direct the behaviour of its members.

2. The function of the parts is the contribution that they make to the maintenance of the social system.

3. Society has functional prerequisites which must be met in order for the system to operate effectively.

4. For Durkheim, the most important prerequisite is social order. This is met by establishing 'essential similarities' that provide the basis for a 'collective conscience' and 'social solidarity'.

5. Talcott Parsons argues that social equilibrium is necessary for society. It is provided by value consensus, which is established by socialisation and social control.

6. Parsons identifies four functional prerequisites – adaption, goal attainment, integration and pattern maintenance.

7. Parsons sees social change as a response to disturbances in the system in order to restore it to equilibrium.

8. Robert Merton questions the view that all parts of the social system perform positive functions. He argues that some parts may be either dysfunctional or non-functional.

9. Merton distinguishes between manifest and latent functions.

10. Criticisms of functionalism include:

    » Its explanations are teleological.

    » It is extremely difficult to establish whether the net effect of any institution is beneficial to society.

    » The stability of society may owe more to the absence rather than the presence of value consensus.

    » It gives a deterministic view of human behaviour.

    » It tends to ignore conflict and coercion in society.

Unit 1.1.2 Marxism

Functionalism is sometimes called a **consensus theory** because of its view that value consensus is essential for the wellbeing of society. Value consensus is seen to benefit all members of society. As a result, they share a common interest in maintaining this consensus.

Like functionalism, Marxism is a structural theory. It sees society as divided into two main parts – a ruling class and a subject class. Unlike functionalism, Marxism sees a basic conflict of interest in society. From a Marxist view, the ruling class exploit and oppress the subject class. For this reason, Marxism is sometimes called a **conflict theory**.

Marxism takes its name from its founder, the German-born philosopher, economist and sociologist Karl Marx (1818–1883). Marx saw human society as beginning when people joined together to produce their food and shelter; in his words, 'The first historical act is the production of material life.' The production of material life is a social enterprise – people work together to produce goods and services. The way they produce them shapes the society they live in. In Marx's words, their society 'coincides with their production, with *what* they produce and *how* they produce it'.

Marx believed that at the dawn of human history people lived in a state of 'primitive communism'. Food and shelter were communally owned – owned by all members of society. Each member of society produced both for themselves and for society as a whole. As a result, there were no conflicts of interest. Everybody worked for everybody else.

Things changed with the emergence of private property, in particular with the private ownership of the **forces of production** – the materials and technology used in the production of goods and services. For example, in feudal society, the main force of production was land – for growing crops and feeding domesticated animals. In industrial society, the main forces of production are factories and raw materials for producing goods. When the forces of production are owned by a minority, for example the lords in feudal society and the factory owners in industrial society – conflicts of interest arise. Through its ownership of the forces of production, a minority are able to control, exploit and enjoy the fruits of the labour of the majority.

Ruling and subject classes

When members of society produce goods and services, they enter into social relationships that Marx called the **relations of production**. In primitive communism, everybody had the same relations of production – they all worked together to produce goods and services that they all shared. However, with the private ownership of the forces of production, this equality in the relations of production ended. The relations of production now consisted of two main classes – a **ruling class** and a **subject class**. The ruling class owned the forces of production. This ownership gave them the power to oppress and exploit the subject class, to use them for their own gain.

According to Marx, in industrial society the forces of production – the factories and raw materials – are owned by a rich and powerful capitalist ruling class – the bourgeoisie. The workers – the subject class or proletariat – produce the goods but their wages are only a small part of the value of those goods. Most of the value is taken away in the form of profits by the capitalists. Marx saw this as exploitation. (Capitalism is an economic system in which businesses are privately owned – by capitalists – and run, using wage labour, for the purpose of profit.)

Infrastructure and superstructure

Taken together, the relations of production and the forces of production form the economic base, the **infrastructure**, of society. Marx believed that the infrastructure largely shapes the rest of society, the **superstructure**. This means that the economic relationships between the ruling and subject class will be reflected in the superstructure. For example, the state will support the ruling class, passing laws to legalise the private ownership of industry and the right of owners to take any profits which might be made. Other parts of the superstructure will also reinforce the position of the ruling class. The education system will produce the kind of workers that capitalism requires. Religion, which Marx called the opium of the people, will produce false happiness and delusions of pleasure. In doing so, it will ease the pain of exploitation and this will keep the subject class in their place.

Activity

A view of capitalist society.

In what ways does this picture illustrate Marx's view of class in capitalist society?

Activity

The following verse is taken from the Victorian hymn 'All Things Bright and Beautiful'. 'Estate' means position in society.

> *The rich man in his castle,*
>
> *The poor man at his gate,*
>
> *God made them high and lowly,*
>
> *And ordered their estate.*

How can this verse be seen as a justification of the class system?

According to Marx, members of both social classes are largely unaware of the true nature of their situation, of the reality of the relationship between ruling and subject classes. Members of the ruling class assume that their particular interests are those of society as a whole. Members of the subject class tend to accept this view of reality and regard their situation as part of the natural order of things. Marx referred to this false and distorted set of beliefs as **ruling class ideology**. It reinforces, legitimises and justifies the social order. It disguises the true nature of class society and conceals the exploitation on which it is based. In Marx's words, it produces a **false class consciousness**.

Alienation

Marx saw work as the most important human activity. He argued that in class societies people are alienated or cut off from their work. As a result, they are alienated from the things they produce, from themselves and from others. **Alienation** will only end when the forces of production are communally owned. Alienation reaches its height in capitalist society where labour is dominated by the requirements of capital, the most important of which is the demand for profit. These requirements determine levels of employment and wages, the nature and quantity of goods produced and their method of manufacture. Workers see themselves as prisoners of market forces over which they have no control. They are subject to the laws of supply and demand. They are at the mercy of the periodic booms and slumps which characterise capitalist economies. As a result, workers lose control over the goods and services they produce and become alienated from both their products and the act of production. Their work becomes a means to an end, a means of obtaining money to buy the goods and services necessary for their existence. In the process, workers become alienated from themselves. The more they produce, the more they lose themselves. In Marx's words, 'the greater this product, the less he is himself'.

Activity

Alienation.

In what ways does this picture illustrate Marx's view of alienation?

From capitalism to communism

Given the priority Marx gives to economic factors, an end to alienation, oppression and exploitation involves a total change in the economic infrastructure. In particular, it requires the abolition of private property and its replacement by communal ownership of the forces of production, that is, the replacement of capitalism by communism. Marx saw communism as 'the positive abolition of private property and thus of human self-alienation… as the complete and conscious return of man himself as a social, that is human being'. As a member of communist society, each person contributes to the wellbeing of all and so expresses both their individual and social being. The goods and services produced are owned and controlled both by the individual and by all members of society.

For Marx, 'The history of all hitherto existing society is the history of the class struggle.' He saw the intensity of class conflict steadily increasing as capitalism developed, with a growing **polarisation** – an increasing gap – between the two main classes as intermediate groups sink down into the proletariat – the subject class. Capital is concentrated more and more into fewer hands, a process accompanied by the growing poverty of the proletariat. Production is increasingly social and cooperative as larger and larger groups of workers are concentrated in factories. At the same time, the wealth produced by their labour is taken from them

by fewer and fewer individuals as greater competition drives all but the largest companies out of business. Such processes magnify and illuminate the conflicts of interest between the ruling and subject classes. It is only a matter of time, he believed, before members of the proletariat recognise the reality of their situation. This awareness will lead to 'a revolt to which it is forced by the contradiction between humanity and its situation, which is an open, clear and absolute negation of its humanity'.

Evaluation of Marxism

Judging from the constant reinterpretations, impassioned defences and vehement criticisms of Marx's work, his ideas are as alive and relevant today as they ever were. This section looks at some positive and negative assessments of his ideas.

Class in capitalist society Critics argue that the growing intensity of class conflict which Marx predicted in capitalist society has not occurred. Instead, class conflict has been institutionalised. It has become a standard part of society with political parties representing various classes in a democratic system.

Rather than polarisation of classes, a steadily growing middle class has emerged between the so-called bourgeoisie and the proletariat. Class divisions are becoming less clear-cut and, as a result, less apparent.

Communist society Turning to communist society, critics have argued that history has not borne out the promise of communism contained in Marx's writings. Significant social inequalities were present in communist regimes, and there were few, if any, signs of a movement towards equality. The collapse of communism in Eastern Europe and the Soviet Union in the late 1980s and early 1990s suggests that the promise of communism has been replaced by the desire for Western-style democracies.

Social change Particular criticism has been directed to the priority that Marx gave to economic factors, to changes in the forces and relations of production, in his explanation of social change. Max Weber's (1958) study of ascetic Protestantism in the 16th and 17th centuries argued that religious beliefs provided the rationale, attitudes, ethics and direction for the development of capitalism. (Ascetic means severe self-discipline and abstaining from pleasure and fun.) Weber believed that ascetic Protestantism developed before capitalism. He argued that at certain times and places, aspects of the superstructure, in this case religious beliefs, can play a primary role in directing change (see pp. 14–16).

Economic determinism Critics have accused Marx of **economic determinism** – of arguing that economic factors determine and shape human behaviour and the structure of society. It is possible to select passages from Marx's 40 years of writing that appear to support this criticism. At certain times, Marx has claimed that:

» The superstructure is 'determined' by the infrastructure.

» Economic forces beyond human control shape human consciousness.

» History is directed by economic forces which follow 'iron laws'.

» Conflicts of interest between the ruling and subject classes will inevitably lead to revolution, to the downfall of capitalism and the establishment of communism.

However, as the next section indicates, the above criticisms may well go too far.

In defence of Marx

Although Marx gave priority to economic factors, he did not see them as the only cause of social change. He did describe the economic infrastructure as the 'ultimately determinant element in history'. Yet he added:

> *If somebody twists this into saying that the economic element is the only determining one, he transforms that proposition into a meaningless, abstract and senseless phrase. The economic situation is the basis, but the various elements of the superstructure... also exert their influence upon the course of the historical struggle and in many cases preponderate in determining their form.*   Marx and Engels, 1950

Marx consistently argued that 'man makes his own history'. Human behaviour is not simply determined by forces beyond human control. In Marx's words, 'History is nothing but the activity of men in pursuit of their ends.' Because people make society, only people can change society.

Globalisation and multinational corporations The US economist John Cassidy (1997) claimed that Marx would reappear as 'The next big thinker'. Writing with Engels in 1848, Marx predicted that capitalism would spread throughout the world as capitalists sought to find new markets to maintain profitability. Cassidy believes that Marx correctly identified the dynamic behind the present process of globalisation. He also praises Marx for recognising that even in the highly productive world of advanced capitalism, some workers would still be extremely poor. This is certainly true, particularly in less developed countries where capitalists often employ workers on extremely low wages.

Cassidy also agrees with Marx's view that as capitalism developed, more and more wealth and power would be concentrated in the hands of capitalists. The growth of giant multinational corporations with a bigger turnover than the gross domestic product of many nation-states provides support for Marx's view.

Capitalism, crises and growing inequality Marx saw capitalism as an unstable system moving from crisis to crisis in its drive to accumulate more and more capital and ever greater profits. The British Marxist geographer/sociologist David Harvey (2010) sees the recurring financial crises, for example the crises of the early 1970s and 2007/08, as providing support for Marx's view.

Marx predicted that in capitalist society income and wealth would be increasingly concentrated in fewer and fewer hands. Again, Harvey finds support for Marx's view. He notes that, 'In the United States, for example, household incomes since the 1970s have generally stagnated in the midst of an immense accumulation of wealth by capitalist class interests' (Harvey, 2010).

For Harvey, Marx remains relevant and offers possible solutions to today's inequalities of capitalist society. Like Marx, David Harvey believes 'We need revolutionary politics to replace capitalism with a fair and just society.'

Activity — Occupy Wall Street

In 2011, over 20 000 people occupied Wall Street, the financial district of New York, protesting against what they saw as corporate greed and corruption, and social inequality.

The Occupy Movement stated that 'The one thing we have in common is that we are the 99% that will no longer tolerate the greed and corruption of the 1%.' (Gautney, 2011). Estimates indicate that the top 1 per cent own around 40 per cent of the nation's wealth and receive about 25 per cent of the income. The protest was partly about the financial crisis of 2007/08, the effects of which were still being felt by millions of people.

The posters carried by the protesters on Wall Street give some idea of their concerns. Typical statements read:

- NEED NOT GREED
- TAX THE FILTHY RICH
- OVERTHROW CAPITALISM
- WE ARE THE 99%

- GET $ $ OUT OF POLITICS
- IT'S A CLASS WAR
- PEOPLE BEFORE PROFITS
- WALL STREET WHERE CRIME PAYS

Question

How might a Marxist explain the Occupy Wall Street Movement?

Neo-Marxism

Neo-Marxism or 'new Marxism' refers to followers of Karl Marx who have taken his theories in new directions. This section looks at two neo-Marxists, the Italian, Antonio Gramsci (1891–1937) and the Frenchman, Louis Althusser (1918–1990).

Antonio Gramsci

Gramsci's (1971) main development of Marxist theory is his concept of **hegemony** – the means by which the ruling class maintains its dominance and control over the subject class. Hegemony has certain similarities to Marx's view of ruling class ideology and false class consciousness. It consists of political and moral beliefs and values which justify and maintain ruling class power. Hegemony broadcasts the idea that the interests of the ruling class are those of society as a whole. It provides ways of seeing and thinking which tend to be taken for granted, which appear normal and reasonable, but which distort reality and present a false consciousness.

However, where Marx sees ruling class ideology as ultimately shaped by economic infrastructure, Gramsci claims that hegemony is not simply a by-product of the economy, nor is it just a reflection of the forces and relations of production. As such, hegemony has a degree of autonomy – to some extent it is independent of other aspects of society. According to Gramsci, the beliefs that form hegemony can prevent a proletarian revolution. But it follows that a different set of beliefs can reveal a true picture of society and promote a true consciousness – and this can lead to a proletarian revolution.

Gramsci argues that ruling class hegemony never completely blinds the proletariat to the reality of their situation; it never completely indoctrinates them. As a result, members of the subject class have a **dual consciousness**, seeing two views of the world side by side. On the one side they see the world in terms of ruling class hegemony; on the other side they have glimpses of the true picture of society. To some extent their daily experience of poor working conditions, low wages, poverty and powerlessness leads them to see through ruling class hegemony and opens their eyes to the truth of their situation.

Where Marx sees economic crises as leading to revolution and the downfall of capitalism, Gramsci argues that this can result from a rejection of ruling class hegemony and its replacement by a set of beliefs which provide a true picture of society. This can happen, in Gramsci's words, by 'intellectuals of a new type which arise directly from the masses, but remain in contact with them' and who present a set of beliefs in direct opposition to ruling class hegemony. These views must become fashionable, they must dominate the media and spread throughout popular culture in order to lead to a proletarian revolution.

Traditional Marxists have criticised Gramsci's separation of hegemony from the economy arguing, like Marx, that changes in society are ultimately based on economic changes. However, Gramsci's ideas have had an important influence on the development of Marxist theory.

Louis Althusser

According to Louis Althusser (1972), capitalist society is divided into three levels – the economic, the political and the ideological. Although each level affects the other levels, the economy is 'determinant in the last instance'. However, the political and ideological levels are not simply reflections of the economy, as they have 'relative autonomy' – a degree of independence. The importance of each level varies in different historical periods. For example, in the feudal era the landlords had to make sure that the serfs, who farmed the lords' land, handed over the surplus they produced. To do this, they relied on the church (God states that disobedience is a sin) and the state (the threat of military intervention). Under feudalism, the ideological and political levels were particularly important.

Althusser identifies two main systems of control in class societies – the **Repressive State Apparatus (RSA)** and the **Ideological State Apparatus (ISA)**. The RSA consists of the government, the army, the police, the courts and the prisons. Control is ultimately based on violence. The ISA includes the educational system, religion, the family, political parties, trade unions and the mass media.

How does the ISA operate? In Althusser's phrase, it says 'Hey, you there' to individuals, hails them, seizes their attention and shapes their identities. People's day-to-day involvement with ISAs, such as their family, religion, school and the media, tells them who they are, where they belong and gives them an identity. In the process, this puts them in their place, makes them subservient and enforces their 'submission to the ruling ideology'.

Althusser sees religion as the main ISA in pre-capitalist societies. In capitalist society, it has been largely replaced by education, which teaches workers to accept and submit to their oppression and disguises their exploitation.

Althusser argues that no class can hold power for any length of time simply by the use of force. Ideological control provides a far more effective means of maintaining class rule. If members of the subject class accept their position as normal, natural and inevitable, and fail to realise the true nature of their situation, they will be unlikely to challenge ruling class dominance. Physical force is an inefficient means of control compared to winning over hearts and minds.

Althusser's views on the influence of the ISA on identities raises interesting questions. However, as Anthony Elliott (2009) states, 'what is lost by Althusser is an understanding of the complex, contradictory ways in which people inculcate [learn to accept, are ingrained with] dominant forms of ideology… as well as how people come to dis-identify with, and in turn contest, existing societal arrangements'.

Althusser pictures society as a structure with people behaving in terms of their position in the structure. According to Elliott, people are presented as 'cultural dopes', who are 'serenely subjugated through ideology and just passively adapt to processes of socialisation'. There is no indication of any opposition to the ruling class and 'no sense of the politics of ideological struggle'.

Key terms

Consensus theory A theory that sees consensus – agreement – about values as essential for the welfare of society.

Conflict theory Sociological theory, suggested by Marx, which views society as consisting of groups with conflicting interests vying for dominance. This can be contrasted with consensus theories such as functionalism, which see societies as essentially harmonious.

Forces of production The materials and technology used in the production of goods and services.

Relations of production The relationships people enter into in order to produce goods and services.

Ruling class The class who own the forces of production.

Subject class The class who are subject to the rule of the ruling class and who are oppressed and exploited by them.

Infrastructure The economic base of society made up of the forces and relations of production.

Superstructure The rest of society that is largely shaped by the infrastructure.

Ruling class ideology A set of beliefs that present a false picture of society and justify the position of the ruling class.

False class consciousness A false picture of the class system that conceals the exploitation on which it is based.

Alienation The cutting off of people from their work, the things they produce, from others and from their true selves.

Polarisation The growing gap between the two classes in terms of income and wealth as intermediate groups sink down into the subject class.

Economic determinism The idea that economic factors determine and shape human behaviour and the structure of society.

Hegemony The means by which the ruling class maintain their dominance and control over the subject class.

Dual consciousness The idea that the subject class have two views of society, one based on ruling class hegemony, the other a true picture.

Repressive State Apparatus (RSA) Social institutions, such as the government, police and army, that control the population by the use or threat of force.

Ideological State Apparatus (ISA) Mechanisms that transmit ruling class ideology, which enforces the submission of the subject class. They include the educational system, religion and the family.

Summary

1. According to Marx all societies, with the possible exception of the societies of pre-history, have a ruling class and a subject class.

2. The ruling class exploits and oppresses the subject class.

3. Their power comes from the ownership of the forces of production.

4. The subject class are largely unaware of their exploitation as this is disguised by ruling class ideology.

5. The class system and the exploitation it brings will only end when the forces of production are communally owned.

6. Marx predicted that as capitalism developed, class conflict would intensify, class polarisation would occur and a revolution would result in the end of class division and an equal society. Critics argue that there is no sign of this happening.

7. Marx has also been criticised for what some see as economic determinism. Marx rejected this criticism.

8. Marx's supporters argue that there is some evidence, for example, the growth of multinationals, to support his view of the development of capitalism.

9. Gramsci argues that to some extent hegemony is independent from the economy and its rejection by the subject class could lead to revolution.

10. Althusser argues that there are two main systems of control in class societies – the Repressive State Apparatus and the Ideological State Apparatus.

PART 2 SOCIAL ACTION THEORIES

Contents

This part looks at a number of theories which can be grouped under the heading of social action theories. Although they differ in many respects, they have one thing in common – they focus on meanings that they see as directing human action. It follows that one of the main jobs of a sociologist is to identify and interpret these meanings. As a result, social action theories are sometimes called interpretivist theories.

Some social action theories, for example symbolic interactionism, are largely based on the meanings that operate in small-scale interaction situations. Others take a much broader sweep. For example, Max Weber's social action theory looks at the meanings that he claims precede and direct the rise of capitalism.

Unit 1.2.1 Social action theory – Max Weber (1864–1920)

Max Weber (1964) defined sociology as 'a science which attempts the interpretive understanding of social action to arrive at a causal explanation of its course and effects'. To Weber, an action is social if it takes account of the actions of others. The job of the sociologist is to interpret the meanings that direct social action – the meanings people give to their own actions and to the actions of others. Weber was particularly concerned with motives – the intentions and purposes used to achieve goals.

The Protestant ethic

Weber's approach is illustrated by his most famous work, *The Protestant Ethic and the Spirit of Capitalism* (1958, first published in 1904). Weber was interested in the meaning and motives – the 'spirit of capitalism' – which, he believed, led to the rise of capitalism. On the basis of a wide range of historical documents, he claimed that these meanings developed from early forms of Protestantism in the 16th century, which he called 'ascetic Protestantism' – ascetic means abstaining from worldly pleasures and entertainment.

According to Weber, the 'Protestant ethic' saw work as a religious calling. Success in business showed that a person had not lost favour in the sight of God. Ascetic Protestantism banned luxuries and frivolous entertainment. As a result, the early capitalist had little else to do with their profits other than re-invest them in their businesses. All these factors focused the mind and activity on building businesses, expanding businesses, making profits and reinvesting those profits.

Weber argues that from ascetic Protestantism came the Protestant work ethic, which led to the 'spirit of capitalism', which in turn provided the meanings and motives that led to the development of capitalism. (See pp. 226–228 for a more detailed examination of *The Protestant Ethic and the Spirit of Capitalism*.)

Activity – The Protestant ethic

'The Godly and diligent man shall have prosperity in all his ways, but he that followeth pleasures and voluptuousness shall have much sorrow before he die … Avoid overmuch familiarity amongst men, for it makes thee spend much loss of time.'

(John Browne, a 16th-century Protestant merchant, quoted in Kitch, 1967)

'Religion must necessarily produce both industry and frugality. We must exhort all Christians to gain what they can and to save all they can; that is, in effect, to grow rich.'

(John Wesley, 1703–1791, the founder of Methodism, quoted in Weber, 1958)

Question

Use the above quotations to 1) support Weber's argument about the rise of capitalism, and 2) to illustrate his social action approach.

Types of social action

Weber identified various types of **social action** that are distinguished by the meanings and motives on which they are based. These include 'affective' or 'emotional action', 'traditional action' and 'rational action'.

Affective or emotional action stems from an individual's emotional state at a particular time. A loss of temper that results in verbal abuse or physical violence is an example of affective action.

Traditional action is based on established custom. Individuals act in a certain way because of habit, because things have always been done that way. They have no real awareness of why they do something; their actions are simply second nature.

Rational action involves a clear awareness of a goal. It is the action of a business manager who wishes to increase productivity – the goal is clearly defined. Rational action also involves a systematic assessment of the various means of attaining a goal and the selection of the most appropriate means to do so.

Weber believed that rational action had become the dominant mode of action in modern industrial society. He saw it expressed in a wide variety of areas: in state administration, business, education, science, and even in Western classical music.

Bureaucracy and rational action

Weber saw bureaucracy as the prime example of rational action. A bureaucratic organisation has clearly defined goals. It involves precise calculation of the means to attain those goals. In Weber's words, it is 'designed to coordinate the work of many individuals in the pursuit of large-scale administrative tasks and organisational goals'. Bureaucracies combine the work of specialists based in several different departments – for example, in a large business organisation, marketing, finance, design, legal, personnel, administration, health and safety, and research and development departments. Compared to other types of organisations, Weber claimed that bureaucracies performed with greater efficiency, speed and precision, and with lower costs.

Weber saw bureaucratic organisations as the dominant institutions of industrial society. Marxists see fundamental differences between communist and capitalist societies. To Weber, these differences are minimal compared to the similarities in the bureaucratic organisations that these societies share. He saw bureaucracies as the institutionalisation of rational action and the defining characteristic of modern industrial society.

'Iron cages' and 'irrational societies'

Despite recognising that bureaucracies are capable of 'attaining the highest degree of efficiency', Weber had serious concerns about what he saw as their downside. Bureaucracies have strict rules, specialised tasks and highly organised routines. Weber was afraid that rational action in a bureaucratic structure would imprison workers in an 'iron cage' and reduce them to 'cogs in a bureaucratic machine'. Rules, regulations and standardised procedures may prevent spontaneity, initiative and creativity. Workers may become trapped in their specialised routines – 'specialists without spirit', experts without vitality.

Weber saw the danger of bureaucrats becoming preoccupied with uniformity and order, of losing sight of all else and becoming dependent on the security provided by their highly structured niche in the bureaucratic machine. He believed that it is as if 'we were deliberately to become men who need "order" and nothing but order, become nervous and cowardly if for one moment this order wavers, and helpless if they are torn away from their total incorporation in it'. To Weber, the process of rationalisation, of which bureaucracy is the prime expression, is basically irrational. It is ultimately aimless because it tends to destroy the traditional values which give meaning and purpose to life. To Weber, the 'great question' is 'what can we oppose to this machinery in order to keep a portion of mankind free from this parcelling-out of the soul, from this supreme mastery of the bureaucratic way of life'.

Despite his forebodings, Weber believed that bureaucracy was essential to the operation of industrial society. In particular, he believed that the state and large business enterprises could not function effectively without bureaucratic control.

Disenchantment and rationalisation

As noted above, Weber believed that **rationalisation** has its costs. Rational action and rational thinking replace faith. Religion no longer provides a foundation for world views. The world is 'demystified', its richness, mystery and magic are disappearing. It is no longer the 'great enchanted garden' of traditional society. The result is **disenchantment**, although a more literal translation of Weber would be 'driving out the magic from things'.

Weber was fearful that the growing replacement of emotion with reason would drive the warmth and feeling out of social relationships – the very things which give meaning and depth to human existence. Social life would become increasingly impersonal and cold. People would become disillusioned and cynical.

Weber saw material prosperity as a major goal in a rational world. This prosperity has become an end in itself, stripped of its 'religious and ethical meaning'. Shops are steadily replacing churches and other places of worship. In Weber's view, 'material goods have gained an increasing and finally inexorable power over the lives of people as at no previous period in history'.

Evaluation of Weber

Along with Marx and Durkheim, Weber is regarded as one of the three founding fathers of sociology. His social action theory, with its emphasis on 'the interpretive understanding of social action' and the importance it gives to the meanings and motives directing behaviour, has been particularly influential. His focus on meanings gave direction to the various interpretivist theories. His view that the meanings embedded in ascetic Protestantism led to the rise of capitalism provided a real alternative to Marxist theory with the priority it gave to economic factors.

Weber's view of the process of rationalisation has influenced a number of theories and research projects. For instance, George Ritzer's *The McDonaldisation of Society* uses the example of McDonald's fast-food restaurants to argue that rationalisation has become increasingly global and extended into more and more areas of society (Ritzer, 1996, 2012).

There have been a number of criticisms of Weber's view. They include the following:

1. Weber has been criticised for failing to provide an overall theory of how society works, of failing to recognise social systems and social structures. However, Weber regards structural views of society as deterministic, for example he sees Marxism as economic determinism.

2. Weber is seen to place too much emphasis on individuals rather than on social groups. In Weber's words, social action starts with and must be studied in terms of 'the particular acts of individual persons'. Many sociologists argue that human

Contemporary issues: The McDonaldisation of society

McDonald's in Tokyo, Japan.

McDonald's has over 36 000 restaurants in more than 115 countries (Investopedia, 2017). George Ritzer identifies four basic aspects of McDonald's restaurants that he sees as reflecting the process of rationalisation (Ritzer, 1996, 2012):

Efficiency Fixed rules, regulation and procedures designed to produce efficient organisations.

Calculability Goals and products are quantified – for example, speed in a 'fast-food' restaurant, weight for standardised burgers.

Predictability Products, settings, employee and customer behaviour are totally predictable – the same products and the same service.

Control by means of technology The technology used to make uniform products. For example, the French fry machines always produce exactly the same French fries.

Like Weber, Ritzer sees a downside to rational action. Rationality and the fixed procedures it produces can lead to irrationality – long queues of people at the counters, long queues of cars at the drive-through windows. Fixed procedures are inflexible and, as such, unlikely to deal effectively with sudden increases in demand. Like Weber, Ritzer believes that the 'iron cage of rationality' can crush initiative and dehumanise workers, who are bound by strict rules and regulations.

Questions

1. Name some other organisations based on rational action that are found in many countries.

2. What support does Ritzer's study of McDonald's provide for Weber's view of the positive and negative aspects of rationalisation?

behaviour is largely shaped by social groups rather than individual acts. In his defence, Weber does recognise the importance of social groups. This can be seen from his theory of social stratification where he identifies class, status and power groups.

3. Weber did not see an alternative to bureaucracy, which he saw as 'completely indispensible'. However, some sociologists have argued that organisations are becoming increasingly flexible and far less rigid than the 'iron cages' that Weber described (Clegg, 1992).

4. Weber stated that, 'we are trapped in an increasingly meaningless and disenchanted world'. Unlike Marx, who looked forward to a communist utopia, Weber offered no hope of escaping from the negative society he pictured. Weber has been criticised for not offering an alternative to this 'disenchanted world'. However, as George Ritzer (2012) states, 'It is shortsighted to criticise someone who points out your cage, if in fact you are in one'.

Key terms

Social action To Weber, action that takes account of the actions of others.

Affective or emotional action Action directed by emotion, often regardless of the consequences.

Traditional action Action directed by custom.

Rational action Action directed by reason with a clearly defined goal and a selection of the most appropriate means to do so.

Rationalisation The process by which actions are increasingly governed by trying to use the most efficient means to achieve given goals and not by, for example, tradition or emotion.

Disenchantment To Weber, the removal of religion, 'magic', warmth and humanity in an increasingly rational society.

Summary

1. Weber argued that in order to understand and explain social action, it is necessary to discover the meanings that people give to their own actions and to those of others.

2. Weber saw ascetic Protestantism and the Protestant work ethic as producing the 'spirit of capitalism' and directing the rise of capitalism.

3. Weber identified various types of action. They included affective or emotional action, traditional action and rational action.

4. Weber saw bureaucracy as the main example of rational action in industrial society.

5. He was concerned about the negative aspects of bureaucracy, which he saw as 'iron cages' stifling initiative, creativity and spontaneity.

6. Despite this, he saw no alternative to bureaucratic organisations.

7. Weber saw rational thought and action as leading to disenchantment.

8. Weber's focus on meaning provided a real alternative to structural theories.

9. Criticisms of Weber's social action theory include:
   » what some see as his failure to recognise social structure
   » his emphasis on individuals as opposed to social groups
   » his failure to see an alternative to bureaucracy and to the disenchanted society he pictures.

Unit 1.2.2 Symbolic interactionism

Symbolic interactionism is a theory that focuses on the meanings people use to direct their actions. It usually examines small-scale interaction situations rather than the wider society. It looks at the meanings that people use to interpret, define and make sense of the social world.

Symbolic interactionists ask questions such as: How do you see yourself? How do others see you? How do these views of yourself affect your actions? How do you interpret the actions of others?

George Herbert Mead (1863–1931)

The American philosopher George Herbert Mead is one of the founders of symbolic interactionism.

In Mead's view, human thought and action are essentially social. They are based on the fact that human beings interact in terms of **symbols**. A symbol stands for and gives meaning to an object or event and indicates how to act towards it. For example, the symbol 'chair' gives meaning to a particular object and indicates the action of sitting.

Social life can only proceed if the meanings of symbols are largely shared by members of society. Symbolic interaction is only possible if those involved are able to interpret the meanings and intentions of others. This is accomplished by a process that Mead calls **role-taking**, which involves placing yourself in the position of others. For example, if you see a person smiling, crying, waving a hand or shaking a fist, you will put yourself in their situation in order to interpret their meaning and intention. On the basis of this interpretation, you will respond — you may return their smile, indicate sympathy for their crying and so on. In this respect, social interaction can be seen as a process of interpretation with each taking the role of the other.

Activity

Interpreting actions.

You are a spectator. Take the role of the man with the red headband.

1. How do you do this?

2. In what ways might you interpret his action?

3. If you were a player on the opposing team, how might you respond in terms of these interpretations?

The self

Mead argued that through the process of role-taking, a person develops a concept of **self**. By placing themselves in the position of others, they are able to look back on themselves. Mead (1967) claimed that

the idea of self can only develop if an individual can 'get outside himself (experimentally) in such a way as to become an object to himself'. To do this, a person must observe themselves from the standpoint of others. For example, a child can develop a sense of self by playing roles that are not their own — for instance, playing a mother or a father. In doing so, the child becomes aware that there is a difference between themselves and the role they are playing. This is one way that the idea of self is developed — by taking the role of a make-believe other.

Mead saw the development of a sense of self as an essential part of the process of becoming human. It provides the basis for thought and action. Without an awareness of self, an individual cannot direct their own actions or respond to the actions of others. By acquiring a concept of self, a person can take the role of self. In this way thought is possible because, in Mead's view, the process of thinking is simply an 'inner conversation' — a conversation with yourself.

Herbert Blumer (1900–1987)

Blumer (1962), a student of Mead, developed the views of his teacher. He argued that symbolic interactionism is based on three key ideas.

1. Individuals act on the basis of meanings and interpretations rather than simply reacting to external stimuli such as social structures.

2. Meanings arise from the process of interaction rather than simply being present at the outset and shaping future action. To some degree, meanings are created, modified, developed and changed within interaction situations rather than being fixed and pre-formed. In the process of interaction, people do not slavishly follow pre-set norms or mechanically act out established roles.

3. Meanings are the result of interpretive procedures employed by individuals within interaction contexts. By taking the role of the other, they interpret the meanings and intentions of others. By means of 'the mechanism of self-interaction', individuals modify or change their definition of the situation, rehearse alternative courses of action and consider their possible consequences. Thus, the meanings that guide action arise in the context of interaction via a series of complex interpretive procedures.

Blumer is particularly critical of functionalism, which he argues pictures action as a response to the requirements of the social system, as shaped by the demands of norms and values, which are constrained by the structure of society. Despite this criticism, Blumer accepts that to some degree action is structured and standardised. He states that, 'In most situations in which people act towards one another they have in advance a firm understanding of how to act and how other people will act.' However, such knowledge offers only general guidelines for conduct. It does not provide a precise and detailed recipe for action that is mechanically followed in every situation. Within these guidelines, there is considerable room for manoeuvre, negotiation, adjustment and interpretation.

Erving Goffman (1922–1982)

In *The Presentation of Self in Everyday Life* (1959) the Canadian sociologist Erving Goffman compared social interaction with a performance in a play. As social actors, we give performances to different audiences on a variety of stages using appropriate props; we play parts, adopt fronts and create believable impressions. Goffman's approach is known as a **dramaturgical analogy**, as a correspondence to and comparison with a theatrical performance.

Impression management

Impression management is a key idea developed by Goffman. It refers to attempts by individuals to give a particular impression of themselves to others in order to receive a desired response. This can be done in a variety of ways:

- Clothing – for example, uniforms – can help to provide an appropriate believable performance as it often indicates the part a person is playing, as a nurse, police office, soldier and so on.

- Titles – Mr, Mrs, Ms, Sir, Dame, Duke, Duchess – all convey an impression of a person's expected role.

- Body language – for example, facial expressions such as a smile, a stare or a frown – can be selected to give a particular impression.

- Hiding negatives – drug addiction, time spent in prison or academic failure can be hidden so as not to negate a positive impression and an otherwise successful performance.

Activity

Impression management.

Identify aspects of the picture that might confuse the patient.

The importance of self

Something of the importance of impression management for a person's self-concept can be seen from Goffman's (1968) study of **total institutions** – places such as prisons and some mental hospitals where people are confined, usually under strict supervision, for 24 hours a day. Isolated from the wider society, a person may lose their picture of self as a parent, friend and workmate. Their impression of self, formerly embedded in their name, appearance, clothes and personal possessions may be lost by a name change or number, a shaven head, an inmate's uniform and a lack of personal possessions. Their sense of self might also be weakened or lost by the strict rules and regulations applied by those in authority. In total institutions, the threat to a person's identity means that self-direction and breaking rules, such as stealing food from the kitchen and conning those in authority, can assume great importance to the inmate. According to Goffman, such actions say that 'he is still his own man, with some control of his environment', that to some extent he can still manage his own impression of self.

Labelling theory

Labelling theory is one of the most influential ideas developed by symbolic interactionists. The most famous statement of labelling was made by the American sociologist Howard S. Becker (1963) in his study of **deviance** – action defined as abnormal and/or criminal. In Becker's words, 'the deviant is one to whom that label has successfully been applied; deviant behaviour is behaviour that people so label'. This means that a deviant is a person labelled as such and deviant behaviour is behaviour labelled as such. In each case, the label has been 'successfully applied'.

A **label** defines an individual as a particular kind of person. Others tend to see and respond to them in terms of the label and assume that the person has the characteristics associated with the label.

A person's self-concept, their picture of self – comes in part from their perception of the way others see them. This is known as their **looking-glass self**. A person's looking-glass self can lead to a **self-fulfilling prophecy** – a prediction that comes to pass. A person may then act in terms of the way that others define them. Becker outlines the following possibility:

A person is released from prison and publicly labelled as a criminal. As a result, employers may refuse to give them a job. The ex-convict may then return to crime for their livelihood. They may find support from others in a similar situation and join an organised criminal group. In this social context, the person might see themselves as a professional criminal and act accordingly. Becker argues that this process is by no means inevitable. Ex-convicts do 'go straight' and re-enter conventional society. But, once labelled, there is pressure to act in terms of the label.

However, there are instances of just the opposite happening – people acting in direct opposition to the way the label defines them. The actions of Black female students in two London comprehensives provide an example. Being labelled as unlikely to succeed spurred the young women on to academic success. They achieved higher exam results than Black boys and White boys and girls in the two schools (Mirza, 1992).

Evaluation of symbolic interactionism

Symbolic interactionism usually focuses on small-scale interaction situations. This has been seen as a strength, because of the insights it provides, and a weakness, because it tends to ignore the wider society. Concepts such as self, role-taking, impression management, labelling and the self-fulfilling prophecy have provided valuable insights into social interaction. The focus on small-scale groups, meanings and interpretations offers a real alternative to society-wide explanations of human action. Compared to what some see as the determinism of structural approaches, the creative freedom pictured by symbolic interaction is seen as a more realistic view of human action.

Symbolic interactionists have often been accused of examining human interaction in a vacuum. They have tended to focus on small-scale, face-to-face interaction with little concern for its historical or overall social setting. They have concentrated on particular situations and encounters with little reference to the historical events that led up to them or the wider social framework in which they occur. Because these factors influence the particular interaction situation, the scant attention they have received has been regarded as a serious omission.

Interactionists have also been criticised for failing to explain the origin of the meanings that direct action. Critics argue that such meanings are not spontaneously created in interaction situations. Instead, they are systematically generated by the social structure – for example, by inequalities in class, ethnicity and gender. Thus, Marxists have argued that the meanings that operate in face-to-face interactions are often the product of class relationships. From this viewpoint, interactionists have failed to explain one of the most significant things about meanings – their origin.

Key terms

Symbol Something that stands for and gives meaning to an object or event.

Role-taking Placing yourself in the position of others.

Self A person's individuality and essence as seen by themselves and others.

Dramaturgical analogy A comparison of human actions with a theatrical performance.

Impression management The process by which people try to influence the impressions others form of them by regulating or controlling information in social interaction.

Total institutions Places where people are confined, usually under strict supervision, for 24 hours a day.

Deviance Actions that are seen to depart from standard and accepted ways of behaving.

Label A definition of an individual as a particular kind of person.

Looking-glass self A picture of self provided by others.

Self-fulfilling prophecy A prediction of an individual's action which comes to pass.

Summary

1. Symbolic interactionism focuses on the meanings that people use to direct their action in interaction situations.

2. Social interaction can be seen as a process of interpretation with people taking the roles of others.

3. Through role-taking, individuals develop a concept of self.

4. A concept of self is seen as the basis for thought and action.

5. There are various ways for projecting a positive impression of self. They include clothing, titles, body language and hiding negative aspects of self.

6. Labels can result in a self-fulfilling prophecy, though this is by no means always the case.

7. Symbolic interactionism has been praised for providing valuable insights into social interaction.

8. It has been criticised for what some see as its failure to take account of the historical and society-wide context of social interaction and for failing to explain the origin of meanings.

Unit 1.2.3 Phenomenology and ethnomethodology

This unit looks at theories that see meanings as the only social reality. As human beings, we construct meanings to make sense of the social world. There is no reality apart from or beyond these meanings.

Phenomenology

Phenomenology is a part of a European philosophical tradition that looks at the way human beings make sense of their experience of the world. It was applied to the social world by the Austrian sociologist Alfred Schutz (1899–1959).

Alfred Schutz started from the assumption that we are all unique individuals with different experiences and different memories. However, this does not mean that we each create our own particular reality. Instead, we see the world in terms of a *social* reality, a view that we share with other members of our society.

Our **lifeworld** – the world we live in on a daily basis – is a world of meaning. It exists only through our consciousness. It is based on **typifications** – concepts and ideas used to construct a shared social reality. Typifications include objects such as tables and chairs, activities such as posting a letter and having a drink, and ideas such as justice and democracy. Typifications build up into a stock of what Schutz calls **common-sense knowledge**. Common-sense knowledge makes communication possible. It creates an illusion of shared experience, of a sense of order in society and an impression of shared understanding.

Schutz argues that things and events have no meaning in themselves. Meaning is a social construction based on common-sense knowledge. In our everyday lives we take this knowledge for granted, and we see the picture of life it produces as normal and natural. We need this knowledge as we have experienced very little of what we know about. Schutz gives the following example of common-sense knowledge. We take it for granted that our action of addressing an envelope, sticking a stamp on it and placing it in a post box will lead to someone else – a postal worker – recognising it as a letter and delivering it to the addressee within a reasonable period of time.

According to phenomenologists, the job of the sociologist is to study how a meaningful social world is constructed, how illusions of a stable, ordered society become a social reality, how events and things known only through our consciousness are seen to have an existence of their own in a real and objective world, and how unique individuals have a common sense of supposedly shared experiences in everyday life.

Ethnomethodology

Ethnomethodology was influenced by Alfred Schutz's phenomenological approach. The term was coined by its founder, the American sociologist Harold Garfinkel, whose *Studies in Ethnomethodology* was published in 1967. Roughly translated, ethnomethodology means the study of the methods used by people – the methods they use to construct and give meaning to the social world.

Following Schutz, ethnomethodologists start with the view that in reality social order does not exist. It only appears to exist because people believe it exists. Social order, therefore, becomes a convenient fiction, an appearance of order constructed by members of society. This appearance allows the social world to be described and explained and so made knowable, reasonable, understandable and accountable to its members. The methods used by members for creating a sense of order form the subject matter of ethnomethodological enquiry. Zimmerman and Wieder (1971) state that the ethnomethodologist is 'concerned with how members of society go about the task of *seeing, describing,* and *explaining* order in the world in which they live'.

The documentary method

Harold Garfinkel (1967) argued that members of society employ the '**documentary method**' to make sense of and account for the social world, and to give it an appearance of order. This method consists of selecting certain aspects of the infinite number of features contained in any situation or context, defining them in a particular way, and seeing them as evidence of an underlying pattern. The process is then reversed and particular instances of the underlying pattern are used as evidence for the existence of the pattern.

Garfinkel claimed to have demonstrated the documentary method by an experiment conducted in a university department of psychiatry. Students were invited to take part in what was described as a new form of psychotherapy. They were asked to summarise a personal problem on which they required advice and then ask a counsellor a series of questions. The counsellor sat in an adjoining room. The student and the counsellor could not see each other and communicated via an intercom. The counsellor was limited to responses of either 'yes' or 'no'. Unknown to the student, the 'counsellor' was an actor and the answers received were evenly divided between 'yes' and 'no', their sequence being predetermined by a table of random numbers. One of the experiments is illustrated in the following activity.

Students in this experiment found the 'counsellor's' answers helpful, reasonable and sensible. Garfinkel drew the following conclusions. Students made sense of the answers where no sense existed, imposing an order on the answers where no order was present. When answers appeared contradictory or surprising, the students assumed that the counsellor was

Activity

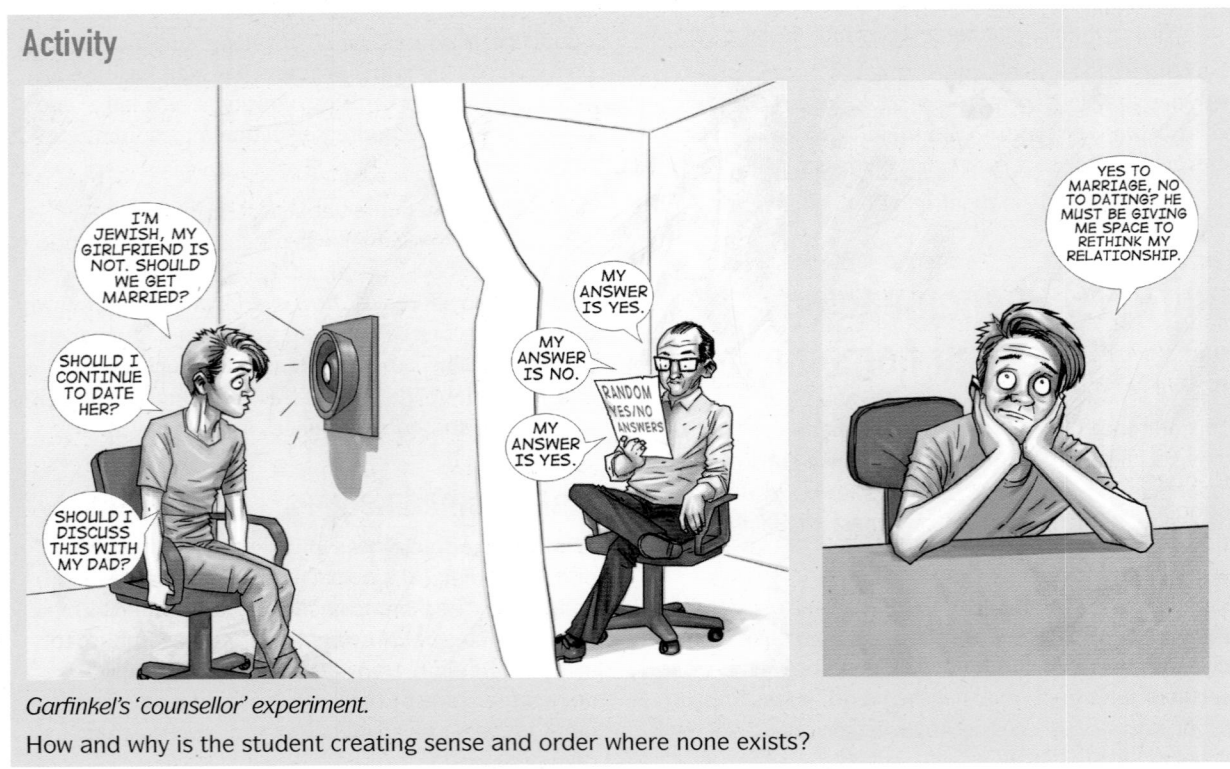

Garfinkel's 'counsellor' experiment.

How and why is the student creating sense and order where none exists?

unaware of the full facts of their case. The students constructed an appearance of order by using the documentary method. From the first answer, they perceived an underlying pattern in the counsellor's advice. The sense of each following answer was interpreted in terms of this pattern, and each answer was seen as evidence for the existence of the pattern.

Garfinkel claimed that the counselling experiment highlighted and captured the procedures that members of society are constantly using to construct the social world in their everyday lives.

Indexicality

This experiment can also be used to illustrate the idea of **indexicality**, a central concept employed by Garfinkel and other ethnomethodologists. Indexicality means that the sense of any object or activity is derived from its context − it is 'indexed' in a particular situation. As a result, any interpretation, explanation or account made by people in their everyday lives is made with reference to particular circumstances and situations.

Thus, the students' sense of the counsellor's answers was derived from the context of the interaction. From the setting − a psychiatry department − and the information they were given, the students believed that the counsellor was what he claimed to be and that he was doing his best to give honest and sound advice. His answers were interpreted within the framework of this context. Garfinkel argued that the sense of any action is achieved by reference to its context. People's sense of what is happening depends on the way they interpret the context of the activity concerned.

Disrupting the social world

Garfinkel encouraged his students to disrupt the social world in order to reveal the way that people made sense of it and reached understandings. For example, he suggested they go into supermarkets and haggle over the price of goods, or go back to their own homes and act as if they were lodgers. In such ways, they would demonstrate the fragile nature of social order. The victims of these experiments found it difficult if not impossible to index them in the situation in which they took place. Thus parents, faced with a child acting as a lodger in their own home, became perplexed or angry, and desperately tried to make sense of their child's actions by, for example, believing that the child must be ill. Garfinkel called these experiments **breaching experiments** because they breached expected ways of behaving.

Activity

Garfinkel's breaching experiment.

1. How is the student disrupting social order?

2. How is her mother attempting to restore order and manufacture sense?

The nature of social reality

Garfinkel argued that mainstream sociology has typically portrayed people as 'cultural dopes' who simply act out the standardised directives, the norms and values provided by the culture of their society. In place of the 'cultural dope', the ethnomethodologist pictures the skilled member of society who is constantly attending to the particular, indexical qualities of the situation, giving them meaning, making them knowable, communicating this knowledge to others and constructing a sense and appearance of order. From this perspective, members of society construct and accomplish their own social world rather than being shaped by it.

Ethnomethodologists argue that 'conventional' sociologists have misunderstood the nature of social reality. They have treated the social world as if it has an objective reality that is independent of people's meanings and interpretations. Thus, they have regarded aspects of the social world such as suicide and crime as facts with an existence of their own. They have then attempted to provide explanations for these 'facts'.

By contrast, ethnomethodologists argue that the social world consists of nothing more than the constructs, meanings and interpretations of its members. The job of the sociologist is, therefore, to explain the methods and procedures that people employ to construct their social world. According to ethnomethodologists, this is the very job that mainstream sociology has failed to do.

Evaluation of ethnomethodology

The positive views of ethnomethodology have been presented in the previous section. They include the identification of the procedures that people use to make sense of the social world, the lengths they go to in their attempts to create order and the strategies they employ to construct social reality. Ethnomethodologists use interesting and original methods to produce data which, for some, support their claims.

Ethnomethodology has come under a barrage of criticism from mainstream sociology. This includes the following points:

> It ignores the wider society, examining only small-scale interaction situations.

> It focuses on the trivial and insignificant rather than major issues.

> It fails to examine power differences in the wider society and to consider that some may have the power to impose their constructions of reality on others.

> Critics argue that there is an objective reality out there that can have a real and dramatic effect on people's lives. As John Goldthorpe (1973) pointedly remarked in his criticism of ethnomethodology, 'If for instance, it is bombs and napalm that are zooming down, members of society do not have to be orientated towards them in any particular way, or at all, in order to be killed by them'.

Whatever its shortcomings, however, ethnomethodology asks interesting questions and offers interesting answers.

Key terms

Phenomenology The theory that sees the social world as comprising sets of social meanings that constitute reality for the members of society. Phenomenological sociologists reject the idea that there is an objective social reality underlying or hidden behind this subjective social reality.

Lifeworld The world people live in on a daily basis.

Typifications Common-sense ideas about the nature of individuals or groups which see them as sharing particular sets of characteristics.

Common-sense knowledge The shared knowledge constructed to make sense of the social world.

Ethnomethodology The study of the methods that people use to make sense of the social world.

Documentary method The method that people use to give the social world an appearance of sense and order.

Indexicality Deriving sense of an object or activity by seeing it in terms of its context.

Breaching experiments Experiments that go outside social norms to see how people will react.

Summary

1. Phenomenology states that objects and events have no meaning in themselves. People construct meaning based on common-sense knowledge.

2. People construct illusions of a stable, ordered society, which becomes their social reality.

3. Ethnomethodology states that social order is a convenient fiction that creates a world which appears knowable, reasonable and understandable.

4. The documentary method is used to create this appearance. It gives an impression of an underlying pattern that makes sense of objects and activities.

5. Indexicality indexes an object or activity in a particular situation or context. The context is used to make sense of the object or activity.

6. Garfinkel argues that mainstream sociology presents people as 'cultural dopes' who simply act out the directives of the culture of their society. Instead, he sees people as skilled operators who are constantly constructing their social world rather than being shaped by it.

7. Ethnomethodology has been criticised for:

   > ignoring the wider society

   > focusing on the trivial

   > ignoring power differences between members of society

   > rejecting the existence of an objective reality.

Unit 1.2.4 Structure and action

The sociological theories examined so far in this chapter have been divided into two main types – structural theories and social action theories. Functionalism and Marxism are often seen as structural theories.

Weber's social action theory, symbolic interactionism, phenomenology and ethnomethodology are sometimes known as social action or interpretivist theories. This division is not clear-cut. It is more a question of emphasis. No theory completely ignores either structure or action. However, they tend to focus on one or the other.

Structural theories emphasise the structure of society and the way it influences behaviour. Social action theories focus on meanings, how they are constructed and how they direct action. Critics of structural theories sometimes see them as deterministic – as implying that the structure of society determines the behaviour of its members. Critics of some social action theories, particularly symbolic interactionism and ethnomethodology, state that these theories largely ignore the influence of the wider society on human action. However, this criticism does not necessarily apply to Weber's social action theory, which he used to study the influence of religious beliefs on the rise of capitalism. This hardly ignores the wider society.

Many sociologists argue that theories that combine structure and action would provide a fuller understanding of human behaviour. This unit looks at an attempt to do so by British sociologist Anthony Giddens. He calls his theory **structuration**.

Anthony Giddens and structuration

For Giddens (1984, 2009), structure and action are two sides of the same coin. The actions of individuals are influenced by social structure but social structure is the result of human action. Giddens (2009) summarises his structuration theory in the following quotation.

> *'Structure' and 'action' are necessarily related to one another. Societies, communities or groups only have 'structure' insofar as people behave in regular and fairly predictable ways. On the other hand, 'action' is only possible because each of us, as an individual, possesses an enormous amount of socially structured knowledge.*

Giddens uses the example of language to illustrate his view. To exist at all, language must be 'socially structured'. Language is based on grammatical rules which speakers must follow in order to communicate. However, these structural rules are not fixed for all time. New words and phrases are introduced and become standard, and old words and phrases drop out – they are forgotten or no longer fashionable. In this way, human beings act in terms of the structure,

and change the structure by their actions. In Giddens' words, 'Language is constantly in the process of structuration.'

Giddens argues that much of human action is directed by structures. Most of the time people draw on stocks of shared, common-sense knowledge with little conscious thought. By acting in terms of structures, they reproduce structures. In Giddens' words, 'structure depends on regularities of human behaviour'.

Given that structures direct action and are reproduced by action, how does change occur? First, it can result from the 'reflexive monitoring of action'. Individuals can look back and reflect on their own actions and the consequences of those actions. In view of these reflections, they may choose new courses of action. Second, change can occur from the unintended consequences of actions. Giddens gives the following example. A person goes home at night and switches on the light. This alerts a burglar who runs away, is caught by the police, goes to court and receives a prison sentence. This is an unintended consequence of switching on a light to illuminate a room.

Giddens refers to 'the duality of structure', which summarises his view that human action is influenced by structure but that structure is the result of human action. In this respect, Giddens presents a theory that combines structure and action.

Giddens' theory of structuration has received positive and negative criticism. On the positive side, it has been seen as a brave attempt to produce a theory which combines structure and action. On the negative side, Giddens has been criticised for failing to recognise the extent to which structures can prevent change. For example, Margaret Archer (1982) states that often structures constrain actions that aim to produce change and prevent people from doing what they want to do.

Key term

Structuration A theory that attempts to combine structure and action.

Summary

Anthony Giddens' structuration theory combines structure and action by arguing that the actions of individuals are influenced by the structure of society and that structure is the result of human action.

PART 3 FEMINIST THEORIES

Contents

According to Pamela Abbott, Claire Wallace and Melissa Tyler (2005), feminist sociological theory is 'concerned with enabling women (and men) to understand the subordination and exploitation of women'. Feminists brought women into mainstream sociology. They catalogued the inequalities between women and men, examined how women were oppressed by men, developed theories to explain unequal gender relationships and suggested routes to equality.

Until the 1970s, nearly all sociologists were men, and male perspectives and concerns dominated sociology. Times have changed but female sociologists remain in a minority and men are still more likely to set sociological agendas. According to Pamela Abbott *et al.*, 'feminist arguments still tend to be ignored or marginalised in many areas of sociological thought'.

This part examines some of the main theories that have been developed to explain gender inequality and women's oppression. It also examines the contribution made by feminism to sociology as a whole.

Unit 1.3.1 Feminist perspectives

There are a variety of theories that attempt to explain the subordination of women in society. This unit looks at the following: liberal feminism, Marxist feminism, radical feminism, dual system theory and intersectionality theory.

Liberal feminism

Liberal feminists argue that gender equality can be achieved by reforms within the existing institutions and structures of society. In the UK laws have discriminated against women, denied them from having the same opportunities as men and maintained them as second-class citizens. For example, laws have prevented women from voting, owning property and receiving higher education. Liberal feminists argue that one of the main ways that gender equality can be achieved is by changes in the legal system – by removing laws that prevent equal opportunity and introducing laws that aim to guarantee equal rights for women and men.

In the UK, the Equal Pay Act (1970) and the Sex Discrimination Act (1975) are examples of laws designed to provide equal treatment for women and men. However, enforcing such laws is easier said than done. For instance, the Equal Pay Act has probably reduced the gender pay gap but, over 45 years after the act was passed, women still earn significantly less than men. In 2017, the difference in average pay for male and female full-time employees was 9.1 per cent. One estimate states that at this pace the pay gap will not be eradicated until 2069, that is 99 years after the Equal Pay Act (*The Guardian*, 28.02.2018; 02.04.2017).

Liberal feminists argue that changes in culture are also needed to produce gender equality. This would involve ending traditional stereotypes of women and men, such as the view that women embody emotion and men reason (Jones, P. *et al.*, 2011). Changing stereotypes would require changes in socialisation, in role models, in children's toys and books, and in the media.

In sociology, research by liberal feminists has presented the reality of women's lives. This has been seen as essential for changing attitudes; and changing attitudes is seen as necessary in order to end gender inequality in the job market, in politics and in life chances generally.

Evaluation of liberal feminism

Liberal feminists have been praised for revealing the injustices of women's lives, for helping to change attitudes and for promoting gender equality. Sylvia Walby (2011) has argued that liberal feminists have contributed to **gender mainstreaming**, a process in which, 'Feminist projects are becoming embedded in institutions of civil society and of the state and are being placed on the mainstream agenda of government.'

Criticisms of liberal feminism include the following.

1. It has failed to identify the causes of gender inequality and, as a result, a failure to develop effective strategies for ending it.

2. The view that gender inequality can be removed within the existing social framework has been questioned. Critics argue that the changes required are too fundamental to be made within the present society. Revolution rather than reform is needed.

3. Liberal feminists have been criticised for what some see as ignoring the intimate and emotional side of women's lives – their relationships in marriage and in family life.

Marxist feminism

From a Marxist feminist perspective, women in capitalist society are exploited and oppressed. Revolutionary change, not reform, is seen as the only way to end this situation, in particular the abolition of capitalism and its replacement by a communist society.

Marxist feminists see women's subordination as essential to capitalism. Women's labour, both paid and unpaid, provides support for the entire capitalist system. First, as mothers, women provide and socialise new generations of workers at no cost to the capitalists. Second, as housewives, they provide domestic services and support for male workers, again at no cost to capitalists. Third, as partners, they give emotional support to male workers, yet again at no cost to capitalists. Fourth, women provide a reserve army of labour which can be called upon when needed by capitalist employers – for example, if there is a shortage of workers in a time of rapid economic expansion. As women's work is seen as secondary to that of men, they can be paid less and channelled into and out of low-status and part-time work as required.

According to Michelle Barrett (1988) the subordinate position of women is justified and reinforced by ideologies that present a picture of the loving mother, the caring partner and the dutiful housewife.

Evaluation of Marxist feminism

While accepting that the subordination of women can be seen as beneficial to capitalism, critics argue that this does not explain its cause. Women's subordination preceded capitalism and, if capitalism is overthrown, it may well continue. There is evidence of women's oppression in non-capitalist societies and also in former communist societies such as China and countries in Eastern Europe.

Critics argue that it is not just capitalism that benefits from female oppression but also men; and that, because of the benefits they receive, men may continue to oppress women if capitalism is overthrown.

Radical feminism

Where liberal feminists see gender inequality, radical feminists see gender oppression. Where Marxists blame capitalism, radical feminists blame men. They claim that **patriarchy** – male domination and control – shapes and colours every detail of women's lives, in the past, the present and, all indications suggest, in the future, across the globe in all cultures, and in societies from hunter-gatherers to those at the forefront of change. Patriarchy exists in the most private, personal and intimate situations to global organisations such as the World Bank, the World Trade Organization and multinational companies.

Radical feminists have suggested a number of reasons for the origins and maintenance of patriarchy. An early radical feminist, Shulamith Firestone (1974) argues that patriarchy is based on the fact that only women bear children. Women will only escape from male control when they are free from reproduction – when it is possible to conceive and nurture children outside the womb.

Some radical feminists argue that the origins and maintenance of patriarchy are ultimately based on the actual and threatened violence of men against women. Elizabeth Stanko (1985) refers to the constant threat of men's physical and sexual aggression and violence.

Women know about the unpredictability of men's physical and sexual intimidation. We plan our lives around it: finding the right street to walk down when coming home, cooking the eggs the way the husband likes them, and avoiding office parties are examples of strategies designed to avoid male sexual and physical intimidation and violence.

Radical feminists see the intimate and private world as just as important for maintaining patriarchy as the wider society. They sometimes use the phrase, 'the personal is political' to describe this view. In Mary Maynard's (1989) words:

Politics occur in families and between individuals when one person attempts to control or dominate another. It is in the personal and private sphere that women are particularly vulnerable to the power of men.

It is in men's interests to maintain patriarchy – using women to satisfy their sexual desires, give them emotional support, provide domestic services and to raise their children.

According to Sara Delamont (2003) radical feminists have a bleak and pessimistic view of the future. They see patriarchy as the oldest form of oppression and it is unlikely that men could change even if they wanted to. As a result, some radical feminists see that 'women's best chance of safety and fulfilment lies in avoiding men, and male institutions. It is better to live in all female groups, and try to minimise all contact with patriarchal institutions'. In Adrienne Rich's words, women should look to other women for 'the sharing of a rich inner life, the bonding against male tyranny, the giving and receiving of practical and political support' (quoted in Jones, P. *et al.*).

Rather than living in an all-women world, some radical feminists argue that women must value their gender, come together in trust and mutual support, present a united front, grow in confidence and confront patriarchy directly (Ritzer, 2012).

Evaluating radical feminism

Critics of radical feminism argue that it focuses on negative experiences and tends to ignore the positive side of relationships with men – there are happy marriages. They see it as presenting women as essentially good and men as essentially bad. Men are pictured as people who cannot be trusted as fathers, friends and partners (Bryson, 1999). Radical feminists have also been criticised for dividing humanity into women and men. This fails to consider differences between women in terms of factors such as culture, class, ethnicity and sexual orientation and how these differences might affect the oppression of women (Dill and Zambrana, 2009). These points will be developed in the section on intersectionality – see pp. 28–29.

Dual system theories

Dual system theories combine radical feminism and Marxist feminism in order to explain what Zillah Einstein (1979) calls **capitalist patriarchy** – the form that patriarchy takes in capitalist society. According to Heidi Hartmann (1981), 'As feminist socialists, we must organize a practice which addresses both the struggle against patriarchy and the struggle against capitalism.' The end of capitalism does not mean the end of patriarchy as 'men have more to lose than their chains'. Hartmann argues that women must actively oppose both capitalism and patriarchy. To do this, 'We must have our own organisations and our own power base.'

Intersectionality theory

Over the past 10 years, intersectionality theory has become, in the words of Bonnie Thornton Dill and Ruth Enid Zambrana (2009), 'the most celebrated theoretical innovation within women's studies'. Intersectionality states that various factors intersect – combine and work together – to produce women's experience of oppression. These factors include gender, social class, 'race', ethnicity, culture, nationality, sexual preference, physical ability and age.

Contemporary issues: Patriarchy and male violence

The Crime Survey for England and Wales estimated that for the year ending March 2016, 7.7 per cent of women (1.2 million women) experienced 'domestic abuse'. 78 per cent of the cases of domestic abuse reported to the police were violence against women (Office for National Statistics, 08.12.2016). These figures probably underestimate the extent of domestic violence.

Question

It has been claimed that in this day and age patriarchy is on the way out. Comment on this view in the light of the above evidence.

Thousands of women march through London in 2014 demanding an end to male violence against women.

Activity

Not all women are the same.

What support do these pictures provide for intersectionality theory?

This view can be seen from the personal experience and theoretical position of the American sociologist, Patricia Hill Collins (2000). She grew up in a Black, working-class family in Philadelphia. She uses her ethnicity, class and gender to understand the experience of African-American, working-class women. In terms of intersectionality theory, she argues that they suffer under a distinctive 'matrix of domination', a particular array of elements that intersect to shape their experience of oppression. For example, they are discriminated against because they are 1) Black, 2) working-class, and 3) women.

Intersectionality theory developed partly because many women could not relate to theories of female oppression which they saw as reflecting the experiences of White, middle-class, heterosexual women. Intersectionality theory states that different combinations of factors can produce different experiences of being a woman. This variation and diversity must be taken into account when developing theories to explain women's oppression.

Key terms

Gender mainstreaming Embedding feminist projects in the institutions of society and the agendas of governments.

Patriarchy Male domination and oppression of women.

Capitalist patriarchy The form that patriarchy takes in capitalist society.

Summary

1. Feminist theories aim to explain gender inequality and the oppression of women.

2. Liberal feminism focuses on gender inequality, arguing that it can be ended by reforms to the existing society.

3. Marxist feminism sees the capitalist system as the main cause of women's oppression. It can only end with the overthrow of capitalism and its replacement by communism.

4. Radical feminism states that the oppression of women is based on patriarchy which predates capitalism.

5. Dual system theory combines radical feminism and Marxism to explain women's oppression.

6. Intersectionality theory states that various factors intersect to produce women's oppression. Different combinations of factors can produce different experiences of being a woman.

Unit 1.3.2 Feminist contributions to sociology

This unit starts with a look at '**malestream sociology**', a sociology dominated by men, based on men's concerns and men's issues, a sociology that largely ignores women. At best women are in the background; at worst they are invisible.

The unit then considers the contribution that feminists have made to sociology – to the theories and content, perspectives and priorities of sociology as an academic discipline.

Malestream sociology

Sara Delamont (2003) and Pamela Abbott, Claire Wallace and Melissa Tyler (2005) list some of the main criticisms of malestream sociology made by feminist sociologists.

1. There is a tendency to see a single society made up of women and men. On this basis, generalisations are made about all members of society. However, women and men may well live in different social worlds.

2. Even when research has been based on all-male samples, generalisations are still made about all members of society.

3. Women and girls are often ignored. For example, until the 1970s, most studies of education were based on men and boys.

4. Topics and concerns focusing on women were usually overlooked and seen as unimportant. For example, when Ann Oakley's *The Sociology of Housework* was published in 1974, some of her male colleagues wondered why she had chosen to study something so insignificant.

5. When women did appear in ethnographic studies, they were often little more than part of the scenery. For example, Lyn Lofland's (1975) study of the presence of women in American urban sociology research found that they were presented as 'largely irrelevant', as 'fuzzy, shadowy background figures', as part of the scenery for male action.

6. When women were included in research, they tended to be presented in a sexist and stereotypical way. For example, early studies of female criminality sometimes suggested that there was something wrong with women who committed crime, meaning that they had psychological problems. In terms of the stereotype, women were passive and law-abiding.

7. Conventional sociological theories fail to consider the possibility that gender inequality may be a fundamental aspect, if not the most important aspect, of social inequality.

Pamela Abbott *et al.* summarise what they see as the inadequacies of malestream sociology.

> *At best there is no recognition that women's structural position and consequent experiences are not the same as men's and that sexual difference is therefore an important explanatory variable; at worst women's experiences are deliberately ignored or distorted. Furthermore, the ways in which men subordinate and dominate women are either ignored or seen as natural.*
> Abbott *et al.*, 2005

Contributions of feminist sociology

Feminist sociologists have made major contributions to sociology in terms of theory, content and research methods. As the previous unit has shown, feminists have introduced new theories and modified existing theories. They have developed theories which state that gender inequality is a basic structural feature of all societies. They have argued that gender should be a part of sociological theories of every aspect of society. In addition, intersectionality, an important new theory, was partly developed from studies of gender inequality.

In terms of topics, feminists have added gender to traditional areas of study and added a number of new areas including:

> Housework
> Domestic violence
> Caring

> Food, drink and cooking
> Emotional 'work'
> Childbirth

In terms of research methods and approaches to research, feminists have developed **feminist methodology**, which has provided a real alternative to traditional methodology. This is examined on pp. 51–52.

In terms of publications, feminists have produced a number of academic journals. These include *Feminist Theory*, *Gender & Society* and *Feminist Review*. In addition, they have written a wide range of books, many of which deal with women's issues and concerns.

In conclusion, Pip Jones, Liz Bradbury and Shaun Le Boutillier (2011) state that feminists have 'successfully challenged some of the deep-rooted assumptions of traditional social theory and made visible to sociological analysis the impact of gender in all areas of social life'.

Key terms

Malestream sociology A term involving a play on words ('mainstream') coined by feminist sociologists to draw attention to the way in which sociology had marginalised and ignored women's lives. Malestream sociology is characterised by its focus on exclusively men's issues and men's concerns.

Feminist methodology A methodology designed to reflect feminist ideals and values.

Summary

1. Malestream sociology focuses on men's issues in terms of theory, content and research methods.

2. Feminists have made major contributions to sociology. They have brought women into mainstream sociology.

PART 4 MODERNITIES AND POSTMODERNITY

This part looks at the ways that sociologists have pictured the past 250 years. The term **modernity** has been used to describe this stage in the development of society. Modernity has been the main focus of sociological research. For Marx its defining characteristic was the development of capitalism; for Weber it was rationalisation and the rise of bureaucracy.

More recently, some sociologists have argued that during the past 30 or 40 years, society in the West has entered a **postmodern** era, a period after modernity. Other sociologists have seen this time period as an extension of modernity. It has been variously referred to as late modernity, the second modernity and liquid modernity. These and further views of the development of society will now be examined.

Modernity

There have been various views of modernity. Colin Bell and Howard Newby (1983) outline some of the main aspects of this historical period that sociologists have identified. They state that modernity has involved four major transformations of society. These are:

1. Industrialism The Industrial Revolution, which started in the late 18th century, transformed Britain and, later, other societies from mainly agricultural to manufacturing economies.

2. Capitalism Closely connected with industrialism was the development of capitalism – privately owned companies run for profit in a market economy employing wage labour. New classes emerged – a class of business owners and a working class of wage labourers.

3. Urbanism A massive movement from rural to urban areas accompanied the development of industry. In Britain in 1750, before the Industrial Revolution, only two cities had populations of over 50 000 – London and Edinburgh. By 1851, 29 British cities had a population of more than 50 000, with people increasingly concentrated in the centres of capitalist industry.

4. Democracy The overthrow of the monarchy in France by the revolution of 1789 and the American War of Independence (1775–1783) indicated that people were increasingly demanding a say in the way they were governed. This led to the development of political parties and democratic systems of government.

Modernity also involves a new ethos – new perspectives, new outlooks on life. These include beliefs in the possibility of human progress; in rational planning to achieve objectives; in the superiority of reason over emotion, faith and tradition; in the ability of technology and science to solve human problems and of industry to improve living standards; in the right and capability of humans to shape their own lives.

Postmodernity

Postmodernity means 'after modernity'. Some sociologists argue that we are now living in the postmodern era, which differs in important respects from the modern era. Book 1 outlined what they see as the main aspects of postmodernity – see p. 17. This section examines the ideas of two of the main postmodern theorists, the French philosophers/sociologists Jean-François Lyotard and Jean Baudrillard.

Jean-François Lyotard (1924–1998) Lyotard (1984) states, 'I define *postmodern* as incredulity towards metanarratives'. Incredulity means disbelief. **Metanarratives** are 'grand stories' which claim to present the truth. Lyotard argues that in postmodern society people no longer believe the grand stories presented by science, religion and political ideologies.

Science is an example of a metanarrative. In the modern era, people believed that science provided answers and explanations which were based on evidence. Science was seen as the key to solving human problems, for example scientific advances in medicine. Science was seen as the key to human progress, for example the development of nuclear energy. Lyotard claims that in the postmodern era people are increasingly sceptical of the explanations provided by science and the promises it offers. As a result, they are turning to alternative medicines and they are wary of the dangers of producing nuclear energy.

According to Lyotard, in the postmodern era certainty has been replaced with uncertainty. There are now a multitude of answers, none of which can be shown to be definitively true or untrue. Knowledge is relative to time and place and to particular cultures. Truth and falsehood, right and wrong are defined in different ways by different cultures.

Lyotard welcomes the downfall of metanarratives. From his perspective, grand stories laid down the law, presenting a single version of the truth and of right and wrong. He believes that this led to intolerance and prevented many voices from being heard. Lyotard argues that postmodern society provides an opportunity to hear the voices of a wide variety of groups who were largely silenced in modern society – for example, the voices of ethnic minorities and the voices of those with a range of sexual orientations.

Jean Baudrillard (1929–2007) Baudrillard (1983) states that in postmodern society we live in a world of simulacrum. A **simulacrum** is a simulation – an image and imitation which we see as real. In postmodern society, illusions become real and simulations become authentic. Baudrillard describes our view of the world as **hyperreality**, as an inability to distinguish simulation from reality, which results in an artificial and distorted vision of the world.

According to Baudrillard, we are flooded with media images which remove 'any distinction between the real and imaginary'. We are presented with imaginary worlds that glue millions to TV screens. Our views of what actually is are rarely directly observed. They are presented on and mediated by mobile phones, social media, websites and TV. In Baudrillard's (1983) words, 'TV watches us, TV alienates us, TV manipulates us, TV informs us'. TV dissolves and decomposes into our lives and our lives dissolve and decompose into TV. In this age of 'simulacra and simulation', reality is presented in

Contemporary issues: Hyperreality

Gondola rides at the Venetian Resort Hotel, Las Vegas.

Las Vegas is famed for its themed hotels. The picture shows gondola rides at the Venetian Resort Hotel. The Paris Las Vegas has a half-size replica of the Eiffel Tower; the Luxor Hotel is built in the shape of a pyramid with copies of ancient Egyptian statues in its grounds; and the New York-New York Hotel has a replica of the Statue of Liberty and part of the skyline of New York City. An American tourist at the Venetian Resort Hotel was overheard saying, 'Why would we want to go to Europe when we've got it all here?'

Question

How can the themed hotels in Las Vegas be seen as hyperreality?

a myriad of different ways – in news, in adverts, in films, in documentaries, in images, in words, via a growing range of electronic media. As a result, there cannot be a single truth or universally accepted knowledge.

Evaluation of Lyotard and Baudrillard

Greg Philo and David Miller (2002) have made the following criticisms of Lyotard and Baudrillard's views of postmodernist society:

❯ People are aware that there is a reality beyond the images broadcast by the media. They recognise that media images are often one-sided, partial and distorted.

❯ As a result, people do not simply absorb media images and see the world in terms of them.

❯ There are often shared views of what's right and wrong. For example, the majority of people still condemn Nazi ideology and the slaughter of millions of Jews, gypsies and homosexuals in Nazi death camps.

❯ Lyotard and Baudrillard tend to ignore how social structures such as the class system can shape world views.

Despite these criticisms, the picture of postmodernity provided by Lyotard and Baudrillard is reflected, albeit in a less extreme form, in the various views of modernity that will now be examined.

Late modernity

Like most sociologists today, the British sociologist Anthony Giddens (1991, 2000, 2009) does not accept the view that we are now living in a new era, postmodernity, which has replaced modernity. Instead, he sees a new phase, a later stage of modernity, which he calls **late modernity**.

Giddens (1991) sees late modernity as a 'world of rapid change'. It is like a 'juggernaut, a runaway engine of enormous power which, collectively as human beings, we can drive to some extent but which also threatens to rush out of our control'. The ride can be exhilarating but never entirely secure as it is 'fraught with risk'. People recognise the risks of living in late modernity – financial crises, climate change, nuclear catastrophes. This 'fuels a general climate of uncertainty', which produces anxiety and concern.

In late modernity, custom and tradition are less likely to guide behaviour. As a result, people become increasingly **reflexive**. They reflect on society and their situations, they question their actions and decisions, they choose between a range of alternatives.

In the rapidly changing society of late modernity, identity ceases to be clearly defined. The self becomes 'something to be reflected on, altered, even "moulded"'. For example, the body becomes 'a visible carrier of self-identity', as people transform their appearance with diet, exercise, tattoos, piercing, cosmetic surgery, hairstyles and clothes. They also become increasingly dependent on experts to help them do this. In Giddens' (1991) words, 'the self becomes a reflexive project', the body becomes 'a visible carrier of self-identity'.

According to Giddens (1991), the two key factors in late modernity are 'transformations in self-identity and globalisation'. He claims that 'For the first time in human history, "self" and "society" are interrelated in a global milieu' where 'information and images are routinely transmitted across the globe'. The self is now created in a global context. For example, people are increasingly aware of how women are seen in a variety of societies across the world. These views, pictures and notions of women can influence an individual's definition of self wherever they happen to live (Giddens, 2000).

Giddens (2000) believes 'There is a global revolution going on in how we think of ourselves and how we form ties and connections with others.' In terms of partnerships, late modernity is seeing the development of **pure relationships**. These relationships are based on **confluent love** – on 'intimacy', 'emotional communication', 'disclosure – opening oneself up to the other', 'equality' and 'mutual respect'. Relationships often fall short of these 'ideals' but Giddens sees them heading in this direction. However, if confluent love does not exist, a relationship is likely to end.

As noted above, Giddens sees globalisation as a key feature of late modern society. Globalisation can be defined as the increasing interconnectedness of countries, people and institutions across the world. For Giddens, 'Globalisation influences everyday life as much as it does events happening on a world scale.' In *Runaway World* (2000), he lists some of the main aspects of globalisation. They include a global economy and market-place, global financial transactions, multinational companies such as Coca-Cola and McDonald's, global risks such as global warming, political decisions that have world-wide effects, a growing awareness of world events and other cultures that influence family life and travel down to individual identity.

Although his book *Runaway World* pictures an insecure world 'fraught with anxieties' and 'scarred by deep divisions', Giddens is, on balance, optimistic. He believes that we can take control of this runaway world

Activity

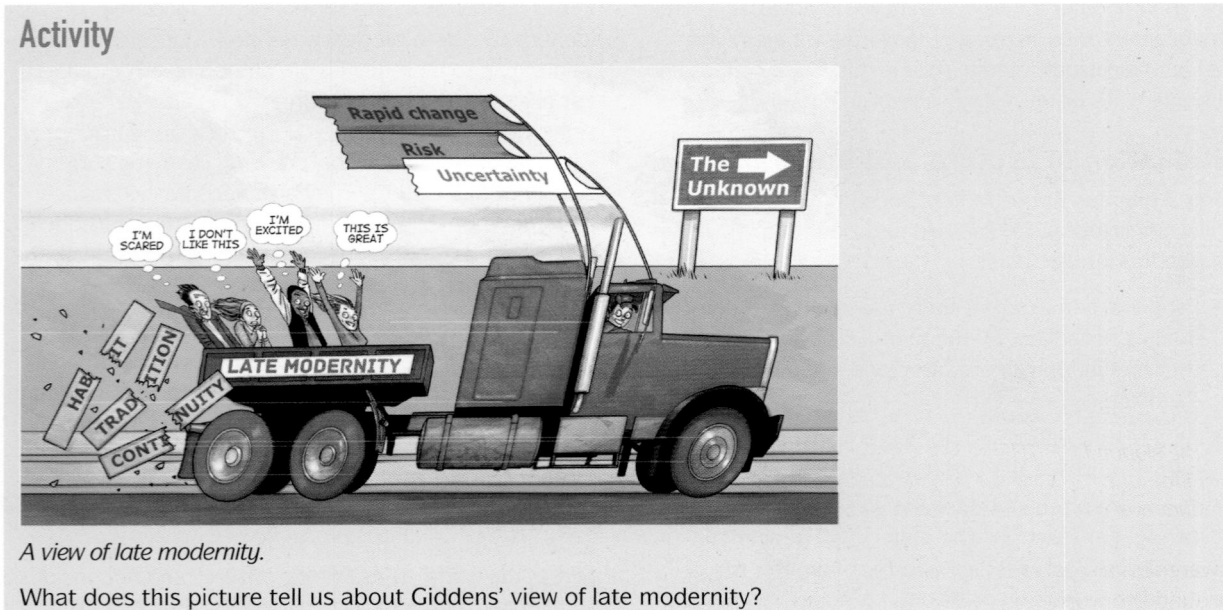

A view of late modernity.

What does this picture tell us about Giddens' view of late modernity?

and create new institutions that will eventually benefit the human race.

Evaluation of Giddens

Giddens' picture of late modernity is seen as a landmark that has influenced more recent views of contemporary society. Like all the views of modernity, Giddens has been criticised for exaggeration. For example, some critics argue that he overemphasises 'the extent to which traditional values have been left behind' (Jones, P. *et al.*, 2011). Others argue that he places too much emphasis on confluent love as the basis of intimate relationships. They point to the importance in many relationships of home-building and raising children.

The Danish sociologist Lars Bo Kaspersen (2000) states that Giddens has failed to recognise the extent to which differences in class and ethnicity within societies, and of cultures between societies, might affect people's behaviour in late modernity. For example, class differences may well influence people's freedom of action and their ability to construct their own identities. Despite the above criticisms, Giddens' views of late modernity have inspired many sociologists. Looking back on his work, Giddens (2009) concludes:

Ideas I have developed have been taken in fruitful directions by other sociologists and, in that sense, it is satisfying to have provided a theoretical framework and some conceptual tools for younger generations to take forward and develop.

The second modernity, the world risk society

The German sociologist Ulrich Beck (1944–2015) believes that we have entered a new phase of modernity which he calls the **second modernity**, or more usually, the **world risk society**. In *The Metamorphosis of the World* (2016), he paints a rather frightening picture of the world today. In Beck's words, **metamorphosis** is a 'radical transformation in which the old certainties of modern society are falling away and something quite new is emerging'. In a global risk society 'what was unthinkable yesterday is real and possible today'. These real and possible events include 'the September 11 terrorist attacks, catastrophic climate change all over the world, the Fukushima (nuclear) reactor disaster, and the financial and euro crises to the threats to freedom by totalitarian surveillance in the age of digital communication'.

Events such as these have led to a growing sense of **risk** across the world. Beck (2009) defines risk as 'the anticipation of catastrophe'. As such, risk refers to 'the possibility of future occurrences'. Beck claims that risk has now become global, hence the term 'world risk society'.

A key feature of the metamorphosis of the world is **globalisation**, which involves a drawing together of human beings across the world. People who have never left their villages, never boarded a train or plane are linked by international news media, social media and mobile phones. They are also linked by an

Contemporary issues: Global risks

The slogan FOR THE PLANET projected onto the Eiffel Tower in Paris during the United Nations Climate Change Conference in 2015.

The Paris Climate Agreement was signed by 196 countries. Its aim was to combat global warming, limit the temperature increase to 1.5°C above pre-industrial levels, and reduce the risks involved with climate change.

Question

How does the Paris Agreement illustrate Beck's view that risk has 'become a political force which transforms the world'?

awareness of global risks that these media broadcast around the world.

Risks are becoming increasingly visible. They can be seen in airport security where people and their belongings are scanned, and in major cities where surveillance cameras record life on the streets, revealing crime and terrorist activity. In parts of the world, climate change is becoming more and more apparent with rising sea levels, melting glaciers and major changes in the weather.

Beck (2009) argues that risk 'permeates and transforms the foundations of social life and action in all spheres, national and global'. This produces fear and a belief that security is increasingly important.

According to Beck, risk has now become a 'political force which transforms the world'. There is a new 'political realism' that 'no nation can master its problems alone', that cooperation and working together are now necessary for a country's survival.

Evaluation of Beck

In his assessment of Beck, Anthony Elliott (2009) begins with praise, stating that 'risk is an idea whose time has arrived'. However, he questions whether the risks that Beck identifies are significantly different from those of past eras. He points to the risks of bubonic plagues and syphilis epidemics from the past and suggests that they 'functioned in much the same manner' as today's risks. Elliott recognises that some risks have a global awareness today but questions whether risk has become 'the exclusive worry in the plight of contemporary women and men. Are we really so worried about risk?'

Paul Ransome (2010) accepts the increase in global risks but asks whether people are more concerned

with local risks, in their day-to-day lives – for example, the 'quality of local housing, health care and social amenities'.

Alan Scott (2000) argues that Beck has not given sufficient consideration to the effect of class on people's experience of risk. In recent years, the gap between rich and poor in terms of income and wealth has widened in Western society. People's class position has an important effect on the way they experience risk. For example, those in lower classes are more likely to be unemployed and unemployment can be cushioned with money; the moneyed classes are more able to avoid risks – for instance, moving away from polluted areas. As Alan Scott in *Risk Society or Angst Society* (2000) argues, 'Money can give far more protection from risks'.

The network society

The Spanish sociologist Manuel Castells (2000, 2004, 2012) believes that we now live in a new type of society – the **network society**. There have always been social networks. The difference today is that these networks have been transformed by information technology and the internet. 'Digital networks are global as they know no boundaries. Thus the network society is a global society' (Castells, 2004).

The availability of mobile phone and internet use has grown at a tremendous rate. In 2017:

> Nearly two thirds of the world's population has a mobile phone.

> More than half the world's web traffic now comes from mobile phones.

> More than half of all mobile connections around the world are now 'broadband' (wearesocial.com, 2017).

35

Today's economy is increasingly based on information technology. In Castells' (2000) words, 'The new economy is organised around global networks of capital, management and information. Access to technological know-how is at the roots of productivity and competitiveness.' These networks are 'enacted by light-speed-operating information technologies'.

Those at the centre of global economic networks tend to grow richer, while those excluded grow poorer. The gap between them is widening. The poor are increasingly drawn into global crime networks – for example, drug networks, which include poppy and coca growers, traffickers, street gangs, money launderers and drug barons.

In *Networks of Outrage and Hope: Social Movements in an Internet Age* (2012), Castells argues that digital communication plays a crucial part in social movements. They have helped to create and organise networks of protest, they have challenged the powerful and 'turned fear into outrage and outrage into hope for a better humanity'. For example, in the Tunisian revolution of 2011, which overthrew the ruling dictatorship, Twitter, Facebook, YouTube, websites and smart phones were used to record, publicise and organise demonstrations. However, digital communication can also be an effective weapon in the hands of those who many people would regard as terrorists.

Evaluation of Castells

According to Anthony Elliott (2009), Castells has provided 'brilliant insights' into the importance of digital networks in 21st-century global society. However, Elliott believes that Castells has overstated the significance of digital networks. He questions whether 'identities and social relations are really as fully permeated by networks as Castells suggests'. He argues that 'Castells expands the notion of "networked communications" to breaking point'.

Elliott states that Castells focuses on the 'expensive, technologically sophisticated cities of the West'. Although Castells recognises that networks can exclude as well as include, Elliott argues that he tends to neglect the poor and those in developing countries, the 'many millions disconnected from our age of informationalism'.

Liquid modernity

Born in Poland and living in England since 1971, Zygmunt Bauman (1925–2017) was Professor of Sociology at the Universities of Leeds and Warsaw. He calls the latest stage of modernism **liquid modernity** – it is fluid, flowing and flexible. 'Change

is *the only* permanence and uncertainty *the only* certainty' (Bauman, 2012).

Modern society has moved from 'solid' to 'liquid'. In liquid modernity, relationships are frail and fractious, jobs are often temporary and insecure, nothing is certain. Change is constant. In Bauman's (2007) words, 'social forms … decompose and melt faster than the time it takes to cast them'. As a result, uncertainty is ever present. This generates anxiety, insecurity and fear.

This fear extends from an individual to a global level. We live in an increasingly global society in which people experience **negative globalisation**. This 'brings to most minds the terrifying experience of a heteronomous, hapless and vulnerable population confronted with, and possibly overwhelmed by forces it neither controls nor fully understands; a population horrified by its own undefendability' (Bauman, 2007). As a result,

> *Living under liquid modern conditions can be compared to walking in a minefield: everyone knows that an explosion might happen at any moment and in any place, but no one knows when the moment will come and where the place will be. On a global planet, that condition is universal – no one is exempt and no one is insured against its consequences.*
> Bauman, 2012

Bauman (2003) sees **individualisation** as a key feature of liquid modernity. People are increasingly defining themselves as individuals rather than as members of social groups. They see themselves taking responsibility for their own future rather than joining others in collective action to improve their situation. Relying on oneself can result in pride for success but it can also produce self-blame for failure. For the poor and powerless, especially, who have few resources to fall back on, the loss of a job or a partner can lead to self-blame and 'broken, loveless and prospectless lives'.

Individualisation, Bauman believes, leads to a desire for individual freedom. However, in a society 'saturated with insecurity' people also look for security. There is a conflict between the need for freedom and the need for security. This can result in fragile bonds between partners. People need partners for emotional security. However, the demand for freedom means that bonds have to be 'loosely tied so they can be untied with little delay', should the partnership prove unsatisfactory. The result is 'semi-detached couples' in 'top-pocket relationships'. People can pull their partners out of their top pockets when required but they also have the freedom to live their own lives as individuals. However, this is not a recipe for stable, long-lasting relationships.

The picture that Bauman paints of liquid modernity is not optimistic. He argues that nation states are clearly inadequate to solve global problems. He believes that to move forward humans require 'a model of a *global* society, global politics and a global jurisdiction. Instead, we react to the latest trouble, experimenting, groping in the dark' (Bauman, 2012).

Evaluation of Bauman

Bauman's views of liquid modernity have been highly praised. For example, Anthony Elliott (2009) describes them as having 'enduring significance to social theory'. However, Bauman's views have also been criticised. As Elliott notes:

1. Bauman tends to see everything through the lens of liquidisation. As a result, he has exaggerated the extent to which society has become 'liquid'. Not everything is liquidising and dissolving. In addition, liquidisation is too broad and vague a concept to fully capture the detail and complexity of contemporary society.

2. Bauman's focus is too narrow. It is largely based on life in North America and Europe, on societies with high rates of divorce and remarriage for which the process of individualisation is particularly applicable.

3. Despite the increasing change and diversity in society, traditional views remain important. For instance, marriage is still a 'cultural ideal'. Individualisation is occurring but it has not led to the ending of this ideal (Elliott, 2009).

The reinvention society

In his short, entertaining and illuminating book *Reinvention* (2013), Anthony Elliott draws together the ideas of sociologists such as Giddens and Bauman and takes them a step further. He links the personal and the global, examining how individuals respond to global processes. In particular, he looks at how the demands of globalisation for endless reinvention, transformation and improvement shape individuals' priorities, emotions and concerns.

Elliott sees the **reinvention** of persons, bodies, careers, corporations, networks and places as a wide-ranging and fast-growing global trend. He argues that this process is largely directed by globalisation – by the demands of a global economy for constant innovation and change. In his words, 'globalisation spells endless reinvention'. This reaches down to the individual level – to self-concepts, relationships, appearances and redefinitions of self. The result is 'the reconstruction and reinvention of self'.

Buying new and fashionable clothes is an obvious example of transforming the self. Diet, gym membership and personal trainers promise to re-sculpt, remould and enhance the body. Cosmetic dentistry, cosmetic surgery and makeovers provide opportunities to redesign and reconstruct appearance. Therapy offers a 'new you' with a positive and dynamic outlook. Self-help books provide recipes for self-improvement; and speed dating and dating websites offer possibilities for a fresh start and a new and exciting relationship. In Elliott's words, 'the self becomes a site for endless improvement'.

Reinvention also applies to jobs and careers. People are increasingly hired for projects on short-term contracts. As a result, they must be flexible, learn new skills, be ready to 'embrace change' and keep pace with a rapidly changing job market.

The global economy is increasingly competitive, changeable and turbulent. This requires corporations to constantly reinvent – 'redesign, rebrand, refinance' and restructure their business practices.

According to Elliott, today's reinvention reflects 'a culture obsessed with having the biggest, best, largest, shiniest and newest of everything'. The prime example is Dubai, with its 'monumental architecture, mega-shopping malls for excessive consumption, lavish hotels, and blockbuster sports and entertainment events'.

Activity – Dubai: City of the Future

The Palm Jumeirah in Dubai – luxury hotels, restaurants and apartments built on land reclaimed from the sea in the shape of a palm tree.

Dubai now calls itself 'City of the Future'.

Recent projects include the Museum of the Future, the Dubai Eye – the world's largest Ferris wheel, Aladdin City inspired by tales of Aladdin and Sinbad, the Dubai Design District, and by 2030 an estimated 25 per cent of Dubai's buildings will be 3-D printed.

Question

How does Dubai reflect today's 'reinvention culture'?

Modernities and postmodernity – conclusion

The views of contemporary society presented by the various theories in this part of the chapter have all been criticised for overstating their case and understating the importance of factors relevant to the arguments they present. In a sense the authors of these theories are like artists painting with a vision that colours the entire picture; and this leads to both overstatement and understatement.

Despite this, the authors are widely recognised as important social theorists. Their views are fresh and exciting. Their pictures are painted with broad brushstrokes – at times they lack hard evidence, but they have impact, and they make points which have real significance to all our futures.

Key terms

Modernity A term often used to describe the period from the Industrial Revolution to the present.

Postmodernity A term used by some sociologists for what they see as a new period following modernity.

Metanarratives Grand stories that claim to explain things.

Simulacrum A simulation. (The plural is simulacra.)

Hyperreality The blurring of reality and illusion.

Late modernity The term used by Anthony Giddens for what he sees as a late phase of modernity.

Reflexivity In the context of research, reflecting on yourself, looking back at your research, and examining how your values and background might have influenced your feelings.

Pure relationships Relationships based on confluent love.

Confluent love Intimacy, emotional communication and mutual disclosure.

The second modernity/world risk society The terms used by Ulrich Beck for what he sees as a late phase of modernity.

Metamorphosis A radical transformation from one thing to another.

Risk The possibility of danger. As used by Ulrich Beck, 'the anticipation of catastrophe'.

Globalisation An increasing interconnection between various parts of the world.

The network society Manuel Castell's term for his view of the latest phase of modernity.

Liquid modernity Zygmunt Bauman's term for his view of the latest phase of modernity.

Negative globalisation A negative experience of globalisation.

Individualisation A growing emphasis on the individual rather than the group.

The reinvention society Anthony Elliott's term for his view of the latest phase of modernity.

Summary

1. Modernity involves industrialism, capitalism, urbanism and democracy.

2. Postmodernism involves a rejection of metanarratives, a state of uncertainty and a blurring of reality and illusion.

3. Late modernity involves rapid change, risk and uncertainty, reflexivity, transformations in self-identity and globalisation.

4. The second modernity, also known as world risk society, involves global risks, which extend to the personal level.

5. The network society involves global digital networks.

6. Liquid modernity involves constant change, insecurity and fear and an experience of negative globalisation. Bonds between people are often fragile and temporary.

7. The reinvention society mirrors the demands of a global economy for innovation and change. Reinvention extends from the global to the individual.

PART 5 METHODOLOGY

Contents

This part looks at methodology – the study of methods. Research methods were outlined and evaluated in Book 1. This part examines the theories and assumptions underlying these methods. It looks at the different views of human behaviour and society and considers which methods are appropriate for each view. It asks whether the methods used in the natural sciences are suitable for the study of human behaviour. It raises the question of objectivity and value freedom. Can sociology be free from the values of the researcher? Will the researcher's culture, gender, social class and political views affect their observations, interpretations, analysis and conclusions?

These are important questions. They question what we think we know. This part looks at various answers to these questions.

Unit 1.5.1 Positivist and quantitative methodologies

Sociology has often been referred to as a social science. Whether or not it can be seen as a scientific discipline has been one of the major debates within the subject (see pp. 54–57). The founding fathers of sociology in the 19th century were, however, in no doubt. By following the rules and logic of the scientific method, sociology could discover the laws underlying the development of human society. In this respect, it was a science just like the natural sciences of physics and chemistry, which seek to discover the laws underlying the behaviour of matter.

Auguste Comte – positivism

Auguste Comte (1798–1857) is credited with inventing the term 'sociology'. He argued that sociology should be based on the methodology of the natural sciences. According to Comte, this would produce a 'science of society', which would reveal the 'invariable laws' that governed the evolution of human society. Comte's approach is known as **positivism**.

Comte insisted that only directly observable 'facts' were acceptable in a positive science of society. This ruled out anything that could not be directly observed, such as meanings. Positivism assumes that behaviour in the natural and social world is based on similar principles. The behaviour of matter is a reaction to external factors such as temperature and pressure. In much the same way, human behaviour is a reaction to external forces beyond the individual, such as economic and political systems. Behaviour in both the natural and social worlds is determined by external stimuli. As a result, natural science methodology is appropriate for the study of human behaviour.

Scientists explain the behaviour of matter in terms of cause and effect relationships. In order to discover these relationships, behaviour must be objectively quantified. It must be measured in the form of numbers and these measurements must be **objective** – they must be unbiased and **value-free**. They must not be affected by the values, morality or the politics of the researcher.

Statistical analysis of quantitative data can then be used to discover possible **correlations** – links or connections – between social facts. Correlations may indicate relationships between social facts. Theories can then be developed to explain these relationships. In this way, the 'positive science of sociology' may uncover the 'invariable laws' governing human behaviour.

Émile Durkheim – the rules of sociological method

Social facts

The French sociologist Émile Durkheim (1858–1917) is one of the founders of sociology. His approach illustrates many of the aspects of positivism.

In *The Rules of Sociological Method*, first published in 1895, Durkheim outlined the logic and methods to be followed for sociology to become a science of society. The starting point, 'the first and most fundamental rule is: Consider social facts as things'. Social facts are the institutions, norms and values of society. As 'things', social facts can be treated in the same way as the material objects of the natural world. They can be objectively measured, quantified and subjected to statistical analysis. Correlations can be drawn between social facts, cause and effect relationships established and theories developed to explain those relationships. In this way 'real laws are discoverable' in the social world as in the natural world.

However, can social facts be treated as things? Aren't beliefs, for example, part of human consciousness? Also, aren't human beings, because they have consciousness, fundamentally different from the inanimate objects that make up the natural world? In view of this, is natural science methodology appropriate for the study of human behaviour?

Durkheim accepted that social facts form part of our consciousness – they have to for society to exist. Without shared norms and values, for example, society could not operate. However, although they are a part of us, social facts also exist outside of us. In Durkheim's words, 'collective ways of acting and thinking have a reality outside the individuals'. Members of society do not simply act in terms of their own particular psychology and personal beliefs. Instead they are directed and constrained to act by social facts, by values and beliefs that are over and above the individual and part of the wider society. In this respect, social facts 'have a reality outside the individuals' and can therefore be studied 'objectively as external things'.

Thus, just as matter is constrained to act by natural forces, so human beings are constrained to act by social facts. Given this, social facts can be studied using the methodology of the natural sciences.

The social fact of suicide

Durkheim's *Suicide: A Study in Sociology* was published in 1897. This study exemplified his rules of sociological method. Durkheim argued that the causes of suicide rates (the number of suicides per million of the population) are to be found in society, *not* in the psychology of individuals. Suicide rates are social facts. They are also a product of social

facts, of 'real, living, active forces which, because of the way they determine the individual, prove their independence from him'.

Durkheim examined official statistics on suicide from a number of European countries. He found that 1) suicide rates within each country were fairly constant over a number of years and 2) there were significant differences in the rates both between societies and between social groups within the same society.

Durkheim found correlations between suicide rates and a wide range of social facts. For example, he found statistical relationships between suicide rates and religion, age and family situation. Some of these are illustrated in the following table. In each of the pairs, the group on the left had a higher suicide rate than the group on the right.

Higher suicide rate	Lower suicide rate
Protestants	Catholics
City dwellers	Rural dwellers
Older adults	Younger adults
Unmarried	Married
Married without children	Married with children

Having established correlations between social facts, Durkheim's next task was to see whether he could discover causal connections. He argued that variations in suicide rates were caused by variations in levels of social integration, that is the extent to which individuals are part of a wider social group. In the case of the examples given above, the groups on the left have lower levels of social integration than the groups on the right. For example, older adults are less socially integrated than younger adults because their children have grown up and left home, many of their friends and relatives have died, and if they have retired from work they may well have lost touch with their workmates. Using examples such as this, Durkheim claimed that 'suicide varies inversely with the degree of integration of the social groups of which the individual forms a part' – that is, the higher an individual's social integration the less likely they are to take their own life.

Durkheim's final task was to explain why suicide rates vary with levels of social integration. Part of his explanation runs as follows. As members of society, people are social beings – they have been socialised to play a part in society. The greater their social isolation, the less they can participate in society. Their lives lack meaning and purpose unless they are shared with others. In Durkheim's words, 'The individual alone is not a sufficient end for his activity. He is too little.' In a situation of social isolation, 'the individual yields to the slightest shock of circumstances because the state of society has made him ready prey to suicide'.

Durkheim doesn't claim to explain all aspects of suicide. For example, he does not explain why only a small minority of socially isolated individuals commit suicide. He sees this as the job of the psychologist because it concerns individual behaviour rather than social facts.

Durkheim believed that his research on suicide proved that scientific methodology was appropriate for the study of society, because it had shown that 'real laws are discoverable'. (For further discussion of Durkheim's study of suicide see pp. 42–44. For a broader discussion of Durkheim's view of society, see pp. 101–103.)

Activity

Unmarried

Married

Married without children

Married with children

Older adults

Younger adults

Some of the groups Durkheim studied with regard to suicide.

According to the data available to Durkheim, those on the left-hand side had higher suicide rates than those on the right-hand side. Use Durkheim's methodology to explain why this might be the case.

Quantitative methodology

Today the term 'positivism' is sometimes used to cover quantitative approaches and methods. As the following summary of **quantitative methods** indicates, these are often influenced by traditional positivist approaches.

Quantitative research, as its name suggests, is largely based on quantitative data, that is data in the form of numbers. It aims to produce objective measurements of human behaviour. This allows patterns found in the data to be precisely described, for example in terms of percentages. Numerical data makes it possible to use statistical tests to measure the strength of relationships between two or more factors.

Some research methods are more likely than others to produce quantitative data. It can be fairly easy to translate the answers to a questionnaire or a structured interview into numbers. As a result, sociologists who prefer quantitative approaches tend to use these methods.

Quantitative approaches usually aim to make generalisations about human behaviour. A generalisation is a statement about a whole group based on the findings from a relatively small number of members of that group. To do this, a researcher needs to study a sample of people who are representative of the larger group, who have the same characteristics as the larger group.

Sociology has been described as the study of people in social groups. Some sociologists who prefer quantitative methodology argue that without data in the form of numbers it is not possible to provide accurate descriptions of social groups.

Key terms

Positivism According to Comte, a method of study based on directly observable facts, which can be objectively measured and quantified, and from which it is possible to identify cause and effect relationships.

Objective/value free Research findings that are free from the values of the researcher.

Correlation A statistical link between data.

Quantitative methodology An approach to research which states that human behaviour should be quantified, i.e. put in the form of numbers.

Summary

1. Comte assumed that behaviour in the natural and social worlds is determined by external stimuli. As a result, natural science methods are appropriate for the study of human behaviour.

2. According to Durkheim, social facts are external to individuals, they become part of human consciousness, and they direct and constrain behaviour.

3. Sociologists who base their research on quantitative methodology argue that numerical data are necessary to analyse and explain human behaviour.

Unit 1.5.2 Interpretivist and qualitative methodologies

Interpretivism is a term used to cover various **qualitative research methodologies**. Some sociologists argue that understanding human behaviour involves seeing the world through the eyes of those being studied. People give meaning to their own actions and to the actions of others, they interpret what they see and hear, they define situations in certain ways and act accordingly. To understand their behaviour, it is essential to discover the meanings and definitions that guide their actions. The sociologist's job is to discover these meanings and definitions.

Interpretivists reject the view that the methods and assumptions of the natural sciences are applicable to the study of human beings. Matter simply reacts to external stimuli such as temperature and pressure. Human beings act in terms of meanings, which they use to direct their behaviour.

Interpretivists tend to favour particular research methods. Some see participant observation as one of the best ways to discover meanings. This provides researchers with the opportunity to observe people in their normal, everyday situations, to see life as it is lived. Interpretivists also favour in-depth, unstructured interviews that allow research participants to express their own view of the world and define situations in their own way. Interpretivists see these methods as more likely to provide qualitative data, which they believe is richer and more meaningful than quantitative data.

Suicide and the construction of meaning

The following research provides a comparison of Durkheim's approach to the study of suicide with two of the several interpretivist approaches. This comparison illustrates some of the differences between positivist/quantitative and interpretivist/qualitative methodologies.

Discovering suicide

In *Discovering Suicide*, J. Maxwell Atkinson (1978) asks, 'How do deaths get categorised as suicide?' Atkinson sees suicide as a meaning. He rejects the view that the suicide rate is a 'social fact', arguing that there is no such thing as a 'real' or objective suicide rate.

Atkinson's research attempts to discover the meanings used by coroners to classify deaths as suicide. He held discussions with coroners, attended inquests, observed a coroner's officer at work and analysed a coroner's records. He argues that coroners have a 'common-sense theory of suicide' which they use to both classify and explain deaths as suicide. In terms of his theory, the following evidence is seen as relevant for reaching a verdict:

1. Whether suicide threats have been made or suicide notes have been left.

2. The type of death – hanging, gassing and drug overdose are seen as typical suicide deaths.

3. The location of death – death by gunshot at home is more likely to be seen as suicide than in the countryside where it may well be interpreted as a hunting accident.

4. The biography of the deceased – a recent divorce, the death of a close friend or relative, a history of depression, problems at work, financial difficulties, lack of friends are seen as typical reasons for suicide.

The closer the deceased fits this common-sense theory of suicide, the more likely their death will be defined as suicide. In Atkinson's words, coroners 'are engaged in analysing features of the deaths and of the biographies of the deceased according to a variety of taken-for-granted assumptions about what constitutes a "typical suicide", "a typical suicide biography", and so on'.

According to Atkinson, suicides are not objective 'social facts' with causes that can be explained, they are meanings. To try and discover the 'causes' of suicide will simply result in uncovering the meanings used to classify a death as suicide. Thus it comes as no surprise that the 'typical suicide biography' – the friendless, divorced loner – is very similar to Durkheim's socially isolated individual. For Atkinson, suicides, like any other aspect of social reality, are simply constructions of meaning.

Activity

The maniac father and the convict brother are gone – the poor girl, homeless, friendless, deserted, destitute, and gin mad, commits self murder. (From a series of illustrations entitled 'The Drunkard's Children' drawn by George Cruikshank in 1848.)

How might this picture and its original caption be used to illustrate both Durkheim's and Atkinson's explanation of a 'suicide death'?

The social meanings of suicide

Compared to Atkinson, Jack Douglas (1967) takes a less extreme interpretivist view of suicide. He argues that suicide is not simply a meaning, that it has a reality. He claims that it is possible for researchers to discover whether a death actually was suicide.

In *The Social Meanings of Suicide* Douglas (1967) argues that suicide is an act that is defined and given meaning by the victim, their family, friends and acquaintances and the coroner. The job of the sociologist is to discover these meanings and to judge whether or not they indicate actual suicides. To do this, Douglas suggests three steps.

Step 1 Examine the meanings victims give to their possible suicide. This involves:

› an analysis of suicide notes if available
› an examination of diaries if kept
› interviews with families and friends
› building up a biography of the victim.

Step 2 Look for the meanings that appear common to a number of possible suicides. These might include:

› a 'cry for help' suicide when all else has failed
› a self-punishment suicide for one's misdeeds
› an escape suicide when life becomes unbearable.

Step 3 Link these patterns of meaning with the wider beliefs of the culture. For example:

› In Western culture, suicide is often seen as an act of desperation when all else fails.
› In some nomadic hunter-gatherer bands, such as the traditional Inuit, older people who can no longer physically keep up with the band leave the encampment to die.

Douglas argues that suicide statistics are the result of negotiated meanings and social interactions. For example, the family and friends of the deceased, who they believe has committed suicide, may do their best to conceal his or her 'suicide'. This, in turn, may lead the coroner to deliver a verdict of accidental death or death by natural causes.

Douglas argues that only by discovering meanings by following steps 1, 2, and 3 can the researcher have a chance of judging whether or not a death is suicide.

Qualitative methodology

In recent years qualitative methodology has become increasingly popular. Academic journals are now devoted to it. There are growing numbers of books on qualitative research methods. Qualitative methodology has become a major focus in various disciplines – in particular, sociology and psychology. There are books applying it to the study of a range of occupations from nursing and social work to business and management. Qualitative methodology is often seen in a very positive light. In the words of Virginia Braun and Victoria Clarke (2013), authors of *Successful Qualitative Research*, 'We're about to introduce you to the wonderful world of qualitative research. We hope you'll learn to love and feel as passionate about it as we do.'

The aim of qualitative research is to see the world through the eyes of the research participants, to discover their meanings and definitions of the situation. This means avoiding the imposition of the researcher's categories, classifications and frameworks. In the works of David Silverman, author of *Doing Qualitative Research* (2013) and *Interpreting Qualitative Data* (2015), 'Qualitative research gives deeper understanding. It provides naturally occurring data rather than data structured by the researcher.'

Obtaining 'naturally occurring data' often means studying research participants in their normal, everyday settings. Participant observation provides this opportunity. It allows the researcher to observe people acting on their own terms and directing their own actions. The researcher can stand back and watch and listen rather than organising and directing research participants.

Interviews are one of the main methods used in qualitative research. In *What Is Qualitative Interviewing?* Rosalind Edwards and Janet Holland (2013) state that qualitative interviews should be fluid and flexible, open and non-directed, informal and conversational. Research participants should have the freedom to say what they want, to direct the interview into areas which concern them, to deal with issues they see as relevant to their lives and compose answers in terms of their own meanings.

Researchers recognise that qualitative interviews are social events in which both parties are personally involved and that the data are a joint production. Both the researcher and the research participant bring their own values, ideas and experiences to the interview. This inevitably influences the course of the interview and the resulting data. Researchers must bear this in mind when analysing interview data.

Whatever methods they use, qualitative researchers tend to let what they observe and hear direct their research. They are more likely than quantitative researchers to develop categories and ideas from the data they collect rather than inserting that data into pre-defined categories based on the researcher's ideas before collecting their data. Qualitative researchers tend to be more open and flexible, developing descriptions and explanations during the course of their research rather than testing pre-conceived hypotheses (Hammersley, 2013).

Supporters of qualitative research methods argue that they are more likely than other methods to produce rich, detailed and valid data and more likely to lead to the discovery of the meanings research participants use to direct their actions.

Mixed methods

So far, this chapter has divided sociological methodology into two parts – positivist/quantitative and interpretivist/qualitative. To some extent, this division reflects real differences in the assumptions and theories underlying these two approaches and the research methods favoured by each. However, this division has been criticised by some sociologists. According to Ray Pawson

(1989), instead of two approaches there is a whole range of different approaches with different assumptions and different emphases.

A second criticism states that an examination of actual research indicates that sociologists have often used a mixture of qualitative and quantitative methods and combined the different kinds of data that each produces. This is known as a **mixed methods** approach – for example, using participant observation and questionnaires on a single research project. The mixed methods approach has become increasingly popular. It has been seen as providing the benefits of two or more methods to give a fuller and more detailed picture.

Social action theories and research methods

Some sociologists have spelt out the research methods they see as appropriate for their theories of social action.

Max Weber and *verstehen*

Weber stated that sociology is based on 'the interpretive understanding of social action'. This involves interpreting the meanings and motives that direct action. Weber calls his method **verstehen**, which roughly translates as empathetic understanding. It involves researchers putting themselves in the place of those they are researching and attempting to see the world through their eyes. Weber used this method when studying a range of historical documents in his famous work *The Protestant Ethic and the Spirit of Capitalism* (see p. 14 and p. 226).

Herbert Blumer – symbolic interactionism

In order to discover the meanings in interaction situations, Blumer (1962) stated that this involves 'feeling one's way inside the experience of the actor' in order to 'catch the process of interpretation through which they construct their action'. Blumer is refreshingly honest when discussing how this might be achieved. 'It is a tough job requiring a high order of careful and honest probing, creative yet disciplined imagination, resourcefulness and flexibility in study, pondering over what one is finding, and constant readiness to test and recast one's views and images of the area.'

Harold Garfinkel – ethnomethodology

Garfinkel designed various experiments to discover the methods that people used to make sense of the social world. One experiment was to illustrate the importance of context. Students made sense where there was no sense when they thought the person giving them advice was a counsellor in a university psychology department. A second method was the 'breaching experiment' where students went into familiar situations and behaved in unexpected ways – for example, behaving like a lodger in front of their parents in the family home (see p. 23). These experiments revealed the 'practical common-sense reasoning' used to create sense and order where none existed.

Key terms

Interpretivist and qualitative methodologies
Approaches which state that understanding human action involves seeing the world through the eyes of those being studied.

Mixed methods Using different methods for the same research project, often mixing qualitative and quantitative methods.

Verstehen As used by Weber, a method for interpreting the meanings and motives that direct behaviour.

Summary

1. According to interpretivist and qualitative methodologies, the job of the sociologist is to discover the meanings used to direct action.

2. Participant observation and in-depth, unstructured interviews are the favoured methods for discovering meanings.

3. Qualitative methodology attempts to avoid imposing researchers' categories and frameworks on research participants.

4. The supporters of qualitative methodology claim it provides richer, deeper and more valid data.

5. Sociologists often use mixed methods in the same research project.

Unit 1.5.3 Objectivity, values and reflexivity

The founders of sociology saw the subject as an objective science of society. **Objectivity** means value-free, impartial and unbiased. It means that the research process and findings are not influenced by the values of the researcher, by their moral, political or religious beliefs, by their gender, ethnicity, social class, nationality, sexual orientation, by their world view or their personality. **Subjectivity** is the opposite of objectivity. It refers to a personal viewpoint based on a particular individual's values and beliefs.

Until the mid-1950s, many sociologists believed that an objective, value-free sociology was possible. Since then, growing numbers have questioned this view. The American sociologist Alvin W. Gouldner (1975) stated that 'a value-free sociology is a myth', that it is 'absurd' to claim that it is possible. He believed that his political views lead him to condemn the system of social inequality which generates poverty and powerlessness. Gouldner argued that this belief will inevitably influence his choice of research project, the research process, his findings and his conclusions.

The American sociologist Howard S. Becker (1970) shared this view. He stated that it is impossible to conduct research and produce findings that are 'uncontaminated by personal and political sympathies'. He argued that, 'There is no position from which sociological research can be done that is not biased in one way or another.' Becker saw society divided into the powerful and the powerless. He believed that 'we cannot avoid taking sides' and he sides with powerless 'underdogs'.

Activity

'*We cannot avoid taking sides.*'

How does this picture reflect Becker's views?

45

Does the view that a value-free sociology is impossible mean that sociologists should no longer be concerned about objectivity? For many sociologists, the answer is No! They see the pursuit of objectivity as essential. Howard Becker puts it this way. 'Our problem is to make sure that, whatever point of view we take, our research meets the standards of good scientific work, that our unavoidable sympathies do not render our results invalid.'

What does this mean in practice? According to Becker, it means 'we must not misuse the tools and techniques of our discipline'. It means we should avoid asking leading questions, avoid advertising our sympathies to research participants or encouraging them to give the response we'd like to hear. We should not reject findings that go against our sympathies. Becker argues that we should be as objective as possible, guard against our 'personal and political commitments' and do our best to 'avoid the distortion' they might bring to our findings.

Today, most sociologists recognise that complete objectivity is impossible. However, this does not mean giving up on objectivity. Clifford Geertz (1973) made the following case for the pursuit of objectivity. 'I have never been impressed by the argument that, as complete objectivity is impossible, one might as well let one's sentiments run loose. That is like saying that as a perfectly aseptic (germ free) environment is impossible, one might as well conduct surgery in a sewer.'

Reflexivity

Sociologists are increasingly looking at themselves, at their values, beliefs and concerns and their position in society, to see how these factors might influence their research. This process is known as reflexivity. It means reflecting on yourself, how you as a person might have affected the findings you produce and the conclusions you reach. The importance of reflexivity can be seen from the following example. Two American researchers conducted investigations of the same Mexican village with very different results. They reflect on the reasons for these differences.

In the 1920s, Robert Redfield (1930) studied the village of Tepoztlán in Mexico. He found a warm, generous and close-knit community. Oscar Lewis (1951) studied the same village 17 years later. He saw a community divided by envy, distrust and conflict. Redfield and Lewis reflected on themselves and their research to try to explain why their pictures of Tepoztlán were so different (Critchfield, 1978).

They agreed that the 17 years between their research projects could not account for the different pictures. According to Redfield, the main reasons were 'personal differences between the investigators' – 'differences in interests and values' which resulted in 'different questions asked' and different conclusions drawn. Redfield clearly liked the people of Tepoztlán. He found them friendly, generous and welcoming – 'I found doors were open to me.' Lewis did not appear to like them. He wrote that the kindness, generosity and

Activity

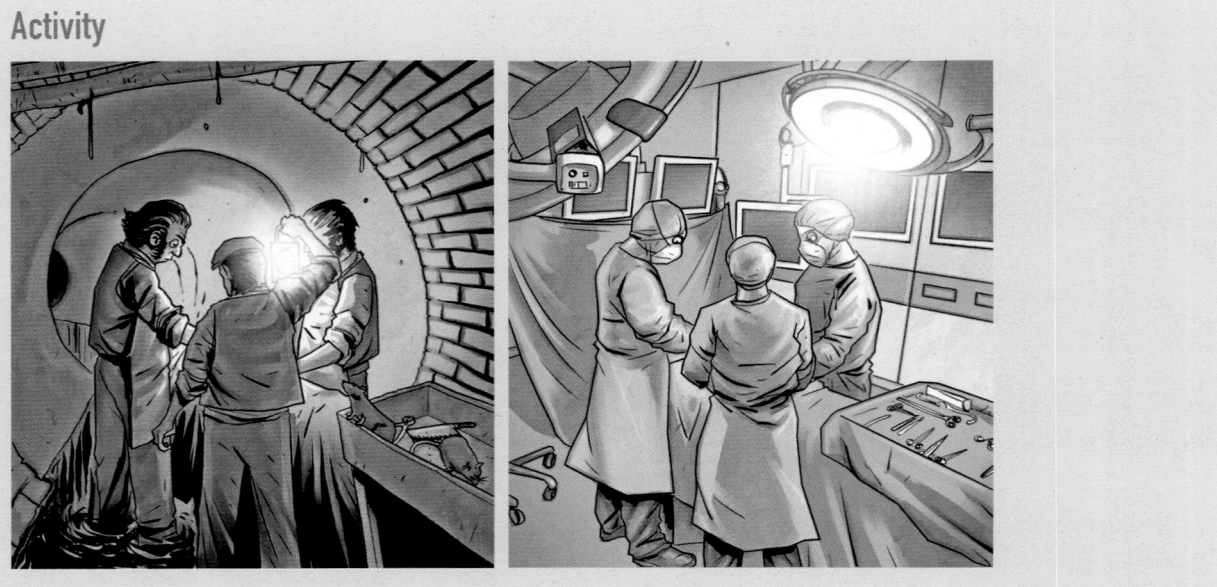

How do these pictures reflect the arguments of Becker and Geertz?

joy described by Redfield 'appeared much less often than anger, hate, irritability, jealousy, fear and envy'.

The studies of Tepoztlán indicate the importance of reflexivity. Looking at themselves and looking back at their research, Redfield and Lewis recognised what a difference the personal characteristics of the researcher can make to the results of research.

Assessing reflexivity

The following examples indicate how reflexivity can be used to assess research, to improve research and provide lessons for others to apply their own research.

Gaining acceptance and assessing validity Meghan Hollis (2014) used participant observation to study female and ethnic minority police officers in the USA. As part of her research, she observed a fight on a Saturday night outside a club in a New England city. The police officer she was with accidentally pepper-sprayed her. Despite her discomfort, Hollis spent a further four hours on patrol with the officer. She had proved herself in a male-dominated occupation. As a result she gained the trust, respect and cooperation of the police.

Looking back on her research, she notes that 'after this incident, the officers were increasingly likely to talk to me and accept me as part of the group'. Reflexivity allowed her to assess the quality of the data she collected. Gaining acceptance from the police officers probably indicated to Hollis that her data were more likely to be valid.

Activity

Meghan Hollis outside the club.

1. Why was it important for Meghan to 'prove herself'?
2. How might reflexivity help her to judge the validity of her data?

Identifying with the researcher In a study of mixed-race women, Minelle Mahtani reflects on interviews she conducted. Minelle was of Indian and Iranian descent. This had both advantages and disadvantages for her interviews with mixed-race women. On the plus side, the research participants identified with her and felt comfortable and at ease in her presence. However, in many interviews this led to 'the phrase "you know what I mean Minelle" followed by a knowing glance or smile'. This 'created a more comfortable space for these women to tell their stories – but also prevented them from divulging further detail'. This was one of the drawbacks of research participants identifying with the researcher. In this example, reflexivity allows the researcher to judge the quality of the data, and the appropriateness of the research method used (discussed in Edwards and Holland, 2013).

Activity – Alice Goffman: reflexivity and self-awareness

Alice Goffman.

Alice Goffman is a well-educated White woman from a middle-class, well-off family. She spent her twenties conducting a participant observation study of young Black men, 'dipping and dodging the police' in a low-income African-American neighbourhood in Philadelphia.

Her early months in the neighbourhood were difficult. 'I often felt like an idiot... I couldn't seem to follow events and conversations... There was a language barrier... I misinterpreted people's gestures and actions.' Mike, one of the young men, adopted and presented her as his sister, which helped with her acceptance.

Where possible, Alice tried to 'take up as little social space as I could using social shrinkage to reduce the impact of my difference'. This approach had its pluses – the young men often treated her as if she wasn't there and behaved normally – but it also had its minuses. The young men often made promises to beat up or shoot someone who'd injured or insulted them. 'I sat quietly by, like a fly on the wall, waiting to see what would happen... Months later, I realised that as a friend, sis or cousin, men were expecting me to hold them back; to fail to do this would put them in danger of having to make good on their promises. So after a time I learned that taking someone's car keys or hiding a gun wasn't changing the outcome of events as much as sitting idly by would be. Blocking the door was the way to blend into the walls.'

As the years went by, Alice Goffman became as much a friend and companion as an observer of the men she was studying. However, despite this, she notes that 'my background and identity were so different from those of the people I was observing that I couldn't always trust my reactions to events and situations that I did experience first-hand. That is, I had to be cautious in generalising from my reactions to the feelings or experiences of others. With all these frustrating barriers, a lot can be said for sustained observation and involvement. Certainly, I came closer to understanding than when I started out.'

Adapted from Alice Goffman (2014) *On the Run: Fugitive Life in an American City*.

Question

How does Alice Goffman's research indicate the importance of reflexivity, self-awareness and an understanding of research participants?

Doing reflexivity In *Doing Reflexivity*, Jon Dean (2017) provides a recipe for being reflexive and addresses the various issues that reflexive investigators face. He argues that 'autobiographical reflexivity is a vital part of the production of qualitative research'. As a

researcher, he conducted an autobiographical profile of himself, examining his social class and political position and interviewing his parents about his upbringing. He states that, 'It is now accepted and normal to write the researcher into the world they investigate. More than that, as this book argues, it is necessary.'

Standpoint theory, values and experience

Should researchers guard against their background and experience from influencing their research? No, according to **standpoint theory**. In fact, standpoint theory argues that background and experience can provide valuable insights and more valid data.

Standpoint theory conducts research from the standpoint of a particular group. These groups are often oppressed and experience negative discrimination – for example, women, ethnic minorities, gay men and women and people with disabilities. Standpoint theory rejects the view that researchers must necessarily guard against their background as a source of bias and distortion. Instead, standpoint theory researchers embrace their background and welcome the insights it may bring. For example, a researcher's gender as a woman gives them a particular vantage point which may provide a distinctive viewpoint and special knowledge. In Sandra Harding's (2004) words, 'Starting off research from women's lives will generate less partial and distorted accounts not only of women's lives but also of men's lives and of the whole social order.'

Evaluation

Critics of standpoint theory argue that it has been developed largely by White, heterosexual middle-class women and tends to ignore the many differences in background and experience between women (Alvesson and Sköldberg, 2009). However, not all versions of standpoint theory limit themselves to one standpoint. For example, the American sociologist Patricia Hill Collins (1990, 1998) combines three standpoints – gender, ethnicity and class. She grew up in a Black, working-class family in Philadelphia and uses these standpoints to research African-American, working-class women (see p. 29).

While this widens the focus of standpoint theory, critics still point to what they see as its narrow viewpoint. For example, they argue that to understand women's oppression it is important to have a male viewpoint. As oppressors, men have access to different sorts of knowledge that may provide insights into the nature of male oppression (Hammersley, 2011).

Key terms

Objectivity A value-free, impartial, unbiased view.

Subjectivity A personal view based on an individual's values and beliefs.

Standpoint theory The view that a researcher's position in society, their background and experience, can provide valuable insights.

Summary

1. Most, if not all, sociologists now recognise that complete objectivity is not possible. However, many see objectivity as an important aim for sociological research.

2. Reflexivity is increasingly seen as an important part of the research process.

3. Standpoint theory argues that a researcher's background and position in society can be used rather than guarded against when conducting research.

Unit 1.5.4 Postmodernist methodology

Many postmodernists directly challenge the entire basis of research methodology in sociology. They reject the whole idea of collecting data to support or reject hypotheses or theories. They question the possibility of making any definite statements about social reality. They reject the idea that there is an objective reality 'out there' waiting to be discovered. They argue that the 'facts' and 'knowledge' that fill sociological research reports and textbooks are nothing of the sort, but are simply sociologists' constructions of reality rather than a valid description and analysis of the social world 'out there'.

A postmodernist view of reality

The following discussion of postmodernist methodology is partly based on Mats Alvesson's excellent book *Postmodernism and Social Research* (2002).

From a postmodernist perspective, any description, analysis, view or picture of the social world is simply one view among many. This applies to sociologists as much as anybody else.

Nothing is certain – everything is tentative, doubtful, indeterminate. Take yourself. In one sense you are one person, in another sense you are lots of people. In one sense you have one identity, in another sense you are made up of multiple identities. In various situations you adopt different identities, see things in different ways, operate with different meanings. What you see or say in one situation may contradict what you see or say in another situation.

This applies both to the sociologist and to the research participants. Nothing is fixed, everything is fluid; nothing is whole, everything is fragmented; there is no single reality, only multiple realities.

Objectivity and research

Most sociologists aim to be objective, to present the social world of those they are studying as it really is, to give us the 'facts'. Many sociologists accept that complete objectivity is an ideal that is unattainable. However, they do their best to get there; and they believe their research reports are a lot better than the view of the person in the street.

From a postmodernist view, objectivity is a myth. Research findings are constructions that are designed to persuade, to give the impression of rational, analytical thinking, and to convince the reader that the researcher's view is 'the truth'. Often, the persuasion works. Sociologists are a bit like conjurers. They deceive, they play tricks, they create illusions. For example, they skilfully present an illusion of objectivity where none exists.

This view is an extreme version of relativism, the idea that all knowledge is relative to time, place, culture and the individual. There is no such thing as objective knowledge because everything is seen through the lens of our values and experience, the time we live in, and our culture.

Sociological categories

Think of the following terms – 'culture', 'subculture', 'norm', 'value', 'social class', 'ethnicity', 'social structure', 'social status', 'social role'. These are all categories used by sociologists to order, organise and make sense of the social world. According to postmodernists, the social world is forced into these categories, wedged into these pigeonholes. In this respect, the social world becomes a construction built by sociologists. In this way, researchers impose their own order and framework on the social world.

From a postmodernist viewpoint, the social world is ambiguous rather than clear-cut, fluid rather than fixed, open rather than closed. It cannot be rammed into fixed, predetermined categories.

Is there any alternative to researchers imposing their reality on the social world? Do they have to make sense of human action by using pre-set categories?

Categories as problematic A starting point is to see all categories as problematic, to be aware that they create order where none may exist, that they impose a particular view of reality, that they structure the social world in a particular way.

Defamiliarisation This offers the possibility of getting away from a sociological construction of the social world. **Defamiliarisation** means looking at the familiar in new and novel ways. Instead of assuming that human action is natural, rational, patterned, ordered, the observer should try to see it from other viewpoints — as exotic, random, irrational, contradictory, arbitrary, crazy. For example, look back on your schooldays and family life and try to look at them in a fresh and novel way — for instance, look at them as if you were an alien from another planet or somebody from the distant past or future.

Multiple interpretations

From a postmodernist viewpoint, there are multiple, if not infinite, interpretations of the social world. Who is to say which is 'right' or the 'best'? Where does this take us? Some would say nowhere — what's the point of doing research if it's no better or worse than any other view — for example, no better or worse than the view of the journalist, novelist, comedian, child or grandparent?

For some, there is a halfway house. Sociologists should be more humble. They should accept the idea of **multiple interpretations**. They should look at the social world from different vantage points, in terms of different perspectives. Also, they should allow other voices to be heard in their research publications, particularly the voices of those they are researching.

Evaluation of postmodernist methodology

Much of what postmodernism has to say about sociological methodology is negative. Taken to its extreme, it suggests that sociological research is a waste of time. Worse, research findings can be seen as an illusion that distorts the social world and deceives the audience.

However, have postmodernists got it right? Using their arguments, there's no way of judging whether they're right or wrong. The voice of postmodernism is simply one voice among many — neither better nor worse.

Despite this criticism, postmodernism has made sociologists more aware of the problems and pitfalls of research. It has made many researchers more sensitive, more questioning and more humble. Mats Alvesson (2002) presents the following evaluation. Postmodernism 'offers a challenge and an inspiration to revise and make qualitative research more sophisticated and creative. This is not bad, and a strong reason for taking it seriously. But not too seriously.'

Activity – Defamiliarisation

Body ritual among the Nacirema

The Nacirema spend a large part of the day in ritual activity. The main concern of this activity is the human body. The basic belief underlying their rituals is that the human body is ugly and prone to ill-health and disease.

Every household has a shrine where the body rituals take place. Within the shrine is a box that contains potions and charms with magical powers. Beneath the charm box is a font which contains purifying water. The Nacirema perform their daily mouth ceremonies in the font. Without rituals of the mouth they believe that their teeth would rot, their gums would become diseased and their breath would smell. If this happened, their friends would be repelled and their lovers would desert them.

The Nacirema's fear of tooth, gum and mouth disease leads them to see the holy-mouth-man twice a year. He performs a painful ceremony bordering on ritual torture. His clients have great faith in his powers. Despite continuing mouth problems they return to his holy shrine year after year.

Source: based on Miner, 1956.

Questions

The above is an adapted extract from an article by Horace Miner, an American anthropologist. Nacirema is American spelt backwards.

1. How is this description an example of defamiliarisation?

2. Do you find it useful? Explain your answer?

3. Write a brief defamiliarised description of an aspect of everyday behaviour.

Key terms

Defamiliarisation Looking at the familiar in new and novel ways.

Multiple interpretations Seeing the social world from different vantage points and in terms of different perspectives.

Summary

1. From a postmodernist perspective, any description or analysis of the social world is simply one view among many.

2. As a result, it is not possible to make any definite statements about social reality. Sociological research is not, and cannot be, objective.

3. Researchers impose their own order and framework on the social world by using pre-set categories.

4. Researchers should regard all categories as problematic, and they should defamiliarise themselves from the social world in order to open their eyes to a variety of interpretations.

5. Using their own arguments, there is no way of judging whether postmodernists are right or wrong.

6. Postmodernism has made sociologists more aware of the problems and pitfalls of research; and it has encouraged them to be more creative and innovative.

Unit 1.5.5 Feminist methodology

Feminist methodology starts from an awareness that sociology is gendered, a belief that women are oppressed, and a view that sociology and sociological methodology reflect male dominance. Given this, the job of a **feminist sociologist** is to reveal the extent of gender inequality and conduct research that seeks to end this inequality.

A rejection of 'malestream' sociology

Mainstream sociological research was traditionally, and to some extent still is, male dominated. Pamela Abbott, Claire Wallace and Melissa Taylor (2005) give the following examples of so-called 'malestream sociology'.

1. Sociology has been largely concerned with research on men conducted by men.

2. Research findings were mainly based on all-male samples and generalised to the whole population.

3. Issues of concern to women were frequently ignored and seen as insignificant.

4. When included in research, women were presented in a stereotypical way and tended to be simply an 'add-on' to the males who were seen as more important.

Examples of the above include the study of crime and deviance which, until the late 1970s, was almost exclusively based on males, the view of social class which was based on the male 'head of household' and the bewilderment of male colleagues that Ann Oakley should choose something as 'insignificant' as housework for her *Sociology of Housework* (1974). Although things have changed, Oakley (2014) still sees the abolition of 'malestream sociology' as unfinished business.

Feminist research methodology

Feminists have also attacked what they regard as masculine research methodology. This can be seen from Ann Oakley's (1981) ground-breaking article entitled *Interviewing Women: A Contradiction in Terms*.

Oakley argues that the standard approach to interviewing has the following characteristics. '(a) its status as a mechanical instrument of data-collection; (b) its function as a specialised form of conversation in which one person asks the questions and another gives the answers; (c) its characterisation of interviewees as essentially passive individuals and (d) its reduction of interviewers to a question asking and rapport-promoting role'.

Oakley sees this approach as clinical, manipulative, exploitative and hierarchical. The interviewer 'uses' the respondent for 'his' purposes, controlling the content and direction of the interview. The relationship is unequal – the interviewer takes and the respondent gives. A feminist methodology would replace this by a non-hierarchical relationship, with the researcher giving as well as receiving. For example, an interviewer must 'be prepared to invest his or her personal identity in the relationship' which means honesty, sincerity, understanding and compassion between equals. It means that both parties have a say in the

51

content and direction of the interview. Only with this personal involvement will 'people come to know each other and admit others into their lives'.

This example argues for a change in research methods – a new type of interviewing. It claims that research techniques are so imbued with male assumptions and practices that they must be radically changed. These changes are not only morally correct, they will also result in better data.

One reaction to Oakley's views is summed up by Ray Pawson's (1992) query, 'What's new?' There is a long tradition of interviewing which emphasises sensitivity and non-directive approaches. He questions whether Oakley's views are significantly different from this.

Feminist politics and methodology

Some feminists argue that the 'women's struggle' and feminist methodology are inseparable. 'Malestream' sociology is so saturated with assumptions of male dominance that a feminist alternative is required. Maria Mies (1993) provides an example of this approach. She argues that a feminist methodology must have the following features.

1. **Conscious partiality** The idea of so-called value-free research has to be replaced by conscious partiality, which in practice means that female researchers must positively identify with the women they study.

2. **View from below** This replaces the 'view from above', with its assumptions of male dominance, which supports the existing power structure. Researchers must take the 'view from below' because it is more likely to reflect women's experiences and more likely to empower women in their struggle for liberation.

3. **Action research** Rather than being a detached spectator, a dispassionate observer, the researcher should actively participate in the struggle for women's liberation.

4. **Changing the status quo** From this involvement in their own emancipation, both researchers and the women they study will develop a better understanding of their situation. This is based on the idea, 'If you want to know a thing, you must change it.' Only by challenging and changing patriarchy will its true nature be revealed.

5. **Raising consciousness** Both researchers and the researched must raise their consciousness – become aware of their oppression. In particular, it is the job of the researcher to give women the means to gain insight into and change their situation.

6. **Individual and social history** Part of the process of raising consciousness requires a study of women's individual and social history. This will allow women to reclaim their history from its appropriation by men.

7. **Collectivising experience** Women must collectivise their experience and join together and cooperate in their struggle for liberation. They must overcome the individualism, competitiveness and careerism which characterise the male world.

In terms of these propositions, Maria Mies is claiming that valid knowledge can only emerge from the struggles waged by the oppressed against their oppressors. The journey to truth involves just the opposite of value freedom. In Mies' case it requires a wholehearted commitment to women's liberation.

The primacy of experience

A number of feminists have argued that the only way to know something is to experience it. Given this, it is crucial for feminist research to capture the experience of women and to express it as directly as possible with a minimum of reinterpretation on the part of the researcher.

Too often researchers see the experience of others in terms of their own values and preconceptions. In particular, they force this experience into theoretical frameworks and categories that only serve to distort it. This argument was put forcibly by Kaluzynska (1980) when she rejected the whole Marxist debate about domestic labour – whether it was 'productive' or 'non-productive', whether it created 'surplus value', whether it was 'alienating' and so on. She objects to the imposition of such concepts which, she argues, distort the experience of housework. In her words, 'Why did we have to get to grips with value theory to appreciate what a drag housework was?'

Standpoint theory

As noted earlier, standpoint theory emphasises the shared experience of the female researcher and the female research participant. From their standpoint as women, female researchers have a special vantage point which gives them an insider's view. Sharing the experience of being a woman with the women they observe provides them with valuable insights, relevant questions and common concerns, all of which may well produce more valid data. In this respect, allowing their background and experience to influence their research is often seen as an asset by feminist researchers.

Postmodern feminism

Feminism is not a single perspective. In its early days, things were fairly simple. Women were the oppressed, men were the oppressors, the target was patriarchy, the aim to liberate women. There was a tendency to see women as a single, undifferentiated category. Groups of women objected to this approach – for example, Black women and lesbian women. Okay, they were women, but, they argued, their experiences and social situation distinguished them from women in general. As a result, many of the generalisations about women did not apply, or only partly applied, to them.

Postmodern feminism takes this argument a step further. It rejects the view of women as a homogeneous, undifferentiated category. It even rejects categories which subdivide the category 'women', such as Black women, lesbian women and working-class women. Instead, postmodern feminists emphasise diversity and variation. They argue that researchers should be open to this diversity rather than approaching it with pre-set, preconceived categories.

Evaluation

This approach has been criticised by a number of feminists. Breaking down or rejecting the category 'women' prevents the possibility of making generalisations which apply to most or all women. It also blunts the force of feminist protest and threatens the unity of women as a group. Emphasising variation and uniqueness may lead to 'divide and conquer', so serving male dominance (Alvesson, 2002).

Activity

Four women, four different religions.

How can this picture be used to support postmodern feminism?

The research process

Postmodern feminists favour interpretivist research methods such as participant observation. They are particularly aware that the results of research are a social construct – they are largely constructed by the researcher from field notes which document their observations. This awareness leads them to revisit, reopen and reinterpret their field notes. As Sara Delamont (2003) states, 'fieldnotes are not a closed, completed, final text: rather, they are indeterminate, subject to reading, rereading, coding, recording, interpreting, reinterpreting'. This is in line with the postmodernist view that there are multiple interpretations of any observation.

Postmodernists argue that researchers should allow the voices of those they research to be heard. In Sara Delamont's (2003) words, this means 'the text will reproduce the actors' own perspectives and experiences. This may include extended biographical and autobiographical accounts, extended dialogues between the researcher and informants, and other "documents of life".'

Conclusion

Sociology used to be a male subject, run by men and concerned with men. Women were largely absent from sociology departments and in a minority among research participants. When sociologists studied workers, they usually studied male workers. When they studied social mobility, it was men who went up and down the class system – women didn't even make it into the supposedly representative sample. In addition, women's concerns and issues were unlikely to be heard and researched. Today, women are no longer invisible. Feminists are steadily bringing them into mainstream sociology.

Feminists have been in the forefront of recent developments in methodology. Many have argued that sociology is not, should not and cannot be value-free. They have emphasised the importance of capturing the experience of research participants and of expressing that experience directly. They have argued that emotion has an important part to play in the research process, and they have opened up, questioned, and presented alternatives to, established research methodology.

Key terms

Feminist sociology A viewpoint which states that society is gendered, that women are oppressed and that sociology mirrors male dominance in the wider society.

Feminist methodology A methodology designed to reflect feminist ideals and values.

Summary

1. Ann Oakley states that interviews should be based on equality, honesty and sincerity.

2. Some feminists argue that feminist politics and feminist methodology are inseparable and that true knowledge can only emerge from the struggle between the oppressed and their oppressors.

3. Standpoint theory states that female researchers have a special vantage point which gives them an insider's view.

4. Postmodern feminists argue that there is no universal essence of womanhood. Women differ widely. No single theory can explain this diversity.

5. Feminists are bringing women into mainstream sociology.

Unit 1.5.6 Sociology and science

For many years sociologists have been debating whether sociology is a science, could be a science or should be a science. Answers to these questions depend on a number of factors – how science and scientific methodology are defined and how human beings and society are seen. This unit looks at the sociology and science debate.

Positivism and natural science methodology

As outlined in Unit 1.5.1, p. 39, the early positivists saw sociology as a 'positive science of society'. As such, they argued that natural science methodology was appropriate for the study of human behaviour. Its use would reveal the 'invariable laws' that governed society. Data consist of observable facts that could be directly measured and quantified. The research process would be objective – free from the values of the researcher.

Positivism aims to discover cause and effect relationships that are seen to underlie human behaviour. Statistical techniques are applied to numerical data in order to identify and measure possible cause and effect relationships. A hypothesis or prediction is developed. A hypothesis translates the theory into a form that can be tested. Observation and measurement are then used to accept or reject the hypothesis. This, in turn, can result in a confirmation, modification or rejection of the theory.

This process is known as a **deductive approach**. It is sometimes known as a 'top down' approach as it starts at the top from a theory and moves downwards as shown in Figure 1.5.1.

Today, few quantitative researchers would call themselves positivists. This is partly because the term 'positivist' is sometimes used in a negative way, partly because quantitative sociologists do not look for 'laws' underlying human behaviour as few, if any, now believe that such laws exist. Nor do they necessarily start their research with a hypothesis. They do, however, attempt to make generalisations from quantitative data based on representative samples.

Figure 1.5.1 A deductive approach

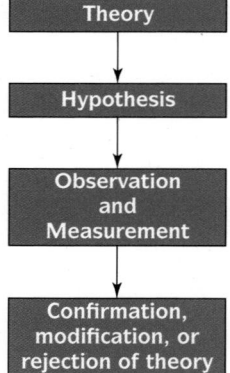

Karl Popper and falsification

Like positivists, the philosopher of science Karl Popper (1902–1994) used a deductive approach though in a rather different way. He started with a theory and used data to test that theory. However, instead of looking to confirm theories, Popper argued that scientists should look for evidence to disprove or **falsify** theories. This means that theories must be constructed in such a way that falsification is possible, that theories can be shown to be untrue.

Theories that survive falsification tests, however, are not necessarily true. They have simply not been falsified. The following oft-quoted example illustrates this point. 'All swans are white' is a scientific statement because it can be falsified. But, however many times it is confirmed by observation, it cannot be accepted as true because the very next swan might be black, red, blue or yellow. In this respect, there are no absolute truths in science.

Popper sees no reason why the methodology of the natural sciences cannot be applied to the social sciences. Theories of human behaviour which are open to the possibility of falsification can be developed.

However, not all sociological theories are open to falsification. For example, Popper argues that Marx's theory of history cannot be falsified and is therefore non-scientific. In particular, it fails to specify precisely what has to happen before the proletarian revolution occurs in capitalist society. So when the revolution does not happen, Marxists simply push its coming further and further into the future, thus preventing the possibility of falsification.

Grounded theory and induction

Grounded theory, as its name suggests, starts from 'concrete data' 'on the ground'. It then builds upwards to theory. This is known as an **inductive approach**. As shown in Figure 1.5.2, it moves in a 'bottom up' direction as opposed to the 'top down' direction of the deductive approach. Starting with data, an inductive approach moves on to an analysis of the data looking for connections, patterns and relationships. From this, it develops a theory to explain these relationships.

Figure 1.5.2 An inductive approach

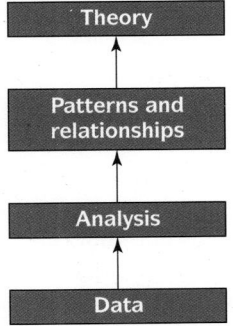

Inductive grounded theory does not start with a hypothesis to test. It tends to start with a largely blank sheet without preconceptions. In *The Rules of Sociological Method*, first published in 1895, Émile Durkheim argued that sociological research should be based on an inductive approach. He stated that researchers should start with recognition of their 'complete ignorance' and that 'all preconceptions have to be eradicated'.

Today, participant observation and in-depth qualitative interviews are the main methods used in grounded theory. Participant observers often begin their research by looking and listening with no fixed ideas about what they might find and no hypotheses to test. Their observations lead to the discovery of patterns and relationships from which theories are developed. This was the starting point for Sudhir Venkatesh's (2009) participant observation study of the Black Kings, an African-American gang in Chicago. In his words, 'I had little exposure to African-American culture at all, and no experience whatsoever in an urban ghetto.' 'Just another day as an outsider looking at life from the inside.'

In practice, many researchers combine inductive and deductive approaches. For example, Durkheim began his research on suicide with an inductive approach. He examined official statistics on suicide from 11 European countries. He found patterns in the statistics from which he moved towards theories that may explain them. He then tested these theories by using a deductive approach (Swedberg, 2011).

Thomas Kuhn – normal science

For Durkheim, science consists of accumulating evidence and developing theories from that evidence. For Popper, science consists of creating testable theories and attempting to falsify them. For Thomas Kuhn, **normal science** – the vast majority of work that is called science – differs from both these views. Kuhn's *The Structure of Scientific Revolutions* (1962) argues that the way science has developed bears little relationship to conventional views of the scientific method.

Paradigms

According to Kuhn, most of the time scientists are busily preoccupied with 'normal science'. Normal science operates within a **paradigm**. A paradigm is a framework of concepts and theories which states how the natural world operates. It identifies appropriate methods for studying that world and specifies what questions to ask and how to answer them. A paradigm is shared by members of the scientific community. It shapes the way they see the world they study.

Normal science operates within the confines of a paradigm – developing and refining it but not challenging it. For example, until the 16th century Western astronomy was based on the theory of terracentricity – the idea that planets and the sun move around the earth. It is perfectly possible to confirm this idea with observations and measurements; and it is also possible to ignore or explain away contradictory evidence that might challenge it. So committed are scientists to the existing paradigm that they operate within it rather than attempting to falsify it.

Scientific revolutions

Kuhn rejects the conventional view that sees science as a progressive accumulation of knowledge based on the testing and proving and disproving of hypotheses. Change does occur, but only when one paradigm is replaced by another. Kuhn calls this process a **scientific revolution** – it is sudden and revolutionary as a whole way of thinking about the world is swept away within a relatively short period of time. An example is the replacement of Newton's paradigm in physics with Einstein's. Once a new paradigm is established, normal science resumes and any real change has to wait until the next scientific revolution.

Scientific revolutions occur when evidence accumulates that cannot be explained in terms of the existing paradigm. This evidence accumulates to the point where it cannot be ignored, dismissed as an anomaly or as the result of incorrect observation and measurement.

Sociology and paradigms

In terms of Kuhn's view of science, it has been argued that sociology is in a pre-paradigmatic and therefore pre-scientific situation. There is a range of competing sociological perspectives and there is little indication that this variety will develop into a single paradigm which will be acceptable to the sociological community.

However, Kuhn's view of paradigms and scientific revolutions has been criticised as a distortion of the history of science. For example, Imre Lakatos (1970) rejects the view that normal science is dominated by a single paradigm. Instead, he sees the development of science as a history of constantly competing paradigms. In terms of Lakatos' view, this does not disqualify sociology from being a science. In fact,

sociology's history of competing perspectives largely accords with his view of the history of science.

The realist approach to science

The **realist** view of science, while accepting that there are basic differences between the social and natural worlds, maintains that a social science is possible. It argues that events in both the social and natural worlds are produced by underlying structures and mechanisms. According to Roy Bhaskar, the essential task of realism is to uncover and explain these structures and mechanisms (Bhaskar, 1978).

Open and closed systems

Andrew Sayer (1992) distinguishes between open and closed systems as arenas of study. The laboratory is the prime example of a **closed system**. Sciences like physics and chemistry have the advantage of being able to create closed systems in which conditions can be fixed and variables controlled. This allows them to reveal 'more clearly the operation of mechanisms' (Sayer, 1992).

However, a large body of scientific research takes place within **open systems** where it is not possible to control variables. Meteorology is an example of a natural science where closed systems are rare. As a result, it is unable to predict the weather with any degree of accuracy, as weather forecasts indicate. However, it is able to offer an explanation of the weather after the event in terms of underlying mechanisms. In much the same way, geology is able to provide explanations for the occurrence of oil deposits. However, geologists' attempts to predict its presence have only limited success as the billions of dollars spent on unsuccessful oil exploration show.

One of the most famous non-predictive explanations is the theory of evolution, which specifies mechanisms such as natural selection and mutation, which are seen to underlie the evolutionary process. However, because evolution takes place within an open system it is not possible to predict its future.

Human behaviour takes place in open systems. Because of this, it is not possible to predict its course with any degree of accuracy. There is no way of controlling all the variables that affect human action. However, from a realist viewpoint, this does not rule out a social science. It is still possible to explain human behaviour in terms of underlying structures and mechanisms, just as meteorologists, geologists and evolutionary biologists explain behaviour in the natural world.

Realism, sociology and science

From a realist viewpoint, events in both the natural and social worlds are produced by structures and mechanisms. Given this, social science is based on the same principles as natural science. Both are concerned with the identification and explanation of structures and mechanisms. In this respect, the social scientist's job is the same as the natural scientists'. So just as an evolutionary biologist identifies mechanisms such as natural selection to account for biological change, so a sociologist identifies mechanisms such as the class struggle to account for social change.

Interpretivism and natural science methodology

Interpretivism starts from the view that the subject matter of the natural and social sciences is fundamentally different. The natural scientist investigates the behaviour of matter. Matter reacts in predictable ways to extrinsic stimuli. Human beings act rather than react. Their actions are directed by meaning. Any understanding of human action must therefore involve an understanding of those meanings. For many researchers, this means employing methodologies that are very different from those used in the natural sciences.

The job of the sociologist is to discover meanings. This involves observation and interpretation. Qualitative methods, in particular participant observation and in-depth interviews, are seen as the main ways of discovering meanings. The research process is viewed as an art rather than a science.

Interpretivists accept that objectivity is not possible. The discovery of meanings cannot be value-free. It is inevitably affected by the researcher who becomes personally involved and immersed in their research.

Two research methodologies offer a particularly extreme rejection of natural science methodology. Many postmodernists argue that there is no objective reality beyond the meanings in terms of which human beings view the world (see pp. 49–50). And standpoint theorists state that the researcher's values can be a necessary part of the research process (see p. 48 and p. 52).

There are many views of science and scientific methods. As a result, there are many views about the relationship between sociology and science, and about the appropriateness of applying the assumptions and methods of the natural sciences to the study of human behaviour.

Key terms

Deductive approach Starting with a theory and using evidence to test that theory.

Falsification Looking for evidence to disprove a theory.

Grounded theory Starting from the systematic collection of 'concrete data' and building upwards to theory.

Inductive approach Starting with evidence and developing a theory from that evidence.

Normal science Science that operates within an established paradigm.

Paradigm A framework of concepts and theories that states how the natural world operates.

Scientific revolution The overthrow of an established paradigm by a new paradigm.

Realist approach Assumes that events in both the natural and social worlds are produced by underlying structures and mechanisms.

Closed system A system in which all the variables can be controlled.

Open system A system in which it is not possible to control all the variables.

Summary

1. The early positivists assumed that natural science methodology was appropriate to the study of human society. As such, sociology was seen as a 'positive science of society'.

2. According to Popper, natural science methodology can be applied to explain human behaviour. However, he argued that not all sociological theories are 'scientific' because they cannot be falsified.

3. According to Kuhn, 'normal science' operates within a paradigm. A scientific revolution occurs when the existing paradigm is overthrown by a new paradigm.

4. Sociology has a range of competing perspectives rather than a single paradigm. In terms of Kuhn's view of science, it is in a pre-paradigmatic and, therefore, pre-scientific situation.

5. From a realist viewpoint, events in both the social and natural worlds are produced by underlying structures and mechanisms. In view of this, there is no reason why sociology cannot be a science.

57

6. Human society is an open system. So is the world that sciences such as meteorology and geology study. In this respect, there is no reason why sociology cannot be a science.

7. In view of the differences between the natural world and the social world, between inanimate objects and human beings, interpretivists argue that natural science methodology is inappropriate for the study of human society.

PART 6 SOCIOLOGY AND SOCIAL POLICY

Social policy refers to government policy on a range of social issues. Social issues include education, health, housing, families and employment. They also include social problems – for example, poverty, homelessness and unemployment. This part examines the relationship between sociology and social policy. In particular, it looks at the influence of sociology on social policy.

It is difficult to assess sociology's effect on social policy. Government policy is influenced by a range of factors from the state of the economy to the personal experiences of particular ministers. Governments are faced with a variety of interest groups from the Confederation of British Industry to Families Need Fathers, Oxfam and Crisis. Governments are influenced by current ideologies such as social democratic perspectives and neoliberalism. Their social policy is partly shaped by the politics of the particular political party in power. It is also shaped by the concerns of the day such as child abuse, migration and modern slavery.

As a result of the many influences on social policy, it is difficult to isolate the influence of sociology.

Social problems, sociological problems and social policy

Social problems Peter Worsley (1977) makes a distinction between **social problems** and **sociological problems**. He defines a social problem as 'social behaviour that causes public friction and/or private misery and calls for collective action to solve it'. Examples include poverty, unemployment, hate crime and racism. They cause public friction as indicated by demonstrations against austerity and against the physical and verbal abuse of ethnic minorities, they produce private misery and they require collective rather than individual action to provide solutions – for example, government legislation based on appropriate social policy.

Sociological problems By comparison, Worsley defines sociological problems as 'any pattern of relationships that calls for explanation'. Sociological problems include social problems – for example, the inequality of educational opportunity discussed in Book 1. However, they also include a variety of topics such as family life, religious behaviour and the mass media, which do not necessarily involve social problems.

Social policy After World War II (1939–1945), social policy became an academic subject offered by most universities. This followed the establishment of the welfare state, which was created to deal with the five 'giant' social ills – poverty, ill-health, poor housing, inadequate education and unemployment. Social policy is a multidisciplinary subject often taught within sociology departments by sociologists. Sociologists have studied the range of social problems dealt with by social policy. In view of this, it has been argued that sociologists should be among the main advisors for government social policy, should be present on appropriate government working parties and be involved in government research projects.

Sociologists and social policy

Many of the early sociologists believed that sociology had a central part to play in society – in reforming social institutions, solving social problems and improving the human condition.

Auguste Comte (1798–1857) Comte saw sociology as a practical subject. He believed that it shouldn't remain in the universities, but should be applied to the wider society. Comte believed in order and progress – he saw sociology providing the ideas to reinforce social order and direct social progress. In his words, the purpose of sociology is 'to know, in order to predict, in order to control'.

Émile Durkheim (1858–1917) Like Comte, Durkheim focused on the question of order in society. He was concerned with political upheaval and civil unrest, which he believed resulted from industrialisation and a weakening of value consensus. He saw sociology as providing ways or restoring order and strengthening the integration of society. Durkheim believed that sociology pointed to a need for a new moral order in industrial society, whereby people would be bound together by a sense of duty and obligation to the community as a whole.

Karl Marx (1818–1883) Where Durkheim saw sociologists working with governments to improve existing societies, Marx looked forward to the overthrow of governments and the replacement of capitalist societies with communist societies. Marx hoped that his work would inspire and direct working-class movements to overthrow capitalism. Judging by his statue in Moscow, his ideas inspired the Russian revolution of 1917 and the establishment of a communist state.

David Harvey Today, the Marxist geographer/ sociologist David Harvey (2011, 2014) also looks forward to the downfall of capitalism. In his words, 'we need revolutionary politics to replace capitalism with a just and fair society'. Harvey supports and advises the Occupy Movement in the USA and similar anti-capitalist, pro-equality movements across the world (see p. 11 for information on the Occupy Movement). To achieve his aim of a just and fair society, Harvey argues that it's no good trying to reform the policies of existing governments. They are too involved with and committed to the capitalist system. What's needed is a mass movement outside the existing political process.

Harvey (2011) states that, 'The movement must above all reach out to all the alienated, the dissatisfied and the discontented, all those who … feel in their gut that there is something profoundly wrong.'

Activity

A statue of Karl Marx in Moscow.

Do you think David Harvey will ever have his statue in New York, London and other cities? Give reasons for your answer.

Peter Townsend (1928–2009) In recent years, sociologists have tended to look to reform rather than revolution – to improve government policy rather than replace governments. This is not to diminish their work. The British sociologist Peter Townsend spent over 60 years making a magnificent contribution to ending poverty and social inequality. In his words, 'social justice is an unending struggle'. His *Poverty in the United Kingdom* (1979) based on 10 years' research brought poverty to the forefront of social policy. He co-founded the Disability Alliance and the Child Poverty Action Group. From 1955 to 1989, he sat on Labour Party subcommittees and working parties. Throughout his career Peter Townsend persuaded, cajoled, encouraged and worked with governments to end poverty and social inequality.

Shaping social policy

David Donnison, one of the UK's leading experts on poverty, makes the following points about how social policy is shaped.

> *As in all debates about important issues of social policy, the questions posed and the concepts used in debates about poverty are shaped partly by changing circumstances and growing knowledge, but also by the changing political agendas of the societies concerned.*   Donnison, 2001

Changing circumstances Societies change. To some extent social policy is shaped by changes in society. This is illustrated by the following example.

The aftermath of a war often brings changes. People have made great sacrifices, their lives have been disrupted and they are often not prepared to accept their old status – they want something better. This can be seen in the expansion of social services after World War I (1914–1918) when the then Prime Minister, Lloyd George, promised the troops 'homes fit for heroes'.

During World War II (1939–1945), a committee chaired by Sir William Beveridge produced the famous *Beveridge Report on Social Insurance and Allied Services*. Published in 1942, it became an immediate bestseller. Popular support for its principles was widespread both at home and among the troops abroad. Its recommendations appeared to embody the very things being fought for – democracy, freedom and equality.

The Beveridge Report's recommendations were put into effect by a series of Acts from 1944 to 1948. Together, they created the modern welfare state in the UK.

Changing economic circumstances can have a major effect on social policy. The Coalition government of 2010 and the Conservative government of 2015 responded to the results of the financial crisis of 2007/08 with a policy of **austerity** that involved deep cuts in government spending. This brought to an end the reduction in levels of child poverty (Jones, 2016).

Growing knowledge Social policy is also shaped by a growth in knowledge. The following evidence illustrates this point.

During the 19th century, the dominant view of poverty saw it resulting from some form of character defect — the poor lacked moral fibre, they were work-shy, lazy and idle. In other words, the poor were to blame for their poverty.

In 1899, Seebohm Rowntree conducted a systematic study of poverty in York. In terms of his definition of poverty — insufficient food, fuel and clothing to maintain good health — 28 per cent of York's population were poor. In many cases, there was no evidence of individual blame. In some instances, the breadwinner's wages were simply too low to keep the family out of poverty, and in other instances, people were too old or sick to work.

Research such as this influenced governments. For example, Liberal governments in the early 1900s were increasingly likely to see poverty as a social rather than an individual problem, and as a problem for which the state should accept some responsibility. This view is reflected in their social policies. For example, the 1908 Old-Age Pensions Act provided pensions for those over 70, and the 1911 National Insurance Act provided sickness benefit to all manual workers below a certain income level.

Changing political agendas This is the third major influence on social policy identified by Donnison. Sociologists can sometimes change political agendas with new concepts and new ideas. Rowntree's study of poverty in York, discussed earlier, was based on the idea of **absolute poverty**. People were defined as poor if they were unable to meet basic needs such as adequate food and shelter. In terms of this concept, it appeared that, by the 1960s, poverty was a small and dwindling problem. Then, two British sociologists, Brian Abel-Smith and Peter Townsend, developed a new concept — **relative poverty**.

Relative poverty was defined as the inability to afford an acceptable standard of living and a reasonable style of life. The concept of poverty was extended to include things that most people would see as reasonable — for example, an annual holiday and Christmas presents for the children. In terms of relative poverty, 7.5 million people, that is 14.2 per cent of the population, were now defined as poor — a massive jump from previous estimates (Abel-Smith and Townsend, 1965). Earlier studies had seen the elderly as the largest group in poverty. This now changed to the low paid with dependent children. This suggested a change in social policy — direct more resources to the low paid with young children. Since then, governments have seen poverty in relative terms and focused on child poverty.

Sociology and social policy

Labour governments, 1997–2010 The influence of sociology on social policy was probably greatest in the Labour governments led by Tony Blair (1997–2007) and Gordon Brown (2007–2010). When Labour came to power in 1997, they offered a '**Third Way**' in politics — new directions and new solutions to social problems.

Much of this was influenced by one of Britain's leading sociologists, Anthony Giddens, who has been described as Tony Blair's favourite guru. Giddens' *The Third Way: The Renewal of Social Democracy* was published in 1998. In *The Third Way*, Giddens stressed the importance of social solidarity. He saw **social exclusion** as the main threat to social solidarity. In the case of the poor, Giddens argued that social exclusion could be prevented by raising welfare benefits, improving public services — especially health and education — and providing opportunities to move out of poverty.

Giddens' Third Way is reflected in Labour's social policy. In their first year in government, Labour set up the Social Exclusion Unit to find solutions to the problem of exclusion. The Unit was directly responsible to the Cabinet and it attempted to ensure that all policies — health, education, poverty, crime, urban renewal — were part of a coordinated strategy to deal with social exclusion (MacGregor, 2001).

Living in poverty means exclusion from many of the activities that most people take for granted. The largest group in poverty are low-paid workers and their dependent children. Labour's policy to reduce poverty focused on this group. It introduced the following:

» a minimum wage
» the Working Families Tax Credit to top up the wages of low-paid workers
» a significant increase in Child Benefit allowances
» the National Childcare Strategy, which provides money for the development of childcare centres
» the Sure Start programme, which provides health and support services for low-income families with children under four
» the Child Poverty Unit set up to eliminate child poverty and jointly run by the Department for Work and Pensions, the Department for Education and the Treasury (Donnison, 2001; Page, 2001).

In 1997, around 4 million or nearly 30 per cent of all children in the UK were in relative poverty. By 2010, this figure was reduced to 20 per cent, some 2.6 million children (Sutherland *et al.*, 2003; BBC News online, 12.05.2011). This reduction was largely due to Labour governments' spending on benefits and tax credits (Institute of Fiscal Studies, 06.06.2013).

The Coalition and Conservative governments
Judging from the social policies of the largely Conservative Coalition government (2010–2015) and the Conservative government from 2015 onwards, priorities have changed. Austerity was the response to the economic downturn following the financial crash of 2007/08. Cutbacks in government spending and pay freezes for government employees ended the trend towards decreasing poverty. In 2015/16, some 4 million children were in poverty, nearly 30 per cent of all children. On the basis of these figures, it appears that the Conservatives were taking little notice or were not aware of the recommendations of sociologists such as Anthony Giddens.

Abolition of the Child Poverty Unit

In 2016, the Conservative government abolished the Child Poverty Unit set up by Tony Blair in 1999. Many MPs and charities feared that the focus on child poverty had been abandoned by Theresa May. Jointly run by three government departments, the Unit's work was transferred to the Department for Work and Pensions. According to Alison Garnham, head of the Child Poverty Action Group, 'A move to restrict the unit to just one department would be worrying and could potentially downgrade the unit's status and weaken its reach, influence and effectiveness right across government' (quoted in *The Guardian*, 20.12.2016). In addition, 'Sure Start centres have closed, homelessness is rising, inequality is widening and now the unit tasked with drawing up a strategy has gone' (Yvette Cooper, quoted in *The Guardian*, 21.12.2016).

Activity – Social policy and sociology

Anthony Giddens (left) and Tony Blair.

Quotes from Tony Blair:

» 'Our historic aim will be for ours to be the first generation to end child poverty, and it will take a generation.'
» 'The sight of a rough-sleeper bedding down for the night in a shop doorway or on a park bench is one of the most potent symbols of social exclusion in Britain today.'

How do the quotes from Tony Blair suggest that his social policy was influenced by the sociologist Anthony Giddens?

Contemporary issues: The Trussell Trust

A Trussell Trust foodbank.

The Trussell Trust is the largest foodbank provider in the UK. In the year ending 31 March 2017, it provided nearly 2 million three-day emergency food supplies to 'people in crisis' with nearly 444 000 going to children, numbers that have grown rapidly since 2010 (Trussell Trust, 25.04.2017). A study commissioned by the Trussell Trust looked at over 400 households using its foodbanks. Lone parents with children made up the largest number of users. All users faced extreme financial insecurity. Over 78 per cent of households were 'severely food insecure, meaning that they had skipped meals, gone without eating, or even gone days without eating in the past 12 months. For a majority of households, this was a chronic experience, happening every month or almost every month over the past 12 months' (Loopstra and Lalor, 2017).

Question

What does the information in this activity suggest about the social policy priorities of the Conservatives and the influence of sociology on their policy?

Personal experience and hunches

As noted earlier, it is difficult to uncover exactly what influences governments' social policy and, in particular, to identify the possible influence of sociology. This section indicates that government ministers may actually be unaware of the existence of sociological research that is directly relevant to the decisions they make. In some instances, they may simply base their decisions on personal experience and/or hunches.

David Laws was a Liberal Democrat in the Coalition government. He served as Schools Minister under the Education Secretary, Michael Gove. In 2016, he became head of the Education Policy Institute, a think tank aimed at improving educational policy. Judging by his experience at the Department for Education, sociology appears to have had little influence on educational policy. He describes policy making as 'poor'. He states that, 'A lot of decision-making is not based on evidence but on hunch ... politicians are prone to make decisions based on ideology and personal experience ... All politicians have that weakness, but Michael [Gove] particularly so' (quoted in *The Guardian*, 01.08.2017).

The same might be true of Theresa May's wish to reintroduce grammar schools. Part of her education was spent in a grammar school. She gives no indication of having read the widespread sociological research on grammar schools, social mobility, and inequalities of educational opportunity (see Book 1, Chapter 2, Unit 2.2.5, pp. 58–65).

An evidence champion Former Education Secretary Michael Gove is famously quoted as saying, 'People have had enough of experts.' Justine Greening, who was replaced as Education Secretary in January 2018, does not appear to be one of those people. According to David Laws, 'Justine Greening seems a more pragmatic, nuts-and-bolts person who doesn't start with the presumption of where she should end up'. In 2017, she created the post of '**evidence champion**' and appointed Sir Kevan Collins to the position to ensure that changes to education policy were based on research evidence. In his words, 'Let's start with what we know rather than what we think we know' (BBC News online, 12.08.2017). Maybe now the considerable evidence of sociological research will help to guide educational policy decision making.

Conclusion

Sociology has at times influenced government policy. Today, sociologists often sit on government committees and working parties. They are sometimes employed to carry out research for government departments such as the Home Office and the Department for Education. However, sociologists tend to be asked to do particular projects and provide specific expertise rather than giving more general advice and direction for government policy.

Sociologist after sociologist has stated that reducing inequalities of educational opportunity cannot be left to schools and to the Department for Education. It can only come from a reduction of inequality in the wider society. With the present increase in child poverty, with the widening income gap between top and bottom and the almost complete lack of upward social mobility, it can be argued that social policy and government policy in general should be directly aimed at reducing social inequality. Here, the influence of sociology is crucial in order to inform and direct governments.

Key terms

Social policy Government policy on social issues such as poverty, education and health.

Social problems According to Worsley, 'social behaviour that causes public friction and/or private misery and calls for collective action to solve it'.

Sociological problems According to Worsley, 'any pattern of relationships that calls for explanation'.

Austerity A policy based on reducing government spending as a solution to economic and social problems.

Absolute poverty The inability to meet basic needs such as adequate food and shelter.

Relative poverty An inability to afford a reasonable standard of living according to the standards of the day.

The Third Way A new direction in Labour Party policy based in part on the ideas of the sociologist Anthony Giddens.

Social exclusion Exclusion from mainstream society.

Evidence champion A position in the Department for Education to ensure that policy decisions are based on evidence.

Summary

1. Many early sociologists believed that sociology had a part to play in changing society for the better.

2. According to David Donnison, social policy is shaped by a variety of factors. These include:

   > changing circumstances in society

   > a growth in knowledge

   > changing political agendas.

3. In view of the many factors affecting social policy, it is difficult to isolate the influence of sociology.

4. The influence of sociology varies from government to government.

5. It is most evident in Tony Blair's Labour government which was influenced by Anthony Giddens' views of the Third Way and the priority he gave to the problem of social exclusion.

6. Since 2010, the influence of sociology on social policy appears to have declined. Coalition and Conservative social policy has tended to focus on austerity as a solution to social problems.

7. David Laws suggests that Coalition and Conservative education policy since 2010 has been based in part on personal experience and hunches. This leaves little room for sociological research.

EXAM PRACTICE QUESTIONS

A-LEVEL PAPER 3
THEORY AND METHODS

| 0 5 | **(Example 1)** Outline and explain **two** advantages of using questionnaires in sociological research. **[10 marks]**

| 0 5 | **(Example 2)** Outline and explain **two** advantages of following ethical guidelines when conducting sociological research. **[10 marks]**

| 0 6 | **(Example 1)** Read **Item C** and answer the question that follows.

> **Item C**
>
> Many sociological theories have based their ideas on the assumption that society has a structure. This means that human behaviour and identity can be explained by examining the structure of society, which is sometimes known as a 'top down' approach. However, other perspectives have challenged this idea. They see the individual as having a more active role to play in shaping their own behaviour and identity. Human beings are not always shaped by the structure of society but through their interaction with other individuals. This is sometimes described as a 'bottom up' approach. The focus of studying society should be to analyse the actions and interactions of social actors.

Applying material from **Item C** and your knowledge, evaluate the usefulness of social action approaches in understanding society. **[20 marks]**

| 0 6 | **(Example 2)** Read **Item C** and answer the question that follows.

> **Item C**
>
> Classic social theory was concerned with the changes in society produced through industrialisation and urbanisation, particularly in the 19th century. Many assumed that western societies had entered an era of modernity which would continue indefinitely. However, by the late 20th century important changes were taking place in UK society in science, technology and many areas of social life including education, the media and family life. These have meant there have been significant changes to UK society. There has also been increasing globalisation as countries became more interdependent and national boundaries became less important. Because of these changes, some sociologists argue we are now in the era of postmodernity and therefore classic sociological theories are out of date.

Applying material from **Item C** and your knowledge, evaluate the usefulness of postmodern approaches in understanding society. **[20 marks]**

2 CRIME AND DEVIANCE

Chapter contents

Social life is beset by rules. These rules take many different forms. Some – social norms – are generally not written down anywhere, but nevertheless regulate virtually all aspects of social interaction, from appropriate forms of greeting to how to behave at funerals. Then there are the more formal rules associated with organisations and associations – school rules and the off-side rule in football or netball, say. Finally, there are the rules encoded in a society's laws: criminal law, which sets out rules designed to ensure that social order is maintained, and civil law, which sets out rules regulating the relationships between individuals and between the individual and the state.

In sociology, 'deviance' refers to behaviour that breaks social norms, while 'crime' refers to behaviour that breaks criminal laws. The two overlap, but are not the same. Only a fairly limited range of behaviours are regulated by the criminal law. Burping, picking your nose in public and swearing may all be socially disapproved, but they are not illegal, whereas stealing, assault and murder are. On the other hand, some acts that are technically criminal may be so widespread in society – driving over 70 mph on a motorway, say, or paying for certain services in cash to avoid VAT – that the label 'deviant' becomes problematic.

This chapter is mainly concerned with those deviant acts that are also criminal, and explores the light that can be thrown on this topic by viewing it from a sociological perspective. Sociology focuses on *social variations* in crime, offending, victimisation and so on: how these vary from one society (or one group) to another and how they change or remain the same over time. Among the questions we will be exploring are the following: Is the amount of crime in society rising, falling or staying the same? Can we know for sure? Why are only some of the things that are socially harmful criminalised? Is offending – and victimisation – distributed more or less evenly throughout society or is it more heavily concentrated among some groups than others? How can we explain social patterns in offending and victimisation? Does the criminal justice system treat everyone the same, irrespective of class, ethnicity or gender or is it biased? Does the mass media simply reflect crime or does it play a role in its causation?

PART 1 THE MEDIA AND CRIME

Contents

Our perception of crime in the wider society – who commits it, how much there is, who the victims are, what happens to offenders and so on – is heavily dependent on the mass media (TV, radio, film, newspapers, magazines, the internet and so on).

In Unit 2.1.1, we look at the picture of crime that emerges from the media, both factual – such as newspapers and documentaries – and fictional – such as crime dramas on TV and in the cinema. How does the picture correspond with what we know about crime from other sources of information, such as official statistics? What types of crime are over-represented and which under-represented? What picture emerges of criminals, of the police and of victims?

As we shall see, the picture that emerges is highly skewed, with crimes of violence and sex crimes over-represented. In Unit 2.1.2 we look at the consequences of this for individuals and for society as a whole. Can media representations of violence lead to violent behaviour? Does the media's portrayal of crime produce heightened levels of fear of crime among its audience? What other effects can we identify?

In Unit 2.1.3, we look in more depth at two kinds of consequences that have been extensively researched by sociologists: moral panics (heightened levels of public anxiety around particular categories of crime) and deviancy amplification (the idea that media attention can unintentionally exacerbate a particular crime problem).

Finally, in Unit 2.1.4 we look at the impact of the new media (digitally enabled forms of communication) on the rapidly expanding area of cybercrime.

Unit 2.1.1 Representation and reality

As Geoffrey Pearson (1983) has argued, the public are both fearful of and fascinated by crime and the media has sought to satisfy the public's apparently near-insatiable appetite for stories about crime more or less since its inception in the form of 18th-century news sheets. For example, at the time of writing (May, 2017), six of Amazon's 20 best-selling TV box-sets are crime dramas and the final episode of Series 4 of the police-corruption drama *Line of Duty* attracted an estimated 9.92 million viewers on its transmission.

The common-sense view of the role of the media is that it acts like a mirror, reflecting back to its audience more or less accurately what is happening in society. While there is clearly some truth in this notion, sociologists argue that what is really happening is more complex in at least two significant respects.

Activity

A still from the BBC crime drama Line of Duty.

How many of Amazon's 20 best-selling TV box-sets are crime dramas in the week you are reading this?

First, media coverage of crime is highly *selective*. Not all the crime that takes place in society is reflected in the media and certain types of crime are given priority over others, even if this varies both within and between different mediums. For example, crimes of violence and sexual crimes are heavily reported in tabloid newspapers while white-collar and corporate crime are under-represented.

Second, the media don't simply tell us about what's happening, but offer us particular ways of understanding what they have selected – what Stuart Hall (1973) called '**interpretative frameworks**' or '**frames**'. Framing refers to the way an issue is presented to the public or the 'angle' it is given by the news media. It involves calling attention to certain aspects of an issue while ignoring or obscuring other elements. One of the ways in which this is done is through the media's use of language. Thus, for example, rapists are routinely dubbed as 'beasts' or 'sex fiends' in tabloid press rape reports, implying that rape is the product of animalistic passions or abnormal sexual appetites rather than something that 'ordinary' men might do.

Activity

Get hold of a selection of tabloid newspaper crime stories and analyse the language used to describe the perpetrators. What emotional responses do you think the language is designed to provoke?

Crime and the news media

Galtung and Ruge (1970) suggested that journalists' decisions about what stories to report were dependent on 'news values' – their ideas about what made something newsworthy – such as being out-of-the-ordinary, involving élite persons, negativity, unambiguity and so on. Reiner (2010) argues that deviance is the essence of news because it contains many elements that journalists regard as newsworthy, such as immediacy, **dramatisation**, **personalisation**, titillation and novelty. The presence of these news values in crime stories explains the priority given, in both tabloid newspapers and broadcast news, to sexual and violent crimes. In contrast, stories about crime rarely focus on economic crimes, although references to business crimes might be featured in the business sections of the quality broadsheet newspapers. Reiner notes that treatment of this kind of crime that is mainly committed by high-status wealthy individuals or by corporations has resulted in this type of deviance being 'marked off from real crime'.

Williams and Dickinson (1993) note that, on average, 12.7 per cent of newspaper space is devoted to crime stories. However, they also note that the further **down-market** the newspaper, the greater the space devoted to crime and deviance, and vice versa. For example, they found that 30.4 per cent of space in *The Sun* newspaper was devoted to crime, compared with only 5.1 per cent of the content of *The Guardian*.

Cumberbatch *et al.* (1995) found that crime reporting was also a major feature of broadcast news. For example, their research found that 40 per cent of news on BBC radio was focused on crime, while crime stories constituted 53 per cent of all stories on Sky News, compared with 42 per cent of ITN and 38 per cent of BBC TV news output.

Reiner notes that crimes of violence, especially homicide, are disproportionately reported across the news compared to their incidence in the official crime statistics or victim surveys. For example, Soothill and Walby (1991) found that rape and sexual crime were over-reported – sometimes these stories occupied as much as 45 per cent of newspaper coverage of crime despite only accounting for a minority of violent incidents. On the other hand, Reiner found that property crime was significantly under-reported, considering that such crimes constituted the majority of crimes reported to the police and victim surveys.

Some sociologists argue that the emergence of mobile digital forms of communication and the proliferation of internet sites that enable various forms of 'citizen journalism' (blogs, podcasts and so on) have democratised news production and altered the relationship between crime and the media. However, Jewkes (2015) argues that most people continue to rely on traditional news media in relation to crime.

Press reporting of rape and sexual assault

Marhia (2008) analysed a random sample of 136 news articles about rape and sexual assault of girls and women by men and boys that appeared in UK national newspapers and on the BBC Online news site during 2006. She argues that, overall, the way in which these offences are reported constructs rape as 'an outdoor crime at the hands of a monstrous or bestial deviant stranger, who may be "foreign" and uses extreme violence to overpower a victim'. This construction is way out of line with the picture that emerges from social research:

'Rape cases which led to a conviction account for 48.5% of news reports about rape, but in reality only 5.7% of reported rapes result in a conviction.

Attacks by strangers account for over half – 54.4% – of press reports about rape, despite the fact that only 8–17% of rapes in the UK are stranger rapes.

The majority – 56% – of rapes are perpetrated by a current or former partner, but these cases are almost invisible in the press, accounting for only 2% of stories about rape.

Although only 13% of rapes take place in public places, these account for 54% of press reports of rape.

The press disproportionately covers rape cases involving excessive additional violence including grievous bodily harm and murder, the use of a weapon or intoxicants, abduction and kidnapping and/or multiple assailants.

Attacks against underage girls are over-reported in the press, while attacks against adult women are under-reported compared with recorded crime statistics.'

Marhia argues that this distorted representation of rape not only leads to public misperceptions of sexual offences in general, but also has significant effects on both the willingness of victims to report rape and on the conviction rates for rape (see Unit 2.1.2).

Activity

1. Identify the main features of the distorted picture of rape and sexual violence that press and TV reporting produces.

2. How do you think this distorted picture can be explained?

Crime fiction

Crime is extremely popular as a source for novels, films and television drama. Reiner estimates that one in five movies exclusively focus on a crime theme, while 50 per cent of Hollywood and British films and between 20 and 40 per cent of television drama output have significant crime content.

Reiner argues that fictional narratives about crime over-represent murder and violence in an even more disproportionate way than news reporting. Moreover, scenes of severe suffering often accompany the depiction of fictional violence. Murder is portrayed as mainly being the result of greed and calculation (although in real life, most murders are the result of spontaneous brawls between young men or are the outcome of domestic disputes). When storylines do focus on property crime, these are frequently portrayed as tightly planned, high-value thefts that require a degree of violence, despite the fact that the overwhelming majority of such crimes in real life are opportunistic, involve little loss and certainly involve little or no physical threat or harm to the victim. Finally, Reiner notes how fictional policemen nearly always 'get their man'. However, Reiner also notes that the last decade has seen a clear trend towards criticism of the police in contemporary fiction, with the appearance of more novels, films and TV series about police corruption, as in *Line of Duty*. This is partly because writers need constantly to find new angles to prevent established genres from becoming 'tired' and partly because increasingly sophisticated audiences would reject police procedurals that presented a sanitised version of the police. Nevertheless, it is still the honest cops who win out in the end.

Key terms

Interpretative frameworks/frames Ways in which the media represent the topics they cover to their audience.

Dramatisation Turning mundane events and situations into something dramatic.

Personalisation Reducing complex issues to a matter of the personalities involved.

Down-market Aimed at lower status social groups.

Summary

1. The public are both fascinated by and fearful of crime.

2. Crime features prominently in the media.

3. The media provide a distorted picture of crime because their coverage is highly selective.

4. The media offer particular interpretations of crime to their audience through, for example, their choice of language.

5. News media coverage of rape provides a dramatic illustration of 4.

6. Fictional representations of crime over-represent violence and murder.

Unit 2.1.2 Media effects

Having looked at how crime is (mis-)represented in the media, we turn in this unit to the effects of this media coverage. However, before doing so we need to recognise that the relationship between media content and audience response is not straightforward.

Early media theorists suggested that there was a direct relationship between content and response, likening it to the effect of a drug being injected into someone's veins – the so-called '**hypodermic syringe model**' – so that, for example, violence on screen would lead to violent behaviour by the audience. Subsequent theorists have increasingly challenged this model arguing that:

》 The effects are indirect rather than direct and are mediated by people's social relationships with others. Katz and Lazarsfeld (1965) in their **2-step flow model** of media influence suggested that people discuss what they see/hear/read in the media with others whose opinions they value ('opinion leaders') who consume a range of media before accepting/rejecting media messages.

》 Audiences are active rather than passive, selecting which media messages to expose themselves to (**selective exposure**) and interpreting media messages in light of their pre-existing attitudes, values and knowledge

(**selective interpretation**) rather than simply absorbing them. For example, Morley (1980) argued that while some people who watched a popular current-affairs programme at that time called *Nationwide* accepted the intended message of an item, others queried elements of it (producing a 'negotiated reading') or rejected it completely (producing an 'oppositional reading').

》 Effects may vary in terms of intensity and duration.

The cumulative effect of these qualifications has led some theorists to go so far as to suggest that 'if, after over sixty years of a considerable amount of research effort, direct effects of media upon behaviour have not been clearly identified, then we should conclude that they are simply *not there to be found*' (Gauntlett, 1998). However, few media theorists would agree with such an extreme position and, indeed, it rather implausibly implies that, for example, the £20 billion spent on advertising in the UK annually is a complete waste of money!

In this unit, we examine four examples of (alleged) effects of media representations of crime: media violence and real-life violence; fear of crime; ideological effects; and effects on the criminal justice process.

Media violence and real–life violence

One area that has been the focus of extensive research over a long period of time is the possible relationship between the portrayal of violence in the media and violent behaviour in the real world, particularly by children and adolescents.

Early studies of the relationship between the media and violence focused on conducting experiments in laboratories. For example, Bandura *et al.* (1963) looked for a direct cause-and-effect relationship between media content and violence. They showed three groups of children real, film and cartoon examples of a self-righting doll ('bobo doll') being attacked with mallets, while a fourth group saw no violent activity. After being introduced to a room full of exciting toys, the children in each group were made to feel frustrated by being told that the toys were not for them. They were then led to another room containing a bobo doll, where they were observed through a one-way mirror. The three groups who had been shown the violent activity – whether real, film or cartoon – all behaved more aggressively than the fourth group. On the basis of this experiment, Bandura and colleagues concluded that violent media content could lead to imitation or 'copycat' violence.

In a similar vein, McCabe and Martin (2005) argued that imitation was a likely outcome of media violence, because often it is the hero who uses violence to deal with a problem, violence which not only goes unpunished but also brings rewards to its perpetrator. Consequently, it is argued that such media violence has a '**disinhibition effect**' – it convinces children that in some social situations, the 'normal' rules that govern conflict and difference can be suspended – that is, discussion and negotiation can be replaced with violence.

McCabe and Martin's views are supported by Kevin Browne (a consultant to the Home Affairs Committee investigation of knife crime, 2009), who argued that there are 'well-established short-term effects of children or teenagers watching violent video films, DVDs or playing violent computer games and then behaving aggressively in the hours and weeks afterwards'. Moreover, he argues that children who grow up in a violent environment and witness real violence in their community or family were particularly prone to copy what they see on screen.

Activity

According to Kevin Browne, what effect can watching violent video games have?

A third alleged consequence of media violence is **desensitisation**. Newson (1994) noted that children and teenagers are subjected to thousands of killings and acts of violence as they grow up, through viewing television and films. She suggested that such prolonged exposure to media violence may have a 'drip-drip' effect on young people over the course of their childhood and result in their becoming desensitised to violence – they become socialised into accepting violent behaviour as normal, especially as a problem-solving device. Newson concluded that, because of this, the latest generation of young people subscribe to weaker moral codes and are more likely to behave in antisocial ways than previous generations.

There can be no disputing the claim that real-life violence can and does mimic media violence. Numerous examples are available. For example, in 1995 two 18-year-olds, Sarah Edmondson and her then-boyfriend, Benjamin Darras, went on a violent crime spree in the southern USA following repeated viewings of the film *Natural Born Killers*. Darras shot and killed a businessman in Mississippi and Edmondson shot and wounded a store clerk in Louisiana. Similarly, in 2014, 16-year-old Steven Miles stabbed his girlfriend to death in his bedroom in Surrey and then dismembered her body, mimicking the actions of *Dexter*, a vigilante serial killer in a cult US TV series.

However, the claim that these screen depictions of homicidal violence *caused* real-life killings needs to be treated with caution. First, correlation does not necessarily prove causation. That is to say, just because two variables are associated, it doesn't follow that one is causing the other. The direction of cause and effect could be the other way round – homicidally inclined people may be attracted to watching screen violence – or a third factor, mental instability, say, or childhood abuse may lead to *both* a taste for screen violence *and* murderous tendencies. Second, recognising that the violent acts mimicked those viewed on screen still leaves unexplained why these specific people acted in this murderous way when the vast majority of viewers of *Dexter* and *Natural Born Killers* didn't subsequently kill others. Finally, the question has to be asked: Would these or similarly fatal actions have been carried out at some point by those convicted *whether or not they had viewed these instances of screen violence?* Clearly, we can never know for sure, but – at the very least – it has to count as a distinct possibility.

Overall, the evidence for a direct causal relationship between screen violence and violence in real life is quite weak. For example, studies that have looked at how children are affected when television first arrives

Activity

DRIVEN TO KILL BY CALL OF DUTY?

Maniac spent 18 hours a day playing violent video games.

KILLER'S CALL OF DUTY OBSESSION.

Massacre loner addicted to controversial vid game.

Summaries of the front pages of the Daily Mirror (18.09.2013) reporting on the shooting dead of 12 people by Aaron Alexis at an American naval base in Washington and The Sun (18.12.2012) reporting on the high school massacre of 20 children in Newtown, Connecticut carried out by Adam Lanza.

Both headlines imply that playing *Call of Duty* was causally linked to the subsequent shootings. Suggest reasons why this claim needs to be treated with caution.

in a society have found little change. The last study was in St Helena, a British colony in the South Atlantic Ocean, which received television for the first time in 1995. Before-and-after studies showed no change in children's social behaviour (Charlton *et al.*, 2000). Similarly, Rhodes (2000) found that violent crime rates in Europe and Japan either stayed the same or declined in the years following the introduction of television. Nevertheless, it may well be the case that certain children who have grown up in a violent environment are more vulnerable to being negatively influenced by screen violence.

Guy Cumberbatch (2004) looked at over 3500 research studies into the effects of screen violence, encompassing film, TV, video and, more recently, computer and video games. He states that: 'If one conclusion is possible, it is that *the jury is still out. It's never been in.* Media violence has been subjected to lynch mob mentality with almost any evidence used to prove guilt.' In other words, there is still no conclusive evidence either way that violence shown in the media influences or changes people's behaviour.

The media and fear of crime

Another suggested effect of the representation of crime in the media is the production of heightened states of fear of, and anxiety about, the risk of being a victim of crime in real life, particularly a victim of those crimes disproportionately covered in the media such as crimes of violence.

Gerbner and Gross (1976: 419), for example, argue that because television overstates both the seriousness and the risk of criminal victimisation, portraying the world as 'mean and scary', heavy viewing (more than four hours a day) is associated with higher levels of fear of crime.

Research examining this alleged link between media consumption and fear of crime, however, has been inconclusive. Ditton *et al.* (1999), drawing on a literature review carried out by Sarah Eschholz in 1997, note that 'of a total of 73 attempts to establish a connection between media consumption and fear of crime, only 27 per cent of studies find a positive relationship, while 73 per cent do not'.

Jewkes (2015) argues that this is hardly surprising given that there are a wide range of factors beside the media that are likely to impact on people's level of fear, including the '[a]ctual risk of victimisation, previous experience of victimisation, environmental conditions, ethnicity and confidence in the police and the criminal justice system' to name just a few. Additionally, the British Crime Survey/Crime Survey for England and Wales has found significant variations in levels of fear associated with both age and gender, with fear increasing with age among both men and women and women generally having higher levels of fear than men (or, possibly, women simply being more willing to *acknowledge* their fears).

The 2013/14 CSEW shows that 12 per cent of adults were classified as having a high level of worry about violent crime, 11 per cent about burglary, and 7 per cent about car crime. All of these measures were at a similar level to the previous year and the general trend has been flat for a number of years. However, all measures are significantly lower than in the mid-to-late 1990s when crime measured by the BCS/CSEW was at much higher levels than today (if one excludes cybercrime figures). It would seem unlikely that there have been dramatic changes in the nature of media coverage of crime since the mid-nineties, so the changes in fear levels suggest that factors other than media consumption must be involved. Hence, while the selective coverage of crime by the media must inevitably play a part in people's fear of victimisation, the relative significance of this factor compared to others remains uncertain.

Ideological effects of media representations of crime

Marxist and critical criminologists (see Unit 2.6.3) see the media as playing an **ideological** role in society. By presenting a skewed picture of reality, or a partial account as the whole story, the media help to justify the present social arrangements. For example, by presenting crime as the product of people who are innately 'bad' or 'evil', the social and economic roots of crime are left unexplored, as is the role of political decisions in shaping these social and economic arrangements.

The national press in Britain is predominantly right-wing in orientation and therefore openly supports **neoliberal policies** in its editorials and comment pages. However, Marxists and critical criminologists argue that through their selection and presentation of news stories they also *covertly* promote support for these same policies. The reporting of benefit fraud in recent years provides a striking example.

Baumberg, Bell and Gaffney (2012) examined a database of national daily newspapers from 1995–2011 and located about 6600 articles concerned with benefit and working-age claimants. They found an 'extraordinarily disproportionate' focus on benefit fraud, with 29 per cent of news stories referencing fraud over this time period despite the fact that the Department of Work and Pension's own estimate of fraud across all benefits is just 0.7 per cent.

The authors also conducted focus groups and commissioned a *Mori* survey of public opinion to examine public attitudes towards benefit claimants. The survey asked respondents to estimate the

Activity – Press coverage of benefit fraud

Below is an example of one of the kinds of stories that Baumberg, Bell and Gaffney identified, taken from the on-line site of the *Daily Mail* (03/03/2017)

All I Want For Xmas is… a CRUISE! Caribbean-loving benefits cheat who claimed £150 000 by saying she couldn't walk and needed an oxygen tank is JAILED after being caught on video dancing to Mariah Carey's festive hit

- Investigators found clip of Lisa White dancing to All I Want For Christmas Is You
- She was receiving disability payments after claiming she needed oxygen tanks
- Mrs White was jailed for 18 months while her husband received a suspended term
- They even went on a 28-night £9000 New York and Caribbean cruise after arrest
- Judge: 'I see why she's happy; if I was getting money for nothing, I'd be happy'

Questions

1. How might such stories affect audience attitudes towards benefit claimants?
2. How might such stories affect attitudes towards disabled people?
3. How might such stories affect attitudes towards benefits in general?

proportion of claims that were fraudulent. Their estimate was one in four, a proportion pretty much in line with the proportion of news reports about benefits that focused on fraud. The hypothesis that the newspapers were largely responsible for these estimates is further strengthened by their finding that there was a strong relationship between the amount of news coverage of fraud in particular newspapers and the estimates provided by the readers of those titles.

Clearly, if the general public believe that a significant minority of benefit claimants make claims fraudulently, this will undermine their support for social security in general. Since the 2008 financial crisis, governments have been seeking to reduce their budget deficit and the Coalition government elected in 2010 made it a priority to cut the benefits bill, as did the Conservative government elected in 2015. The news media have arguably played an important role in legitimising significant reductions in a range of social security benefits by reinforcing the idea that benefit claimants are claiming fraudulently or are, more generally, undeserving 'scroungers'.

One further effect of such coverage is worth noting. Recorded rates of disability hate crime in England and Wales have been rising since 2008 when official records began. The Home Office estimated in 2012 that 65 000 occur each year, while disability charities put the figure even higher and − according to *The Guardian* (14.08.2012) − disability charities 'have little doubt that the deteriorating situation is being driven by "benefit scrounger" abuse'. This would appear to provide a much more plausible example of the media causing violence than the claim that media portrayals of violence cause real-life violence.

Activity

Earlier research by Barnes (1992) found that a number of negative stereotypes of disabled people regularly appear in the media: as pitiable and pathetic, as sinister and evil, as 'super-cripples' and as incapable of participating fully in community life. How might such stereotypes also contribute to disability hate crime? Can you think of any positive representations of disability in mainstream media today?

Impacts on the criminal justice process

As we saw earlier (p. 68), press reporting of rape produces a distorted picture of this offence in the public's mind as, **stereotypically**, a crime carried out by a monstrous or bestial stranger, outdoors, using excessive violence.

Kelly (2001) argues that the reporting generates a host of myths about rape in addition to these, such as that 'anyone facing the possibility of rape will resist' and 'all victims react in the same way if they have really been raped'. In fact, she points out, while many do resist, many freeze through fear or shock, or decide that resistance would be futile and/or dangerous, and victims in practice display a wide range of responses, from extremely distressed through to quiet and controlled.

This set of myths and stereotypes combine to form what Kelly calls the '**real rape template**' and this template, she argues, plays a crucial role throughout the criminal justice process in influencing:

》 whether a victim is likely to report a rape to the police

》 whether the police are likely to believe the complainant and refer the case to the Crown Prosecution Service (CPS)

》 whether the CPS prosecute

》 whether a jury finds the defendant guilty or innocent.

The closer an actual case conforms to the 'real rape' template, the more likely it is to progress through each of these stages; the further away it is, the less likely. Thus, for example, if the victim tells the police that she did not put up any resistance to her attacker and appears quiet and controlled rather than extremely distressed, the police are more likely to doubt the truthfulness of her complaint.

Marhia (2008) argues that the 'real rape' template contributes to the high rate of **attrition** in rape cases, with only about 5−7 per cent of reported rapes in England and Wales resulting in convictions since 2000. Her conclusion is that the press 'continues to propagate harmful myths which feed back into the criminal justice system, perpetuating a vicious cycle of under-reporting, attrition and low conviction rates'.

Key terms

Hypodermic syringe model A theory of media effects that likens the impact of the media to that of an injection of a drug into a vein.

2-step flow model A theory of media effects that claims that the effects are mediated through people's relationships with informal 'opinion leaders'.

Selective exposure People select which media messages they will consume.

Selective interpretation People interpret media messages in light of their pre-existing knowledge, values and predispositions.

Disinhibition effect An effect that reduces the power of in-built barriers to acting in a deviant or criminal way.

Desensitisation An effect that dampens the emotional impact of something which would otherwise be distressing, such as viewing violent behaviour.

Ideological An ideology is a belief system that reflects the vested interests of a particular group or groups in society.

Neoliberal policies Policies based on a belief in the efficiency of the market and the desirability of a minimal role for the state in running an economy.

Stereotypically A stereotype is a simplified picture of the members of a group which paints them as all possessing the same set of – usually, negative – characteristics.

Real-rape template A set of misguided beliefs about rape that are nevertheless used to judge the truthfulness of rape claims made by victims.

Attrition The loss of cases recorded by the police as rapes from the criminal justice process before they reach court.

Summary

1. Media effects are conditioned by factors such as selective exposure and selective interpretation, but nevertheless the media's (mis)representation of crime has real effects.

2. The claim that media violence leads to real-life violence is not well supported by the evidence, but the issue remains unresolved.

3. Nevertheless, the misrepresentation of crime by the media can be seen as having a number of effects:

   » raising the level of the public's fear of crime
   » ideological effects
   » exacerbating hate crime
   » impacting on the criminal justice process, for example, the distorted coverage of rape produces a false 'real rape template' whose use contributes to high attrition rates in the prosecution of rapists.

Unit 2.1.3 Moral panics and deviancy amplification

Two further alleged effects of the media's representation of crime and deviance have received considerable attention by sociologists and it is to these we turn in this unit. The first, **moral panic**, is to do with how the media can affect public opinion. The second, **deviancy amplification**, is concerned with how the media can affect behaviour.

The term 'moral panic' was popularised by Stanley Cohen (1972) in his classic work *Folk Devils and Moral Panics: The Creation of the Mods and Rockers*. The term refers to widespread feelings of anxiety and concern held by the general public that develop when – in Cohen's words – 'a condition, episode, person or group of persons emerges to become defined as a threat to societal values and interests'.

According to Goode and Ben-Yehuda (1994), there are five distinguishing features of moral panics:

» **Concern** – the belief that the behaviour of the group or activity deemed deviant is likely to have a negative effect on society

» **Hostility** – hostility towards the group in question develops, and they come to be seen as '**folk devils**'

» **Consensus** – there must be widespread agreement that the group in question poses a real threat to society

» **Disproportionality** – the level of anxiety and concern is disproportionate to the actual threat posed by the accused group

» **Volatility** – moral panics are highly volatile (unstable) and tend to disappear as quickly as they appear due to a waning in public interest or news media turning their attention elsewhere. (Note though that Cohen himself argued that 'sometimes the panic passes over and is forgotten, except in folk-lore and collective memory; at other times it has more serious and long-lasting repercussions and might produce such changes as those in legal and social policy or even in the way society conceives itself' (Cohen, 1972).)

Moral panics are closely linked to the concept of deviancy amplification. The concept was coined by Wilkins (1967) and draws upon the **labelling theory** (see Unit 2.5.2) notion that the social reaction to deviant behaviour can unintentionally – and ironically – actually make it worse. It could, for example, attract more people to engage in this form of deviancy or encourage those already involved to become more deviant.

Deviancy amplification needs to be distinguished from what Jock Young (1971) called a '**fantasy crime wave**', which occurs when there is no *real* increase in the deviant behaviour, but where there *appears* to be an increase, either because the police devote more effort to detection, thereby uncovering more instances, or because the public become more willing to report instances as victims or witnesses, thereby inflating the crime statistics.

Moral panics go through a number of stages, with the media implicated at every stage:

1. The news media (especially, the tabloid press) report on a particular activity/ incident or social group, using sensationalist and exaggerated language and headlines.

2. **Moral entrepreneurs** – for example, politicians, religious leaders and so on – react to media reports and make statements condemning the group or activity; they insist that the police, courts and government take action.

3. The media oversimplifies the reasons why the group or activity has appeared (e.g. young people out of control, a lack of respect for authority, a decline in morality and so on), and follow-up articles demonise the group as a social problem or 'folk devils' – that is, the media gives them particular characteristics, focusing particularly on their dress and behaviour, which helps the general public and police to identify them more easily.

4. The authorities stamp down hard on the group or activity – this may take the form of the police stopping, searching and arresting those associated with the activity, the courts severely punishing those convicted of the activity, or the government bringing in new laws to control the activity or group.

5. The reporting of incidents associated with the group or activity to the police by the general public rises as the group or activity becomes more visible in the public consciousness.

6. The media reports the arrests and convictions that result from the moral panic, thereby fulfilling the initial media prophecy or prediction that the group or activity would be a social problem.

7. The group may react to the moral panic, over-policing and so on, by becoming more deviant in protest, or the activity may go underground, where it becomes more difficult to police and control.

Examples

Three empirical studies carried out in the 1960s and 1970s illustrate the process outlined above.

1 The mods and rockers

The 'mods' and 'rockers' were two working-class youth subcultures that emerged in Britain in the 1960s. Stanley Cohen argued that the media itself played a part in crystallising the distinctive identities of these two subcultures by exaggerating their differences from each other (in terms of such things as dress, musical preferences, preferred mode of transport and so on) and, at the same time, generated a moral panic around their activities.

Activity

Rockers and their preferred mode of transport.
Are there any equivalent youth subcultures today?

Cohen focused on the media's reaction to youth 'disturbances' beginning on Easter Monday 1964. He demonstrated how the media blew what were essentially small-scale scuffles and vandalism out of all proportion by carrying stories on their front pages and using headlines such as 'Day of Terror by Scooter Gangs' and 'Wild Ones "Beat Up" Margate'.

He argued that the media tapped into what it saw as a social consensus – it assumed that decent law-abiding members of society shared their concerns about a general decline in the morality of the young symbolised by the growing influence of youth culture. Subsequently, groups labelled 'mods' and 'rockers' by the media were presented and analysed in a distorted and stereotyped fashion as a threat to law and order. A **deviancy amplification spiral** was set in train, with the news media eager to 'expose' new examples of delinquency, increasing numbers of working-class youths identifying with one or other group, further run-ins between the youth groups and calls by moral entrepreneurs to 'do something' about this growing menace to social order and civility.

2 Youth and drugs

Around the same time as Cohen was studying mods and rockers, Jock Young carried out a study of marijuana use among young people in Notting Hill, London – published in 1971 as *The Drugtakers: The Social Meaning of Drug Use.*

If Cohen's book was about the moral panic associated with working-class youth in the sixties, Young's study was about the moral panic provoked by middle-class youth.

The sixties saw the emergence of a 'hippy' **counter culture** protesting against the Vietnam War and the 'military-industrial complex'. Their motto was 'make love, not war', their means of protesting was via 'flower power', and marijuana use was seen as facilitating a relaxed and convivial state of mind.

If hippies today are seen as largely harmless 'oddballs', this is not how they were viewed by the authorities in the sixties and there were a series of newspaper exposés of drug use on university campuses and elsewhere and of the sexually permissive attitudes of hippies, designed to both shock and titillate their readers. For example, *The People* on 21 September 1969 reported 'Hippie Thugs – The Sordid Truth: Drug taking, couples making love while others look on, rule by a heavy mob armed with iron bars, foul language, filth and stench, THAT is the scene inside the hippies' fortress in London's Piccadilly.' Such stories helped to generate a moral panic around drugs and youth and led to the formation of Regional Drugs Squads who proceeded to arrest and charge significant numbers of young people.

Young clearly sympathised with the young people who subsequently ended up with a police record and, in extreme cases, a prison record and suggested that criminalisation might exacerbate rather than solve the problem. He argued that police reaction to marijuana users can 'fundamentally alter and transform the social world of the marijuana smoker' and in his book identified a number of deviancy amplification spirals that were set in train by the punitive societal response. For example, because of the perceived injustice of the police's response, many of the young people involved saw marijuana use as a symbolic expression of resistance and it took on a more central role in their lifestyles. Also, as police action made it more difficult to acquire marijuana from friends and associates as young people become more wary of arrest, youths were brought into contact with professional drug dealers who would have encouraged them to try harder drugs.

3 Mugging

See Unit 2.10.2 below for another influential early study of a moral panic: the study of mugging in the early seventies by Stuart Hall, Chas Critcher and colleagues (*Policing the Crisis,* 1979).

Contemporary issues: Online grooming: moral panic or genuine cause for concern?

In the last couple of decades, there has been widespread concern regarding children and the internet. One of the issues that has received considerable attention is online 'grooming'.

Grooming refers to actions deliberately undertaken by an adult with the aim of befriending and establishing an emotional connection with a child, in order to lower the child's inhibitions in preparation for sexual abuse. Child grooming is also used to lure children into sexual exploitation such as child prostitution or the production of child sexual abuse images.

Most sexual abuse of children is carried out by relatives, neighbours or friends of the parents; in other words, by adults whom the child knows rather than strangers.

However, BBC online (15.12.2016) reported that of the 702 children that children's charity Barnado's had supported over the previous six months at five specialist units across the UK, 297 (42 per cent) had been groomed online. Of these, 182 had met their online groomer and suffered sexual abuse.

Section 67 of the 2015 Serious Crime Act makes it illegal for an adult to communicate with a child for the purpose of sexual gratification. The section became operational in March, 2017.

Question

Do you think it is appropriate to call public concern over online grooming a moral panic?

The decades since the seventies have seen a succession of further moral panics around such issues as 'bogus asylum seekers', 'raves', 'predatory paedophiles', 'dangerous dogs', 'road rage', 'girl gangs', 'hoodies', 'scary clowns' and so on.

Moral panics and deviancy amplification: a critique

A number of issues have been raised about moral panics and deviancy amplification:

» The key feature of a moral panic is the disproportion between the level of public concern and the real threat that the deviant behaviour poses to society. However, estimation of whether the level of concern is disproportionate hinges on a value-judgement and so is not a simple matter of fact.

» Analyses of deviancy amplification usually leave the original causes of the initial deviant behaviour unexplored and unexplained.

» The appearance of interactive new media, according to McRobbie and Thornton (1995), has radically changed the relationship between the media and its audience and has consequently undermined the overall impact of moral panics. Audiences are allegedly now more sophisticated in terms of how they interpret media content. Competition between different types of media – newspapers, television, 24-hour rolling satellite news channels, Facebook, Twitter, blogs and other internet gossip websites – means that audiences are exposed to a wider set of interpretations about potential social problems and are consequently more likely to be sceptical of their moral panic status.

» These points notwithstanding, both concepts continue to provide powerful ways of understanding two significant features of the relationship between crime/deviance and the media.

Key terms

Moral panic Widespread public anxiety about a particular kind of crime or deviance.

Deviancy amplification A social process in which actions intended to reduce deviance have the opposite effect.

Folk devils Groups seen by the public as irredeemably evil.

Labelling theory A theory of deviance drawing upon symbolic interactionism and pluralism.

Fantasy crime wave An imaginary increase in crime.

Deviancy amplification spiral A social process in which actions intended to reduce deviance have the opposite effect. A deviancy amplification spiral can occur when attempts to control deviance feed back on themselves, producing increased deviance.

Moral entrepreneurs Individuals or groups who make moral judgements and seek to bring about social change in line with these judgements.

Counter culture A subculture opposed to a society's dominant culture.

Summary

1. Two well-attested media effects in relation to crime are moral panics and deviancy amplification.

2. Moral panics are characterised by concern, hostility, consensus, disproportionality and (arguably) volatility.

3. Deviancy amplification needs to be distinguished from a fantasy crime wave.

4. The media play a crucial contributory role in the process of deviancy amplification.

5. Early studies looked at mods and rockers, marijuana use and mugging.

6. Moral panics often focus on young people either as folk devils or as victims.

7. The key feature of moral panics is that the level of public concern is disproportionate to the real threat. Whether the level of public concern is disproportionate in a particular case involves making a value judgement, so is not a simple matter of fact.

Unit 2.1.4 The 'new media' and crime

'New media' refers to means of mass communication that use digital technologies such as the internet. It also includes social media such as Facebook, Twitter, WhatsApp, Instagram and Flickr, in which people communicate with others online.

The reach of such media has grown spectacularly in recent years. According to the ONS, 90 per cent of households in Great Britain in 2017 had internet access and, according to Ofcom, roughly three-quarters of internet users in the UK in 2017 had a social media profile.

New media have offered criminals the opportunity to commit old crimes in new ways (such as terrorist offences), but also opportunities to commit a wide range of entirely new types of crime (such as computer hacking).

Such offences are known as cybercrimes. The term refers to any type of criminal activity conducted through, or using, an Information and Communications Technology (ICT) device. The UK government's National Cyber Security Strategy (2016) distinguishes between the following:

- **Cyber-dependent crimes** – crimes that can be committed only through the use of ICT devices, where the devices are both the tool for committing the crime, and the target of the crime

- **Cyber-enabled crimes** – traditional crimes that can be increased in scale or reach by the use of computers, computer networks or other forms of ICT.

Cyber-dependent crimes fall into two main categories: illegal intrusions into computer networks such as hacking (where criminals gain entry to computers or computer networks in order to gather personal data or information that they can then exploit in some way) or the disruption or downgrading of computer functionality and network space, such as malware and Denial of Service (DOS) attacks.

Cyber-enabled crimes take many forms:

- economic-related cybercrimes including fraud and intellectual property crime such as piracy, counterfeiting and forgery

- malicious and offensive communications, such as cyber-bullying and trolling offences that specifically target individuals, such as cyber-stalking and harassment

- child sexual offences, such as online grooming (See Contemporary issues on p. 76)

- extreme pornography and obscene publications.

It is difficult to know whether such cyber-enabled crimes have simply replaced more traditional types of criminal harm or have added a further layer of offending, but according to the National Crime Agency, the scale of cybercrime is being underestimated because many cases are not reported to the police. (See also Unit 2.2.1.)

Summary

1. The new media, associated with digital technologies, have produced new ways of committing traditional crimes as well as entirely new types of offences.

2. It is possible to distinguish between cyber-dependent crimes (where ICT devices are both the means for committing offences and the target of such offences) and cyber-enabled crimes (where the use of ICT facilitates the commission of offences that can also be carried out without the use of ICT).

PART 2 PATTERNS AND TRENDS IN CRIME

In Part 1, we saw that the media produce a distorted picture of crime, criminals and victims in the public mind. For example, while the level of crime measured by the British Crime Survey (BCS)/Crime Survey for England and Wales (CSEW) has been *falling* since a peak in 1995, the survey has consistently found – since it first started asking the question in 2008/09 – that most people perceive that crime across the country as a whole has been *rising*. Thus the 2013/14 survey found 61 per cent of adults thought crime had gone up nationally in the last few years.

However, this raises the question of the accuracy of official measures of crime such as the BCS/

CSEW. How sure can we be that they offer a **valid** (accurate) and **reliable** (consistent) measure of the true extent of crime in society and that the amount of crime really has been falling since the mid-1990s?

In this part, we will try to get closer to the true picture by looking at the available evidence relating to crime in society, though it should be noted that some sociologists (those who adopt an interpretivist or phenomenological perspective) reject the whole idea that there is an objectively knowable crime total (see p. 83, Official crime statistics: sociological debate). Unit 2.2.1 focuses on police recorded crime and the BCS/CSEW. Unit 2.2.2 looks at white-collar crime and a type of crime not covered by the official statistics: corporate crime. Finally, in Unit 2.2.3, we look at a growing category of crime associated with globalisation: transnational organised crime.

Unit 2.2.1 Official crime statistics

Official crime statistics are those produced by government departments and non-governmental agencies. Official crime statistics for England and Wales are produced by a range of organisations including the Office for National Statistics (ONS), the National Fraud Intelligence Bureau, the Home Office, the Ministry of Justice and Her Majesty's Inspectorate of Constabulary. (Scotland and Northern Ireland have separate court and police systems and produce their own crime statistics.)

There are two principal sources of information about crime in England and Wales:

» police recorded crime (PRC)

» the Crime Survey for England and Wales (formerly, the British Crime Survey).

Information from these two sources is published four times a year by the ONS and headline figures are widely reported in the news media, drawing attention to apparent rises or falls.

Police recorded crime (PRC)

Figure 2.2.1 shows long-term trends in crimes recorded by the police in England and Wales from 1898 to 2010. It shows that rates remained very low until the 1950s, but increased rapidly for most of the second half of the 20th century. However, there were some falls in recorded crime during the late 1990s, with steeper falls since the turn of the millennium.

A more up-to-date picture is provided by Figure 2.2.2, which also incorporates figures from the BCS/CSEW. As you can see, PRC (as indicated by the bars) was falling from the early years of this century until around 2014, since when it has been slowly rising again, reaching nearly 5 million offences in the year ending March 2017.

PRC statistics provide a far from complete record of crimes committed. First, they exclude less serious offences known as **summary offences** – such as most motoring offences, minor criminal damage, being drunk and disorderly – which the police are not required to notify the Home Office about. Second, they inevitably exclude crimes that have not been reported to, or detected by, the police. Third, not all

Activity

Figure 2.2.1 Recorded crime statistics, England and Wales, 1898–2009

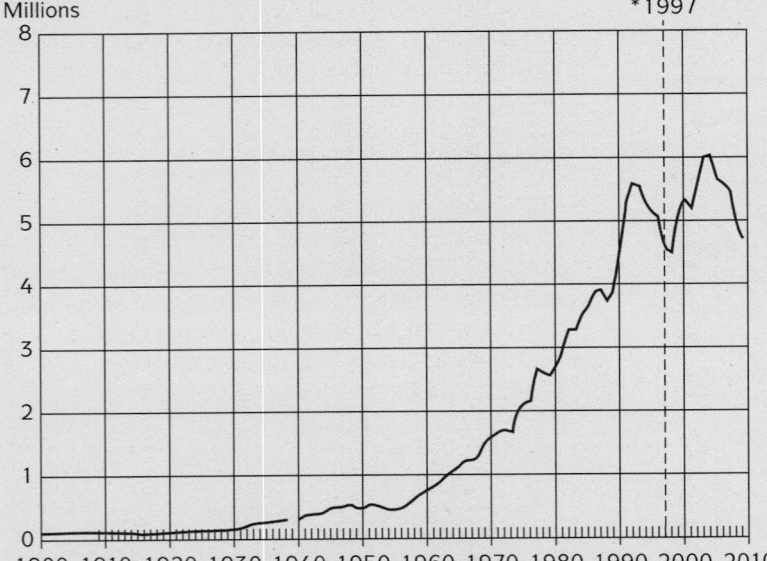

Source: 'Recorded Crime Statistics in England and Wales 1898–2002' and 'Recorded Crime Statistics in England and Wales 2002–2010, Home Office, © Crown copyright

Why do you think recorded crime started to rise steeply in the 1960s?

Activity

Figure 2.2.2 Trends in Crime Survey for England and Wales and police recorded crime (PRC), year ending December 1981 to year ending March 2017

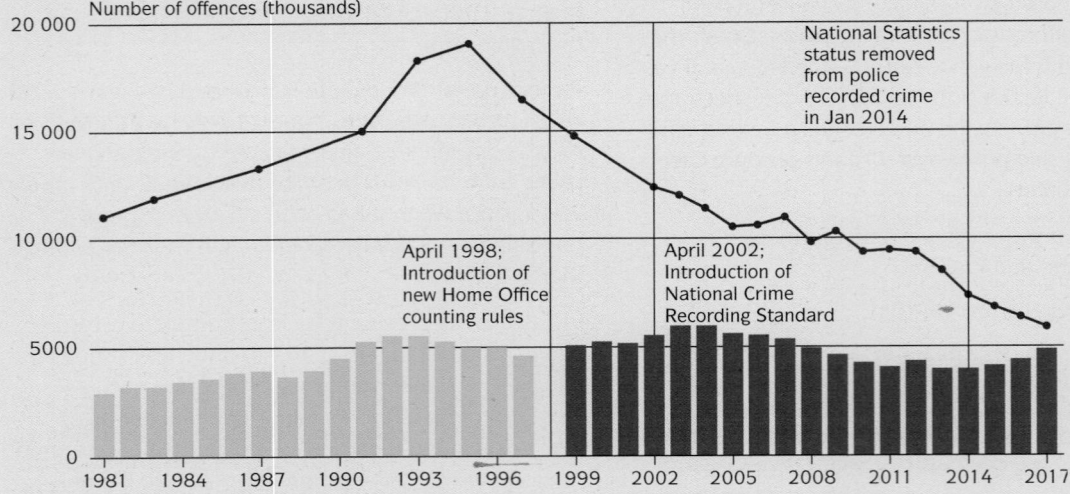

Source: Crime in England and Wales: year ending Mar. 2016, July 2016

Suggest reasons why in recent years CSEW estimates show crime continuing to decline while PRC shows it increasing.

crimes reported to the police are recorded by them. An HM Inspectorate of Constabulary report in 2014 estimated that 1 in 5 reported offences had not been recorded.

A useful metaphor is to think of crime as an iceberg. The police statistics represent the visible tip of the iceberg: those crimes which the police both know about and which they have decided to record. An almost certainly much larger number of crimes remain invisible, hidden beneath the surface of the water − the so-called 'dark figure' of crime.

Activity

Figure 2.2.3 The dark figure of unrecorded crime

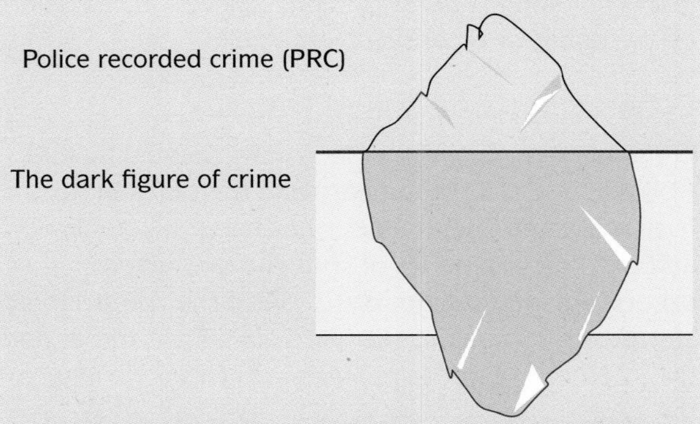

Police recorded crime (PRC)

The dark figure of crime

Explain what elements make up the dark figure of crime.

As a result, the validity of police recorded statistics (in terms of providing an accurate picture of crime overall) is low, though this does vary according to the category of crime considered. For example, it is likely that most of the domestic burglaries and thefts of cars that take place are reported to the police, because if victims wish to claim on their insurance (assuming that they *are* insured) they must provide proof to their insurers that they have reported it. So, for *these* crime categories the statistics are likely to be relatively accurate. However, for many other categories of crime, such as sexual assault or criminal damage, validity is likely to be relatively low because many victims don't report the offence. Victims of sexual assault, for example, may be too embarrassed or too frightened of the possible consequences. Victims of criminal damage may see it as too trivial, say, or think the police would not be able to identify the perpetrator.

Neither are the police statistics seen as particularly reliable. Following an assessment by the UK Statistics

Authority, published in January 2014, PRC data was found not to meet the required high standard for designation as 'National Statistics' because it was insufficiently reliable (and this remains the case at the time of writing). PRC data reliability is compromised by:

> changes in recording practices, for example Home Office counting rules were changed in 1998 and again in 2002

> changes in police activity, for example, focusing efforts at detection on different crimes at different times

> changes in the public's willingness to report different categories of crime as victims or witnesses.

As a result, trends apparently revealed by PRC data will not necessarily reflect changing levels of criminal activity. According to the ONS, 'apparent increases in police recorded crime seen over the last 2 years may reflect a number of factors, including tightening of recording practice, process improvements, increases in reporting by victims and also genuine increases in the levels of crime. It is often difficult to disentangle these different factors' (Crime in England and Wales: year ending Dec. 2016).

British Crime Survey/Crime Survey for England and Wales

Recognition of such weaknesses in PRC data led to the establishment of an alternative set of data in the early 1980s based on surveying potential victims of crime.

Since it began in 1981, the British Crime Survey, which changed its name to the Crime Survey for England and Wales (CSEW) in 2012, has become steadily more sophisticated. Today, the CSEW involves a large representative sample (currently around 35 000) of adults living in private households who are interviewed at home and asked about their experience of being a victim of crime in the previous 12 months. They are also asked about whether they have reported any crimes that they have experienced as victims to the police. The survey is now carried out annually and, since 2009, an additional sample (currently around 3000) of those aged 10−15 has been interviewed. At the end of the main interview, there is a self-completion element (via a tablet computer), where adults aged from 16 to 59 are asked about their experience of domestic abuse and sexual violence, and these results are reported separately.

The main strength of the CSEW is that it picks up on crimes that have not been reported to the police or that have been reported but not recorded. This is why the estimates of total crime that it produces are always higher than the PRC figures.

As a measure of crime, the CSEW therefore has some marked advantages compared to the PRC. Moreover, its validity is enhanced by the high **response rates** (over 70 per cent) that it consistently achieves and by the transfer of responsibility from the Home Office to the independent Office for National Statistics (ONS) in April 2012 – making it more or less impossible for governments of the day to manipulate the figures.

However, this does not mean that the CSEW provides a valid picture of crime overall. Newburn (2007) points out a number of limitations:

1. It does not include some crimes, such as murder (for obvious reasons given that it is a victim survey) or **'victimless' crimes** such as certain drug offences (e.g., using rather than supplying illegal drugs).

2. Most types of corporate crime, environmental crime and offences that are regulated by organisations other than the police (such as the Inland Revenue) are not included.

3. People living outside households, such as the homeless, those in hostels and those in prison, are not part of the sample and they are likely to have high rates of victimisation.

4. Crimes against businesses and commercial premises are also not covered by the survey (although the ONS does carry out a small-scale Commercial Victimisation Survey annually).

Moreover, there are also limitations that are inherent in survey research using face-to-face interviews identified by Hope (2005, cited in Newburn). These include:

> Respondents may deliberately withhold information (e.g., to protect family members).

> Poor memory may result in them forgetting incidents.

> They may believe that incidents happened in the previous 12 months, when in reality they happened earlier.

> The interview conditions, such as where and when the interview takes place and the characteristics of the interviewer might influence the responses.

However, none of the factors identified by Hope are likely to seriously compromise the findings of the CSEW and the picture it presents *of the crime categories it covers* is likely to be more accurate than the police figures. Moreover, the CSEW data are significantly more reliable as a source of information about crime trends than PRC data because the methodology employed in the main count of crime has remained broadly consistent since the survey began and is not subject to fluctuations in levels of reporting by the public or recording by the police.

Cybercrime and online fraud

In the past, the 'high volume' crimes covered by the BCS and CSEW were burglary and theft of vehicles. In recent years, their number has fallen substantially and two new categories of crime have emerged: **cybercrime** and **online fraud.** When the crime survey started, fraud was not seen as a significant threat and the internet had yet to be invented. This is no longer the case.

Consequently, questions on fraud and computer misuse were added to the CSEW in October 2015 and the results indicated an estimated 3.5 million cases of fraud and 1.9 million computer misuse offences in the year ending December 2016. The enormous extent of these offences is demonstrated by the contrast between the CSEW estimated crime total *excluding* these crimes – which was 6.1 million over this

Activity

An FBI poster used to draw attention to the risks of cybercrime.

What criminal stereotype is represented here?

period – and the total when they are *included,* which was 11.5 million – getting on for double the number!

Estimates produced by *Get Safe Online* and *Action Fraud* suggest that cybercrime and online fraud cost the UK economy nearly £11 billion in 2015/16.

Official crime statistics: sociological debate

The discussion above of issues surrounding the validity and reliability of crime statistics takes for granted that, in principle at least, it should be possible to gain an accurate picture of crime in society. This, in turn, assumes that sociologists can produce a picture of crime that is objectively true, just as – if they work hard enough – they can establish objective truths about society as a whole.

Interpretivist/phenomenological sociologists (such as labelling theorists) reject this view. For them, sociology is limited to studying the interpretations of the world held by the members of society and these interpretations are irremediably subjective. We cannot know whether there is any objective reality lying beyond these interpretations. Indeed, sociological accounts are themselves simply the interpretations of sociologists and there is no basis for claiming that they are superior to any other interpretations.

From this perspective, crime statistics are simply a record of occasions when the police, victims, witnesses and so on have interpreted certain actions as crimes. Consequently, for interpretivist/phenomenological sociologists, questions about the validity or reliability of official statistics are beside the point, as there is no way of knowing what the 'true' picture of crime might be (if, indeed, such a thing exists).

Positivist/realist sociologists, (such as functionalists and Marxists) by contrast believe both that society exists as an objective reality and that it is possible to discover what this reality is. The fact that people interpret the world differently doesn't mean that statements about the world that are objectively true cannot be made. For example, the fact that some youths might interpret throwing a stone through someone's window as 'a bit of a laff' doesn't mean that they have not, objectively, committed an offence of criminal damage. Hence, for positivist/realist sociologists, questions about the validity and reliability of crime statistics are both legitimate and important.

Official crime statistics: political and policy implications

The CSEW and PRC taken together, despite their many limitations, are widely seen by the mainstream media, politicians and the general public as providing a more or less accurate and reliable picture of both the total amount of crime in society and how it is changing over time. This view is disputed by many sociologists and criminologists.

First, as Richard Garside (2015) has argued, even when the two types of statistics are taken together, they do not offer an accurate guide to all the behaviours that can be classified as crimes. Indeed, as Garside pithily observes, 'talk of "overall crime" is best reserved for crime involving overalls'. Where, he asks, are the official measures of corporate crime or environmental crime?

Second, Tim Hope (2015) argues that the CSEW conceals as much as it reveals. In particular, it fails to draw attention to significant *inequalities* in the risk of being a victim of crime. For example, while roughly 80 per cent of the population absorb less than a quarter of all household property crime, 20 per cent suffer from all the rest, with a small percentage of this 20 per cent 'chronically victimised'. Hope maintains that there is a need to 'rebalance' the CSEW in favour of victims by selecting samples that include those facing a high probability of victimisation, encouraging respondents to be honest about crimes that they may find difficult to talk about and by trying to find ways of engaging more of those people who decline to take part in the survey.

Hope is also critical of the fact that the CSEW usually places an arbitrary cap on the number of incidents of victimisation that respondents can report in order that estimates based on the sample findings are not skewed by a small number who report an extremely high number of incidents. When the cap is removed there is a 70 per cent increase in violent crimes against women, a 70 per cent increase in violent crime committed by family members and a 100 per cent increase in violent crimes committed by acquaintances.

Finally, the dominance of the PRC and CSEW data in discussion of crime in the public domain means that politicians adopt a narrow focus on just those crimes covered in these data sets when discussing 'crime' policies. If, for example, the data suggest that ('total') crime is falling, crime is unlikely to figure prominently on the political agenda (it was pretty much absent from the 2017 General Election campaign, for instance). It also means that politicians can safely ignore those crimes not covered by the official statistics (or that rarely make an appearance), such as corporate and environmental crime. Yet, in terms of the economic costs alone, such crimes have an enormous impact on society.

It is to these categories of crime that we now turn.

Key terms

Valid Data are valid if they represent a true and accurate description or measurement.

Reliable Data are reliable when different researchers using the same methods obtain the same results. Data can be reliable without being valid.

Summary offences Offences in England and Wales are divided into three categories: summary, triable either way and indictable. Indictable offences are seen as the most serious and must be tried in a Crown Court rather than a Magistrates' Court. Summary offences are seen as the least serious.

Response rate The percentage of the sample that participates in the research.

Victimless crimes Crimes where there is no apparent victim because the act is consensual or because the perpetrator and 'victim' are one and the same person.

Cybercrime and online fraud Cybercrime refers to crime involving computer networks and online fraud is fraud facilitated by the internet.

Summary

1. Official crime statistics are those produced by government departments or agencies.

2. The two main types are police recorded crime (PRC) and the Crime Survey for England and Wales (CSEW, formerly the British Crime Survey). Both have strengths and limitations. Cybercrime and online fraud have recently been added to the CSEW.

3. The 'crime problem' is often thought about in terms of crimes covered by the official statistics, but they don't cover all crimes. In particular, they exclude corporate crime, state crime and much green crime.

Unit 2.2.2 White–collar and corporate crime

The term 'white-collar crime' was coined by the American sociologist Edwin Sutherland in 1939. He defined it as 'crime committed by a person of high social status and respectability in the course of his occupation'. Sutherland introduced the term in order to draw attention to what he felt was the unjustifiable neglect within sociology of crimes committed by middle- and upper-class people as opposed to '**blue-collar**' crime committed by the working class.

The term was used, and still is used by some, to describe both crimes committed by individuals seeking personal gain and crimes committed by organisations. However, today sociologists increasingly distinguish between these two categories. Gary Slapper and Steve Tombs (1999) argue that the term 'white-collar crime' should be reserved to describe 'crimes by the individually rich or powerful that are committed in the furtherance of their own interests, often against corporations or organisations with, for or within which they are working'. 'Corporate crimes', on the other hand, are crimes committed by or for corporations, which act to further the interests of the corporation rather than those of the individual employee.

While in principle these two types of crime are distinct, in practice the boundary between them may be blurred. There are two main reasons for this. First, corporations may exist as legal entities, but they cannot 'act': it is individuals within those corporations who do things that are, or are not, illegal. Second, in promoting the interests of the corporation by illegal means, individuals are likely to be promoting their own interests at the same time. For example, individuals may receive advantages through bonuses, promotion or salary rises if they engage in illegal activities which promote the profitability of a company.

White–collar crime

White-collar crime covers a wide range of crimes including fraud, bribery, **embezzlement**, **insider trading** and individual tax evasion. These crimes are generally hidden from public view and, on those infrequent occasions when perpetrators are caught, receive little media publicity unless they involve people in the public eye such as politicians or celebrities or unless the sheer scale of the crimes results in media attention.

One of the most widely publicised examples of white-collar crime in Britain in recent years was the expenses scandal, affecting members of the House of Commons and the House of Lords. The scandal broke in 2009 when the *Daily Telegraph* got hold of and published details of expenses claimed by MPs (including claims for a duck house, which cost over £1500, and the cost of clearing a moat). Many MPs were required to repay excessive claims for expenses, although their actions were not deemed illegal. However, four MPs and two members of the House of Lords were charged with the crime of false accounting and were sent to prison for fraud.

Activity

CAN'T I JUST HAND IT BACK...LIKE AN MP?

SWAG

FRAN.

In what way is this cartoon not an entirely accurate take on the MPs' expenses scandal?

Corporate crime

Pearce and Tombs (1998) define corporate crime as 'illegal acts or omissions, punishable by the State under administrative, civil or criminal law, which are the result of deliberate decision making or **culpable negligence** within a legitimate formal organisation'. In simpler terms, corporate crime involves members of corporations doing things that are against the law or not doing things that the law requires them to do.

Like white-collar crime, corporate crime is generally hidden from view and under-reported in the news media. Moreover, when it *is* reported, it is rarely treated as criminal. Instead, the frames used by the media represent corporate crimes as, say, 'errors of judgement', 'accounting mistakes', 'oversights' or – at worst – 'scandals'. However, in recent years thanks to the campaigning of anti-austerity groups such as UK-uncut and Occupy and to investigative journalists, at least some types of corporate wrong-doing such as tax avoidance (Google, Starbucks), dubious employment practices (Amazon, JD Sports) and phone-hacking (*News of the World*, the *Sun*, the *Mirror*) have been widely publicised.

Tombs (2013) identifies four main types of corporate crime:

» *Financial offences,* such as illegal share dealings, mergers and takeovers; tax evasion; bribery; and illegal accounting practices. For example, the US company Enron was one of the world's major electricity, natural gas, communications and pulp and paper companies, with claimed revenues of nearly $101 billion in 2000. In 2001, it was revealed that its reported financial position was sustained by fraudulent accounting practices. The company was forced into bankruptcy and had to sell assets to try to meet some of the claims of creditors who were owed around $50 billion.

» *Offences against consumers*, such as illegal sales/ marketing practices; the sale of unfit goods; conspiracies to fix prices and/or carve up the market for particular goods and services; and various forms of false/illegal labelling. For example, the pharmaceutical company Chemie Grünenthal of Germany manufactured the drug Thalidomide in the late 1950s, which was used as a sleeping pill or tranquilliser. However, the use of the drug by pregnant women led to over 10 000 seriously deformed babies being born throughout the world. The drug was not tested for its effects during pregnancy before it was launched, yet was marketed with advertising proclaiming that it was 'completely safe'. The company was slow to withdraw the product even when the drug's disastrous effects were known.

» *Offences against employees,* such as sexual and racial discrimination, violations of wage laws, of rights to organise and take industrial action, and various occupational health and safety offences. For example, in 1984 an escape of poisonous gas from a pesticides plant at Bhopal in India killed nearly 3000 people (both employees and local residents) and caused permanent injury to a further 20 000. Moreover, campaigners say that nearly 20 000 others have since died from the effects of the leak. The escape of gas was caused by inadequate safety procedures at the plant, which was owned by a subsidiary of the US multinational corporation Union Carbide. In 1989 a settlement was reached between Union Carbide and the Indian government in which, in return for exemption from criminal charges, the company agreed to pay $470 million in compensation to victims and their families.

» *Offences against the environment*, such as illegal emissions to air, water, and land; hazardous waste dumping; and illegal manufacturing practices, for example the revelation in September 2015 that the car manufacturer Volkswagen had been using special software to cheat emissions-testing checks on their diesel cars thereby allowing them to emit nitrogen oxide pollutants up to 40 times above legal limits (*The Guardian*, 23.09.2015). According to Tombs (2016), an estimated 29 000 deaths each year in the UK are attributable to the effects of airborne pollution. (See also Unit 2.3.4 Green crime.)

There are no official statistics on corporate crime, so estimating its extent is extremely difficult. However, Tombs claims that, on the basis of the data that are available, two 'unequivocal conclusions' can be drawn. The first is that corporate crime entails enormous costs, both physical and financial, which far outweigh those associated with 'conventional' or 'street' crime. The second is that corporate offending is not a rare occurrence, the product of a few 'bad apples', but 'routine and pervasive'.

Key terms

Blue collar An alternative label for the working class based on the typical colour of the shirts worn by people doing manual work in the past (ditto, white collar).

Embezzlement Theft or misappropriation of funds placed in one's trust or belonging to one's employer.

Insider trading (or dealing) Making use of confidential information to buy or sell stocks and shares illegally.

Culpable negligence A failure to do something that is legally required, for example, protecting employees from health hazards.

Summary

1. White-collar crime is crime committed by people in higher-status positions and includes fraud, embezzlement, workplace theft and individual tax evasion.

2. Corporate crime is crime committed by organisations. The main categories are financial crime, crimes against consumers, crimes associated with employment relationships and environmental crimes. There are no official statistics for corporate crime.

Unit 2.2.3 Globalisation and transnational organised crime

Corporate crime is sometimes referred to as 'organisational crime'. Organis*ational* crime should not be confused with 'organis*ed* crime'. The UK's **National Crime Agency** defines organised crime as 'serious crime planned, coordinated and conducted by people working together on a continuing basis'.

The popular image of organised crime groups (OCGs) in Europe and America – informed by Hollywood block-busters like *The Godfather* – is of Italian mafia groups such as La Cosa Nostra, 'Ndrangheta and the Camorra: tightly structured, hierarchical groups based on family and ethnic ties. Such images are increasingly dated. Following globalisation, organised crime is now international in nature.

Transnational organised crime (TOC) is organised crime coordinated across national borders, involving groups or networks of individuals working in more than one country to plan and execute criminal activities. According to Europol (the Europe-wide police support organisation), 30 per cent to 40 per cent of the OCGs operating on an international level today feature loose network structures and members who don't share the same ethnic origins. Moreover, approximately 20 per cent of these networks only exist for a short period of time and are set up to support specific criminal ventures.

Recognition of the growing problem of TOC led to the establishment of the United Nations Office on Drugs and Crime (UNODC) in 1997. The UNODC estimates that in 2009 TOC generated $870 billion of revenue – an amount equal to 1.5 per cent of global GDP. The final report of a research project sponsored by the European Commission – the Organised Crime Portfolio research project (2015) – estimated that organised crime costs the EU economy about €110 billion annually.

Main types of Transnational Organised Crime (TOC)

TOC takes a number of forms. The main ones according to UNODC are as follows:

> drug **trafficking**, particularly of heroin and cocaine, which accounts for over one third of the total annual value of TOC

» human trafficking of men, women and children for sexual or labour-based exploitation

» smuggling of migrants, particularly from Latin America to North America and from Africa to Western Europe

» illegal trading in firearms, particularly handguns and assault rifles

» trafficking in natural resources such as diamonds, rare metals and hardwoods

» illegal trading in wildlife, such as animal skins, ivory and rhino horns

» supply of fraudulent medicines that don't work or may actually be dangerous to health

» cybercrime, including **phishing**, **hacking** and identity theft.

Most of these offences would appear in the official crime statistics, provided they were detected, though they wouldn't be distinguished as TOC offences.

The resulting global flows of goods, people and wildlife are shown in Figure 2.2.4.

Explaining the growth of TOC

The growth of transnational organised crime is directly linked to the growth of globalisation since the 1980s. Globalisation involves all parts of the world becoming increasingly interconnected, so that national borders – in some respects at least – become less important. TOC can be seen as part of the 'dark side of globalisation' (Brittain-Catlin, 2005).

Activity

Figure 2.2.4 Main global transnational organised crime flows

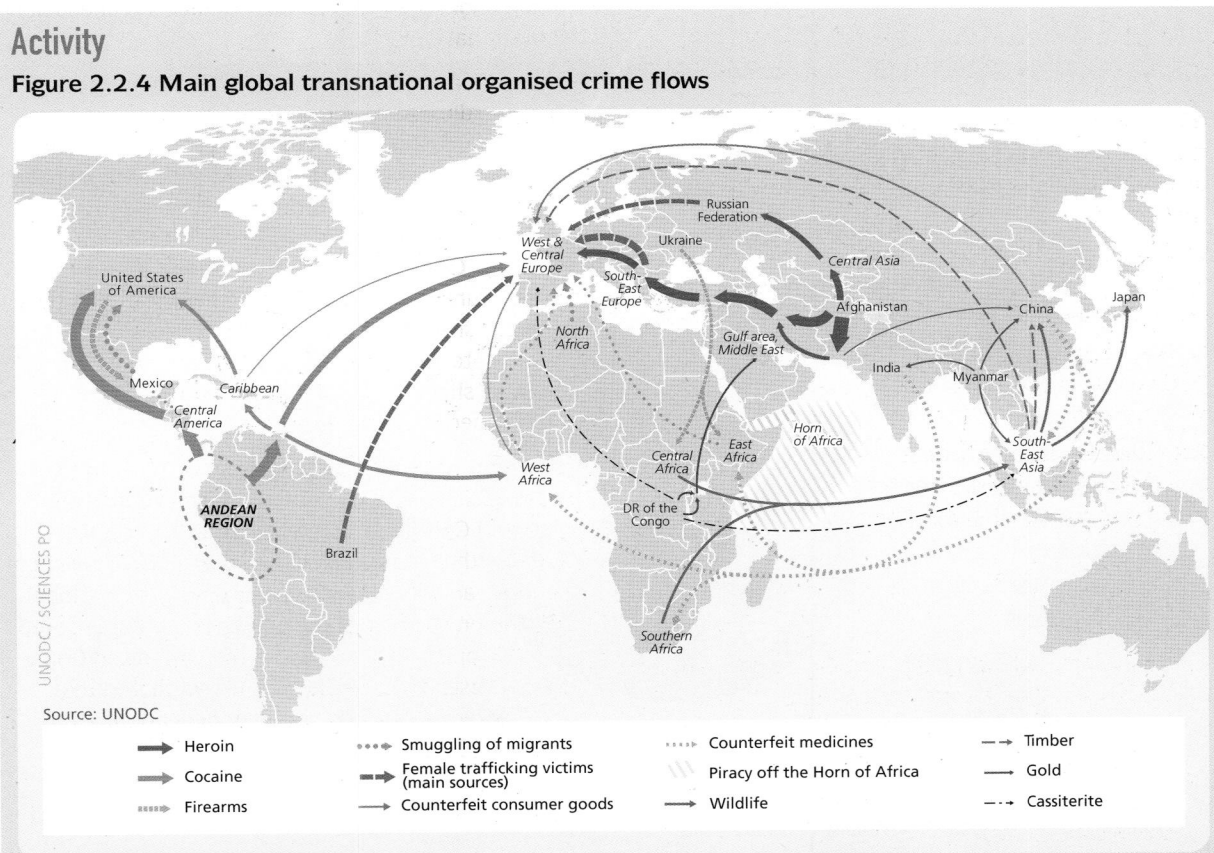

Source: UNODC

Heroin	Smuggling of migrants	Counterfeit medicines	Timber
Cocaine	Female trafficking victims (main sources)	Piracy off the Horn of Africa	Gold
Firearms	Counterfeit consumer goods	Wildlife	Cassiterite

UNODC / SCIENCES PO

Source: *The Globalisation of Crime: A Transnational Organised Crime Threat Assessment*, United Nations, 2010

How can the TOC flows be seen as reflecting global inequalities?

A number of features of globalisation are relevant here:

» the development of cheaper and faster international transport (e.g., cheap international flights) facilitating the trafficking of illegal products as well as legal ones

» the deregulation of the financial sector facilitating **money laundering**

» the explosion in computer and electronic communications facilitating communication between OCGs based in more than one country as well as opening up a whole new range of criminal opportunities in terms of cybercrime

» the collapse of the **Iron Curtain** allowing OCGs in the former Soviet Union countries the opportunity to move into new territories

» the growth of tax havens or 'secrecy jurisdictions', which tend not to be too worried about where the money passing through them has come from

» the growth of world trade, providing cover for illegally traded goods.

Contemporary issues: Transnational Organised Crime (TOC) – The 'Global Laundromat'

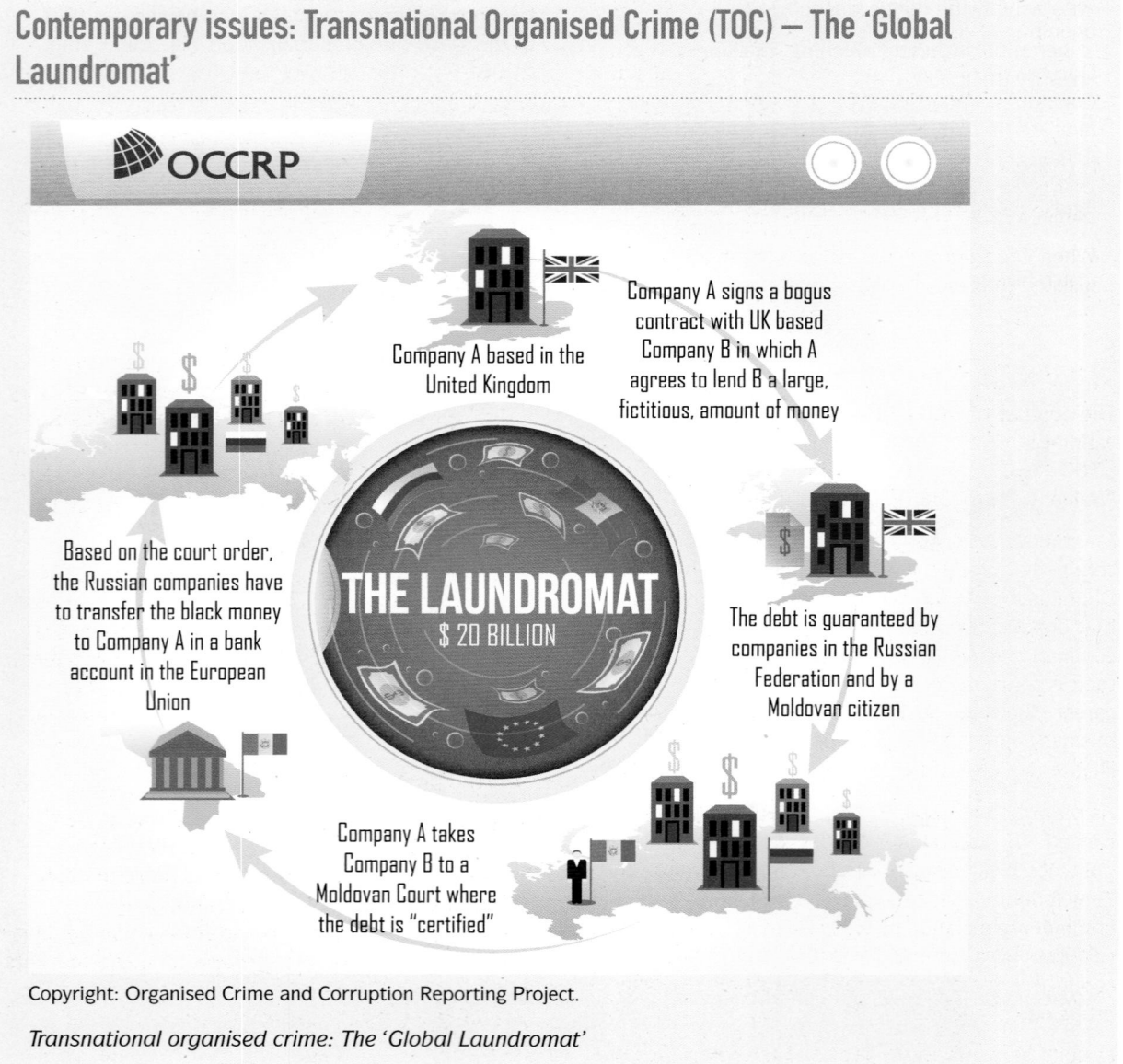

OCCRP

Company A based in the United Kingdom

Company A signs a bogus contract with UK based Company B in which A agrees to lend B a large, fictitious, amount of money

THE LAUNDROMAT
$ 20 BILLION

Based on the court order, the Russian companies have to transfer the black money to Company A in a bank account in the European Union

The debt is guaranteed by companies in the Russian Federation and by a Moldovan citizen

Company A takes Company B to a Moldovan Court where the debt is "certified"

Copyright: Organised Crime and Corruption Reporting Project.

Transnational organised crime: The 'Global Laundromat'

A recent example of TOC – dubbed the 'Global Laundromat' – suggests that weak oversight of suspicious financial flows allowed nearly $740 million of suspect Russian funds to be laundered through UK high street banks, and foreign banks with offices in London, between 2010 and 2014.

A three-year investigation led by police in Latvia and Moldova covering 96 countries has uncovered a conspiracy that involved at least $20 billion being sent from suspected criminals in Russia via accounts held in Latvian and Moldovan banks to anonymously owned **shell companies**, most of them registered at Companies House in London. Most of the 21 core companies under scrutiny have since been dissolved.

Documents obtained by the Organised Crime and Corruption Reporting Project and Novaya Gazette indicate that HSBC processed about $543 million in Laundromat cash, RBS about $113 million and Coutts $33 million, though virtually all the major UK banks were implicated to some degree.

When *The Guardian* contacted these banks, they all insisted that they had strict anti-money-laundering policies as required by the Financial Conduct Authority. However, an international financial investigator – L Burke Files – interviewed by *The Guardian* said that compliance checks at many western banks were half-hearted: 'Typically the compliance and investigations department is treated like an unwanted step-child. The directors of a bank see compliance as an expense without any return.'

Investigators are still trying to identify some of the estimated 500 Russians involved who include oligarchs, Moscow bankers and figures working for, or connected to, the FSB (the successor to the KGB).

(Adapted from 'British banks handled vast sums of laundered Russian money,' *The Guardian* 20.03.2017)

Questions

1. How does this case illustrate some of the characteristic features of TOC?

2. How culpable (blameworthy) do you think British banks were in facilitating money laundering in this case?

Organised crime in the UK

The number of OCGs operating in the UK was estimated by the National Crime Agency to be around 5300 in 2013, comprising about 36 600 individuals (Wall and Christyakova, 2015).

An ethnographic study of organised crime in Britain conducted during the 1990s by Dick Hobbs and Colin Dunningham (1998) provides support for the idea that organised crime increasingly involves individuals, coming together in loose-knit networks, who treat their criminal career rather like they would a business career. They are constantly on the lookout for new business opportunities, and often mix legitimate and illegitimate enterprises.

As part of their study, Hobbs and Dunningham carried out research in an economically depressed post-industrial town, which they called Downtown. They found no evidence that there was any large criminal organisation in the area. Instead, individuals with extensive criminal contacts acted as 'hubs', connecting the diverse activities of different loose groupings of criminals.

Despite globalisation, Hobbs and Dunningham see criminal activities as being firmly rooted in local contexts. Criminal entrepreneurs develop their careers, at least initially, in local areas. They rely very much on networks of contacts to find opportunities to make money. Eventually, some become involved in wider networks – for example, those involving drug smuggling. They may even emigrate, but generally they retain strong local links.

Hobbs and Dunningham do not believe that organised crime in the UK is increasingly dominated by large multinational or even global criminal organisations (such as the Mafia). Instead, it works as a **glocal** system. That is, there are some global connections involved but it remains locally based.

Wall and Christyakova agree. Moreover, they argue that OCGs in the UK are shifting towards 'less risky and less violent – but still lucrative – market niches where detection is more difficult'. According to their research, fraud, drug trafficking, counterfeiting and tobacco smuggling are currently the largest organised illegal markets in the UK, with trafficking for sexual exploitation and organised vehicle crime following close behind.

Key terms

National Crime Agency (NCA) The NCA was established in 2013 to tackle serious organised crime in the UK. It replaced SOCA (the Serious Organised Crime Agency).

Trafficking Either the transportation and dealing of illegal products or the transportation and dealing of legal products illegally acquired.

Phishing The sending of emails from supposedly reputable companies asking the recipients to reveal personal details such as passwords.

Hacking Gaining unauthorised access to data in a system or computer.

Money laundering The crime of moving money that has been obtained illegally through banks and other businesses to make it seem as if the money has been obtained legally.

Iron Curtain The Iron Curtain was the name coined by Winston Churchill for the boundary dividing Europe into two separate areas from the end of World War II in 1945 until the end of the Cold War in 1991. The term symbolised the efforts by the Soviet Union to block off itself and its satellite states from open contact with the West and non-Soviet-controlled areas.

Shell companies Companies set up purely for purposes such as tax avoidance or evasion.

Glocal A word formed by combining 'global' and 'local', drawing attention to the two-way relationship between the local and the global.

Summary

1. Another category of crime is serious organised crime (SOC). Globalisation has been associated with the growth of transnational serious organised crime (TOC), estimated by the UNODC to be worth $870 billion dollars in 2009.

2. TOC involves crimes such as drug trafficking, human trafficking, illegal trading in firearms and wildlife and cybercrime.

3. TOC is increasingly carried out by relatively loose-knit social networks of criminals acting across national boundaries.

PART 3 HUMAN RIGHTS, STATE CRIME AND GREEN CRIME

Contents

In Part 3 we complete our overview of patterns and trends in crime begun in Part 2 by turning our attention to two categories of crime that were largely ignored by criminologists until recent decades: state crime and green crime.

Globalisation has been associated with the development of a global capitalist system incorporating regions and countries (the former 'communist' states) that had previously operated outside its scope and made scrutiny difficult – China, the former USSR, Angola, Mozambique and others.

At the same time, a global human rights movement has developed – examined in Unit 2.3.2. Together, these developments have led to increasing scrutiny of how states treat their citizens and the harms they can and do inflict – which we examine in Unit 2.3.3.

Recent decades have also seen a growing global concern with environmental issues such as the depletion of natural resources, ecological disasters and global warming. This has led to the development of a new branch of criminology focused on environmental harms – green criminology – which we examine in Unit 2.3.4.

Finally, the examination of state and green crime has led some criminologists to question the very foundations of their discipline. The motivation of many practitioners for studying crime is a concern with social justice. But what if the category 'crime' excludes many clear social and ecological harms? We begin with an examination of this issue.

Unit 2.3.1 Crime vs. harm

Both crime and deviance can be seen as **social constructs** in that what counts as 'deviant' and what counts as 'criminal' varies from one society to another and from one time to another. Euthanasia, for example, remains illegal in the UK, but has been legalised in the Netherlands, Belgium, Colombia and Luxembourg. Gay sex was, until relatively recently, illegal in the UK, but in 1967 homosexual acts conducted in private between consenting male adults over the age of 21 were made legal in England and Wales and, since then, the age of consent has been reduced so that it is now in line with that for heterosexual sex. Hence, there is nothing intrinsic about certain acts or omissions (failures to act) that make them criminal. 'Crimes' are defined by what particular states at particular times choose to criminalise.

Some sociologists – functionalists – see the criminal law in liberal democracies as reflecting a consensus about those harms that are so serious that the state should seek to prevent them or punish those who commit them. However, others – conflict theorists – argue that the law is a reflection of the relative power of different groups in society and that it therefore inevitably reflects the interests of the powerful. Consequently, many things that are harmful to *society*, but are in the interests of the powerful are not criminalised.

Zemiology

Writing from a conflict theory perspective, in *Beyond Criminology: Taking Harm Seriously* (2004), Hillyard *et al.* argue, not that the harms defined by the criminal law are unimportant, but that an exclusive focus on crime provides a 'highly partial, biased and distorted view of the nature and extent of harms people experience during their lifetime'.

In place of criminology, they advocate the development of a new discipline called **zemiology** (from the Greek z*emia,* meaning harm). They argue that such a discipline would have a number of advantages over criminology including providing the basis for a more accurate picture of the harms that people are likely to experience during their lives, identifying where responsibility for the production of these harms lies and devising policies to tackle them.

Activity

We often hear people say 'there ought to be a law against it'. Try to identify half-a-dozen things that you consider to be harmful, but which are currently legal in the UK. Compare your list with a classmate. Assuming your lists differ, do you nevertheless agree with each other's list? If not, why do you think this is? What do you think are the chances of the acts you list being criminalised?

Some green criminologists have also argued for the adoption of a wider harm approach, but they would extend the notion of harm beyond social harm to include harm caused to non-human species and harm to the environment more generally.

Zemiology: for and against

Critics have raised a number of objections to the suggestion that criminology should be replaced by a new discipline focused on harm. One is that 'harm' is no easier to define than crime and, in some ways, more difficult. Another is that deciding what counts as 'harmful' inevitably entails making value-judgements and would therefore simply reflect the ideological preferences of those making such judgements. For example, people with left-wing views would see gross inequalities in pay as socially harmful, while people with right-wing views would see any attempts to limit by law what people can be paid as a harmful infringement of liberty.

Activity

How does this cartoon illustrate the distinction between crime and social harm?

Hillyard *et al.* acknowledge these objections, but argue that the process of debate involved in trying to reach agreement about what constitutes unacceptable harms and how they could best be measured would be a positive one. Rightly or wrongly, they view these objections 'more as technical issues *in*, rather than as **insuperable** obstacles *to*', the development of a new discipline.

One possible solution to the problem posed by the **relativistic** nature of judgements about what counts as 'harmful' would be the identification of a generally accepted standard against which such judgements could be gauged. The concept of universal human rights constitutes just such a standard in the view of some social scientists and so it is to this topic that we turn next.

Key terms

Social construct Something which has the appearance of being a straightforward and inevitable feature of human existence, but is actually a product of social processes.

Zemiology The study of harm.

Insuperable Too great to overcome.

Relativism The idea that all knowledge is relative to time, place, culture and the individual, and that no one set of ideas reveals the whole truth.

Summary

1. Critical social scientists have sought to extend the scope of criminology to include the examination of acts that may not be illegal, but nevertheless produce harm.

2. The term 'zemiology' has been suggested to cover such an extension of the scope of criminology.

3. Critics have argued that focusing on harm rather than on illegality would raise difficulties because harm is difficult to define and would produce ideologically biased analyses.

4. The concept of 'human rights' could offer a standard against which harm could be measured relatively objectively.

Unit 2.3.2 Human rights

The idea that human beings have innate rights simply by virtue of being human has deep historical roots, but it was the horrific events connected with the slaughter of millions of Jewish people (and other minority groups including gypsies, homosexuals and disabled people) during World War II – the Holocaust – that provided the impetus for a global effort to formulate what these might be.

Activity

Auschwitz in southern Poland was the most notorious of the concentration camps built by the Nazis during World War II.

Carry out research to find out what role concentration camps such as Auschwitz played in the Holocaust.

The United Nations (UN) was established immediately following the end of the war in 1945 and one of the first concerns of its 50-odd member states was to produce a document that would identify the fundamental rights and freedoms that all human beings should enjoy. The result of their efforts was the Universal Declaration of Human Rights, adopted in 1948.

In 30 'Articles', it sets out a range of freedoms and rights that (should) apply to all. For example, Article 3 states that 'Everyone has the right to life, liberty and security of person' and Article 5 that 'No one shall be subjected to torture or to cruel, inhuman or degrading treatment or punishment'. The Declaration formed the basis for the European Convention on Human Rights, adopted in 1950, and the Human Rights Act 1998 made these rights part of UK domestic law.

Activity

The Universal Declaration of Human Rights.

Access a copy of the UN Universal Declaration of Human Rights. Are there any of the 30 Articles you disagree with?

In principle, as nearly every state in the world has signed up to the Declaration, it would appear to provide a standard against which social harms could indeed be judged. In practice, however, things are more complicated.

For a start, the Declaration has been adapted by some countries so that it is in line with deeply held religious beliefs. For example, in 1990 the member states of the Organisation of the Islamic Conference issued the Cairo Declaration on Human Rights in Islam (CDHRI), which argues that Sharia law takes precedence over secular law and, for example, states that men and women do not have equal rights to marry more than one person or to divorce their spouse.

Second, as Eric Posner (2014) has argued, while virtually all governments today use the language of human rights, they use it to make radically different arguments about how countries should behave:

China cites 'the right to development' to explain why the Chinese government gives priority to

economic growth over political liberalisation. Many countries cite the 'right to security', a catch-all idea that protection from crime justifies harsh enforcement methods. Vladimir Putin cited the rights of ethnic minorities in Ukraine in order to justify his military intervention there, just as the United States cited Saddam Hussein's suppression of human rights in order to build support for the Iraq war.

Finally, statements of human rights do not necessarily provide clear-cut guides to action: does the right to 'freedom of expression', for example, extend to saying hateful things about ethnic groups or sexual minorities or, indeed, about the ex-boyfriend or girlfriend who has just dumped you?

Nevertheless, the notion of human rights has played a significant role in sociologists' examination of state crimes and it is to these we now turn.

Summary

1. The slaughter of millions of Jews (and other minorities) by the Nazis in World War II led to the Universal Declaration of Human Rights.

2. In 30 Articles, it identifies a wide range of rights and freedoms that all humans should enjoy.

3. Using human rights as a standard for judging whether acts are harmful faces problems as there are competing lists of human rights, they may conflict with each other and they don't necessarily provide clear-cut guidelines for judging harm.

Unit 2.3.3 State crime

On a narrow definition, state crimes are acts that are initiated, committed or approved by government officials or agencies that violate domestic or international law. However, many social scientists wish to extend this definition to include acts that, while not formally illegal, nevertheless cause social harm. Thus, the International State Crime Initiative (based at Queen Mary College, University of London), for example, draws upon the notion of human rights to argue that the term 'state crime' should 'include all violations of human rights that are deviant in the sense that they infringe some socially recognized norm' (ISCI, *About state crime*).

In defining state crime thus, ISCI is following the lead of Herman and Julia Schwendinger (1975), who argued that we should define state crime as the violation of people's human rights by the state or its agents. Sociologists should not simply accept the laws as passed by national governments, but go beyond these to explore the harm perpetrated by governments in the name of having to maintain social control.

On this basis, McLaughlin (2001) identifies four main categories of state crime:

- *political criminality*, including corruption, intimidation and censorship

- *criminality associated with security and police forces*, including war-making, genocide, **ethnic cleansing**, torture, terrorism

- *criminality associated with economic activities*, including **monopolisation practices**, health and safety violations, illegal collaboration with multinational corporations

- *criminality at cultural and societal levels*, including material impoverishment of sections of the community, institutional racism, cultural vandalism.

State–corporate crime

The reference in bullet-point three above to 'illegal collaboration with multinational corporations' draws attention to a hybrid category that has been called *'state-corporate crime'* by Kramer and Michalowski (1991) – crime or serious social harm that results from the interaction of political and economic organisations.

Kramer and Michalowski identify two basic types of state-corporate crime:

State-initiated corporate crime occurs when corporations, employed by the government, engage in organisational deviance at the direction of, or with the tacit approval of, the government.

State-facilitated corporate crime, on the other hand, occurs when government regulatory institutions fail to restrain deviant business activities, either because of direct collusion between business and government or because they both share goals whose attainment would be hampered by effective regulation (Kramer *et al.*, 2002).

Kramer (1992) gives the example of the space shuttle *Challenger* explosion in 1986, which killed seven astronauts, as an example of state-initiated corporate

Activity

The explosion of the space shuttle Challenger, *which took off despite safety concerns.*

Explain why this can be seen as an example of state-corporate crime.

crime. The official inquiry into the disaster found NASA's organisational culture and decision-making processes had been key contributing factors to the accident, with the agency violating its own safety rules. NASA managers had known since 1977 that contractor Morton Thiokol's design of the rocket boosters contained a potentially catastrophic flaw, but they had failed to address this problem properly. They had also ignored warnings from engineers about the dangers of launching posed by the low temperatures on the morning of the launch.

In a more recent study of the nuclear industry in the USA, Bruce and Becker (2007) argue that these two types of state-corporate crime are not necessarily discrete and that one can merge into the other. In their case-study of the Paducah Gaseous Diffusion Plant (PGDP) in Paducah, Kentucky, they found that the role of the state evolved from that of instigator to facilitator of state-corporate crime.

Bruce and Becker argue that the US government made the decision to locate a nuclear plant at the Paducah site in 1950 and subsequently encouraged a generally lax attitude towards safety with the result that as many as 400 PDGP workers received an annual radiation dose up to 20 times the limit now considered safe between 1952 and 1985. Over the life of the plant, the state took deliberate steps to transfer plant ownership and operation to private corporations and transformed its role to that of regulator. However, the authors draw attention to many failings in the subsequent regulatory regime and argue that the government's role 'clearly change[d] from that of instigator to facilitator of state-corporate crime'.

Genocide and war crimes

Perhaps the most extreme examples of state crimes are genocide and war crimes. The term 'genocide' was coined in 1944 and is defined by the UN Convention on the Prevention and Punishment of the Crime of Genocide (CPPCG) as 'acts committed with intent to destroy, in whole or in part, a national, ethnical, racial or religious group'. The convention came into force in 1951 and has since been ratified by more than 130 countries. However, it appears to have made little difference in terms of genocidal acts.

Between 1975 and 1979, the Khmer Rouge regime killed roughly 1.7 million Cambodians. In 1992, the government of Bosnia-Herzegovina declared its independence from Yugoslavia and Bosnian Serb leaders targeted both Bosnian Muslim and Croatian civilians resulting in the deaths of some 100 000 people by 1995. From April to mid-July 1994, members of the Hutu majority in Rwanda murdered some 500 000 to 800 000 Tutsis.

War crimes fall into two main categories: illegal wars and acts carried out during a war that breach the **Geneva Conventions**, such as intentionally directing attacks against the civilian population, pillaging, rape, sexual slavery, forced pregnancy or any other form of sexual violence.

The legality of the Iraq War which Britain fought in alongside the USA starting in 2003 is still hotly contested. The invasion was never approved by the UN. Indeed, then General Secretary of the UN, Kofi Annan, said in 2004, 'I have indicated it was not in conformity with the UN charter from our point of view, from the charter point of view, it was illegal' (BBC, 16.09.2004).

The US and UK governments justified their invasion on the basis that Iraq had violated United Nations Security Council Resolution 1441 (passed in November 2002), which required Iraq to disarm, by continuing to produce weapons of mass destruction. However, the Chilcot inquiry into the Iraq War, published finally in 2016, stated that Saddam Hussein did not pose an urgent threat to British interests, that intelligence regarding Iraq's alleged possession of weapons of mass destruction was presented with 'unwarranted certainty' and that peaceful alternatives to war had not been exhausted before the invasion took place. Its damning conclusion was that a war in 2003 was 'unnecessary'.

Activity

The two leading non-governmental organisations (NGOs) campaigning on behalf of human rights globally are Amnesty International (AI) and Human Rights Watch. Access their websites and make notes on current examples of state crimes that you could use in answering exam questions on this topic.

Contemporary issues: Disabled rights in the UK

A demonstration in support of disabled people.

In 2007, the UK (Labour) government signed up to the UN Convention on the Rights of Persons with

Disabilities (UNCRPD). In 2015, the campaigning organisation Disabled People Against Cuts submitted evidence to the associated UN Committee on the Rights of Persons with Disabilities (CRPD) that disabled people had been disproportionately harmed by the Coalition government's austerity policies.

This triggered an investigation by CRPD, which reported in October 2016. The report found that government reforms had led to 'grave and systematic' violations of the rights of disabled people. The report emphasises the impact of changes to Housing Benefit entitlement, eligibility criteria for Personal Independence Payment (PIP) and social care, and the closure of the

Independent Living Fund. It also said that the **bedroom tax** and other cuts to housing support had led disproportionately to debt and eviction, criticised the way that work capability assessments for Employment and Support Allowance had been carried out, and stated that disabled people had suffered from a climate in which they were portrayed as 'lazy and putting a burden on taxpayers'.

In a formal response, the UK government rejected the report, arguing that it presented an inaccurate picture of life for disabled people in the UK: 'While the government continues to improve and build on the support available to disabled people, it stands by and is proud of its record.'

Like other UN human rights conventions, the UNCRPD does not contain any mechanism that allows the Committee to enforce its recommendations. As the government's response to the report rejected all the recommendations made, there are no more official steps that the CRPD can take.

Questions

1. Do you think that this is an example of a 'state crime'?

2. How does this example illustrate the UN's limited ability to force governments to change their policies?

Key terms

Ethnic cleansing The UN defines ethnic cleansing as 'rendering an area ethnically homogeneous by using force or intimidation to remove from a given area persons of another ethnic or religious group'.

Monopolisation practices A monopoly exists where one company dominates the market for a particular good or service.

Geneva Conventions International rules – dating initially from 1864 – that apply only in times of armed conflict and seek to protect people who are not, or are no longer, taking part in hostilities.

Bedroom tax The 'bedroom tax' is the colloquial name for a reform contained in the Welfare Reform Act 2012, which means that people receive less in housing benefit if they live in a housing association or council property that is deemed to have one or more spare bedrooms.

3. Genocide and war crimes are two extreme examples of state crimes.

4. The UK government was accused by the UN CRDP of gross violations of the rights of disabled people in 2016.

Unit 2.3.4 Green crime

Running parallel to the growing interest in state crime within criminology has been a growing concern with green crime. This reflects a developing awareness over recent decades of how human actions are impacting negatively on global eco-systems and has led to the formation of both environmental pressure groups such as Greenpeace and Friends of the Earth and 'green' political parties in countries throughout the world. (In the UK, the 2010 general election saw the first elected Green Party MP – Caroline Lucas.)

Ulrich Beck's *Risk Society*

These developments in criminology were foreshadowed by the publication in 1986 of a book by the German sociologist Ulrich Beck, translated and published in English in 1992 as *Risk Society*.

Beck argued that, during the period of modernity, societies were faced with issues of scarcity, and social conflict was based on gaining access to these scarce resources. Beck suggested that, out of this conflict, social class and many modern political structures developed.

Summary

1. Narrowly defined, state crimes refer to acts or omissions by states that infringe domestic or international law; broadly defined, they include acts or omissions that violate human rights.

2. State-corporate crimes are criminal acts involving collusion between states and corporations. They can be divided into state-initiated and state-facilitated crimes.

However, technologically advanced and socially complex 'late modern' societies have resolved this issue of scarcity. There are adequate resources for all – in the developed world – and consequently class conflict declines. One outcome of the production of goods and services, though, has been massive damage to the environment, which has, in turn, generated new forms of dangers or 'risks' that humanity has never had to face before.

Beck pointed out that although nuclear energy has produced adequate power output, we are faced with the threat that a malfunctioning nuclear power station can represent, as demonstrated by the nuclear accidents at Chernobyl in Ukraine in 1986 and Three Mile Island in the USA in 1979. Beck also pointed to pollution through toxins in the environment and the health dangers of processed foodstuffs. He argued that these risks are different from those faced by humanity throughout history in that past global risks were not manufactured by humans themselves but were the outcome of natural processes (forest fires, earthquakes, volcanic eruptions and so on).

Beck suggested that despite the clear evidence that catastrophe may well occur as a result of technological pollution and environmental degradation, there was still a failure to grasp the true causes, and that there was a 'loss of sociological thinking' about the environment. He argued that the definition of harm and the causes of this harm were generally regarded as 'matters of nature and technology or of economics and medicine' (Beck, 1992).

Beck's warnings have since been heeded and there is now no shortage of sociological (and criminological) thinking about the risks posed by environmental harm.

Green criminology

As with the study of state crimes, some green criminologists feel that they should restrict their focus to environmentally harmful acts outlawed by domestic or international law, while others feel that such an approach ignores the fact that the law reflects inequalities in social power and that many environmental harms are not criminalised.

Thus, Beirne and South (2007) define green criminology as the study of 'those harms against humanity, against the environment (including space) and against non-human animals committed both by powerful institutions (e.g. governments, transnational corporations, military apparatuses) and also by

ordinary people'. This definition clearly goes beyond what is currently defined as unlawful.

This is the approach favoured, for example, by Nigel South (1998) who suggests a twofold framework for understanding green crimes.

Primary crimes

Primary crimes consist of harm done to the environment and people by activities such as:

Air pollution The burning of fossil fuels releases about 6 billion tons of carbon into the air each year, which, by the time it settles, increases the existing levels by 3 billion tons. Industrial output, vehicles and planes cause this increase. According to South, potential criminals here are governments, big business and consumers.

Deforestation Between 1960 and 1990, approximately 20 per cent of the world's tropical forest was lost. This is important, not just because of the role of forests in converting carbon dioxide to oxygen, but because between 75 and 95 per cent of all living species live in these forests. According to South, the world is losing about 10 million hectares of forest each year, which is an area approximately the size of South Korea. He suggests that 'new crimes and criminals would include those who deal in the destruction of rainforests and valuable lands'.

Species decline South notes that we lose 50 species a day, with 46 per cent of mammal species and 11 per cent of bird species said to be at risk. By 2020, 10 million species are likely to become extinct. South also points to how over-fishing has depopulated the oceans of the world.

Water pollution 25 million people die each year as a result of contaminated water and 500 million people lack access to fresh, clean drinking water. The seas of the world are also polluted, with one-third of all fish at risk. Since 1990, over 1.1 million tons of oil have been leaked or spilled into the world's oceans.

All the activities described above are currently legal under international law, but South is suggesting that the amount of harm they cause should allow these issues to be debated under the umbrella of criminology rather than as solely 'environmental' concerns.

Secondary crimes

Secondary crimes are those which develop out of 'the flouting of rules that seek to regulate environmental disasters' and therefore involve activities that are defined as illegal. According to South, these include hazardous waste and organised crime, and state violence against oppositional groups.

Hazardous waste and organised crime The disposal of hazardous waste is an extremely lucrative business, given its complexity and the care that must be taken. Because of lax international controls, this area has attracted organised crime. In Italy, there are currently investigations involving the Mafia's control of waste contracts, and earlier reports cited by South suggest that illegal dumping pollutes significant parts of the Gulf of Naples. The situation is so bad that it has been estimated that authorised dumping accounts for only 10 per cent of all disposal outflows into the gulf.

Illegal dumping is a huge international trade, with illegal transports of waste travelling from richer countries to poorer ones, where the material is simply dumped with no regard for human or animal lives.

Ruggiero (1996) points out that as the people in richer nations become more aware of the problems of pollution caused by hazardous waste, and the requirements imposed upon legal disposal firms by governments grow, the greater the potential profits of the illegal dumpers.

State violence against oppositional groups South points out that although governments condemn 'terrorism', some are prepared to use illegal and violent methods when they need to. One famous example was the blowing up of the Greenpeace ship *Rainbow Warrior* by French secret services operatives in 1985, in which one of the crew was murdered. South cites Day (1991), who argues that the *Rainbow Warrior* case was unusual in that it became public. According to Day, there have been numerous other examples of government interference that have never been uncovered.

Contemporary issues: Green criminology and fracking

A demonstration against fracking.

'Fracking' refers to the process of extracting shale gas from solid rock deep underground using hydraulic fracturing of the rock. Its potential development in the UK has provoked fierce debate.

In the UK, the Conservative Party is the only one of the main parties that supports fracking. Decisions on its use have been devolved to the Scottish Parliament and the Welsh Assembly and both currently prohibit the development of fracking.

As of summer 2017, exploratory drilling is taking place at a number of sites in England with the support of the Conservative government. Both the Royal Society and Royal Academy of Engineering have reviewed the health, safety and environmental risks associated with fracking and have concluded that these can be managed effectively in the UK by

implementing and enforcing best operational practice. The government argue that the exploitation of shale gas will create jobs, reduce the need to import liquid natural gas from abroad, heighten our energy security and allow us to reduce the burning of coal, which produces more **greenhouse gases** than burning gas.

Opponents of fracking argue that fracking involves unacceptable environmental risks including earthquakes, air pollution and surface and groundwater contamination. They also argue that exploitation of shale gas on a large scale would not be compatible with the UK's commitment to reducing its greenhouse gas emissions and that the tax incentives offered by the government to companies looking to extract shale gas would be better spent on subsidising the development of renewable energy sources.

In *Green Criminology and Fracking in the UK: An Application of Utilitarian Ethics*, Lampkin (2016) argues that the government's promotion of fracking can be seen as an example of a state-corporate trade-off between possible public and environmental health risks on one hand and the potential for economic development and expansion on the other. However, using a **utilitarian** costs-benefits analysis, he argues that fracking should not be instigated by the UK government on the basis that the potential for harm outweighs the potential benefits.

Questions

1. Fracking is not illegal in the UK, so on what basis can it be explored by green criminologists?

2. Explain why it would be contentious to view fracking as an example of 'state-corporate crime'.

3. Evaluate Lampkin's conclusion.

Key terms

Greenhouse gases Greenhouse gases are a group of compounds that are able to trap heat (longwave radiation) in the atmosphere, keeping the Earth's surface warmer than it would be if they were not present. The main one is carbon dioxide, which is released when fossil fuels such as coal and gas are burned.

Utilitarian Utilitarianism is the philosophical doctrine that an action is right in so far as it promotes happiness, and that the greatest happiness of the greatest number should be the guiding principle of conduct.

Summary

1. Growing concern in recent decades about issues to do with the environment has seen the development of a global 'green' movement. This has produced a green criminology.

2. Green criminology focuses on acts or omissions that damage the environment and both human and non-human species. Some restrict themselves to legally defined crimes, others go beyond this to include harms to the environment and human and non-human species.

3. Primary green 'crimes' are legal acts that harm the environment; secondary green 'crimes' are acts that are illegal under international law.

4. Fracking is currently legal in England, but some green criminologists see it as an example of state-corporate collusion that risks environmental damage for the sake of economic growth.

PART 4 EXPLAINING CRIME: FUNCTIONALIST, STRAIN AND SUBCULTURAL THEORIES

Contents

The next five parts of this chapter explore the major sociological perspectives that have been developed to explain the types and patterns of crime described in parts two and three. Some of these will be perspectives with which you are already familiar, such as functionalism, Marxism and interactionism. Others are focused more or less exclusively on crime and deviance and represent perspectives that you are unlikely to have come across yet, such as left and right realism and critical criminology.

Unit 2.4.1 is designed to help you understand what can sometimes seem like a random set of unrelated theories, whose origins are unclear and that seem to talk past each other rather than engage in any meaningful dialogue.

Unit 2.4.2 looks at the contribution made by the founding father of functionalism, Émile Durkheim. Unit 2.4.3 covers the contribution of an influential American functionalist, Robert Merton and Unit 2.4.4 focuses on subcultural theories.

Unit 2.4.1 Understanding sociological perspectives on crime

Students studying social science are confronted by what can appear to be a bewildering variety of discrete theories competing for their attention. If these theories are all studying the same topic, how can there be so much disagreement? Are they really completely unrelated to each other?

The first step in making sense of this variety is to recognise that facts are open to different interpretations (contrary to the common-sense idea that 'the facts speak for themselves'). For example, when functionalists look at countries such as the USA and the UK, they see modern *industrial* societies. When Marxists look at the same societies, they see modern *capitalist* societies. For functionalists, the key feature is the level of technology; for Marxists, it is the pattern of ownership of that technology. Both ways of characterising these societies are valid, but the theoretical implications are quite different.

Second, all theories are based on sets of underlying assumptions that tend to be more or less taken for granted by the theorists concerned. For example, some sociologists see people's behaviour as a product of the way that societies are organised, so in order to explain social behaviour they focus on the structure of society (structural theories). Other sociologists see society as a product of people's actions and believe that people's actions depend on how they interpret the world around them. So in order to explain social behaviour, they focus on the meanings people give to their own and to other's actions (action theories).

Thus, functionalists and Marxists, for example, tend to see crime as a product of the structure of society. Labelling theorists, by contrast, see crime as a product of the way in which certain acts and actors are interpreted ('labelled') by those with the power to get their labels accepted by others.

Third, theories – arguably – inevitably reflect the values and perceptions of those producing them, however much they strive for objectivity. As we shall see, for example, while left and right realists share the perception that conventionally defined crime needs to be addressed, the theories they produce reflect the opposed ideological positions from which they begin their theorising. Similarly, some of the early theories developed by positivist victimologists

(explored in Part 11) strike the modern-day reader as clearly sexist.

Fourthly, social theories do not emerge from a social vacuum, from nowhere. They emerge from within particular societies at particular times and inevitably reflect what is happening in those societies and the wider social, political and economic issues that people in those societies are facing. Thus, the dominance of functionalist theories in the 1940s and 1950s reflected the relative social and economic stability of those decades in the West, while the 1960s saw widespread social conflict connected with the Vietnam War, Black civil rights, the emergence of feminist and Gay Rights movements and so on, which functionalism was ill-equipped to explain. **Conflict theories** (such as Marxism, Weberianism and feminism) by contrast, see societies as inherently unstable as they comprise groups with conflicting interests, so were well placed to address such social conflict. Hence, in trying to understand theories it is helpful to locate them historically.

Finally, new theories tend to emerge out of the questioning of earlier theories, for example, out of challenges to their underlying assumptions or recognition of what they fail to explain. In science, nothing is ever settled for all time. Instead the job of scientists – including social scientists – is to keep probing and challenging the received wisdom in order to try to get closer to the truth. This means engaging with existing theories. Thus, it is helpful to see theories, not as distinct sets of ideas, but as related to each other in terms of the features they agree on and those over which they disagree.

Key terms

Capitalist societies Industrial societies based on private ownership of the means of production and a market economy.

Conflict theories Sociological theories such as Marxism which view societies as comprising groups with conflicting interests vying for dominance. They can be contrasted with consensus theories such as functionalism which see societies as essentially harmonious.

Summary

1. Theories are based on facts, but facts don't speak for themselves.

2. All theories are based on sets of underlying assumptions, for example, about the nature of society and about the relationship between people and society.

3. Theories seek to be objective, but arguably can't escape the values and preconceptions of those who produce them.

4. Theories tend to reflect the times and places which produce them.

5. Competing theories are engaged in a dialogue with each other.

Unit 2.4.2 Durkheim

Émile Durkheim (1858–1917), one of the 'founding fathers' of sociology (alongside Marx and Weber), adopted a functionalist perspective. He saw society as like a living organism in which the different parts – social institutions – functioned to keep the whole arrangement going. Social order depended on people conforming to social rules – laws, organisational rules and social norms – whose function was to regulate social life. Crime and deviance, therefore, threatened social order, but their level could be restrained through mechanisms of social control – both formal (courts, prisons and so on) and informal (ridicule, gossip and so on) – which functioned to restore order. These involved the use of positive and negative sanctions (rewards and punishments) to encourage conformity.

Activity

Copy the table below. Thinking about the school or college in which you are studying, try to provide two or three examples in each of the boxes to illustrate the social control mechanisms that are in use. One example has been provided in each category to help get you started.

	Positive sanctions	Negative sanctions
Formal sanctions	Certificates	Suspension
Informal sanctions	Praise from teacher	Reprimand by teacher

Like Marx and Weber, Durkheim wanted to understand the new industrial societies that had emerged in Europe in the 19th century. In *The Division of Labour in Society* (1947, orig. 1883), he argued that such societies were more prone to crime than traditional societies.

Traditional societies were held together by a strong, religiously based 'conscience collective' (or value consensus) which impeded criminal and deviant behaviour. Moreover, communities were smaller and there was little geographical mobility so people knew each other in the round, making informal social control more effective.

Industrialisation led to urbanisation – the growth of towns and cities – in which people were strangers to each other, so informal social control became less effective. Additionally, the division of labour became ever more complex and jobs ceased to be automatically passed down from father to son. Instead, people were in competition with each other for work, changing the nature of social relationships. People were no longer so closely bound together. Moreover, as societies grew in both size and complexity, so the power of religion waned – societies became more **secular**. Both these developments, Durkheim believed, made crime more likely. Finally, increased geographical mobility and urbanisation brought together people from many different backgrounds with different outlooks on life and rapid social change undermined existing norms. Industrial societies were, therefore, more prone to what Durkheim called '**anomie**' (or normlessness) where social norms were unclear or conflicting, again making crime more likely.

Activity

The Peasant Wedding *by Pieter Brueghel the Elder, 1566–1569.*

Why did Durkheim think that crime would be lower in communities like the one illustrated in Brueghel's painting?

Crime as inevitable

In *The Rules of Sociological Method* (1938, first published 1895), Durkheim argued that crime is an inevitable and normal aspect of social life. It is inevitable because not every member of society can be equally committed to the collective sentiments (the shared values and moral beliefs) of society. Because individuals are exposed to different influences and circumstances, it is 'impossible for all to be alike'. Therefore not everyone is equally reluctant to break the law.

Durkheim imagined a 'society of saints' populated by perfect individuals. In such a society there might be no murder or robbery, but there would still be deviance. The general standards of behaviour would be so high that the slightest slip would be regarded as a serious offence. Thus the individual who simply showed bad taste, or was merely impolite, would attract strong disapproval from other members of that society. Such behaviour would likely be criminalised. Hence, crime would be present even in this 'perfect cloister of exemplary individuals'.

Crime as functional

Crime is not only inevitable; it can also be functional. Durkheim argued that it only becomes dysfunctional (harmful to society) when its rate is unusually high or low. He argued that all social change begins with some form of deviance. In order for change to occur, yesterday's deviance must become today's normality. As a certain amount of change is healthy for society (so that it can progress rather than stagnate), so is deviance. If the collective sentiments are too strong, there will be little deviance, but neither will there be any change or progress. Therefore, the collective sentiments must have only 'moderate energy' so that they do not crush originality, both the originality of the criminal and the originality of the genius. In Durkheim's words:

To make progress, individual originality must be able to express itself. In order that the originality of the idealist whose dreams transcend this century may find expression it is necessary that the originality of the criminal, who is below the level of his time, shall also be possible. One does not occur without the other. (The Rules of Sociological Method, *1938, first published 1895*)

Consider the example of Nelson Mandela. Nelson Mandela was imprisoned as a terrorist in South Africa for leading the African National Congress in its campaign against apartheid; a system under which Black Africans, Whites and 'Coloureds' (people of mixed descent) had to live separate lives. Mandela was released in 1990 and he went on to become the first president of post-apartheid South Africa. He was praised for his achievements throughout the world and awarded the Nobel Peace Prize in 1993. He went from being condemned as a terrorist to being a globally respected statesman.

Activity

Nelson Mandela, 1918–2013.

Explain how Mandela illustrates the functionalist claim that criminality can be functional.

Hence for Durkheim, crime is 'an integral part of all healthy societies'.

Punishment too was seen as functional for society. Durkheim argued that its function was not to remove crime in society, but to maintain the collective sentiments at their necessary level of strength. A criminal trial helps to remind people where the boundary lies between acceptable and unacceptable behaviour and punishment 'serves to heal the wounds done to the collective sentiments'. Without punishment, the collective sentiments would lose their power to control behaviour, and the crime rate would reach the point where it became dysfunctional. Thus, in Durkheim's view, a healthy society requires both crime and punishment; both are functional.

Evaluation

> Durkheim provided a convincing explanation of why crime is higher in industrial societies than traditional societies and why crime is inevitable in any society. His claim that both crime and punishment can be functional is plausible.

> Arguably, Durkheim underplayed the dysfunctional consequences of crime and offers no way of gauging

what would count as 'too high' or 'too low' in terms of crime rates.

» Durkheim's view that the law is an expression of 'society's' moral sentiments would be challenged by conflict theorists, who would see it more as an expression of the interests of powerful groups.

» Interactionists would argue that Durkheim's theory is too **deterministic,** underplaying people's agency – their ability to choose to behave in certain ways, including criminal ways.

Key terms

Secular Societies in which religious institutions, beliefs and practices have declined in social significance.

Anomie A situation where social norms are unclear, conflicting or unintegrated.

Deterministic Social theories assume that people have little or no choice in their social behaviour – they are like puppets with society pulling the strings.

Summary

1. Durkheim adopted a functionalist perspective.

2. He thought that industrial societies were more prone to crime than traditional societies because informal social control was less effective in urban settings, religious beliefs were weaker and anomie was more likely.

3. He believed that crime was an inevitable feature of all societies and that it could be functional. Crime was dysfunctional only if its rates were too high or too low.

4. Formal punishment was functional in demonstrating what happened if people broke the law and reaffirming the boundary between acceptable and unacceptable behaviour.

5. Critics of Durkheim argue that he underplayed the dysfunctional features of crime, assumed wrongly that the law is a reflection of a society's collective conscience and failed to acknowledge the role of human agency in the commission of crime.

Unit 2.4.3 Merton

Robert Merton was a functionalist sociologist who drew upon Durkheim's concept of anomie to explain crime in American society. Anomie occurred because people found themselves in a situation where they could not realise the goals of American society by legitimate means, but the norms of society failed to offer guidance about how they should respond to this situation. As a result, they experienced *strain* to find a solution to this dilemma (hence the name '*strain theory*', which is sometimes used to refer to theories such as Merton's).

Merton (1968, orig. 1938) argued that the members of American society share the major values of American culture. In particular they share the goal of success, for which they all strive and which is largely measured in terms of wealth and material possessions. The 'American Dream' embodies the idea that anyone can 'make it' in the USA: anyone, supposedly, can own a Cadillac, a Beverly Hills mansion and have a substantial bank balance.

Activity

An image conveying the idea that the American Dream is an integral part of American identity.

How far do you think people across society in the UK today share the goal of financial success?

In all societies, there are institutionalised means of reaching culturally defined goals. In the USA, the accepted ways of achieving success are through educational qualifications, talent, hard work, drive, determination and ambition. However, since members of society are located in different positions in the social structure (e.g., they differ in terms of class position), they do not have the same opportunity of realising the shared values. This situation can generate deviance. In Merton's words, 'the social and cultural structure generates pressure for socially

103

deviant behaviour upon people variously located in that structure'.

Adaptations to strain

Merton outlined five possible ways in which members of American society could respond to success goals:

1. The first and most common response is *conformity*. Members of society conform both to success goals and to the normative (that is, socially approved) means of reaching them. They strive for success by means of accepted channels.

2. A second response is *innovation*. This response rejects normative means of achieving success and turns to deviant means, in particular, crime. Merton argues that members of lower social classes are most likely to select this route to success. They are least likely to succeed via conventional channels, so there is greater pressure upon them to deviate. Their educational qualifications are usually low and their jobs provide little opportunity for advancement. In Merton's words, they have 'little access to conventional and legitimate means for becoming successful'. Since their way is blocked, they 'innovate', turning to crime, which promises greater rewards than legitimate means.

   Merton stressed that membership of the lower classes is not, in itself, sufficient to produce deviance. Only in societies such as the USA, where all members share the same success goals, does the pressure to innovate operate forcefully on the lower classes. Merton argues that those who innovate have been 'imperfectly socialized so that they abandon institutional means while retaining success-aspirations'.

3. The third possible response is *ritualism*. Those who select this alternative are deviant because they have largely abandoned the commonly held success goals. The pressure to adopt this alternative is greatest for members of the lower-middle class, whose occupations provide less opportunity for success than those of other members of the middle class. However, compared with members of the working class, they have been strongly socialised to conform to social norms. This prevents them from turning to crime. Unable to innovate, and with jobs that offer little opportunity for advancement, their only solution is to scale down or abandon their success goals.

   Merton paints the following picture of typical lower middle-class 'ritualists'. They are low-grade bureaucrats, ultra-respectable but stuck in a rut.

They are sticklers for the rules, follow the book to the letter, cling to red tape, conform to all the outward standards of middle-class respectability, but have given up striving for success. Ritualists are deviant because they have rejected the success goals held by most members of society.

4. Merton terms the fourth, and least common, response, *retreatism*. It applies to 'psychotics, autists, pariahs, outcasts, vagrants, vagabonds, tramps, chronic drunkards and drug addicts'. They have strongly internalised both the cultural goals and the institutionalised means, yet are unable to achieve success. They resolve the conflict of their situation by abandoning both the goals and the means of reaching them. They are unable to cope, and 'drop out' of society, defeated and resigned to their failure. They are deviant in two ways: they have rejected both the cultural goals and the institutionalised means. Merton does not relate retreatism to social-class position.

5. *Rebellion* forms the fifth and final response. It is a rejection of both the success goals and the institutionalised means, and it replaces them with different goals and means. Those who adopt this alternative, wish to create a new society. Merton argues that 'it is typically members of a rising class rather than the most depressed strata who organize the resentful and rebellious into a revolutionary group'.

Activity

How might Merton's categories of conformity, innovation, ritualism, retreatism and rebellion be applied to the activities of pupils in schools faced with the goal of achieving academic success? For example, what category would copying someone else's homework fit into? How about truancy?

Evidence to support Merton

Hannon and Defronzo (1998, cited in Jones, 2009) provided some empirical support for Merton. In a study of 406 metropolitan counties in the USA, they found that those with higher levels of welfare provision had lower levels of crime. They argued that the welfare provision reduced the level of strain felt by those ill-placed to achieve material success through legitimate means and therefore reduced anomie and the crime that could result from it.

Joachim J. Savelsberg (1995) argued that Merton's strain theory can help to explain the rapid rises in the crime rate in post-communist Poland, Czechoslovakia, East Germany and Russia. Poland is an example of how dramatic these rises sometimes were. Poland had its first free elections in 1989. Between 1989 and 1990 the official crime rate in Poland increased by no less than 69 per cent. The culture of communist societies emphasised collective responsibility rather than individual financial success. However, with the collapse of communism and its replacement with free market capitalism, people's material expectations were suddenly raised, only to be frustrated in most cases. This resulted in anomie and a strain towards criminal innovation.

Evaluation

> Sociologists are sometimes criticised for dressing-up common sense in obscure technical language. It might seem that this is what Merton has done by stating that criminals are seeking financial success by illegitimate means. However, this ignores two powerful features of Merton's theory: his recognition of the fact that the American Dream is such a central feature of American culture and that the class structure militates against equal opportunities to be financially successful.

> Critics have attacked Merton's work for neglecting the power relationships in society as a whole, within which deviance and conformity occur. Laurie Taylor (1971), writing from a conflict perspective, criticised Merton for not carrying his analysis far enough: for failing to consider who makes the laws and who benefits from the laws:

It is as though individuals in society are playing a gigantic fruit machine, but the machine is rigged and only some players are consistently rewarded. The deprived ones either resort to using foreign coins or magnets to increase their chances of winning (innovation) or play on mindlessly (ritualism), give up the game (retreatism) or propose a new game altogether (rebellion). But in the analysis nobody appeared to ask who put the game there in the first place and who takes the profits.

> Merton can be criticised for ignoring white-collar, corporate and state crime. However, Reiner (1984) notes that 'Merton was well aware both of the extensiveness of white-collar crime in the suites, and of the way that official statistics disproportionately record crime in the streets'. Merton explained white-collar crime by suggesting that American society placed no upper limit on

success: however wealthy people were, they might still want more.

> Merton's theory does not offer any explanation for non-acquisitive crime, such as crimes of violence, vandalism, public order offences and so on.

Summary

1. Merton drew upon the concept of 'anomie' to devise a theory of crime known as 'strain theory'.

2. He identified a variety of responses to the situation where people could not achieve success by legitimate means: innovation, ritualism, retreatism and rebellion.

3. The lower level of crime in societies that offer social security to those who are not financially successful and the explosion of crime in Eastern European countries following the collapse of communism both provide support for Merton's theory.

4. Conflict theorists criticise Merton for not questioning the structure of American society, for restricting his analysis to conventionally defined crime and for ignoring non-acquisitive crime.

Unit 2.4.4 Subcultural theories

Subcultural theories explain deviance in terms of the subculture of a social group. They argue that certain groups develop norms and values which are to some extent different from those held by other members of society. For example, some groups might develop norms that encourage and reward criminal activity. Other members of society would regard such activities as immoral, and strongly disapprove of them.

Albert K. Cohen – the delinquent subculture

The American sociologist A.K. Cohen (1955) sought to understand the distinctive features of youth criminality or what was then known as 'juvenile delinquency'. The theory he developed was a modification and development of Merton's position. From his studies of delinquency, Cohen made two major criticisms of Merton's views on working-class deviance:

> First, he argued that delinquency is a collective rather than an individual response. Whereas Merton saw individuals responding to their position

in the class structure, Cohen saw individuals joining together in a collective response.

) Second, Cohen argued that Merton failed to account for **non-utilitarian crime** – such as vandalism and joyriding – which does not produce monetary reward. Cohen questioned whether such forms of offending were directly motivated by the success goals of the mainstream culture.

Cohen began his argument in a similar way to Merton. Lower-working-class boys initially share the success goals of the mainstream culture, but, due largely to educational failure and the dead-end jobs that result from this, they have little opportunity to attain those goals. This failure can be explained by their position in the social structure. Cohen supported the view that cultural deprivation (See Book 1, Chapter 2, Part 3) accounts for the lack of educational success of members of the lower working class.

Stuck at the bottom of the stratification system, with avenues to success blocked, many lower-working-class boys suffer from **status frustration** – that is, they are frustrated and dissatisfied with their low status in society. Status frustration engenders **unconscious** feelings of guilt, shame and resentment. With great originality, Cohen turned to Freudian ideas to suggest what then happened.

Freud suggested that the unconscious mind has a number of **defence mechanisms** that are brought into play when faced with troubling thoughts. One of these is what he called *reaction formation* where the mental tension is unconsciously resolved by exaggeration of the directly opposing tendency. So, the values of mainstream society are not simply rejected, but treated as a guide to how *not* to behave. The delinquent subculture therefore represents an *inversion* of mainstream culture: whatever is valued in mainstream culture is denigrated (looked down upon) in the delinquent subculture and the subculture positively celebrates acts that would outrage respectable members of society.

Hence, they resolve their frustration, not by turning to criminal paths to success, as Merton suggested, but by rejecting the success goals of the mainstream culture. They replace them with an alternative set of norms and values, in terms of which they can achieve success and gain prestige: a delinquent subculture. Thus, truancy, cheeking teachers, destroying property through vandalism and so on offers the opportunity for recognition and prestige in the eyes of their peers.

Cohen argued that, in this way, lower-working-class boys 'solve' the problem of status frustration. As

a result of an unconscious process (of reaction formation), they reject mainstream values, which offer them little chance of success, and replace them with deviant values, in terms of which they can be successful. Cohen thus provides an explanation for delinquent acts that do not appear to be motivated by monetary reward.

Activity

Bike vandalism.

How could Cohen's theory be applied to explain the image above?

Evaluation

) Cohen's theory helps to make sense of acts that would otherwise appear to be senseless, such as vandalism, by explaining how they emerge out of a process that leads to the inversion of mainstream values.

) By combining sociology with **psychoanalysis**, Cohen broke new ground.

) Walter Miller (1962) argued that delinquency was not a product of status frustration, but a reflection of the emotional attachment of lower-class boys to six focal concerns of the 'lower-class culture' into which they had been socialised: trouble, toughness, smartness, excitement, fate and autonomy.

) David Matza (1964) questioned the view that most delinquents are strongly opposed to mainstream values and strongly committed to delinquent gangs. Matza's research in the USA suggested that the majority of youths who were seen as delinquent accepted most of the mainstream values of society and only occasionally and in special circumstances committed offences. Few were strongly involved in a delinquent subculture; they simply 'drifted' into delinquency from time to time without any commitment to delinquent values or a delinquent way of life.

Richard A. Cloward and Lloyd E. Ohlin – Delinquency and Opportunity

In *Delinquency and Opportunity*, the American sociologists Cloward and Ohlin (1961) combined and developed many of the insights of Merton and Cohen. However, they argued that neither writer recognised that delinquency took a number of different forms: some delinquency centred on vandalism and violence – as Cohen argued – but some centred on acquisitive crime, for example.

Cloward and Ohlin argued that Merton had only dealt with half the picture. He had explained deviance in terms of the legitimate opportunity structure, but he failed to consider what they called **'illegitimate opportunity structures'**. In other words, just as the opportunity to be successful by legitimate means varies, so does the opportunity for success by illegitimate means. Differential access to, and performance in, these two different opportunity structures led to three different types of delinquent subcultures:

1. *Criminal subcultures* tend to emerge in areas where there is an established pattern of organised adult crime. In such areas a 'learning environment' is provided for the young: they are exposed to criminal skills and deviant values, and presented with criminal role models. Those who perform successfully in terms of these deviant values have the opportunity to rise in the professional criminal hierarchy. Criminal subcultures are mainly concerned with acquisitive crime – crime which produces financial reward.

2. *Conflict subcultures* tend to develop in areas where young people have little opportunity for access to illegitimate opportunity structures. There is little organised adult crime to provide an 'apprenticeship' for the young offenders and opportunities for them to climb the illegitimate ladder to success. Such areas usually have a high turnover of population and lack unity and cohesiveness. This situation tends to prevent a stable criminal subculture from developing. Thus access to both legitimate and illegitimate opportunity structures is blocked. The response to this situation is often gang violence. This serves as a release for anger and frustration, and a means of obtaining prestige in terms of the values of the subculture.

3. *Retreatist subcultures* are a product of a double failure. Cloward and Ohlin suggested that some lower-class adolescents form retreatist subcultures, organised mainly around illegal drug use, because they have failed to succeed in both the legitimate and illegitimate structures. As failed criminals or failed gang members, they retreat, tails between their legs, into drug use.

Evaluation

> Cloward and Ohlin's application of strain theory offers a plausible way of understanding how strain can lead to a variety of delinquent responses.

> Their concept of 'illegitimate opportunity structures' broadens our understanding of the pathways into crime and delinquency.

> The criticisms made of A.K. Cohen's theory of delinquency by Miller and by Matza apply equally to Cloward and Ohlin's theory.

> Arguably, their more or less exclusive focus on male delinquency reflects the era when they put forward their theories. Whether their theory could be adapted to explain female delinquency is unclear.

Applications of Cloward and Ohlin

In his study of changing masculinities in Sunderland, Simon Winlow (2001) draws upon the work of Cloward and Ohlin to explain the existence of a working-class subculture that values 'hardness' among men. He argues that in the modern industrial era there were few opportunities to make a living out of crime. There was little in the way of organised crime and therefore no significant illegitimate opportunities. In these circumstances a conflict subculture developed, characterised by petty crime and the use of violence to gain status. Winlow says, 'Violence was ... a crucial signifier of self-image, a reflection upon a culture that favourably judged those who maintained a credible use of force.' This subculture was evident still in post-industrial Sunderland.

Nigel South (1997), writing about the supply of illegal drugs in towns and cities in the UK, argued that the drug trade is largely based around disorganised crime (which can be compared to Cloward and Ohlin's conflict subcultures), although some of the trade is based around professional criminal organisation (more akin to criminal subcultures). Moreover, some drug users themselves could be seen as part of a retreatist subculture. While experimentation with illegal drugs does not appear to vary much between social groups, addiction and regular use are more likely to develop among young people from lower social classes.

Research by Sudhir Venkatesh (2009) into drug gangs in the housing projects of Chicago found evidence of a hierarchical and quite organised criminal subculture, similar to that described by Cloward and Ohlin. It included different levels of management backed up by large numbers of street-level dealers, with gangs heavily involved in the running of the 'projects' – social housing in some of Chicago's poorest areas. Venkatesh found that the particular gang leader he studied, J.T., was gradually developing his criminal career and gaining status among the interlinked networks of criminal gangs in the city.

Contemporary issues: Post-industrial gangs

UK gang members.

Source: GTA forums

We define a gang as a relatively durable, predominantly street-based group of young people who (1) see themselves (and are seen by others) as a discernible group, (2) engage in a range of criminal activity and violence, (3) identify with or lay claim over territory, (4) have some form of identifying structural feature and (5) are in conflict with other, similar, gangs.

Gangs are not a new phenomenon in Britain, but a number of criminologists have identified the growth in many of Britain's largest cities of a new form of street gang since the 1980s: the 'post-industrial gang'.

These are semi-organised, violent and criminal gangs born out of acute deprivation. The 1980s witnessed massive economic and social change with an economic boom but growing inequality: while many people prospered, those in the most deprived communities got poorer.

In today's global cities, wealth is highly visible: those living in acute deprivation have a daily reminder, sometimes just by walking to the end of their street, of what they don't and can't have. It is no coincidence that in Britain the highest prevalence of gangs is found in London, Manchester, Liverpool, Birmingham and Glasgow.

In this environment of intense and overt consumerism coupled with profound social breakdown, those excluded from access to legitimate opportunity structures often seek alternative routes:

(The growth of post-industrial gangs) is the result of a widening economic and social divide, of a housing policy that throws together the victim and the victimiser, and of marginalisation. Excluded from mainstream society, but with mainstream hopes and desires for material possessions and status, an alternative societal structure is established. (p. 81)

(*Dying to Belong: An In-depth Review of Street Gangs in Britain*. Centre for Social Justice, February, 2009.)

Question

How could the strain theories examined in this section of the chapter be applied to explain the development of post-industrial gangs in Britain?

Key terms

Non-utilitarian crime Crime that appears to serve no useful purpose, and has no monetary gain, for example joyriding or vandalism.

Status frustration Feelings of annoyance and distress generated by the inability to acquire social respect.

Unconscious Below the level of a person's awareness.

Defence mechanisms In psychoanalysis, defence mechanisms are unconscious mental processes initiated to avoid experiencing psychic conflict or anxiety.

Psychoanalysis A branch of psychology associated with Sigmund Freud.

Illegitimate opportunity structures Illegal routes to financial success.

Summary

1. Subcultural theories focus on the formation of delinquent subcultures.

2. A.K. Cohen saw delinquent subcultures as a product of status frustration experienced by lower-class boys.

3. Cloward and Ohlin introduced the concept of illegitimate opportunity structures and argued that differential access to, and success within, both legitimate and illegitimate opportunity structures led to three types of delinquent subcultures: criminal, conflict and retreatist.

4. Cloward and Ohlin's theory has been used to illuminate contemporary examples of criminal and violent behaviour in run-down urban areas.

5. Walter Miller suggested that delinquent subcultures are not a response to status frustration, but an expression of a set of focal concerns characteristic of lower-class culture that manifest themselves in delinquency.

6. David Matza argued that most young men drift in and out of delinquency rather than being committed to it.

PART 5 EXPLAINING CRIME: LABELLING THEORY

Contents

The theories examined in Part 4 share a number of assumptions: that criminals and delinquents are different from other people, are mainly drawn from lower social classes and that the way society is organised generates delinquent and criminal responses to the strain such people experience.

'Labelling theory', which came to prominence in the 1960s and 1970s, challenged all of these assumptions and offered a new way of thinking about crime and deviance, drawing upon a different set of sociological perspectives and developing new concepts with which to think about crime and delinquency.

The theoretical roots of these new ideas were symbolic interactionism – commonly shortened to just 'interactionism' – and **pluralism**. Rather than seeing society as a *structure*, interactionists see it as a *process* of social – or *symbolic* – interaction in which people interpret the behaviour of others and act according to the meaning they give to that behaviour. A raised fist, for example, could be interpreted as a threat, but – depending on the social context – it could equally symbolise achievement (a tennis player punching the air after winning a point), solidarity (a raised fist salute was a symbol of **Black power** in the 1960s) or a joke! Moreover, these meanings, interactionists claim, are not simply enshrined in the society's culture, but emerge from the interaction process itself.

The theories examined here also moved the focus away from law-breaking to ask questions about law-enforcement and law-making (or **criminalisation**). This required a consideration of issues of power, which was implicitly viewed from a *pluralist* political perspective. Pluralists see power in **liberal democracies** as spread out between different social groups with conflicting interests, some with more power than others, with the state acting as a kind of neutral mediator seeking to resolve these conflicts in the 'public' interest.

The key theorists were again American sociologists: Edwin Lemert, Howard Becker and Aaron Cicourel. We will begin with Lemert.

Unit 2.5.1 Lemert

Labelling theorists take seriously the idea that, as just about everyone breaks the law at some point in their lives, what distinguishes criminals from non-criminals is not the fact that they have violated social rules. Instead, such theorists follow Erving Goffman who argued in **Stigma**: *Notes on the Management of Spoiled Identity* (1963) that the real difference is between the *discreditable* and the *discredited*. All of us have done things in our lives that, if they were public knowledge, would be discrediting, but through luck, cunning, deception or other means we have been able to conceal these acts. Hence, we are discreditable, but not discredited. Criminals, by contrast, have had the bad luck of being caught and have been subjected to a penal process that has produced a 'spoiled' identity. They have been discredited.

Activity

A popular image of a convict?

How might the label 'ex-con' affect someone's future prospects?

On this basis, Edwin Lemert (1951) distinguished between what he called *primary and secondary deviation*.

Primary deviation

Primary deviation consists of deviant acts before they are publicly labelled. In Lemert's view, any number of causes of primary deviation exist and it is largely a fruitless exercise to enquire into them. Moreover, those who have been convicted of a particular crime are unlikely to be a representative sample of all those who have committed that act, so theories based on known offenders are unlikely to be valid. Indeed, Lemert suggested that the only thing that 'known' deviants have in common is the fact that they have been publicly labelled as such.

In Lemert's view, not only is the search for the causes of primary deviation largely fruitless, but also primary deviation itself is relatively unimportant. Lemert argued that it 'has only marginal implications for the status and the psychic structure of the person concerned'. The odd deviant act has little effect on individuals' self-conception and status in the community, and does not prevent them from continuing a normal and conventional life.

Secondary deviation

The important factor in 'producing' deviance in the view of labelling theorists is *societal reaction* – the public identification of the deviant, and the consequences of this for the individual concerned. Secondary deviation is the deviant behaviour engaged in subsequently as a result of being labelled.

Lemert argued that studies of deviance should focus on secondary deviation, which has major consequences for the individual's self-concept, status in the community and future actions. In comparison, primary deviation has little significance: 'In effect the original "causes" of the deviation recede and give way to the central importance of the disapproving, **degradational,** and isolating reactions of society.'

Thus, Lemert claimed that societal reaction can be seen as the major cause of deviance. This view, he argued, 'gives a proper place to social control as a dynamic factor or "cause" of deviance'. In this way, Lemert controversially reversed traditional views of deviance: the blame for deviance lies with the agents of social control rather than with the deviant.

Stuttering and societal reaction

Lemert (1952) was particularly convincing in his paper entitled 'Stuttering among the North Pacific Coastal Indians', which examines the relationship between societal reaction and deviance.

Previous research had indicated a virtual absence of stuttering among what we would now call Native Americans. Indeed, most tribes did not even have a word for this speech irregularity. However, Lemert's investigation of deviance among various tribes living in the North Pacific coastal area of British Columbia revealed evidence of stuttering both before and after contact with whites. In addition, the languages of these tribes contained clearly defined concepts of stutterers and stuttering.

The North Pacific Coastal Indians had a rich ceremonial life, involving singing, dancing and speech-making. Their legends and stories were filled with references to famous orators and outstanding speeches. From an early age, children were initiated into ceremonial life, and parents stressed the importance of a faultless performance. There were rigorous and exacting standards to be met; rituals had to be performed exactly as they should be. If they did not meet these standards, children shamed their parents and suffered the ridicule of their peers. In particular, there was a highly developed sensitivity to any speech defect. Children and parents alike were anxious about any speech irregularity and responded to it with guilt and shame.

Lemert concluded that stuttering was actually produced by societal reaction. Some children in any society will display developmental speech irregularities, but usually these are not seen as an issue, their occurrence does not provoke sanctions and children are expected to grow out of them. However, among the North Pacific Coastal Indians even minor speech defects were noted and responded to. They were, if you like, 'labelled'. This generated anxiety in the children concerned and the anxiety increased the likelihood of stuttering.

In other Native American societies, where such concerns were largely absent, stuttering was unknown. Thus, Lemert argued, societal reaction, prompted by a concern about particular forms of deviance, can actually produce those forms of deviance.

Activity

Lemert provides a plausible explanation for stuttering, but how far do you think the logic of his analysis can be applied to explain other forms of deviance and crime?

Key terms

Pluralism A theory of political power in liberal democracies which argues that power is spread out among numerous different interest groups and that the state mediates between these interests in the national interest.

Black power A social movement that developed out of the Black Civil Rights movement in the USA in the 1960s dedicated to Black empowerment.

Criminalisation Making an act or omission against the criminal law.

Liberal democracies Countries such as those in Western Europe and North America with political systems based on representative democracy in which individual rights and freedoms are officially recognised and protected.

Stigma Characteristics that are seen as socially discrediting.

Degradational Designed to reduce an individual's social status.

Summary

1. Labelling theory came to prominence in the 1960s and 1970s.

2. Labelling theory argues that everyone breaks social rules, but only some are publicly identified as deviants or criminals. They distinguish between the discreditable and the discredited.

3. Lemert distinguished between primary and secondary deviation. Primary deviation was widespread but had little importance for the individual's self-conception. Societal reaction to primary deviance, however, had a major impact and led to secondary deviance.

4. Lemert backed up his claims with a study of stuttering among the North Pacific Coastal Indians (Native Americans) in which he argued that it was the societal response to children's speech defects that produced stuttering through raising children's anxiety levels.

Unit 2.5.2 Becker

The best known presentation of labelling theory was provided by Howard Becker in his book *Outsiders: Studies in the Sociology of Deviance* (1963).

The nature of deviance

In a much-quoted statement, Becker argued:

Social groups create deviance by making the rules whose infraction constitutes deviance, *and by applying those rules to particular people and labelling them as **outsiders**. From this point of view, deviance is* not *a quality of the act the person commits, but rather a consequence of the application by others of the rules and sanctions to an 'offender'. The deviant is one to whom the label has successfully been applied; deviant behaviour is behaviour that people so label.*

111

Becker is suggesting that in one sense there is no such thing as a deviant act. An act only becomes deviant when others perceive and define it as such.

The act of nudity in Western society provides an illustration. Nudity in the bedroom, where the actors involved are husband and wife, is generally interpreted as normal behaviour. Should a stranger enter, however, nudity in his or her presence would usually be considered deviant. Yet, in particular contexts, such as nudist camps or certain holiday beaches, the participants would see nudity in the presence of strangers as perfectly normal. A male spectator at a cricket match who 'streaked' across the pitch might be viewed as 'a bit of a lad', but, if he stood and exposed himself to the crowd, he might be regarded as 'some kind of a pervert'. Thus there is nothing intrinsically normal or deviant about the act of nudity. It only becomes deviant when others label it as such.

Activity

A streaker at the Lord's cricket ground in August 1975 during an England v Australia test match.

Explain why most people see streaking as a bit of a laugh rather than as a seriously deviant act. Why is 'flashing' not viewed similarly?

Whether or not the label is applied will depend on how the act is interpreted by the audience. This in turn will depend on who commits the act, when and where it is committed, who observes the act, and the negotiations between the various actors involved in the interaction situation.

Becker illustrated his views with the example of a brawl involving young people. In a low-income neighbourhood, it may be defined by the police as evidence of delinquency; in a wealthy neighbourhood, as evidence of youthful high spirits. The acts are the same but the meanings given to them by the audience differ. In the same way, those who commit the act may

view it in one way; those who observe it may define it in another. The brawl in the low-income area may involve a gang fighting to defend its 'turf' (territory). In Becker's words, they are only doing what they consider 'necessary and right, but teachers, social workers and police see it differently'. If the agents of social control define the youngsters as delinquents and they are convicted for breaking the law, those youngsters then become 'delinquents'. They have been labelled as such by those who have the power to make the labels stick. Thus, Becker argued, 'Deviance is not a quality that lies in behaviour itself, but in the interaction between the person who commits an act and those who respond to it.' From this point of view, deviance is produced by a process of interaction between the potential deviant and the agents of social control.

Possible effects of labelling

Becker then examined the possible effects upon an individual of being publicly labelled as deviant. A label defines an individual as a particular kind of person. A label is not neutral: it contains an evaluation of the person to whom it is applied. It is a **master status** in the sense that it colours all the other statuses possessed by an individual.

If individuals are labelled as criminal, mentally ill or sexually deviant, such labels largely override their status as parent, worker, neighbour and friend. Others see them and respond to them in terms of the label, and tend to assume that they have the negative characteristics normally associated with such labels. Moreover, because individuals' self-concepts are largely derived from the responses of others, they are likely to come to see themselves in terms of the label. This may produce a **self-fulfilling prophecy** whereby 'the deviant identification becomes the controlling one'. Becker outlined a number of possible stages in this process:

1. Initially, the individual is publicly labelled as deviant. This may lead to rejection from many social groups. Regarded as a 'junkie', a 'troublemaker', a 'nutter', a 'wino' or a 'tearaway', he or she may be rejected by family and friends, lose his or her job and be forced out of the neighbourhood.

2. This may encourage further deviance. For example, drug addicts may turn to crime to support their habit as 'respectable employers' refuse to give them a job.

3. The official treatment of deviance may have similar effects. Ex-convicts may have difficulty finding employment and be forced to return to crime for

their livelihood. Becker argued: 'The treatment of deviants denies them the ordinary means of carrying on the routines of everyday life open to most people. Because of this denial, the deviant must of necessity develop illegitimate routines.'

4. The **deviant career** is completed when individuals join an organised deviant group. In this context, they confirm and accept their deviant identity. They are surrounded by others in a similar situation who provide them with support and understanding.

5. Within the group, a deviant subculture develops. The subculture often includes beliefs and values which rationalise, justify and support deviant identities and activities. For example, Becker states that organised male homosexual groups provide the individual with a rationale for his deviance, 'explaining to him why he is the way he is, that other people have also been that way, and why it is all right for him to be that way'. (Remember that Becker was writing before the advent of the Gay Rights movement.)

Jock Young's 1971 study of 'hippie' marijuana users in Notting Hill in London, which we examined in Unit 2.1.3, provides an illustration of the application of Becker's theory. Young examined the *meanings* that influenced the police view of the hippies, how their reaction to the hippies was directed by these meanings and the effects upon the hippies of this reaction.

Activity

Explain how labelling theory could be used to make a case for the decriminalisation of drug use.

The process of law-making

Labelling theorists focus heavily on societal reaction to deviance, but Becker did offer some insight also into the process of law-making.

New laws, he suggested, were a product of the efforts of moral entrepreneurs, individuals or groups who sought to translate widely held values into specific social rules – or laws – which would outlaw behaviour that violated those values. This involved the moral entrepreneur enlisting the support of other like-minded groups or organisations and using the mass media to arouse public opinion on the need for legislation by engaging in what he called a **moral crusade.**

Becker (1963) used the example of the federal Marihuana Tax Act of 1937 in the USA designed to stamp out marijuana use by regulating its importation, cultivation, possession and/or distribution. Becker identified the Treasury Department's National Bureau of Narcotics as the moral entrepreneur in this case and the prohibition of marijuana use as being in line with three traditional American values: disapproval of behaviour that could cause loss of self-control, disapproval of behaviour whose only purpose was to achieve states of ecstasy and a humanitarian desire to protect people from their own weaknesses. As to the Bureau's motivation, Becker wrote: 'While it is, of course, difficult to know what the motives of Bureau officials were, we need assume no more than that they perceived an area of wrongdoing that properly belonged in their jurisdiction and moved to put it there.'

Key terms

Outsiders People who are seen as living outside the boundary of respectable society.

Master status A social status that overwhelms all the other statuses that a person has.

Self-fulfilling prophecy A prediction that comes true because it provokes people to act in ways that produce the predicted outcome.

Deviant career A life-path based on pursuing socially disapproved activities.

Moral crusade The campaign waged by moral entrepreneurs in order to get the law changed.

Summary

1. Becker argued that societies create deviance by identifying certain acts as deviant and labelling those who commit them as outsiders.

2. Deviant labels act as master statuses, overwhelming all the other statuses an individual occupies. Others and the individual concerned come to see the person solely in terms of this master status.

3. Labelling produces a self-fulfilling prophecy in which the labelled individual adopts a deviant identity and embarks on a deviant career.

4. New laws are a result of the efforts of moral entrepreneurs who engage in moral crusades to get the law changed.

Unit 2.5.3 Cicourel

Strictly speaking, Cicourel is a **phenomenological** sociologist rather than an interactionist, but both perspectives give great importance to social meanings: how people interpret their own and other's behaviour. In his study of juvenile justice (1968), Cicourel analysed how such interpretations generated a set of youths officially classified as 'delinquent'.

Two cities compared

Cicourel based his research on two Californian cities, each with a population of around 100 000. The socio-economic characteristics of the two populations were similar. In terms of structural theories, the numbers of delinquents produced by the pressures of the social structure should be similar in each city. However, Cicourel found a significant difference in the numbers of delinquents arrested and charged. He argued that only the size, organisation, policies and practices of the juvenile and police bureaux can account for this difference.

For example, the city with the highest rate of delinquency employed more juvenile officers and kept more detailed records on offenders. In the second city, the delinquency rate fluctuated sharply. Cicourel argued that in this city the response of the police to delinquency 'tends to be quite variable depending on publicity given to the case by the local paper, or the pressure generated by the mayor or chief or Captain of Detectives'. Thus, societal reaction can be seen directly to affect the rate of delinquency.

The social production of 'delinquency'

The process of defining a young person as a delinquent is not simple, clear-cut and unproblematic. It is complex, involving a series of interactions based on sets of meanings – or typifications – held by the participants. These meanings can be modified during the interaction, so each stage in the process is negotiable.

The first stage is the decision by the police to stop and interrogate an individual. This decision is based on meanings held by the police of what is 'suspicious', 'strange', 'unusual' and 'wrong'. Such meanings are related to particular geographical areas. Inner-city, low-income areas are seen as 'bad areas' with a high crime rate; consequently, behaviour in such areas is more likely to be viewed as suspicious. Interrogation need not lead to arrest. The process is negotiable but depends largely on the picture held by the police of the 'typical delinquent'. If the appearance, language and demeanour of the young person fits this picture, he or she is more likely to be arrested.

Once arrested, the young person is handed over to a juvenile officer (probation officer) who also has a picture of the 'typical delinquent'. If the suspect's background corresponds to this picture, he or she is more likely to be charged with an offence. Factors assumed to be associated with delinquency include 'coming from broken homes, exhibiting "bad attitudes" toward authority, poor school performance, ethnic group membership, low-income families and the like'.

It is not surprising, therefore, that Cicourel found a close relationship between social class and delinquency. Most young people convicted of offences had fathers who were manual workers. On a seven-class occupational scale, Cicourel found that one-third came from class 7.

Cicourel explained the numerical dominance of working-class delinquents by reference to the meanings held by the police and juvenile officers, and the interactions between them and the juveniles. When middle-class juveniles were arrested, there was less likelihood of them being charged with an offence: their background did not fit the standard picture of the delinquent. Their parents were better able to negotiate successfully on their behalf.

Middle-class parents can present themselves as respectable and reasonable people from a 'nice' neighbourhood, who look forward to a rosy future for their child. They promise cooperation with the juvenile officers, assuring them that their son or daughter is suitably remorseful.

As a result, the middle-class juvenile who breaks the law is often defined as ill rather than criminal, as accidentally straying from the path of righteousness rather than committed to wrongdoing, as cooperative rather than obstructive, as having a real chance of reforming rather than being a 'born loser'. He or she is typically 'counselled, warned and released'.

Thus, in Cicourel's view, the over-representation of lower-class youths in delinquency statistics is not the result of their delinquent adaptation to social strain, but the outcome of a biased law enforcement process. Delinquents are produced by the agencies of social control. Certain individuals rather than others are selected, processed and labelled as deviant. In Cicourel's words, 'what ends up being called justice is negotiable'.

Activity

An example of disintegrative shaming.

Disintegrative shaming is illustrated in the photo at left issued by the Bradford County Sheriff's Department in Pennsylvania, USA who have adopted a 'name-and-shame' policy towards certain categories of offenders. Critics argue that such policies encourage vigilantism and make it less likely that offenders will be able to reintegrate into society once their punishment is over.

Drawing on labelling theory, explain why disintegrative shaming policies such as 'naming-and-shaming' could be counter-productive in terms of protecting the public.

Contemporary issues: Reintegrative shaming and sex offenders

Volunteers and convicted child sex offenders at a Circles meeting in Newcastle. Mark Pinder

Since the early 2000s throughout England and Wales a number of 'Circles of Support and Accountability' (Circles) have been established with the aim of making communities safer by engaging with sex offenders.

A Circle is a group of volunteers from a local community which forms a Circle around an offender. In Circles, the sex offender is referred to as the 'Core Member'. Each Circle consists of four to six Volunteers and a Core Member.

Circles are based on an initiative begun by the Mennonite Church in the USA. They aim to provide a supportive social network that also requires the Core Member to take responsibility (be 'accountable')

for his or her ongoing risk management. The Circle can also provide support and practical guidance in such things as developing their social skills, finding suitable accommodation or helping the Core Member to find appropriate hobbies and interests.

Offenders must be prepared to enter voluntarily into a contract with a Circle, must have some understanding of their offending behaviour and be committed to developing a positive, non-offending lifestyle.

The umbrella organisation representing these projects is Circles UK, which works to support their development and effective operation and has been funded by the Ministry of Justice to ensure that projects across England and Wales are of a high standard.

Circles UK's 2015/16 Annual Report identified 137 Circles throughout England and Wales run by 16 schemes. Evidence of their success is that, out of the 137 'core members', only 4 had been recalled to prison, 3 had been charged, 5 had been convicted and 0 cautions had been issued in relation to sexually recidivist behaviour. (Note: individuals may be counted in more than one category.)

Questions

1. Identify the ways in which Circles conform to Braithwaite's description of 'reintegrative shaming'.

2. What difference do you think it makes that these projects are run by volunteers rather than state agencies or commercial companies?

Policy implications of labelling theory

An important implication of labelling theory is that the stigmatisation brought about by labelling can produce a self-fulfilling prophecy in which the labelled individual adopts a deviant master status and goes on to reoffend.

John Braithwaite (1989) has suggested a policy response that could avoid this consequence, which he calls '**reintegrative shaming**' and which he contrasts with conventional penal approaches, which he calls '**disintegrative shaming**'.

Reintegrative shaming is accomplished when shaming: 1) maintains social bonds between the person being shamed and the person/people doing the shaming,

2) is directed at an evil act rather than an evil person (in other words, it labels the act rather than the person), 3) is delivered in the context of social acceptance of the offender, 4) is terminated with gestures or ceremonies of acceptance and forgiveness.

Such an approach is illustrated by projects in certain USA states, in Canada and in the UK which have sought to reintegrate sex offenders into the community once they have been released from prison. (See Contemporary issues: Reintegrative shaming and sex offenders).

Key terms

Phenomenological Phenomenological sociologists see the social world as comprising sets of social meanings that constitute reality for the members of society. They reject the idea that there is an objective social reality underlying or hidden behind this subjective social reality.

Reintegrative shaming Treating offenders in a way that allows them to remain a part of society while making clear that they have done something morally wrong.

Disintegrative shaming Penal policies based on the idea that the way to reform offenders is to publicly shame them.

Summary

1. Cicourel compared rates of delinquency in two American cities with similar social structures and found that the official rates of delinquency were not the same.

2. He argued that this was because of differences in the juvenile justice processes in the two cities.

3. Youths who broke social rules were treated differently according to whether they did or did not fit the picture held by relevant officials of the typical delinquent. Only those who fitted the picture ended up being identified as delinquents.

4. Consequently, Cicourel argued that 'what ends up being called justice is negotiable'.

5. Recognition of the possible negative consequences of labelling has led to the adoption of policies of reintegrative shaming in some social contexts.

Unit 2.5.4 Labelling theory: an evaluation

By **problematising** the nature of deviance, labelling theory opened up a range of important questions that had previously been largely ignored, questions about law enforcement and law-making rather than just law-breaking. It also drew attention to the ways in which law enforcement, by impacting on people's self-conception, might inadvertently cause the very behaviour it was intended to stamp out.

However, labelling theory has been subjected to a number of criticisms.

First, if Becker was right that 'deviant behaviour is behaviour that people so label', the notion

of 'primary deviancy' becomes problematic because, by definition, it has not been labelled. From a positivist or realist perspective, there is no contradiction in talking about behaviour that breaks social norms as deviant, whether it has been publicly recognised or not, because, *objectively*, that's what it is. However, because labelling theory emphasises *subjective* definitions, it places itself in a logical bind by talking about unacknowledged 'deviancy'.

Second, even if we put this problem to one side, its view that primary deviancy requires no explanation because it is so widespread and, allegedly, has little impact on the individual's self-conception has also been challenged. Critics claim that, while it is true that everyone is likely to break the law at some point in their lives, serious criminal behaviour is not spread evenly either within or between societies and it is therefore worthwhile trying to explain its social and historical distribution. Also, critics challenge the view that primary deviancy does not impact on a person's view of themselves. As Taylor *et al.* (1973) argued, even if people keep their deviancy secret, they are still going to be aware that they are flouting social norms or laws and are therefore likely to see themselves as rule-breakers.

Third, critics have argued that labelling theorists, by focusing on a fairly narrow range of victimless crimes or forms of deviance (prostitution, homosexuality, disability, marijuana-use and so on) and on juvenile delinquency, sought to promote sympathy for the '**underdog**'. But they were only able to do this by ignoring more serious crimes such as rape, burglary, robbery, grievous bodily harm and so on. It is easier to feel sympathy for the 'underdog' if one restricts one's gaze to youths and those seemingly unfairly stigmatised by a morally conservative outlook.

Fourth, critics have argued that labelling theory ends up being just as deterministic as the earlier theories it criticised by implying that labelling inevitably produces secondary deviance. Becker defended himself against this accusation in *Labelling Theory Reconsidered* (1974), where he acknowledged that at any point following labelling an individual could choose to reverse their progress towards a deviant career, but nevertheless insisted that societal reaction makes this unlikely to happen.

Fifth, some critics argue that it oversimplifies the possible responses to labelling. Labelling may lead to secondary deviance, but it might also lead to people ceasing to be deviant, or to people individually or collectively challenging the label of 'deviant'. That is to say, it may lead to what has been called '**deviance disavowal**'. For example, the Gay Rights and Disability Rights movements challenged the view of homosexuals and disabled people as deviant through political action.

Finally, while labelling theory introduced the concept of power into discourses around crime and deviance, Marxists reject the implicitly pluralist view of power with which labelling theorists operated, arguing that power is concentrated, directly or indirectly, in the hands of the wealthy.

It is to an examination of Marxist views of crime and deviance that we turn next.

Key terms

Problematising Identifying something as in need of examination rather than as something to be taken at face value.

Underdog Individuals or groups who are treated as inferior by society.

Deviance disavowal To 'disavow' something is to claim that it is untrue, so deviance disavowal involves the rejection of a deviant label.

Summary

1. Labelling theory pointed out that both crime and deviance are social constructs and that therefore there was a need to examine which acts and which actors were identified as deviant or criminal and why others were not.

2. It opened up the study of both rule-enforcement and rule-making beside rule-breaking.

3. Labelling theory has been subject to a number of criticisms. Among them are its view that primary deviancy does not require any explanation; that primary deviancy has no impact on people's self-concept; that labelling theory oversimplifies the range of possible responses to being labelled; that it is ideologically biased in treating deviants and criminals as 'victims' of an unfair society and that it operates with an inadequate understanding of society's power structure.

PART 6 EXPLAINING CRIME: MARXIST, NEO-MARXIST AND CRITICAL CRIMINOLOGICAL THEORIES

Contents

The same social currents that gave rise to labelling theory in the 1960s and 1970s – the Women's Liberation movement, the Black Power movement, student protest, the Gay Rights movement and so on – led to a resurgence of interest in another theoretical tradition, Marxism.

Marxism is both a political ideology and a social theory. Most Marxist sociologists see Marxism as a powerful tool for analysing capitalist societies without necessarily buying into its associated theory of history which predicts an inevitable movement from capitalism, through socialism to communism.

Marxism, like functionalism, is essentially a structural theory which seeks to explain social behaviour by locating it within a structure, or system, of social institutions. However, whereas functionalists see society as essentially harmonious, Marxists see capitalist societies as organised around an inevitable conflict between those who own the means of production and those who provide the labour. These 'social relations of production' (or class relations) are seen by Marxists as central to understanding crime.

Neo-Marxists draw upon Marxist ideas but adapt them to analyse contemporary capitalist societies. For example, they challenge the idea that the owners of capital still constitute a 'ruling class' and that the state is simply an instrument of this class, passing into law whatever this class demands. Additionally, neo-Marxists accept that the class structure in modern capitalist societies is more complicated than the picture offered by a simple division into 'bourgeoisie' (owners) and 'proletariat' (workers). They also challenge the idea that behaviour is straightforwardly determined by the economic structure of society, seeing crime as 'the product of conscious action by individual actors' (Taylor, Walton and Young, 1973).

Closely related to Marxist perspectives is a perspective called 'critical criminology', which also had its origins in the 1970s. Critical criminologists are not necessarily Marxists, but all adopt a conflict rather than consensus perspective. They are 'critical' of what they see as a global economic order propelled by neoliberal, pro-capitalist ideas and are interested in a much wider range of criminal behaviour than that conventionally focused on by Marxists, including gendered and racialised violence, war, environmental crime, state crime and crimes against humanity.

Unit 2.6.1 Conventional Marxist theories

Unlike Durkheim, Marx said little about crime or criminals. Marx saw criminals as part of the **lumpenproletariat,** a sub-section of the proletariat not involved in legitimate employment who Marx viewed negatively, seeing them as living off the honest labours of the true proletariat. Nevertheless, he also suggested that capitalism itself played a key role in generating crime: 'There must be something rotten in the very core of a social system which increases its wealth without diminishing its misery, and increases in crimes even more rapidly than in numbers' (Marx, 1859).

This theme was taken up by the Dutch Marxist Willem Bonger (1916, orig. 1905) in *Criminality and Economic Conditions,* who argued that crime is caused by the capitalist mode of production because economic conditions in capitalist societies exert strong pressures towards criminal behaviour. A capitalist system encourages people to compete with each other in order to survive – capitalists for profit, workers for jobs. The consequence is the promotion of an **egoistic** outlook, in which each person looks out for him or herself first, and *demoralisation* (the loss of moral feelings for other human beings) leading to crime throughout the class structure.

Work such as Bonger's was rediscovered in the 1970s by sociologists such as William Chambliss, Milton Mankoff, Frank Pearce and Laureen Snider in the USA and Paul Walton, Ian Taylor and Jock Young in the UK. They set out to develop a Marxist criminology that would address all three elements of crime: law-breaking, law enforcement and law-making.

Willem Bonger, 1876–1940.

Law-breaking

Many Marxists see crime as a natural 'outgrowth' of capitalist society, arguing that capitalism is **criminogenic** (that is, it generates crime).

Chambliss (1976) argued that the greed, self-interest and hostility generated by the capitalist system motivate many crimes at all levels within society. Members of each stratum use whatever means and opportunities their class position provides to commit crime. Thus, in low-income areas, the mugger, the petty thief, the pusher, the pimp and the prostitute use what they have got to get what they can. In higher-income brackets, business people, lawyers and politicians have more effective means at their disposal to grab a larger share of the cake.

Given the nature of capitalist society, and particularly American society, David Gordon (1976) argued that crime is rational – it makes sense. In a 'dog-eat-dog' society, where competition is the order of the day, individuals must fend for themselves in order to survive. This is particularly true for the American poor, because the USA has minimal welfare services compared to other advanced industrial societies. Gordon concludes: 'Most crimes in this country share a single important similarity – they represent rational

responses to the competitiveness and inequality of life in capitalist societies.'

Mankoff (1976) argued that the lower crime rate in Western Europe compared to the USA was a result of the fact that the criminogenic effects of capitalism had been moderated by the existence of comprehensive state welfare systems, reflecting the existence of strong trade union movements and socialist political parties, neither of which existed in the USA.

Laureen Snider (1993) argues that figures suggest that corporate crime costs more, in terms of both money and lives, than street crime. Street crime involves losses of around $4 billion each year in the USA. However, losses from corporate crime are more than 20 times greater. She referred to 312 US savings and loan companies that had been unable to pay their debts, due to fraudulent activities such as insider dealing, failing to disclose accurate information in accounts, and racketeering. The General Accounting Agency estimated the total cost of bailing out these companies as a minimum of $325 billion and, more probably, around $500 billion. This means that it is likely to have cost every household in the USA $5000.

Law enforcement

If Marxists are right and capitalism exerts pressure on people throughout the class structure to break the law, one would expect the social class profile of the prison population to roughly match that of society at large. This is not the case. Instead, the prison population is heavily skewed towards those from deprived backgrounds.

A Social Exclusion Unit Report in 2002 found that over a quarter of prison inmates in England and Wales had been in care, roughly half had run away from home as children, two thirds had been unemployed before imprisonment, half of male inmates and nearly three-quarters of female inmates had no qualifications and a third had been homeless.

In *The Rich Get Richer and the Poor Get Prison* (2009), Reiman and Leighton argue that the criminal justice system in the USA is biased against the poor, starting from the definition of what constitutes a crime and continuing through the process of arrest, trial and sentencing. This is reflected in the fact that the criminal justice system is more lenient towards white-collar offenders than non-violent property offenders and in the fact that affluent offenders are less likely to serve prison sentences than poor offenders even when they have committed the same offence.

Activity

"THE DEFENDANT— IS HE RICH OR POOR?"

Differential law enforcement.

How does this cartoon illustrate a Marxist view of law enforcement?

Similarly, Snider argues that despite the enormous costs of corporate crime, both the penalties and the chances of prosecution for those involved in it are small. She argues that enforcement agencies are expected to balance the costs of enforcing regulations (e.g., in lost profits or jobs) with the benefits. Prosecutions are normally used as a last resort, and it is more likely to be small businesses that are taken to court rather than the big corporations that do most harm.

Snider's claims are supported by the recent example of the treatment of HSBC by tax authorities both here and in the USA. (See Contemporary issues: HSBC — One law for the rich and another for the poor?)

Ideological functions of selective law enforcement

Gordon (1976) argued that the selective enforcement of the law serves to maintain ruling-class power and to reinforce ruling-class ideology. The occasional prosecution of ruling-class crime perpetuates the fiction that the law operates for the benefit of society as a whole, that the state represents the public interest and that the extent of ruling-class crime is small. Conversely, frequent prosecution of members of the subject class supports the capitalist system in three ways:

Contemporary issues: HSBC — One law for the rich and another for the poor?

HSBC headquarters in London.

In the USA, a Senate report in 2012 identified multiple failures by HSBC and its US affiliates to comply with anti-money-laundering laws over a

number of years, which involved it handling billions of pounds of funds from drug cartels, terrorist groups and third-world dictators (Murphy, 2013).

In December 2012, the Department of Justice announced that a $1.9 billion fine had been imposed but that there would be no criminal prosecutions of HSBC personnel because 'had the U.S. authorities decided to press criminal charges, HSBC would almost certainly have lost its banking license in the U.S., the future of the institution would have been under threat and the entire banking system would have been destabilised'.

Senator Elizabeth Warren, commenting on this outcome in February 2013 said: 'You know, if you're caught with an ounce of cocaine, the chances are good you're going to go to jail. If it happens repeatedly, you may go to jail for the rest of your life. But evidently, if you launder nearly a billion dollars for drug cartels and violate our international sanctions, your company pays a fine and you go home and sleep in your own bed at night, every single individual associated with this. I think that's fundamentally wrong'.

In the UK in 2010, Her Majesty's Revenue and Customs (HMRC) were passed files obtained by a whistle-blower from HSBC's Swiss subsidiary on 3600 high net-worth individuals who were potentially using the bank to evade tax in the UK (Syal, 2016). Of the 1100 cases where HMRC identified people as owing tax, most were settled under a special agreement – the Liechtenstein disclosure facility – which offered reduced penalties of up to 30 per cent. One hundred and fifty cases were identified as serious candidates for criminal prosecution, but only one person was in fact prosecuted.

In January 2016, HMRC informed a public accounts committee hearing that its criminal investigation had been wound up. A few days earlier, it had been revealed that HSBC would not face any formal action from the financial services regulator, the Financial Conduct Authority (FCA). During the time HMRC were carrying out their investigations, HSBC had announced that it was considering relocating its headquarters from London to Hong Kong. In February 2016, the *Financial Times* reported that HSBC is now 'leaning towards keeping its headquarters in London'.

(Adapted from Dylan Murphy, *Global Research*, 08.05.2013 and Rajeev Syal, *The Guardian*, 13.01.2016.)

Questions

1. How does the treatment of HSBC in the USA and UK support Marxist views of the process of law enforcement?

2. How might HSBC's announcement that it was considering relocating its headquarters to Hong Kong have impacted on the investigations by HMRC and the FCA?

1. By selecting members of the subject class and punishing them as individuals, it protects the system that is primarily responsible for their criminal deviance. Individuals are defined as 'social failures' and as such they are responsible for their criminal activities. In this way, blame and condemnation are directed at the individual rather than at the institutions of capitalism.

2. The imprisonment of selected members of the subject class 'legitimately' neutralises opposition to the system. For example, Black Americans are heavily over-represented among those arrested for 'street crimes' such as robbery and aggravated assault.

3. Defining criminals as 'animals and misfits, as enemies of the state' provides a justification for incarcerating them in prisons. This keeps them hidden from view. In this way, the most embarrassing extremes produced by the capitalist system are neatly swept under the carpet. If something were really done to help those who broke the law, if their problems were made public, the whole system might be questioned.

Law-making

For functionalists, the law reflects the collective conscience of a society and it holds all to account equally, irrespective of their class position. For labelling theorists, the law is a product of the actions of moral entrepreneurs operating in a pluralist social structure. For Marxists, the law is essentially an expression of ruling-class interests made possible through their control of the apparatus of the state and the formal equality of the law is an illusion. As the French novelist, Anatole France, put it (ironically) in *Le Lys Rouge* (*The Red Lily*) in 1894: 'The majestic quality of the law which prohibits the wealthy as well as the poor from sleeping under the bridges, from begging in the streets, and from stealing bread.'

Many sociologists have noted the large number of laws dealing with property in capitalist society. For example, Hermann Mannheim (1965) wrote: 'the history of criminal legislation in England and many other countries, shows that excessive prominence was given by the law to the protection of property'. According to William Chambliss (1976), such laws were largely unnecessary in feudal society, where land – unmovable property – was the main source of wealth, and landowners were 'the undisputed masters of the economic resources of the country'.

However, the increasing importance of trade and commerce (which involve movable property) and the eventual replacement of feudalism by capitalism resulted in a vast number of laws protecting the property interests of the emerging capitalist class. Chambliss argues: 'The heart of a capitalist economic system is the protection of private property, which is, by definition, the cornerstone upon which capitalist economies function. It is not surprising, then, to find that criminal laws reflect this basic concern.'

Chambliss provides two examples to support his claim that the law reflects the interests of the dominant class. The first relates to the Vagrancy Laws passed in England in 1349. At that time, there was a chronic shortage of labour following the Black Death, which had wiped out about half the population. The law made it illegal to give money to any person of sound mind or body who was unemployed, thus forcing such people to work for landowners in order to survive. Moreover,

Activity

Vagrancy laws still operate in the UK. In the period from 2006 to 2014, the number of court cases for vagrancy-related offences in England shot up by 70 per cent (Cooper and McCulloch, 2017).

How could such laws be seen as supporting a Marxist view of criminal law?

vagrants were threatened with imprisonment if they refused offers of work from landowners.

Chambliss' second example relates to the introduction of a Poll Tax (levied on every head of household) by British colonisers in their East African colonies. The native economy of these colonies was not based on money so the only way that the migrant workers could earn the money needed to pay the tax was by working on the tea and coffee plantations. Moreover, wages were kept low so that the workers could not earn sufficient to quit working on the plantations before the harvest season was over.

Where laws exist that do appear to benefit the working class, Marxists argue that indirectly they also benefit the ruling class. Thus Pearce (1976) wrote 'The majority of laws in Britain and America work in favour of the capitalists, yet many laws do also benefit the other social classes, not only because the system needs a healthy, safe population of producers and consumers, but also because it needs their loyalty.'

Equally important for Marxists as the nature of the laws that are passed is the fact that many activities that are potentially socially harmful are *not* covered by the criminal law.

Laureen Snider (1993) notes that the capitalist state is often reluctant to pass laws which regulate large capitalist concerns and which might threaten their profitability. She points out that capitalist states often spend vast sums of money trying to attract investment from corporations. They offer new investors tax concessions, cheap loans and grants, and build expensive infrastructures to help companies operate successfully. Having tried so hard to attract inward investment, the state is unwilling to risk alienating large corporations. Snider says: 'The state is reluctant to pass – or enforce – stringent laws against pollution, worker health and safety, or monopolies. Such measures frighten off the much sought-after investment and engender the equally dreaded loss of confidence.'

Activity

An example of the absence of legislation relates to the pay of chief executives. While there are laws relating to minimum wages in the UK, there are no laws limiting how much someone can be paid (for example, by setting a maximum ratio between the lowest and the highest paid in an organisation). According to an analysis published by the Equality Trust in 2017, the average Financial Times Stock Exchange 100 (the 100 biggest companies listed on the London Stock Exchange) chief executive earns 386 times more than a worker on the National Living Wage (NLW). This is justified on the basis that such laws would represent an unjust infringement on the freedom of businesses to set the pay rates they choose. However, Marxists would see such justifications as ideological – reflecting the interests of the rich. In other words, they would see them as an example of ruling-class ideology.

Question

Do you think that the law has a role to play in regulating the level of (pre-tax) income inequality or would this be an undue infringement on people's liberty?

Evaluation of conventional Marxist theories

Compared with functionalism, Marxist theories of crime have the virtue of recognising that the law can reflect sectional interests rather than the public interest. Also, they avoid functionalism's narrow focus on law-breaking by giving equal attention to law-enforcement and law-making. Compared with labelling theory, Marxist theories have the virtue of considering a wider range of crimes including corporate crime. In addition, there is compelling evidence that law enforcement in relation to white-collar and corporate crime is considerably less punitive than in relation to conventional crime.

However, Marxist theories have come in for heavy criticism from a number of quarters:

1. Feminist sociologists have argued that Marxist theories put undue emphasis upon class inequality. From their point of view, Marxist theories ignore the role of patriarchy in influencing the way the criminal justice system operates. In a similar way, Marxists have also been accused of neglecting the importance of racism in the enforcement of laws.

2. Marxists have been criticised for assuming that a socialist system could eradicate crime. Before the end of communism in the Soviet Union and Eastern European **state-socialist societies**, crime had not been eradicated.

3. Both the idea of a 'ruling class' and the idea that the state is a mere 'instrument' of this alleged class are problematic in representative democracies where, whatever their democratic shortcomings, wealth does not automatically translate into power. Neo-Marxist theories which recognise that the state has some autonomy, are more plausible in this regard. Stephen Jones (2009) points out that the activities of capitalists are sometimes criminalised. He gives the example of insider trading. If it were not illegal, capitalists would be free to make substantial profits out of their knowledge about proposed mergers and takeovers. Similarly, there are laws relating to health and safety, pollution, monopolies and so on. The illegality of such activity suggests that capitalists cannot always get the laws they want.

4. Many laws in capitalist societies clearly are in the general interest, for example laws relating to robbery, burglary, assault, rape, incest and traffic laws.

5. While conventional Marxist theories recognise that crime rates vary between capitalist societies according to their levels of welfare provision by the state, both variations in crime between capitalist societies and over time are under-theorised.

6. Left realists (see Part 7) tend to see Marxist theories as putting undue emphasis on corporate crime, at the expense of other types of crime, and as being largely indifferent to the suffering of the victims of crime. Left realists argue that crimes such as burglary, robbery and other violent crimes cause greater harm than Marxist theories seem to recognise. The victims of such crimes are usually working class, and the consequences can be devastating for them.

Key terms

Lumpenproletariat Literally, the 'proletariat of rags' (from the German *lumpen* meaning rag), Marx's disparaging term for a class of people living on the margins of society and not in regular employment.

Egoistic Self-centred individualism.

Criminogenic Generating crime.

State-socialist societies Societies with a centrally planned economy organised by the state, known as 'communist' societies because power was monopolised by a single party – the Communist Party.

Summary

1. Marxist theories of crime cover law-breaking, law-making and law enforcement.

2. Marxists see capitalism as criminogenic – that is, as generating crime.

3. Crimes are carried out by people in every social class, but the criminal justice system focuses its efforts on working-class crime and treats white-collar criminals more leniently.

4. The occasional prosecution of wealthy people helps to maintain the fiction that the law treats everyone the same.

5. Laws in capitalist societies reflect the interests of the capitalist class.

6. Conventional Marxist theories of crime have been criticised, among other things, for ignoring patriarchy, oversimplifying the nature and role of the state in modern capitalist societies and ignoring crime under socialist societies.

Unit 2.6.2 Neo-Marxist theories of crime

In 1973, the British sociologists Ian Taylor, Paul Walton and Jock Young published *The New Criminology*. It was intended to provide a radical alternative to existing theories of crime and deviance, including to labelling theory and conventional Marxism. They were critical of labelling theory because they thought that crime needed to be located within a structural framework and they were critical of conventional Marxism because they saw it as economically determinist. They nevertheless incorporated elements from both in their own theory.

Taylor, Walton and Young shared the view of conventional Marxists that capitalism was criminogenic, but they saw criminals as having agency (or choice). In their view, crimes are often deliberate and conscious acts with political motives. Many crimes against property involve the redistribution of wealth: if a poor resident of an inner-city area steals from a rich person, the former is helping to change society. Deviants are not just the passive victims of capitalism: they are actively struggling to alter capitalism.

Another distinctive feature of Taylor *et al.*'s outlook was their view — relatively uncommon at the time — that social diversity should be celebrated. They opposed the fact that groups such as hippies, ethnic minorities, disabled people and homosexuals were, at the time they were writing, often socially stigmatised and seen as deviant. Such views, they felt, were characteristic of the '**correctional criminology**' they sought to distance themselves from.

For these reasons, *The New Criminology* can be characterised as neo-Marxist.

A 'fully social theory of deviance'

The aim of *The New Criminology* was to produce what the authors called a 'fully social' theory of deviance. They identified seven aspects of crime and deviance that they believed an adequate theory needed to cover:

1. The wider origins of the deviant act: The criminologist first needs to understand the way in which wealth and power are distributed in society.

2. The immediate origins of the deviant act: He or she must consider the particular circumstances surrounding the decision of an individual to commit an act of deviance.

3. The actual act: It is necessary to consider the deviant act itself, in order to discover its meaning for the person concerned. Was the individual, for example, showing contempt for the material values of capitalism by taking drugs? Was he or she 'kicking back' at society through an act of vandalism?

4. The immediate origins of social reaction: Taylor *et al.* proposed that the criminologist should consider in what ways, and for what reasons, other members of society react to the deviance. For example, how do the police or members of the deviant's family respond to the discovery of the deviance?

5. The wider origins of social reaction: The reaction then needs to be explained in terms of the social structure. This means that the researcher should attempt to discover who has the power in society to make the rules, and to explain why some deviant acts are treated much more severely than others.

6. The impact of social reaction on the deviant's subsequent actions: Taylor *et al.*, then, turn to labelling theory. They accept that it is necessary to study the effects of deviant labels. However, they emphasise that labelling may have a variety of effects. The amplification of deviance is only one possible outcome. Deviants may not even accept that the labels are justified: they may see their actions as morally correct and ignore the label as far as possible.

7. The nature of the deviant process as a whole: Finally, Taylor *et al.* say that the relationship between these different aspects of deviance should be studied, so that they fuse together into a complete theory.

There have been few attempts to put a 'fully social theory of deviance' into practice. However, one such attempt is the work of Stuart Hall and colleagues on the moral panic that emerged in Britain in the 1970s over mugging (see Part 10).

Evaluation of The New Criminology

In seeking to develop a theory that gave due weight to both social structure and human agency and which provided a more sophisticated view of the power structure than that embodied in labelling theory, *The New Criminology* broke new ground. It has nevertheless been criticised on a number of counts:

1. Some of the criticisms outlined above of conventional Marxist theories apply equally to *The New Criminology*. For example, despite the fact

that the Women's Liberation movement was highly visible at the time, Taylor *et al.* more or less ignored both female criminality and the impact of crime on women.

2. Roger Hopkins Burke (2009) believes that *The New Criminology* is both too general to be of much use in explaining crime and too idealistic to be of any use in tackling crime. He says:

    The 'new criminology' provides a generalised prescription for a crime-free, socialist 'good society' and from the standpoint of the twenty-first century, it can be seen as **utopian**, *reflecting the optimistic nature of the times in which it was written, while, the generality of the work itself meant that it could offer very little to substantive theory at all.*

3. *The New Criminology* has also been criticised for romanticising working-class criminals as modern-day Robin Hoods. Criminals were viewed as **proto-revolutionaries** – people who, although they might not realise it themselves, foreshadowed the socialist revolution to come.

4. Finally, *The New Criminology* has been criticised for neglecting the impact of working-class crime on its victims, who are typically from the same class rather than higher classes. This was a criticism which, to his credit, Jock Young took on board in developing left realist criminology (See Part 7).

Contemporary issues: Bank robbers – villains or modern-day Robin Hoods?

Noel 'Razor' Smith today.

The following extract is taken from *A Few Kind Words and a Loaded Gun: The Autobiography of a Career Criminal* by Noel 'Razor' Smith (2004). Smith wrote the book while serving a long prison sentence for bank robberies and this extract comes towards the end of the book where he reflects on having attended the funeral of his son.

Joe's death had a profound effect on me. In the weeks and months after his funeral I did a lot of thinking, and I was forced to face up to the frightening fact that choices I had made in my life had not only affected me but had consequences for many other people, including my children.

I had been strutting about in a dream world, full of myself and too busy with macho posturing to notice other people. What was I? I wasn't some heroic Robin Hood figure. Yes, I stole from the rich, but I didn't give the money to the poor. So what if I had morals about the crimes I committed? Did that make me any less a thief and a thug?

Joe dying so young made me realize just how I had squandered my own life. And for what? So that other criminals could say, 'There goes Razor Smith, he's a diamond geezer. One of our own'. Did I really give a shit how I was perceived by others of my ilk? We classed straight-goers as mugs and told each other stories of how we had outsmarted straight society while sitting in top-security prisons with real life passing us by. Who were the real mugs, I now wondered.

I had chosen this life. And though, once my choice had been made, no serious effort had ever been made to show me any other path, it was my own stubbornness and stupidity that led me to where I am today. In some ways, I was a 'product of the system', but I had entered that system with my eyes wide open and of my own free will. I have to admit it, I liked committing crimes, I liked my status as one of the Chaps and I loved fighting the system. As John McVicar once said, 'Being a criminal is a great life. The only trouble is they put you in prison for it'.

Questions

1. What is Smith's view of the idea that he is a kind of modern-day Robin Hood?

2. What is Smith's view of the idea that criminality is a choice rather than a product of forces outside the individual's control? Do you agree?

3. What are the implications of Smith's comments for *The New Criminology*?

Key terms

Correctional criminology A label applied by critics to criminological approaches which take for granted that the purpose of criminology is to find out what's wrong with criminals so that they can be reformed.

Utopian Imagining that a perfect (in this case, crime free) society is possible.

Proto-revolutionaries People at the earliest stage of developing a revolutionary consciousness.

Summary

1. Neo-Marxist theories seek to update Marxism so that it better fits modern capitalist societies.

2. *The New Criminology* sought to offer a 'fully social' theory of deviance by drawing on Marxism and labelling theory and argued that some criminals could be seen as proto-revolutionaries.

3. Hall *et al.*'s *Policing the Crisis* can be seen as an attempt to apply Taylor *et al.*'s theory.

4. Critics have argued that *The New Criminology* romanticises working-class crime, ignores patriarchy and naively thinks that crime would not occur under socialism. It also ignores the impact of conventional crime on the working class.

Unit 2.6.3 Critical criminology

Ian Taylor, one of the authors of *The New Criminology*, saw himself as a critical criminologist. In a later book *Crime in Context: A Critical Criminology of Market Societies* (1999), he sought to understand how the changes that had taken place in global capitalism since the late 1970s had impacted on crime.

For most of the 20th century, capitalism was organised on a nation-state basis, but in the 1970s this system was faced with a crisis of stagnant growth and rising prices ('stagflation') and falling profits. Over the next two decades capitalism was reorganised on a global scale with the growth of transnational corporations under the influence of neoliberal ideas.

The key feature of neoliberalism is the idea that the 'market' can do no wrong. Politicians who try to intervene – 'interfere' – in the market only make things worse. For example, as Charles Murray argued, by setting up welfare states they – allegedly – create an underclass who are happy to live off the state and supplement their benefits by working for cash.

The global reorganisation of capitalism involved a number of mechanisms. One was the promotion of a new set of capital-labour relations based on the notion of labour flexibility to be achieved by weakening trades unions through legislation. Another involved the intensification of capitalism itself via policies of privatisation (selling off nationalised industries) and commodification (that is, widening the range of things that could be bought and sold) – a process collectively referred to as **marketisation**. A third was the deregulation of financial markets, that is the loosening or removal of rules that limited the freedom of finance capital to make money.

The impact on crime

Against this backcloth of the rise in what he called 'market society', Taylor then proceeded to offer an analysis of a wide range of criminal activity and judicial responses, including youth and crime, crime in the city, drug crime, white-collar crime, the use of firearms and the growth of imprisonment:

> *Marketisation and opportunities for criminality*
> The reorganisation of capitalism has produced new opportunities for criminal activity. For example, the deregulation of financial markets has encouraged the development of tax havens, such as the Cayman Islands and the British Virgin Islands,

which are not just used for avoiding tax but also for laundering and hiding money gained through criminal activities.

According to Taylor, marketisation has also increased the opportunities for various types of crime based directly upon the growth of consumer societies. Examples include insurance fraud by claimants and salespeople, and VAT, customs and pension scheme fraud.

Activity

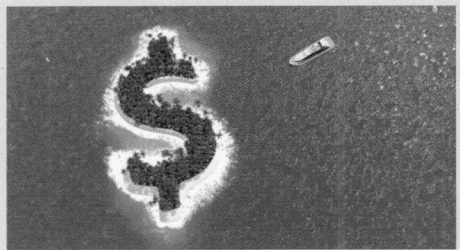

There are 60–70 tax havens globally, which in 2010 held an estimated $21 trillion (equivalent to about one-third of annual world income) according to John Urry (2014).

Carry out research into the 'Panama Papers' and the 'Paradise Papers'. How have they shed light on tax havens?

⟩ *Changes in employment and unemployment*
Other crimes are related to the changing nature of employment and unemployment. Both mass manufacturing and the public sector have experienced substantial job losses and many of the new jobs that have been created are flexible, temporary or part time.

These changes have two main effects. First, in the areas most affected by unemployment, lack of opportunity and an absence of hope lead some to turn to crime as does the increasing insecurity associated with new forms of employment. Second, changing patterns of work have created more opportunities and incentives for criminal activity based on work. For example, subcontracting facilitates the employment of people who are working illegally, such as illegal immigrants, those who are fraudulently claiming benefit, and those who can be paid below the minimum wage.

⟩ *Materialism and inequality*
While the precise nature of employment opportunities is related to particular types of crime, Taylor links the overall increase in criminality to the effect of growing inequality combined with the growth of a popular culture that celebrates designer labels, the lifestyles of the rich and famous and shopping in general. He cites *Hello!* magazine and the growth in theft of and from cars as symbolic of these developments.

⟩ *Drugs and globalisation*
Perhaps the area of crime where globalisation and marketisation have had the biggest impact is the drugs trade. Drawing on Mike Davis' book *City of Quartz* (1990), Taylor argues that cities such as Los Angeles have been badly affected by deindustrialisation and lack of opportunities for young working-class men. At the same time, the culture of **entrepreneurship** has encouraged many young Black men, who confront the additional problem of racism, to pursue illegitimate opportunities in the drugs business.

However, it was not just poverty and inequality in inner cities and the culture of entrepreneurship that encouraged the drugs trade – factors connected to globalisation were also important. In a globalised economy, countries such as Peru, Colombia, Sri Lanka and Burma have been left behind. Some 'third-world' countries such as Brazil, Mexico, South Korea and Taiwan have developed substantial industries, but other countries have not. Peasants in the less successful countries have turned to the production of drugs, because crops from which drugs are derived require little technology or investment, and can command high prices when used to produce drugs. Meanwhile, the massive profits of the global drugs trade can be hidden in the growing offshore tax havens.

Evaluation of *Crime in Context*

Taylor's work has the great merit of trying to explain crime in the context of important changes in capitalist societies linked to marketisation and the growth of globalisation.

Robert Reiner (2007) offers broad support for Taylor's views. He says that 'The emergence of a globalised, neoliberal political economy since the 1970s has been associated with social and cultural changes that were likely to aggravate crime'.

However, Taylor does tend to produce rather generalised arguments that lack a detailed examination of criminal motivation. It is, therefore, difficult to evaluate how directly any increase in criminality can be linked to the changes he discusses.

Key terms

Marketisation The process of subjecting the supply of goods and services to the forces of demand and supply.

Materialism The belief that money and possessions are the most important things in life.

Entrepreneurship The taking of risks in order to set up a business. Both Thatcher and Reagan sought to encourage an 'enterprise culture'.

Summary

1. *Crime in Context* seeks to explain the impact of the changes that have taken place in global capitalism since the late 1970s on crime.

2. The main areas that Taylor focuses on are: marketisation and new opportunities for criminality; changes in the labour market; the impact of growing materialism combined with growing economic inequality, and globalisation and illegal drugs.

3. *Crime in Context* provides a wide-ranging overview of how a globalised capitalism underpinned by a neoliberal ideology has impacted on crime, but criminal motivation is under-theorised.

PART 7 EXPLAINING CRIME: LEFT AND RIGHT REALISM

Contents

In the final decades of the 20th century, the seemingly unstoppable rise in recorded crime meant that issues of 'law and order' were high on the political agenda and the Conservative and Labour Parties in the UK vied with each other for who could appear to be tougher on crime.

Traditionally, the Conservative Party had been seen as the party of law and order with its support for traditional morality, the police and prisons. By contrast, the Labour Party were perceived as 'soft' on crime because of their recognition of the impact of social conditions on criminality, which some saw as merely 'making excuses' for criminal wrongdoing. Electorally, this posed a problem for Labour, but an article published by Tony Blair when he was Shadow Home Secretary in 1993 signalled a change of direction when he wrote that 'We should be tough on crime and tough on the underlying causes of crime.'

This formulation owed a good deal to a criminological perspective developed in the 1980s at a time when criminology became more politically engaged and, arguably, more politically polarised. This perspective was known as 'left realism' and had been developed in response to the failure of the perspectives examined in Part 6 to offer any practical policies to tackle conventional crime based on the assumption that crime was an inevitable feature of capitalism and that there was little that could be done short of a revolution.

'Realist' criminologies were so-called because they took seriously the crimes covered by official crime statistics and sought to develop policies that could reverse the upward trend. The counterpart to **left** realism was **right** realism and the theories developed under these two headings, as we shall see, reflected very different underlying assumptions about the nature of society, the motivations of criminals and the role of the criminal justice system.

Unit 2.7.1 Left realism

Left realism originated in Britain in the early 1980s and is associated particularly with Jock Young, John Lea, Roger Matthews and Richard Kinsey. Left realist criminologists are critical of perspectives that see longer sentences and more prisons as the solution to crime, but they also oppose the views of what they term 'left idealists'. In their view, this includes a variety of Marxists and neo-Marxists, whom they criticise for romanticising working-class crime and underplaying the significance of conventional crime – or 'street crime' – such as burglary, robbery, theft and assault.

In focusing on street crime, left realists did not deny the importance of white-collar and corporate crime, but argued that left-wing criminologists had failed to take seriously the kinds of crimes that ordinary people worry about the most.

Left realists point out that, while the average chances of being a victim of street crime are small, particular groups face high risks. It is not the rich who are the usual targets of muggers or thieves, but the poor, the deprived, minority ethnic groups and inner-city residents. For example, Lea and Young (1984) calculated that unskilled workers are twice as likely to be burgled as other workers. In some of the poorer areas of London, the chances of being mugged are four times the average for the city as a whole. In the USA, figures indicate that Black men and women are more likely to be murdered than to die in a road accident. Young (1997) has calculated that in the mid-1990s Black Americans were 8.6 times as likely to be murdered as White Americans. It is the deprived groups in society who are most likely to be harmed by these crimes; it is also these groups who suffer most if they are the victims of some of these offences. For example, those with low incomes suffer more if they are robbed or burgled: crime adds to and compounds the other problems that they face.

Crime is widely perceived as a serious problem in urban areas and this perception has important consequences. Left realists have carried out a considerable number of local victimisation studies, examining such issues as the extent of crime and attitudes towards crime. These studies have been conducted in, among other places, Merseyside, Islington, Hammersmith and Fulham. In the Second Islington Crime Survey (1990), no less than 80.5 per cent of those surveyed saw crime as a problem affecting their lives. Fear of crime was widespread. Some 35 per cent sometimes felt unsafe in their own homes. Many people altered their behaviour to avoid becoming victims of crime. This was particularly true of women. The authors said, 'women are not only less likely to go out after dark, but also stay in more than men because of fear of crime'.

The explanation of crime

In *What is to be Done about Law and Order?* (1984), John Lea and Jock Young based their attempt to explain crime around three key concepts: relative deprivation, subculture and marginalisation.

Relative deprivation

Lea and Young rejected the idea that poverty itself generates crime, arguing instead that deprivation will only lead to crime where it is experienced as **relative deprivation**. A group experiences relative deprivation when it feels deprived in comparison to other similar groups, or when its expectations are not met. It is not the fact of being deprived as such, but the feeling of deprivation that is important. Thus, in modern societies, the media (and particularly advertisers) stress the importance of economic success and the consumption of consumer goods. All individuals are exposed to values that suggest that people should aspire to middle-class lifestyles and patterns of consumption.

Rather like Merton, Lea and Young argued that rising crime is partly the result of rising expectations for higher standards of living, combined with restricted opportunities to achieve this success because, for example, of educational barriers, discrimination and unemployment.

Moreover, in *Ten Points of Realism*, Jock Young (1992) stressed that relative deprivation is experienced in all social strata. Anybody can feel deprived and 'crime can, therefore, occur anywhere in the social structure and at any period, affluent or otherwise'. It can explain the theft of luxuries as well as necessities, and crimes committed by white-collar criminals who crave the lifestyles of those better off than themselves. To Young, relative deprivation can also help explain violent crime: relative deprivation can cause frustration, which in turn can cause violence.

Subculture

The second key concept Lea and Young used is that of subculture. They saw subculture as the collective solution to a group's problems. Thus, if a group of individuals share a sense of relative deprivation, they will develop lifestyles that allow them to cope with this problem. However, a particular subculture is not an automatic, inevitable response to a situation.

Human creativity will allow a variety of solutions to be produced.

For example, Ken Pryce in his book *Endless Pressure* (1979), based on a participant observation study of the inner-city area of St Paul's in Bristol, which has a large African-Caribbean community, argued that the response of some of the second generation to what they saw as 'slave labour' and 'shit work' was to develop a subculture organised around delinquency ('hustling'), while others turned to Rastafarianism and various forms of black consciousness. Both subcultures offered solutions to their felt deprivation: one by offering a way of making a lot of money (illegally), the other by reassuring them that they were God's chosen people.

Marginalisation

The third and final key concept is that of marginalisation. Marginal groups are those that lack organisations to represent their interests in political life, and which also lack clearly defined goals. Lea and Young argue that marginal groups in society are particularly prone to the use of violence and riots as forms of political action.

Activity

Police officers in riot gear block a street near the Hackney neighbourhood of London during the 2011 riots.

Left realists see rioting as a form of political protest adopted by the marginalised. Suggest how right realists would see rioting.

Lea and Young believed that 'participation in the process of production' is the key to a group avoiding marginality. Workers have clearly defined objectives, such as higher wages and improved working conditions. Furthermore, they may have membership of unions, which provide them with involvement in pressure-group politics. Thus they have no need to resort to violence.

In contrast, the young unemployed do not have clearly defined aims, or pressure groups to represent them. Rather than precise grievances, they feel a general sense of resentment that the future does not seem to offer an interesting, worthwhile and rewarding life.

The square of crime

While explaining the behaviour of offenders is seen as important by left realists, it is not seen as sufficient to fully explain crime. The offender and their actions are seen as just one part of a bigger picture that left realists call the 'square of crime'.

As Figure 2.7.1 shows, the square of crime involves four elements:

1. The state and its agencies
2. The offender and their actions
3. Informal methods of social control (sometimes called 'society' or 'the public')
4. The victim.

Activity

Figure 2.7.1 The square of crime

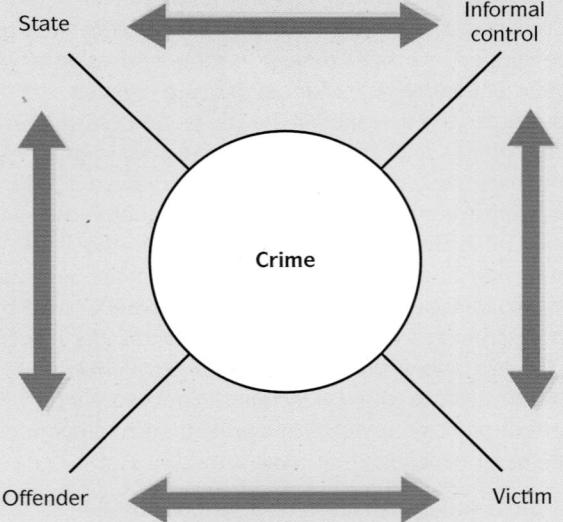

Source: Sociology Review, February 1993, p. 28.

Identify the contribution of each of the four elements to a left realist explanation of crime.

Whatever the type of crime, left realists believe that each of these four elements is crucial, and together they determine what crime is, as well as what causes it and how it might be dealt with. Young called this the principle of **multiple aetiology** – that is, crime is caused by several different factors. Crime by its very nature is a product of formal and informal rules, of actions by offenders, and of reactions by victims and the state and its agencies. It is therefore important to try to understand not only why people offend, but also what makes the victims vulnerable, the factors that affect public attitudes and responses to crime, and the social forces that influence the police.

From inclusive to exclusive society

In two more recent works, *The Exclusive Society* (1999) and *The Vertigo of Late Modernity* (2007), Young argues that various changes connected with the development of capitalist societies combined with neoliberal policies have exacerbated feelings of relative deprivation and led to increasing numbers feeling socially excluded.

He contrasts the present day with what he describes as the 'Golden Age' of the 1950s and 1960s when most members of the working class could find secure employment, the state was committed to trying to maintain full employment, or something near to it, and the welfare state provided important citizenship rights for all members of society. Women were increasingly included in the formal economy as large numbers of married women found paid employment. Compared to today, family life was relatively stable, with much lower rates of divorce and fewer lone-parent families.

Core values shared by most of the population centred around work and family life. A sense of community was stronger than today. All of these characteristics together produced an 'interwoven and buttressed structure' in which most people felt included.

By the 1970s, however, this structure was beginning to unravel. According to Young, this was brought about by a shift from **Fordist** to **post-Fordist production**. Post-Fordism moved away from the mass production of standardised products towards more specialist production of a wider range of products. It brought with it greater economic insecurity as unemployment became more common. It led to more people being employed in insecure work in the secondary labour market. There were more short-term contracts and fewer 'safe' careers where you could expect a job for life. The number of male manual jobs available declined as manufacturing shifted to the 'third world', where wages were much lower. All of this increased the amount of economic exclusion.

Young uses the ideas of the British writer Will Hutton to suggest that Britain had developed into a '40:30:30 society'. In such a society, '40 per cent of the population are in tenured secure employment, 30 per cent in insecure employment, and 30 per cent marginalised, without paid work or working for poverty wages'.

Consequently, in late modernity many people experience their lives as unstable, unpredictable and precarious, characterised by widespread feelings of vertigo or fear of falling – falling behind others in terms of consumption, falling into poverty, falling into debt and so on.

Alongside this growing economic exclusion, Young argues that people have been increasingly drawn into the culture of consumption and the belief that not having the latest consumer goods – for example the latest mobile phone, fashionable trainers or designer clothes – is tantamount to a kind of social death. He calls the resulting society a **bulimic society** where 'massive cultural inclusion is accompanied by systematic structural exclusion. It is a society which has both strong **centrifugal and centripetal** currents: it absorbs and it rejects' (Young, 2007, p. 32).

As a result, Young argues, crime becomes both more widespread and nastier. In the 1950s, most burglaries were directed at commercial property in Britain but by the 1990s, most burglaries were directed at domestic property. There is also a considerable increase in hate crime directed at people because of their age, sexuality, gender, ethnicity, or simply because they are poor. Much of this is encouraged by what Young calls 'relative deprivation downwards' – feelings of resentment towards those who are seen as unfairly benefiting from policies of (what those on the right call) **'political correctness'** or from 'too generous' social security benefits.

Evaluation of left realism

By recognising that the impact of conventional crime falls most heavily on those who are already disadvantaged and by giving victims a prominent place in their analysis of crime, left realism represented a significant advance on earlier theories. It also had a much more significant impact on criminal and social policy than most previous theories: policies adopted by Labour governments between 1997 and 2010 such as Community Safety Partnerships, the Social Exclusion Unit, neighbourhood policing, Police and Community Together (PACT) meetings, the introduction of Police Community Support Officers (PCSOs), the Communities that Care initiative, Sure Start and others can all be linked to aspects of left realism's analysis of crime.

Contemporary issues: Hate crime

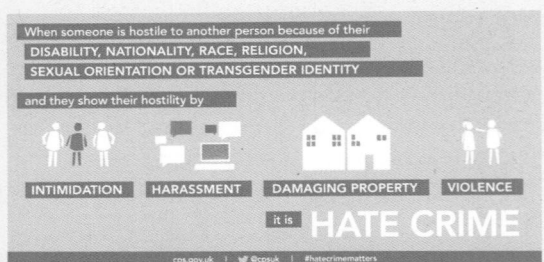

CPS hatecrimematters campaign poster.

The police and the CPS have agreed the following definition for identifying and flagging hate crimes: 'Any criminal offence which is perceived by the victim or any other person to be motivated by hostility or prejudice, based on a person's disability or perceived disability; race or perceived race; or religion or perceived religion; or sexual orientation or perceived sexual orientation or transgender identity or perceived transgender identity.'

Beginning with the 1998 Crime and Disorder Act, legislation has been passed which requires that enhanced sentences should be given to offenders in England and Wales who commit offences which involve a demonstration of hostility based upon the victim's race, religion, sexual orientation, disability or transgender identity, or which are motivated by such hostility.

In 2015/16, there were 62 518 offences recorded by the police in England and Wales in which one or more hate crime strands were deemed to be a motivating factor. This was an increase of 19 per cent compared with the 52 465 hate crimes recorded in 2014/15. However, the true extent of

hate crime is almost certainly considerably higher. The Home Office, drawing on the Crime Survey for England and Wales, estimated in 2013 that the total figure was about 280 000 annually.

Research (e.g., Iganski, 2008) suggests that very few perpetrators – perhaps 1 in 20 – are what might be called 'extremists': people whose lives centre around the desire to inflict pain and suffering on the members of a particular out-group and who plan their crimes beforehand.

Instead, hate crime can be seen as the product of three main social factors:

> ideologies of oppression (racism, heterosexism, disablism and so on) that cast some people as 'other' and inferior

> unequal social structures which generate status anxieties, frustrations and resentments

> situational triggers that lead to the expression of these frustrations and resentments.

Source: Adapted from Davies, T. (2014) 'What is hate crime?', *Sociology Review*, vol. 24, no. 1.

Questions

1. How might Young's concept of 'relative deprivation downward' link to hate crime?

2. In the three months of July to September 2016 following the EU referendum in June, racially and religiously motivated recorded hate crimes rose by 25 per cent compared with the previous three months. Why do you think the referendum result proved to be a trigger for a spike in hate crimes?

However, there are nevertheless various weaknesses that have been identified.

The period when left realism was being developed – the 1980s and 1990s – coincided with the period that saw a continuing growth in recorded crime and consequently the claims that left realists made about the criminogenic features of late modernity (growing relative deprivation, instability, individualism, hyper-consumerism and so on) seemed to be validated. However, since that time, there has been a persistent fall in recorded crime in Britain, North America and elsewhere and left realists have failed to provide convincing explanations of what has changed. The

issue was directly addressed by Roger Matthews in a paper published in 2016 in which he talks about the impact of mass immigration and associated cultural shifts, changes in gender relations and in notions of masculinity and changes in the nature of social control and modes of governance, but it is not entirely clear how these might link with a fall in recorded crime, nor is any evidence offered to support the claimed link.

Indeed, a lack of supporting evidence is also evident in relation to a number of the claims made by Young in his later work, for example his claim that the fear of falling – vertigo – is a pervasive feature of late modern societies. It is also unclear in what way

Activity

A PACT meeting in Burnham-on-Sea, Somerset in April 2010.

Find out when the next PACT meeting covering your neighbourhood is taking place and try to arrange to attend it.

Young's notion of late modern society as a bulimic society goes beyond Merton's strain theory.

Gordon Hughes (1991) attacks left realism on a number of counts, but argues that its major failing is in its attempts to explain the causes of street crime. This is largely because left realists have simply failed to carry out the necessary research. The concentration on victimisation studies has prevented left realists from gathering their own data on the motives of offenders. The data they have collected are largely quantitative and statistical and cannot reveal the subjective states of offenders. Thus, according to Hughes, left realism 'offers no empirical account of the subjective worlds of the street criminal but, instead, appears to rely for the most part on speculation'.

Key terms

Left and **right** Shorthand terms used to describe two opposed political outlooks.

Left Those on the left are in favour of greater equality and see the state as having an important role intervening in the operation of capitalist economies (e.g. by providing unemployment benefit) or believe in replacing capitalism with socialism.

Right Those on the right emphasise freedom over equality and see a 'big state' as a threat to such freedom. They also favour private enterprise over state-provided goods and services.

Relative deprivation Deprivation felt when people compare their situation with that of others.

Multiple aetiology Aetiology is the study of the cause or causes of sickness or disease, so the term is being used metaphorically to refer to the many causes of social ills or social problems.

Fordist/post-Fordist production In the first part of the 20th century, manufacturing industry was based on high-volume, assembly line production such as that pioneered by the Ford Motor Company. Towards the end of the century, manufacturing turned to more flexible methods of production aided by advances in automation and ICT.

Bulimic society Bulimia is a medical condition in which the sufferer binges on food and then induces vomiting to expel it. Young is using the term metaphorically to describe a society that both draws people in culturally (to consumerism) and at the same time expels them economically through increasingly poorly paid and insecure employment.

Centrifugal and centripetal Centrifugal forces draw people in; centripetal forces push them out.

Political correctness A term coined by those on the political right to undermine efforts by oppressed minority groups to challenge their oppression by painting supporters of such efforts as overzealous and humourless do-gooders.

Summary

1. Left realism originated in the 1980s in Britain.

2. It focuses on conventional or street crime on the basis that local victim studies reveal that this is what concerns people and that the burden of such crimes falls mostly on the already disadvantaged.

3. Key concepts are relative deprivation, subculture and marginalisation.

4. Left realists argue that crime needs to be understood in terms of the interaction of four elements: the state, offenders, victims and social control agencies – the 'square of crime'.

5. Young argues that late modern societies are characterised by high levels of crime because they are bulimic and vertigo inducing.

6. Left realism has had a significant impact on criminal policy, but has been criticised for a lack of empirical research on offenders, for merely recycling earlier strain and subcultural theories and for failing to account for the drop in recorded crime since the late 1990s.

Unit 2.7.2 Right realism

Around the same time that left realist ideas were being developed in the UK, an approach which also took conventional crime seriously was being developed in the USA, but by criminologists who viewed the issues from a right-wing perspective. Rather than seeking explanations in the overall structure of society and the distribution of rewards, right realists focused more on the individual offender as a rational actor and on the role of formal and informal social control.

Rationality, community and crime

An early influential publication from a right realist perspective was *Thinking about Crime* (1975) by James Q. Wilson.

Wilson saw crime as being the result of rational calculations. People will commit crime if the likely benefits exceed the likely costs. This might suggest that harsher sentences and more police are the answer to crime. If punishments were greater and there was more chance of being caught, then people would commit fewer crimes. However, Wilson believed that such an approach can have only a limited impact. In reality, the chances of getting caught for a particular crime are quite small. If offenders do not believe they are going to get caught, or if punishments take place a long time after offences, then even severe penalties will not deter people. Certain and swift penalties are likely to be effective, but, until they can be assured by the criminal justice system, other types of measure are also needed.

There are other ways of changing the balance between the gains and losses of committing crimes. One example is the prescription of methadone to heroin addicts. This offers addicts an alternative and less destructive substitute drug, which helps to limit the side effects of giving up heroin. Combined with a clampdown on the supply of heroin, leading to an increase in price, the heroin problem can be contained in this way. The costs of taking the drug are increased, while the difficulties of giving up are reduced. At the same time, former addicts have more chance to enjoy the benefits of a conventional lifestyle.

Another effective way of dealing with crime is to try to prevent communities from falling apart. This is more effective than trying to rely upon deterrent sentencing. Where strong communities exist, they can deter crime, because people who are disgraced by being found to be involved in crime will lose their standing in the community. Where a community is strong, this loss will be important to people and they will try to avoid it. The problem is that crime itself undermines communities. Wilson (1975) says:

> *Predatory crime does not merely victimize individuals; it impedes and, in the extreme case, prevents the formation and maintenance of community. By disrupting the delicate nexus of ties, formal and informal, by which we are all linked with our neighbours, crime atomizes society and makes its members mere individual calculators estimating their own advantage.*

This tends to lead to even higher crime rates. In the absence of a community, people no longer gain by conforming to the community's values.

Broken windows

In a later article, Wilson and George Kelling (1982) spelled out how to avoid the collapse of community as a consequence of criminality. They believed that it is crucial to try to maintain the character of neighbourhoods and prevent them from deteriorating. If a single window broken by vandals goes unmended, if incivilities such as rudeness and rowdiness on the streets go unchallenged, then problems will quickly grow. More windows will be vandalised, unruly youths will start hanging around on the streets, and law-abiding citizens will become afraid to go out. Freed from close observation by respectable members of the community, those inclined to criminality will commit more and more street crimes.

On the other hand, if residents believe that attempts are being made to maintain law and order, they will be more likely to report crime and discourage incivilities and anti-social behaviour in public places. Informal social controls will be maintained, and street crime will not get out of hand.

The crucial role of the police, then, is to stop an area from deteriorating by clamping down on the first signs of undesirable behaviour. They should try to keep drunks, prostitutes, drug addicts and vandals off the streets. They should try to make law-abiding citizens feel safe. Their role is to maintain public law and order in areas where it has yet to break down.

Controversially, Wilson and Kelling believed it is a waste of valuable resources to put much effort into the worst inner-city areas. Once law and order have broken down, the police are unlikely to be able to restore it by arresting people. Their time is better spent concentrating on those areas where there is still hope.

Activity

Caption: Broken windows theory suggests a single broken window left unrepaired will soon lead to others and result in the deterioration of the whole neighbourhood.

What do you think are the strengths and weaknesses of broken windows theory?

Crime and human nature

In a later book written with Richard Hernstein called *Crime and Human Nature*, Wilson's work took a slightly different tack. Wilson and Hernstein (1985) claimed that crime has a biological basis. They argued that some people are born with a predisposition towards crime. Their potential for criminality is more likely to be realised if they are not properly socialised. If parents fail to teach them right from wrong, and particularly if they fail to punish them immediately for misbehaving, those who are prone to crime become much more likely to commit criminal acts in later life.

In close-knit nuclear families, children can be conditioned to have a conscience, which will keep them out of trouble with the law. Where such families are absent (e.g., single-parent families), Wilson and Hernstein believed that effective socialisation is unlikely. Furthermore, they believed that the quality of socialisation has declined with the development of a more permissive society in which anything goes.

Despite the role they saw for biology and socialisation, Wilson and Hernstein still believed that people possess free will. Ultimately, people choose whether to commit crimes, by weighing up the costs and benefits. Unfortunately, in their view, an over-generous welfare system discourages people from putting in the hard work necessary to hold down a job. It is too easy to live off benefits. At the same time, in an increasingly affluent society, the potential gains from crime are constantly increasing. For many people, the benefits of crime come to outweigh the costs, and the crime rate rises.

The underclass

The view that an over-generous welfare system contributes to crime was taken up forcefully by the American social scientist Charles Murray who claimed in 1989 that an underclass exists in the USA and Britain consisting of people 'at the margins of society, unsocialised and often violent…and who cannot provide for themselves'.

Murray argued that the underclass was characterised by three distinctive features:

- *Crime:* a very high proportion of violent and property crime in society is carried out by the underclass
- *Illegitimacy:* a high proportion of children in the underclass are born outside marriage, particularly to never-married women, and the fathers feel no obligation to support their children
- *Economic inactivity:* men in the underclass are happy to draw down state benefits and work in the **shadow economy**.

In an update published in 2000, Murray claimed that this alleged underclass was continuing to grow and was responsible for a high proportion of violent and property crime.

Routine activity theory

The idea that crime is the result of a rational calculation made by a potential offender was taken up and developed by Cohen and Felson (1979). In their routine activities theory, they argued that three elements need to be present for a crime to occur: a motivated offender with criminal intentions and the ability to act on these inclinations, a suitable victim or target, and the absence of a 'capable guardian' (such as a neighbour or police officer) who can prevent the crime from happening.

These three elements must come together in time and space for a crime to occur. Hence, the same place can be safe during the day, but can become an area of crime in the evening and night (it could also be that different crimes are committed at different times). The best example of this is the high street of any town. During the day there will be relatively few crimes, but those that occur are likely to be offences such as theft. In the evening, when large numbers of young people are out drinking, the crime level may well increase, including the number of violent crimes.

Thus Cohen and Felson's approach helps explain why most violent offences occur in the evenings and at weekends in city centres, and why burglaries are most likely to occur in poorer areas and in areas adjacent to them. Furthermore, it throws light on the fact that those who are most likely to be victims of violence tend to be young males, who go out three or more times a week, who drink alcohol and who are themselves most likely to commit offences — as they are the ones whose routine activities place them in the most likely situation to be victims/offenders.

Evaluation of right realism

Right realism, like left realism, has had a significant impact on criminal and social policy. For example, the adoption of **situational crime prevention strategies** such as installing alley-gates in areas of back-to-back housing to make it more difficult for burglars to enter from the rear of properties, or for drug dealers to carry out their trade hidden from view, picks up on the notion of guardianship in routine activity theory.

Another policy, linked to the broken windows theory, is that of 'zero tolerance' policing in which even minor offences are addressed as speedily as possible in order to try to stop neighbourhoods sliding into disorder. It was most famously applied in New York City in the early 1990s, but has also been used in the UK in the King's Cross area of London, Hartlepool, Middlesbrough and Strathclyde.

A third policy initiative that could be linked to right realism is the attention now paid to anti-social behaviour by community safety partnerships across England and Wales. Anti-Social Behaviour Orders (ASBOs) were introduced by the Labour government in the 1998 Crime and Disorder Act, which defined anti-social behaviour as any kind of behaviour that

Activity

Alley-gates

What do you think are the strengths and limitations of alley-gating as a situational crime prevention strategy?

'caused or was likely to cause harassment, alarm or distress to one or more persons not of the same household as himself'. They were civil orders, but if they were breached this constituted a criminal offence. Since March 2015, ASBOs have been replaced by Injunctions to Prevent Nuisance and Annoyance (IPNAs), Community Protection Orders (CPOs) and by Criminal Behaviour Orders (CBOs), which can be issued when a person is convicted of a criminal offence at the same time as being involved in persistent anti-social behaviour.

Nevertheless, as a theoretical perspective on crime, right realism has been subjected to a number of criticisms.

First, the idea that offenders are rational actors has been challenged both on the grounds that it ignores the role of the emotions in criminal behaviour (particularly violent behaviour) and because it assumes that offenders typically consider the legal consequences of their actions before acting. Much offending is impulsive and focused on immediate rewards rather than on the long-term consequences if caught. Indeed, interview research with prisoners by Tunnell (1996) found that all 60 respondents reported that they simply did not think about the legal consequences of their actions. Moreover, though they knew their actions were criminal, and therefore tried to avoid capture, more than half were unaware of the severity of the punishment for the offence.

Second, routine activity theory focuses on individuals and their choices while ignoring the social constraints and conditions that shape an individual's circumstances, thought processes and life chances. These exert a considerable influence on people and offer alternative possible targets for efforts to control crime.

Third, Wilson and Hernstein's theory has been criticised for being self-contradictory. On the one hand they claim that some people are born with a biological predisposition to commit crime, but on the other they claim that criminals are rational actors who choose to offend on the basis of rudimentary cost/benefit calculations. Such a combination of determinism (that behaviour is a product of factors over which the individual has no control) and voluntarism (that individuals choose how to behave) is problematic to say the least!

Fourth, Murray's claim that a self-reproducing, criminally inclined underclass exists in Britain and the USA has been fiercely contested by left-wing sociologists. Empirical evidence does not support the idea that there are generations of workless or workshy families. For example, research by Lindsey Macmillan (2011) based on the government's Labour Force Survey found that in households with two or more generations of working age, there were only 0.3 per cent where neither generation had ever been in legitimate employment. Moreover, the idea that high rates of illegitimacy are a distinctive feature of an underclass is undermined by evidence which shows that the proportion of children born outside marriage/civil partnerships in England and Wales in 2012 was 47.5 per cent.

Finally, right realist explanations of the falling recorded crime rate over the last couple of decades have been as scarce as those of left realists. An exception is an article by Hough and Mayhew (2006) in which they suggest that some forms of 'guardianship' over property have increased, such as greater use of home security hardware, car immobilisers and CCTV. Also, that comparatively low levels of unemployment, more targeted and proactive policing and increased attention to delivering crime prevention at the local level might have played a part. In addition, they suggest that demographic changes (a decline in the number of young men) and changes in youth lifestyles and aspirations might have made a difference, claiming that 'a steady, legitimate income rather than misbehaviour is now the fashion' for the young (though no evidence is provided to support this claim).

Key terms

The shadow economy Economic activity that is both unregulated and out of sight of the tax authorities where work is done for cash-in-hand.

Situational crime prevention strategies Strategies designed to reduce the vulnerability of crime targets or increase the likelihood of being caught.

Summary

1. Right realism originated in the USA in the 1970s and 1980s.

2. Right realists see offenders as rational actors who have been inadequately socialised and choose to commit crime when the potential benefits outweigh potential costs.

3. Right realism traces the growth in crime in the second half of the 20th century to a decline in morality and in self-reliance promoted by over-generous state welfare provision. Some see this as having created a crime-prone underclass.

4. The broken windows theory argues that anti-social behaviour such as vandalism and graffiti needs to be speedily addressed to forestall community decline.

5. Routine activities theory argues that crime occurs when there is a motivated offender, a vulnerable victim and the absence of a capable guardian.

6. Right realism has had a significant impact on criminal policy, but critics have questioned the idea that offenders act rationally, that crime can be divorced from the broader societal context in which it occurs and argue that it fails to explain the drop in recorded crime over the last two decades.

PART 8 EXPLAINING CRIME: CORPORATE, STATE AND GREEN CRIME

Contents

Corporate crime has been a topic of study for criminologists since the middle of the 20th century, while the study of both state and green crime dates from the final decade of that century.

Most of the perspectives we have looked at in Parts 4–7, other than Marxism and critical theory, are focused on conventionally defined crime. Nevertheless, as we shall see in Part 8, criminologists have drawn on some of these theories, as well as developing new ones, to analyse corporate, state and green crime.

The categories of corporate, state and green crime are not completely distinct from each other. As we saw in Unit 2.3.3, sociologists have coined the term 'state-corporate crime' to identify crimes in which both corporations and states are implicated. Moreover, the study of state crime grew out of the work of critical criminologists studying corporate crime who were struck by the many links between the corporate world and the state in capitalist societies. It is also the case that much environmental crime is perpetrated either by corporations or by states (or both together), so explanations of corporate and state crime take us a long way towards explaining many cases of green crime.

Nevertheless, conceptually the three categories are distinct, so can be examined separately. We will begin with corporate crime.

Unit 2.8.1 Explaining corporate crime

As we saw in Unit 2.2.2, corporate crime includes financial offences, offences against employees and consumers and offences against the environment. Various theoretical perspectives and concepts have been drawn on by sociologists to explain corporate crime.

Marxist and critical criminological perspectives

For Marxists and critical criminologists, capitalism is criminogenic, generating crime at all levels of society, so corporate crime is neither surprising nor exceptional. In a competitive economic environment, companies are under pressure to minimise their costs in order to stay in business and make profits. Moreover, many senior managers' pay packages are tied to the company's performance on the stock exchange (in terms of its share price) and therefore they have a personal incentive to maximise profits.

Consequently, especially if the company is struggling, managers will be under pressure to 'innovate' – in

Merton's term – that is, adopt criminal methods to achieve their goal of profit maximisation. There are many illegal methods that can be used to achieve this goal, such as price-fixing agreements (where competitors agree to sell their products at a fixed price), paying staff below the minimum wage, tax evasion and corporate fraud. In 2013, the Serious Fraud Office launched a criminal investigation to discover whether G4S and Serco had been charging the Ministry of Justice millions of pounds for the electronic monitoring ('tagging') of convicts who were either dead or in prison. At the time of writing, four years later, the investigation is still ongoing and no criminal charges have been made, while G4S has been awarded a new six-year tagging contract.

Organisational culture and personality types

Another area that merits attention, according to Tombs (2013) is the organisational culture of corporations and the kinds of personality types such cultures reward. Snider (1993) suggested that the personality characteristics favoured by corporations included being innovative, ambitious, shrewd, aggressive, impatient, and 'morally flexible',

Activity

A fitted electronic monitoring device.

Get an update on the G4S and Serco overcharging case by visiting the SFO's website.

characteristics which might well lead to people prioritising business goals over moral scruples. Indeed, Babiak and Hare (2006) have suggested that commercial businesses provide a setting in which people with psychopathic tendencies can flourish. Psychopaths – or people with **anti-social personality disorder** – are goal-driven, tend to act impulsively and recklessly and lack a moral conscience. They also tend to believe that only the strongest survive and that one must do whatever it takes to be successful. Moreover, given that such characteristics may also favour the achievement of promotion (psychopaths are unlikely to be too concerned about who they trample on in their route to the top), people displaying these characteristics may be especially likely to be in a position to shape the organisation's culture.

Differential association and techniques of neutralisation

Related to the issue of organisational culture, Tombs also suggests that Edwin Sutherland's theory of differential association can be used to explain corporate crime. Differential association theory explains crime as a product of learning and the nature, range and intensity of the associations we have with others. If those associations result in our acquiring an excess of definitions favourable to law violation over definitions that condemn it (that is, we internalise more opinions suggesting that it is all right to break the law than ones which say that it is not) offending is likely to result.

People spend a significant amount of time at work, so if the occupational culture emphasises 'getting the job done' over how this is achieved, illegality becomes an

option. Tombs provides the example of retail butchery and suggests that it is common knowledge that frozen poultry can be defrosted in a way which makes it resemble fresh poultry. The meat can then be sold at a higher price, thereby defrauding the customer. Moreover, various '**techniques of neutralisation**' (Sykes and Matza, 1957) serve to make it seem that such strategies are legitimate – 'everyone does it', 'the meat still tastes the same', 'it doesn't harm anyone' and so on.

Rational actor theory: corporate regulation and the punishment of corporate crime

The activities of corporations, whether commercial, public or charitable, are generally subject to official regulation in advanced industrial societies. A wide range of regulatory bodies exist in the UK, for example, such as Her Majesty's Revenue and Customs, the Financial Conduct Authority, the Health and Safety Executive, the Environment Agency, the Care Quality Commission, the Office of Fair Trading, the Food Standards Agency, and many more. Some of these regulatory bodies also have the power to initiate criminal prosecutions.

If crime is the result of rational action, as some criminologists argue, then three considerations above all others are likely to enter into such rational calculations on the part of corporations: the likelihood of being caught, the likelihood of being prosecuted if caught and the likely severity of any resulting punishments. Marxists and critical criminologists argue that, on all three counts, the scales are balanced in favour of corporate illegality. According to Snider, non-enforcement is the most frequently found characteristic; where enforcement is pursued it tends to focus upon the smallest and weakest organisations; and the punishments following regulatory activity are typically light.

Neoliberal governments tend to equate regulation with unnecessary 'red tape'. Indeed, the 2010–2015 UK coalition government introduced a 'one in, two out rule' for regulation, under which the introduction of any new regulation, would require two existing ones to be removed. This, combined with austerity policies, has resulted in widespread cuts to the funds given to regulatory agencies by government with inevitable knock-on effects on their ability to oversee corporate activity. Tombs and Whyte (2013), for example, note that between 1990/2000 and 2012/13 there was a 37 per cent decline in the number of inspection visits made by the Health and Safety Executive (HSE) to business premises. Hence, the chances of getting caught for breaches of regulations are low and declining.

Activity

Health and safety signage on an industrial site.

What message do you think each circle seeks to convey? (Answers can be found on the HSE website.)

It is also the case that regulatory authorities tend to seek cooperative relationships with corporations, rather than pursue a punitive strategy towards regulatory violations. According to Tombs, 'regulators seek to enforce through persuasion – they advise, educate, and bargain, negotiate and reach compromise with the regulated'. When violations become known, the usual response of regulatory authorities is to enter into a dialogue with the company, not to prosecute them.

Finally, when prosecutions are pursued, they are usually against the company rather than named employees and typically result in relatively low fines. For example, Tombs found that the average fine for all HSE health and safety convictions for 2010/11 was £27 420. Occasionally, the fines imposed are much higher, but even so, as a proportion of turnover or profits, they are rarely punitive. The record fine for a health and safety offence in the UK was £15 million, levied on Transco Plc in August 2005 following the deaths of Andrew and Janette Findlay and their two children when a gas explosion destroyed their home. Yet this fine represented less than 2 per cent of Transco's after-tax profit in the previous year and just 0.16 per cent of their turnover – the equivalent, as Tombs points out, of fining someone earning £25 000 a year just £36.

Activity

The 2003 American documentary 'The Corporation' provides a radical analysis of the development of multinational corporations and highlights their involvement in crime. It can be watched for free on various websites. Which of the various explanations of corporate crime examined above does the documentary support?

Key terms

Anti-social personality disorder A personality disorder is a type of psychiatric disorder in which people habitually display abnormal patterns of thoughts, feelings and behaviour. People with ASPD lack empathy and are generally callous, manipulative, impulsive and irresponsible.

Techniques of neutralisation A term coined by Matza and Sykes (1957) to describe a number of ways in which delinquents sought to deny that they had done anything wrong by reframing their behaviour in ways that made it seem reasonable or legitimate.

Summary

1. Marxist and critical criminological explanations of corporate crime emphasise that the pressure to maximise profits puts pressure on corporations to act illegally.

2. Corporate crime can also be explained by reference to the organisational culture of corporations and the personality types that the culture rewards.

3. Another line of explanation draws on differential association theory, emphasising that people spend a lot of time at work and that the organisational culture of some firms may produce an excess of definitions of reality that justify criminal actions to achieve corporate goals.

4. A final line of explanation focuses on the regulatory environment within which firms operate. This approach emphasises that firms which engage in corporate crime are a) unlikely to be caught, b) if caught, are unlikely to be prosecuted, c) if prosecuted, are unlikely to face heavy penalties.

Unit 2.8.2 Explaining state crime

For many people living in the world today, state crime, often of the most brutal kind, is an everyday reality. People living in what are known as representative or liberal democracies, such as the UK, take many freedoms and rights for granted – freedom of speech and freedom of association, for example, and rights such as the right to life, the right to a fair trial and the right to vote. In many states, however, these rights and freedoms are, at best, severely curtailed, at worst virtually absent. For example, in 2016, homosexual behaviour was illegal in 74 countries and punishable by execution in 13 countries (*The Independent,* 17.05.2016).

This is not to say that state crimes are absent from liberal democracies. Far from it, as we saw in Part 3. Indeed, at the time of writing, a story which looks likely to become an iconic example of state harm, if not state crime, dominates the news: the Grenfell Tower tragedy where the local authority and the Kensington and Chelsea Tenant Management Organisation (the company responsible for the upkeep of the tower block) failed to take seriously numerous warnings by the Grenfell Action Group residents' association of fire risks in the years preceding the fatal fire.

However, as we shall see, most explanations of state crime focus not on the type of state, but on the mechanisms that lead ordinary people to carry out criminal acts on behalf of the state.

Types of state and state crime

Hazel Croall (2011) argues that state crimes occur in most states, but are more common in one-party states than in advanced democratic states because of the power of civil society in the latter. In democratic states, non-governmental organisations, the media, religious groups and others can mount serious protests against dubious actions by the state by means of media campaigns, petitions, protest meetings, demonstrations and so on. There is also a degree of transparency in the operation of formal state institutions which means that corruption is more difficult to hide.

This approach to explaining state crime is similar to **control theory**. Control theory turns the conventional approach to explaining crime on its head by asking, not why people break the law, but why the law isn't broken more often! Given the power possessed by states with their control of the military and police (and, in some states, control of the media and judiciary as well), this approach assumes that the curious thing is not why states use such power to engage in illegal activities, but why they don't do so more often. From this perspective, the level of state crime is a product of the degree of independence of the media, the level of power of civil society organisations, the degree of political transparency and so on.

The Economist Intelligence Unit (linked to *The Economist* magazine) produces an annual estimation of how democratic countries are: the 'democracy

index'. It covers most of the countries of the world and uses 60 indicators to allocate each country to one of four categories: full democracies, flawed democracies, hybrid regimes and authoritarian regimes. In 2016 it looked at 167 countries and categorised 19 as full democracies, 57 as flawed democracies, 40 as hybrid regimes and 51 – covering roughly one-third of the world's population – as **authoritarian regimes**.

In authoritarian regimes, infringements and abuses of civil liberties are commonplace, government criticism is suppressed, the judiciary is not independent of the government and the media is often state-owned or controlled by groups associated with the ruling regime. Those who actively oppose the regime are likely to find themselves imprisoned or 'disappeared' (as happened to over 3000 Chilean citizens under the dictatorship of General Pinochet between 1973 and 1990).

Activity

Participants in a 2013 demonstration in Santiago, Chile on the 40th anniversary of the Pinochet coup carry photos of the murdered and disappeared.

Where does Chile rank in the 'democracy index' today?

The lowest-ranked country in the 2016 democracy index was the – so-called – Democratic People's Republic of Korea (North Korea). A report by a UN Commission of Inquiry on human rights in North Korea, released in 2014, concluded that the gravity, scale, and nature of the human rights violations in North Korea are 'without parallel in the contemporary world'. The commission documented widespread forced labour, deliberate starvation, executions, torture, rape, and infanticide against the up to 120 000 men, women and children detained in North Korea's political prison camp system.

In North Korea, state crime is a product of an all-powerful, **totalitarian**, political regime. In some other poor countries, such as Afghanistan, state crime is associated with the relative lack of power of central government, which means that various forms of corruption are endemic.

In 2001, following the September 11 twin-tower attacks, the USA began a bombing campaign in Afghanistan designed to oust the **Islamic-fundamentalist** Taliban regime. This was successful and in December, Hamid Karzai was sworn in as head of an interim power-sharing government. Karzai remained in power until 2014, but according to Adel (2016), his rule depended heavily on patronage and **clientelism**. Local warlords and wealthy landowners were given government posts and other favours in return for political and electoral support.

While not on the same scale as in Afghanistan, it should be noted that clientelism is far from absent in liberal democracies. For example, because there is no limit on the size of donations that can be made to political parties in the UK, wealthy individuals and corporations make donations in the hope or expectation of some kind of payback, for example in terms of policies that promote their interests or rewards such as peerages.

Integrated theory and the obedience model

Penny Green and Tony Ward (2012) have examined different ways of explaining state crime. They distinguish two main approaches:

1. The *integrated theory* of state crime was developed in the USA by Ron Kramer and colleagues (Kramer and Michalowski, 1990, cited in Green and Ward, 2012). This theory argues that crime results from a combination of a motive, the opportunity to commit crime and the failure of control mechanisms that might prevent crime. The third element is particularly important because states consist of organisations that provide the context in which crimes might take place and which can also prevent crime. One example examined by Kramer is the way in which the 1986 space shuttle *Challenger* was allowed to blast off, with disastrous consequences when it exploded, despite awareness of safety risks (Kramer, 1992, cited in Green and Ward, 2012). (See Unit 2.3.3.)

2. The second approach is known as the *obedience approach* (Kelman and Hamilton, 1989, cited in

Green and Ward, 2012) and argues that many of those who commit crimes on behalf of the state do so out of conformity and obedience to those in authority. This follows the findings of a famous series of psychological experiments which found that subjects were willing to administer apparently fatal levels of electric shock on the basis of instructions by an authority figure – a white-coated supervisor (the shocks were not real and the recipient of the shocks was an actor) (Milgram,1974, cited in Green and Ward, 2012), as discussed in Book 1, Chapter 3, Unit 3.1.2.

Green and Ward argue that both approaches have some merit, and they illustrate how they can be combined with reference to a study of genocide in Rwanda, where hundreds of thousands were killed in the space of one month in1994 (Straus, 2006, cited in Green and Ward, 2012). In Rwanda, the Hutus, who were the ethnic group who controlled the government, slaughtered the Tutsis, a less powerful ethnic group. Straus found that in Rwanda, the opportunity for genocide was created by war and political crisis following the shooting down of a plane carrying the Hutu president. A long history of inter-ethnic conflict and the scapegoating of Tutsis for the poverty experienced by many young Hutu men provided the motivation; and the lack of rule of law within the country resulted in a failure of control mechanisms. The state, indeed, endorsed the genocide so that it became the norm for Hutu men to take part, and not taking part would have carried the risk of being killed for being a 'sympathiser'.

Spiral of denial and culture of denial

Earlier in this chapter (Unit 2.1.3), we looked at the work of Stanley Cohen on the mods and rockers. Later in his career, Cohen turned his attention to state crimes and crimes against humanity. Cohen (2001) argued that since the establishment of the United Nations in 1945 and the adoption of the Universal Declaration of Human Rights in 1948 – which virtually all countries have signed up to – while human rights violations have continued to take place, states engaged in such actions feel the need to justify them in some way.

Cohen identifies two main forms that such 'justifications' take. The first is what he calls a 'spiral of denial', which plays out in three stages:

» Stage 1: The typical first response of governments is to deny that a human rights violation has taken place.

» Stage 2: Faced with proof that such an event has occurred, governments seek to claim that it is not what it appears by redefining what has happened. Thus, forced removals of people from their land become merely 'population transfers' and civilian deaths as a result of bombing 'collateral damage'.

» Stage 3: Finally, governments resort to a tactic which involves claiming that what took place was justified by some higher purpose, for example, that the action was necessary to protect national security or to advance the war against terrorism.

This spiral of denial takes place within a broader 'culture of denial' in which governments use techniques of neutralisation to rationalise their human rights violations:

» the denial of injury by claiming, for example, that their victims 'exaggerate', 'don't feel it', 'are used to violence'

» the denial of the victim by claiming, for example, 'they started it', 'they are the terrorists', 'we are the real victims'

» the denial of responsibility by claiming, for example, that 'we were only obeying orders' or that 'events were out of our control'

» the condemnation of the condemners by claiming, for example, that those condemning the government in question have themselves acted immorally (e.g. that those opposing Israel's occupation of Palestinian land are **anti-Semitic**)

» the appeal to higher loyalties by claiming that the government's actions were justified in pursuit of a greater good, for example: 'it was Allah's/ God's will', 'the defence of the free world is at stake', 'the forces of evil must be defeated'.

Key terms

Representative or liberal democracies Types of states in which the government is made up of people elected by citizens to represent them in a parliament and in which citizens, in principle, enjoy a wide range of rights and freedoms.

Control theory A theory of delinquency developed by Travis Hirschi (1969) that explains non-delinquency in terms of the existence of a bond between the individual and society based on four elements: attachment, commitment, involvement and belief.

Authoritarian regime A type of state in which elections are absent or merely serve a cosmetic function (i.e. take place merely to make the regime *appear* to be democratic) and in which political power is concentrated in an authority not responsible to the people.

Totalitarian A type of state in which every aspect of citizens' lives is monitored and regulated by the government and there is an absence of citizenship rights and freedoms.

Islamic fundamentalist Individuals or groups who favour a literal interpretation of the Qur'an and who see their religious duty as the establishment of a caliphate (a territory ruled by a person seen as a successor to Muhammad).

Clientelism A political or social system based on the relation of a client to a patron with the client giving political or financial support to a patron (e.g. in the form of votes) in exchange for some special privilege or benefits.

Anti-Semitic Characterised by hostility or prejudice against Jews.

Summary

1. One approach to explaining state crime follows control theory in seeking to identify the mechanisms which discourage crime rather than motivate it. State crime is discouraged where civil society groups have power and state decision-making processes are open to public scrutiny. This is not the situation in many authoritarian states.

2. Integrated theory explains state crime in terms of three elements: motive, the opportunity to commit crime and the failure of control mechanisms that might prevent crime.

3. The obedience model explains state crime by examining the pressure that state agents are under to obey instructions issued by those in authority.

4. Cohen explains state crime in terms of a spiral of denial engaged in by states that have committed crimes against humanity and a culture of denial.

Unit 2.8.3 Explaining green crime

While the identification of what should count as corporate crime or what constitutes state crime is not always straightforward, the identification of green crime is even more problematic. White (2008) identifies three 'theoretical tendencies' within green criminology, each of which understands green crime differently: one in terms of environmental justice, another in terms of ecological justice, and the third in terms of species justice:

> *Environmental justice* is a human-centred (or '**anthropocentric**') approach that is concerned with the impact of green crimes such as toxic dumping, chemical spills, industrial pollution, nuclear testing and contamination of drinking water on human beings. It is also concerned with the fact that such crimes often impact disproportionately on the poor and marginalised social groups.

> *Ecological justice* is concerned with the impact of green crimes on the **ecosystem**, understood as the complex network of connections linking all living things (plants and animals) to the environment (water, soil, rocks and air).

> *Species justice* is a non-human or biocentric approach that is concerned with the impact of green crime on non-human species. It asserts that human beings are not the only creatures with rights and that humans are not superior beings. Beirne and South (2007) argue that to treat non-human creatures as of lesser standing to humans within the natural environment denies the value and worth of those species.

Activity

A tranquilised rhino is dehorned by a researcher in Zimbabwe to make the animal less attractive to poachers.

According to Save the Rhino, 'rhino poaching has escalated in recent years and is being driven by the demand for rhino horn in Asian countries, particularly Vietnam. It is used in Traditional Chinese Medicine but more and more commonly now it is used as a status symbol to display someone's success and wealth.'

Which of the theoretical tendencies in green criminology would see the trade in rhino horn as an example of green crime? Justify your answer.

Green crimes are carried out by a wide range of social actors: individuals, organised crime networks, corporations, states, and states and corporations acting together (state-corporate crime). Green criminologists have not generally sought to develop novel theories of their own, but instead draw upon theories that have been previously developed to explain the actions of these different types of offenders.

Contemporary issues: Toxic waste dumping in the Third World

Toxic waste dumping in Côte d'Ivoire.

In 2006, the cargo ship the Probo Koala reached the end of a four-month journey that resulted in toxic waste being dumped illegally in a country in West Africa.

Multinational oil trading company Trafigura produced the toxic waste on board the ship as a result of refining a dirty petroleum product called coker naphtha to mix with gasoline and sell it on as petrol. Trafigura knew the waste was hazardous, but hadn't figured out how to dispose of it safely.

Trafigura tried and failed to get rid of the waste in five countries: Malta, Italy, Gibraltar, The Netherlands and Nigeria. Its attempt to dispose of the waste in Amsterdam sparked an environmental incident when residents complained of the overwhelming smell and experienced nausea, dizziness and headaches after some of the waste was unloaded. Trafigura rejected an offer from a disposal company to deal with the waste safely in The Netherlands for the equivalent of US$620 000.

Instead, the toxic waste was finally dumped illegally in and around the city of Abidjan in Côte d'Ivoire by a local company – Compagnie Tommy – that

Trafigura hired to dispose of it for just US$17 000 – a fraction of the price quoted in the Netherlands.

On 20 August 2006, the people of Abidjan woke up to the appalling effects of the dumping. Tens of thousands of people experienced a range of similar health problems, including headaches, skin irritations and breathing problems. Over 100 000 people sought medical assistance and extensive clean-up and decontamination was required. Côte d'Ivoire authorities also recorded about 15 deaths.

In February 2007, Trafigura agreed to pay the Côte d'Ivoire government around US$200 million under a settlement agreement that granted Trafigura sweeping immunity from prosecution. In a civil claim in the UK, brought on behalf of 30 000 victims, Trafigura reached another settlement of £30 million (around £1000 per claimant) with no admission of liability for the dumping.

In 2008, a Dutch court found Trafigura guilty of illegally exporting the waste from the Netherlands and fined it €1 million. But Dutch authorities decided not to prosecute Trafigura for the dumping in Côte d'Ivoire because they said it appeared impossible to do so after various attempts to conduct an investigation in Côte d'Ivoire.

As a result, Trafigura has never been properly held to account (*in the view of Amnesty International*) for its role in the actual dumping of the waste in Côte d'Ivoire. Many of those affected are still waiting for an adequate remedy and justice.

Trafigura denies responsibility for the toxic waste dumping and maintains that it believed the local company would dispose of the waste safely and lawfully.

Source: Adapted from Amnesty International, *Trafigura: a toxic journey* (accessed 11.07.2017)

Questions

1. How might criminologists explain this example of (alleged) corporate green crime?

2. How might criminologists explain the fact that Trafigura has not faced a criminal prosecution for the dumping in Côte D'Ivoire?

Key terms

Anthropocentric An outlook that places the concerns and interests of human beings above those of all other creatures.

Ecosystem A community of interdependent animals, plants and micro-organisms, together with the habitat where they live.

Summary

1. White (2008) identifies three competing theoretical tendencies within green

criminology: a concern with environmental justice in terms of human well-being; ecological justice in terms of crimes that damage the ecosystem; species justice in terms of crimes that damage any and all species.

2. Green crimes are carried out by a wide range of actors: individuals, organised crime networks, corporations, states, and states and corporations working in concert.

3. Explanations of green crimes draw on theories developed to explain the illegal actions of the offenders listed in point 2.

PART 9 GENDER AND CRIME

Contents

Arguably, the most significant single factor predicting criminality, both in the UK and globally, is gender. In England and Wales, women constitute about 5 per cent of the prison population; globally, the figure is about 7 per cent (World Prison Population List, 2015).

The gender gap in relation to other aspects of the criminal justice process is not quite as pronounced as the prison figures, but there are still clear-cut differences. For example, in 2015, just 16 per cent

of those arrested by the police in England and Wales, 27 per cent of those prosecuted in criminal courts and 27 per cent of those convicted were women. Moreover, this pattern is apparent not only globally, but historically as far as we can tell.

Official figures such as these have raised four main questions about gender and crime:

1. Do women really commit fewer crimes than men, or are the figures misleading?

2. If women do commit fewer crimes, how can we explain this gender gap?

3. Why do those women who do break the law commit crimes?

4. How can we explain the relationship between men and crime?

In the following sections, we examine the answers that sociologists have given to these questions.

Unit 2.9.1 Gender bias in criminal justice?

The suggestion that the official statistics seriously underestimate female criminality was first made in 1950 by Otto Pollak. He argued that women were involved more than men in crimes that are unlikely to be reported/detected (such as shoplifting, prostitution-related offences and illegal abortions); that they are more adept than men at deception and that they are treated leniently by the police, magistrates and judges because the men who dominate these roles have been taught to be chivalrous.

Pollak provided little in the way of evidence to support his claim that female offenders are less likely to be detected and his view that women are more skilled than men at deception is now dismissed as prejudice. However, the idea that female offenders may be treated more leniently has been examined in the intervening years.

The chivalry thesis

One type of study that has been used to support such claims is the self-report study, in which individuals are asked about what crimes they have committed. Although such studies have their methodological limitations, they do give some indication of the extent of unreported crime and the chances that different groups have of escaping the discovery and prosecution of their offences.

These studies suggest that the gender gap in relation to offending is much narrower than official statistics suggest and that, for some unknown reason or reasons, females are more likely to escape detection and/or prosecution. For example, the 2006 Offending, Crime and Justice Survey (Roe and Ashe, 2008) interviewed 5353 respondents in England and Wales aged between 10 and 25. It covered 20 core offences but excluded homicide and sexual offences. Figure 2.9.1 shows the proportion of male and female offenders for different types of crime in the previous 12 months. The graph shows that there was a gap between the proportion of males committing any offence (26 per cent) and the proportion of females (17 per cent), but this is much smaller than the gap in officially recorded crime. A similar picture was found in relation to serious crimes (12 per cent of males and 8 per cent of females admitted these). There was a bigger difference for frequent offenders (8 per cent of males but 3 per cent of females). For those individuals most likely to come to the attention of the authorities – frequent offenders who had committed serious offences – the figures were 5 per cent of males and 3 per cent of females.

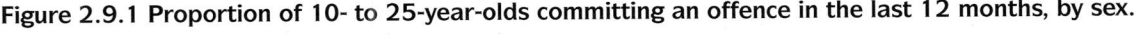

Figure 2.9.1 Proportion of 10- to 25-year-olds committing an offence in the last 12 months, by sex.

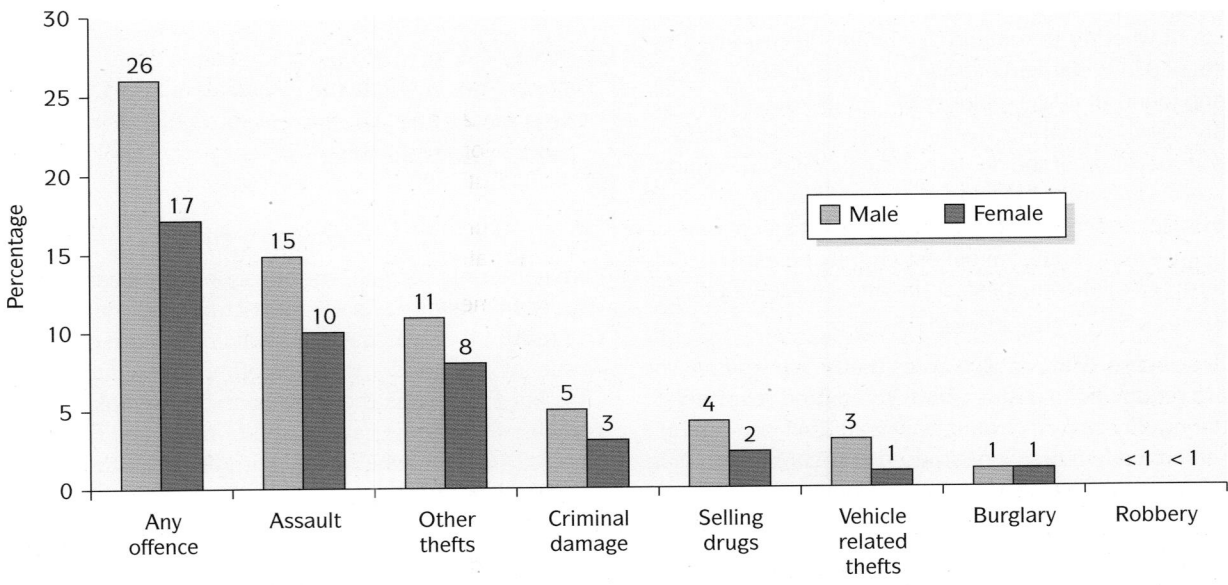

Source: Roe, S. and Ashe, J. (2008) *Young People and Crime: Findings from the 2006 Offending, Crime and Justice Survey*, Home Office, London, p. 13.

Statistics relating to whether defendants awaiting trial are remanded in custody (or granted bail) and statistics relating to sentencing also support the chivalry thesis. Recent data from the Ministry of Justice (*Women and the criminal justice system statistics, 2015*) indicates the following.

» Women are less likely to be remanded in custody than men: at magistrates' courts the percentages were 1 per cent for females and 5 per cent for males; at crown courts 19 per cent for females, 38 per cent for males.

» Women are less likely to be given a custodial sentence than men: for indictable offences, the figures were 15 per cent for women and 28 per cent for men; for all offences, the figures were 2 per cent for women and 10 per cent for men.

» Women receive shorter sentences than men: for indictable offences the average sentence for women was 10.5 months, for men 19.7 months; for all offences, 9.5 months for women and 16.9 months for men.

Evidence against the chivalry thesis

Despite the apparent strength of the evidence supporting the chivalry thesis, relatively few criminologists support the theory today. Raw statistics, even those broken down by broad offence type, do not take account of the exact nature of individual crimes and how serious they are. Research that does this is much less likely to find support for the chivalry thesis.

For example, Kate Steward (2006) studied decisions about whether to remand defendants in custody. She studied 103 remand hearings in magistrates' courts, and found that 'the majority of remand decisions are based primarily on offence seriousness, without consideration of the defendant's gender'. Furthermore, Steward discusses Home Office research that suggests that differences in the chances of males and females being granted bail can almost entirely be explained in terms of the seriousness of the offence (Home Office, 2003, cited in Steward, 2006).

In any case, Steward also notes that many women who are remanded in custody have committed relatively minor offences. For example, in 2002, 41 per cent of remanded females were accused of theft and handling. In the same year, 59 per cent of women who were kept in custody prior to their trial were ultimately not given custodial sentences.

Sentencing is another area where the chivalry thesis has been subject to critical scrutiny. In 1983, David P. Farrington and Alison Morris conducted a study

of sentencing in magistrates' courts. Although men received more severe sentences than women, the research found that the differences disappeared when the severity of offences was taken into account.

More recently, the Home Office stated that 'the evidence suggests that courts are imposing more severe sentences on women for less serious offences' (Home Office, 2004, cited in Heidensohn and Silvestri, 2012). Indeed, rates of imprisonment have been rising for women and they rose significantly faster than those for men in the 1990s and early years of the 21st century (Heidensohn and Silvestri, 2012).

This point is also made by Carol Hedderman (2010), who notes that the number of women in custody rose by 68 per cent between 1997 and 2008, while the number of men rose by only 35 per cent. This, she says, is despite the evidence that 'women's involvement in crime has become only a little more prevalent, and the seriousness of their offending has either increased marginally or remained static'. Hedderman argues, therefore, that far from being chivalrous, the criminal justice system is becoming increasingly severe on women.

One reason for this could be that the increasingly harsh treatment of offenders generally has had a particularly strong impact on women. The tough climate has led to significant increases in the penalties for relatively minor offences, particularly theft and handling stolen goods, which make up a high proportion of female offences.

Activity

Overall, do you think the evidence supports or weakens the chivalry thesis as an explanation of the gender gap in offending?

Evaluation of the chivalry thesis

While there are significant questions to be asked about the validity of self-report studies, there is no reason to think that their validity is more of an issue for one gender than the other. Consequently, it is hard to escape the conclusion that females are less likely to be caught and/or convicted than males. However, whether this has anything to do with chivalry is unclear.

The evidence on remands and sentencing is ambiguous. Clearly, women are generally less likely than men to be remanded in custody in recent years in England and Wales, less likely to be given custodial sentences and, if they do get custody, are likely to be given shorter sentences than men. However, some research suggests that this is not because of their gender, but because of the nature of the offences committed and because of gender differences in conviction history, which is taken into account when courts consider sentencing (men are more likely to have a record of repeat offending).

Indeed, Heidensohn (1985) has argued, not that women are treated more leniently by courts, but that female offenders are punished more harshly because they are seen as 'double deviants' – not only have female offenders broken the law, but they have also offended the 'more fundamental norms which govern sex-role behaviour' (Heidensohn, 1985, p. 47).

Additionally, some sociologists, particularly feminists, have argued that it is not female but male offenders who are sometimes treated more sympathetically. This is particularly the case with rape trials. Carol Smart (1989) argues that such trials 'celebrate the deep-seated notions of natural male sexual need and female sexual capriciousness'. She provides a number of egregious examples of comments by judges in rape cases in support of this claim, such as the following by Judge Bertrand Richards in 1982: 'It is the height of imprudence for any girl to hitch-hike at night. That is plain, it isn't really worth stating. She is in the true sense asking for it.'

Since that time, judges have tended to be more circumspect in their comments, though Walklate (2004) argues that it is still the case that, in effect, it is the female victim rather than the male suspect who ends up on trial. Women have to establish their respectability if their evidence is to be believed. It also remains the case that only a tiny fraction of alleged rapes end up in convictions – in 2015/16, the figure for England and Wales was 7.5 per cent. (See also the coverage of rape trials in Unit 2.1.2.)

Two final points are worth making. First, much of the empirical research on the chivalry thesis was carried out in the 1970s and 1980s. Section 95 of the 1991 Criminal Justice Act, requires governments to publish statistical information annually on the functioning of the criminal justice system (CJS) in relation to its statutory duty to avoid discriminating 'against any persons on the ground of race or sex or any other improper ground'. Now, this does not, of course, mean that discrimination will not happen, but it does mean that were discrimination of a systematic type to take place it would be difficult to conceal it. Second, the CJS is no longer overwhelmingly male:

in 2016, roughly three out of ten police officers and judges in England and Wales and over half of magistrates were female.

Activity

New magistrates being sworn in.

Do you think it matters what the gender composition of the magistracy is? Why?

Summary

1. Women in all countries are convicted of fewer crimes than men and it is thought that this has been true throughout history.

2. The chivalry thesis suggests that this is not because women commit fewer crimes, but because they are treated more leniently.

3. Self-report studies suggest that the gap between male and female offending is narrower than official statistics indicate.

4. Recent data indicate that women in England and Wales are less likely to be remanded in custody, less likely to be sent to prison, and get shorter sentences.

5. Critics of the chivalry thesis argue that this is because of the lesser seriousness of women's crimes and the different offending histories of men and women.

6. Critics also argue that in some cases (e.g. rape) it is men who are treated more leniently.

7. Since 1991, UK governments have had to publish information that would reveal systematic discrimination in the CJS. Also, the CJS is now much less male-dominated in terms of its staff.

Unit 2.9.2 Explaining the gender gap in criminality

Even if official statistics under-represent female criminality, it remains the case that, in relation to virtually every category of criminal activity, male offenders significantly outnumber female offenders. Various theories have been put forward to account for this fact.

Biological theories

Some of the earliest attempts to explain criminality identified alleged biological differences between criminals and non-criminals. In the 19th century, Cesare Lombroso and William Ferrero, for example, argued that criminals were 'atavistic beings' – throwbacks to an earlier stage of human evolution – who could be identified through the presence of 'stigmata' or physical abnormalities, such as having an extra toe or nipple. They found few examples of such abnormalities among female offenders, leading them to conclude that most female offenders were not true 'biological' criminals.

Lombroso and Ferreros' work is now seen as fanciful. However, this is no reason for dismissing out of hand the idea that there could be a biological basis to the gender gap in criminality. Indeed, the fact that this gap is universal (that is, as far as we can tell, found in all societies and throughout history) provides strong grounds for arguing that there is likely to be a biological component.

Activity

Sociologists are generally reluctant to concede that there could be a biological basis to variations in social behaviour. Why do you think this is?

A relatively new branch of criminology called 'biosocial criminology' seeks to explain crime and antisocial behaviour by exploring the interaction between biological and environmental factors, drawing on genetics, neurophysiology and evolutionary psychology as well as sociology. Biosocial criminologists argue that the gender gap in crime is a product of evolutionary forces that have led women to develop higher levels of fearfulness and empathy than males – which serve to deter them from offending – as a result of the different roles men and women play in sexual reproduction. (See Contemporary issues: A biological basis for the gender gap in criminality?)

Sex-role theory

Sociologists associated with functionalism emphasised the importance of primary and secondary socialisation in shaping the behaviour of boys and girls and men and women, including their involvement in criminal behaviour.

(Functionalists were writing at a time before Ann Oakley had introduced the conceptual distinction between 'sex' (to refer to biological differences) and 'gender' (to refer to cultural differences) between men and women, so they talked about 'sex-roles' and 'sex-role socialisation' where sociologists today would talk about 'gender roles' and 'gender role socialisation'. We will use the latter terms here.)

Gender role socialisation, gender roles and gendered identities were all seen as reducing the likelihood of female criminality while making male criminality more likely.

For example, Talcott Parsons (1955) argued that the primary socialisation of girls in the nuclear family prepared them for their 'expressive' role as mothers and housewives in which caring for, and the ability to empathise with, others were key characteristics. Moreover, aggression and rule-breaking were perceived as 'unfeminine'. Such attributes were inconsistent with criminality, unless women's circumstances were such that crime was the only way they could see to support their family. Boys, by comparison, were prepared for their 'instrumental' role as breadwinners and encouraged to be active, tough, risk-taking and oriented towards the world beyond the family. Indeed, attributes such as gentleness, tenderness and emotionality were actively discouraged as 'unmanly'.

Many psychologists, particularly those influenced by Freudian ideas, believe that early childhood experiences have a profound impact on people's future lives. However, it might be argued that the segregated sex-roles that existed in the 1940s and 1950s no longer exist and that therefore gender socialisation no longer sheds any light on the gender gap in criminality.

Gender roles have certainly undergone significant changes in the last 50 or so years, with most adult women now employed outside the home and adult men taking a much larger role in childcare, for example. Nevertheless, traditional notions of 'femininity' and 'masculinity' arguably continue to exert an influence on society and therefore on socialisation.

Recent research on young men aged 18–30 in the USA, UK and Mexico (Heilman, Barker and Harrison,

2017) argues that many still feel pushed to live in what the researchers call the 'Man Box' – a rigid construct of cultural ideas about male identity – even while personally distancing themselves from the ideas associated with such traditional notions of masculinity (which only about a third directly subscribed to). These include being self-sufficient, acting tough, looking physically attractive, sticking to rigid gender roles, being heterosexual, having sexual prowess and using aggression to resolve conflicts.

Contemporary issues: A biological basis for the gender gap in criminality?

'Cross-cultural, evolutionary, hormonal, genetic and neurological data all converge on the conclusion that we should strongly *expect* to see the low rate of criminal offending among females in comparison to males. There is no mystery about it; the gender ratio problem is only a problem for those who refuse to look beyond traditional sociological factors for explanation of human behaviour. A profound mystery would exist if we actually found a culture in which we *did not* find large sex differences in antisocial behaviour. If there were no deep biological differences between the sexes, and if socialisation practices alone accounted for gendered behaviour, we would see some cultures in which female rates were close to or even surpassed male rates. No such culture has ever existed, thus it is a fool's errand to continue to explore gender differences in criminal behaviour in terms of such things as socialisation and sex roles.

If forced to boil down the proximate foundational reasons for the universal sex differences in criminal behaviour to their bare minimum, it would have to be differences in empathy and fear. Empathy and fear are the natural enemies of crime. Empathy is other-oriented and prevents one from committing acts injurious to others because one has an emotional and cognitive investment in the well-being of others. Fear is self-oriented and prevents one from committing acts injurious to others out of fear of the consequences to oneself. Many other prosocial tendencies flow from these two basic foundations, such as a strong conscience, altruism, self-control and agreeableness. These sex-differentiated levels of empathy and fear have evolved in response to sex-differentiated reproductive roles of males and females. Empathy assured the rapid identification and provision of infant needs, and nourished social relationships. Fear kept both mother and child out of harm's way and provided a sturdy scaffold around which to build a conscience.'

Source: Walsh, A. and Bolen, J.D. (2016) *The Neurobiology of Criminal Behaviour: gene-brain-culture interaction*, p. 150.

Questions

1. On what basis do Walsh and Bolen reject sex-role theory as an explanation for the gender-gap in offending?

2. What do they argue is the evolutionary basis for the gender gap?

3. What arguments could be used to challenge this theory?

Control theory

Feminist explanations of the gender gap in criminality draw on control theory. Frances Heidensohn (1985) argues that male-dominated patriarchal societies control women more effectively than they do men, making it more difficult for women to break the law. Control operates at home, in public and at work.

Being a housewife directly restricts women by limiting their opportunities for criminality. Heidensohn describes domesticity as 'a form of detention'. The endless hours spent on housework and the constant monitoring of young children leave little time for illegal activities. A 'very pervasive value system' persuades women that they must carry out their domestic responsibilities dutifully or they will have failed as mothers and wives.

In public, women are controlled by the male use of force and violence, by the idea of holding on to a 'good' reputation, and by the 'ideology of separate spheres' (the idea that women's lives should be centred on the home and men's on the world beyond the home).

At work, male superiors in the hierarchy usually control women, and men also dominate workers' own organisations – trade unions. Women may also be intimidated by various forms of sexual harassment that discourage female employees from asserting themselves or from feeling at home at work. Sexual harassment 'ranges from whistles and catcalls and the fixing of pinups and soft porn pictures, to physical approaches and attacks which could be defined as possibly indecent and criminal'. Heidensohn quotes surveys that find that up to 60 per cent of women have suffered some form of sexual harassment at work.

The significance of patriarchal control over women's lives in restricting their opportunities to engage in criminal behaviour is illustrated by a study of British Asian girls. Sunita Toor (2009) argues that their low rates of criminality are the result of 'key dynamics embedded in Asian cultures that effectively preclude female activity in criminal and deviant spheres'. These dynamics involve a strong emphasis upon the idea of honour (or *izzat*) and shame (*sharam*).

However, in the wider society, successive waves of feminist activism, including the second-wave associated with the Women's Liberation movement that began in the 1960s, have brought about significant changes in the lives of men and women, even if there is disagreement over just how far those changes have taken society towards a situation of gender equality.

At least some features of the society that Heidensohn described in the 1980s are no longer with us. For example, the notion of 'separate spheres' for men and women and that 'a woman's place is in the home' would now be widely seen as distinctly 'old-fashioned'. On the other hand, women – particularly mothers – still spend more time than men on domestic chores and the widespread revelations of sexual harassment in the workplace that have emerged following the Harvey Weinstein scandal in the USA, suggest that this form of patriarchal control is still an everyday feature of many women's lives. Hence, the continuing relevance of control theory as an explanation of the gender gap in criminality in today's society is very much an open question.

Summary

1. There are three main competing explanations of the gender gap in criminality: biological theory, sex-role theory and control theory.

2. Lombroso and Ferrero's biological theory has been discredited, but biosocial criminologists argue that evolution has produced differences in the biological make-up of men and women that explain the gender gap.

3. Sex-role theory points to differential gender socialisation to explain the gender gap.

4. Feminists explain the gender gap as a product of differential social control of men and women associated with patriarchy.

5. Sunita Toor's study of offending among British Asian young women provides support for control theory. Its continuing relevance in the wider society remains an open question.

Unit 2.9.3 Explaining female criminality

We now turn our attention from the gender gap in criminality to work that has sought to shed more light on the nature of the relationship between femininity and crime and masculinity and crime. We begin with femininity and crime.

The liberation thesis

Writing in the 1970s, Freda Adler (1975) suggested in *Sisters in Crime: The Rise of the New Female Criminal* that women's liberation was resulting in increasing levels of female criminality and creating new and more serious types of female criminal. As women's lives became less restricted to the domestic sphere, so their access to both legitimate *and* illegitimate opportunity structures increased, resulting in increased female criminality.

In support of her thesis, Adler drew on arrest statistics published by the FBI that, she claimed, demonstrated dramatic increases in serious female criminality alongside an increase in female labour force participation. For example, from 1960 to 1972, arrests of female robbers grew by 277 per cent, arrests of female burglars by 168 per cent and arrests of female embezzlers by 280 per cent. She also claimed that there were similar trends in Western Europe, New Zealand, Japan and other countries.

Heidensohn and Silvestri (2012) argue that in the 21st century the idea that women's liberation and increased involvement of women in crime are connected is alive and well. They argue that this perception is linked to widespread media portrayal of the 'ladette' – the girl who wants to be just as hard-drinking, delinquent and criminal as lads. The media have carried numerous reports of female 'binge drinking', fighting and involvement in gangs. Indeed female involvement in violence has been a particular focus of concern. According to Tara Young (2009), this has included concern over the apparent emergence of the 'shemale gangster'. Young says that, according to media reports, 'teenage girls are no longer spectators hovering on the periphery of street gangs but are hard core members actively engaging in the kind of extreme violence that is usually the preserve of men'.

Activity

Ladettes?

Why should one be cautious about drawing conclusions about changes in female criminality from news reports of 'ladettes'?

Evaluation of the liberation thesis

Adler's work has been subjected to a number of criticisms. One line of criticism has focused on her use of percentage changes to support her theory. Given that the base line figures for recorded female crime in these categories would have been low, small numerical increases produce large and dramatic percentage changes. For example, if arrests increase from 2 to 10 that is a 400 per cent increase, but in absolute terms the numbers remain low. Another is that arrest statistics may not be a valid indicator of the actual amount of male and female crime taking place.

Evidence of changes in official statistics relating to gender and crime in the UK raise similar issues. On the surface, there appears to be some evidence to support Adler's argument. Gilly Sharpe and Loraine Gelsthorpe (2009) note that between 2002/03 and 2005/06 recorded offences committed by young females rose by 38.7 per cent, while offences committed by young males rose by just 6.6 per cent. Heidensohn and Silvestri (2012) point out that the number of women and girls arrested for violence against the person rose from 37 100 in 1999/2000 to 88 100 in 2007/08.

Nevertheless, Heidensohn does not support the theory that female liberation has been the cause of this apparent increase in female criminality. She comments:

> *Criminal women are amongst those least likely to be affected by feminism (and those most affected by it, middle-class white women, are the least likely to be criminal). Moreover, criminal women tend to score highly on 'femininity' scores, whereas 'masculine' scoring women are less delinquent.*   Heidensohn, 2002

Furthermore, there is strong evidence that the apparent rise in female crime, particularly violent crime, is more to do with the operation of the criminal justice system than actual changes in behaviour. Sharpe and Gelsthorpe (2009) have found evidence that there is an increasing tendency for minor assaults by females, such as playground fights and relatively trivial domestic incidents, to be recorded as violent offences. Sharpe (2009, cited in Heidensohn and Silvestri, 2012) found evidence that the idea that women were becoming more violent had begun to influence professionals in the criminal justice system. This raised the possibility that women were more likely to be prosecuted for violent offences because female violence was seen as a growing social problem.

Heidensohn and Silvestri (2012) therefore argue that it is highly debatable whether there has been any real and substantial increase in female criminality. They point out that over the long term the ratio of female/male offending, in terms of reported crime, remains quite stable and men are still four times more likely than women to be arrested for violence.

Activity

How would you explain the fact that men are far more likely than women to be arrested for offences of violence?

Women, crime and poverty

In 1985, Pat Carlen (1988) conducted a study of 39 women aged 15–46 who had been convicted of one or more crimes. She carried out lengthy and in-depth unstructured taped interviews with each of the women. Most were from the London area and 20 were in a prison or youth custody centre at the time of interviewing. Most of the women were working class (as are most women with criminal convictions) and they had committed a range of offences.

Carlen does not believe that liberation has resulted in an increase in crimes by women. Most of her sample had been touched little by any gains that women had experienced in, for example, access to a wider range of jobs. Instead, most had experienced their opportunities becoming increasingly restricted.

Like Heidensohn, Carlen adopted control theory as her theoretical approach. According to Carlen, working-class women have been controlled through the promise of rewards stemming from the workplace and the family. Such women are encouraged to make what she calls the 'class deal' and the 'gender deal'. The class deal offers material rewards such as consumer goods for those respectable working-class women who work dutifully for a wage. The gender deal offers 'psychological and material rewards ... emanating from either the labours or the "love" of a male breadwinner'. When these rewards are not available, or women have not been persuaded that these rewards are real or worth sacrifices, the deals break down and criminality becomes a possibility.

Carlen found that the women she studied attributed their criminality to four main factors. These were drug addiction (including alcohol), the quest for excitement, being brought up in care, and poverty.

She places particular emphasis on the last two factors: very often the abuse of drugs and the desire for excitement were the consequence of being brought up in care or of being poor.

In all, 32 of the women had always been poor, 4 of the remaining 7 were unemployed at the time of being interviewed, and only 2 had good jobs. A majority of the women (22) had spent at least part of their lives in care.

Poverty, familial abuse and being brought up in care led to the women rejecting the class and gender deals. Few of the women had experience of the possible benefits of the class deal. They had never had access to the consumer goods and leisure facilities that society portrays as representing the 'good life'. Similarly, their experiences of family life – sexual or physical abuse and periods spent in care – meant that they also rejected the gender deal:

When young girls have been brought up in situations where absolutely no rewards (and many severe disabilities) have been seen to emanate from families, when, too, the technologies of gender discipline have been unusually harsh or oppressive, women's adult consciousness has been constituted within an immediate experience of the fundamental oppression inherent in the gender deal ... they have resisted it.
Carlen, 1988

Consequently, having rejected the idea that domesticity could offer happiness and being ill-equipped to secure well-paid work, the women Carlen studied had little to lose by breaking the law. Crime appeared to offer a possible alternative route to some sort of economic security. In effect, the failure of a patriarchal, capitalist society to 'deliver' on the deals it offered to women who conformed pushed these women towards crime.

Carlen's study was based upon a small sample of mainly working-class women involved in fairly serious crimes. It is, therefore, dangerous to generalise from her findings. However, there is support from other studies for the finding that deprivation and disadvantage are typical of female offenders.

For example, the Corston Report (Corston, 2007), which studied women in prison, found that 40 per cent had not worked in the five years prior to entering prison, 61 per cent had no qualifications (compared to 18 per cent in the general population), 10 per cent had problems with reading, writing or understanding instructions, and 20 per cent had no permanent accommodation before entering prison; 60 per cent of women in prison were single and over a third (34 per cent) were lone parents.

Activity

A woman in a UK prison.

An update to the Corston Report was published in 2017 by Women in Prison. What are its findings?

Summary

1. The liberation thesis put forward by Freda Adler argued that women's liberation was leading to higher rates of female offending as liberation increased women's access to illegitimate opportunity structures.

2. Media references to 'ladettes', 'girl gangs' and 'shemale gangsters' appear to provide support.

3. Critics of the liberation thesis have questioned Adler's use of arrest statistics and argued that most of the women who commit crime are the ones least likely to have benefited from liberation.

4. They also suggest that a kind of self-fulfilling prophecy may have operated where professionals involved in dealing with female offenders have been sensitised by the media to apparently new forms of female offending and have begun to respond more punitively.

5. Carlen's work links female offending to poverty and other kinds of deprivation. She argues that women offend when the 'class deal' and 'gender deal' fail to pay out.

6. Statistics on the characteristics of female prisoners support Carlen's thesis.

Unit 2.9.4 Masculinity and crime

Before feminist perspectives began to impact on what they characterised as '**malestream**' sociology in the 1960s and 1970s, most studies of crime were actually studies of crimes committed by men, but the issue of gender was left unexamined. However, in recent years some sociologists and criminologists have begun to consider what it might be about masculinity which leads to men committing more crimes than women.

James W. Messerschmidt

Messerschmidt (1993), like Connel (1995), argues that a variety of ideas about what constitutes masculinity – a variety of 'masculinities' in the plural – coexist in societies today, but that traditional conceptions remain **hegemonic.** Hegemonic masculinity is based on the idea that men need to be powerful, economically self-sufficient, strong, sexually active, heterosexual and in control of both themselves and others – particularly of women.

He also argues that masculinity is not a characteristic that men possess, but something that is 'accomplished'. Manliness has to be demonstrated through one's actions. The importance of this for crime is that criminal behaviour can be used as a resource for asserting masculinity. Indeed, Messerschmidt goes so far as to argue that: 'Crime by men is a form of social practice invoked as a resource, when other resources are unavailable, for accomplishing masculinity'.

Different men are not equally well-placed to demonstrate masculinity through legitimate means. The opportunities to do so vary with social class, ethnicity, sexual preference and age. Consequently, Messerschmidt argues, different groups of males turn to different types of crimes in their attempts to demonstrate their masculinity.

For example, Messerschmidt argues that White middle-class youths adopt an **accommodating masculinity** in school so as not to jeopardise their chances of academic success, but outside school may engage in pranks, acts of vandalism, excessive drinking and minor thefts in order to demonstrate they're not 'soft' or 'girly'. White working-class youths have less chance of academic success and so cannot easily access the type of masculinity based on academic success available to middle-class youth. They therefore tend to construct masculinity around the importance of physical aggression. It is important to be tough or hard and to oppose the imposition

155

of authority by teachers and others. Messerschmidt quotes the 'lads' in Paul Willis' study of anti-school peer groups as an example.

In addition, Messerschmidt suggests that various types of crime can be understood as attempts to demonstrate aspects of hegemonic masculinity. For example, pimping enables lower-class Black men 'to transcend class and race domination' because they can assert their ability to earn money through work and their power to exercise authority and control by getting the prostitutes they 'run' to turn most of their earnings over to them. He also explains both white-collar crime and domestic violence as expressions of hegemonic masculinity: the former as a way of demonstrating economic success, the latter as a way of demonstrating control over others (what Dobash and Dobash (1979) termed 'coercive control').

While Messerschmidt's work does offer a way of understanding why most crime is committed by men, there are a number of problems with it. First, the concept of hegemonic masculinity is being made to do an awful lot of work as he uses it to explain a vast range of criminal activity. As Collier (1998) states 'to account for such a diversity is, clearly, asking a great deal of the concept of masculinity'.

Second, Messerschmidt's line of reasoning can be seen as circular. Crime is a way for men to demonstrate their masculinity. How do we know this? Because it is men who are doing it!

Third, Messerschmidt insists that there is a range of 'subordinate masculinities' that coexist with hegemonic masculinity, but it is unclear what role these play in relation to male crime.

Finally, while Messerschmidt may be right that it is difficult to understand male crime without reference to masculinity (or masculinities), he may be wrong to assume that it can be explained by this alone.

Simon Winlow

Simon Winlow's study *Badfellas* (2001) has already been referred to briefly in Unit 2.4.4 in relation to his use of Cloward and Ohlin's concepts of conflict and criminal delinquent subcultures.

In the late 1990s, Winlow conducted an ethnographic study of bouncers and associated criminal activity in and around Sunderland in the north-east of England. He argued that Sunderland, like many other areas once associated with heavy industries like mining, steel making and shipping, had undergone a process of rapid deindustrialisation. As a result, there had

been a shift to a post-industrial economy in which employment in the service and leisure-related sectors of the economy had grown. He also argued that what was happening in Sunderland was increasingly linked to global changes that had opened up new opportunities for entrepreneurship in both legitimate and illegitimate markets. Winlow's study focused on one aspect of this: the night-time economy of pubs, clubs and bars.

Putting all these changes together, Winlow describes and explains a major shift in masculine identities in the north-east of England.

Before the decline in heavy industry, working-class men were able to prove their masculinity through hard physical labour and supporting a wife and family. Alongside this, Winlow argues that the culture of working-class men in Sunderland also incorporated violence and 'an immediate aggressive style of behaviour', most evident in conflict subcultures.

Being a hard man continues to be a way of gaining status. However, in the changed circumstances it assumes a new significance and becomes a way of earning a living, an entrepreneurial activity, as well. Working as a bouncer, Winlow found that the other door staff increasingly saw their work as more of a career than a hobby (as it had been in the past for those engaged in industrial work during the day). They were paid for their efforts in maintaining order and used it as a springboard for getting involved in potentially rewarding criminal activities. For example, some door staff started selling drugs, or importing and selling cheap duty-free beer and spirits to licensees and publicans.

To sum up, Sunderland had now developed a thriving criminal subculture in which crime was not just important for status, but also as a way of earning a living. There was a considerable degree of organisation in this subculture, with various legal businesses and illegal activities being interlinked. For example, legitimate security firms were connected to protection rackets and apparently legal businesses were used to launder money from illegal activities.

The criminal subculture was developing international and global connections, particularly those related to importing cheap alcohol and drugs. For those involved in these activities, it was vital that they maintained their reputation as hard men. Any sign of weakness could encourage rivals to challenge them. With little in the way of legitimate job prospects, the men involved used their **bodily capital** to earn a living. Many of the doormen and other 'hard' men would actively try to develop their physique through body building.

Winlow's study provides an interesting account of the centrality of a particular conception of masculinity in the lives of men making a living through acting as door staff. However, the link here between masculinity and crime would appear to be **contingent** rather than inevitable. That is to say, being a bouncer could be seen as a way of demonstrating a conception of masculinity involving being courageous and physically hard *with or without* being involved in criminal activity. Also, it is unclear just how central such notions of masculinity are to performing this role effectively: roughly 40 per cent of door supervisors and other security staff today are female (*Call on Security Ltd.* blog post, 15.03.2015).

Activity

Door staff outside a nightclub in London.

How do you think female door staff are viewed? Why do you think this is?

Then and now: Simon Winlow, *Badfellas* (2001)

"If I were to write *Badfellas* today, it would be a very different book. The book is based on my PhD research, and I was still in my early twenties when I wrote it. I've come a long way since then. If I was to write the book now, it would be much more theoretical. Since the book's publication, I've written a lot about male violence, and much of this work has drawn upon theoretical psychoanalysis and recent developments in continental philosophy. In recent years, my goal has been to identify more precisely which men are likely to go on to forge careers in violence, and this has meant moving from a cultural analysis to an analysis of individual biographies and psychological processes.

The book is really about what neoliberalism has done to the organised working-class communities that were such a key feature of the industrial age. This is still one of my great concerns. The central thesis – that the fundamental economic shift that took place in the 1980s greatly affected working-class culture and patterns of working-class criminality – still holds up to scrutiny. We lost something with the shift to neoliberalism. Our communities began to break apart, and we have yet to produce a sufficiently robust plan to put them back together again. The certainties of the old world disappeared into the distance, and many people felt themselves set apart from the world, with little or no practical purpose. Many men and women who occupy these zones of permanent recession feel they've been forgotten, and they're right to think this way. We are as a nation richer than we were during the heyday of industrial modernity. We are also unhappier. All the indicators of social regression lie scattered around post-industrial Britain. We have gained the petty trinkets of mass consumerism, but we have lost something in our collective life that has prompted the widespread loneliness, depression, anxiety, cynicism and anger that are such important features of culture today. I'm still in touch with some of the characters who appear in *Badfellas*. At the time the book was published, they were mostly young men, full of optimism, seeking profit in the illegitimate economy. Only a very small number have managed to keep their heads above water. An up-to-date description of their activities would not make for pleasant reading: drug problems, mental health problems, failed relationships, alcoholism, prison, underemployment, poverty. *Badfellas* to me offers a snapshot of a moment in time when everything appeared to be changing. Now that change has played out; the optimism that accompanied the end of the Thatcher years and the dawning of Blair's new Third Way was, quite clearly, misplaced."

157

Key terms

Malestream A term involving a play on words ('mainstream') coined by feminist sociologists to draw attention to the way in which sociology had marginalised and ignored women's lives.

Hegemonic Culturally dominant.

Accommodating masculinity One that does not challenge the power differential between teachers and pupils.

Bodily capital Aspects of people's bodies that can be used to generate an income.

Contingent Dependent on something else, accidental or arbitrary.

Summary

1. Messerschmidt argues that crime can be a way of demonstrating masculinity, but different groups of men have different opportunities to do this.

2. These opportunities vary with class, ethnicity, sexuality and age.

3. Critics have argued that the concept of masculinity is being over-extended in terms of the wide range of offending it is being used to explain and that Messerschmidt employs a circular line of argument.

4. Winlow argues that de-industrialisation and globalisation have opened up new opportunities for young men to demonstrate masculinity and commit crimes by acting as door staff in the night-time economy.

5. Critics have questioned the nature of the link between being a doorman and acting criminally.

PART 10 'RACE', ETHNICITY, CRIME AND CRIMINAL JUSTICE

Contents

Issues of 'race', ethnicity, crime and criminal justice are rarely out of the headlines both in the UK and further afield. At the time of writing, for example, the campaigning organisation Black Lives Matter features prominently in its fight against what it claims is police and state violence against Black people in the USA and Britain.

Moreover, in recent years the accumulation of evidence pointing to the possibility, if not probability, of the existence of systematic biases against ethnic minorities in the operation of the criminal justice system (CJS) has been acknowledged by UK governments.

In July 2015, the then-Home Secretary, Theresa May, set up an inquiry into deaths in police custody with a particular focus on deaths of Black, Asian and Minority Ethnic (BAME) people. A few months later, in January 2016, the then-Prime Minister, David Cameron, asked David Lammy MP to chair an independent review of the treatment of, and outcomes for, BAME individuals in the CJS.

Part 10 examines sociologists' attempts to shed some light on this highly charged area of social life. We begin by examining what various sources of data reveal about the relationship between ethnicity, crime and criminal justice in the UK.

Unit 2.10.1 Disproportionality in the CJS

Before examining the relevant data, we need to clarify some terms. The term 'race' is placed in inverted commas in the Part title above because scientists today are in general agreement that the idea that human beings can be categorised into biologically distinct groups has no empirical basis. Geneticists believe that all human beings have evolved from a single set of African ancestors who spread out across the globe and that race as a scientific concept is 'well past its sell-by date' (Steven and Hilary Rose, 2005). Nevertheless, the term continues to be used to refer to people distinguished by characteristics such as skin colour – 'Black', 'Brown', 'White' and so on. Note, though, that these are social, not biological, classifications.

The term 'ethnicity' has, today, largely replaced that of 'race' in sociology. Ethnic groups are groups defined by 'race', religion and/or national origin who share a common cultural heritage. In the UK, the ethnic majority is officially classified as 'White', but there are numerous minority ethnic groups. Such groups are conventionally referred to either as Black and Minority Ethnic (BME) groups or, more recently, as Black, Asian and Minority Ethnic (BAME) groups.

The data available indicate that ethnic minority groups are generally over-represented in the CJS, although the picture is not uniform when age, gender and ethnic differences are taken into account. (In the data below, the population is divided into five self-identified ethnic groups: White, Black, Asian, mixed ethnic and other ethnic, including Chinese.)

For example, according to the Ministry of Justice (2015) in 2014:

> Stop and search rates were higher for all ethnic minority groups than for White groups apart from those for 'other ethnicity, including Chinese', with Black groups over four times as likely to be stopped and searched and mixed ethnic groups twice as likely.

> The same picture holds true for arrest rates, with Black groups three times as likely to be arrested as White groups and those of mixed ethnicity twice as likely.

> Black and mixed ethnic defendants had the highest number of prosecutions per 1000 members of the population for indictable offences, with Black groups three times as likely and mixed groups twice as likely to be prosecuted, though Asian and other ethnic groups had a lower prosecution rate than White groups.

> A similar picture emerges in relation to sentencing. The average length of custodial sentences was higher for all ethnic minority groups, with an average length of 17 months for White groups and 25 months for Black and Asian groups.

> Rates of imprisonment were higher for all ethnic minority groups than White groups with the exception of those of other ethnicity. Black groups were roughly four times as likely to be in prison; those of mixed ethnicity three times as likely.

Disproportional outcomes were particularly apparent in certain categories of offences. For example, for every 100 White women handed custodial sentences at crown courts for drug offences, there were 227 Black women. For Black men, the figure was 141 for every 100 White men. Similarly, of those convicted at magistrates' courts for sexual offences, 208 Black men and 193 Asian men received prison sentences for every 100 White men.

However, the disparities were not all one way. BAME females, both young and adult, were less likely to be charged by the Crown Prosecution Service than comparable White groups. BAME men were about 10 per cent less likely to be convicted at crown court than the comparable White group, and Asian women were about 20 per cent less likely to be convicted at crown court than White women.

The Lammy Review, published in September 2017, confirms the general picture outlined above. Its findings indicate, for example, that 25 per cent of adult prisoners and 41 per cent of youth prisoners are from ethnic minority backgrounds although they constitute only roughly 13 per cent of the population of England and Wales, and that BAME males are almost five times more likely to be housed in high-security prisons for public order offences than White men. The report concludes that 'BAME individuals still face bias, including overt discrimination, in parts of the justice system. Prejudice has declined but still exists in wider society – it would be a surprise if it was entirely absent from criminal justice settings'.

Activity

Feltham Young Offenders Institution.

Over 40 per cent of the inmates in YOIs in England and Wales are from BAME backgrounds although they represent only roughly 13 per cent of the general population. How do you think this can be explained?

It should be noted that the issue of ethnic minority overrepresentation in the CJS is by no means unique to the UK. In the USA, for example, African-Americans have an incarceration rate in state prisons (where the vast majority of inmates are held) of five times that of White Americans and Hispanics have an incarceration rate of 1.4 times that of White people (The Sentencing Project, 2016). In Australia, 28 per cent of the adult prison population in 2016 were Aboriginal people although they only make up roughly 2 per cent of the population (Australian Bureau of Statistics, 2016).

Summary

1. BAME groups are generally over-represented in the CJS.

2. Those of Black and mixed ethnicity are more likely than other BAME groups to be over-represented.

3. Over-representation is particularly pronounced in relation to imprisonment with 25 per cent of adult prisoners and 41 per cent of youth prisoners in England and Wales from BAME backgrounds in 2015.

4. The disparities are not all one way.

5. This situation is not unique to the UK.

Unit 2.10.2 Explaining the patterns

Broadly speaking, there are two possible alternative explanations for these patterns: that rates of offending differ along lines of ethnicity or that ethnic minorities are subject to discriminatory treatment within the CJS. It is unlikely that either explanation alone can adequately account for the patterns, but there is disagreement among sociologists about where the balance lies.

Neo–Marxist perspectives

Neo-Marxist sociologists have supported the idea that the over-representation of Black people in CJS statistics is a product of criminalisation by the police and courts rather than of higher levels of criminality.

One influential study that propounded this view was *Policing the Crisis: Mugging, the State, and Law and Order* (1979). Stuart Hall *et al.* argued that in the 1970s a moral panic developed around 'mugging' and that young Black men served as scapegoats for an economic and political crisis faced by the British state in that decade.

In the 13 months between August 1972 and August 1973, 60 events were reported as muggings in the national daily papers. These stories highlighted an apparently new and frightening type of crime in Britain, allegedly perpetrated predominantly by Black youths. Judges, politicians and the police lined up with the media in stressing the threat that this crime posed to society. Many commentators believed that the streets of Britain would soon become as dangerous as those of New York or Chicago. The Home Secretary in the House of Commons quoted an alarming figure of a 129 per cent increase in muggings in London in the previous four years.

Hall *et al.* note that there is no legally defined crime called mugging. Because in law there is no such crime, it was not possible for the Home Secretary accurately to measure its extent. Hall *et al.* could find no basis in the criminal statistics for his figure of a 129 per cent rise over four years. From their own examination of the statistics, there was no evidence that violent street crime was rising particularly fast in the period leading up to the panic. Using the nearest legal category to mugging – robbery, or assault with intent to rob – the official statistics showed an annual rise of an average of 33.4 per cent between 1955 and 1965, but only a 14 per cent average annual increase from 1965 to 1972. This type of crime was growing more slowly at the time the panic took place than it had done in the previous decade.

Nevertheless, the media-fuelled public concern led to changes of operational procedure and priority on the part of the police, which led to more arrests as well as to more offences being classified as muggings and longer sentences being handed down by the courts. An amplification spiral was thus set in motion (See Unit 2.1.3, pp. 76–77).

Crises

At the same time, the British state was facing both an **economic crisis** and a **crisis of legitimacy**. From 1945 until about 1968, there had been what Hall *et al*. called an **inter-class truce**: there was little conflict between the ruling and subject class. Full employment, rising living standards and the expansion of the welfare state secured support for the state and acceptance of its authority by the working class. As unemployment rose and living standards ceased to rise rapidly, the basis of the inter-class truce was undermined. It became more difficult for the state to govern by consent.

The authority of the state was under threat from a number of different sources: the activities of the IRA in Northern Ireland, student militancy, the Black Power movement and trades union militancy (in 1972 there were more workdays lost because of strikes than in any year since 1919).

As the government was no longer able to govern by consent, Hall *et al*. claim, it turned to the use of force to control the crisis. It was in this context that street crime became an issue. Mugging was presented as a key element in a breakdown of law and order. Violence was portrayed as a threat to the stability of society, and it was the Black mugger who was to symbolise the threat of violence.

In this way, the public could be persuaded that 'immigrants' rather than the faults of the capitalist system caused society's problems. The working class was effectively divided on racial grounds, as the White working class was encouraged to direct its frustrations towards the Black working class.

Explaining mugging

Although *Policing the Crisis* concentrated on the moral panic about crime, Hall *et al*. also made some attempt to explain African Caribbean criminality. Many immigrants to Britain from the Commonwealth arrived in the 1950s and early 1960s. They were actively encouraged to come to the country during a period of full employment and labour shortage. London Transport, for example, recruited large numbers of West Indians to fill low-paid jobs that might otherwise have remained vacant.

The recession in the early 1970s hit immigrant groups hard. They became a 'surplus labour force', many of whom were not required for employment. Those who remained in employment often had to do menial and low-paid jobs, which some referred to as 'white man's shit work'. Some opted out of the employment market altogether. They turned to 'hustling' for money, using petty street crime, casual drug dealing, and prostitution to earn a living. Street crime was a survival strategy employed by an unwanted reserve army of labour.

Nevertheless, the main thrust of *Policing the Crisis* was that African Caribbeans were much more likely to be labelled as criminals than Whites, that at least certain sections of the police were racist and that concern about street crime, particularly mugging, was an unjustified moral panic that served the interests of a state in crisis.

Then and now: Chas Critcher, *Policing the Crisis: Mugging, the State, and Law and Order* (1978)

" *Policing the Crisis* is a sprawling, multi-faceted book. While we are here concerned with its relevance to the sociology of crime and deviance, it has elsewhere been examined for its contribution to other sociologies: of the media, of Black culture, of policing and even of modern conservative politics. 'Mugging', a term unknown in Britain before being imported from the USA in the early 1970s, was never legally defined. However, it implied the gratuitous use of violence during street robberies. As the book title implies, the argument was designed to explain how the advent of this apparently new type of crime resonated throughout the main institutions of society. We claimed to identify what kind of a crisis this was, as well as how and why 'mugging' came to symbolise what had been going wrong with British society in the early to mid-1970s.

That period is now over 40 years ago. Much has happened in the meantime to many aspects of British society, which were the focus of the book. The media, crime, policing, race relations, political issues – all these have changed, perhaps beyond recognition. This was before the digital media revolution: no internet, much less social media, no mobile phones, not even satellite TV. Immigration as an issue had a different resonance. Migrants had arrived from the West Indies, India and Pakistan and a few from Africa, but migrants from Europe, East or West, were few and far between. Consequently, 'immigrant' usually referred to somebody who was not White. By

161

contrast, police forces were almost entirely White and in their day-to-day actions demonstrated a pattern of what would later be called institutionalised racism.

So many changes have happened and yet, as any historian will concede, even the most profound changes usually involve some elements of continuity from the past.

The possession and use of recreational drugs was widespread in inner cities and elsewhere. Their illegal status gave rise to constant tension between young people on the streets and the police who patrolled them. Looking for drugs became the most frequent justification offered by the police for stopping and searching young, and often Black, men who regarded this treatment as racial harassment. Lifestyles of inner city youth revolved around the street and reflected their alienation and exclusion from the education and employment systems of White society.

This is a pattern recognisable today and is not the only similarity between then and now. *Policing the Crisis* argued that crime in general, and some violent and apparently random crimes in particular, were taken to signify a breakdown of law and order which, in turn, indicated a moral decline. Society, it appeared, was threatened to its very core by the daily criminal behaviour of a small but dangerous minority who would use any means at their disposal to steal and rob passers-by. Though it was sometimes coded and sometimes not, this minority was, at the height of the mugging scare, characterised as Black.

If *Policing the Crisis* was right, and the authors have recently reassessed its accuracy (Hall *et al.*, 2013), a wide range of fears coalesced into the figure of the Black mugger: unpredictable, violent and on the loose. Like many basic and widespread fears, these were open to exploitation by those with their own political agenda. The need to defend law and order required a package of authoritarian measures: more police on the beat with enhanced powers to stop and search; new laws and penalties recognising the 'special' nature of mugging as a crime; courts willing and able to hand down exemplary sentences; the message loud and clear that 'we' – respectable society – would no longer tolerate this sort of thing. Conspicuously absent were any measures to address the social conditions of the inner city, aimed at improving access to and experience of education, employment or housing. Even palliative measures, to divert alienated youth away from a life of crime by providing alternative activities and identities in the local neighbourhood, were way down the list of priorities. The aim was to make the streets safe – by cracking down hard.

For mugging then, read gun or knife crime – even acid attacks – now. *Policing the Crisis* was criticised for implying that mugging was a media-inspired myth yet at the same time offering a complex explanation of why young Black men were attracted to street crime. We don't necessarily have to choose between myth and reality. One virtue of the model of a moral panic is that it allows for something to have really happened but for it to be misrecognised in a process of exaggeration and distortion which then produces a policy reaction which is misdirected and/or disproportionate. These are difficult judgements – who decides what is 'real', 'exaggerated' or 'proportionate'? – but they are not impossible. The debate, if that is what it is, about inner city crime, has for 40 years or more been long on punishment and short on social reform. *Policing the Crisis* identified and challenged this pattern as it emerged around 'mugging'. It has continued unabated since. **"**

Evaluation of *Policing the Crisis*

Policing the Crisis has been subjected to a number of criticisms. For example, David Downes and Paul Rock (1988) criticised the book for contradicting itself. It appeared to claim simultaneously that African Caribbean street crime was not rising quickly, that it was being amplified by police labelling, and that it was bound to rise as a result of unemployment. According to this criticism, Hall *et al.* were trying to have their cake and eat it too. They changed their view on whether these crimes were rising or not, according to how it fitted their argument. It is also unclear exactly how the crisis faced by the state and the moral panic over mugging were related to each other: Was the occurrence of the moral panic at the same time as the crisis purely fortuitous or did the crisis somehow *cause* the moral panic? If the latter, then *how* it did this remains obscure. Finally, the authors showed little interest in, let alone sympathy for, the victims of mugging. Rather, young Black men were conceived of as the victims of an oppressive state over-reacting to a relatively 'minor' type of criminal activity.

Gilroy: the 'myth of black criminality'

Another neo-Marxist perspective that supports the idea that Black over-representation in CJS statistics is a product of racism is that associated with Paul Gilroy.

Writing a few years later, but when there were still heightened levels of public anxiety about Black street crime, Gilroy (1983) argued that Black criminality was a myth. He rejected the view that Black criminals belonged to an 'alien culture' or that minority ethnic groups were poorly socialised and therefore became criminals. Instead, he saw minority ethnic groups as defending themselves against a society that treated them unjustly.

Both British Asians and African Caribbeans originate from former colonies of Britain and the original migrants to Britain carried with them 'the scars of imperialist violence'. The **anti-colonial struggles against British imperialism** − such as the non-violent mass protests led by Mahatma Gandhi in India and the Mau Mau rebellion in Kenya − allowed these ethnic groups to learn how to resist exploitation.

Activity

Mahatma Gandhi leading the Salt March in March 1930, an act of nonviolent civil disobedience in colonial India.

Research the purpose and outcome of the Salt March.

Once they arrived in Britain, they used the same techniques they had first developed in Asia and the Caribbean: marches, demonstrations and riots. In areas such as Southall and Brixton in London, Toxteth in Liverpool, Handsworth in Birmingham and St Paul's in Bristol (all scenes of inner-city rioting in the late 1970s and early 1980s), they hit back against police harassment, racially motivated attacks and discrimination.

Although Gilroy saw minority ethnic crime as part of a political struggle, he denied that minority ethnic groups were any more prone to crime than other groups. He claimed that the myth of Black criminality had been created as a result of the police having

negative stereotypes of African Caribbeans and Asians. African Caribbeans were seen as 'wild and lawless' and more specifically as potential 'muggers'. Asians were also regarded with suspicion and were often at that time seen as possibly being illegal immigrants.

Gilroy (1983) provided some evidence to support such views. He referred to a police officer in Brixton saying to a reporter: 'We are here to give our coloured brethren all the help we can − all they need to go somewhere else.' Gilroy also pointed out that the Police Federation magazine claimed that Jamaica had deliberately shipped convicts to Britain during the early period of migration in order to export its crime problems.

For these reasons, Gilroy argued that statistics that showed a disproportionate involvement of African Caribbeans in street crime could not be trusted. They reflected the prejudice of the police rather than any real tendency for this group to be more criminal than White British people.

Left realist perspectives

Left realists challenge the idea that the ethnic disparities in the CJS statistics are simply a product of discrimination by law enforcement agencies. John Lea and Jock Young (1984) argued that it is not entirely a myth that certain types of crime are more common among minority ethnic groups than among Whites. They were particularly critical of Paul Gilroy, but by implication they also rejected the main thrust of the argument put forward by Stuart Hall and his colleagues.

Lea and Young attacked Paul Gilroy for suggesting that the disproportionate number of Black males convicted of crimes in Britain was caused by police racism. Lea and Young quote figures showing that 92 per cent of crimes known to the police are brought to their attention by the public, and only 8 per cent are uncovered by the police themselves. In such circumstances, they argued, it was difficult to believe that the preponderance of Black people in the official figures was entirely a consequence of discrimination by the police.

Lea and Young also made use of statistics on 'race' and crime produced by the Home Office researchers, Stevens and Willis. Lea and Young calculated that the differences in offending between ethnic groups found by Stevens and Willis could only be explained entirely in terms of police racism if the police had arrested a substantial majority of African Caribbean offenders but a small minority of White offenders. Thus, 66 per cent of all African Caribbean offenders and just 21 per cent of all White offenders would have to have been arrested for the figures to be explicable entirely in terms of racism. Lea and Young believed discrimination on such a scale was unlikely. They saw it as more plausible to believe that there were real differences between offending rates, with African Caribbeans having a higher offending rate than Whites for some crimes.

They also pointed to a number of aspects of criminal statistics that could not be explained by police racism alone. The recorded rate for crimes committed by Whites was consistently slightly higher than that recorded for Asians. Lea and Young maintained that 'police racism would have to manifest itself very strangely indeed to be entirely responsible for such rates'.

Furthermore, in the 1960s the recorded rates for crimes committed by first-generation African Caribbean immigrants were lower than the national average. Even today, the official statistics for offences such as burglary show the rate for African Caribbeans to be lower than that for Whites. If these statistics were produced by police racism, then the police must have exercised positive discrimination in favour of some minority ethnic groups at times.

Lea and Young accepted that policing policies and police racism exaggerate the minority ethnic crime rate. Nevertheless, they believed there had been a real increase in the number of certain crimes (particularly robbery) committed by African Caribbeans. They found it hard to understand why writers such as Gilroy could not bring themselves to believe that unemployment and racial discrimination might result in minority ethnic groups committing more street crime than others.

Lea and Young were even more critical of Gilroy's claim that such African Caribbean crime as there was resulted from a continuation of the 'anti-colonial struggle' conducted in the former colonies. They pointed out that most young West Indians were second-generation immigrants who had lived in Britain since birth. Most of their parents appear, from the statistics in the 1950s and 1960s, to have been highly law-abiding. It is hard to see how they could have passed down the tradition of the 'anti-colonial struggle' to their children.

In any case, most of the victims of crimes committed by African Caribbeans were also African Caribbeans. How, Lea and Young enquired, could crimes committed against members of their own community be seen as a political attack on the White racist state? To them, it was far more plausible that street crime was a reaction to the oppression that African Caribbeans had experienced in Britain. They saw their criminality as a response to relative deprivation (they had less experience of material success than their White peers), a sense of marginalisation (produced partly by unemployment) and the formation of subcultures that were supportive of some types of criminal activity in some areas.

The debate between neo-Marxists and left realists remains unresolved, but in the 1990s arguments about police racism were propelled to the forefront of public attention by the tragic death of a Black student at the hands of a group of White racist thugs in London.

Institutional racism

The concept of 'institutional racism' originated with the Black Power movement in the USA in the 1960s, but it was its use in the Macpherson Report in 1999 that brought the concept to the attention of the general public in the UK.

In 1993 an 18-year-old African Caribbean student, Stephen Lawrence, was stabbed to death in London by a gang of White youths as he waited at a bus stop with a friend. Despite tip-offs by local residents identifying the youths involved, the Metropolitan police failed to collect sufficient evidence against them and although two of the five were charged, the CPS halted proceedings. Furious over this failure, Stephen Lawrence's parents – Doreen and Neville Lawrence – pursued a private prosecution, but this too failed in 1996. The eyewitness evidence of Stephen's friend, Duwayne Brooks, was ruled unreliable and Neil Acourt, Gary Dobson and Luke Knight were formally acquitted.

However, thanks to the tenacity of Stephen's parents and support from the *Daily Mail* in particular, when a Labour government was elected in 1997 the new Home Secretary Jack Straw ordered a public inquiry, chaired by Sir William Macpherson.

The Macpherson report concluded that 'There is no doubt whatsoever but that the first Metropolitan Police Service investigation was palpably flawed and deserves severe criticism.' Macpherson explained the failure as a product of 'institutional racism', which he defined as:

The collective failure of an organisation to provide an appropriate and professional service to people because of their colour, culture, or ethnic origin. It can be seen or detected in processes, attitudes and behaviour which amount to discrimination through unwitting prejudice, ignorance, thoughtlessness and racist stereotyping which disadvantage minority ethnic people.

The inquiry prompted Parliament to introduce two important changes to the law on equality and justice. The first, the Race Relations Amendment Act 2000, imposed a duty on public bodies to promote equality. The second, the Criminal Justice Act 2003, scrapped double jeopardy – the legal principle that prevented someone being tried twice for the same crime after being cleared at the first hearing.

This legislation, combined with the further determined public campaigning of the Lawrence family and continuing pressure from the media (including a hard-hitting BBC documentary), led to the Metropolitan police reopening the case and eventually, thanks to advances in forensic science, two of the original five – Gary Dobson and David Norris – were finally convicted of Stephen Lawrence's murder in 2012.

Activity

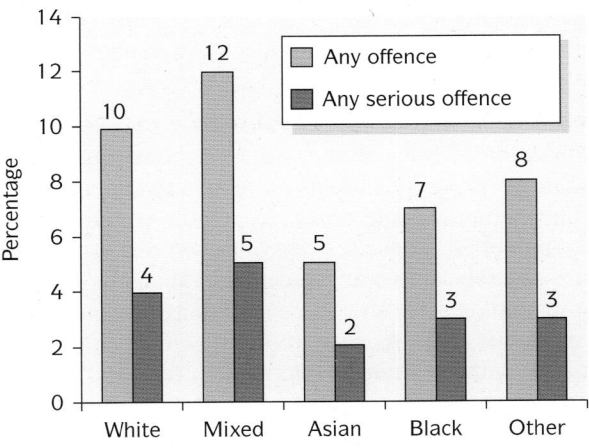

Stephen Lawrence's parents, Neville and Doreen Lawrence.

Why do you think it took so long for Neville and Doreen Lawrence to gain some justice in relation to the death of their son?

While the Macpherson report was focused on one police force, there is no reason to suppose that its findings could not apply also to other police forces and other branches of the CJS. Hence, the notion of institutional racism provides another possible explanation for the over-representation of certain ethnic minority groups in the CJS.

Ethnicity and self-reported offending

A final way of examining ethnic differences in rates of offending is to use self-report data.

The largest study of ethnicity and self-reported offending resulted from the government's Crime and Justice Survey of 2003, with data analysed by Clare Sharp and Tracey Budd (2005). This was based upon 12 000 respondents aged 10–65, with respondents from minority ethnic groups over-sampled to make ethnic comparisons more reliable. It examined property offences, violent offences and drug offences and collected data both on offending in the previous 12 months and on offending over the lifetime of the respondents. It produced some striking findings, as shown in Figures 2.10.1 and 2.10.2.

Figure 2.10.1 Self-reported offending in the last year, by ethnic group, in the Crime and Justice Survey of 2003

Source: Sharp, C. and Budd. T. (2005) *Minority Ethnic Groups and Crime: Findings from the Offending, Crime and Justice Survey 2003,* 2nd edition, Home Office, London, p. vi.

Figure 2.10.1, which relates to offending in the 12 months preceding the survey, shows that the group with the highest self-reported rate of offending in terms of any offence was the mixed ethnicity group followed by the White group, other ethnicity, Black and Asian respectively. Roughly the same picture holds true for serious offences.

Figure 2.10.2, which relates to offending over the whole of the respondents' life span, shows the highest rate of offending (in terms of 'any offence') was admitted to by the White group followed by those of mixed ethnicity, Black, other ethnicity and Asian in that order. For serious offences

165

Figure 2.10.2 Self-reported offending during their lifetime, by ethnic group, in the Crime and Justice Survey of 2003

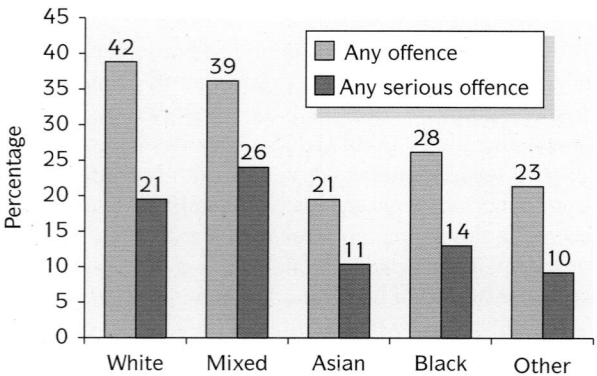

Source: Sharp, C. and Budd, T. (2005), *Minority Ethnic Groups and Crime: Findings from the Offending, Crime and Justice Survey 2003*, 2nd edition, Home Office, London, p. 10.

over someone's life span, the order was mixed ethnicity followed by White, Black, Asian and other ethnicity respectively.

Self-report studies do, of course, have significant limitations, relying as they do on respondents' honesty. However, there is no reason to suppose that this limitation would apply to one ethnic group more than another. Consequently, while self-report studies are severely limited as measures of absolute levels of offending, they should be less limited as measures of relative rates. As such, there is a clear mis-match between the relative positioning of Black and Asian groups in the CJS statistics examined above and their positioning in the self-report data. In particular, the self-report data would suggest that White offenders are under-represented in the CJS statistics and Black offenders severely over-represented in relative terms, pointing to the possibility of institutional racism.

Conclusion

Phillips and Bowling (2007) conclude that it is impossible to calculate the extent to which the over-representation of some minority ethnic groups among those convicted of crime is due to racism. It is impossible because some studies are contradictory and none of the evidence is perfect, and because of the complex nature of criminal justice itself.

However, Phillips and Bowling still argue that the research suggests there is racism and discrimination in the criminal justice system, influenced by prevailing

stereotypes of race and ethnicity, but that these stereotypes and the associated discrimination change over time. They say:

In our view, conceiving of racism as a complex and socially situated phenomenon can explain the criminal justice experience of different ethnic groups. Thus, patterns of selective enforcement and harsher criminal justice outcomes are consistent with unjustified heightened suspicion of black people (and more recently Asians, especially Muslims) based on stereotypes. For this reason, we reject notions of the uniform, static, and monolithic form of racism in favour of one rooted in historical and spatial specificity. (Phillips and Bowling, 2012)

Key terms

Economic crisis In the 1970s the UK economy was under pressure from falling profits, faltering economic growth, rising prices and growing unemployment.

Crisis of legitimacy A situation where people start to question the government's right to govern.

Inter-class truce A situation where class conflict is limited because both sides are prepared to make concessions.

Anti-colonial struggles against British imperialism The resistance to the colonial rule of one country by another, in this case the British Empire. Many of the post-World War II immigrants to Britain came from countries such as those in southern Asia and the Caribbean that had once been colonies of the British Empire.

Summary

1. Neo-Marxist sociologists explain BAME over-representation in the CJS as a product of criminalisation of young Black men (particularly) by the police and courts.

2. Left realists argue that, given the social and economic marginalisation of BAME groups in British society, higher levels of criminality are to be expected.

3. The Macpherson Report (1999) identified the existence of institutional racism within the Metropolitan police force.

4. Self-reported offending rates do not explain BAME over-representation in the CJS.

Contemporary issues: Overrepresentation of young Black people in the CJS

Police officers searching a group of Black men.

In 2006/7 the Home Affairs Select Committee investigated the over-representation of young Black people in the CJS. Below is their conclusion on the causes of this over-representation.

'Many of the causes of overrepresentation among young black people are similar to those which predispose a minority of young people from all communities to involvement in the criminal justice system. Social exclusion, educational underachievement and school exclusion interact to form a web of disadvantage, bringing young black people disproportionately into contact with crime and the criminal justice system as both victims and offenders.

However, our evidence suggested there are issues which are particular to young black people which need to be tackled. Many but not all of these stem from the social exclusion described above. We heard that a lack of father involvement may have a negative impact on the development of young black males in particular. Our evidence also suggested there is a culture amongst some young black people, fuelled by the media and popular culture, in which

"success" or credibility is built on young people's willingness and ability to break the law or exercise power through force.

Young black people are more likely than other young people to come to the attention of the police because they are more at risk of factors such as social exclusion, living in rented accommodation or being homeless, which are associated with arrest. The types of crimes they commit may also bring them more readily to the attention of the police. In addition, the particular relationship between black communities and the police leads to greater involvement in the criminal justice system – in some instances due to discrimination, and in other cases because suspicion or mistrust of criminal justice agencies leads young people to take the law into their own hands to protect themselves or exact redress.

Our evidence suggests that, in addition to addressing the underlying causes of overrepresentation, any response to overrepresentation needs to tackle those causes which are specific to black communities.'

Source: House of Commons Home Affairs Committee Young Black People and the Criminal Justice System Second Report of Session 2006–07, p. 53.

Questions

1. What factors common to a minority of young people from all ethnic groups are identified as relevant to explaining the over-representation of young Black people in the CJS?

2. What factors specific to young Black people are identified as relevant?

3. The report states: 'We were acutely aware of the sensitivities in undertaking such an inquiry.' What do you think they meant by this?

Unit 2.10.3 Ethnicity and victimisation

Table 2.10.1 shows the risk of victimisation by ethnic group according to data from the British Crime Survey/Crime Survey for England and Wales of 2010/11 to 2014/15. It shows that members of all minority ethnic groups are more likely to be victims of

personal crime than other groups, with the exception of 'other, including Chinese' – where the pattern is inconsistent – and the figure for Asian or Asian British in 2014/15. However, the assumption that this is directly related to ethnicity has been questioned by a number of studies.

For example, according to Clancy *et al.* (2001), much of the difference in victimisation can be explained in terms of social factors, such as the areas in which

Table 2.10.1 Trends in the percentage of adults who were victims once or more of a British Crime Survey/Crime Survey for England and Wales personal crime, by ethnicity, England and Wales, 2010/11 to 2014/15

	2010/11	2011/12	2012/13	2013/14	2014/15
% victimised once or more					
ALL	**5.9**	**5.9**	**5.2**	**4.9**	**4.1**
White	5.6	5.7	5.0	4.7	3.9
Mixed	10.8	13.1	11.1	12.9	10.8
Asian or Asian British	7.0	7.0	6.4	5.5	3.9
Black or Black British	6.9	6.9	7.2	6.3	5.6
Chinese or other	8.5	5.6	4.2	3.1	5.0
ALL	*46 754*	*46 031*	*34 880*	*35 371*	*33 350*

Source: Ministry of Justice (2015) Statistics on Race and the Criminal Justice System 2014, Ministry of Justice, London.

minority ethnic groups live, the higher rates of unemployment among minority ethnic groups, and the younger age structure of minority ethnic groups compared to Whites. Indeed, their statistical analysis suggests that such factors are more important than ethnicity.

Such is not the case with hate crimes (See Unit 2.7.1), where prejudice and hostility towards others is linked directly to their perceived race or ethnicity. In 2014/15, there were 52 580 hate crimes recorded by the police in England and Wales of which 42 930 (82%) were recorded as race hate crimes. The majority of these take the form of 'public order offences' where victims are caused fear, alarm or distress, followed by violence against the person offences and, finally, criminal damage or arson to the victim's property.

However, many hate crimes go unreported because victims believe the police would not – or could not – do much about them. Estimates based on combined data from the 2012/13 to 2014/15 CSEW put the figure of race hate crimes at 106 000 annually during this period. Adults in non-White ethnic groups were much more likely to be victims of a racially motivated hate crime than White adults (e.g. 1.0% of Asian and 0.7% of Black adults compared with 0.1% of White adults).

In recent years, the growth of Islamophobia means that Muslims have been particularly likely to be targeted. Religion is one of the five 'protected

categories' recognised in hate crime legislation, although 'racial' and 'religious' hate crime are far from being discrete categories. As Sadiq Khan, the current Mayor of London, has ruefully observed: 'When we were growing up, we weren't defined by faith. You were white or black, and I was black, then Asian and now it's religion. Identity is very complex.' (Observer Weekend, 30.07.2017.) Analysis of racially motivated hate crime by religion shows that Muslim adults or those whose religion was coded as 'other' were more likely to be a victim of racially motivated hate crime (1.2%) than other adults (e.g. 0.1% of Christian adults or those with no religion).

Hate crimes are likely to have particularly damaging effects on people emotionally. According to the 2012/13 to 2014/15 surveys, victims of hate crime were more likely than victims of CSEW crime overall to say they were emotionally affected by the incident (92% and 81% respectively) and more likely to be 'very much' affected (36% and 13% respectively). Among the effects listed by victims were a loss of confidence, feelings of vulnerability, difficulty sleeping, anxiety or panic attacks and depression. These feelings are likely to be exacerbated where victims who do contact the police feel let down by their response. It is, therefore, a matter of concern that while 52 per cent of the victims interviewed were very or fairly satisfied with the police's handling of the matter, 35 per cent were very dissatisfied.

Summary

1. Members of BAME groups, according to the BCS/CSEW, are generally more likely to be victims of personal crime than White groups.

2. Factors other than ethnicity, such as residential location, age-structure and unemployment rates, are relevant in explaining this pattern.

3. BAME groups are far more likely to be victims of racial and religious hate crime than White groups.

4. Hate crime is more prevalent than police-recorded figures suggest. It has damaging effects, not only on its immediate victims, but on the wider community to which its victims belong.

PART 11 CRIME CONTROL, PREVENTION, PUNISHMENT AND VICTIMS

Contents

In this, the final part of the chapter, we turn our attention to the various ways in which societies seek to control crime and the efforts they make to prevent it. We also look at what were for a long time the forgotten figures in criminology: the victims of crime.

We begin by focusing on the increasingly diverse ways in which contemporary societies have become proactive rather than merely reactive in trying to prevent crime by identifying ways in which it may be able to stop people developing criminal dispositions, making it more difficult for potential offenders to commit crimes, organising communities to reduce crime or using the criminal justice system (CJS) to deter criminals.

Next, we look at the different perspectives that sociologists have developed to understand the role of punishment in society and, in particular, the growing trend towards locking people up in prison in countries such as the UK and the USA.

Finally, we look at how victimhood is not distributed randomly throughout society but – like criminality – is socially patterned and examine the insights provided by a growing sub-discipline within criminology known as 'victimology'.

Unit 2.11.1 Crime control and crime prevention

Crime prevention strategies can be categorised in a number of different ways. One classification system was suggested by Tonry and Farrington (1995), who distinguished four main categories:

» *Developmental prevention*: interventions designed to prevent the development of criminal motivations in children and young people through identifying, and acting on, risk and protective factors.

» *Situational prevention*: interventions designed to prevent the occurrence of crimes by reducing opportunities and increasing the risk and difficulty of offending.

» *Community prevention*: interventions designed to change the social conditions and institutions that influence offending in communities.

» *Criminal justice prevention*: actions by CJS agencies designed to deter, incapacitate or rehabilitate offenders.

We will look at each of these in turn.

Developmental crime prevention

One of the most famous studies of risk factors associated with the development of criminal careers is the Cambridge Study in Delinquent Development, a longitudinal survey of 411 South London males first studied at age eight in 1961 (Farrington *et al.*, 2006).

The study found that the most important childhood risk factors at age 8–10 for later offending were:

1. disruptive child behaviour (troublesomeness or dishonesty)

2. criminality in the family (a convicted parent, a delinquent sibling)

3. low intelligence or low school attainment

4. poor child rearing (poor discipline, poor supervision or separation of a child from a parent)

5. impulsiveness (daring or risk taking, restlessness or poor concentration)

6. economic deprivation (low income, poor housing, large family size).

According to Welsh and Farrington (2007), four types of programmes have proved particularly successful in addressing such risk factors: parent education (in the context of home visiting), parent management training, child skills training, and pre-school intellectual enrichment programmes.

An example of an intervention aimed at parent education and child management skills is parenting orders. These were introduced under the Crime and Disorder Act 1998 as a means of responding to non-attendance at school, serious misbehaviour at school or where children have got into trouble with the police. They are court orders that require parents to attend parenting programmes for up to three months designed to help parents manage their child's/children's behaviour more effectively.

The best known pre-school programmes are Head Start, launched in 1965 (and adopted by the federal government in 1981) in the USA and Sure Start launched in 1998 in England and Wales. Research into their effectiveness has generally found positive outcomes, although that into Sure Start has been more variable.

For example, research into the Perry pre-school project in Ypsilanti (Michigan) found that it had long-term benefits in terms of crime reduction. One hundred and twenty-three children aged 3–4 were allocated randomly to an experimental and a control group with the experimental group attending a daily pre-school programme, backed up by weekly home visits, lasting

two years. The most recent follow-up of this project, at age 40, which included 91 per cent of the original sample, found that the programme continued to make an important difference in the lives of the participants (Schweinhart *et al.*, 2005, in Welsh and Farrington, 2012). Compared to the control group, experimental participants had significantly fewer lifetime arrests for violent crimes (32% vs. 48%), property crimes (36% vs. 58%), and drug crimes (14% vs. 34%), and were significantly less likely to be arrested five or more times (36% vs. 55%).

Activity

Children in a pre-school setting.

What do you think are the strengths and limitations of such developmental crime prevention strategies?

Due to cuts in central government grants to local councils, the Sure Start programme has struggled to keep going in many areas. For example, in February 2017, all 44 Sure Start children's centres in Oxfordshire were closed after High Court appeals against the measure failed. Central government has instead invested heavily in the Troubled Families programme introduced by the Coalition government following the 2011 riots. (See Unit 2.7.1.)

Research conducted by the National Institute for Economic and Social Research into the first phase of the programme, which lasted from 2012–2015, concluded that 'participation in the programme had no significant or systematic impact' on the families involved. Nevertheless, the programme is continuing and in 2017 involved around half a million families. (See Contemporary issues: The Troubled Families programme.)

Contemporary issues: The Troubled Families programme

'Troubled Families is a programme of targeted intervention for families with multiple problems, including crime, anti-social behaviour, truancy, unemployment, mental health problems and domestic abuse.

Local authorities identify "troubled families" in their area and usually assign a key worker to act as a single point of contact. Central Government pays local authorities by results for each family that meet set criteria or move into continuous employment. £448 million was allocated to the first phase of the programme, which ran from 2012 to 2015.

Local authorities worked with around 120 000 families, and "turned around" 99%. However the independent evaluation of the programme found no evidence that the programme had made any significant impact across its key objectives.

The second phase of the Troubled Families programme was launched in 2015, with £920 million allocated to help an additional 400 000 families. The second phase will run until 2020,

with annual progress reporting until 2022. The programme was championed in part as a way to reduce public spending on families who require support from multiple parts of the state.

No formal analysis has yet been published on the extent of any savings from the programme as a whole. The Troubled Families programme is administered by the Department for Communities and Local Government, and covers England only.'

Source: House of Commons Briefing Paper CBP 07585, April 2017, The Troubled Families programme (England).

Questions

1. Given that the independent evaluation of the first phase found no evidence of its effectiveness, why do you think the government is continuing with it?

2. How valid do you think it is to locate the family as the source of the 'crime problem' in society?

Evaluation

Developmental crime prevention strategies are based on the idea that criminal tendencies are a product of early childhood experiences and that if such tendencies can be 'nipped in the bud' the level of crime in society can be reduced. There is a wealth of evidence that childhood experiences have a significant impact on later behaviour, including involvement in crime and delinquency (although Farrington and West identified a minority of 'late-onset offenders' whose future criminality was not well predicted at age 8–10).

Most developmental interventions target children from deprived backgrounds. However, Marxist and critical criminologists would argue that programmes based on this approach to crime prevention merely tackle the symptoms rather than the root cause of criminality: structural disadvantage and economic insecurity. If this isn't tackled, the system will continue to churn out successive generations of children with criminal tendencies. It is also doubtful whether such interventions are likely to have any impact on white-collar, corporate or state crime.

Situational crime prevention

Situational crime prevention strategies are based on rational action and routine activity theories of crime that see crime as the product of circumstances where a motivated offender, the opportunity to offend and the absence of a capable guardian come together in one place. (See Unit 2.7.2.)

Situational crime prevention is associated particularly with the criminologist Ronald V. Clarke. In 1983, Clarke identified three key components of situational crime prevention: surveillance, target hardening measures and environmental management. These remain at the core of situational crime prevention, but a number of other techniques have been added to this list over the years.

A Scottish government review of crime reduction strategies in 2014 identified seven situational crime prevention strategies:

▶ increasing formal surveillance using electronic alarms, CCTV, private security patrols or neighbourhood watch

▶ increasing natural surveillance by removing obstacles to line of sight or improving street lighting

171

> increasing access or exit controls to residential areas or buildings

> concealing or removing targets (such as lightweight, high-value goods that tend to be easy to steal: jewellery; cash; iPods; mobile phones)

> erecting or strengthening physical barriers such as window locks, double-pane glass – which is both more difficult and noisier to break – and deadbolt locks on doors

> restricting access to the tools of crime (such as spray paints)

> reducing provocation (e.g. by segregating rival fans in stadiums).

The review also includes an example of an early project that made use of a number of these techniques – the Kirkholt burglary-reduction project that ran between 1987 and 1990 on a deprived housing estate near Rochdale in Northern England. The estate was chosen because it had twice the rate of burglaries characteristic of high crime areas, had clearly defined boundaries and because residents indicated a willingness to participate in the project.

The project was divided into two phases. Phase one ran for the first year and involved the removal of pre-payment fuel meters, improved household security (target hardening), a community support team (primarily to provide support to victims of burglary) and a 'cocoon' neighbourhood watch scheme (where close groupings of dwellings keep an eye on each other's properties). Phase two ran for the second and third years and involved offenders engaging in community work on the estate (such as cleaning up public spaces under the supervision of probation), the introduction of a credit union and schools providing recreational activities for youths outside school hours. The annual number of residential burglaries compared with the level before the project began fell by 38 per cent in the first year, by 67 per cent in the second and by 72 per cent in the final year.

The Kirkholt burglary-reduction project was implemented on an existing estate, but increasingly situational crime prevention strategies are taken into account at the planning and design stage when new housing is being considered. 'Crime Prevention Through Environmental Design' (CPTED) – or 'Secure by Design' (SBD) as it is also known – forms part of a commitment to 'designing out crime' which is now part of the UK government's crime prevention strategy.

Activity

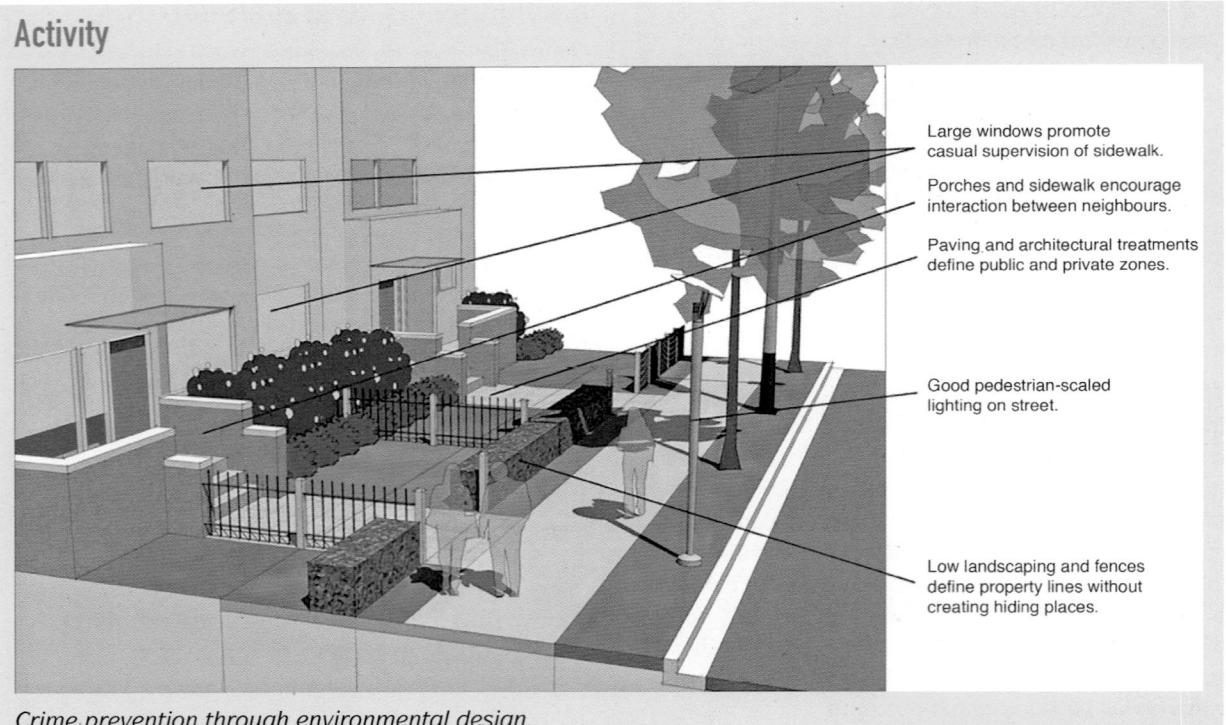

Large windows promote casual supervision of sidewalk.

Porches and sidewalk encourage interaction between neighbours.

Paving and architectural treatments define public and private zones.

Good pedestrian-scaled lighting on street.

Low landscaping and fences define property lines without creating hiding places.

Crime prevention through environmental design.

What kinds of crimes does CPTED target?

CCTV

Probably the most visible evidence of the adoption of situational crime prevention strategies is provided by the presence of **CCTV** cameras in town centres, shopping malls, sports grounds and other public and private spaces.

According to the BBC, the UK has one of the largest CCTV networks in the world. The British Security Industry Association (BSIA) estimated in 2015 that there were between 4 and 6 million cameras installed in the UK, mostly in private locations.

CCTV systems vary according to whether they involve 'active' or 'passive' monitoring. 'Active monitoring' involves operators monitoring the cameras in real time, which can both increase the threat of identification and increase the likelihood of arrest as operators can alert the police to an incident while it is happening. 'Passive monitoring' refers to CCTV systems that regularly scan an area and produce a filmic record that can later be examined, thereby assisting with the collection of evidence.

CCTV surveillance is meant to deter crime by increasing the perceived likelihood that offenders will be identified, thereby making them think twice about actually committing an offence. A systematic review and meta-analysis carried out by Welsh and Farrington (2009) estimated that overall, for every 100 crimes, an average of 16 crimes were prevented with CCTV (based on 41 studies) and specifically for vehicle crime, for every 100 crimes, an average of 26 crimes were prevented (based on 22 studies). They concluded that CCTV has been highly effective in reducing vehicle-related crime, has had a limited, positive impact on other types of acquisitive crime and no impact on violent crime.

Evaluation of situational crime prevention strategies

There is strong evidence that situational crime prevention strategies can help to reduce the incidence of certain types of crime or crime in specific locations. The reduction in thefts of and from cars and in domestic burglaries in recent years almost certainly owes much to the introduction of target hardening measures by car manufacturers and householders and to the introduction of CCTV.

Proponents of such measures, moreover, challenge the idea that they don't reduce the motivation for crime on the basis that 'opportunity makes the thief' (that is, that easy targets will tempt people to steal who would otherwise be law-abiding). They also challenge the claim that situational crime prevention strategies simply 'displace' offending from one place to another, from one time to another, from one target to another, or from one kind of crime to another. An example of such a claim is Chaiken *et al.* (1974), who evaluated the effect of a massive increase in the number of Transit Police employed during the night on the New York underground in 1965, designed to tackle high rates of night-time robbery. The immediate effect was to reduce the number of robberies on the underground at all times of day, but after an eight-month 'honeymoon' period it appeared that the higher staffing rates at night had simply displaced robberies on the subway to the daytime.

However, Clarke (1998) refers to a meta-analysis of 55 studies of displacement undertaken for the Ministry of Justice in Holland (Hesseling, 1994). In 22 of the studies, no evidence of displacement was found. In the remaining 33 studies some evidence was found, but the displacement was often relatively small. In no case did the crime displaced elsewhere equal the crime prevented.

On the other hand, while there may be some truth in the idea that 'opportunity makes the thief', this is only likely to apply to opportunistic offenders and to acquisitive crime. It is unclear how situational crime prevention strategies would prevent white-collar, corporate or state crime. Moreover, it assumes that offenders act rationally. While this may be true of some offenders in relation to some offence categories, it is far from true of all, particularly in relation to crimes of violence.

Community crime prevention

Community crime prevention is based on two key ideas. First, that crime prevention should not simply be left to the police, but should involve a range of agencies including the health service, the fire service, local councils, probation, housing authorities and so on working in partnership. Second, that policies should seek to engage the wider public by, for example, consulting them about what they see as priority issues.

Broken windows theory

One influential spur to the development of community crime prevention efforts was Wilson and

173

Kelling's 1980s broken windows theory. (See Unit 2.7.2.) Broken windows theory suggests that signs of disorder such as broken windows, graffiti and litter induce other types of disorder and petty crime, so to prevent the escalation of crime and disorder such early signs of community breakdown needed to be addressed.

In the mid-1990s, the mayor of New York and his police commissioner adopted a 'Quality of Life' campaign modelled on broken windows theory. Attention was focused on addressing signs of disorder: graffiti was removed, streets were kept clean and signs of vandalism were dealt with. A policy of '**zero tolerance policing**' was also implemented.

After the introduction of the campaign, crime rates in New York dropped significantly. However, it is unclear whether this was a product of the campaign or merely coincidental. Some critics argue, for example, that crime had already started dropping before the introduction of the campaign and that crime also fell in other US cities that had not adopted such approaches.

Broken windows theory was, then, very influential, but studies aiming to test the theory provided mixed results and the US National Research Council concluded in 2004 that the research done up to that point did not provide strong support. However, more recent experimental research conducted in Groningen in the Netherlands has provided some robust evidence supporting the theory.

Keizer, Lindenberg and Steg (2008) designed six ingenious field experiments in which they manipulated situations in public spaces so that they could see whether subjects were more likely to commit minor offences (such as littering, trespassing and stealing) if there were visible – or, in one case, auditory – signs of contextual disorder (such as the presence of litter or graffiti) in the immediate environment. For example, in one experiment they examined whether an envelope hanging out of a mailbox which visibly contained a €5 note would be stolen more often if the mailbox was covered with graffiti or if the space around the mailbox was littered.

In all six experiments, there were statistically significant differences in the level of petty offending where contextual signs of disorder or rule-breaking were present. For example, in relation to the visible €5 note, 13 per cent of passers-by stole it when there were no contextual signs of disorder/rule-breaking, whereas 27 per cent stole it when the mailbox was covered with graffiti and 25 per cent stole it when the surrounding area was littered.

Community safety partnerships

Community crime prevention in the UK is associated most strongly with what were initially called Crime and Disorder Reduction Partnerships, but are now more generally known as Community Safety Partnerships (CSPs) set up by the 1998 Crime and Disorder Act.

Over the years CSPs have evolved through legislation and practice. Thus, the 2006 Police and Justice Act expanded the number of 'responsible authorities' who should be engaged in CSPs – besides the local council and police service – to include the Fire Service, Probation Service, Health Service, local Police Authority and a representative of Registered Social Landlords (Housing Associations). It also required local authorities to put in place arrangements for scrutinising the work of the CSP. Further changes were introduced by the 2011 Policing and Social Responsibility Act, which replaced local police authorities with elected Police and Crime Commissioners (PCCs). CSPs were required to cooperate with the PCC within whose area they were located to reduce crime and disorder.

Currently there are about 300 CSPs in England and 22 in Wales. Each CSP has to carry out a 'Strategic Intelligence Assessment' of crime and disorder in their area and then produce a strategy document (which usually covers the upcoming three-year period), following public consultation, in which it sets out its priorities and how it intends to tackle the problems identified. This has then to be sent to the PCC.

To provide an illustration, the Blackpool CSP – known as BSafe Blackpool – Plan for 2016–2019 identifies five priority areas: Antisocial Behaviour, Domestic Abuse, Violence against the Person, Sexual Offences and Rape, and Child Sexual Exploitation. The Plan itself explains how these priorities came to be chosen, how they were endorsed by a survey of Blackpool residents and outlines in some detail how the CSP intends to tackle each of these issues.

Activity

CSPs often make use of volunteers. Street Pastors are people who volunteer to patrol city-centre streets in order to offer support to night-time revellers who might need it.

1. Street Pastors operate in Blackpool and many other CSP areas. Find out more about them at http://www.streetpastors.org

2. Find out the name of your local CSP and examine its current Community Safety Plan. What are the priorities identified and how do they compare with BSafe Blackpool's?

Evaluation of community crime prevention

Community crime prevention should not be seen as distinct from other types of crime prevention, such as situational crime prevention. For example, over the years Blackpool's community safety plans have incorporated alley gating, the use of CCTV, improved street lighting, town centre exclusion orders, bans on street drinking and the substitution of traditional drinking glasses with polycarbonate glasses in bars and nightclubs.

Rather, community crime prevention can be understood as an approach to tackling crime and disorder that allows local areas to enjoy some autonomy from central government and attempts to respond to local concerns by drawing on a wide range of professional knowledge and expertise through partnership working. Moreover, the fact that plans have to be published and successes and failures acknowledged, offers a much higher level of transparency than was the case before the establishment of CSPs.

While broken windows theory has been subjected to extensive evaluation, there is a lack of research literature examining CSPs. Nevertheless, a Home Office Research Report published in 2011, based on nine studies conducted in the USA, concluded that the principle of applying partnership working as a component of initiatives to tackle complex crime problems 'is effective'. Also, research by Caroline Thwaites (2013) which examined two CSPs in London, noted that if effectiveness was measured solely on recorded crime rates, 'both partnerships had some impact'.

On the other hand, Thwaites also found that neither partnership was clear about how to measure 'effectiveness', that an undue burden was placed on the local authorities and that governance structures needed to be streamlined. It is also the case that, to the extent that CSPs respond to the public's perception of the 'crime problem', certain categories of crime are likely to be absent from their plans, such as corporate and environmental crime.

Crime prevention and the CJS

According to the Home Office's *Modern Crime Prevention Strategy* (March 2016), the CJS can prevent crime through four principal mechanisms:

- *Deterrence*: the idea that the prospect of being caught and punished should deter people from offending.

- *Legitimacy*: the idea that by engaging positively with people and treating them fairly, those working in the CJS can increase the system's legitimacy in the eyes of the public and foster greater compliance with the law.

- *Incapacitation*: the idea that 'prison works' by locking people – particularly, prolific offenders – up, thereby preventing them from committing further crimes.

- *Rehabilitation*: the idea that offenders' lives can be turned around by targeted interventions such as treatment for drug addiction and programmes improving offenders' cognitive skills, or anger management programmes for domestic violence perpetrators.

Sentencing and rehabilitation

While most media attention is focused on imprisonment, most of the sentences handed down by magistrates and crown courts do not involve imprisonment. An overview of sentencing in England and Wales is provided by figures released by the Ministry of Justice in 2013 giving a breakdown of the 1 230 000 sentences issued in 2012:

- Fines 67%
- Community sentences 12%
- Immediate custody 8%
- Absolute or conditional discharge 7%
- Suspended sentence 3.5%
- Otherwise dealt with 2%

(Note: figures do not add up exactly to 100% due to rounding.)

Critics of imprisonment point to the high rates of recidivism (reoffending) among those released from prison. Currently, nearly half of adult prisoners are reconvicted within one year of release and the figure for those serving sentences of less than 12 months is even higher at about 60 per cent.

Community punishments provide an alternative for offenders other than those who have committed the most serious kinds of crimes (such as murder, manslaughter, rape, grievous bodily harm and so on). Community sentences combine punishment with activities carried out in the community such as up to 300 hours of unpaid work, adhering to a curfew (which may require electronic tagging), rehabilitation activity requirements (such as attending anger management courses), residency requirements and so on. They may also mean that the offender is required to undertake alcohol or drug treatment programmes. Around one third of adults given a community sentence reoffend within a year.

Evaluation of the CJS and crime prevention

The CJS has an important role to play in crime prevention in terms of deterrence, incapacitation and rehabilitation. However, critics argue that currently in England and Wales a lack of funding and overcrowding in the prison estate militates against effective rehabilitation and that (as we saw in Part 10) there is evidence of bias against BAME groups.

Activity

Alongside its Modern Crime Prevention Strategy (2016), the Conservative government published a 12-page summary: Modern Crime Prevention Pamphlet, which can be accessed online. Read the Pamphlet and answer the following questions:

1. What does it see as the 'six key drivers of crime' and what prevention strategies are associated with each?

2. List the types of crimes that the Pamphlet identifies as targets for preventative action.

3. What types of crime are missing from the Pamphlet?

Key terms

Longitudinal survey A research method that involves following the same sample of people over an extended time period.

CCTV Closed-circuit television.

Zero tolerance policing A policing strategy that involves treating even minor infringements of the law harshly.

Summary

1. Developmental crime prevention seeks to prevent the development of criminal dispositions by intervening in the early lives of children at risk of becoming offenders.

2. Situational crime prevention strategies are based on rational action and routine activity theories of crime and include the use of surveillance, target hardening measures and environmental design measures.

3. Community crime prevention was initially associated with broken windows theory and involves efforts to prevent crime by local partnership working between the police, local authorities and other agencies. In the UK, it is particularly associated with Community Safety Partnerships.

4. The criminal justice system can also be seen as playing a role in crime prevention through deterrence, incapacitation and rehabilitation.

Unit 2.11.2 Sociological perspectives on punishment

Sociologists share the view that the nature of punishment reflects the society in which it occurs, but differ in their view of the role it plays in society.

Functionalist perspectives

For Durkheim, punishment had an important expressive role, giving voice to society's outrage at the violation of strongly held **social mores** as expressed in the law. Moreover, punishment was functional in that it reassured people that social mores could not be violated with impunity and reaffirmed the power and authority of the moral order of society. Without punishment, both social order and social solidarity would be undermined. (See also Unit 2.4.2.)

Durkheim distinguished between two types of justice: retributive and restitutive. Retributive justice, characterised by cruel and vengeful punishments, was characteristic of traditional societies, while restitutive justice (characterised by reparation – making amends through the payment of fines, say, or by losing one's liberty through imprisonment) was more characteristic of modern societies. Indeed, in Durkheim's view, retributive justice was dysfunctional in that it destroyed an important basis of social solidarity, the ability to empathise with others, even with those who have broken the law.

The functionalist view assumes that the society within which law-breaking takes place is essentially harmonious and that punishment is an expression of the collective will. Such a view is not shared by Marxists as for them the notion of genuine harmony in a class-divided society is a deception or delusion.

Marxist perspectives

For Marxists, the CJS is part of what Althusser called the repressive state apparatus of capitalist societies and the purpose of punishment is the ongoing maintenance of class domination by means of coercive force. Moreover, the idea that all are equal under the law is little more than an ideological justification for a penal system that disproportionately punishes those at the bottom of the class system.

The classic statement of a Marxist perspective on punishment was provided by Rusche and Kirchheimer (1939), who argued that the types of punishments used by a society were determined by what was in the economic interests of the dominant class and that changes in penal policy reflected changes in the mode of production. Thus, in the early Middle Ages the landowners needed the labour power of peasants so neither imprisonment nor execution were favoured. Instead, religious penances and fines were used. In the late Middle Ages, there was no shortage of labour, but the ruling class were concerned about social order so were prepared to use barbaric forms of treatment to deter social unrest, such as branding, mutilation, torture and execution. By the 17th century, labour was again scarce so the ruling class devised ways of exploiting the potential labour power of convicts through punishments such as galley slavery, transportation and penal servitude with hard labour. By the 20th century, it was becoming difficult to use the labour power of prisoners effectively, because, for example, of the difficulties of employing modern production techniques in a prison setting. Consequently, other considerations became more central to the formation of penal policy, in particular the concern to minimise expenditure. Hence, fines became the most frequently employed penal measure.

This preoccupation with the labour market implications of penal policy also, in Rusche and Kirchheimer's view, set severe limits on the extent to which prison regimes could be more humane or rehabilitative. Prisons had to operate on the 'less eligibility' principle, a principle embodied in the 1834 Poor Law Amendment Act which stated that conditions in workhouses had to be worse than conditions available outside so that paupers would be deterred from claiming poor relief. Similarly, prison regimes had to be less attractive than the conditions of life experienced by the lowest levels of the non-convict proletariat in order that criminality didn't appear to be an attractive proposition. They also needed to be places that reinforced the work ethic, so even when such labour could no longer be economically profitable, inmates were required to work in prison in order to prepare them for employment on their release.

Garland (1991) made a number of significant criticisms of Rusche and Kirchheimer's **economic determinist** view of penal policy. In particular, he argued that they exaggerated the explanatory power of economic factors in explaining penal policy, overlooking the important role played also by professional interests (such as those of lawyers

177

and probation officers), institutional dynamics (such as changes of government), criminological conceptions (of the purpose of imprisonment, say) and religious and humanitarian reformers. They also failed, in Garland's view, to explain the mechanisms through which ruling-class interests are translated into penal policies, particularly in liberal democracies, and are unable to explain why, if penal policy simply serves dominant class interests, it commands such a wide degree of support among all classes.

Michel Foucault

Another influential sociological perspective on punishment is associated with the French philosopher and historian of ideas Michel Foucault. In *Discipline and Punish: the Birth of the Prison* (1977), Foucault sought to account for the change from the barbaric kinds of punishments associated with the Middle Ages to those associated with modern society in which imprisonment has become the standard form of severe punishment.

Foucault argued that the change can be understood in terms of a change in the nature of state power, from what he calls sovereign power to **disciplinary power**. Sovereign power – the power of the king or monarch – involved punishment which took the form of public spectacles in which the body of the criminal was subjected to horrific acts of violence: the book begins with a description of the public torture and execution of Robert-Francois Damiens in 1757 who had attempted to kill King Louis XV. Disciplinary power, by contrast, involved punishments which sought to 'correct' the criminal, not by inflicting pain on their bodies, but by altering their minds.

Foucault used the panopticon or correction house designed by the British philosopher Jeremy Bentham in 1791 (though never built) as a symbol of this new kind of punishment. The panopticon is a circular building with prisoners' cells arranged around its perimeter with a central observation tower from which a supervisor could see into every cell. In this way, the inmates could be kept under constant surveillance, but could not see into the tower so did not know whether or not they were being observed. Foucault argued that over time the inmates would come to regulate their own behaviour for fear that they were being watched. Imprisonment was thus intended to discipline the inmate and bring them into line.

Activity

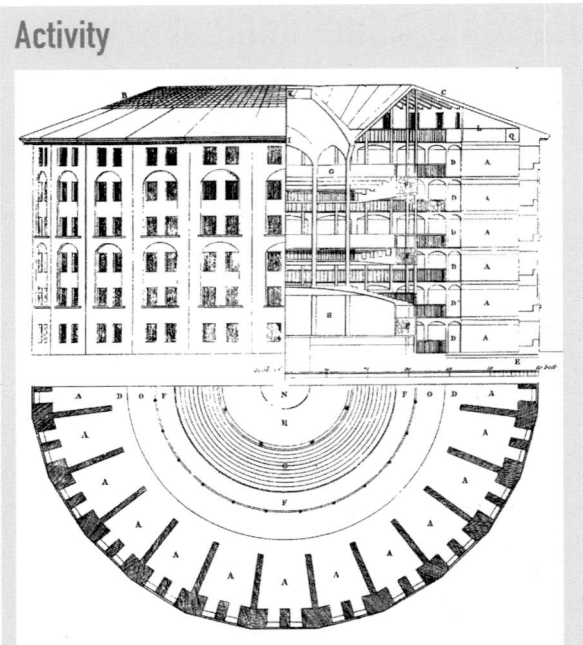

Bentham's design for the panopticon.

Do you think the fact that Bentham's design was never implemented weakens Foucault's thesis?

Critics have pointed to a number of problems with Foucault's thesis. First, Foucault arguably wants both to have his cake and eat it. He places enormous importance on the idea that prison seeks to correct inmates' behaviour through surveillance and discipline, but acknowledges that it often fails in this endeavour. This does not matter, he says, because prison is not really concerned with rehabilitation, but with controlling the working class. However, if this is the case, then why use imprisonment in the first place, given its expense? Second, his focus on 'correction' ignores the other functions that imprisonment can be seen as performing, such as incapacitation, deterrence and retribution. Finally, Garland (1986) argued that Foucault's attempt to explain punishment and penal history solely in terms of control seriously oversimplifies the extent to which penal policy is inevitably an uneasy compromise between the wishes and interests of a number of social actors, including the judiciary, politicians, penal reformers and the general public.

Update

Discipline and Punish was written before the digital age really took off. Technologies of surveillance have become far more sophisticated today with the ability to monitor people's online life: emails, texts, internet searches, online financial transactions and so on – leading to the claim that we now live in a '**surveillance society**'. Moreover, in 2013 the whistle blower Edward Snowden revealed that both the NSA in America and GCHQ in the UK had secretly been collecting massive amounts of personal data on their citizens.

The principal impetus behind the collection of such data is the hope that they can be used to identify and forestall potential terrorist attacks. In 2013, the White House claimed that more than 50 terror plots had been uncovered by the NSA's bulk collection of Americans' phone metadata (that is data about the origin and recipient of the call, the duration of the call, the location of both phones if mobile phones and so on). However, according to David Lyon (2015), two independent reviews published in 2014 showed that of 225 cases of terrorism investigated by the NSA, only 4 were prompted by the use of the phone metadata and none of these prevented attacks.

Lyon – drawing on the work of Eric Dahl – argues that research into planned terrorist attacks that have been successfully thwarted shows that what worked in these cases was not *mass* surveillance, but *targeted* surveillance of suspects identified by conventional police work, community tip-offs and informants.

The Investigatory Powers Act was passed in the UK in 2016 to regulate both mass and targeted surveillance activities of the police and security services, but critics argue that there are insufficient safeguards to protect individuals' rights to privacy.

Activity

Explain the joke.

David Garland

A more recent examination of crime control and punishment in the USA and the UK is provided by David Garland (2001), writing at a time when crime and criminal justice were at or near the top of the political agenda on both sides of the Atlantic. He argues that in the 1950s and 1960s penal policies in both countries took the form of 'penal welfarism' where the main goal of punishment was the rehabilitation of offenders. However, since the 1970s, Garland argues, a new 'culture of control' has developed which takes a more *punitive* (that is, punishing harshly) line in relation to offenders and is mainly concerned with reassuring the public that the (then) rapidly growing crime rate was under control.

These developments, Garland suggests, have been shaped by two underlying social forces: the distinctive features of late modern society and the growth of a free-market, socially conservative politics (neoliberalism). Late modern society is characterised by increasing individualism, greater insecurity (the end of a job for life for most people) combined with a weakening of social ties and growing anxiety about rising levels of (recorded) crime. These characteristics help explain a turn to what he calls '**popular punitivism**', associated with the anti-welfare politics of neoliberalism and a conception of the poor as an undeserving underclass.

Garland identified three main ways in which the state sought to reassure the public that crime was under control:

> The use of developmental crime control strategies where groups at risk of becoming criminals are identified at an early age and intervention strategies are implemented.

> 'Mass incarceration' – locking more people up in prison. Indeed, Garland argues that offenders are increasingly likely to spend much of their lives locked up because of this culture of control, moving from growing up in care, to young offender institutions, then to prison as adults with time also spent by some in mental hospitals in between: a process he calls 'transcarceration'.

> Politicians talking about being tough on crime as an electoral strategy to gain votes.

Roger Matthews (2005) challenged Garland's view that criminal policy had become more punitive in the UK and USA, arguing instead that it had become increasingly complex, opaque and diverse. Nevertheless, there can be no disputing the significant rise in the prison population that

179

has occurred in both the UK and the USA with the number in prison in the USA more than quadrupling between 1980 and 2010 and that in England and Wales nearly doubling between 1990 and 2015. Moreover, it is worth noting that the USA has the highest rate of incarceration in the world of any substantial nation at 666 per 100 000 and England and Wales the highest in Western Europe at 146 per 100 000, according to World Prison Brief (2017).

Key terms

Social mores Shared ideas of morally proper conduct.

Economic determinist The view that what happens in society is ultimately determined by economic factors.

Disciplinary power Power that seeks to get people to follow social rules by threatening them with sanctions if they do not and by encouraging the development of self-discipline.

Surveillance society A society where surveillance technology is widely used to monitor people's everyday activities.

Popular punitivism The idea that the general public want politicians to be tough on criminals and will vote for those who promise to be so.

Summary

1. Durkheim saw restitutive punishment as performing an important role in modern society by reaffirming the value consensus and demonstrating the consequences of infringing social mores.

2. Marxists see punishment as functioning to maintain class domination by the use of coercive force and argue that it is mainly inflicted on lower social classes.

3. Foucault saw the development of the prison as symbolic of the spread of disciplinary power in modern capitalist societies and saw its main function as an instrument of social control.

4. Garland argues that, in the final decades of the 20th century, the apparently unstoppable rise in (recorded) crime was associated with the development of a culture of control which relied increasingly on mass incarceration to try to reassure the public that crime was being tackled.

Unit 2.11.3 Victims and victimology

The idea that crime produces victims who suffer real physical, emotional and psychological harm and that this needs to be acknowledged is a relatively recent feature both of the operation of criminal justice and of criminology. Moreover, ironically, when victimology – the scientific study of victims – first emerged this fact was far from being the main focus of interest.

Patterns in victimisation

Victim surveys (see Unit 2.2.1) have helped shed light on the unequal distribution of victimisation within society. Analysis of the 2014 and 2015 Crime Surveys for England and Wales by Victim Support (Rossetti, Dinisman and Moroz, 2016) found the following, in relation to violent crime and theft.

> Gender: Men have a significantly greater risk of being victims of violence than women (though, it should be added, women are far more likely to be victims of domestic violence, sexual assaults and stalking).

> Age: Young people are at a greater risk of being victims of both theft and violence than older groups.

> Ethnicity: Those of mixed ethnicity are at greater risk of being victims of both violence and theft.

> Relationship status: People who are separated and single have the highest rates of victimisation in terms of violent crime and personal theft.

> Health status: Adults with limiting disability or longstanding illness had a higher risk of being a victim of violence with injury than adults with non-limiting disability/illness and those without any disability or illness.

> Household income: Those living in households with an income of under £10 000 are at the greatest risk of all forms of violence and form the second highest risk group for personal theft.

Theoretical perspectives in victimology

The theoretical perspectives that have been developed within victimology are less clear-cut than those within criminology itself, but two main perspectives are currently conventionally distinguished: positivist victimology and critical victimology.

Positivist victimology

Positivist approaches within victimology seek to identify and explain social patterns in victimisation while treating the category 'victim' as a given. According to David Miers (1989), positivist victimology has traditionally pursued three major concerns:

» identification of factors in individuals or their environment that make them more likely to be victims

» an understanding of the dynamics of inter-personal crimes of violence

» identification of the processes through which victims may contribute to their own victimisation.

Victim-precipitation theories

The first theory that is usually identified with positivist victimology was the '**duet theory**' put forward by Hans von Hentig (1948). He classified victims into 13 categories according to the over-riding factor that precipitated their victimisation, categories that included *the young, females, the mentally defective and deranged, the depressed, the lonesome or heartbroken and the tormentor*. He then identified the various ways in which they, in his view, 'invited' their own victimisation:

> *The inexperienced businessman, for example, invites embezzlement; the nagging wife is flirting with murder; the alcoholic is a natural for robbery. Thus the victim becomes the 'tempter'.*

Another early study was conducted by Marvin Wolfgang who investigated police homicide records in Philadelphia between 1948 and 1952. He concluded that in just over a quarter of the cases the victim had contributed in some way to their own death. Wolfgang identified three factors common to victim-precipitated homicides: (1) The victim and offender had some prior interpersonal relationship, (2) there was a series of escalating disagreements between the parties, and (3) the victim had consumed alcohol.

Some years later, a student of Wolfgang's, Menachem Amir (1968), used a similar research methodology and similar explanatory framework to examine 'forcible rape'. Based on his reading of police records of rapes that had taken place in Philadelphia between 1958 and 1960 he claimed that 1 in 5 were victim-precipitated. Among the characteristics he identified that distinguished victim-precipitated from non-victim-precipitated rapes were these:

» both victim and perpetrator were white

» victims were between 15 and 19 years of age

» either the victim or both the victim and offender had been consuming alcohol

» the victim had a 'bad' reputation

» the victim had met the offender in a bar or at a picnic or party.

Routine activities and lifestyle theories

More recently, Cohen and Felson's (1979) routine activities theory has been combined with a focus on victims' lifestyles to explore the risk factors for victimisation. Hindelang, Gottfredson and Garofalo (1978) used data from victimisation surveys conducted in 1972 in eight American cities to explore the lifestyle factors associated with an increased risk of being a victim of rape, robbery, assault or theft and particularly with the risk of multiple victimisation.

They identify five demographic factors that are particularly relevant: age, gender, marital status, family income and race – pointing out, for example, that married people are less likely to spend time alone in public and people on low incomes are more likely to use public transport and live in high crime areas. They also put forward a number of propositions regarding relevant lifestyle factors. For example, they suggest that the more time individuals spend in public places (especially at night and weekends) the more likely it is that they will be victimised and that the chances that individuals will be victims of crime increase as a function of the proportion of time that they spend among non-family members.

Evaluation of positivist victimology

Positivist victimology provides useful insights into the social patterning of victimisation and how the interaction between the victim and offender in some cases can affect the outcome of an attempted crime. Also, in identifying risk factors, it can suggest ways in which such risks can be reduced. However, critics have pointed to a number of weaknesses:

» The notion of victim-precipitation can easily shade into victim-blaming in which description becomes conflated with moral judgement and the victim is blamed for causing the offence. Studies such as von Hentig's and Amir's have been attacked by feminists for doing just this.

> It has largely ignored the victims of corporate, green and state crimes.

> It fails to recognise that powerful groups are able to influence whether the status of victimhood is conferred on, or withheld from, victims (see below).

> Because it tends to focus on the immediate situational context of offending, it misses the larger structural features that shape crime and which would offer alternative targets for crime reduction efforts, such as patriarchy and social inequality.

Activity

Suggest how feminists might respond to von Hentig's suggestion that *the nagging wife is flirting with murder*.

Critical victimology

Critical victimology can be seen as a direct counterpart to critical criminology (see Part 6). It locates victimisation within the wider structural features of a society divided along lines of class, gender, ethnicity, ability and sexuality. Spencer and Walklate (2016) identify three main ways in which critical victimology challenges positivist victimology:

> by analysing the role played by power (particularly in terms of the power of the state) in the identification or non-identification of crime victims

> by focusing on the 'hidden victims' of corporate and state crime

> by analysing processes of victim blaming, particularly – though not only – in relation to female victims.

Just as labelling theorists identify 'deviant' as a label applied to some, but not all, rule-breakers by those with power, so critical victimologists argue that the label 'victim' is applied to some, but not all those who are victims of crime, by those in positions of power.

Whyte (2007) argues that whether or not people are identified as victims depends on how closely they resemble the category of an **'ideal victim'**. Drawing on the earlier work of Christie (1986), he lists the characteristics that victims need to possess in order to gain public and media sympathy:

> the victim is weak

> the victim is involved in a respectable project

> the victim is in a place where they could not be blamed for being

> the offender is physically dominant and 'bad'

> the offender is unknown to the victim

> the victim needs to be unopposed by 'counter-powers' strong enough to silence the victim

> the victim is a victim of an interpersonal crime.

Victims of corporate and state crime

Victims of corporate and state crime are consequently often denied victimhood because they do not possess these characteristics. For example, following the 7 July bombings in London in 2005, Jean Charles de Menezes, was shot and killed on the London underground by armed police officers who had mistaken him for a fugitive terrorist suspect. Despite the obvious injustice of his killing, de Menezes was not officially defined as a victim. The Crown Prosecution Service decreed that there was too little evidence to prosecute the officers involved, and the coroner who chaired the inquest into de Menezes' death refused to allow a verdict of unlawful killing, resulting in an open verdict.

Similarly, research by Barr *et al*. (2016) suggested that since the introduction of Work Capability Assessments by the DWP in 2008 (designed to assess whether people should continue to receive the main out-of-work benefit for disabled people) as many as 590 additional suicides had occurred as a result of the stress generated by the tests. The government's response was to claim that 'this report is wholly misleading', thereby denying that people could have been victims of government policy.

In relation to victims of corporate crime, Whyte argues that the number of people killed by injuries and illnesses caused by work, by air pollution and by food poisoning far exceeds the number of people who die each year as a result of murder or manslaughter, but these victims remain largely hidden from view.

Victim-blaming

Critical victimologists argue that not only do many victims remain hidden from public view, but sometimes victims are blamed for their own victimisation. We have already seen in Unit 2.9.1 that this can be the case with female victims of rape, but it can also happen in relation to any group lacking social power. A noteworthy example is provided by the case of the Hillsborough disaster.

On 15 April 1989, 96 Liverpool FC supporters died as a result of being crushed at Sheffield's Hillsborough football stadium. For much of the time since then, those who died, alongside other Liverpool fans present on the day, were blamed for bringing the tragedy upon themselves. The South Yorkshire Police's match commander claimed on the day that Liverpool fans had broken through an exit-gate, rushed down a steep tunnel into the already packed central pens and thereby caused a fatal crush at the front of the pens. The media followed the next day with stories and editorials condemning 'yobbism at its most base' and 'uncontrolled fanaticism and mass hysteria', while *The Sun*'s front page, headlined 'THE TRUTH', claimed that some fans had picked the pockets of the dying, had urinated on police officers and had beaten up a police man attempting to resuscitate a dying fan.

It was not until 27 years later that a new inquest into the deaths ruled on 26 April 2016 that there had been no behaviour on the part of the Liverpool fans that had caused or contributed to a dangerous situation and that those who had died in the disaster had been 'unlawfully killed'. The second inquest was a product of the remarkable persistence of the Hillsborough Family Support Group and many other concerned Liverpool councillors, the MP Andy Burnham and religious leaders to gain justice for the dead fans.

Activity

A vigil in Liverpool city centre commemorating the victims of the Hillsborough disaster, held following the publication of the second inquest.

What parallels can be drawn between the Hillsborough cover-up and the Stephen Lawrence case examined in Unit 2.10.2?

The critical criminologist, Phil Scraton, who played a significant part in producing the research that led to the second inquest, argues that:

Hillsborough raises fundamental questions about institutional power and, to acknowledge the work of Michel Foucault, how the state mobilises **'regimes of truth'** *to deflect, diminish and defeat oppositional discourses.*
Times Higher Education, 01.12.2016

Evaluation of critical victimology

Critical victimology has played a useful role in drawing attention to the fact that the status of victimhood is not automatically conferred on the victims of crime and to the many 'hidden' victims of crimes of the powerful. However, as Spencer and Walklate acknowledge, it has not as yet produced a substantial body of work. Arguably, as yet, it may more reasonably be seen as complementing rather than replacing more positivistic approaches.

Key terms

Duet theory The theory that it is the interaction between the victim and offender that produces the offence.

Ideal victim Someone who fits the ideal type (or stereotype) of a victim (not 'ideal' in the sense of preferable).

Regimes of truth Descriptions of the world that claim the status of being true and, by doing so, serve the interests of the state.

Summary

1. Victimology is a relatively recent sub-discipline of criminology.

2. Victims are not distributed randomly throughout society and some are likely to experience multiple victimisation.

3. Positivist victimology explains victimhood as a product of victim precipitation or of the lifestyles adopted by people.

4. Critical victimology argues that victimhood is not an objective fact, but a status that can be conferred on or withheld from people and reflects power differences. It focuses on the process through which some people but not others become labelled as victims, on the victims of corporate, state and green crime and on the process of victim blaming.

EXAM PRACTICE QUESTIONS

A-LEVEL PAPER 3
CRIME AND DEVIANCE

0 1 Outline **two** ways in which laws may benefit the ruling class.　　　**[4 marks]**

0 2 Outline **three** reasons why official crime statistics may not give a true representation of crime.　　　**[6 marks]**

0 3 Read **Item A** and answer the question that follows.

> **Item A**
>
> Feminists have argued that women's involvement in crime has been ignored. Women have always offended, yet we know very little about the reasons why they offend. Much sociological crime literature has focused on the male offender, exploring the reasons for men's higher involvement in criminal and deviant behaviour. One argument for this is because official crime statistics show us that women do not participate in high levels of criminal behaviour and therefore explanations with regard to gender focus on the lack of criminal involvement of women. Different theorists have attempted to explain this by exploring both culture and control.

Applying material from **Item A**, analyse **two** reasons for the lesser involvement of women in criminal and deviant behaviour.　　　**[10 marks]**

0 4 Read **Item B** and answer the question that follows.

> **Item B**
>
> Most sociological theories have assumed that crime and deviance are harmful to society. They have concentrated on explaining why crime and deviance occur and have assumed that something must have gone wrong in society to cause the criminality and deviance. They have therefore tended to advocate new policies to reduce deviance and offending.
>
> However, other sociological theories have suggested that crime and deviancy can be functional for a society and help a society to evolve.

Applying the material from **Item B** and your own knowledge, evaluate the view that crime can be functional for a society.　　　**[30 marks]**

3 BELIEFS IN SOCIETY

Chapter contents

If you asked a representative sample of people in the UK what they believe in, the answers are likely to reveal a wide range of beliefs. On a global level, millions of people identify themselves as Muslim, Jewish, Hindu or Christian while less conventional beliefs include Spiritualism, Scientology and Paganism. This chapter explores the role of beliefs in society. It begins by examining different ways of defining religion. It asks why science often enjoys higher status than other sources of knowledge and belief. It then focuses on sociological accounts – both positive and negative – of the role of religion in society. How far do religious beliefs bind people together? To what extent does religion promote social stability? What are the links between religion, conflict and violence?

The chapter moves on to examine different types of religious organisation such as churches (for example, the Church of England) and sects (for example, the Branch Davidians in the USA). How does a church differ from a sect? What motivates people to join sects? Spiritual beliefs can thrive outside established religious organisations such as churches, and this chapter also looks at New Age movements, which include, for instance, belief in witchcraft or tarot card readings. Sociologists are interested in the relationship between religion and social class, gender, ethnicity and age. Are young people, for example, less likely to participate in religion than older people? A main focus of the chapter concerns whether religion is becoming less significant in the modern world. Is religion declining in importance or are different things happening in different societies within a global context? This chapter suggests answers to these and other important questions.

PART 1 IDEOLOGY, SCIENCE AND RELIGION

Contents

In diverse societies such as Britain, people's beliefs vary enormously. A particular individual's beliefs may be based on, for example, science, faith, tradition, common sense, personal experience or any combination of these. Some people believe in ghosts, astrology or telepathy. Others believe in the teachings of a particular faith such as Christianity, Hinduism, Islam or Judaism. Yet others place their faith firmly in science and rational thought.

Sociologists are interested in understanding the different belief systems in society. A belief system is a set of ideas held by individuals or groups that help them to interpret and make sense of the world. Examples include religious and scientific belief systems. But what do we actually mean by religion and science? Are these belief systems completely different from each other? Is scientific knowledge really superior to religious beliefs? Part 1 of this chapter looks at contrasting sociological definitions of religion. It also explores different views on science as a belief system. It then examines the concept of ideology and how this contributes to an understanding of belief systems.

Unit 3.1.1 Definitions of religion

Religions are important examples of belief systems. Religious **beliefs** exist in every known society and, on a global scale, their variety is immense. In order to study and explain **religion** from a sociological approach, it is necessary to define it. Any definition of religion must take account of this rich diversity. However, sociologists disagree on the question of what religion means and how to define it. What are the sources of this disagreement? Is there necessarily a clear-cut boundary between religious and non-religious phenomena? Is it essential to agree on a single definition? This unit looks at some of the issues and problems involved in defining religion.

Different types of definition of religion

Initially, defining religion might seem to be a fairly straightforward task. Belief systems such as Judaism, Islam and Christianity are clear examples of world religions. Each of these has its own set of beliefs and values that followers are expected to stick to. Each one also has its own practices, **rituals** and symbols.

One problem that sociologists face when defining religion is that of devising a definition that is broad enough to encompass the wide variety of beliefs without also including phenomena that are not usually considered to be religious, such as astrology or fortune telling. The different sociological definitions of religion can be divided into three types: substantive definitions, functional definitions and social constructionist approaches.

Substantive definitions of religion

Substantive definitions of religion focus on the substance or content of religion and are concerned with what religion is. They can take several forms. Émile Durkheim (1961, first published 1912) defined religion in terms of a distinction between **the sacred and the profane**. In his view, religion is 'a unified system of beliefs and practices relative to sacred things', that is to say, things 'set apart and forbidden'. Sacred objects – such as the cross in Christianity – produce a sense of awe, veneration and respect. Profane objects, by contrast, are ordinary or mundane. However, critics point out that not all cultures distinguish between the sacred and the profane. They also argue that, in some cases, religious objects are not always treated with respect. In Southern Italy, for instance, the statues of Catholic saints who do not respond to prayer may be turned upside down or replaced (Hamilton, 2001). Another problem is that people such as political leaders and objects such as national flags could be seen as sacred in that they inspire deep respect even though they are not connected to any religions.

A substantive definition may also define religion in terms of a belief in the supernatural, in divine forces, powers or spiritual beings such as a god or gods that are above the laws of nature. Malcolm Hamilton (2001) argues, however, that such definitions are problematic because some belief systems which are commonly regarded as religions, such as forms of Buddhism, do not necessarily include a belief in supernatural beings. This highlights the potential problem of defining and using the concept of religion from a Western perspective.

Functional definitions of religion

Functional definitions view religion in terms of the functions or roles it performs for individuals or society rather than in terms of its substance. In other words, they focus on what religion does rather than what it is (Hamilton, 2001). Durkheim's definition of religion includes a substantive element by referring to sacred things. However, it also contains a functional element by focusing on the role or function of religion in uniting its followers in a community of believers and reinforcing **social cohesion**.

J. Milton Yinger adopted a functional definition of religion as 'a system of beliefs and practices by means of which a group of people struggles with the ultimate problems of human life' (1970, quoted in Hamilton, 2001). However, Hamilton notes several problems with such a definition. First, it is too broad and would encompass a wide variety of belief systems in the category 'religion'. For example, by this definition, a political belief system such as communism could be seen as a religion because of the function it performs even though it explicitly rejects religious beliefs. Second, Yinger's definition is based on prejudgements about the roles and purposes of religion in all societies when in fact these roles and purposes might vary between societies. Rather than making assumptions about what the roles are before starting a study, sociologists should actually undertake research in order to uncover them. In this case, a definition of religion would emerge only after the study has been completed rather than at the outset. Third, phrases such as 'the ultimate problems of human life' are open to interpretation. Hamilton points out that, for many people, the ultimate problems of life might be 'simply how to enjoy it as much as possible, how to avoid pain and ensure pleasure'. Many other aspects of social life, apart from religion, address such issues – for example, medicine and leisure.

Inclusive and exclusive definitions of religion

All definitions emphasise some aspects of religion and exclude others. Alan Aldridge (2007) distinguishes between more inclusive and more exclusive definitions. With **inclusive definitions**, it is relatively easy for a belief system to qualify as a religion if, for example, it promotes unity or reinforces social cohesion. Religion is defined broadly and could include devotion to a football team, loyalty to a rock band, hip hop or rap artist, or a deep commitment to one's country. (See also Unit 3.2.1 for an account of civil religion.) Generally, functional definitions of religion tend to be more inclusive.

Broad or inclusive definitions would include political belief systems such as nationalism, fascism and communism. One potential problem with using broad definitions is that they would result in religion being found everywhere. With more narrow or **exclusive definitions**, the criteria are more restrictive and the focus is on the content of religion, for example a belief in a supernatural power such as a god or gods. Substantive definitions of religion tend to be more exclusive.

Activity

Inclusive, functional definitions would classify devotion to a football team as a religion.

1. How far does football support involve the following characteristics:

   a) rituals

   b) sacred symbols

   c) faith

   d) a sense of group identity and being bound together?

2. To what extent would you see loyal devotion to a football team as a religion?

Social constructionist approaches to the study of religion

Social constructionist approaches are sometimes referred to as 'definitions in use' (Giddens and Sutton, 2013). They focus on how the term 'religion' is used by different individuals, groups and organisations. Research in this area explores what people say and mean when they talk about religion and participate in practices that they consider to be religious. This approach places more emphasis on whatever passes for religion in society and the meanings that people give to it rather than on questions about what religion is or what it does.

James Beckford (2003) adopts a social constructionist approach in order to understand religion. In his view, religion does not have 'a single, common sense meaning in everyday life'. Religion is a **contested concept** and there are disputes about what counts as religion. Powerful interest groups are prepared not only to defend 'their definition of religion against opponents' but also to enforce it. This can be seen, for example, in the measures taken by anti-witchcraft movements around the world. Today, there are controversies about whether Scientology is a religion. Such disputes suggest that religions are not taken-for-granted phenomena within societies.

Beckford challenges the view that religion can be easily defined. The search for a 'correct' conceptualisation of religion is 'unwise in view of the immense variation in the meanings attributed to the term in everyday life'. Furthermore, it is neither possible nor necessary to produce a definition of religion that all social scientists would accept. Instead, Beckford focuses on the uses that individuals, groups and agencies such as the mass media, schools and the state make of religion in everyday life.

The assumptions behind the different definitions of religion

When considering the different approaches to the issue of defining religion, it is important to bear in mind that they tend to reflect the theoretical assumptions and specific arguments being put forward by individual sociologists. For example, the argument that religion is becoming less important in society (part of the secularisation debate) is usually based on traditional church religion (see Part 6). In practice, however, there is general agreement that belief systems such as Hinduism, Islam, Christianity, Buddhism and Judaism are religions. The disputes tend to occur over phenomena that can be seen as on the fringes of

religion such as the **New Age movement**. Examples of New Age beliefs include paganism as well as interest in clairvoyance or different types of meditation.

Key terms

Beliefs Ideas or convictions that individuals or groups hold to be true even when they are not based on evidence.

Religion Often defined narrowly as a belief system related to supernatural beings or divine forces. However, there are several ways of defining religion including substantive, functional and social constructionist approaches.

Rituals Religious practices or ceremonies comprising a set of actions that are carried out in an established order.

Substantive definitions (of religion) Definitions that focus on the substance or content of religion, or what religion is rather than what it does.

The sacred and the profane The distinction that Durkheim made between things that are set apart and inspire reverential attitudes among followers (the sacred) and ordinary, everyday things (the profane).

Functional definitions (of religion) Definitions that focus on the functions or roles of religion, or what religion does rather than what it is.

Social cohesion The idea that members of society should share a set of values that unite them into a body of citizens.

Inclusive definitions (of religion) Broad definitions that could include traditional religions and other belief systems such as nationalism, communism and humanism.

Exclusive definitions (of religion) Narrow definitions that include traditional religions but exclude other belief systems.

Social constructionist approach (to defining religion) Rather than trying to provide a single definition that all sociologists would accept, this approach focuses on how religion is used in daily life.

Contested concept A concept or key idea such as religion for which there is no agreement on its meaning; it means different things to different theorists.

New Age movement Diverse and loosely organised groups within which people seek spiritual experiences, inner peace or growth through, for example, meditation, crystal healing and/or aromatherapy.

Summary

1. Sociologists disagree on how to define religion and there are several different definitions of the concept.

2. Substantive definitions focus on what religion is and its content such as belief in supernatural forces or supreme beings.

3. Functional definitions focus on what religion does and the purposes, functions or roles that it performs.

4. Durkheim's definition of religion contained both functional and substantive elements.

5. Inclusive definitions define religion in broad terms. Exclusive definitions are narrower in focus.

6. Rather than searching for a correct or agreed definition of religion, social constructionist approaches focus on the uses that individuals, groups and agencies make of religion in everyday life.

7. Any definition of religion is likely to reflect particular theoretical assumptions and arguments.

Unit 3.1.2 Science as a belief system

In many societies, scientific knowledge is often seen as superior to other types of knowledge such as religious beliefs. Science earns its high status because of the methods it uses to provide knowledge that is generally considered to be objective and based on evidence. This knowledge is often utilised for the benefit of humankind. For example, medical research has led to the eradication of smallpox, the control of leprosy and the development of a vaccine against polio. However, does science really deserve its high status? Is scientific knowledge genuinely superior to other sources of knowledge and beliefs in society? This unit looks at contrasting views of science and questions some of the **knowledge claims** of science. It also explores the relationship between scientific and religious belief systems.

Auguste Comte and the stages in the development of knowledge

Auguste Comte (1986, first published in the 1940s) saw science as superior to religion and superstition as a form of knowledge. He identified three stages that a society would move through in its development of knowledge: the theological, metaphysical and positive stages.

Table 3.1.1 Three evolutionary stages of society and human thought

Stage	Period in European history	Description of the stage
Stage 1: Theo -logical	Up to the 14th century	People thought in supernatural terms. They explained the natural and social worlds in terms of supernatural forces or the actions of gods.
Stage 2: Meta- physical	From the 14th century to around 1800	Supernatural forces were still an important source of explanations. However, these explanations became more systematic and consistent. They focused more on abstract forces rather than on God as a concrete individual.
Stage 3: Positive or scientific stage	Began in the early 19th century	Science and reason replaced religion and superstition as means of explaining the world.

Comte saw the social changes associated with **industrialisation** as involving the progressive triumph of scientific rationality. As a result, scientific investigation would be based on rational thinking, reason, logic and evidence. Comte believed that modern society would be dominated by science. The influence of religion and superstition would be replaced by 'positivist' science that uses objective, scientific methods. Supporters of positivism (see Chapter 1, Unit 1.5.1) argued that science was the only valid form of knowledge.

Science and the Enlightenment

The **Enlightenment** refers to a range of scientific, social and philosophical beliefs that developed in Western Europe in the 17th and 18th centuries. Enlightenment thinking rejected belief in the supernatural and in superstition as ways of understanding the world. It argued that knowledge could only come from reason and rational ways of thought. (See also Chapter 1, Unit 1.2.1 for a discussion of Weber's account of rational action.) Enlightenment thinking is seen as the foundation of modernity. Modernity is a phase in human history during which faith is placed in science. For example, it is believed that humankind can use scientific knowledge to bring about progress, improve people's lives, fight disease and tackle natural disasters.

Open and closed belief systems

Science and religion are both sources of knowledge and beliefs but they differ in important respects. Some sociologists, anthropologists and philosophers distinguish between **open belief systems** and **closed belief systems**. (Bear in mind that these are not the same as Andrew Sayer's open and closed systems discussed in Chapter 1, Unit 1.5.6) Robin Horton (1993), for example, highlighted differences between open and closed systems of ideas. He argued that science is an open system as its knowledge claims are based on evidence. Science operates in an open environment and is characterised by questioning, testing and the subsequent revision of ideas. As a result, science is constantly developing. By contrast, closed systems of ideas such as magic and religion are not open to criticism or to alternative views. Consequently, religion is conservative and does not change or develop its ideas over time.

Horton argued, however, that religion and magic are in some respects similar to science. Each tries to make sense of the world and understand how it operates in order to control it for human purposes. Critics disagree, arguing that religion and magic are fundamentally different from science. For example, scientific propositions are testable whereas religious beliefs are based on faith and cannot be tested. Unlike non-scientific belief systems, science enables people to explain, predict and control the world. It can also confirm its explanations in terms of its practical results, for example by eradicating diseases or predicting when a volcano will erupt. Religion, however, is unable to confirm its explanations in this way.

Bryan Wilson (1966) identified a shift away from religious thinking towards rational thinking. He argued that the development of rational thinking was encouraged partly by a greater knowledge of the physical and social world. This resulted from the development of the natural and social sciences. Scientific knowledge is based on reason and the testing of arguments and beliefs. By contrast, religion is based on faith and, as such, is non-rational. Its **truth claims** cannot be tested by rational procedures.

Karl Popper

Karl Popper (1959) argued that science is an open belief system. Scientists put forward statements and then test them systematically by observation and experiment. Scientific theories are open to scrutiny, criticism and testing by peers.

However, Popper challenged the traditional view that scientific discovery and knowledge are based on verification or proof (see Chapter 1, Unit 1.5.6). He argued that it is impossible to verify a theory or show it to be completely accurate. It is always possible that a theory will be falsified or proved wrong at some point in the future. For example, 'No matter how many instances of white swans we may have observed, this does not justify the conclusion that all swans are white.' (Popper, 2002). It only takes one observation of a black swan to disprove the idea that all swans are white.

So Popper argued that all scientific knowledge is provisional, 'for the time being', (Popper, 1979) rather than certain or true for all time. Science is based on falsification rather than verification. Science progresses by gradually building on the achievements of other scientists. Good science involves a process of conjecture and refutation (or trial and error). In other words, scientists put forward hypotheses and test them to try to prove them wrong. The aim of the scientist is 'not to discover absolute certainty, but to discover better and better theories ... capable of being put to more and more severe tests'. These 'theories must be falsifiable. It is through their falsification that science progresses'.

According to Popper, scientific knowledge is distinctive because it is not absolute or sacred truth and can be questioned and tested. By contrast, with non-scientific thought such as religion or magic, explanations are not tested. Popper argues that subjective experiences or strong feelings of conviction 'cannot be accepted by science' (Popper, 2002). Someone may be completely convinced of the truth of something but this conviction cannot be seen as an objective scientific statement if it cannot be tested. For example, statements such as 'God exists' are not scientific because they cannot be tested or falsified. Scientific statements must be open to testing, falsification, criticism and revision.

Activity

In Popper's view, we only need one observation of a black swan to falsify the idea that all swans are white.

1. To what extent do you agree with Popper's view that all scientific knowledge is provisional?

2. Drawing on Popper's ideas, explain one difference between scientific knowledge and religious thought.

Merton's contribution to the sociology of science

Robert K. Merton (1973) showed that natural scientists, like everyone else, were subject to social influences. In his view, science was a social activity in that it took place within institutional settings. Merton examined how science as an institution organised and regulated itself. He examined the ethos of modern science and identified four key norms that guided scientists' actions and behaviour within scientific organisations. These norms – which enabled science to be carried out – were communism, universalism, disinterestedness and organised scepticism. They are sometimes referred to as CUDOS for short.

Communism Scientific knowledge and findings are common property; they are publicly or collectively owned resources. Scientists are expected to communicate their findings, publish their work and, in this way, openly share it with others in the scientific community. As a result, other scientists can use it to build and advance the body of scientific knowledge.

Universalism New scientific knowledge is to be judged solely in terms of universal, objective and impersonal criteria (for example, by testing it). This means that truth claims about the world are not accepted or rejected depending on the personal or social characteristics of the people making the claims (for example, their nationality, class, gender, ethnicity or age). The norm of universalism also means that scientists advance their careers solely in terms of their talent.

Disinterestedness Scientists are expected to be objective and impartial in their approach to their work. If they cheated or exaggerated, this would threaten the great respect that the public gives to scientific knowledge.

Organised scepticism All aspects of the real world, all ideas, beliefs and knowledge claims are seen as open to scientific scrutiny and objective analysis.

People's faith in science and in the high-status, rational knowledge that scientists produce is based on these norms. However, critics argue that Merton's account of the norms governing scientists is idealistic rather than realistic. They also point out that scientific knowledge is a social construction rather than a description of an objective reality.

Critical views of science as an open system

One view is that science is an open belief system and that religion is a closed belief system. However, sociologists and philosophers now question how far science is an open system. This implies that scientific knowledge may not be as trustworthy as is usually assumed.

Thomas Kuhn and paradigm shifts

Thomas Kuhn (1962), a historian and philosopher of science, examined the way that science is practised, and identified the social processes involved in the practice of science. As a result, he challenged the view that scientific discovery is based on rational and critical enquiry (see Chapter 1, Unit 1.5.6). Rather than being open minded, scientists tend to be closed and conservative as a community.

Kuhn saw science as a closed system of ideas and argued that progress in science is neither linear nor gradual. Science is committed to a particular scientific paradigm or a set of beliefs shared by a group of scientists. Kuhn did not accept that scientists are completely objective or that they accept or reject a paradigm on the basis of evidence alone. For example, they may ignore any evidence that contradicts the paradigm and resist new ideas. Change in scientific knowledge comes about via the replacement of one scientific paradigm by another during a scientific revolution. For instance, the shift from Newtonian to Einsteinian science can be seen as an example of a paradigm shift.

The distinction between reconstructed logics and logics in use

Positivists and Popper claim that science uses established methods and procedures. However, Kaplan (1964) pointed out that it is necessary to distinguish between 'reconstructed logics' and 'logics in use'. Reconstructed logics consist of the methods and procedures that scientists claim that they use when, for example, they present their work at conferences or in academic papers and books. Both positivism and Popper's methodological approaches represent reconstructed logic. There is no guarantee, however, that scientists do actually follow such procedures in practice. By contrast, logics in use refer to what scientists actually do during their research and the methods and procedures they use. According to Kaplan, their logics in use may depart considerably from their reconstructed logics.

Laboratory-based studies of science

Over the last 50 years, traditional views about science have been challenged and ideas have changed significantly. For example, studies of science now question how far scientists produce objective knowledge. One area of scrutiny is the practice of science, the way that scientific knowledge is produced, rather than the content of science. Research focuses on the way that scientific knowledge is manufactured or constructed inside the natural settings of laboratories.

Michael Lynch (1983) conducted research in a psycho-biological laboratory and his findings suggested that scientists may be less objective than they claim. The scientists studied brain functioning by examining thin slices of rats' brains under microscopes. Photographs and slides of the brain slices were examined to see how useful they were in developing theories of brain functioning.

Sometimes, unexplained features were found in the photographs. Very often, these were put down to some error or glitch in the production of the photograph or slide. They were seen as **artefacts** rather than as real features of rats' brain. Some of these features were held to be an error in staining. Others were believed to be the result of scratching of the specimen when it was being sliced.

There was much discussion in the laboratory about whether these features were artefacts or not. In reaching their conclusion, the scientists were influenced by their existing theories, and the types of feature they were looking for and expected to find. If the visible marks on the slide or photograph did not fit the scientists' theories of how rats' brains functioned, they were much more likely to dismiss the marks as errors. Their interpretations of the data were guided by their theories.

Far from following Popper's methodology and striving to falsify their theories, the scientists tried to use the evidence to confirm them. Many scientists may be reluctant to dismiss perhaps years of intellectual effort and research because a single piece of evidence does not support the theory that they have developed.

Steve Woolgar (1988) pointed out that science influences all aspects of modern life and enjoys high status as a way of producing reliable knowledge. However, he was sceptical about the knowledge claims of sciences. Woolgar saw science as a social activity and focused on the social context of science. He was interested in what goes on in science on a daily basis and what scientists do in laboratories. In his view, there is little to separate science from other social activities. He took issue with the concept of science and argued that science is not, in fact, distinct from other forms of social activity or knowledge production. There is nothing inherently special about 'the scientific method' and, in practice, scientists do not necessarily stick to it. In Woolgar's view, science activities are constructive (in that scientific 'facts' are constructed in laboratories) rather than descriptive.

In *Laboratory Life: The Construction of Scientific Facts*, Latour and Woolgar (1986) drew on their data from an ethnographic study of the work carried out by scientists in a laboratory setting. Latour and Woolgar were interested in 'the way in which the daily activities of working scientists lead to the construction of facts'. By working as a laboratory technician, Latour observed at first hand 'daily encounters, working discussions, gestures, and a variety of guarded behaviour'. He was able to explore the daily processes of routine scientific work, laboratory life and how scientific knowledge is produced. Through overt participant observation, he collected information that does not appear in scientists' research reports or in other accounts of their work.

Latour and Woolgar illuminated the social construction of scientific knowledge and facts by focusing on 'the process by which scientists make sense of their observations'. They analysed conversations and informal discussions between scientists at work in the laboratory and highlighted the scientists' construction of facts. They saw scientific activity as 'just one social arena in which knowledge is constructed'.

Along similar lines, Karin Knorr Cetina (2005) undertook an ethnographic study of a science laboratory and concluded that science is constructive rather than simply descriptive. She refers to this approach as constructionism. For example, laboratories are artificial settings and the 'nature' found in them is also artificial. In these settings, scientists do not deal with 'nature-in-the-raw (like weather conditions, seasonal and temporal constraints on plant growth...).' Instead, they deal with '... a nature miniaturized and remodeled in other ways such that it can be processed in a rationalized and accelerated manner.'

Activity

Sociologists who undertake laboratory-based studies explore how scientists construct scientific knowledge.

1. Explain two advantages of using an ethnographic approach to study the work carried out by scientists in laboratories.

2. Outline and explain two arguments for the view that science is an open belief system.

3. Outline and explain two arguments against the view that science is an open belief system.

Postmodernism and science

Most postmodernists are sceptical about all claims to absolute or objective knowledge. They challenge the objectivity and truth of science and other belief systems. Truth is not something that exists 'out there' waiting to be discovered through the use of objective scientific methods. Instead, truth is created or constructed by people.

Postmodernists argue that people no longer place their trust unquestioningly in science or scientists. People increasingly question the power of science to solve global problems such as famine or natural disasters and to produce a better world. In fact, science and technology have negative side effects. For example, the use of vehicles such as cars and aeroplanes contributes to air pollution and global warming; the use of fertilisers can produce nitrous oxide, a greenhouse gas associated with global warming. Rather than being linked to human liberation and progress, science has been involved in the development of weapons of mass destruction. Rather than providing truth, the truth claims of science have been challenged by sceptical philosophers and historians of science.

Jean-François Lyotard (1984) argued that science and religions rest on 'metanarratives' – grand theories, 'big stories' or myths – that give meaning to other narratives or stories. For example, science provides a metanarrative or a big story about evolution by natural selection. Metanarratives give a sense of purpose to scientific endeavour and a sense of direction to social life. They suggest that humans can progress, through science, towards defeating ignorance and oppression, and that science can help humans to conquer nature.

According to Lyotard, postmodernist views have undermined scientific and other metanarratives. An 'incredulity towards metanarratives' develops. People no longer put their faith in these big, all-embracing theories about how the world works. They become sceptical that any set of beliefs can provide a means of understanding and resolving the problems of humanity. They no longer believe that reason can conquer superstition.

Lyotard's critics point out, however, that nationalist and religious metanarratives are still powerful forces in some countries. They also argue that although Lyotard dismisses the possibility of objective knowledge, he nonetheless claims to have accurately described key changes in society such as an increased scepticism about science. However, if objective knowledge is not possible, then there is no reason to believe that Lyotard's claim about science is any more 'true' than claims made by sociologists who disagree with him.

Contemporary issues: Labelling obesity as a disease

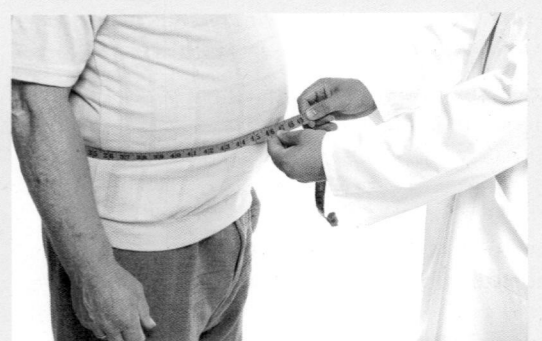

The issue of whether obesity should be regarded as a disease is controversial.

The Obesity Society based in the USA commissioned a panel of experts from among its members to review the issue of labelling obesity as a disease. Whether obesity should be declared a disease is controversial, and thoughtful arguments have been made on both sides of the issue. The panel reviewed several approaches to the issue of whether obesity should be classified as a disease.

One, the scientific approach, proceeds by firstly identifying the characteristics that entities must have in order to be considered diseases. Secondly, it examines empirical evidence (data based on observation or experience rather than on theory) to determine whether obesity possesses those characteristics. The scientific approach would be well suited to answering the question 'Is obesity a disease?' However, the panel concluded that this question cannot be answered. This is not because of a lack of agreement or understanding about obesity. It is due to the lack of a clear, widely accepted, and scientifically applicable definition of 'disease' that allows one to objectively and empirically determine whether specific conditions are diseases.

Another approach to this issue was termed the utilitarian approach and it asks 'Should obesity be considered a disease?' This is an ethical and moral question. It recognises that there is no clear agreed-on definition of disease with precise, assessable criteria. It seems that conditions that produce adverse health outcomes come to be considered diseases as the result of a social process when it is assessed to be beneficial to the greater good that they be so judged. Such judgements about likely benefit to the greater good are utilitarian judgements that may involve empirical evidence but must also assume certain values.

The panel concluded that considering obesity a disease is likely to have far more positive than negative consequences. It is likely to benefit the greater good by soliciting more resources into prevention, treatment, and research of obesity; and by reducing the stigma and discrimination heaped on many obese people. The panel felt that this utilitarian analysis was a legitimate approach to addressing the topic. It is also the approach used for many other conditions labelled diseases, even if not explicitly so. One cannot scientifically prove either that obesity is a disease or that it is not a disease. However, a utilitarian approach supports the position that obesity should be declared a disease.

Source: Adapted from Obesity as a Disease: A White Paper on Evidence and Arguments Commissioned by the Council of The Obesity Society. *Obesity,* vol. 16, no. 6, pp. 1161–1177. June 2008. Authors: The Council of The Obesity Society.

Questions

1. According to this article, why is it not possible to answer the question 'Is obesity a disease?' from a scientific perspective?

2. What is meant by the 'utilitarian approach' in this context?

3. Explain why an answer to the question 'Should obesity be classified as a disease?' would involve making a value judgement.

Feminism, Marxism and science

A number of feminists reject Robert K. Merton's view that universalism is a key norm in science and question how far scientists' careers are influenced by their gender. They argue that women are under-represented in science, for example in scientific occupations, in well-paid, higher-level positions in science departments within universities and in terms of their access to resources to carry out research.

Activity

Some feminists see Western science as dominated by privileged White men while others argue that the culture of science is gendered.

1. Which research method or methods would you use to investigate how far Western science is dominated by White men from privileged backgrounds?

2. Why would you use your chosen method or methods to investigate this particular topic?

3. Which method or methods would you use to investigate how far the culture of science is gendered?

4. Explain why you would use the method or methods you have selected to investigate this topic.

Some feminists see Western science as dominated by White men from privileged social backgrounds. Science is therefore influenced by such men's perspectives. Others argue that the culture of science as well as its institutions, language, methods and interpretations are gendered. They argue that scientific knowledge is not objective or neutral because sexist ideas about gender contribute to its construction. This can be seen, for example, in some scientific claims about differences between female and male brains (see Unit 3.1.3).

Marxists, like feminists, are critical of science and its role in society. In their view, science and technology serve the interests of capitalism rather than those of humankind. Science is geared towards generating profits for the bourgeoisie (the ruling class in capitalist society) rather than improving the lives of the proletariat (the subject class). For example, many developments in industry, such as mass production in factories, were introduced to increase the profits that the capitalist class made. Similarly, developments in agriculture, such as genetically modified crops that are resistant to pests, are designed with profits in mind. Big businesses fund scientific research but are only likely to invest in research projects that will increase their profit margins. More recent innovations such as computerisation and the internet are geared towards ensuring the spread and profitability of global capitalism (see Unit 3.1.3 for feminist and Marxist accounts of ideology).

The relationship between scientific and religious belief systems

Some commentators see science and religion as compatible belief systems that can exist together without tension. Others see the two as competing with each other in terms of how they explain the nature of the world. In this view, they are completely incompatible because their ideas clash.

Science and religion as compatible

Science and religion can be seen as compatible for a number of reasons.

1. Stephen Jay Gould (1999, cited in Bainbridge, 2009) was a scientist who argued strongly for evolutionary theories of biology. Evolutionary theories support the idea of natural selection and argue that those organisms that were well adapted to their environment survive and breed, leading to the gradual development of increasingly complex organisms. Gould dismissed biblical claims that the world was created by God in six days. Nevertheless, he argued that there is no conflict between science and religion because they are concerned with different aspects of human life and human needs. Gould claimed that one type of human need is the need to understand the facts about how nature works. Science has the authority and power to teach about this. However, humans also have a drive to give meaning to their own lives and to find a basis for their moral views. Because meaning and morality cannot come from facts – they are too subjective – religion can fulfil this purpose without being in direct conflict with science.

2. Following Weber's ideas on the Protestant ethic (see Unit 3.3.1), it can be argued that Calvinist Protestantism encouraged the development of rational thought, which in turn encouraged the development of science.

3. Some religions, particularly Scientology, claim to be based upon scientific knowledge. Scientologists believe that their founder (the science fiction writer L. Ron Hubbard) uncovered the science of Dianetics. This revealed that people's minds were blocked by engrams. A device known as an e-meter could detect these and the blockages could then be removed.

4. Steve Bruce (2011) argues that science and religion can exist together quite easily. Not many people have a great deal of knowledge about scientific methods and discoveries. In his view, science is unlikely to disprove religious faith if that faith is backed up and supported by a strong religious community.

Science and religion as incompatible

An alternative view is that science and religion are fundamentally incompatible. For example, Richard Dawkins (2006) argues that belief in all 'supernatural gods' is simply a delusion completely at odds with all scientific beliefs. Dawkins rejects Gould's idea that religion can provide answers to questions that science cannot. Although he accepts that science may not have answers to questions such as the meaning of life, he sees no reason why religion should be seen as offering any expertise in such areas.

Dawkins dismisses a wide range of arguments for the existence of God, using a combination of rational argument and evolutionary biology. For example, he argues against the idea of **intelligent design** (the argument that the natural world is so complex that it must have been designed by a God). In his view, the development of ever-more complex life-forms was the result of the evolutionary process of natural selection.

Dawkins claims that religion is based on faith. In his view, faith is an inadequate and positively harmful basis for believing in something. It is harmful because it involves believing something without question despite the lack of any evidence to back it up. This can lead, for example, to acts of terror being carried out on religious grounds.

Problems with viewing science and religion as compatible

Many sociologists and natural scientists believe in scientific technology while also believing in a god or gods, or the supernatural. This suggests that there may be a greater variety of relationships between science and religion than might be indicated by those who see them as fundamentally incompatible. One possibility is that religion and science may accommodate each other. However, Bainbridge identifies a number of problems with the idea that religion and science can easily exist together.

1. Religion tends to interpret the world and the universe from a human standpoint (an **anthropocentric view**). For example, Christianity originally saw the earth as the centre of the universe. However, Galileo undermined this view by demonstrating that the earth orbited the sun rather than vice versa. Anthropocentric views have been further undermined by later developments in science. For instance, the argument that God created the earth specifically for the benefit of humans is undermined by the realisation that intelligent life could have emerged on some of the many diverse planets in the universe simply by chance (Bainbridge, 2009).

Activity

EVERY MORNING THE SUN COMES UP IN THE SAME PLACE, MOVES ACROSS THE SKY AND GOES DOWN ON THE OTHER SIDE. CLEARLY, THE SUN GOES ROUND THE EARTH.

People used to believe that the sun goes round the earth. In the 17th century, Galileo, an Italian astronomer, was convicted of heresy by the Roman Catholic Church for his hypothesis that the earth revolves around the sun.

1. Drawing on Galileo's experience, explain one way in which religion can be seen as a closed belief system.

2. Explain one way in which science can undermine beliefs based on religion.

2. There is an increasing tendency towards the unification of science into a single science as scientists seek a theory of everything. If such a theory is achieved, this will make it difficult for religion to find any gaps in knowledge that it can claim to fill. In this case, the conflict between science and religion is likely to grow.

3. Religion might not fulfil positive functions in society and therefore it may be difficult to provide scientific justification for maintaining religious beliefs. For example, Stark and Bainbridge (1985) suggest that religion acts as a form of deception. If this is the case, it might prove difficult to justify the continued existence of religion.

Despite these points, Bainbridge does not believe it is impossible for religion to continue to be popular alongside increasingly sophisticated scientific beliefs. The results of survey research in the USA suggest that it is perfectly possible for a high percentage of the population to continue to hold beliefs that are incompatible with science (for example, the belief that astrology has some scientific truth). People are able to hold both religious and scientific beliefs, even when they directly contradict one another.

Key terms

Knowledge claims Information or statements (such as claims about what the world is like) that a particular individual, group or belief system believes to be true but are nonetheless open to debate.

Industrialisation The process involving the introduction of mechanised methods of mass production in, for example, the manufacture of goods in factories and the use of machines in agriculture to increase productivity.

Enlightenment The period from the 17th century in Europe that emphasised reason, was sceptical about religious belief systems and put its faith in natural science and progress.

Open belief system A set of ideas that makes knowledge claims based on the testing of evidence. As a result, its beliefs develop over time. Science is seen as an open belief system that tests evidence through observation and experimentation.

Closed belief system A set of ideas that is not open to testing or criticism so its beliefs tend not to change. Religion and magic are seen as examples of closed belief systems. Religion, for instance, is based on faith rather than on the testing of evidence.

Truth claims Statements or ideas that particular individuals, groups or belief systems (such as religions or science) hold to be true.

Artefacts Things produced by the research process (resulting from, for example, a technical glitch or error) that do not exist in the phenomenon being studied.

Intelligent design The argument that the natural world is so complex that it must have been designed or created by an intelligent entity such as God rather than by chance or natural selection.

Anthropocentric view An argument that sees humankind rather than, for example, animals or gods, as the most important element in the universe.

Summary

1. Comte identified three stages that societies move through: the theological, metaphysical and positive. The positive stage is characterised by science and reason.

2. Science is seen as an open system of ideas because its knowledge claims are based on testing so it constantly moves forward. Religion is seen as a closed system as its beliefs are based on faith and it is not open to testing.

3. Merton identified four norms that guided scientists' behaviour: communism, universalism, disinterestedness and organised scepticism.

4. Popper saw science as an open belief system that is based on falsification. Religious beliefs are not scientific statements because they cannot be tested.

5. Kuhn saw scientists as conservative rather than as completely objective. Progress in science comes about during a scientific revolution when one paradigm is replaced by another.

6. Kaplan distinguishes between reconstructed logics (what scientists say they do during their research) and logics in use (what they actually do).

7. Research inside science laboratories highlights the processes involved in the manufacture of scientific knowledge.

8. Postmodernism suggests that science is a metanarrative rather than the truth. Lyotard argues that people have lost faith in science and scientists.

9. Feminists question universalism in science. Western science is male dominated and influenced by male perspectives. Marxists see science as serving the interests of capitalism.

10. Science and religion are seen by some as compatible because they are concerned with completely different aspects of human life. They are seen by others as incompatible because belief in gods conflicts with scientific beliefs.

Unit 3.1.3 Different accounts of ideology

Ideology is a key concept in sociology and refers to a set of ideas that present a partial view of reality. An ideology also includes value judgements not only about the way things are but also about how things ought to be. So an ideology is a set of shared ideas, beliefs or values that provide a way of seeing and interpreting the world that results in a partial view of reality. The term 'ideology' is often used to suggest a false or distorted picture of reality. In practice, an ideology often legitimises or justifies the position and actions of powerful groups in society such as the ruling class or men. Religion and science can both be seen as examples of ideologies. This unit explores different sociological accounts of ideology. It begins with Marxist perspectives on the ideological role of religion and neo-Marxist accounts of ideology. It then looks at feminist perspectives on patriarchy and how this operates within science.

Marxist accounts of ideology

Marxists refer to the ideology of the ruling class. In this sense, ideology is a viewpoint that distorts reality and justifies the position of a particular social group. Marxists see ruling-class ideology as a set of beliefs and values that express the interests of the bourgeoisie in capitalist society. Ruling-class ideology legitimises existing power relationships in society.

Religion as an ideology

Karl Marx saw religion as an ideology in that religious beliefs uphold the interests of the ruling class and justify inequalities of wealth and power. (See also Unit 3.2.2.) This can be seen in Christian teachings such as 'blessed are the meek' and 'the meek shall inherit the earth'. Religious beliefs also make the social order appear not only natural and acceptable but also inevitable. Marxists link religion to false class consciousness suggesting that religious ideas keep the subject class from recognising its own interests and disguise the true extent of its exploitation.

By justifying the status quo, religion distorts reality. False class consciousness blinds members of the subject class to their true situation and their real interests. In this way, religion diverts people's attention from the real source of their oppression and so helps to maintain the power of the ruling class.

Activity

Religious beliefs and practices can be seen as a way of justifying social inequality. In this sense, religion has an ideological role.

From a Marxist perspective, ruling classes adopt religious beliefs to justify their position both to themselves and to others. Have another look at the verse from the Victorian hymn 'All Things Bright and Beautiful' in Chapter 1, Unit 1.1.2.

Briefly explain how the lyrics of this hymn could be used to show that religion has an ideological role.

Neo-Marxist accounts of ruling-class ideology

Antonio Gramsci (1971) uses the term 'hegemony' to describe ruling-class control that is achieved by gaining the consent and approval of members of society. In other words, hegemony refers to the ruling class's ideological domination of society. Hegemony is largely achieved not by using force (for example, by mobilising the army or the police) but by persuading people to accept the political and moral values of the ruling class. In Gramsci's view, a group's power could be based on its control over people's ideas. The ruling class only maintains its control to the extent that it can command people's beliefs through, for example, religion, the mass media and education.

Gramsci argued that the ruling class is unable to completely control the population's ideas. Ruling-class hegemony could never be complete. In his view, members of the proletariat have dual consciousness in capitalist societies and their ideas are contradictory rather than consistent. For example, they might support the monarchy but disagree with the principle of hereditary peers and see the practice of tax avoidance among 'fat cats' as unfair. Some of the proletariat's ideas come from the ruling class's control over institutions such as the church, schools and the mass media. The ruling class is able to use these institutions to persuade people to accept that capitalism is natural, desirable and legitimate. However, people's beliefs are also the product of their own experiences. To a limited extent, they are able to see through the capitalist system and realise that their interests lie in changing it. For example, their daily experiences of oppression and exploitation at work, poor working conditions and low wages contradict the false class consciousness that the bourgeoisie fosters. This means that people are unlikely to fully accept capitalist ideology. They can partly see through the capitalist system and realise that it does not necessarily operate in their interests.

Like Marx, Gramsci looked forward to a **proletarian revolution** and the end of capitalism. In his view, this would only be possible when individuals have been made to realise the extent to which they are being exploited and see through the ideas and beliefs of the ruling class. For this to happen, 'intellectuals' have to emerge within the subject classes to mould their ideas and overcome ruling-class hegemony.

Critics, however, disagree with Gramsci's account of why people do not engage in action to change the capitalist system. They argue that factors such as the fear of unemployment and poverty prevent people from rebelling against capitalism.

Raymond Williams (1978), another neo-Marxist, rejects the idea that there is a totally dominant ruling-class ideology in society. While there may be a **dominant ideology**, it is always likely to be challenged by other ideologies. There may be **residual ideologies** (the ideology of a class which is declining but still important). There may also be **emergent ideologies** (the ideologies of new groups that are outside the ruling class). Residual and emergent ideologies may be either oppositional (opposed to the dominant ideology) or alternative (coexisting with the dominant ideology without challenging it). In Williams' view, groups outside the ruling class may accept the dominant ideology but they may also reject it – both responses are possible. Furthermore, people may accept some aspects of the dominant ideology but reject others.

Feminist accounts of ideology

Some feminists highlight the significance of patriarchy (male power, control and dominance over women) as an ideology. For example, the socialisation process can be ideological if it indoctrinates people into accepting patriarchy and gender inequality as reasonable and acceptable. Radical feminist accounts see patriarchy as both an ideology and a system that is based on 'male domination and female submission' (Clare Chambers, 2013).

Patriarchal ideology within science

Some feminists argue that sciences are patriarchal and based on masculine assumptions. In this view, sciences are designed to preserve male power rather than to seek truth. Consequently, science can be seen as ideological rather than as gender neutral and objective. A number of feminists see science as an attempt to justify the oppression of

women by men. For example, Anne Fausto-Sterling (2000) believes that scientific theories of gender differences are influenced by patriarchal ideology. The assumptions that scientists make, the sort of research that gets done and the way that results are interpreted are all influenced by wider social and political factors including the nature of gender in society. For instance, scientific claims that differences in the corpus callosum (part of the brain) led men and women to think differently were based on highly debatable and ambiguous evidence. Fausto-Sterling does not completely reject the possibility of objective scientific knowledge. It may be difficult, however, to separate objective knowledge from distorting, male ideological influences.

Other feminists see the whole process of science, not just the study of issues such as gender differences, as thoroughly distorted by patriarchal assumptions. For example, the topics that are studied in science are often based on what men see as important and men usually have the power to determine research priorities.

Deboleena Roy (2004) sees male-dominated science as shaped by ideology in several ways, including the selection of issues and topics for research. In biology, for example, patriarchal values are revealed in the emphasis on controlling and medicalising women's reproduction. Research into the genetic screening of embryos reflects dominant ideologies that you should control nature and screen for the 'perfect' foetus. Roy argues that, in doing so, it devalues the lives of people with disabilities. By contrast, feminist research would examine ways of overcoming the oppression of women rather than ways of further controlling and medicalising pregnancy.

In Roy's view, male-dominated approaches to science influence how far a genuine understanding of scientific phenomena can be achieved. For example, biological research often explains whether a woman conceives or not purely in terms of certain physical, biological processes. It does not take into account wider social factors such as diet or stress, which can affect hormones and influence fertility. By contrast, feminist science takes these factors into account and can achieve a deeper understanding of issues such as fertility. However, Roy accepts that some aspects of science are not influenced by power differences between females and males. For example, the actual methods that scientists use are generally gender neutral.

Activity

Laboratories are not ivory towers and scientific research is influenced by social and political factors.

1. On what grounds might science be seen as producing objective knowledge?

2. Why might some sociologists see science as an ideology?

Darwin, evolution and ideology

Darwin claimed that species evolved by a process of natural selection which was initiated by sudden genetic changes or mutations. Most of Darwin's followers believed this process took place gradually. However, Roger Gomm (1982) argued that Darwin himself did not believe that evolution was a gradual process. Gomm claims that the popularity of 'gradualism' was not the result of careful interpretation of the evidence. Instead, he argues that the theory was popular because it fitted more closely with the ideologies of dominant social groups in Victorian Britain. For example, the idea of evolution and natural selection allowed species to be seen as superior or inferior. It enabled Victorians to place groups within the human species on an evolutionary ladder. Australian Aboriginal peoples were placed at the bottom (as the least evolved) while Victorian intellectual men were placed at the top.

Key terms

Ideology A set of dominant ideas in society that distort reality and serve the interests of a particular group such as men or the ruling class.

Proletarian revolution A period of radical change in society during which the proletariat overthrows capitalism and replaces it with communism.

Dominant ideology In Marxist terms, this refers to the ideological power of the ruling class in society. In capitalist societies, for example, the ideas of the bourgeoisie are the ruling ideas.

Residual ideologies Ideologies of a social class that, although still important, is declining.

Emergent ideologies The ideologies of new groups that are outside the ruling class.

Summary

1. The term 'ideology' refers to a set of shared beliefs and values which provide a way of seeing and interpreting the world that results in a partial – and usually distorted – view of reality.

2. Marxists focus on ruling-class ideology – a set of beliefs and values that justifies the position of the bourgeoisie in capitalist society.

3. Marxists link religion to false class consciousness in that religious ideas keep the proletariat from recognising its true interests in capitalist society and help to maintain ruling-class power.

4. Antonio Gramsci refers to hegemony as ruling-class control over ideas achieved through consent rather than force. However, ruling-class hegemony is partial rather than complete.

5. Raymond Williams accepts that there may be a dominant ideology in capitalist society but rejects the idea that there is a totally dominant ruling-class ideology.

6. Many feminists focus on patriarchal ideology in society and some see the sciences as patriarchal, as designed to preserve male power rather than to seek truth.

7. Roger Gomm argues that the popularity of 'gradualism' and natural selection fitted the ideologies of dominant groups in Victorian Britain.

PART 2 DIFFERENT THEORETICAL VIEWS ON THE ROLE AND FUNCTION OF RELIGION

Contents

Religions, one of the most important belief systems in contemporary societies, are a key area of sociological interest. Sociologists are not concerned with evaluating different religious beliefs or assessing the competing truth claims that religions make. Instead, they focus on the social aspects of religion, the way religion affects social life and the significance of religion in society. What is religion really about beneath the surface? How does it shape relationships between people? Does religion perform a positive or a negative role in society? Sociologists do not necessarily agree on the answers to such questions. This part examines how the different theoretical perspectives within sociology address questions about the role and function of religion in society.

Unit 3.2.1 Functionalist perspectives

The functionalist perspective sees society as made up of various parts such as religion, the family, the economy, the education and political systems. These parts fit together as a whole to form a complete system. In order to understand any one part of society, such as religion, it must be seen in relation to society as a whole (see Chapter 1, Unit 1.1.1).

In the functionalist view, society has functional prerequisites (basic needs or requirements) such as value consensus. These functional prerequisites must be met if society is to survive over time. Functionalism examines each of the different social institutions such as religion in terms of its functions, that is, the contribution it makes to meeting society's needs and maintaining the social system.

When studying religion, functionalism focuses on questions such as:

» What are the functions of religion for society as a whole?

» How does religion contribute to meeting society's needs?

Functionalism focuses on the positive role of religion and its contribution to meeting society's needs. This unit examines and evaluates some of the main functionalist theories of religion.

Émile Durkheim's account of religion, the sacred and the profane

Émile Durkheim (1912) has had a huge influence on the sociology of religion (see Unit 1.1.1 for his definition of religion). He argued that all religious beliefs divide the world into two completely separate parts: the sacred (things that are set apart and forbidden) and the profane (ordinary, everyday things). However, the 'sacred' are not simply things such as gods or spirits. According to Durkheim, anything could potentially be sacred, including 'a rock, a tree, a spring, a pebble, a piece of wood, a house'. In fact, one society's sacred objects could be other societies' everyday objects. There is nothing about the intrinsic qualities of a rock or a tree that make them sacred. What sacred things do have in common is the reverential attitudes (or feelings of great respect and awe) that they inspire among believers.

Durkheim argued that as sacred objects do not have any intrinsic qualities that would make them sacred, they must be symbols, they must represent something else. In order to understand the role of religion in society, he believed that it is necessary to examine the relationship between sacred symbols and what they represent.

Durkheim examined published reports of the religion of various Australian Aboriginal groups to develop his argument. He saw their religion, **totemism**, as the simplest known form of religion. In his view, it would be possible to understand the main elements of all religions by examining this most simple religion.

Aboriginal society is divided into several clans. Each clan has its own unique totem, usually an animal such as a kangaroo or a plant. The totem is a sacred symbol in Aboriginal ritual and ritual observances separate it from profane or ordinary things. A representation of the totem – the totemic emblem or image – is placed or painted on objects or on people. The totemic emblem is also surrounded by rituals and is considered to be more sacred than the totemic object itself. The totem provides the clan with its name and clan members share the same name. This means that the clan members themselves possess sacred qualities because of their sacred name.

Activity

Among many Roman Catholics, statues of angels are seen as sacred.

Sarah Dunlop and Peter Ward (2014) asked young Polish Catholics living in Plymouth to take photographs of what is sacred to them. The photographs they took included images of churches, statues and people.

1. If you were asked to take photographs of what is sacred to you, what would you include?

2. If you were asked to photograph the profane, what images would you include?

Durkheim argued that the totem is the symbol of both god and society. From this, he argued that god and society are, in fact, the same thing. He suggested that, in worshipping a god, people are actually worshipping society. Society is more important and powerful than the individual. Durkheim argued that: 'Primitive man comes to view society as something sacred because he is utterly dependent on it.' People invent a sacred symbol such as a totem because it is easier for someone to

'visualize and direct his feelings of awe toward a symbol than towards so complex a thing as a clan'.

Religion and the collective conscience

Although Durkheim was not personally religious, he viewed religion as performing valuable functions for society. He argued that social life would be impossible without the shared values and moral beliefs that form the collective conscience. Without them, there would be no social order, social control or cooperation. In short, there would be no society. Religion performs a key function by reinforcing the collective conscience. The worship of society strengthens the values and moral beliefs that form the basis of social life. In this way, religion acts like a cement or glue that binds members of society together.

In worshipping society, people are, in effect, recognising the importance of the social group and their dependence on it. In this way, religion strengthens the unity of the group, promotes social solidarity and holds society together.

Durkheim emphasised the importance of collective worship. The social group comes together in religious rituals full of drama and reverence. Together, its members express their faith in their common values and beliefs. In this highly charged atmosphere of collective worship, the integration of society is strengthened. Members of society express, communicate and understand the moral bonds that unite them.

Activity

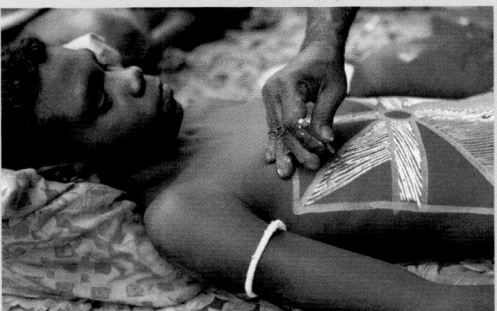

An Aboriginal teenager being painted with his totem for a ceremony to mark his initiation as an adult member of the community.

1. Why do you think that Aboriginal teenagers are painted with a totem as part of their initiation ceremony?

2. What functions might this ceremony perform for the group?

203

Evaluation of Durkheim

Although Durkheim's ideas are still influential today, they have been criticised:

1. Critics argue that Durkheim studied only a small number of Aboriginal groups, which were not typical of other Aboriginal tribes. It may, therefore, be misleading to generalise about Aboriginal beliefs and about religion as a whole from this sample.

2. Andrew Dawson (2011) points out that some of the fieldwork data which Durkheim relied on was of doubtful validity. Other critics argue that totemism is not a religion.

3. Durkheim's views on religion are more relevant to small, non-literate societies whose members share a common belief and value system. They are less relevant to modern, diverse societies which have many subcultures, social and ethnic groups, and a wide range of religious beliefs, rituals, practices and institutions.

4. Most sociologists believe that Durkheim overstated his case. While agreeing that religion can promote social solidarity and reinforce social values, they would not support his view that religion is the worship of society.

5. Durkheim may have also overstated the degree to which the collective conscience shapes the behaviour of individuals. Hamilton (2001) argues that sometimes religious beliefs can be at odds with society's values. As discussed later in the chapter (see Part 3), religion can be a force for change in society. It can also be a cause of conflict and division both within and between faiths. As a result, critics argue that Durkheim focused on the positive role of religion in promoting social order and neglected its links to violence, disorder and social change.

Despite the extensive criticism of Durkheim, many sociologists recognise that he made an important contribution to understanding religion. For example, William E. Paden (2009) argues that Durkheim's observations about the importance of religion for social solidarity remain valid in many circumstances today. The symbolic importance of the Western (or Wailing) Wall in Jerusalem for Jews is an example of the continuing symbolic importance of sacred objects.

Activity

Jewish women praying in the women's section of the Western or Wailing Wall in Jerusalem, a sacred site for prayer and pilgrimage.

1. How might the example of the Western Wall be used to support Durkheim's account of religion?

2. Why might some feminists use this example to support the view that religion is patriarchal?

Bronislaw Malinowski's account of religion in the Trobriand Islands

Like Durkheim, Bronislaw Malinowski (1954) used data from small-scale, non-literate societies to develop his theory on religion. Many of his examples were drawn from his fieldwork in the Trobriand Islands off the coast of New Guinea. Like Durkheim, Malinowski saw religion as reinforcing social norms and values and promoting social solidarity. However, he did not view religious ritual as the worship of society itself.

In Malinowski's view, religion is particularly concerned with situations of emotional stress that threaten social solidarity. Religion is typically involved with two types of event: first, **life crises** and second, activities in which the outcome is important but unpredictable and uncontrollable.

Religion and life crises

Anxiety and tension tend to disrupt social life. Situations that produce these emotions include life crises such as birth, puberty, marriage and death. Malinowski noted that in all societies, these life crises are surrounded by religious ritual. Death is the most upsetting and disruptive of these events because it removes one of society's members. Religion, however, deals with the problem of death. A funeral ceremony expresses the belief in immortality and so comforts the bereaved. Other mourners support the bereaved by being present at the ceremony. This comfort and support checks the emotions that death produces and controls the stress and anxiety that might otherwise disrupt society. When members of the social group unite to support the bereaved at a funeral ceremony, this expression of social solidarity reintegrates society.

Religion, prediction and control

A second category of events – practical activities that cannot be fully predicted or controlled – also produces tension and anxiety. From his observations in the Trobriand Islands, Malinowski noted that such events were surrounded by ritual, and he saw ritual as a form of religious practice.

Fishing is an important subsistence activity in the Trobriand Islands. Malinowski observed that in the calm waters of the lagoon, fishing does not involve danger and uncertainty. In the open sea, however, a storm may result in loss of life and the catch is dependent on the presence of a shoal of fish, which cannot be predicted. In the lagoon, there are no rituals associated with fishing, whereas fishing in the open sea is preceded by rituals to ensure a good catch and to protect the fishermen.

Again, ritual is used in specific situations that produce anxiety. Rituals reduce anxiety by providing confidence and a feeling of control. As with funeral ceremonies, fishing rituals are social events. The group unites to deal with situations of stress, and so the unity of the group is strengthened.

Evaluation of Malinowski

Malinowski's distinctive contribution to the sociology of religion is found in his argument that religion promotes social solidarity by dealing with situations of emotional stress that threaten the stability of society. However, he has been criticised for exaggerating the importance of religious rituals in helping people to cope with situations of stress and uncertainty. Tambiah (1990, discussed in Hamilton, 2001) pointed out, for example, that magic and elaborate rituals are also associated with the cultivation of taro and yams on the Trobriand Islands. Taro and yams are important crops because men must use them to make payments to their sisters' husbands. Men who fail to do so show that they are unable to fulfil significant social obligations. These rituals are, therefore, simply related to the maintenance of prestige in that society. They have little to do with cementing social solidarity or dealing with uncertainty and danger.

Talcott Parsons' account of religion

Talcott Parsons (1937, 1964, 1965) argued that religious beliefs provide guidelines for human action and standards against which people's conduct can be evaluated. In a Christian society, for instance, the Ten Commandments show that many of the norms of the social system can be integrated (or brought together) by religious beliefs. For example, the commandment 'Thou shalt not kill' integrates such diverse norms as the way to drive a car, how to settle an argument and how to deal with the suffering of the aged. The norms that direct these areas of behaviour prohibit manslaughter, murder and euthanasia, but they are all based on the same religious commandment.

In this way, religion provides general guidelines for conduct, which are expressed in a variety of norms. By establishing general principles and moral beliefs, religion helps to provide the value consensus that Parsons believed is necessary for order and stability in society.

Religion and social order

Parsons, like Malinowski, saw religion as addressing particular problems that occur in all societies and disrupt social life. These problems fall into two categories. The first relates to 'the fact that individuals are "hit" by events which they cannot foresee and prepare for, or control, or both'. One such event is death, particularly premature death. Like Malinowski, Parsons saw religion as a mechanism for adjustment to such events and as a means of restoring the normal pattern of life.

The second problem area is that of 'uncertainty'. This refers to endeavours in which a great deal of effort and skill has been invested, but where unknown or uncontrollable factors can threaten a successful outcome. One example is humanity's inability to predict or control the effect of weather upon agriculture. Again, following Malinowski, Parsons argued that religion provides a means of coming to terms with such situations through rituals which act as 'a tonic to self-confidence'. In this way, religion maintains social stability by relieving the tension and frustration that could disrupt social order.

Religion and problems of meaning

Parsons argued that religious beliefs give meaning to life; they answer questions about humanity and the world that people live in. One of the major functions of religion is to 'make sense' of all experiences, no matter how meaningless they appear. One example of this is the question of why some people experience suffering. Religion provides a range of answers to this: suffering tests a person's faith; it is a punishment for sins; and those who endure suffering with strength will be rewarded in heaven. In this way, suffering becomes meaningful. Similarly, the problem of evil is common to all societies and some people profit through their evil actions. Religion solves this contradiction by stating that these people will receive their just desserts in the afterlife.

Parsons (1965), therefore, sees a major function of religion as providing meaning to events that people do not expect or that they feel ought not to happen. This allows them to adjust to these events. On a more general level, this adjustment promotes order and stability in society.

Evaluation of Parsons

Parsons highlights the positive aspects of religion in promoting value consensus, social order and stability. However, there are several criticisms of his work, as follows.

1. Critics argue that Parsons puts too much emphasis on the role of religion in maintaining stability and order in society. He pays little attention to the dysfunctional or negative aspects of religion and its role in generating violence, suffering and conflict between, for example, members of different faiths. (See Unit 3.3.2 for a discussion of the relationship between religion and conflict.)

2. Parsons focuses on religion as a source of social stability but overlooks the role of religion as a force that can bring about change in society. (See Unit 3.3.1 for a discussion of the relationship between religion and social change.)

3. From a feminist perspective, Parsons can be criticised for failing to examine the role of religion in maintaining patriarchy and the oppression of women. From a Marxist perspective, he can be criticised for failing to examine religion's role in maintaining capitalism.

Robert Bellah's account of civil religion

Robert Bellah's work is influenced by both Durkheim and Parsons. Bellah (1967) identified a national **civil religion** in the USA that binds Americans together. Over time, civil religion in America has developed a set of beliefs, symbols and rituals related to sacred things. Although much of this civil religion is based on Christianity, it is not itself Christian. A civil religion performs similar functions to a traditional religion such as Christianity and can be seen as a functional alternative to conventional religions. According to Bellah, the main function of civil religion in the USA is to provide 'symbols of national solidarity' that encourage Americans to attain national goals.

Civil religion is based on secular rituals and symbols. Its secular symbols include the statue of liberty and its rituals include swearing allegiance to the US flag, ceremonies surrounding presidential inaugurations and Memorial Day to remember Americans killed during wars. These celebrations have a sacred significance. Civil religion in the USA also has its own sacred places such as Arlington National Cemetery and the Vietnam War Memorial. It has its own martyrs such as Presidents Washington and Lincoln. It has its own texts such as the Declaration of Independence and the Constitution of the US. The words 'In God we trust' are engraved on coins. American schoolchildren pledge allegiance to 'one nation under God'. So although the church and the state are separate in the USA, political life has a strong religious dimension.

Bellah argued that, in a culturally and socially diverse society such as the USA, civil religion generates powerful feelings of national solidarity, unity and purpose among its people. By contrast, conventional religions such as Protestantism, Catholicism and Judaism do not have the allegiance of all Americans. Unlike civil religion, they do not provide social unity or act as an integrative force in American society.

Activity

Some commentators suggest that the monarchy forms part of a civil religion in the UK.

1. How far would you agree that the royal family provides a symbol of national unity in the UK?

2. To what extent do rituals such as royal weddings, the Coronation, the Monarch's Christmas speech and the State Opening of Parliament affirm a sense of shared national identity?

3. To what extent do such rituals reinforce the moral values of UK society?

Evaluation of Bellah

1. Some critics argue that the concept of civil religion is too vague and unclear to be useful.

2. Others argue that civil 'religion' cannot be seen as a religion. Sociologists who adopt an exclusive definition of religion, for example, reject the idea that a civil religion is a religion because its beliefs do not contain a supernatural element.

Evaluation of the functionalist perspective

1. The functionalist perspective emphasises the positive functions that religion performs for society and for individuals but tends to ignore its dysfunctional aspects. It focuses on value consensus, integration and social solidarity but neglects the many instances where religion can be seen as a divisive and disruptive force. Functionalism ignores the frequent examples of internal divisions within a community over questions of religious dogma and worship – divisions that can lead to open conflict. It gives little consideration to hostility between different religious groups within the same society, such as Catholics and Protestants in Northern Ireland, Shia and Sunni Muslims in Iraq, or Hindus and Muslims in India. In such cases, religion can be seen as a direct threat to social order. (See Unit 3.3.2.)

2. Critics argue that the functionalist approach focuses on religion as a conservative force in society and does not explore religion as a radical force that is linked to social change. (See Unit 3.3.1.)

Key terms

Totemism A form of religion practised by the Australian Aboriginal peoples in which a totem (usually a plant or animal) symbolises the clan and is sacred.

Life crises Situations such as birth, puberty, marriage and death that could produce anxiety and stress.

Civil religion A belief system such as nationalism that provides a functional alternative to conventional religions by fulfilling the same functions, for example by providing shared values and promoting social cohesion.

Summary

1. The different theoretical perspectives in sociology focus on the way that religion affects social life and its significance in society. Functionalism focuses on the positive role of religion and its contribution to meeting society's needs.

2. Based on his research on totemism among groups of Australian Aboriginal peoples, Durkheim argued that, in worshipping God, people are actually worshipping society. Religion is functionally important in reinforcing the collective conscience and promoting social solidarity.

3. Critics question the validity of the data that Durkheim used, the relevance of his views to modern, diverse societies and his account of religion as the worship of society. He also overlooked the role of religion in generating conflict and change.

4. Malinowski studied the Trobriand Islands and argued that, by dealing with situations of emotional stress that threaten social stability, religion promotes social solidarity.

5. Critics argue that Malinowski exaggerated the importance of religious rituals in helping people to cope with stress and uncertainty.

6. Parsons linked religion to value consensus, order and stability in society. According to him, religious beliefs give meaning to life and make sense of all experiences, regardless of how meaningless they appear.

7. Critics argue that Parsons paid insufficient attention to dysfunctional aspects of religion and its role in generating conflict, division and change.

8. Bellah focused on civil religion in the USA and its role in binding people together in a culturally and socially diverse society.

9. Critics argue that civil religion is an unclear concept and that it is not a religion.

Unit 3.2.2 Marxist perspectives

Marxist perspectives on religion provide an interesting contrast to functionalist views. While functionalism focuses on the positive role of religion in society, Marxism is critical of religion in all class-based societies. Marxists identify two main classes in capitalist society: the ruling class and the subject class (see Chapter 1, Unit 1.1.2). The ruling class – the bourgeoisie – own the forces or means of production while the subject class – the proletariat – only own their labour power and are forced to sell their labour to the bourgeoisie in order to survive. The relationship between these two classes is based on exploitation as the proletariat's wage is much less than the profits that the bourgeoisie make.

Marxists see capitalist society as made up of the economic base which largely shapes the superstructure. Beliefs, including religious beliefs, and values in society form a ruling-class ideology. This produces false class consciousness and the subject class are not aware that they are being exploited. At the same time, false class consciousness legitimates the ruling class's position in capitalist society.

This unit examines Marxist perspectives on the role of religion in society. It looks at the key Marxist concepts of alienation, ideology and false class consciousness and how they apply to the study of religion. It also evaluates Marxist perspectives on religion.

Karl Marx's views on religion

As an **atheist**, Karl Marx argued that 'Man makes religion, religion does not make man'. He challenged the Christian belief that God created man in his own image by arguing that man created God in his own image. In Marx's view, people create imaginary beings or forces which stand above them and control their behaviour. People project their own human powers and capabilities onto God, who is seen as all-powerful. As a result, they become detached from themselves. Marx saw religion as a form of alienation in capitalist society in that it disguises the fact that people can take control of their own destiny. This prevents them from realising their own potential such as their power to control their own lives on earth.

Marx saw religion in capitalist society as a series of myths that justify and legitimate the subordination of the proletariat and the domination of the bourgeoisie. Religion is an ideology in that religious beliefs support the bourgeoisie's interests and justify inequalities based on wealth and power. Religion is linked to false class consciousness in that religious ideas distort reality, disguise the extent of exploitation in capitalist society and prevent the proletariat from recognising its own interests. (See Unit 3.1.3.)

Marx believed that in order to achieve true happiness and fulfilment, religion and the social conditions that produce it must be abolished. In Marx's future classless communist society, religion will not be necessary because the social conditions that produce it, such as alienation and exploitation, will no longer exist.

Religion as 'the opium of the people'

Marx described religion as 'the opium of the people' (Marx, in Bottomore and Rubel, 1963). Religion acts as an opiate or a drug to dull the pain produced by oppression. It helps to make life more bearable for the proletariat and therefore dilutes demands for change. As such, religion merely numbs or stuns its followers rather than bringing them true happiness and fulfilment.

From a Marxist perspective, religion can dull the pain of oppression in the following ways:

1. It promises a paradise of eternal bliss in life after death. Engels argued that Christianity appeals to oppressed classes because it promises 'salvation from bondage and misery' in the afterlife. The Christian vision of heaven can make life on earth more bearable by giving people something to look forward to. Some Marxists focus on the role of Hell in reproducing social class relations. Rather than acting as an opiate, the threat of eternal damnation in Hell can operate as a means of social control, inhibiting believers from breaking the rules laid down by Christianity.

2. Some religions see the suffering produced by oppression as a just punishment for sins. Suffering is also seen as a trial set by God, promising rewards for those who endure poverty with dignity and humility. This view is contained in the well-known biblical quotation, 'It is easier for a camel to pass through the eye of a needle, than for a rich man to enter the Kingdom of Heaven.' Religion thus makes poverty more bearable by offering a reward for suffering and promising compensation in the afterlife for injustice.

3. Religion can offer the hope of supernatural intervention to solve problems on earth. Members of religious groups such as the Jehovah's Witnesses wait for the day when supernatural powers will descend from on high and create heaven on earth. Anticipation of this future can make the present more acceptable.

4. Religion often justifies the social order and an individual's position within it. God can be seen as creating and supporting the social structure. The lines from the Victorian hymn 'All Things Bright and Beautiful' (see Chapter 1, Unit 1.1.2 and Chapter 3, Unit 3.1.3) make particular social arrangements appear as God-given and therefore inevitable. This can help the proletariat to accept and come to terms with their situation and make life more bearable for them.

Religion and social control

From a Marxist viewpoint, religion does not simply cushion the effects of oppression; it is also an instrument of that oppression. It acts as a **mechanism of social control**, maintaining the existing system of exploitation and reinforcing class relationships. Marx argued that Christianity preaches 'submissiveness and humbleness' to the proletariat. In doing so, it keeps them in their place. Furthermore, by making unsatisfactory lives bearable, religion tends to discourage people from attempting to change their situation. By offering an illusion of hope in a hopeless situation, it prevents thoughts of overthrowing the system. In this way, it acts as a conservative force in society. (See Unit 3.3.1 for a discussion of the relationship between religion and social change.)

Marx did not believe that religion would last for ever. Religion was rooted in societies that alienated, exploited and oppressed their members. When such societies were replaced, religion would no longer be necessary. Ultimately, the proletariat would remove the need for religion by replacing capitalist society with communism.

In Marx's vision of the ideal, communist society, exploitation and alienation are things of the past. The means of production are communally owned, which results in the disappearance of social classes. Members of society are fulfilled as human beings: they control their own destinies and work together for the common good. Religion does not exist in this communist utopia because the social conditions that produce it have disappeared.

Evidence to support Marxism

There is considerable evidence to support the Marxist view of the role of religion in society.

The caste system of traditional India, for example, was justified by Hindu religious beliefs. In medieval Europe, kings and queens ruled by divine right. The Egyptian Pharaohs went one step further by combining both God and king in the same person. Slave-owners in the southern states of the USA often approved of the conversion of slaves to Christianity, believing it to be a controlling and gentling influence. It has been argued that in the early days of the Industrial Revolution in England, employers used religion as a means of controlling the masses and encouraging them to remain sober and to work hard.

Pentecostalism (a form of Christianity that has grown significantly among poor people in Latin America, Africa and parts of Asia) is a contemporary example of a religion that emphasises sobriety (not drinking alcohol) and hard work. Pentecostal churches have conservative teachings on issues such as abortion, sexuality and the role of women in society and within the church. As

Activity – Religion and social control

SUNDAY.

THE church-bell calls, and we
  obey,

And meet in God's own house to
  pray.

At eve we wander by the brook,

Or ponder o'er some holy book;

And say, when radiant glows the
  West,

"Thanks be to God for Sabbath
  rest."

In Marxist terms, religion acts as a means of social control and keeps people in their place.

Questions

1. From a Marxist perspective, how might religious beliefs and practices act as an opiate?

2. Explain one similarity between Marxist and functionalist theories of religion.

3. What key differences are there between Marxist and functionalist perspectives on religion?

a result, Pentecostals are seen as likely to support the status quo and to work hard in order to try to improve their social position. (See Unit 3.3.1 for a discussion of the relationship between Pentecostalism and social change.) Steve Bruce (1988) discussed another contemporary example that can be used to support Marxism. He pointed out that, in the USA, conservative Protestants – the '**New Christian Right**' – consistently support right-wing political candidates in the Republican Party, and attack more liberal candidates in the Democratic Party. According to Bruce, the New Christian Right support 'a more aggressive anti-communist foreign policy, more military spending, less central government interference, less welfare spending, and fewer restraints on free enterprise'. Although Bruce emphasised that the New Christian Right have had a limited influence on American politics, it is clear that they have tended to defend the interests of the rich and powerful at the expense of other groups in the population.

Evaluation of Marxism

1. There is evidence to suggest that religion does not always legitimate power; it is not simply a justification of privilege, and it can sometimes provide an impetus for social, economic or political change. Weber, for example, saw religious ideas as having the potential to bring social and economic change (see Unit 3.3.1).

2. Meredith B. McGuire (2002) argues that the relationship between religion and social and political actions is more complex and unpredictable than Marx claimed. Although religion can act as an opiate, it can also be linked to social and political change.

3. Marxism does not explain the existence of religion where it does not appear to contribute to the oppression of a particular class.

4. Critics argue that Marxism fails to explain why religion might continue to exist when, in theory at least, oppression has come to an end. Under communism in the USSR after the 1917 revolution, the state actively discouraged religion and many places of worship were closed. The communist state placed limits on religious activity, and the religious instruction of children was banned. Nevertheless, religion did not die out under communism as Marx predicted. Statistical evidence suggests that, although communism had some success in suppressing religion in certain countries, it did not eradicate it. Religious activity increased again once communism had ended. This evidence suggests that Marx was wrong to believe that religion would disappear under communism. It also suggests that there must be other reasons for the existence of religion apart from those put forward by Marx.

5. Functionalist approaches accept that religion may act as a means of social control. However, they see this as functional for society.

6. Some feminists link religion to patriarchy rather than to capitalism. They see religion as legitimising male power rather than ruling-class power.

Engels and neo-Marxists' views on religion as a radical force

Although Marx saw religion as legitimising the status quo, Engels saw it as a potentially radical force in society.

Friedrich Engels' account of Christianity and social change

Friedrich Engels recognised that religion can play an active role in bringing about revolutionary social change (Roger O'Toole, 1984). In one of his papers, he compared some of the early Christian sects that opposed Roman rule to communist and socialist political movements (Engels, 1957). He argued that Christianity originated as a way of coping with exploitation among oppressed groups. However, it could become a source of resistance to the oppressors and a force for change. In his view, groups which turned to religion as a way of coping with oppression could develop into political movements that sought change on earth rather than salvation in heaven. Some contemporary neo-Marxists have followed Engels and developed this idea.

Maduro's account of religion as a revolutionary force

Otto Maduro (1982) was a neo-Marxist. He accepted many aspects of Marx's analysis of religion but denied that religion is always a conservative force and, furthermore, claims that it can be revolutionary. He argued that 'Religion is not necessarily a functional, reproductive or conservative factor in society; it often is one of the main (and sometimes the only) available channel to bring about a social revolution.'

Maduro claims that, up until recently, Catholicism in Latin America tended to support the bourgeoisie and the right-wing military dictatorships, which represented its interests. The Catholic Church has tended to deny the existence of social conflicts between oppressive and oppressed classes. It has recognised some injustices, such as poverty and illiteracy, but has suggested that their solution lies with those who already have power. It has also celebrated military victories but has failed to support unions, strikes and opposition political parties.

On the other hand, Catholic priests have increasingly demonstrated their autonomy from the bourgeoisie by criticising them and acting against their interests. Maduro believes that members of the clergy can develop revolutionary potential where oppressed members of the population have no other outlets for their grievances. The oppressed can pressurise priests to take up their cause. Theological disagreements within a church can provide interpretations of a religion that are critical of the rich and powerful. All of these conditions have been met in Latin America and have led to the development of **liberation theology** (see Unit 3.3.1).

Key terms

Atheist A person who does not believe in the existence of a god or gods.

Mechanism of social control A means by which individuals are persuaded to conform to the rules in society.

New Christian Right A term originating in the USA to describe Christian groups with links to the right-wing Republican Party. They have conservative views on social issues and want religious culture to be central in public life.

Liberation theology A movement of radical Roman Catholic priests in Latin America dating back to the 1960s, who promote political change, fight oppression and support the poor.

Summary

1. Karl Marx argued that people create religion. People project their own powers or capabilities onto superhuman beings and, as a result, become detached or alienated from themselves.

2. In Marx's view, religion is an ideology in that religious beliefs support the ruling class's interests and justify inequalities.

3. Marx saw religion as an opiate – a painkilling drug – which makes life more bearable for the subject class, the proletariat under capitalism. In doing so, religion dilutes demands for radical change in society.

4. Marx linked religion in class-based societies to alienation and exploitation. However, by replacing capitalism with communism, the proletariat would remove the need for religion.

5. Examples such as the caste system of traditional India and the divine right of kings support the Marxist view of the role of religion in society.

6. Critics point out that although religion can inhibit change, it can also bring about social, economic or political change. They also argue that Marx was wrong to believe that religion would disappear under communism.

7. Functionalism sees the social control aspect of religion as functional for society.

8. Feminists see religion as justifying male rather than ruling-class power and as legitimising patriarchy rather than capitalism.

9. Engels and neo-Marxists such as Maduro see religion as a potentially radical force in society. Maduro claims that religion can be a revolutionary force.

Unit 3.2.3 Feminist perspectives

There are several different feminist approaches within the sociology of religion, including radical feminism and liberal feminism. These different approaches agree that power and authority are not distributed equally between women and men within most religious organisations and traditions. Male domination can be seen in many religious teachings about women and men, in the leadership structures of religious institutions and in the practices of religions. Feminist approaches use the term 'patriarchy' to refer to a system of male domination in society and they argue that patriarchy is supported by religious beliefs. But are all religions necessarily patriarchal? Can religion empower women rather than oppress them? This unit looks at the different feminist views on the role of religion in society and its links to patriarchy.

Religion and patriarchy

Feminist theories of religion, like Marxist theories, often argue that religion can be an instrument of domination and oppression. However, they tend to see religion as linked to patriarchy rather than to capitalism. Many feminists see religion as serving the interests of men rather than those of a capitalist class.

Religion is seen as a patriarchal institution that perpetuates gender inequality over time. Feminist sociologists draw on evidence from a variety of religious beliefs and practices to support this view. They highlight four main ways in which religion can be seen as patriarchal.

1. Religious organisations: Most religious organisations are hierarchical in their structures and male-dominated in their leadership. Women continue to be excluded from key roles or positions of power in many religions. The Church of England finally allowed the ordination of female priests in 1992 and female bishops in 2014. Roman Catholic women, however, cannot become priests. This exclusion is despite the fact that women often participate more in organised religion (when they are allowed to) than men (see Unit 3.5.2). Orthodox Jewish women cannot become rabbis and, in Hinduism, only men can become Brahmanic priests. Sikhism is perhaps the most egalitarian of the major religions, as all offices are equally open to men and women. However, even in Sikhism, only a small minority of women have significant positions within the religion.

2. Laws and customs: In most religions, women have fewer rights than men. The Roman Catholic Church, for instance, has strict rules on abortion and contraception. Women often have fewer rights than men regarding divorce and are subject to more rules about what is seen as appropriate

dress when praying. In countries where the cultural norms are influenced by religion, men and women may be treated unequally by, for example, receiving different punishments for adultery.

3. Sacred texts: Sacred texts tend to give women subordinate roles. In most religions, the gods are male, and women are portrayed in minor roles. All the apostles in the New Testament, for example, are men. One explanation for this is that the sacred texts were usually written by men.

   The position of women in many societies across the globe has improved over the last 50 years. Faced with such changes to women's social status, some groups want women's traditional roles (for example, as wives and mothers) to be re-established. Such groups often appeal to sacred texts in order to justify their views on gender.

4. Places of worship: Some places of worship segregate men and women. Women's second-class status is often related to female sexuality. Holm (1994) points out that: 'Menstruation and childbirth are almost universally regarded as polluting. In many traditions women are forbidden to enter sacred places or touch sacred objects during the menstrual period.' For example, Hindu women are prohibited from approaching family shrines when pregnant or menstruating. Muslim women are not allowed to touch the Qur'an, go into a mosque or pray during menstruation.

Activity

BUDDHISM   CATHOLICISM   ISLAM

ORTHODOXY   HINDUISM   JUDAISM

Many feminists see the majority of religious organisations as male-dominated in their leadership.

1. How far do you agree with the view that religions are patriarchal?

2. Can you think of any arguments to counter this view?

Fang-Long Shih (2010) identifies two main feminist perspectives on religion: the radical feminist perspective and the liberal feminist perspective. However, other feminist-inspired viewpoints have developed which challenge the view that religion is necessarily patriarchal.

Radical feminist perspectives on religion

Radical feminist perspectives argue that gender inequality is the central type of inequality in society. Furthermore, a radical transformation of society is necessary to remove gender inequality. Unlike liberal feminists, they believe that piecemeal reform will not be enough to bring about change.

Simone de Beauvoir's account of female oppression within religion

Simone de Beauvoir (1953) argued that religion acts for women in similar ways to those suggested by Marx for oppressed classes. Oppressors (men) can use religion to control the oppressed group (women). Religion also serves as a way of compensating women for their second-class status. De Beauvoir notes that men have generally exercised control over religious beliefs in different faiths and use divine authority to support their dominance over women. The fear of God serves to keep women in a subordinate position.

Religion gives women, like Marx's proletariat, the false belief that they will be compensated for their sufferings on earth by equality in heaven. In this way, the subjugation of women through religion helps to maintain a status quo in which women and men are unequal. Women are also vital to religion because they do much of the work for religious organisations and introduce children to religious beliefs.

Goddess religion and feminist spirituality

Some feminists argue that the subordination of women has not always been typical of the majority of religions. Karen Armstrong (1993), for example, argues that in early history women were at the centre of 'the spiritual quest'. In the Middle East, Asia and Europe, archaeologists have uncovered numerous symbols of the Great Mother Goddess. She is pictured as a naked pregnant woman and seems to represent the mysteries of fertility and life. There were very few early effigies of gods as men. As societies developed religious beliefs in which there were held to be many different gods and goddesses, the Mother Goddess still played a crucial role. However, the final death knell for goddesses came with the acceptance of **monotheism** – belief in a single male god (such as Yahweh, the god of the prophet Abraham) rather than in many gods.

Mary Daly and Goddess religion

Some approaches, such as that of de Beauvoir, assume that religion is inevitably patriarchal and must be abolished. Others accept that religion is patriarchal but do not believe that religion itself needs to be abolished. Instead, they argue that patriarchal religions need to be replaced with feminist religion. In particular, they need to be replaced with **Goddess religion**.

Mary Daly (1973) was one of the earliest advocates of this approach. She was strongly influenced by de Beauvoir and agreed that religion was oppressive to women. She argued that existing religions are based on an 'inadequate God', and women are oppressed in several ways:

1. Religions such as Christianity have often proclaimed that the subordination of women is God's will.

2. God is portrayed as a man and as Father. 'One-sex symbolism' of this sort alienates women and places them in an inferior position to men.

3. Religion tells believers that redemption comes through prayer not through actively trying to change the situation and abolish exploitation. For this reason, it tends to support the continuation of patriarchy.

Daly argued for a new feminist spirituality. This sense of spirituality can come from within women themselves and can lead to the revolutionary overthrow of dominant, male gods. Together, women can 'struggle towards self-transcendence' so that religious and spiritual insight comes from within and not from the teachings of male preachers imposing a male god on women.

In this way, some religions may oppose rather than support male domination. Linda Woodhead (2007) describes the Goddess feminist movement as seeking 'to honour the "divine feminine" in their own lives and in society'. It is committed to the empowerment of women.

Radical feminist approaches which emphasise the importance of Goddess religion have demonstrated that while a belief in God can help to maintain patriarchy, non-patriarchal religions are possible. However, critics argue that Daly's work is rather generalised and, in places, lacks detailed evidence to support her claims. Nevertheless, Shih believes

that this type of research has been significant in developing the sociology of religion in general, by helping to open up female and feminist perspectives. For example, Linda Woodhead (2007a) has discussed how involvement in New Age activities such as Reiki in Kendal, Cumbria can be a way for women to gain self-esteem when their sense of self-worth has been undermined by male partners.

Activity

The Glastonbury Goddess Temple in Somerset.

1. Explain two arguments for the view that religion is inevitably patriarchal.

2. Explain one argument for the view that non-patriarchal religions are possible.

Patriarchy, Islam and the limited role of religion

Both Simone de Beauvoir and advocates of Goddess religion write from the perspective of Western, Christian women. Furthermore, they assume that religion itself is a main cause of patriarchy. However, Nawal El Saadawi (1980), an Egyptian feminist writer, discusses female oppression in the Arab world and elsewhere. She examines the importance of religion in perpetuating oppression but does not see religion itself as the main underlying cause of oppression. Instead, she sees it as just one aspect of a wider patriarchal system which needs to be overthrown.

El Saadawi denies that the oppression of women is directly caused by religion in general, or by Islam in particular. She notes that oppressive practices such as female circumcision have often been attributed to the influence of Islam. However, female circumcision has been practised in a considerable number of countries, not all of them Islamic. In her view, authentic religious beliefs tend to be opposed to any such practices and aim at 'truth, equality, justice, love and a healthy wholesome life for all people, whether men or women'.

Furthermore, other religions, including Christianity, are often more oppressive than Islam. To El Saadawi, female oppression is not essentially due to religion but to patriarchy. Nevertheless, she does see religion as playing a role in women's oppression. Men have often distorted religion to serve their own interests, to help justify or legitimate the oppression of women.

El Saadawi is not hostile to religion itself, but only to the domination of religion by patriarchal ideology.

Evaluation of radical feminism

1. Critics argue that much radical feminism tends to generalise about religion and to see all religions as equally patriarchal. However, some liberal feminists have identified certain religions such as Quakerism that are not clearly or strongly patriarchal.

2. Radical feminists also tend to ignore evidence that progress has been made and aspects of patriarchal ideology within religion have been successfully challenged.

3. In some cases, radical feminists have not backed up their views with detailed research. In other cases, the validity or representativeness of the research may be open to question.

4. Radical feminists are not particularly sensitive to the ways in which women may find space within or use apparently patriarchal religions to further their own interests (see below).

Liberal feminist perspectives on religion

Radical feminists tend to believe that patriarchy is so built into existing religions that only their destruction or replacement with an alternative can lead to the furthering of feminism. However, liberal feminists, while also regarding existing religions as patriarchal, focus more on reforming religions in order to remove patriarchal elements from them. In their view, religion and feminism are compatible. They start off by identifying the aspects of religion which, in their view, need reforming.

Inequalities in major religions

Jean Holm (1994) argued that, while the classical teachings of many religions have stressed equality between men and women, in practice they have usually been far from equal. In Japanese folk religions, for example, women are responsible for organising public rituals but only men can take part in the public performances. In Chinese popular religion, women are associated with Yin and men with Yang. However, Yang spirits are more important and powerful. In Buddhism, both men and women can have a religious role, as monks and nuns, respectively. However, all monks are seen as senior to all nuns. Orthodox Judaism only allows males to take a full part in ceremonies. In Islam, in some regions, women are not allowed to enter mosques for worship, and men have made all the legal rulings.

The limits to patriarchy and progress towards greater equality

Many liberal feminists suggest that the patriarchal oppression of women within religion is not universal. Essays in a book edited by Jean Holm (1994) identified three main reasons for this:

1. Some religions are generally patriarchal but aspects of them can still provide significant opportunities for women. For example, Leila Badawi (1994) noted aspects of Islam that are positive for women. Unlike Christian women, Muslim women keep their own family name when they get married.

2. There are a few religions which do not have a strong tradition of patriarchy and have always been relatively egalitarian. According to Alexandra Wright (1994), some Christian religions, particularly Quakerism, have never been oppressive to women.

3. Patriarchal aspects of some religions are changing, partly as a result of liberal feminists' actions and campaigns for gender equality within religions. For example, some have campaigned for women to hold senior posts within the Church of England hierarchy on equal terms to men. Partly due to such campaigns, women have been consecrated as Bishops within the Church of England since 2015. Others are currently campaigning for the Roman Catholic Church to ordain women as priests.

Evaluation of liberal feminism

1. Although there is evidence of some progress as a result of liberal feminism, the extent of this progress is open to question. Radical feminists tend to believe that patriarchy is so embedded within existing religions that reform will never be enough to significantly improve the position of women within religion and within society in general.

2. Some feminists, while not rejecting liberal feminism altogether, believe it has had only a limited impact. Fang-Long Shih (2010) refers to research which suggests that, even with increasing numbers of

215

women ordained within the Church of England, relatively little has changed and sexist attitudes within the Church remain strong.

3. Statistical evidence suggests that there is still a long way to go before women achieve equality within the Church of England. For example, in 2012, women made up 12 per cent of senior staff (including cathedral clergy, archdeacons and bishops) and in 2015, this figure stood at 19 per cent (Church of England, 2016).

Patriarchy and women in conservative religions

Conservative religions, which tend to support traditional values, are often seen as the most oppressive types of religion for women. **Fundamentalism** and **evangelicalism**, which advocate traditional morality and the importance of the domestic role and modesty for women, seem to be particularly patriarchal. However, some feminist sociologists question whether they necessarily always succeed in oppressing women. A number of researchers have found evidence that women find space within such religions to develop their own ideas or use aspects of these religions to further their own interests. For example, Sophie Gilliat-Ray (2010) points out that some British-born Muslim girls and young women wear the hijab (a scarf covering their head and hair) as a means of negotiating approval from their parents to go into higher education or paid employment. This helps to explain why many conservative religions are embraced with some enthusiasm by a significant number of women. It also suggests that religion might affect different women in different ways so that generalisations about religion are inappropriate.

Islam and the veil

Many feminists view the issue of veiling and modest dress among Muslim women as controversial. Rachel Rinaldo (2010) notes that, as veiling regained popularity in the 1970s and 1980s, 'the reaction from feminists was overwhelmingly negative', seeing the practice as a 'reassertion of patriarchy'. After the Islamic revolution in Iran in 1979, veiling was made compulsory, and some saw this as a direct attack on women's rights. However, these assumptions have been challenged by a number of feminist writers.

Helen Watson (1994) argues that the veiling of Muslim women can be interpreted as beneficial to them. She examines three Muslim women's responses to veiling

and finds that Muslim women in a globalised world can use veils in a positive way. As Western culture tries to influence Islamic countries, and more Muslims live in the Western world, the veil can take on new meanings for women. For example, Nadia, a second-generation British-Asian woman studying medicine at university, actively chose to start wearing a veil when she was 16. She was proud of her religion and wanted others to know that she was Muslim. She felt that 'It is liberating to have the freedom of movement and to be able to communicate with people without being on show. It's what you say that's important not what you look like.' She found that, far from making her invisible, wearing a veil made her stand out, yet it also helped her to avoid 'lecherous stares or worse' from men.

Watson concludes that veiling is often a reaction against an increasingly pervasive Western culture. It can be seen as the assertion of independence, separate identity and a rejection of Western **cultural imperialism**. Rather than seeing the veil as a sign of male oppression, it is 'part of the search for an indigenous Islamic form of protest' against patriarchy in society.

Watson's conclusions, however, should be treated with some caution. Her observations are based on a sample of three women. She appears to have made no attempt to find Muslim women who felt men or patriarchal society forced them into wearing the veil against their will.

Activity

In France, it is illegal for women to wear a niqab in public places but critics argue that this infringes their freedom of expression and religion.

1. Why might some feminists support a ban on wearing a niqab in public?

2. Why might other feminists oppose such a ban?

3. To what extent do you agree that the state should impose rules on what people wear in public?

Key terms

Monotheism The belief in one god rather than in many gods. Islam and Christianity are examples of monotheistic religions.

Goddess religion Religion that honours the Divine Feminine, the female side of the divine.

Fundamentalism A form of religion whose adherents want to return to what they see as the core doctrines of the faith as set out in sacred texts such as the Bible or the Qur'an. Christian fundamentalists, for example, adopt a literal interpretation of Biblical accounts of miracles and the Creation.

Evangelicalism A movement within Protestant Christianity that is seen as conservative in its support of traditional values.

Cultural imperialism The practice of imposing a culture, viewpoint or civilisation on people in another, less powerful country.

Summary

1. Feminist theories see religion as a patriarchal institution in terms of its hierarchical organisations, its laws and customs, its sacred texts and its places of worship.

2. Radical feminists such as de Beauvoir argue that religion is inevitably patriarchal and must be abolished.

3. While accepting that religion oppresses women, some feminists argue that patriarchal religions need to be replaced with non-patriarchal religions such as a new feminist spirituality or a Goddess religion.

4. Nawal El Saadawi sees religion as playing a role in women's oppression but rejects the idea that it is the main cause of oppression. Instead, she sees religion as one aspect of a wider patriarchal system.

5. Critics of radical feminism point out that not all religions are equally patriarchal and that aspects of patriarchal ideology within religions have been successfully challenged. Furthermore, women may use apparently patriarchal religions to further their own interests.

6. Liberal feminist perspectives focus on removing patriarchal aspects from religion and argue that progress has been made towards greater equality. Critics question the extent of this progress and reform.

7. Fundamentalism and evangelical Christianity are seen as particularly patriarchal. However, some feminist sociologists argue that women can find space within such religions to develop their own ideas.

8. Many feminists have reacted negatively to the popularity of veiling among Muslim women. However, Watson argues that wearing a veil in a globalised world can be beneficial to Muslim women.

Unit 3.2.4 Rational choice theory

Rational choice theory is seen as a more recent paradigm (a complete theoretical approach) within the sociology of religion by commentators such as R. Stephen Warner (1993). But what is rational choice theory? In what ways is it distinctive as a way of making sense of religion in contemporary societies? How does it explain the appeal of religion? What are the criticisms of this theory? This unit will examine these and other questions about rational choice theory.

The main features of rational choice theory

Rational choice theory has a number of distinctive features compared to other theories of religion:

1. It originated in the USA (a consumer society) and is largely based on the USA where religion thrives and religious practice is more widespread than in countries such as Britain and other parts of Europe.

2. It assumes that most people are naturally religious.

3. It argues that there are rational reasons behind belief in religion – people are rational and motivated by self-interest. They believe in religion because there is a benefit or reward in it for them. Rational choice theory, therefore, adopts a more individualistic stance than perspectives such as functionalism, Marxism and feminism. Religion is seen as meeting the needs of individuals rather than those of social groups or society as a whole.

4. Economic concepts influence the way that rational choice theory views religion. Religion is seen in similar terms to a market and individual consumer choices are important in determining whether a particular religion is successful in the religious marketplace. Religions that provide people with what they want will be in high demand.

217

5. The overall success of religion depends partly on the 'supply side' – that is, on whether religious organisations offer consumers of religion a good selection of alternative products (religious organisations) to choose from.

6. Rational choice theory generally rejects the view that religion is declining. (See also Part 6 for a discussion of secularisation.)

Activity

Rational choice theory views religion in similar terms to a market.

1. How far do you agree that when people make choices between religions, they act like consumers choosing between different products in the marketplace?

2. In your view, to what extent is religion a matter of individual choice?

Stark and Bainbridge's account of rational choice theory

Rodney Stark and William Sims Bainbridge (1985) are the most influential proponents of rational choice theory. They believe that religion helps to meet universal human needs. In their view, 'humans seek what they perceive to be rewards and try to avoid what they perceive to be costs'. In other words, people do what they believe will be good for them. Although this provides a straightforward basis for human decision-making, individuals still face problems:

1. Many of the things that people desire, for example wealth and status, are scarce and cannot be obtained by everybody.

2. Some things that people strongly desire, such as eternal life or immortality, may not be available at all. Despite the lack of convincing evidence that eternal life is possible, people continue to want it, and this desire provides the basis for religion.

Compensators

Stark and Bainbridge recognise that religion might not actually provide people with eternal life but it does offer them **compensators**. A compensator is a belief that a reward can be obtained at some point in the future. It is a type of IOU – if individuals act in a particular way, they may eventually get their reward. In the absence of immediate rewards, people are likely to seek compensators instead. For example, when a parent persuades a child that working hard now will eventually lead to fame and riches or a well-paid job, they are offering their child a compensator as a substitute for immediate rewards.

Compensators and the supernatural

Sometimes individuals want rewards that are incredibly remote from their everyday experience. One example is immortality and, in this case, the possibility of getting the reward can only be contemplated alongside a belief in the supernatural. People have always asked questions about the purpose of life. They want answers that suggest that life has meaning. Stark and Bainbridge argue that only a belief in a god allows people to have answers to such fundamental questions. According to this viewpoint, religion consists of organisations which offer compensators that are based on supernatural rewards. The promise of eternal life after death is an example of such a compensator.

Religious pluralism and secularisation

Because religion answers universal questions and offers compensators that meet universal human needs, Stark and Bainbridge believe that religion can neither disappear nor seriously decline. Churches that compromise their beliefs in the supernatural become less appealing to consumers as a source of compensators. If this happens, people turn to other religious organisations and particularly to new sects and cults that have a greater emphasis on the supernatural. (See Unit 3.4.2 and 3.4.3 for a discussion of sects and cults.)

According to Stark and Bainbridge, American society has become characterised by increasing religious pluralism as people have sought new sources of compensators. Stark and Bainbridge argue that few people lack any religious or supernatural beliefs. They do not think that secularisation has taken place or that it will take place to any great extent in the future.

Rational choice theory and Latin America

Rational choice theory was first developed in the USA and seems to fit the US experience of religion particularly well. For example, there is no official state religion such as an equivalent to the Church of England in the USA. As a result, different denominations such as Roman Catholicism, Methodism and Pentecostalism have to compete with each other in the religious marketplace in order to attract customers. However, rational choice theory has also been applied to other parts of the world including Latin America.

Anthony Gill (1998, 1999, discussed in Davie, 2007) argued that religious growth in Latin America has resulted from increased competition with the Catholic Church. There has been a rapid growth in Pentecostal groups that actively compete to try to recruit former Catholics.

However, Gill argues that rational choice theory can also be applied to the actions of the Catholic Church itself. In some countries, such as Chile, the dominance of the Catholic Church has been threatened by the existence of a strong socialist movement as well as by evangelical Protestants trying to recruit new supporters. In other countries, such as Argentina, there has been much less threat to the dominance of the Catholic Church. In Chile, the Catholic Church shifted its position, distancing itself somewhat from the state and paying more attention to the wishes and interests of the poor. In Argentina, however, with much less threat to its dominance, the Catholic Church has tended to continue to ally closely with the state.

Gill believes that not only individuals but also religious organisations act rationally in pursuit of what they see as their own self-interest. Rational choice theory can, therefore, be applied to understanding different aspects of religion, not just personal belief and the overall strength of religion.

Evaluation of rational choice theory

Given that rational choice theory has tried to produce a complete new theory of religion and has challenged widely held existing views, it is not surprising that it has been heavily criticised.

1. Bruce (2011) rejects the view that, because all humans seek what religion has to offer, secularisation cannot take place to a significant extent. Instead, he argues that secularisation is taking place and this suggests that the demand for religion can decline over time. Furthermore, if rational choice theorists are correct in seeing religion as yet another consumer choice, this implies that religion has lost its central importance in people's lives and that secularisation is taking place. (See Part 6 for further discussion.)

2. Bruce also attacks the underlying principles on which rational choice theory is based. He does not deny that humans behave, at least in part, rationally. However, he does not believe that in choosing religions, people act in the same way as a consumer choosing which product to buy. When buying soap powder or a pair of jeans, there is a clear way to compare the costs and benefits of rival brands. However, there is no clear way of comparing rival beliefs when choosing a religion. Furthermore, religion is not simply a matter of individual choice but is bound up with people's social identities and culture. In practice, the majority of people in many societies cannot easily switch between different religions. If they do so in places such as Kabul or Baghdad, they may face ostracism or worse. Rational choice theory neglects the cultural and social contexts in which people make decisions.

Some European sociologists, however, do not reject rational choice theory completely. For example, Grace Davie (2007) believes that the theory is more applicable in some parts of the world than in others. In the USA, the lack of a state religion or an established church means that the choice of religion is more fluid and there is more competition between religious organisations for customers. Furthermore, in both Europe and North America, religious belief and practice have begun to shift from 'obligation to consumption' – as social pressure on people to conform to the same religious beliefs as their parents has declined. From Davie's point of view, therefore, rational choice theory is becoming more relevant as time progresses.

219

Malcolm Hamilton (2009) also takes a balanced view of rational choice theory. On the positive side, he argues that it shows that 'religion involves active agency, and is not simply the product of socialization'. As a result, rational choice theory moves beyond some theories, such as functionalism, which tend to assume that people will be socialised into the religious culture of the society in which they live. However, Hamilton also says that 'it goes, perhaps, rather too far in this direction, ignoring structural variables and social constraints'. In other words, it focuses on individual decision-making but neglects factors such as the political and cultural settings that people find themselves in and the influence of class, status and ethnicity on their preferences.

Key term

Compensators Beliefs that rewards can be obtained at some point in the future.

Summary

1. Rational choice theory assumes that people are naturally religious.

2. Rational choice theory suggests that there are rational reasons behind people's belief in religion. Religions that provide people with what they want will always be in high demand in the religious marketplace.

3. Stark and Bainbridge argue that religion helps to meet universal human needs.

4. According to Stark and Bainbridge, people look for rewards and try to avoid costs when making decisions. While people strongly desire immortality, this is unavailable. However, this desire provides the basis for religion. Religions offer compensators such as the promise of life after death.

5. Rational choice theory originated in the USA and seems to fit the US experience of religion particularly well. It has also been used to explain the rapid growth of Pentecostalism in Latin America.

6. Bruce argues that secularisation is taking place. He also rejects the idea that people choose a religion by comparing the costs and benefits of rival beliefs. Furthermore, he argues that religion is not simply a matter of individual choice; it is bound up with people's identities and culture. (See Part 6 for further discussion.)

7. According to Hamilton, one strength of rational choice theory is that it presents people as active actors rather than as passive. However, he argues that it ignores the social constraints on people.

Unit 3.2.5 Postmodernist perspectives

Can religion provide humankind with the truth? Why have people become more sceptical about the idea that any set of beliefs can provide a way of understanding the world or resolving the problems that humanity faces? This unit examines how some postmodernist theorists address questions such as these. It begins with a brief outline of modernist beliefs and goes on to criticise them from a postmodernist perspective. It then explores different postmodernist accounts of religion.

The eras of modernity and postmodernity

Many commentators suggest that modern ways of thinking developed with the Enlightenment in Western Europe from around the 17th century (see Unit 3.1.2). They see the Enlightenment as the foundation of modernity. This phase in the development of society is characterised by the belief in reason or rational scientific thought rather than in faith or tradition as ways of explaining the world. Enlightenment thinking is based on several assumptions. First, it assumes that it is possible and desirable to produce objective and valid knowledge about the natural and social worlds. Second, it takes it for granted that knowledge based on factual evidence can be generated by using systematic methods of research. Third, it assumes that the scientific knowledge that is generated in this way can be used to change and improve the social and natural worlds.

The theory of postmodernism challenges these beliefs. First, postmodernism rejects the idea that it is possible to produce valid knowledge. Instead, many postmodernists take a **relativist stance** on knowledge and argue that all knowledge (including that produced by sociologists and natural scientists) is relative and uncertain rather than absolute. There are many versions of reality, none of which is superior to any of the others. A sociologist's account of religion or education, for example, is no better than anyone else's. As a result, there are no rational grounds for using scientific knowledge to improve the social world.

Second, knowledge and belief are seen as products rather than as absolute truths. Postmodernists use the idea of narratives (or stories) rather than truths. Different people have different backgrounds and, as a result, they will have different narratives. Rather than search for the truth, postmodernism compares these narratives.

Third, postmodernists argue that metanarratives or grand theories (such as functionalism, Marxism or world religions including Islam, Judaism and Christianity) that claim to have discovered the truth are misleading. Postmodernists reject all metanarratives that claim to provide definitive, authoritative or complete guides to the truth.

Jean-François Lyotard (1984) argued that religions rest on metanarratives or big stories that give meaning to other narratives or stories. In his view, postmodernism has undermined these metanarratives. People no longer have faith in big, all-embracing theories about how the world works. They are increasingly sceptical about the claim that any set of beliefs, including religious beliefs, can provide a means of understanding and resolving the problems of humanity. For example, religious wars have had devastating effects on people and societies throughout history.

Activity

Harvard University in Massachusetts, USA, dates back to 1636 and is seen as one of the most prestigious universities in the world. Many of its staff engage in research to develop human knowledge.

Why might the idea of extending human knowledge through research be seen as based on Enlightenment thinking?

Zygmunt Bauman's account of religion and postmodernity

According to Zygmunt Bauman (1992), in modernity people searched for universal truths. Postmodernity, however, tears down any claims to universal truth. Furthermore, people no longer accept that others have authority over them or that they must live their lives according to rules imposed on them by an external authority. People are now free to pursue anything, to choose what to believe and how to behave.

In modernity, people were encouraged to behave in particular ways because the rules or laws of society said they should. The rules and laws were justified on rational grounds as providing the best means for achieving given ends. However, the era of postmodernity has torn away the belief that there can be a rational basis for perfecting society. This leaves individuals with no external rules to govern their lives. As a result, personal ethics and morality become important. Morality becomes privatised, a matter of individual choice.

With individuals now being responsible for their own morality, people turn to experts in morality – religious leaders – for guidance on which rules they should adopt and which beliefs to hold. Unlike previous generations, however, they no longer have to turn to the religious leaders that their parents followed for guidance. They have much more freedom to choose which religious or spiritual leaders to follow.

This leads to a revival of religious and **quasi-religious movements** in postmodernity that all claim expertise in moral values. People can try out a range of different religious, spiritual or New Age beliefs, mix them together or switch between them.

Evaluation of Bauman

Sociologists such as David Lyon draw on aspects of Bauman's ideas in developing their theories of religion and postmodernity. However, Bauman's work on religion has been criticised.

1. James A. Beckford (1996) argues that it is contradictory for Bauman to say, on the one hand, that postmodernity undermines faith in external authorities but to suggest, on the other hand, that postmodernity makes people seek the authority of religious experts for their beliefs.

221

2. Beckford does not agree that there has been a significant religious revival in postmodernity because he does not believe that there was an earlier significant decline in religion. This suggests that Bauman may have exaggerated the extent of any changes in modernity as well as the importance of religious movements in postmodernity.

David Lyon's account of Jesus in Disneyland

David Lyon (2000) sees the move towards postmodernity in terms of two key social changes:

1. Developments in information technology allow ideas to spread throughout the world as part of globalisation. On the internet, for example, it is possible to get information about almost any type of religious or spiritual belief. Information technology, along with increased travel, opens up a wider range of possible beliefs from around the globe. These global flows of information and ideas make it harder for people to maintain fixed and unchanging sets of beliefs. They also make it easier to access beliefs from different religions and New Age ideas.

2. Lyon argues that growing **consumerism** is a feature of postmodernity. People are used to being able to choose what fashions they wear and what cars they drive. They now feel they should be able to choose what to believe in from a wide variety of options including non-traditional religions and New Age beliefs and practices.

To Lyon, these changes do not mean that religion is declining or disappearing. Instead, religion is simply relocating to the sphere of consumption. People have become selective consumers of religion. Individuals can choose their own religion in the postmodern world and it can become an important source of their identity. People still seek a narrative or story in order to put their lives in context, but they are less willing to accept the narrative of an established church.

To illustrate his arguments, Lyon uses the image of 'Jesus in Disneyland'. He refers to a Harvest Day Crusade at Disneyland in Anaheim, California. There were several stages on which a variety of Christian singers and other artists performed, and the evangelist Greg Laurie preached the Christian gospel. According to Lyon, this was an example of religion interacting with the most postmodern of settings, Disneyland.

Disneyland is often considered to be postmodern because it is a fantasy world where the images (such as that of Mickey Mouse) have no connection with reality, but are treated as if they are real. For example, some people get the 'autographs' of Mickey Mouse and other characters (or people in costumes). According to Lyon, the Harvest Day Crusade is an example of how religion is adapting to postmodernity and becoming part of it. Religion has discovered new ways to try to appeal to a wide audience. It is no longer confined to established religious institutions such as churches and can be found anywhere. In the case of Jesus in Disneyland, the difference or boundary between religion and **popular culture** is blurred.

Evaluation of Lyon

Lyon seems to be on strong ground in arguing that religion has spread outside the traditional churches and found new ways of trying to appeal to wider audiences. However, sociologists such as Bruce (2002) see this spread of religion as evidence of secularisation rather than of the continuing vitality of religion. It produces only weak religion that has little impact on the way people live their lives. Critics also argue that, for most internet users, online religion supplements rather than replaces their church-based religious activities.

Paul Heelas (1996) sees the New Age as a product of modernity rather than of postmodernity. In his view, the New Age appears, on the surface, to reject mainstream culture. However, it is, in fact, based on an extreme emphasis on individualism (the importance of the individual rather than the group) that is typical of modernity. This individualism allows New Age beliefs to flourish. For instance, it encourages people to try to maximise their own happiness and material success. This links to those aspects of the New Age that aim to provide people with techniques to make them more successful in business or in their careers.

Activity

A sign outside Downtown Disney, a shopping, dining and entertainment complex next to Disneyland, Anaheim.

1. How might Disneyland be seen as a postmodern phenomenon?

2. Explain one way in which religion may be adapting to postmodernity.

Key terms

Relativist stance A view that sees all knowledge as uncertain rather than absolute and does not accept that one set of ideas reveals the whole truth.

Quasi-religious movements Movements concerned with spiritual issues such as ultimate meaning but which are not overtly religious. Examples include astrology, Transcendental Meditation and New Age spiritualism.

Consumerism An ideology that encourages the acquisition of more and more consumer goods and services.

Popular culture Cultural products such as popular music, reality television, blockbuster films and sport that are accessible to everyone.

Summary

1. Postmodernism challenges modernist beliefs about the natural and social worlds. It sees knowledge as relative rather than absolute. Metanarratives or big stories such as world religions that claim to provide the truth are seen as misleading.

2. Lyotard argues that postmodernism has undermined metanarratives such as Christianity. People are now sceptical about the claim that religious beliefs can provide a way of understanding and resolving humanity's problems.

3. Bauman argues that in postmodernity, people no longer accept that others have authority over them. Morality is a matter of individual choice so people turn to religious leaders for guidance on which beliefs to hold but they can choose which leaders to follow.

4. Postmodernity is characterised by a revival of religious and quasi-religious movements, according to Bauman. People can mix or switch between different religious, spiritual and New Age beliefs.

5. Beckford points out a contradiction in Bauman's account. Bauman argues that postmodernity undermines faith in external authorities but, at the same time, that people seek religious experts' authority for their beliefs.

6. Lyon highlights two features of postmodernity: developments in IT, which allow religious and spiritual ideas to spread globally; and consumerism, which encourages people to choose their beliefs for themselves.

7. In Lyon's view, religion is relocating to the sphere of consumption and people have become selective consumers of religion. Religion can be found in many different settings including Disneyland and has found new ways to appeal to people. However, Bruce sees this as evidence of secularisation.

PART 3 THE RELATIONSHIP BETWEEN RELIGION, SOCIAL CHANGE AND SOCIAL STABILITY

Contents

Sociologists are interested in exploring the relationship between religion and social change. Is religion necessarily a source of stability in society? Can it promote social change and, if so, what sort of change does it bring about? Can changes in society have a significant impact on religion?

In addressing these questions, this part draws on functionalist, Marxist and feminist approaches. It also explores the ideas of Max Weber on the links between religion and social change. Sociologists also investigate the relationship between religion and conflict. What role does religion play in generating conflict? Is conflict between different religions inevitable? Can religious conflict have other roots? This part examines these and other questions about the role of religion in relation to conflict and change.

Unit 3.3.1 Is religion a conservative force or a force for social change?

There are a number of possible relationships between religion, social change and social stability. Religion may be a **conservative force**, a factor that inhibits social change. It may also be a radical force, a factor that helps to promote social change. Another possibility is that changes in society as a whole, such as those linked to globalisation, lead to changes in religion. This unit looks at different sociological accounts of the role that religion plays in relation to social change.

Religion as a conservative force

Religion can be seen as a 'conservative force' in two senses, depending on how 'conservative' is defined. The phrase 'conservative force' is usually used to refer to religion as preventing change and maintaining the status quo. Functionalists, Marxists and feminists generally argue that religion acts as a conservative force in society. However, they disagree in terms of how they interpret this. From a functionalist perspective, religion provides shared beliefs, norms and values. Functionalists claim that religion binds

people together, promotes integration and reinforces the collective conscience (see Unit 3.2.1). It also helps individuals to cope with stresses that could potentially disrupt social life. In these ways, religion facilitates the continued existence of society in its present form and inhibits change. This is interpreted by functionalists in positive terms.

Marx had similar views to functionalism in that he saw religion as maintaining the status quo (see Unit 3.2.2). However, he argued that religion operates in the interests of the ruling class rather than those of society as a whole. By promising its faithful followers rewards in the next life, religion discourages people from demanding radical social changes in this life and acts as an agency of social control.

Many feminists see religion as a patriarchal institution that perpetuates rather than challenges gender inequality. From a feminist perspective, religion can be seen as ideological in that it socialises people into accepting patriarchy and gender inequality as natural and inevitable.

'Conservative' may also refer to traditional beliefs and customs. Usually, if religion helps to maintain the status quo, it will also maintain traditional customs and beliefs. For example, the stance of successive popes has restricted the use of abortion among Roman Catholic women. The Roman Catholic Church also has traditional views on issues such as marriage, divorce, sexuality, contraception and gender.

In some circumstances, however, religion can support social change while at the same time promoting traditional values. This often occurs when there is a revival in fundamentalist religious beliefs within, for example, Christianity or Islam. Such beliefs involve a return to what a group claims are the 'fundamentals' or basic, original beliefs of a religion. Christian fundamentalism in the USA, for example, involves an emphasis on the literal truth of scripture, a literal interpretation of the biblical account of creation and a rejection of evolution. It advocates traditional roles for women in society, and control over female sexuality and reproduction expressed, for instance, it its attitudes to abortion. Bryan Turner (2005) argues that Christian fundamentalism has become an important force in the revival of right-wing politics in the USA.

Fundamentalism involves the reassertion of traditional religious and moral values to counter social changes that have taken place and to oppose the people who support these changes (see Unit 3.6.7). If fundamentalists are successful, they succeed in defending traditional values. At the same time, however, they change society by reversing innovations that took place earlier.

One of the most dramatic examples of fundamentalism causing social change by imposing a return to traditional values has been in Iran. Under the last Shah, Iranian society underwent a process of change. One aspect of this change was the liberalisation of traditional Islamic attitudes to women. In 1979, the Shah was deposed during a revolution that was partly inspired by Islamic fundamentalism. The liberalisation that took place under the Shah was reversed. In this case, it can be argued that religious beliefs contributed to revolutionary changes in society. Religion did not act as a conservative force in one sense of the word (to maintain the status quo). However, in terms of supporting traditional values, it did act as a conservative force. Islamic State (IS) can be interpreted along similar lines. On the one hand, it is a movement that wants to bring about change (the establishment of a state that is governed by Islamic law). On the other hand, IS is seen as an organisation that supports traditional, conservative values. This illustrates the importance of distinguishing between the two meanings of the word 'conservative'.

Activity

A preacher challenges students on an American university campus to abandon evolutionary theory and replace it with Christian beliefs.

1. In what way might religion be seen as a conservative force in society?

2. Briefly explain one similarity between feminist and Marxist views on the relationship between religion and social change.

3. Briefly explain one difference between functionalist and Marxist views on the relationship between religion and social change.

The impact of social changes on religion

Most sociologists argue that changes in the wider society lead to changes in religion rather than the other way round.

1. Talcott Parsons (1937, 1964, 1965) believed that, as society developed, religion lost some of its functions in relation, for example, to the education and legal systems. For instance, religious institutions would lose their educational function as the state took over responsibility for educational provision.

2. Marx believed that a change in the economic base or infrastructure of society would lead to changes in the superstructure, including religion. He anticipated that, when a classless society was established, religion would disappear (Marx and Engels, 1957).

3. Supporters of the secularisation thesis argue that industrialisation and modernisation have led to profound changes that have reduced the importance of religion in society (see Part 6).

4. A number of sociologists have claimed that the advent of postmodernity and globalisation have produced changes in religion. For example, Lyon argues that religion is no longer confined to traditional settings such as churches and can now be found in many different settings including Disneyland (see Unit 3.2.4).

Religion as a change-promoting force

Functionalists and Marxists emphasise the role of religion in promoting social stability and inhibiting social change. By contrast, Weber (1958, first published 1904) argued that in some circumstances, religion can promote social change.

Marx is generally regarded as a **materialist**. He believed that the material world shaped people's beliefs, including their religious beliefs. In his view, the economic system largely determined the beliefs that individuals held. In Marxist terms, the **mode of production** (such as capitalism) determines the type of religion that is dominant in a particular society.

Unlike Marx, Weber rejected the view that religion is always shaped by economic factors. He did not deny that, at certain times and in certain places, economic forces may largely shape religion. However, he denied that this is always the case. In his view, under certain conditions, religious beliefs can have a major influence on economic behaviour and bring about social change.

The relationship between Calvinism and capitalism

In *The Protestant Ethic and the Spirit of Capitalism*, Weber (1958) examined the relationship between the rise of Calvinism (a form of Protestantism) and the development of Western industrial capitalism. Weber tried to demonstrate that Calvinism emerged before the development of capitalism. He also tried to show that capitalism first developed in areas where this religion was influential. In his view, the first capitalist nations emerged among the countries of Western Europe and North America that had Calvinist religious groups. Furthermore, most of the earliest capitalist entrepreneurs in these areas came from the ranks of Calvinists. By comparing religion and economic development in different parts of the world, Weber established a relationship – a correlation – between Calvinism and capitalism. He then went on to explain why this type of religion was linked to capitalism. (See also Chapter 1, Unit 1.2.1.)

The Protestant ethic Calvinism originated in the beliefs of John Calvin in the 17th century. Calvin believed in the doctrine of **predestination**, that God had predestined the world and that a distinct group of people, the **elect**, were destined to go to heaven. The elect had been chosen by God even before they were born. Unlike members of other religions, such as Roman Catholics, Calvinists believed that salvation could not be earned through good behaviour or prayer. Those who were not among the elect could not earn themselves a place in heaven, no matter how well they behaved on earth. They could not change God's decision.

Weber pointed out that Calvinists had a psychological problem: they did not know whether they were among the elect. As a result, they suffered from a kind of inner loneliness or uncertainty about their status. However, they reasoned that only the elect would be able to live a good life on earth. If their behaviour was exemplary, they could feel confident that they were among those chosen by God to go to heaven after death. So their behaviour was not an attempt to earn a place in heaven; instead, it was an attempt to convince themselves that they had been chosen to go there.

The **Protestant ethic** developed first in 17th-century Western Europe amongst Protestants including Calvinists. This ethic was **ascetic**, encouraging abstinence from life's pleasures, an austere lifestyle and self-discipline.

The Protestants attacked time-wasting, laziness, idle gossip and more sleep than was necessary. They frowned on sexual pleasures and believed that sex should remain within marriage and then only for the procreation of children. Sport and recreation were accepted only for improving fitness and health. Going to the pub, dance hall, theatre and gaming house was forbidden. In fact, anything that might distract people from their duty to God to work hard was condemned.

Calvinists saw their work, career or occupation as a **calling**, as something to which they had been called by God. The Protestant ethic produced individuals who worked hard in their callings or careers, in a single-minded manner. Acquiring material wealth provided ascetic Protestants with a clue to their fate. They saw financial success as a sign of God's favour – as a sign that they were one of the elect, saved rather than damned. The money they made, however, could not be spent on luxuries, fine clothes, lavish houses and frivolous entertainment. It had to be spent on the glory of God. In effect, this meant being even more successful in one's calling and, in practice, reinvesting profits in the business. Therefore, the interpretation that the Calvinists put on the original doctrine of predestination contributed to them becoming the first capitalists.

The spirit of capitalism Weber argued that modern capitalist enterprises are organised on rational lines and business transactions are conducted in a systematic manner. Costs and projected profits are carefully assessed. Underlying the practice of capitalism is the **spirit of capitalism** – a set of ethics, values and ideas such as time is money and wasting time loses money. The spirit of capitalism involved seeing the accumulation of capital as an end in itself rather than as a means to an end. It involved dedication to acquiring money through economic activity and avoiding the use of wealth for personal enjoyment.

Weber claimed that the origins of the spirit of capitalism were to be found in the work ethic of ascetic Protestantism. He saw ascetic Protestantism as a vital influence in the creation and development of the spirit and practice of capitalism. In his view, the methodical and single-minded pursuit of a calling encouraged rational capitalism. Making money became both a religious and a business ethic.

Finally, Weber noted that the importance of the creation of wealth and the restrictions on spending it encouraged saving and reinvestment. The ascetic Protestant way of life led to the accumulation of capital, investment and reinvestment. It produced the early businesses that expanded to create capitalist society.

Religion in non-Protestant societies Weber examined the nature of other major world religions in addition to Christianity. He made comparisons between them in order to understand the relationship between religion and changes in society (Weber, 1963, first published 1922). Although other parts of the world possessed many of the necessary preconditions to develop capitalism, they were not among the first areas to develop it. For example, India and China had technological knowledge, labour and individuals engaged in making money. What they lacked, according to Weber, was a religion that encouraged the development of capitalism.

One religion, Jainism in India, had a similar ethic to Calvinist Protestantism. Jainism could potentially produce social change, but, in Weber's view, the economic conditions in India were not fertile ground for capitalism to develop. As a result, capitalism developed first in Europe and North America.

Activity

Weber examined the impact of Protestant religions such as Calvinism on the development of capitalism. Calvinism originated in the beliefs of John Calvin in the 17th century.

Write a summary of Weber's ideas on the relationship between the Protestant ethic and the development of capitalism.

Materialism and Weber's theory Weber argued that he had shown that some religious beliefs could promote economic change. He claimed that he had found a weakness in Marx's materialism, which implied that the economic system always shaped ideas. Weber put much more emphasis than Marx on the influence of ideas in bringing about economic change. However, Weber also recognised the importance of the economy, material factors and technology in making capitalism possible. Material factors were as important as ideas in the development of capitalism. Neither could be ignored in any explanation.

Evaluation of Weber

1. Critics disagree with Weber's interpretation of Protestant theology. Sombart (1907) argued that Weber was mistaken about the beliefs held by Calvinists. According to Sombart, Calvinism opposed greed and the pursuit of money for its own sake. However, Weber pointed out that it was not the Calvinist beliefs in themselves that were important. The doctrine of predestination was not intended to produce the rational pursuit of profit. However, this was one of its unintended consequences in that it led to the Protestant work ethic.

2. A second criticism points to parts of the world where Calvinism was strong, but capitalism did not develop until much later. For example, Switzerland, Scotland, Hungary and parts of the Netherlands all contained large Calvinist populations, but were not among the first capitalist countries. However, Gordon Marshall (1982) argued that Weber did not claim that Calvinism was the only factor necessary for the development of capitalism. Simply finding Calvinist countries that failed to become capitalist comparatively early cannot therefore disprove Weber's theory. In his own study of Scotland, Marshall found that the Scots had a capitalist mentality but were held back by a lack of skilled labour and capital for investment, and by government policies that did not stimulate the development of industry.

3. Kautsky (1953), a Marxist critic, argued that early capitalism came before and largely determined Protestantism. He saw Calvinism as developing in cities where commerce and early forms of industrialisation were already established. This is a chicken and egg question – which came first: Calvinism or capitalism? Defenders of Weber insist that a distinctive rational capitalist entrepreneur did not emerge until after Calvinism.

4. Other critics question whether it was the religious beliefs of Calvinists that led to them becoming business people. According to this view, Calvinists devoted themselves to business because they were excluded from holding public office and from joining certain professions by law. Like the Jews in Eastern and Central Europe, they tried to become economically successful in order to overcome their political persecution. However, Weber's supporters argue that only Calvinists developed capitalist behaviour involving rational planning to accumulate capital. As a result, only they could develop capitalist businesses before capitalism was established.

Despite these criticisms, Weber does successfully highlight the theoretical point that ideas – in this case, religious ideas – can possibly lead to economic change.

Contemporary issues: Pentecostalism

Pentecostal movements are one of the faster growing churches within contemporary world Christianity and have spread rapidly in Latin America and other underdeveloped societies. One interpretation of Pentecostalism regards it as a new form or expression of Max Weber's Protestant ethic (Martin, 2013). The lifestyle of Pentecostals, based on hard work, saving money and self-discipline, is seen as encouraging upward social mobility and effective participation in a modern economy. Consequently, in this view, Pentecostalism can be associated with economic and social change.

Pentecostalism is seen as a modernising movement in underdeveloped societies in Latin America, Asia and Africa in terms of economic behaviour. Its beliefs are compatible with economic and industrial growth. It also seeks to transform family life and the role of women to bring about greater gender equality.

David Martin (2013) points out that Pentecostals believe in bettering themselves and self-help. They are prepared to change their circumstances themselves rather than expecting other people to put right their wrongs for them. He sees Pentecostal pastors as religious entrepreneurs who run small, medium or large enterprises including transnational megachurches that are religious versions of large-scale businesses. Becoming a pastor can provide a route of rapid upward social mobility for some.

Allan H. Anderson (2014) suggests that Pentecostalism can change its believers' values and motivate new economic behaviour. As a result, Pentecostalism has encouraged capitalism and development in, for example, parts of Africa. He agrees with Martin that Pentecostalism can create upward social mobility and adds that it legitimises economic success.

Activity – The Prosperity Gospel in Brazil

The Temple of Solomon in São Paulo, Brazil is the world headquarters of the neo-Pentecostal Universal Church of the Kingdom of God.

Pentecostalism is the fastest growing sector of Protestantism in Brazil, a predominantly Roman Catholic country in Latin America. Many neo-Pentecostal churches have introduced the Prosperity Gospel to Brazil. The Religious Literacy Project argues that one key belief of the Prosperity Gospel concerns the power of Jesus Christ and the gospel to heal not only people's emotional and physical illnesses, but also their financial or economic ills. In effect, having faith, praying and donating money to a Pentecostal church can lead to financial rewards and riches. Wealth and prosperity are seen as signs of God's favour while, by implication, poverty is linked to a lack of faith.

The majority of members of these neo-Pentecostal churches in Brazil are female, black and poor, and most have limited education. The Religious Literacy Project argues that, before liberation theology emerged, the Catholic Church failed to address the interests and needs of the increasing numbers of poor people. Pentecostal churches flourished among these groups. They offered people a community with strict rules against the possible temptations of urban or city life (such as gangs, sex, drugs and alcohol). In more recent times, Neo-Pentecostalism's enthusiastic acceptance and promotion of the Prosperity Gospel associates devotion with upward social mobility. This has contributed to the widespread appeal of neo-Pentecostalism among the urban poor as well as the middle class.

Question

How might Pentecostalism be used as an example to support the view that religious ideas can encourage social and economic change?

Examples of religion as a force for change

There are numerous examples to show that religion can undermine stability or promote change:

1. In Northern Ireland, Roman Catholicism has long been associated with Irish Republicanism and the desire to become part of a united Ireland.

2. In the USA in the 1960s, the Reverend Martin Luther King and the Southern Christian Leadership Council played a leading role in establishing civil rights and securing legislation intended to reduce racial discrimination.

3. In the 1960s, a number of radical and revolutionary groups emerged within the Roman Catholic Church in Latin America. They preached liberation theology, arguing that it was the duty of church members to fight against unjust and oppressive right-wing dictatorships (see Unit 3.2.2). In 1979, Catholic revolutionaries supported the left-wing Sandinistas when they seized control in Nicaragua.

4. In Iran, Islamic fundamentalism played a part in the 1979 Islamic revolution, led by the Ayatollah Khomeini. Meredith B. McGuire (2002) argues that charismatic religious leaders (those with the force of personality to make people follow them) such as Khomeini can sometimes gain sufficient support to produce change.

5. Poland provides another example to show that religion can stimulate change. The Roman Catholic Church opposed the communist state in Poland. It supported the attempts of Solidarity, the free trade union, to achieve changes in Polish society. In 1989, the communist monopoly on power was broken when Solidarity was allowed to contest and win many seats in the Polish parliament.

6. In South Africa, Archbishop Desmond Tutu was a prominent opponent of Apartheid (1948–1994) which was based on a government policy of racial segregation. Archbishop Tutu helped to bring this racist system to an end.

Examples such as these led G.K. Nelson (1986) to conclude that, 'far from encouraging people to accept their place, religion can spearhead resistance and revolution'. In many cases when religion has been a force for change in society, the society that results may be strongly influenced by that religion.

More recent examples of religion as a force for change

More recently, actions that are carried out in the name of religion can be seen as generating political changes including changes in foreign policy and regimes. Karen Armstrong (2014) notes that the hijackers who attacked the World Trade Center in New York on 11 September 2001 saw this atrocity as a religious act. The 9/11 attacks were carried out by al-Qaeda, a militant Islamic group. Osama Bin Laden (al-Qaeda's leader, who was killed in 2011) represented the attacks as a holy war. Other commentators point out that the 9/11 attacks led to President Bush's 'war on terror', which involved the invasion of Afghanistan and changes to the regime in that country.

The term 'political Islam' is used to refer to the attempts of Muslim movements, groups and individuals to rebuild the social, cultural, economic and political basis of their society along Islamic lines (Esposito and El-Din Shahin, 2013). In practice, political Islam is concerned with bringing about changes in society, such as legal changes or a more conservative morality.

Shahram Akbarzadeh (2012) sees Islamism as a 'modern-day ideology' and Islamists as 'active agents of change'. Islamists pursue 'the goal of a perfect world, one that is run in accordance with divine will and in line with a specific reading of Islamic history'. The ultimate objective of Islamism is the establishment of an Islamic state.

John L. Esposito and Emad El-Din Shahin (2013) argue that there are different approaches to bringing about change. Most Islamic movements have engaged in the process of democratisation in the countries in which they are based. Others, such as the military wings of Hamas (a Palestinian Islamist movement) and of Lebanon's Hezbollah movement, have chosen to engage in violence and terrorism in order to generate change. Andrea Teti and Andrea Mura (2009), however, point out that violent Islamists are, in fact, a small minority.

The Arab Spring is another relatively recent example that illustrates the role that religion can play in generating social and political change. This term is used to describe a number of rebellions and protests that challenged undemocratic and corrupt regimes that held power in several Arab countries including Tunisia, Egypt, Libya and Syria. These protests involved Muslims and other groups who used social media networks to exchange views, demand reforms and generate political change.

The first uprising of the Arab Spring began in Tunisia in 2010 and resulted in the overthrow of the Tunisian president in 2011. In October 2011, open elections were held in Tunisia and a democratic government took power. The success of this uprising gave hope to other social movements, and demonstrations and protests led to the resignation of President Mubarak of Egypt in 2011. The Muslim Brotherhood played a part in these protests, and formed a government in Egypt after winning an open and free election in 2012. The example of the Arab Spring suggests that religion can promote social and political change by helping to give a voice to dissent and demands for reform. The democratic reforms introduced, however, may not necessarily be long-term ones. In Egypt, for instance, the army backed the overthrow of Egypt's elected president in 2013 and began a crackdown on critics including the Muslim Brotherhood.

Activity

Anti-government protesters gather in Tahrir Square, Cairo, Egypt on 1 February, 2011.

How far does the example of the Arab Spring illustrate the idea that religion can play a part in bringing about social change?

Factors affecting whether religion promotes or inhibits change

Meredith B. McGuire (2002) argues that religion can often support the status quo and act as a conservative force. In her view: '... religious beliefs that are taken-for-granted truths build a strong force against new ways of thinking. Practices handed down through tradition as the God-approved ways are highly resistant to change.' However, she also acknowledges that religion can be a force for change. She notes that processes causing change in society are complex and that religion may be only one factor linked to change.

For these reasons, it is difficult to isolate the effects that religion can have on change, or even to identify whether religion really is a factor in causing change.

Nevertheless, McGuire is clear that religion can have a significant role in producing change. For example, she believes that the Society of Friends (Quakers) played an important role in the abolition of slavery, in promoting prison reform in the USA and England, and in starting self-help projects in Ireland following the famine in the 19th century.

McGuire argues that religion can be both conservative and radical. She identifies the following factors as being most significant in determining whether religion acts as a conservative force or a force for change.

1. The beliefs of the particular religion. Religions with strong moral codes are more likely to produce members who are critical of society and who seek to change it. If a religion stresses concern with this world, its members are more likely to engage in action that produces change than a religion which is more concerned with sacred and spiritual matters. Consequently, Protestantism can have more impact on social change than Buddhism.

2. The culture of the society in which a religion exists. In societies where religious beliefs are central to the culture (such as Latin American countries), anyone wishing to produce change tends to use religion to justify their actions. In Britain, however, religion plays a less central role in society's culture, so it tends to have a less important role in legitimising social change.

3. The social location of religion. This concerns the part that religion plays in the structure of society. The greater the importance of religion, the greater its potential to play a part in producing change. Where an established church or other religious organisation plays a major role in political and economic life, there is considerable scope for religion to impact on processes of change. Sometimes, the social location of religion changes. For example, in Brazil, from 1964 until 1985, the Catholic Church was a crucial focus of opposition to the military dictatorship in power. However, once the military regime was replaced and the civilian government allowed more protest and dissent, the political significance of the Catholic Church as a source of opposition declined.

4. The internal organisation of religious institutions. Religions with a strong, centralised source of authority have more chance of affecting events. On the other hand, the central authority might try to restrain the actions of parts of its organisation. For example, at the Puebla Conference in Mexico in 1978, the Pope clashed with Latin American Roman Catholic bishops who were advocating liberation theology and the need to bring about political change, fight oppression and support the poor.

Activity

Some religions, such as Buddhism, may have less impact on social change than others.

Explain why the beliefs of some religions may be more likely than others to produce adherents who seek to change society.

Key terms

Conservative force A factor such as religion or the mass media that inhibits rather than promotes social, economic or political change.

Materialist A term to describe someone who believes that material forces (such as economic and technological factors) shape society, including people's beliefs and ideas.

Mode of production Marx used this term to refer to the prevailing system under which people produce the things they need to subsist. Examples include feudalism and capitalism.

Predestination The belief that God has predetermined whether people will be saved or damned after they die.

Elect The people chosen by God to be saved and destined to go to heaven.

Protestant ethic Weber used this term to refer to the value that Calvinists placed on the importance of thrift, abstaining from pleasure and the duty to work hard in one's calling.

Ascetic An austere and self-disciplined lifestyle that does not involve indulging in any of life's pleasures.

Calling The vocation, position in society or particular way of life that some individuals believe they are called to by God.

Spirit of capitalism The essence of capitalism involving the single-minded pursuit of profit as an end in itself.

Summary

1. Religion can be seen as a conservative force in terms of preventing social, political and economic change, and also in terms of maintaining traditional customs and beliefs regarding, for example, abortion and divorce.

2. In the case of fundamentalism, religion can support social change and promote traditional values at the same time.

3. Functionalist, Marxist and feminist approaches see religion as a conservative force but disagree on how to interpret this.

4. One possibility is that changes in society lead to changes in religion. For example, the advent of postmodernity and globalisation has generated changes in religion.

5. Weber saw religion as a force for change and argued that the Calvinist way of life was a key factor in the development of capitalism.

6. While Marx argued that the economic base largely determined the superstructure including religious beliefs, Weber argued that religious beliefs could have a major effect on economic behaviour and bring about social change.

7. Critics question Weber's interpretation of Calvinist beliefs and point out that capitalism preceded Calvinism.

8. There are many examples to show that religion can generate change, such as liberation theology in Latin America and Islamic fundamentalism in Iran during the 1979 revolution.

9. McGuire identifies several factors that affect whether religion promotes or inhibits change. These are the beliefs of a particular religion; the culture of the society within which the religion exists; the social location of religion; and the internal organisation of religious institutions.

Unit 3.3.2 Religion as a source of conflict

Religion is often seen as inherently violent and has been linked to conflicts in many parts of the world including Northern Ireland, Bosnia, the Middle East and the Indian subcontinent. These conflicts include acts of terrorism, civil war and riots. In 2017, for example, ISIS claimed responsibility for terror attacks in cities around the world including Manchester, London, Paris, Kabul and Tehran. But are clashes between different religious groups inevitable? This unit examines some of the contrasting views on the relationship between religion and conflict. It begins by considering the view that there is a strong link between religion and violence, and the claim that it is inevitable that different religions will tend to clash. It also examines the view that conflict between Islam and the West is far from inevitable, but is the product of particular conditions. It then explores the idea that religious conflicts can have other roots as well. Finally, it looks at religious conflict in liberal democracies such as Western European countries.

The connections between religion and violence

Mark Juergensmeyer (2009) points out that 'the idea of nonviolence is central to most religious traditions'. However, he notes that many violent acts in the world today are carried out in the name of religion. He gives the examples of Shiite death squads killing Sunni Muslims in Baghdad; of Jewish settlers who think that parts of Palestine should be 'cleansed' of Arabs; of Christian fundamentalists attacking workers in abortion clinics in the USA; of a Japanese religious cult releasing nerve gas on the Tokyo subway; and of Buddhist monks in Sri Lanka encouraging aggression towards Tamil separatists.

Juergensmeyer argues that far from consistently encouraging peace, 'the histories of most religions have left a trail of blood'. Partly, this is because all the main religions have some beliefs which allow or even encourage violence from their followers. In Christianity, for example, those who support the use of force can refer to the incident in the Bible in which Jesus drove money lenders from the temple, declaring that he had come to bring a sword rather than peace. From the 4th century, Christianity adopted the concept of a 'just war' and rejected the idea of **pacifism**.

Aspects of Islamic beliefs also justify violence. For example, violent punishments are specified in Islam for certain types of wrongdoing. The idea of *jihad* literally means 'striving' (for religious purity) and Islam does not allow violence for personal gain. However, *jihad* is often translated as meaning 'holy war' and it has increasingly been used as a term to justify violence in defence of the Islamic faith.

Why contemporary religions have become violent

According to Juergensmeyer, most major religions allow violence and may encourage it in response to threats to the religion. He argues that religion and violence have always been closely intertwined. In his view, the ultimate aim of religion is to achieve order on earth, which will lead to peace and harmony. However, to achieve this order, violence must sometimes be used.

In the modern world, the religious tendency towards violence to achieve order has become linked with nationalism. Religion has been used to legitimate nationalism in a world in which many groups feel that they need to protect the **nation-state** or achieve independence in order to protect their religion. For example, in Israel, many nationalists believe that

Judaism can only survive if Israel is protected from its enemies. Similarly, in Iran, nationalistic politics is closely allied to Islamic faith in opposition to perceived threats from the West.

Religion is sometimes seen as needing protection on a global scale from the threats posed by cultural and economic globalisation. Modern, rational and **secular beliefs** threaten the very idea of religious faith. These beliefs can give rise to global movements taking up the challenge to defend the faith. In Juergensmeyer's view, al-Qaeda is an example of such a movement.

Evaluation of Juergensmeyer

1. Critics argue that Juergensmeyer over-generalises about religion.

2. Juergensmeyer does not demonstrate convincingly that the quest for order is vital to religion. Furthermore, he does not fully explain why the pursuit of this quest should be through violent rather than non-violent means.

3. Juergensmeyer does not discuss religions such as the Quakers, which remain firmly pacifist and strongly opposed to violence. Nor does he explore the role of different religions in helping to discourage violence, build peace and resolve conflicts.

4. According to critics, Juergensmeyer does not explain in detail why particular religions pursue peaceful means to promote their faith in some circumstances but violent means in others.

5. Other theorists question whether there is actually a strong link between religion and violence.

Contemporary issues: The appeal of ISIS to its recruits

The streets of Raqqa, a former ISIS stronghold, in December 2017.

In October 2017, the Islamic State's final strongholds in Raqqa, Syria (where it had planned to build an Islamic state) fell to Kurdish fighters. In the following extract, Jason Burke (2017), a journalist, discusses his interviews with ISIS recruits and the appeal of ISIS to young people in places such as London, Paris or Berlin.

'In 2014 and 2015, I interviewed young men, and some women, who had found the call of Isis irresistible. They came from Belgium and the Maldives, both thousands of miles from the Levant (a region including Syria, Lebanon, Palestine, Israel and Jordan). A few returned to their homelands to proselytise (attempt to convert people, in this context to Islam) or, in Europe, to carry out some of the most infamous terrorist attacks ever. Isis inspired others who had not travelled to execute their own attacks, too. From Bangladesh to Florida, hundreds died in a new wave of terrorist acts. A dozen or so Isis "provinces" were established, from West Africa to eastern Asia.

Many recruits from the UK, Belgium or France were young men of immigrant background with records for petty, and sometimes serious, crime and a superficial knowledge of the faith they professed to follow. Isis offered everything a street gang does — adventure, status, even financial and sexual opportunity — but with the bonus of redemption from past sins and resolution of a complex identity crisis. A weakened Isis, stripped of its territories, is no longer "the biggest … baddest gang around", as one former Belgian Isis recruit described the group to me two years ago, and so the attraction is no longer there.'

Source: Burke, J., (2017) Rise and fall of Isis: its dream of a caliphate is over, so what now? *The Guardian*. 21.10.2017.

Questions

1. What do you think the author means by 'a complex identity crisis' in this context?

2. According to this article, what is the appeal of ISIS to some young people in Europe?

3. Why does the author believe that ISIS has now lost its appeal?

Cultural difference and conflict

Since the Iranian revolution of 1979, there has been hostility between some Islamic fundamentalists and some Western nations. The 9/11 attacks by Islamic militants highlighted the clash and led to further conflict. President Bush's 'war on terror' was largely directed at Islamic countries such as Afghanistan and Iraq.

Samuel P. Huntington (1993) saw such clashes as more or less inevitable. This is due to cultural differences and the emphasis placed upon them in a world where different cultures come into closer contact. However, Karen Armstrong (2001) argues that there is nothing inherently incompatible about the West and the Muslim world. She sees social, political and economic factors rather than cultural incompatibility or deep-seated religious differences as being behind these increased tensions between Islam and the West.

Steve Bruce's account of the relationship between religion and conflict

Steve Bruce (2000) argues that the role of religion in conflict varies. Sometimes religion is no more than a justification for war or violence that has little to do with religion. At other times, religion is important in its own right. Often, however, religious and non-religious factors are intertwined and cannot be separated. According to Bruce, there are three types of relationship between religion and conflict:

1. Religion is often used to justify 'what are essentially secular national or ethnic conflicts, even when the combatants are the same religion' (Bruce, 2000). According to Bruce, one example of this sort of situation was the civil war in the former Yugoslavia in the 1990s. Croats, Serbs and Bosnian Muslims fought one another and religion must have played some role as each group follows a different faith. (Croats are Roman Catholic and Serbs are Orthodox.) However, the war was largely based on ethnic divisions and concerned control of territories rather than the truth of different faiths.

2. At the opposite extreme, some conflicts are essentially to do with religion. Some participants in conflicts see themselves as engaged in a **crusade** (a Christian mission to spread their religion) or *jihad* (the Islamic equivalent). Bruce believes that Osama bin Laden had largely religious motives for his leadership of al-Qaeda, and that Iranian attempts to export its Islamic revolution have also been religiously motivated.

3. In most cases, however, religious and secular motives are 'inseparably intertwined'. There is often an overlap between religious groups, national boundaries and ethnic divisions, so a war might be fought for religion, country and ethnicity at the same time. In these circumstances, religion 'provides each side with a justification for seeing itself as superior (we obey God) and the enemy as inferior (they are the Infidel)' (Bruce, 2000).

Religion and conflict in liberal democracies

More recently, Bruce (2011) examined the extent to which religion in liberal democracies is a cause of conflict. Liberal democracies such as the USA and Western European countries have a plurality of religious beliefs. Bruce argues that most of these countries have reached a settlement that reduces the likelihood of conflict. The settlement usually involves the following:

1. There is a 'public-private divide' with toleration of 'a great deal of religious variety in private'. However, religion is largely excluded from having a role in public life.

2. The previously dominant churches (for example the Roman Catholic Church in Spain or the Church of England in England) are allowed some privileges as long as they do not push them too far or take advantage of them. For example, Church of England schools funded by the state do not push Christianity. Partly because of this, they are often popular with non-Christian parents including Muslims.

Although this settlement often works well, it can run into problems, leading to conflict in a variety of circumstances:

1. Sometimes a minority of the religious reject the whole idea of a public-private divide, arguing that religious beliefs should shape public policy. For example, in the USA some Christian fundamentalists have argued that evolution should not be taught in government-funded schools. Sometimes a religious group believes that the state as a whole should be run along religious lines.

2. A religious group may accept the principle of a public-private divide but not agree with where the line is drawn. For example, there have been several conflicts between Western societies and Muslims over the extent of free speech allowed in the public sphere. Muslims objected strongly to the publication of cartoons depicting the Prophet Muhammad in Denmark in 2006. This led to protests, demonstrations and conflict, including the bombing of the Danish embassy in Pakistan.

3. What religious groups do in private may contradict shared norms or principles. For example, in the USA, following objections to the practice of polygamy (having more than one spouse) among Mormons and their refusal to allow African Americans to be ordained, the authorities forced Mormons to end both of these practices.

Activity

Many people in the West see religion as inevitably linked to conflict, war and violence. However, the two world wars of the 20th century were not caused by religion. In practice, conflicts are often based on interrelated rather than single factors.

1. Explain two reasons why religion may be a source of conflict.

2. What other factors may be involved in conflicts between the West and the Muslim world?

Key terms

Pacifism The belief that violence, including war, can never be justified and that conflict should be resolved through peaceful means.

Nation-state An independent state where the majority of people are from one national group and share the same language, history and traditions.

Secular beliefs Beliefs that have no connection to religion.

Summary

1. Juergensmeyer argues that many violent acts are carried out in the name of religion today. The ultimate aim of religion is to secure order on earth, leading to peace and harmony but to achieve this, violence must sometimes be used. The religious tendency towards violence today is linked to nationalism and globalisation.

2. Critics argue that Juergensmeyer over-generalises and that his explanation lacks detailed evidence. Others question whether religion and violence are strongly linked.

3. Karen Armstrong challenges the view that the world of the West and Islam are inherently incompatible. She argues that political and economic factors, rather than deep-seated religious differences, are behind the clash between some Muslims and the West.

4. Bruce argues that the role of religion in conflict varies. Religion can be used to justify conflict over secular concerns such as control of territories. Other conflicts are motivated by religion. Often, however, religious and secular motives are interconnected.

5. In Bruce's view, most liberal democracies with a plurality of religious beliefs have reached a settlement based on a public-private divide that reduces the likelihood of conflict. However, this settlement can run into problems, leading to conflict.

PART 4 RELIGIOUS ORGANISATIONS AND THE NEW AGE

Contents

Individuals may have their own religious beliefs without belonging to a religious organisation. However, most people express their religious beliefs through organisations, and those organisations tend to shape their beliefs. Religious organisations come in many different shapes and sizes and this part of the chapter asks whether it is possible to understand this diversity by classifying organisations into different types. Some organisations support beliefs or act in ways that appear inexplicable to non-members, and they may be in conflict with wider society or even outside the law. Yet even religions that are widely seen as highly deviant continue to attract recruits and sometimes grow rapidly. Sociologists, therefore, ask why this happens and what motivates people to join these organisations.

Despite the importance of organisations, in recent decades spiritual beliefs have thrived outside religious organisations. The 'New Age' refers to these types of beliefs. Why have they become more popular and what does this tell us about the significance of religion and spirituality today?

Unit 3.4.1 Types of religious organisation

There have been several attempts by sociologists to categorise religious organisations and in the process to understand their role in society. Do any of these attempts succeed in providing a comprehensive approach? Do they help to make sense of the reasons for the development of different types of organisation? This unit examines these issues. We start with an attempt to classify all types of religious organisation in a relatively simple **typology** (a classification of different types of something) before looking in detail at the four main types of organisation and discussing whether they really can be seen as having clearly distinctive characteristics.

Roy Wallis on types of religious organisation

Building on work by earlier writers such as Ernst Troeltsch (1981, first published in 1931) and H.R. Niebuhr (1929), Roy Wallis (1976) classified religious organisations into different types in terms of whether they were *respectable* because they supported the norms and values of the wider society or *deviant* because they did not. They were also distinguished according to whether they were *uniquely legitimate* (they claimed a monopoly on religious truth as the only true religion) or *pluralistically legitimate* (they accepted that other organisations could have legitimate religious beliefs as well). The typology is illustrated in Figure 3.4.1.

Figure 3.4.1 Roy Wallis on types of religious organisation

	Respectable	Deviant
Uniquely legitimate	CHURCH	SECT
Pluralistically legitimate	DENOMINATION	CULT

Source: Wallis, R., *The Road to Total Freedom: A Sociological Analysis of Scientology*, Heinemann, London, 1976, p. 13.

Each of these types of organisation will now be examined in turn to see how well they fit Wallis' typology and how other sociologists have classified them.

Activity – Church, denomination, sect or cult?

1.

2.

3.

4.

1. *Canterbury Cathedral – the most important Cathedral of the Church of England. The Church of England is the official state religion of England.*
2. *Scientologists administer 'stress tests' using apparatus that they believe can identify engrams or harmful memories which stop the brain working effectively. Scientology draws on a variety of belief systems and combines Eastern philosophy with Western thought. It believes that happiness and spiritual enlightenment can be achieved through the science of Dianetics developed by its founder L. Ron Hubbard.*
3. *A sign for The Peoples Temple, a Christian-based religious group that combined Christianity with communist influences. It was founded by a charismatic leader, Jim Jones, in 1955 and ended in Guyana in 1978 when 918 members died in a mass murder/suicide. Believers lived in a commune, and they had to abandon all other beliefs and most social contacts when joining.*
4. *A Methodist Church in Lancaster, Lancashire. Methodism is one of a number of nonconformist Christian religions with their own way of practising Christianity and which broke away from the established church at the end of the 18th century.*

Question
Using Roy Wallis' typology, suggest which of the above images represents a church, a denomination, a sect and a cult. Explain your reasoning.

The church

The word 'church' is used to refer to a large religious organisation that represents the main religion of a society. Individuals may not need to declare their faith to become members. In some churches, baptism ensures that all the children of members are automatically recruited before they are old enough to understand the faith.

In principle, a church might try to be **universal** – to embrace all members of society and to be, in Wallis' words, 'uniquely legitimate' (the only 'true' religion) – but in practice there might be substantial minorities who do not belong. Because of its size, members of a church are drawn from all classes in society, but the upper classes are particularly likely to join because churches are often closely connected to the established political order. For example, the Roman Catholic Church in the Middle Ages had important political, educational and social functions. Even in contemporary Britain, the monarch is both head of the Church of England and head of state.

Churches are traditionally likely to be ideologically conservative and support the status quo. This type of organisation accepts and affirms life in this world: members can play a full part in social life and are not expected to withdraw from society.

In some circumstances a church will jealously guard its monopoly on religious truth, and will not tolerate challenges to its religious authority. For example, between the 12th and 15th centuries in parts of Europe, the Roman Catholic Church used the Inquisition to stamp out heresy – opinions that differed from the established beliefs of the church.

Churches are formal organisations with a hierarchy of professional, paid officials.

The church as an outdated concept?

Steve Bruce (1996) argued that the definition of a church discussed above is primarily useful in describing pre-modern Christian societies where Catholic, Orthodox or Coptic churches tried to be the only religion. Since the Reformation in the 16th century, there have been a variety of Christian religions, including the Protestant Church of England established by Henry VIII. To Bruce, the development of religious pluralism in societies undermines the dominance of the church type of religious organisation because they are unable to have a monopoly on religious belief.

In the contemporary UK, the Church of England is still the established (official) religion. However, only a minority of people belong to, identify with or worship at the Church of England. For example, in 2015 in a typical week less than a million people (930 000) worshipped in a Church of England church (Church of England Research and Statistics, 2016). The Church of England also tolerates other religions (both Christian and non-Christian) and supports some radical views. For example, Justin Welby, who became Archbishop of Canterbury in 2012, has said that it would be desirable if ultimately the Roman Catholic and Anglican Churches were reunited and he has argued that capitalism should meet the needs of the poor and excluded.

In some circumstances churches are not connected to the state, and may even act as a focus of opposition to it. Before the overthrow of communism in Poland, the Roman Catholic Church opposed the communist government, and, in many parts of Latin America, liberation theology has also led to conflict between the Catholic Church and the state.

There are some societies in which one religion is dominant and continues to claim it is 'uniquely legitimate' or the only true religion. This is more common, however, in non-Christian societies, for example Muslim societies such as Pakistan and Iran. It does, of course, seem inappropriate to refer to non-Christian religions as a 'church', as the term 'church' is associated with Christian worship.

Partly because of some of these issues, Lorne Dawson (2009), argues that it is dangerous to generalise about different types of organisation. She argues that many religious organisations have mixed characteristics at any one point in time and it can be difficult to make them fit neatly into particular categories. This will become more apparent as we look at other types of religious organisation.

Denominations

Roy Wallis (1976) defined denominations as respectable religious organisations that are 'pluralistically legitimate' – they exist alongside and accept other religious organisations and belief systems. They have often broken away from a church and exist alongside the original church and other groups that have broken away.

A denomination has been seen as having the following features:

1. Unlike a church, a **denomination** does not have a universal appeal in society. For example, in 2016 in the UK there were just over 200 000 attendances at Methodist churches each week and in 2015 there were an average of 33 100 attendances at United Reformed Churches (Faith Survey, 2015).

2. Like churches, denominations draw members from all strata in society, but unlike churches they are not usually so closely identified with the upper classes.

3. Usually, a considerable number of denominations exist within a particular society. In the USA, for example, there is no established church, but a large range of denominations.

4. Unlike a church, a denomination does not identify with the state and approves the separation of church and state.

5. Denominations do not claim a monopoly on religious truth. They are prepared to tolerate and cooperate with other religious organisations. Alan Aldridge (2013) points out that for this reason it is quite common for people to switch membership between denominations.

6. Denominations are usually conservative: members generally accept the norms and values of society, although they may have marginally different values from those of the wider society. Some denominations place minor restrictions on their members. For instance, Methodists are discouraged from drinking and gambling, but drinking in moderation is tolerated and drinkers are not excluded from the denomination.

7. In other respects, denominations have the same characteristics as churches: new members are freely admitted, and they have a hierarchy of paid officials.

Activity – The Roman Catholic Church

The Archbishop of Westminster, The Most Reverend Vincent Nichols, leader of the Roman Catholic Church in Britain, is appointed a Cardinal by Pope Francis, the Leader of the Roman Catholic Church worldwide in 2014.

Roman Catholicism was the established religion in Britain until the Reformation, when Henry VIII set up the Church of England as the established church in 1537. Since then, the head of the Church of England is the reigning monarch, and by law the King or Queen cannot be a Roman Catholic. There are estimated to be just over 4 million Roman Catholics in the UK with just under 900 000 attending weekly mass in 2010 (Faith Survey, 2017).

Can the Roman Catholic Church best be classified as a church or a denomination in the UK today? Explain your answer with reference to typologies of religious organisations.

Problems with distinguishing denominations

The blurring of boundaries between religious organisations as they change has made the concept of the denomination as problematic as the concept of the church. A wide and diverse range of organisations have been classified as denominations, from Jehovah's Witnesses to Methodists, and from Pentecostalists to Baptists. Some of these organisations are classified as sects by some sociologists but as denominations by others; it is difficult to decide where the boundary between the two should be.

Alan Aldridge (2000) argues that in some contexts a religious organisation might be seen as a respectable denomination, while in other contexts it may be seen as less acceptable and therefore more like a sect. For example, the Church of the Latter Day Saints (or Mormons) is seen as respectable and more like a denomination in the USA, but in Britain it is sometimes seen as deviant and therefore more like a sect.

Sects

Roy Wallis (1976) saw **sects** as being deviant religions that are in tension with the wider society. This is partly because they claim a monopoly of the religious truth and this heightens the tension between them and the rest of society.

In addition to the claim to a monopoly of the religious truth, other sociologists have seen sects as having the following characteristics:

1. They are both smaller and more strongly integrated than other religious organisations.

2. Rather than drawing members from all sections of society and being closely connected to the state, members are mainly drawn from lower social classes and they are often in tension with the state.

3. Far from being conservative and accepting the norms and values of society, sects are likely to be in conflict with the outside world. They reject the values of the world that surrounds them in favour of their own religious beliefs.

4. Sect members may be expected to withdraw from life outside the sect, perhaps giving up connections with friends and family. Often, this involves living in a commune.

5. Members of a sect are expected to be deeply committed to its beliefs. They may be excluded from the sect if they fail to demonstrate their commitment.

6. Young children cannot usually enter the sect but must join voluntarily as adults, and willingly adopt the lifestyle and beliefs of the sect. In particular, they must sacrifice 'worldly pleasures' in order to devote themselves to their religious life. In this sense, sects exercise a stronger control over individuals' lives than, for example, the modern Church of England.

7. Unlike churches, sects are not organised through a hierarchy of paid officials. If central authority exists within a sect, it usually rests with a single **charismatic leader**, whose personality and perceived special qualities attract the followers.

Problems with the definition of sects

While Wallis' definition of sects is broadly supported by most other sociologists, it is possible to find sects of vastly different sizes, with a wide variety of ideologies, contrasting attitudes to the outside world, varying degrees of control over their membership, and with or without a professional clergy and a charismatic leader. Wallis himself argued that many **new religious movements**, which developed from the 1960s in Europe and the USA, did not neatly fit the above descriptions of sects. Wallis' analysis of these new religious movements will be examined shortly.

Contemporary issues: Sects and violence

The tension between the wider society and sects can sometimes lead to violence. For example, the Branch Davidians, founded by their charismatic leader, David Koresh, established a commune at Waco in Texas. Koresh demanded absolute loyalty from members. In February 1993, the Bureau of Alcohol, Tobacco and Firearms attempted to search their premises, only to be met by gunfire. Four ATF agents were killed and sixteen were wounded. After a lengthy siege, the FBI attempted to arrest those inside using armoured vehicles. A fire started, resulting in the deaths of more than 80 Branch Davidians, including 22 children. A subsequent investigation found that sect members had started the fire themselves, although survivors insist this was not the case.

David Koresh was the charismatic leader of the Branch Davidians, a Christian sect in Texas which met a violent end in 1993.

Question

Suggest reasons why sects often have charismatic leader but do not usually have a bureaucracy of paid officials.

Cults

Many different types of religious organisation and sets of spiritual beliefs have been described as **'cults'**. These range from global organisations such as Scientology and more loosely organised practices such as Transcendental Meditation (TM) to small groups with a communal lifestyle such as the Heaven's Gate Cult. There is, therefore, no single definition of cults that is accepted by all sociologists.

Wallis (1976) saw cults as being deviant (having beliefs at odds with those of most members of society) but 'pluralistically legitimate' – tolerating the beliefs of other religious organisations (see Figure 3.4.1). Although this definition could cover a wide range of religious organisations, it doesn't cover all organisations which have been seen as cults.

Steve Bruce (1995) characterised cults as based on more individualistic sets of beliefs than other religions. They leave more room for individual interpretation of the beliefs and the beliefs themselves are less clear-cut. Bruce saw a cult as a 'loosely knit group organized around some common themes and interests but lacking any sharply defined and exclusive belief system'.

Most cults tend to be more individualistic than other organised forms of religion because they lack a fixed doctrine. Cults tolerate other beliefs and would not exclude people for having heretical beliefs – beliefs that go against the group's teachings. Cults often have customers rather than members and these customers may have relatively little involvement with any organisation once they have learned the basic beliefs around which the cult is based.

Stark and Bainbridge (1985) offered a competing definition of cults: they defined them in terms of their novelty in a particular society (see below). Furthermore, there is overlap between the New Age movement and cults as some aspects of the New Age movement are based around cults (see Unit 3.4.4).

Nevertheless, there have been several useful attempts to classify smaller religious groupings. Some of these will now be examined and in the process competing definitions of cults will be discussed further.

Activity

Yogic flying.

Transcendental Meditation, or TM, is a technique that can be learned on courses in which individuals learn to concentrate on a personal mantra (a word or sound). It was introduced by the Indian Guru the Maharishi Mahesh Yogi (1918–2008) who influenced The Beatles, particularly George Harrison. It is claimed that when successfully practised, meditation can lead to stress reduction, self-development and spiritual awareness. If meditation became widespread, the Maharishi believed that it could combat crime and reduce unhappiness. The most advanced practitioners, who undertake specialist training called the Sidhi Program, claim to be able to levitate while sitting cross-legged. This is known as yogic flying.

In what ways does TM differ from church religions, denominations and sects?

Key terms

Typology A classification of different types of something (e.g. religious organisations) that identifies the distinct characteristics of each type.

Church The dominant religious organisation in a society, which usually claims a monopoly of the religious truth.

Universal Applying to everyone/everywhere.

Denomination A religious organisation that has broken away from the main religious organisation in a society and that accepts the legitimacy of other religious organisations.

Sect A relatively small religious organisation which is in conflict with other belief systems in a society. To Stark and Bainbridge, they are also offshoots of an existing religion.

Charismatic leader Someone who others follow because of their personal characteristics.

New religious movements Religious/spiritual organisations and movements which developed from the 1960s onwards.

Cult There are different definitions of cult. To Wallis, it is a relatively small organisation with non-rational beliefs that are considered deviant by most people but it coexists with other belief systems in society. To Stark and Bainbridge, a cult is an organisation that introduces new religious/supernatural beliefs to a society.

Summary

1. Roy Wallis defined churches as respectable organisations that claim to be uniquely legitimate (they do not accept other religions), sects as deviant organisations that claim to be uniquely legitimate, denominations as respectable organisations that claim to be pluralistically legitimate (they accept other religions), and cults as deviant organisations that claim to be pluralistically legitimate.

2. Churches are generally seen as religious organisations that try to encompass everyone in society and attempt to impose their version of the religious truth on society as a whole. They are usually conservative organisations that tend to support the status quo and to recruit members from all social classes.

3. In most contemporary societies, churches no longer claim a monopoly of the truth and they often coexist with many other religious organisations.

4. Denominations are offshoots of an existing religion. They serve a minority of the population and coexist with many other religious organisations. They are usually conservative but may have minor restrictions on members.

5. The boundary between a denomination and a sect is not clear-cut.

6. Sects are relatively small, deviant religious organisations in tension with the wider society. They generally claim a monopoly of the religious truth and expect strong commitment from their members. They are often led by a charismatic leader.

7. Cults tend to be more individualistic than other organisations and they do not usually have as much influence on followers as churches, denominations and sects. Their beliefs are usually seen as deviant although they tolerate the existence of other belief systems.

8. Stark and Bainbridge defined cults as groups that introduce a novel set of beliefs to a society.

Unit 3.4.2 New religious movements, sects and cults

The typology which distinguished churches, denominations, sects and cults had its origins in the work of Ernst Troeltsch and H.R. Niebuhr in the early decades of the 20th century. By the 1970s, although sociologists, including Roy Wallis, still found this set of categories useful for understanding *some* religious organisations, the typology was beginning to look dated with the growth of many new religious groups. This suggested to some that a new typology was needed to understand these new religious movements. However, other sociologists began to question the whole principle on which typologies were based and suggested new ways of categorising religious organisations. How, then, have sociologists dealt with the problem of categorising the many new types of religions that have grown up in recent decades?

Roy Wallis — *The Elementary Forms of the New Religious Life*

Roy Wallis was among the first sociologists to develop a typology for the growing range of religious groups from the 1960s onwards. He described these groups as new religious movements (Wallis, 1984). His typology relates specifically to Britain in the 1970s and 1980s but it has proved influential and has been applied in other contexts. A version of Wallis's views is illustrated in Figure 3.4.2.

Wallis divides new religious movements into three main groups according to whether the movement and its members *reject*, *accommodate* or *affirm* the world outside the movement. He notes the existence of some groups (those in the middle circle) that do not fit neatly into any single category.

Activity

Figure 3.4.2 Types of new religious movement

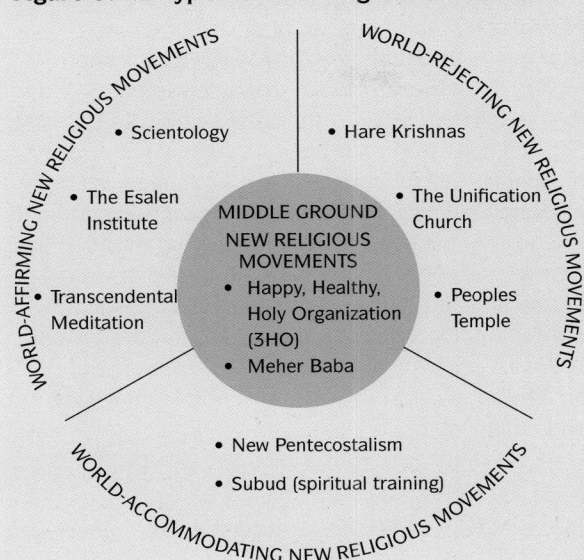

WORLD-AFFIRMING NEW RELIGIOUS MOVEMENTS
- Scientology
- The Esalen Institute
- Transcendental Meditation

WORLD-REJECTING NEW RELIGIOUS MOVEMENTS
- Hare Krishnas
- The Unification Church
- Peoples Temple

MIDDLE GROUND NEW RELIGIOUS MOVEMENTS
- Happy, Healthy, Holy Organization (3HO)
- Meher Baba

WORLD-ACCOMMODATING NEW RELIGIOUS MOVEMENTS
- New Pentecostalism
- Subud (spiritual training)

Using online sources of data, research any **one** organisation in each of the four categories in the figure. Briefly describe their main characteristics and identify some of the main differences between the four movements you have chosen.

World-rejecting new religious movements

The **world-rejecting new religious movements** have most of the characteristics of a sect described by Troeltsch. They are usually unambiguously religious organisations with a definite conception of God but they are highly critical of the outside world and they may seek social change. They often have a communal lifestyle with members living in relative isolation from the outside world and the organisation having a strong influence over their members. Although they are usually radical, there can be conservative elements in the beliefs and actions of such organisations. Many of the movements are morally puritanical, forbidding sex outside marriage, for example. The Unification Church (often referred to as Moonies, due to their founder's name, Sun Myung Moon) are particularly strict about restricting sex to monogamous marriage. World-rejecting new religious movements vary enormously in size: the 'Moonies' have an international following with hundreds of thousands of followers while other groups are small and locally based.

Despite the differences between world-rejecting groups, none of them are content with the world as it is, and they are hostile to competing religions.

World-accommodating new religious movements

The **world-accommodating new religious movements** are usually offshoots of an existing major church or denomination. For example, neo-Pentecostalist groups

are variants of Protestant or Roman Catholic religions, while Subud is a world-accommodating Muslim group.

Typically, these groups neither accept nor reject the world as it is; they simply live within it. They are primarily concerned with religious rather than worldly questions and often want to restore a 'pure' version of the religion that they have split from. The religious beliefs of followers might help them to cope with their non-religious social roles, but the aim of the religion is not to create a new society, nor to improve the believers' chances of success in their lives. Instead, world-accommodating groups seek to restore the spiritual purity to a religion that they believe has been lost in more conventional churches and denominations. An important example of this type of movement is Pentecostalism.

Activity

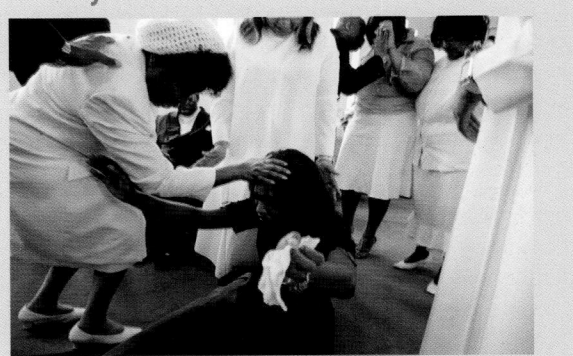

Speaking in tongues at a Pentecostalist meeting.

Pentecostalism is a variety of Christianity followed by many millions of people worldwide. Compared to most Christian belief systems, more emphasis is placed on the importance of the Holy Spirit, being 'born again' and a literal belief in heaven and hell. Pentecostalists live conventional lives. In some Pentecostalist churches, speaking in tongues is practised in which the Holy Spirit is believed to speak through a person's mouth in an incomprehensible language.

In what ways does Pentecostalism conform to the features of a world-accommodating new religious movement?

World-affirming new religious movements

The **world-affirming new religious movements** are very different from all other religious groups, and may not appear to be like a conventional religion. Wallis (1984) said that such a group 'may have no "church", no collective ritual of worship, it may lack any developed theology or ethics'. However, these groups do claim to be able to provide access to spiritual or supernatural powers, and in that sense can be regarded as religions.

World-affirming groups accept the world as it is, and they are not particularly critical of other religions. What they offer the follower is the potential to be successful by unlocking spiritual powers present in the individual. Salvation is seen as a personal achievement and as a solution to personal problems such as unhappiness, suffering or disability. Individuals usually overcome such problems by adopting a technique such as meditation or 'primal screams' that heightens their awareness or abilities.

World-affirming movements are not exclusive groups: they seek as wide a membership as possible. Rather than trying to convert people as such, they try to sell them a service commercially. Followers carry on their normal lives except when undergoing training; often, courses are held at weekends or at other convenient times so as not to cause disruption. There is little social control over the members or customers.

These movements are 'loosely structured, tolerant, and non-exclusive'. They have a rapid turnover in membership and are relatively undemanding on their followers. Examples of world-affirming new-religious movements include Transcendental Meditation (TM) and Erhard Seminars Training (known as est).

The 'middle ground'

Wallis realised that no religious group will conform exactly to the categories he outlines. Some combine elements of different types of movement. One example is the Healthy Happy Holy Organization (3HO). 3HO is like world-affirming movements in that it is an offshoot of an established religion, in this case Sikhism. Like world-affirming movements, it employs techniques including yoga that it is claimed will bring personal benefits, such as happiness and good health. Like world-rejecting movements, the organisation has a clear concept of God and members live in communes or ashrams but hold conventional jobs outside the movement. Occupying as it does the **middle ground**, 3HO allows its followers to combine elements of an alternative lifestyle with conventional marriage and employment.

Roy Wallis — an evaluation

James A. Beckford (1985) criticised Wallis, arguing that:

1. Wallis' categories are difficult to apply. It is not made clear whether the teachings of the movement or the beliefs and outlooks of the individual members distinguish the different orientations to the world.

2. Wallis pays insufficient attention to the diversity of views that often exists within new religious movements.

Nevertheless, Beckford does not deny that a **typology**, or list of types, of new religious movements is useful. In contrast, Rodney Stark and William Sims Bainbridge, whose views we examine next, reject the idea of using a typology to distinguish new religions.

Rodney Stark and William Sims Bainbridge — un-ideal types

Stark and Bainbridge provided a quite different way of categorising religious organisations to those examined so far. They started by criticising the idea of typologies but ended up producing a typology of their own, one which is particularly useful for analysing cults.

The problems of typologies

According to Stark and Bainbridge (1985), none of the typologies of new religious movements, sects, churches and denominations developed by other sociologists are a sound basis for categorisation (see Unit 3.2.4 for Stark and Bainbridge's general theory of religion).

All of them consist of lists of characteristics that each type is likely to have. However, these characteristics are not found in *every* religious organisation placed in each category, just in most of them. There is no clear-cut, definitive way of distinguishing different types of organisation. For example, not all churches try to convert all members of society and not all sects are exclusive.

Stark and Bainbridge, therefore, argued that typologies of religious organisations should be abandoned. They claimed that religious groups can be compared in terms of a single criterion: the degree of conflict that exists between them and the wider society. The use of such a definition allows clear comparisons and also allows changes over time to be clearly described: organisations might change and become more, or less, in tension with the social environment.

Sects and cults

Stark and Bainbridge then went on to argue that there are different kinds (they were careful to avoid using the word 'types') of religious movement in a high degree of tension with their social environment:

1. Sects are groups that are formed as an offshoot of an existing religion as a result of division or schism within that religion.

2. Cults, on the other hand, are new religions, or at least they are new in a particular society. Some result from *cultural importation*, where a religion from other societies is introduced into a society in which it had not previously been practised. Thus, Eastern religions introduced into the USA are examples of imported cults. Some cults, though, are entirely new. These result from *cultural innovation*; they are unconnected to existing religions.

Stark and Bainbridge then suggested that cults exhibit different degrees of organisation and can be divided into three types:

1. **Audience cults** are the least organised and involve little face-to-face interaction. Contacts are often maintained through the mass media and the occasional conference. Many of the members of the audience for such cults may not know each other. Astrology is an example of an audience cult, as is the belief in UFOs.

2. **Client cults** are more organised and usually offer services to their followers. In the past, they tended to offer 'medical miracles, forecasts of the future, or contact with the dead', though more recently they have 'specialized in personal adjustment'. Scientology, for example, offers its clients the opportunity to clear 'engrams' (repressed

Contemporary issues: The Heaven's Gate cult

A well-publicised example that would probably fit Stark and Bainbridge's definition of a cult movement was the Heaven's Gate cult. This was a doomsday cult with an interest in computer technology and science fiction. It started in the mid-1970s in the US and required members to refrain from sex, drugs and alcohol. The leader, Marshall Applewhite, who liked to be addressed as 'Do' or 'The Representative', even had himself castrated so that he did not become distracted by physical pleasures. The group believed that the earth was about to be recycled to become a garden for some future generation. The leader told his followers they needed to leave their earthly bodies in order to get closer to heaven. When the comet Hale-Bopp passed close to earth in 1997, the cult members committed suicide, believing that their spirits would ascend to a spacecraft which was following close behind the comet. They wore a badge declaring they were part of an 'Away Team' leaving both earth and their earthly bodies behind.

Marshall Herff Applewhite, who founded the organisation known as Heaven's Gate.

Questions

1. Why can the Heaven's Gate cult be seen as an example of a cult movement?

2. Why is this group generally classified as a cult rather than a sect?

memories of painful experiences) from the brain with the help of a device called an e-meter, while the Reich Foundation offers the promise of the 'monumental orgasm'.

3. **Cult movements** involve followers much more. They try to satisfy all the religious needs of their members and, unlike client and audience cults, membership of other faiths is not permitted. They do, however, vary considerably in their power. Some require little more than occasional attendance at meetings and acceptance of the cult's beliefs, but others shape the whole of a person's life. The Unification Church (also known as The Moonies) is an example of a cult movement. Many client cults become cult movements for their most dedicated followers, for example practitioners of TM who take the intense Sidhi Program and base their life around the movement.

Conclusion

Stark and Bainbridge offered a different — and they would claim, superior — method of distinguishing religious organisations from that of Wallis. However, basing the typology on a single attribute — the degree of tension with wider society — has its limitations and may result in over-simplification. They undoubtedly made some useful distinctions between different types of cult; however, in doing so, they contradicted themselves by developing a typology of their own, despite having claimed that typologies should be avoided.

David G. Bromley and J. Gordon Melton (2012) are quite supportive of the type of approach adopted by Stark and Bainbridge but argue that *cultural* differences need to be taken into account as well as *social* tensions between religious organisations and society. Traditional typologies in Western societies are generally based on models derived from Christianity but organisations can also be distinguished according to whether they come from the *dominant* religious tradition or an *alternative* religious tradition. For example, in Europe and the USA, Christianity is a dominant religious tradition and Buddhism and Hinduism are examples of alternative religious traditions.

There is, therefore, perhaps no perfect way of classifying religious organisations. However, attempts to classify them can be useful for understanding why these organisations develop and change. These issues are the focus of the next two parts.

Key terms

World-rejecting new religious movements Religious movements that developed after the 1960s and that are hostile to the social world outside the movement.

World-accommodating new religious movements Religious movements that developed after the 1960s and that hold strong religious beliefs but reject mainstream religious doctrine. They nevertheless allow members to have conventional lives outside of their religious practice.

World-affirming new religious movements Religious movements that developed after the 1960s and that are positive about mainstream society and in which the religious practices tend to encourage or facilitate social and economic success.

The middle ground New religious movements which developed after the 1960s and which have a mixture of characteristics that are typical of different types of new religious movement.

Typologies Classification systems identifying different types of something, for example, different types of religious organisation.

Audience cults Cults that involve little commitment by followers and little face-to-face interaction by them.

Client cults Cults that offer services (courses or rituals) to their followers but that require little commitment.

Cult movements Cults that involve followers/ believers fully and act as full religious organisations.

Summary

1. In the 1980s, Roy Wallace distinguished different types of new religious movement that had been developing since the 1960s.

2. World-rejecting new religious movements are generally small organisations that exercise strong control over their members and they are in conflict with the wider society. They usually have a clear concept of God.

3. World-accommodating new religious movements have strong religious beliefs and are usually offshoots of a major religion. Members of these organisations generally live conventional lives apart from their religious practices.

4. World-affirming new religious movements are very different from conventional religions and tend to have more emphasis upon personal spirituality than other religious movements. They often teach techniques that allow people to be more successful in the outside world.

5. Middle ground new religious movements do not fit neatly into any of the above categories.

6. Stark and Bainbridge questioned other typologies of religion and claimed that a single criterion, tension with the wider society, can be used to distinguish different types of organisation.

7. However, Stark and Bainbridge did distinguish three types of cult:

    i. Audience cults that involve little face-to-face interaction

    ii. Client cults that offer services to their members, and

    iii. Cult movements that dominate their followers' lives.

Unit 3.4.3 Growth and change in sects, cults and new religious movements

As the discussion of new religious movements has shown, new religious movements, sects and cults have grown at certain periods of history. They can also decline, disappear, or change from one type of organisation to another. This unit examines the reasons behind the dynamics of change in sects, cults and new religious movements.

Reasons for the growth of sects, cults and new religious movements

Religious sects and cults are not a new phenomenon: they have existed for centuries. Bruce (1995) traced the emergence of the first sects to the Reformation of the church in the 16th century. Despite this, most existing sects and cults originated in the 20th century, and the 1960s and 1970s saw the appearance of many new organisations.

Membership has grown steadily in both Britain and the USA. According to *Religious Trends 3* and *5* (Brierley, 2001, 2005), there were 14350 members of new religious movements in Britain in 1995. By 2005, this had grown to 37412. In 2005, there were 829 individual groups. In addition, in 2005 there were over half a million members of non-trinitarian groups (those not believing in the trinity of 'Father, Son and Holy Spirit'), which are often seen as new religious movements (particularly world-accommodating ones) by sociologists. More recent membership figures are not available but some evidence of recent trends is provided by census figures. The percentage of the population saying that they belonged to the category 'Other religion' rose from 0.36 per cent in 2001 to 0.4 per cent of the population in 2011 – a total of 240000 people. Of these, 57000 were Pagans and 39000 Spiritualists.

The growth of sects and cults can be explained either in terms of why particular individuals choose to join or in terms of wider social changes. In reality, these reasons are closely linked, because social changes affect the number of people available as potential recruits.

Marginality

Max Weber (1963, first published 1922) provided one of the earliest explanations for the growth of sects. He argued that they were likely to arise within groups that were **marginal** in society: members of groups outside the mainstream of social life often feel that they are not receiving the prestige and/ or economic rewards they deserve. One solution to this problem is a sect based on what Weber called 'a **theodicy of disprivilege**' (a theodicy is a religious explanation and justification; disprivilege is a lack of material success and social status). Such sects contain an explanation for the 'disprivilege' of their members and promise them a 'sense of honour', either in the afterlife or in a future 'new world' on earth.

Bryan Wilson (1970) pointed out that a variety of situations could lead to the marginalisation of groups in society, which in turn could provide fertile ground for the development of sects. These situations include defeat in war, natural disaster or economic collapse. Radical and undesirable changes such as these are not the only circumstances that can encourage sect development.

In part, the growth of sects in the USA in the 1960s was accomplished through the recruitment of marginal and disadvantaged groups. The Nation of Islam, for example, aimed to recruit poor and marginalised African Americans, for example those serving a prison sentence. However, for the most part, in the 1960s and 1970s the membership of the world-rejecting new religious movements was drawn from among the ranks of young, white, middle-class Americans and Europeans. Wallis (1984) argued that despite this background most were marginal because they were likely to be involved in alternative lifestyles, such as those related to hippy subcultures, drug use or surfing.

Relative deprivation

However, this does not explain why quite affluent middle-class youth should become marginal members of society in the first place. The concept of 'relative deprivation' can be used to explain their actions. **Relative deprivation** refers to subjectively perceived deprivation: that which people actually feel. Certain members of the middle class may feel spiritually deprived rather than materially deprived in a world they see as too materialistic, lonely and impersonal. According to Wallis (1984), they therefore seek salvation in the sense of community offered by the sect.

Stark and Bainbridge (1985) also employed the concept of relative deprivation in explaining the origin of sects. They defined sects as organisations that break away from an established church, and they believed it is the relatively deprived who are likely to break away. Splits take place when churches begin to compromise their beliefs. When the more successful members of a religion try to reduce the amount of tension between that religion and the outside world, the less successful resent it and split off.

Meredith McGuire (2002) argues that relative deprivation does not directly cause the growth of sects, but that it can produce conditions which make such growth more likely. Other factors also need to be in play for the growth to happen, and these factors may involve social changes.

Social change

Bryan Wilson (1970) argued that sects arise during periods of rapid social change when traditional norms are disrupted and social relationships come to lack consistent and coherent meaning. He gave the example of the rise of Methodism in working-class communities during the early years of the industrial revolution in Britain. Methodism provided the support of a close-knit community organisation, well-defined and strongly sanctioned norms and values, and a promise of salvation.

Similarly, Bruce (1995, 1996, 2011) attributes the development of a range of religious institutions, including sects and cults, to a general process of modernisation and secularisation. He believes that the weakness of more conventional institutionalised religions has encouraged some people to consider less traditional alternatives.

David Bromley (2009) does not deny that factors such as those outlined above *may* play some role in the growth of new religious movements. However, he argues that these types of explanations are rather generalised and that there is little evidence about the motivations of individual members to support them.

The growth of new religious movements

Wallis (1984) pointed to a number of social changes that he believed accounted for the growth of new religious movements in the 1960s. Some of these had important effects on youth in particular. First, the growth of higher education extended the transition between childhood and adulthood giving the young more time to explore different ideas and lifestyles free from work and family responsibilities. Second, the young felt that new technology would lead to the end of economic scarcity, giving the economic freedom to try out new ways of living. Third, radical political movements in the 1960s encouraged the exploration of alternative lifestyles.

Wallis claimed that in these circumstances world-rejecting new religious movements were attractive because of the potential they seemed to offer for a less materialistic lifestyle which enabled the development of deeper and more meaningful relationships than those outside the group.

Steve Bruce (1995, 1996) believed that world-affirming new religious movements are predominantly a response to the **rationalisation** (see Part 6 of this chapter) of the modern world. Modern life does not provide a secure sense of identity for most people. For example, people often stay in jobs for only a short time and work is often seen as a means to an end rather than a vocation or calling. People have, however, been encouraged to value achievement, yet many lack the opportunities to be as successful as they would like. World-affirming movements can offer a solution claiming to bring people both success and a spiritual element to their lives.

The 'supply-side' of new religious movements

Drawing on the work of Stark and Bainbridge (1985, 1987), Dawson (2011) believes that the organisation of new religious movements is important in determining whether or not they are successful and grow. These types of religions will grow when they supply what potential consumers, or converts, want and if they are able to market themselves effectively. This involves using existing members to recruit new members, adapting their beliefs to fit the mood of the times and presenting a positive image of the religion. If there are a number of new religious movements which follow these steps then membership will grow; otherwise, it will tend to fall.

The development of sects and new religious movements

As we have seen, there are a range of reasons why sects and new religious movements enjoy periods when they grow in number and size. What, however, happens to them as time passes? Do most of them survive or do they disappear? Do some of them change into denominations? Sociologists have offered a variety of answers to these questions.

Sects as short-lived organisations

In 1929, H.R. Niebuhr argued that sects could not survive as sects beyond a single generation. Either they would change their characteristics, compromise and become denominations, or they would disappear altogether. He gave the following reasons for this.

1. Sect membership was based upon voluntary adult commitment: members chose to dedicate themselves to the organisation and its religion. Once the first generation started to have children, though, the children would be admitted as new members when they were too young to understand the teachings of the religion. These new members would not be able to sustain the fervour of the first generation. Consequently, the sect might become a denomination.

2. Sects that relied upon a charismatic leader would tend to disappear if the leader died. Alternatively, the nature of the leadership would change: no longer would the charisma of an individual hold the sect together. This would allow the bureaucratic structure of a denomination to emerge, with its hierarchy of paid officials.

3. Niebuhr argued that the ideology of many sects contained the seeds of their own destruction. Sects with an ascetic creed (which involves abstinence from worldy pleasures such as alcohol or excessive consumption) would encourage their members to work hard and save their money. As a result, the membership would be upwardly socially mobile, and would no longer wish to belong to a religious group which catered for marginal members of society. The sect would, therefore, die out or become a denomination.

Many examples support his views. For example, as the Methodist membership rose in status in the 19th century, the strict disciplines of the sect and its rejection of society were dropped and it gradually became a denomination.

A number of sects have also disappeared because of the mass suicide (or murder) of their members. These include the People's Temple, the Branch Davidians and the Heaven's Gate group.

Steve Bruce — sects in secular society

Steve Bruce (2011) generally supports Niebuhr's approach, agreeing that many sects evolve into denominations — an example being the Quakers who were originally a much more radical and egalitarian group than they are now. Bruce believes that rising affluence tends to blunt the radicalism of the members of many sects, encouraging a transition into denominations.

However, Bruce accepts that a few sects manage to survive but only if they can isolate themselves from the secular influences of wider society. One way of doing this is to insist on speaking an archaic language, which makes communication with the outside world difficult; another is to ban the use of modern technology. Bruce gives the example of the Amish to illustrate the point. (The Amish are an American religious group who live simple lives, wear plain dress and decline to use modern technology.)

The life cycle of sects

Bryan Wilson (1966) rejected Niebuhr's view that sects are inevitably short-lived more strongly than Bruce. Wilson pointed out that some sects do survive for a long time without becoming denominations. To Wilson, the crucial factor is the way the sect answers the question: 'What shall we do to be saved?' Sects can be classified in terms of how they answer this question.

> The **conversionist sect** believes that anyone can get to heaven if they convert to the religion. If successful, this type of sect is likely to develop into a denomination because, as it grows by recruiting more and more members, it can become too large to stay as a sect.

> However, **Adventist sects**, which believe in the Second Coming of Christ, who will judge humanity and establish a new world order, tend to be more exclusive because they believe that only a limited number of people will get into heaven. By isolating themselves from the outside world, groups such as Seventh Day Adventists can stay relatively small and free from secular influences and therefore avoid becoming denominations.

Nevertheless, Wilson (2003) does believe that sects will face difficulties. Ever-improving educational standards, opportunities and globalisation make it increasingly difficult for sects to isolate themselves from the outside world. However, globalisation also offers new opportunities for sects to organise and recruit new members in disadvantaged, developing countries. Thus, Wilson predicts that sects will survive, but the branches in Western, developed countries may decline as those in the 'third world' gain in strength.

New Religious movements – internal ideology and the wider society

Roy Wallis (1984) took a more complex view of the paths followed by sects: he thought that the chances of sects surviving, changing or disappearing are affected both by the internal ideology of the sect and by external social circumstances. This can lead to organisations changing rather than disappearing.

World-rejecting sects often change their stance as time passes and become more world-accommodating. Wallis accepts that charismatic leaders have difficulty in retaining personal control over a religious movement indefinitely, and that this may also result in changes. If the organisation grows, a process that Weber described as the **routinisation of charisma** can take place. A more bureaucratic organisation develops so that some of the leader's personal authority becomes vested in his (or untypically her) officials or representatives. Nevertheless, the changes may stop well short of denominationalisation (the process of becoming a denomination).

Wallis also recognised that sects can disappear. The charismatic leader, as in the case of Jim Jones' Peoples Temple, may actually destroy a world-rejecting sect. Social changes may lead to the members becoming less marginal in society, thereby threatening the basis on which the sect was founded. However, as new groups in society become marginal, new sects will arise.

According to Wallis, then, world-rejecting sects tend to be unstable, but new ones emerge, and those that survive may become more world-accommodating while continuing to exist as sects.

World-affirming movements often sell their services as a commodity, so they are vulnerable to a loss of support from their consumers. To the extent that they sell themselves in the market place, they are subject to the same problems as a retailer. If the public no longer needs or gains benefits from their services, they will lose customers. To Wallis, though, world-affirming movements are more likely to change to attract a new clientele than to cease to exist. For example, in the 1970s, Transcendental Meditation (TM) tried to broaden its appeal by emphasising the practical

Activity – The Moonies

The Reverend Sun Myung Moon – founder of The Unification Church (sometimes known as The Moonies) with his wife, blessing couples at a mass wedding.

Reverend Moon founded the church, which reinterprets Christian religion, in Korea in 1955. On his death in 2012, his wife Hak Ja Han became spiritual leader. The Unification Church continues to have hundreds of thousands of followers in a number of different countries, although support may have declined since Moon's death.

Question

What does the example of the Unification Church suggest about the different views of sociologists on the life-cycle of sects?

benefits – the worldly success – that the meditation claimed to offer.

Thus, although Wallis did not agree with Niebuhr that sects inevitably disappear or become denominations, his work does suggest that there may be tendencies in these directions, particularly for world-rejecting movements.

Key terms

Marginality Being outside the mainstream of social life.

Theodicy of disprivilege A set of religious views that provides hope and/or explanations for the position of those who are disadvantaged.

Relative deprivation Feeling disadvantaged in comparison with other groups in society.

Rationalisation The process by which decisions are increasingly based upon calculation of the best way to achieve goals rather than being based upon emotion, tradition or religious belief.

Conversionist sect A sect that tries to convert as many people as possible to its beliefs.

Adventist sect A sect that emphasises that the end of the world is approaching and that there are a limited number of places in heaven for true believers.

Routinisation of charisma The process in which the leadership of a charismatic leader is gradually replaced by leadership through bureaucratic organisation.

Summary

1. Evidence suggests that membership of new religious movements in the UK has grown in recent decades.

2. Max Weber explains the growth of sects in terms of the marginality of its members and the attractions of a 'theodicy of disprivilege' which helps the members cope with their disadvantages.

3. However, much of the growth since the 1960s has been among relatively advantaged groups and this has been explained in terms of relative deprivation and a sense of spiritual deprivation rather than material deprivation.

4. Rapid social changes and secularisation has been used to explain the growth of sects.

5. Roy Wallis argued that the growth of new religious movements is linked to changes affecting young people such as the expansion of higher education.

6. Stark and Bainbridge believed that the growth or decline of religious movements depends upon the ability of organisations to attract new members.

7. Niebuhr argued that sects were inevitably short-lived and either disappear or become denominations.

8. Others argue that there are ways in which sects can and do survive for long periods without changing or disappearing.

9. Roy Wallis suggested that new religious movements can change from one type of movement to another (e.g. world-rejecting to world-accommodating) rather than disappearing or becoming a denomination.

Unit 3.4.4 The New Age

The **New Age** is a term that has been applied to a range of ideas that started to become prominent in the 1980s. The New Age incorporates some world-affirming new religious movements and cults (particularly client cults and audience cults) but it is also present in the wider culture of Western societies in films, shops, seminars, meetings, music, television programmes, public lectures and so on. This lack of a tie to particular organisations makes the New Age distinctive from most other religious and some spiritual belief systems. This unit asks, what exactly is the New Age, why has it grown and what is its significance?

Examples of the New Age

Examples of New Age beliefs include: an interest in clairvoyance, contacting aliens; a belief in 'spirit guides' and 'spirit masters'; various types of meditation and psychotherapy; belief in paganism, magic, tarot cards, ouija, astrology and witchcraft; an interest in self-healing and natural or traditional remedies for ill-health (for example, yoga, aromatherapy, reflexology); spiritually inclined ecology such as a belief in Gaia (the Greek goddess who has been used

251

to represent the sacred and interconnected nature of all life); and so on. The New Age can be found in publications on topics such as feng shui, mysticism and Shamanism; in shops that sell recordings of sounds from nature, which can be used for relaxation or meditation; in communes such as the Findhorn community in Scotland, where communication with nature is used to facilitate personal transformation; and in spiritual groups from Scientology to Buddhism.

Paul Heelas *et al.* (2005) have termed the environment in which the New Age exists the **holistic milieu**. They contrast this with the **congregational domain** in which people attend places of collective worship on a regular basis, typically once a week. The holistic milieu is less visible than the congregational domain, but often involves one-to-one encounters (for example, between a healer and a client) and small group activities (for example, yoga groups).

Activity – the Findhorn community

A community gathering at the Findhorn foundation in Scotland.

Use the internet to research the Findhorn community. (They have their own website at https://www.findhorn.org/about-us/ and there are also interesting films about the community on YouTube.)

Question

Describe the lifestyle of Findhorn and identify the core themes of the community's beliefs. How do they differ from conventional religion?

The core themes of the New Age

What have such a diverse range of activities and beliefs got in common? Paul Heelas (1996) believed that the central feature of the New Age is a belief in **self-spirituality**. People with such beliefs have turned away from traditional religious organisations in their search for the spiritual and instead have begun to look inside themselves. The New Age 'explains why life – as conventionally experienced – is not what it should be; it provides an account of what it is to find perfection; and it provides the means for obtaining salvation'. However, that salvation does not come from being accepted by an external god; it comes from discovering and perfecting oneself. Often, this means going beyond one's conscious self to discover hidden spiritual depths.

There are many different ways to discover these spiritual depths including 'psychotherapies, physical labour, dance, shamanic practices, magic, or for that matter, fire-walking, sex, tennis, taking drugs or using virtual reality equipment' (Heelas, 1996).

According to Heelas, the New Age values personal experience above 'truths' provided by scientists or conventional religious leaders. In this respect, **de-traditionalisation** is a key feature of the New Age: it rejects the authority that comes from traditional sources and sees individuals and their sense of who they are as the only genuine source of truth or understanding.

Activity – Is yoga New Age?

A yoga class.

Yoga combines physical, mental and spiritual exercises and its origins can be traced back to ancient India. It has links with Hinduism, Buddhism and Jainism. It is sometimes claimed to be an effective alternative therapy for some types of physical and mental illness as well as being a useful technique for attaining a sense of well-being.

Question

How well does yoga seem to fit with the core themes of the New Age described by Paul Heelas?

The New Age as a product of postmodernity

Some writers have argued that the appeal of the New Age comes from the failure of the modern world to deliver personal satisfaction. John Drane believes the New Age is:

[a] response to the acknowledged failure of the scientific and materialist worldview to deliver the goods. The great ... vision of a better world for everyone has simply not materialized. Not only has the fundamental human predicament not improved, but as the twentieth century progressed, things actually got worse. Drane, 1999

Drane followed the views of postmodernists in arguing that Western societies are turning against institutions and belief systems associated with modernity. Modern rationality produced such disasters as World War I, the Holocaust, numerous other bloody conflicts, the depletion of the ozone layer and global warming. People have lost faith in institutions such as the medical profession, which is now seen as more interested in 'covering their overheads than in the health and welfare of those they treat'.

Although the churches had 'an uneasy relationship with Enlightenment values', they adapted to and largely adopted those values. The churches are, therefore, viewed with suspicion and distrust. According to Drane, many people believe that, 'because of the dominance of rationalism and reasonableness, the current establishment options ... are pale remnants of the spiritual fire that started them'.

Disillusioned with the inability of the churches to satisfy their craving for spirituality, New Agers seek to develop their own spirituality. Drane saw this change as part of a move towards postmodernity (see Unit 3.2.5 for a discussion of postmodernity and religion).

The New Age as a product of modernity

Both Steve Bruce (1995) and Paul Heelas (1996) argued that the New Age can best be explained as a product of the latest stage in modernity rather than postmodernity.

Bruce – human potential and secularisation

Bruce claims that the New Age appeals most to affluent members of society, particularly the 'university-educated middle classes working in the "expressive professions": social workers, counsellors, actors, writers, artists, and others whose education and work causes them to have an articulate interest in human potential'. They may have experienced personal development themselves and therefore find it plausible to believe that there is the potential for further development for themselves or others. These are also the sorts of people who have been most exposed to a belief in individualism, which is characteristic of modern societies. Modern societies are relatively egalitarian and democratic, so the views and beliefs of individuals are given more credence than was once the case, whereas the views of experts and traditional authorities are regarded with more scepticism. It is this modern emphasis on individualism that gives the New Age its appeal. To Bruce, it is also a symptom of secularisation, particularly the decline of traditional religion, which he also sees as a feature of modernity.

Heelas – individualism and identity

Paul Heelas (1996) reached broadly similar conclusions. He saw the main appeal of the New Age as stemming from aspects of mainstream culture. On the surface it appears to reject mainstream culture, but in fact it is based on an extreme emphasis on the individualism that is typical of modernity. People may have no roots in the locality where they were born or brought up. They no longer have unquestioning faith in political, moral or religious codes, or in the leaders who promote them. People are, therefore, thrown back on their own resources to make sense of the world and to create their own identity.

In the modern world, people have many social roles but no single dominant one. People change jobs frequently and marriage is less stable than it once was. The New Age can help individuals find a unifying identity. Consumer culture encourages people to try to become the perfect person by, for example, wearing the right clothes, but the New Age can offer so much more – discovering your true, inner authentic self.

Heelas – the spiritual revolution

In later work, Paul Heelas *et al.* (2005) argue that the growth of New Age and related beliefs is part of a **spiritual revolution** that is taking place in modern societies. They claim that there has been a **subjective turn** in modern societies. People no longer put such emphasis on carrying out particular social 'roles, duties and obligations'. This involves living 'life – as a member of a community or tradition – whether it takes the form of a kinship system, a feudal system, a nation-state, a class system or a particular religion'. Instead there is an increased emphasis on **subjective life**. This 'has to do with states of consciousness, states of mind, memories, emotions, passions, sensations, bodily experiences, dreams, feelings, inner conscience and sentiments – including moral sentiments like compassion' (Heelas *et al.*, 2005).

In the congregational domain of traditional churches and denominations, religious life is 'life-as' – as a believer and a follower who defers to the authority of religious organisations and their leaders. In the holistic milieu of New Age beliefs, there are few rules and you discover your own spirituality.

The New Age – conclusion

On the surface, the New Age seems to contradict the view of sociologists such as Weber that the modern world would become increasingly rational. There seems to be little rationality in the claim by the New Ager Shirley MacLaine that her daughter was her mother in a previous life (quoted in Heelas, 1996), or that spirit guides, astrology or messages from 'an energy personality essence no longer focused in physical reality' (quoted in Bruce, 1995) can help us to live our lives better. However, if Bruce and Heelas are correct, then the rationality of modernity also brought with it an individualism in which apparently non-rational beliefs could flourish.

Some writers disagree with Bruce and Heelas, seeing the existence of such beliefs as evidence that we have moved beyond modernity into an era of postmodernity (see Unit 3.2.5 on postmodernity and religion). There is no agreement either on whether the New Age is evidence of the resurgence of spiritual belief or a manifestation of secularisation (see Unit 3.6.6). Heelas and Woodhead, however, seem to be on strong ground in arguing that the New Age is related to a decline in traditional beliefs and that it is closely linked with other social and cultural developments in modern societies.

Key terms

New Age A term for a wide range of broadly spiritual beliefs and practices involving non-scientific beliefs that emphasise the discovery of spirituality within individuals more than in external reality. People seek spiritual experiences, inner peace or growth through, for example, meditation, crystal healing and/or aromatherapy.

Holistic milieu The networks of one-to-one encounters, small-group activities and commercial activities in which New Age practices take place.

Congregational domain The site of conventional religious organisations where people meet together to pray in a consecrated place of religious worship.

Self-spirituality The practice of searching for spirituality inside yourself.

De-traditionalisation The rejection of traditional sources of claims about the truth, for example scientists and church leaders.

Spiritual revolution A move away from traditional religions which are practised through attendance at churches or denominations towards spiritual beliefs in the holistic milieu of New Age small-group encounters, commercial products and services, and one-to-one therapies.

Subjective turn/subjective life Concerned with an increased emphasis on discovering your inner feelings and your 'true self' rather than meeting social obligations by performing social roles.

Summary

1. The New Age consists of sets of beliefs involving spiritual or supernatural beliefs. They are not generally organised in the same way as conventional religion and instead involve small-group or face-to-face encounters.

2. This holistic milieu contrasts with the congregational domain of conventional religious worship.

3. Paul Heelas saw the New Age as involving a form of self-spirituality that rejects traditional sources of authority.

4. John Drane saw the New Age as a product of postmodernity and the rejection of modern belief systems.

5. Steve Bruce and Paul Heelas saw the New Age as a product of the individualism of modernity and Heelas linked it to a spiritual revolution in which people are increasingly concerned with subjective life.

PART 5 SOCIAL GROUPS, RELIGION AND SPIRITUALITY

Contents

Religious organisations and movements tend to recruit more members from some social groups than others and this part of the chapter examines the reasons why this occurs. The main social divisions that affect religious belief and participation are gender, ethnicity, age and social class. This part examines these social divisions and discusses how they relate to beliefs and participation. It asks questions such as: How does social class affect religious belief? Why do women appear to participate more than men in most religions and spiritual groups? How closely is ethnicity associated with differences in religious affiliation? Do people get more religious as they age?

Unit 3.5.1 Social class, religion and spirituality

The relationship between social class and religion has been introduced in earlier parts of this chapter, but this unit draws together previous discussion and develops it further. Both Marxist and Weberian theory and sociologists who have studied different types of religious organisation have made a useful contribution to understanding the relationship between social class and religion. Evidence does suggest that different types of religion tend to appeal to different social classes, although the evidence is not clear-cut and there is no simple and straightforward relationship.

Marxist theories of social class and religion

According to Marxists, social class is closely related to religious participation. Karl Marx (1844) described religion in capitalist societies as the 'opium of the masses'. He saw it as acting like a drug by giving its followers a false sense of well-being and distorting reality. Marx claimed that religion started in the subject classes as a way of coping with oppression, but it was later adopted by the ruling classes as a way of justifying their advantaged position in society. Marx, therefore, acknowledged that all classes believed in religion, although for somewhat different reasons. He thought that as the subject class (the proletariat) developed greater class consciousness, they could potentially lose some of their religious beliefs. This leaves open the possibility that higher classes (particularly the ruling class or the bourgeoisie) might become more religious than subject classes.

However, in the UK, figures on religious belief in a 2008 survey by Theos (live from Thessalonica, 2009) found that those from lower social classes were more likely to have a *lifelong* belief in God than people from higher classes. On the other hand, those from higher classes were more likely to have *converted* to believing in God than those from lower classes.

Neo-Marxists such as Otto Maduro (1982) argued that where religious movements become a radical force for change they can become dominated by the subject class. For example, the liberation theology movement among Catholics in Latin America was largely supported by the poor, and Pentecostalism in the UK tends to appeal to people of Black African and Black Caribbean origin.

Max Weber, class and religious beliefs

A variety of theorists have suggested that there are links between social class and different types of religious organisations. This idea originates in the work of Max Weber (1978) who believed that different classes tend to develop different types of religious belief and that this in turn is linked to different religious organisations.

Weber distinguished between different theodicies, or religious explanations for suffering on earth.

> Some religions have a **theodicy of misfortune**, which claims that wealth and worldly success are indicators of evil. Unsurprisingly, this type of belief tends to be associated with religious organisations popular with lower social classes.

> On the other hand, a **theodicy of good-fortune** suggests that worldly success indicates virtue and this is associated more with higher classes.

However, Weber did not believe this was a straightforward relationship and religious beliefs were not simply dictated by class position. Instead, particular classes and status groups played an active role in creating and recreating beliefs. They are influenced by their class position and their class interests, but this does not directly determine their beliefs. (See for example Weber's work on the 'Protestant ethic' in Unit 3.3.1.)

Social class and social mobility

The previous part of this chapter began to explore the relationship between different types of religious organisation and social class. It will be briefly recapped here.

Drawing on research in the USA, Stephen Hunt (2004) notes that generally sociologists have found that upwardly mobile groups and individuals tend to belong to religious organisations that have more liberal beliefs, for example about sexuality. However, conservative or fundamentalist beliefs are likely to be supported by those who have a stake in society and who may feel that they are under threat from upwardly mobile social groups. Lower social classes who feel excluded and marginalised tend to support sects which offer some religious compensation for their low status and which reject mainstream norms and values.

Hunt goes on to argue that New Age beliefs are supported by those 'who have sufficient time and means to pay for a narcissistic journey of self-discovery' (2004), particularly middle-class people in 'expressive professions' (for example artists and writers) who have university-level education. Hunt also claims that in the USA occult practices and superstitious beliefs are more popular with the lower classes, who have low levels of education and live in rural areas.

Activity

A fortune-teller in Blackpool and a Tai Chi class in Kensington, London.

Suggest reasons why the above practices might appeal to different social classes.

Social class and religious organisations

Churches aspire to include members from all classes. However, in contemporary Britain, the upper class and the middle class are over-represented because of an association with the establishment and a generally conservative ideology.

This is supported by a YouGov poll from 2015 (Jones, 2015), which found that over 63 per cent of regular attenders at church were middle class compared with 38 per cent who were working class. Furthermore, 17.4 per cent of married working-class men never attended church compared with 9.3 per cent of married middle-class men. However, another YouGov poll, also conducted in 2015, found that middle-class groups were less likely to believe in God or 'some sort of higher spiritual power' (49%) compared with lower classes (57%) (YouGov, 2015). If this evidence is to be believed, despite being less likely to believe in God, the middle class are more likely to attend church.

Denominations tend to be slightly anti-establishment as they have broken away from the religious mainstream. However, Wallis (1984) noted that they are respectable organisations and therefore they appeal most to the upper-working class and the lower-middle class.

Sects have traditionally recruited the most disadvantaged members of society. They require members to give up their previous life, so those with much to lose are unlikely to join. They tend to appeal to the deprived because it offers them a way of coping with their disadvantages by finding meaning and a sense of self-worth within the sect. Wallis (1984) argued that in the 1960s and 1970s they also began to appeal to the 'relatively deprived' middle class of affluent students who were seeking to compensate for their lack of a spiritual life.

Client cults (Stark and Bainbridge, 1985) or world-affirming new religious movements (Wallis, 1984) appeal to the already successful and affluent who want to become more successful.

Cult movements are similar to sects in being in opposition to mainstream society. They therefore tend to attract the disadvantaged or relatively deprived.

The New Age, according to Paul Heelas (1996), tends to appeal to the middle class (and particularly women). Like Stephen Hunt (2004, see above), Steve Bruce (2002) believes that it appeals to those in expressive professions such as the media, teaching and counselling because they believe in self-improvement.

Evaluation

Unlike the USA, where there is detailed data on social class and religious belief and participation, there is a shortage of such data in the UK. It is, therefore, difficult to be sure how accurate these claims about class and different religious organisations are. General figures on social class and religious belief are not sufficiently detailed or recent to support or undermine more specific arguments, so most of the claims discussed above should be treated as hypotheses rather than well-supported theories. Furthermore, class interacts with other social divisions, particularly gender, ethnicity and age in shaping religious belief and participation. The influence of these other social divisions will now be examined, starting with gender.

Key terms

Theodicy of misfortune A religious explanation for suffering that claims that wealth and worldly success are indicators of evil.

Theodicy of good-fortune A religious explanation for suffering that claims that wealth and worldly success are indicators of virtue.

Summary

1. Marxists believe that religion originates among subject classes to help them cope with oppression, but it is also adopted by the ruling classes to justify their position. Some neo-Marxists believe that religion can become a radical force.

2. Weber argued that different theodicies appealed to different social groups with a theodicy of misfortune attracting lower classes and a theodicy of good-fortune attracting higher classes.

3. Hunt argues that socially mobile groups tend to join a liberal religious organisation but social groups who feel under threat tend to join more conservative organisations.

4. Churches aspire to attract members from all classes but tend to be predominantly middle- and higher-class institutions because they generally support the establishment.

5. Denominations tend to appeal to the upper-working class and lower-middle class.

6. Sects generally attract the disadvantaged or the relatively deprived.

7. Client cults and world-affirming new religious movements appeal to the affluent whereas cult movements tend to appeal to the disadvantaged.

8. The New Age mainly attracts the middle class, particularly women and especially those in expressive professions.

Unit 5.2 Gender, religion and spirituality

An earlier section suggested that women were disadvantaged in many religions (see Unit 3.2.3). However, research suggests that in many groups women are more religiously active than men. Marta

257

Trzebiatowska and Steve Bruce (2012) suggest that on the surface it is surprising that women should be more involved in belief systems that tend to be patriarchal. So just how great are these gender differences and how can they be explained?

Statistics on gender and religion

There is clear evidence that women tend to be more religious than men, both in the UK and around the world.

The Pew Research Center (2016) using its own surveys and other research estimated that in the world as a whole, 83.4 per cent of women identified with a faith group compared with 79.9 per cent of men. Of 192 countries, there were 61 in which women were at least two percentage points more likely than men to express a religious affiliation, and none in which the reverse was true. Furthermore, across 84 countries surveyed, there were 36 in which more women than men said religion was very important to them, 46 in which there was little gender difference and just two (Israel and Mozambique) in which more men expressed this view.

Using various surveys, the Pew Research Center found that the UK was no different in this respect from other parts of the worlds, as shown in Table 3.5.1.

Table 3.5.1 Religious gender gap in the UK. Percentage of each gender who pray daily, consider religion 'very important' and attend religious services weekly

	Women	Men
Percentage praying daily	23%	14%
Percentage saying that religion is 'very important' to them	25%	18%
Percentage attending a religious ceremony weekly	15%	10%

Source: Pew Research Center (2016) 'The Gender Gap in Religion around the World' [online]. Available at http://www.pewforum.org/2016/03/22/the-gender-gap-in-religion-around-the-world/ Accessed 05/04/2018

Activity

1. Briefly describe the patterns shown in Table 3.5.1.

2. Suggest possible reasons for differences in the gender gap in **religiosity** between countries.

The table shows that in the UK women are significantly more likely than men to pray, to see religion as very important and to attend religious ceremonies.

Opinion poll evidence on gender and religious belief also suggests that men are less religious than women. A YouGov survey conducted in March 2011 found that in England and Wales 58 per cent of men and 64 per cent of women identified a religion to which they belonged.

Evidence concerning New Age beliefs suggests that they are overwhelmingly followed or practised by women (see Unit 3.4.4). Data from the 2008 British Social Attitudes Survey found that 40 per cent of women and just 28 per cent of men described themselves as 'very spiritual' or 'moderately spiritual' (BRIN, 2017).

Among minority ethnic groups who are not Christian, the pattern is more complex. The 2008–9 Citizenship Survey (Ferguson and Hussey, 2010) used data from a sample of around 10 000 adults, plus a booster sample of around 5000 adults from minority ethnic groups, to determine the percentages of men and women who practised different religions. In all categories, apart from Sikhs (where there was no difference between males and females), women were more likely to practise the religion than men. However, by far the most significant difference was between males and females practising Christianity, and there were only small differences between males and females practising Muslim and Buddhist religions (see Table 3.5.2).

Activity

Table 3.5.2 Percentages of males and females practising different religions

	Christian	Muslim	Hindu	Sikh	Buddhist	Other religion	All
Males	25	79	65	66	64	46	31
Females	38	82	78	66	69	56	42

Source: Adapted from Ferguson, C. and Hussey, D. (2010) *2008–09 Citizenship Survey: Race, Religion and Equalities Topic Report,* Office for National Statistics, London, Table 17.

1. Briefly describe the patterns shown in Table 3.5.2.

2. How would you account for the differences between religions?

Various explanations have been put forward to account for the apparent greater participation in and commitment to religion among women in most religions.

Alan S. Miller and John P. Hoffmann – 'Risk and religion'

Alan S. Miller and John P. Hoffmann (1995) examined a number of explanations for women's greater religiosity. They argue that other sociologists have put two main types of explanation forward.

1. Many sociologists explain gender differences in terms of **differential socialisation**. According to this view 'females are taught to be more submissive, passive and obedient and nurturing than are males and these attributes are associated with higher levels of religiosity' (Miller and Hoffmann, 1995). These characteristics are more often found in traditional religious beliefs. For example, religions such as Christianity emphasise obedience to God and characteristics such as being loving, which are associated with female gender roles. Male roles place less emphasis on these characteristics. This theory is backed up by research evidence from the USA discussed by Miller and Hoffmann, which shows that men who are submissive, passive, obedient and nurturing tend to be more religious than men who are not.

2. The second explanation argues that the differences result from the **structural locations** of men and women in society. Women are less involved in the labour force than men and more involved in bringing up children. According to this viewpoint, not only do women have more time for church-related activities but their lower level of involvement in paid work also gives them a greater need for the sense of personal identity which religion can provide. Some US research discussed by Miller and Hoffmann suggests that religion is seen as a household activity. Socialising children through taking them to church can be regarded as an extension of female childcare roles.

Activity

A woman and child at church.

1. Suggest as many reasons as you can for women being more likely to take children to church than men.

2. Do you think that this is more likely to make daughters religious in later life than sons? Give reasons for your answer.

The previous paragraph outlined two explanations for gender differences in religious activity – gender differences in socialisation and in structural location. These two explanations are not mutually exclusive and furthermore they are linked. The socialisation of males and females tends to lead to them occupying different social locations, which in turn reinforce gender differences. Despite putting forward these explanations, Miller and Hoffmann argue that they cannot entirely explain the difference between male and female religiosity. They quote research that suggests that even when socialisation and location in the social structure are taken into account, women are still more religious than men. They argue, therefore, that a third factor, attitude to **risk**, is also important.

Not being religious can be seen as risk-taking behaviour. There is nothing to lose by being religious, but not being religious might be seen to involve risks, such as being condemned to hell after death. Using survey research from the USA (*A Continuing Study of the Lifestyles and Attitudes of Youth*), Miller and Hoffmann show that men tend to be less averse to risk than women, and that both men and women who are more averse to taking risks have higher levels of religiosity. They conclude that women's greater concern about risk is an important additional factor alongside socialisation and structural location that may explain women's greater religiosity.

Evaluation

The argument put forward by Miller and Hoffmann that women have more time for church-related activities is very debatable given that a great deal of research suggests that women spend more time on housework and childcare than men. Furthermore, rates of female participation in the labour market are now very high both in the USA and the UK, making it questionable whether women lack a sense of occupational identity. In addition, some other researchers give little credence to their ideas about the role of 'risk' in explaining gender differences in religious activity.

Steve Bruce – religion and secularisation

Unlike Miller and Hoffmann, Steve Bruce (1996) did not see attitudes to risk as being significant in explaining gender differences in religiosity. He does follow Miller and Hoffmann in seeing differences in male and female roles as being important, but he goes beyond their ideas by linking gender differences to **secularisation** and by discussing gender and New Age beliefs. (Secularisation is the theory that religion tends to decline in social significance in modern societies. It will be fully discussed in Part 6.)

Bruce started by suggesting that religion tends to have an affinity with aspects of femininity that make women 'less confrontational, less aggressive, less goal oriented, less domineering, more cooperative and more caring'. This affinity does not just apply to traditional

religion and indeed is particularly strong with spiritual beliefs such as those of the New Age. Women are very attracted to the 'healing, channelling and spirituality' side of New Age beliefs because they are more in keeping with female gender roles. The minority of men involved in the New Age tend to be more interested in the paranormal (for example ghosts and UFOs) than the more feminine aspects of the movement.

Bruce also believed that women are more attracted to traditional religions because 'the churches have always been interested in the control of sexuality and in the instruction of the next generation, both matters which are concentrated on the domestic hearth and in which women have a major role to play'. According to Bruce, there is a sharp division in the modern world between the **public sphere** (of paid work, politics and so on) and the **private sphere** (of the domestic world of the family and personal life). Bruce believed that as a result of secularisation, religion has become less and less important in the public sphere and increasingly confined to the private sphere. Since women are more involved with the private sphere than men, and religion has become a largely private matter, women have tended to become more religious than men. As religion has declined generally, men with their predominantly public-sphere social roles have lost their religiosity more quickly than women.

To Bruce, then, within an overall pattern of decline, religion has declined less among women than among men. However, the type of religion that has retained an appeal for some women varies by social class. Working-class women tend to retain a belief in forms of religion and spirituality in which they are more passive. They believe in a powerful God, or in 'obscure forces beyond their control', such as fortune telling, superstition and charms. Middle-class women, on the other hand, have more experience of controlling and improving their own lives. Consequently, they tend to follow religions that allow more individual autonomy, and forms of spirituality which facilitate personal development. They are attracted to New Age beliefs that promote the growth and development of the self (see Unit 3.4.4 for a discussion of the New Age).

Marta Trzebiatowska and Steve Bruce – 'The sum of small differences'

In more recent writing, Marta Trzebiatowska and Steve Bruce (2012) develop these ideas. They argue that 'the sum of small differences' accounts for the greater religiosity of women.

Like other sociologists, they emphasise the importance of the different roles of men and women in reproduction and, in particular, the greater involvement of women than men in caring and socialising the young. These roles bring women closer than men to religion because the church continues to have a significant role in 'moral teaching', which parents, particularly mothers, still think is important even if they do not have strong religious beliefs themselves.

Although religious beliefs have been declining in significance, an association with churches continued to be a sign of respectability for some time, and men have tended to delegate the job of maintaining this connection to women. This can be linked to patriarchal values. Trzebiatowska and Bruce suggest that patriarchy may play a part in the fact that men sometimes encourage women to be more religious in an attempt to control women's sexuality. They think that their wives are more likely to be faithful if they are religious. Conversely, women in some religious groups may use religion as a way of limiting sexual demand from their husbands if the religion portrays sex primarily as a means of reproduction.

With respect to New Age beliefs, Trzebiatowska and Bruce do not regard them as being particularly religious but as more concerned with 'an interest in physical and psychological well-being'. This is of more concern to women than men because 'dominant notions of masculinity … make health-seeking behaviour (unless it coincidentally involves combat) a sign of weakness'.

Trzebiatowska and Bruce conclude that gender differences in religiosity are likely to shrink in coming decades. More and more women are being freed from the traditional social roles which give them more contact with religion. With no stigma now being attached to a lack of religious beliefs, maintaining ties with religion will become less and less significant for men and women alike.

Linda Woodhead – female religiosity and gendering secularisation

Like Bruce, Linda Woodhead connects gender differences in religiosity to changes in society, including secularisation, and she discusses both traditional religion and New Age and similar spiritual beliefs. However, she develops a more sophisticated explanation of the relationship than Bruce. Furthermore, she does not follow Bruce in arguing that religion and spirituality are simply declining.

Gender and the spiritual revolution

In work with Paul Heelas (Heelas *et al.*, 2005), Woodhead argues that there is a spiritual revolution taking place involving a shift away from the traditional religions of the *congregational domain* (religion based on attending churches and denominations) towards the spiritualities of the *holistic milieu* (involvement in the New Age) (see Unit 3.6.4 for a discussion of these concepts). She believes that, to some extent, religions of the congregational domain are changing as well.

Woodhead (2005) believes that processes of secularisation have had an influence on Western societies, but that they can only be understood if they are related to gender. From the 19th century, modernisation led to a process of **rationalisation** – a process in which people calculate the best/ most rational and logical means to achieve given objectives rather than relying on faith or tradition to guide their actions (see Unit 3.6.5). This had a 'corrosive effect' on religion as it left little room for the non-rational faith required by religion. However, this process largely affected men. The housewife role became increasingly important for middle-class women and this isolated them to some extent from rationalisation. Women were not 'absorbed into rationalized values' and so were not as likely to become disillusioned with the church's teachings as men.

Male church-going declined, but female church-going did not, leading to women becoming the majority of those involved in churches. Churches became 'increasingly feminized or domesticized'. They placed more emphasis on 'love, care and relationships' and less on God as an all-powerful and punitive (punishing) ruler, though they continued to reinforce male power through paternalistic images of God as a 'loving father'. As churches became feminised, they lost prestige and became even less appealing to most men.

Activity

Comforting hands from heaven and dramatic lightning.

1. Explain how these two images above can be seen to represent feminine and masculine views of God.

2. If churches emphasise the message given in the first image, how might that account for gender differences in church attendance?

Religion and different spheres of life

By the 1970s, the process of married women returning to the labour force was well under way. By now the dominance of women as church-goers was well established, reinforced by the 'feminine' nature of the religious beliefs adopted by most churches. However, large numbers of women were increasingly exposed to the rationalised culture of paid work. This led to a rapid decline in church-going by women.

Woodhead believes that it is largely the changes in women's lives that account for the decline of Christian churches and denominations in Western countries since the 1970s. However, women are still more interested than men in religion and spirituality, for a number of reasons:

1. Women are still less involved in the public world of work than men. More women than men work part-time and women are still much more likely than men to have the main responsibility for childcare.

2. Woodhead argues that, contrary to much theory, there are three rather than two spheres in contemporary societies. These are:

   » **Primary institutions** (such as those associated with work and politics)

   » **Secondary institutions** (which are associated with caring for others; these include the family and religion)

   » An **individual sphere** (in which people are concerned with their own autonomous and individual selves).

   Because religion has been feminised, it remains relevant to women, whose lives are based in secondary institutions. Given this, women are still more likely than men to be involved in churches and denominations. Elsewhere, Woodhead (2001) argues that the emphasis on relationships in feminised churches remains more attractive to women than to men. Both church religion and women's lives emphasise 'relationships of love, trust and care'.

3. New Age beliefs or the holistic milieu (Heelas *et al.*, 2005; see Part 6) also tend to be dominated by women. Woodhead argues that this is the case because it helps to resolve a contradiction between 'traditional' female roles in the home and more 'masculine' roles in the workplace. In paid work your sense of self largely derives from your position or job, whereas in family roles your sense of self is more concerned with relationships with others (as wife, parent and so on). The holistic milieu allows this tension to be bypassed because it creates

a new 'type of selfhood in which identity is not dictated by social position and experience, but discovered from within'. The contradiction between roles in primary and secondary institutions is resolved by seeking your identity in the individual sphere.

Conclusion

Woodhead's work is more developed than that of other writers on this topic and adds significantly to the understanding of secularisation as well as of gender differences in religiosity. However, as Woodhead herself admits, gender and religiosity is a somewhat neglected area of research and further investigation is required to make these theories more convincing. Research into gender and religiosity among minority ethnic groups is even less developed, but there have been useful attempts to understand the relationship between ethnicity and religiosity in general, and we will turn to this next.

Key terms

Religiosity The quality of being religious.

Differential socialisation The contrasting ways in which males and females are brought up within and outside the family.

Structural location The position of different social groups within the social structure, for example the greater involvement of men in paid employment than women.

Risk The possibility of danger.

Secularisation The decline in the social significance of religion.

Public sphere The social world outside the family and personal life.

Private sphere The social world inside families and involving personal relationships.

Rationalisation A process in which people calculate the most effective means to achieve given objectives rather than relying on faith or tradition to guide their actions.

Primary institutions Institutions associated with work and politics.

Secondary institutions Institutions associated with caring for others, such as the family and religion.

The individual sphere The sphere of social life concerned with individual identity.

Summary

1. Statistical evidence suggests that women tend to be more religious than men in all types of religious organisations and movements both in the UK and in most countries in the world.

2. Miller and Hoffmann explained gender differences in terms of differential socialisation of males and females, the structural locations of men and women (with women being less involved in the labour force than men), and men's greater willingness to take risks (including risking damnation by not observing religion).

3. Bruce argues that secularisation has led to religion being largely confined to the private sphere in which women are more prominent than men.

4. Trzebiatowska and Bruce attribute gender differences in religiosity to the different roles of men and women in reproduction and the significance of religion in controlling women's sexuality.

5. Woodhead believes that secularisation has impacted on men more than women and this has resulted in churches becoming feminised and appealing to women more than men. New-age beliefs appeal to women because they help women to develop a new sense of selfhood which bypasses the contradiction between their family and work roles.

Unit 3.5.3 Religion and ethnicity

Ethnic groups are groups defined by 'race', religion and/or national origin who share a common cultural heritage. Religion is often one part of this cultural heritage. Minority ethnic groups often develop in a country because of migration and first-generation migrants to Britain have often had stronger religious beliefs than the population as a whole. Over time, with each successive generation, those beliefs may weaken or strengthen. Individuals in minority and majority ethnic groups may also change their religious beliefs. So, how distinctive are the religious beliefs of different minority ethnic groups? What factors shape both the nature and the strength of those beliefs? And is religion becoming less or more important for minority ethnic groups over time? These are the questions which will be addressed in this unit.

Ethnic groups and religion in Britain

There are a number of useful sources of information on religion and ethnicity in Britain, though none of them provides a comprehensive and totally reliable set of data. The census is one important source. However, it only provides information on religious identity and gives no indication of the strength of that identity.

The findings of the 2011 census are shown in Table 3.5.3. Not surprisingly, it shows that there are significant variations in the religious identities of different ethnic groups and on the likelihood of being religious or not. No less than 55.6 per cent of Chinese groups stated that they had no religion, as did 32.3 per cent of those with mixed ethnic backgrounds and 28 per cent of White British groups. Very few members of Indian, Pakistani or Bangladeshi origin said they had no religion. Fewer than one in thirty people of Black African ethnicity said they had no religion, but more than one in eight people of Black Caribbean origin said this.

Both White and Black ethnic groups were predominantly Christian. Pakistani and Bangladeshi groups were predominantly Muslim, and Indian groups were most likely to be Hindu or Sikh (though there were also significant numbers of Muslims and Christians).

Activity

Table 3.5.3 Adults practising different religions as a proportion of the ethnic group, 2008/09

Religion	Christian	Buddhist	Hindu	Jewish	Muslim	Sikh	Other	No religion	Not stated
All categories Total	59.3%	0.4%	1.5%	0.5%	4.8%	0.8%	0.4%	25.1%	7.2%
White: Total	63.9%	0.2%	0.0%	0.5%	0.4%	0.0%	0.4%	27.3%	7.2%
White: English/Welsh/Scottish/Northern Irish/British	63.7%	0.2%	0.0%	0.4%	0.2%	0.0%	0.4%	28.0%	7.2%
Other White	65.1%	0.4%	0.2%	1.6%	5.3%	0.1%	0.5%	18.7%	8.3%
Mixed/multiple ethnic group	46.3%	0.8%	0.8%	0.3%	8.4%	0.4%	0.6%	32.3%	10.1%
Asian/Asian British: Indian	9.6%	0.3%	44.0%	0.1%	14.0%	22.1%	2.3%	3.1%	4.5%
Asian/Asian British: Pakistani	1.5%	0.1%	0.3%	0.0%	91.5%	0.3%	0.1%	1.1%	5.2%
Asian/Asian British: Bangladeshi	1.5%	0.1%	0.9%	0.0%	90.0%	0.2%	0.0%	1.4%	5.9%
Asian/Asian British: Chinese	19.6%	12.6%	0.7%	0.1%	2.0%	0.3%	0.4%	55.6%	8.7%
Black/African/Caribbean/Black British: African	69.9%	0.1%	0.2%	0.1%	20.9%	0.1%	0.2%	2.9%	5.7%
Black/African/Caribbean/Black British: Caribbean	74.2%	0.2%	0.2%	0.1%	1.2%	0.1%	0.7%	12.9%	10.4%
Other ethnic group	19.8%	0.6%	1.4%	2.0%	51.5%	7.2%	0.6%	9.2%	7.6%

Source: ONS (2011) *Social Trends 41*, Office for National Statistics, London, p. 28.

1. Suggest possible reasons for the patterns of religious affiliation for the following groups:

   a Mixed/multiple ethnic group

   b Asian/Asian British: Indian

   c Other ethnic group

2. Briefly suggest possible reasons for the differences between ethnic groups in the proportions saying that they had 'no religion'.

The 2008–09 Citizenship Survey (Ferguson and Hussey, 2010) provided useful information on the strength of religious beliefs. For example, it found that 80 per cent of Muslims actively practised their religion but just 32 per cent of Christians did so. The survey also asked respondents about the extent to which religion affected their day-to-day life. Muslims were most likely to say that religion affected their choice of where to live (39 per cent, compared to 32 per cent of Hindus and 16 per cent of Christians). Muslims were also most likely to say that religion influenced their choice of friends.

Most evidence suggests that members of minority ethnic groups in Britain are more likely than White British people to see themselves as religious; religions that are followed predominantly by minority ethnic groups are more likely to be practised by believers; and their religion is more likely (in most respects) to influence their lives. British people of Chinese ethnicity, however, are generally an exception to these rules.

John Bird — explanations for high levels of religiosity

John Bird (1999) identified five important reasons for the higher levels of religiosity among minority ethnic groups in the UK:

1. Many ethnic groups 'originate in societies with high levels of religiosity'. For example, Bangladesh, Pakistan and, to a slightly lesser extent, India all have high levels of religious observance and belief. Christianity is also strong in former British colonies in the Caribbean such as Jamaica. First generation immigrants tend to bring these high levels of religiosity with them when arriving in the UK.

2. In an environment where people belong to a minority group, religion can 'act as a basis for community solidarity'. Solidarity based on religious affiliation can perform important social functions for new migrants, giving them 'a point of contact in a new country, a source of marriage partners, social welfare and so on'. In this situation, religious buildings such synagogues, mosques and temples can have an important social role.

3. Following on from this point, Bird argues that 'Maintaining a religious commitment is also a way to maintain other aspects of cultural identity such as language, art, patterns of marriage, cooking and so on.' Religion and minority ethnic cultures can be mutually reinforcing.

4. The importance of religion can be maintained through processes of socialisation and 'there is often strong family pressure to maintain religious commitment'. The extent to which this occurs is examined below.

5. Bird also examines the possibility that minority ethnic groups might have strong religious beliefs because it helps them cope with oppression. Disadvantaged minority ethnic groups tend to be working class, and their religious beliefs can be seen as a response to their position in the social structure. Drawing on research by Ken Pryce (1979) in Bristol, and Hinnels (1997), Bird suggests that Pentecostalism may perform a dual function for British African Caribbeans. First, it can be 'a way to adjust to a society in which (they) face discrimination and social injustice'. Bird claims that Pentecostalism can act in the way Marx suggested as the 'opiate of the masses' (see Unit 3.2.2). However, it can also help people to combat disadvantage by improving their social and economic position. Pryce (1979) pointed out that it encouraged hard work and thrift, which could lead to Pentecostalists gaining greater economic security.

In Pryce's study, some African Caribbeans adopted another religion of the oppressed, Rastafarianism. Rastafarianism offers the promise of salvation through a return to Africa and is sometimes associated with radical political views. Bird describes Rastafarianism as 'a typical religious sect based upon material underprivilege'.

Steve Bruce — cultural defence and cultural transition

Steve Bruce (2002) accepts that minority ethnic groups are more likely to engage in religious activity than the ethnic majority, but he argues that this is largely for social reasons. Bruce argues that the vitality of religion is mainly a response to the social situation of minority ethnic groups rather than an expression of deep religious commitment. He sees the strength of minority ethnic religions as caused by either:

1. **cultural defence** (where an ethnic group is protecting its sense of identity and maintaining ethnic pride through religion); or

2. **cultural transition** (where an ethnic group uses religion to cope with the upheaval of migration).

These two processes can work together as immigrant minority ethnic groups try to both adapt and

Activity

A mosque in Bolton, and a Hindu temple in Manchester, UK.

In what ways could mosques and temples act to facilitate or encourage cultural defence and cultural transition for minority ethnic groups in Britain?

defend their religious/cultural heritage. For example, discussing the USA, Meredith McGuire (2002) describes how Vietnamese-American Buddhists attempt to continue socialising their children into their culture but at the same time strive to gain acceptance in US society. She describes how, in 'Houston, Texas, the Vietnamese community has created their temple with many features reminiscent of Vietnam'. However, the temple is also used as a community centre helping the community to integrate into US society, for example by facilitating networking which supports people to find jobs. In such centres, minority ethnic groups can 'negotiate a Buddhist religious identity and work to have it accepted as legitimate in their new community'.

Decline or revival in ethnic minority religions?

Bruce (2002) believes, however, that over time, ethnic groups in Britain and in other Western societies become more integrated and are increasingly influenced by the wider secular society. As a consequence, their religious beliefs will decline.

A more complex view was taken by George Chryssides (1994), who argued that in Britain the religions of immigrant groups and their descendants have had three main paths open to them. The first option is **apostasy**, where a particular set of religious beliefs is abandoned in a hostile environment. The second is **accommodation**, where religious practices are adapted to take account of the changed situation. The third option is **renewed vigour**, where the religion is reasserted more strongly as a response to the actual or perceived hostility towards it.

Examples of all three responses can be found. Chryssides cited the case of Morris Cerullo, a Jew who converted to Christianity, as an example of apostasy. An example of accommodation might be a Sikh who removed his turban because he believed it would improve his chances at a job interview. An example of the third response is those who insist on strong religious orthodoxy from their children.

Chryssides acknowledges that minority ethnic religions have faced difficulties in Britain. They have had to establish places of prayer and deal with situations where religious observation might be difficult. However, he argues that the general pattern has been characterised by accommodation and renewed vigour rather than apostasy. Buildings have been bought and converted into mosques and temples, and religious beliefs and practices have been retained or adapted rather than abandoned. For example, many Islamic women have found ways to dress modestly while incorporating Western elements into their clothing. Religious marriage ceremonies have been adapted to meet the requirements for a legal marriage under British law.

The vigour of minority ethnic religions in Britain is demonstrated by the existence of some first-generation converts to these religions. Chryssides notes that Buddhism has been particularly successful in attracting new followers who have been brought up within the Christian tradition.

Some writers argue that there has been a revival of religion, which directly contradicts the claims

266

of the supporters of the theory of secularisation. For example, Gilles Kepel, in a book called *The Revenge of God* (1994), argues that there has been a resurgence of Judaism, Christianity and Islam in the modern world. According to Kepel, this has affected these religions, whether they are the religion of a minority or a majority in a particular society. Thus, for example, British Muslims have retained or strengthened their faith, not as a way of coping with cultural transition, but because they have been influenced by a worldwide Islamic revival. (For a discussion of Islamic and other faiths in the context of fundamentalism, see Unit 3.6.7.)

Research evidence

Evidence to help evaluate the competing claims is provided by the 2005 English Church Census (Brierley, 2006a). The English Church Census only measures attendance at Christian churches and cannot, therefore, give any indication about the religions of non-Christians. However, it did find that church attendance had gone up among all minority ethnic groups between 1998 and 2005, and among Black British people it had increased by 23 per cent. Brierley accepts that part, but not all, of this increase is due to immigration, but he also thinks that Black churches have been successful because of their 'intense community involvement'.

Research by Lucinda Platt (2014) used survey data from the 2010 Ethnic Minority British Election Study to compare the religiosity of UK-born and non-UK-born members of minority ethnic groups. The research was based on a sample of 2787 and focused on five minority ethnic groups: Indians, Pakistanis, Bangladeshis, Black Caribbeans and Black Africans. It compared the UK-born with those who were born outside the UK to examine whether religious identities had strengthened or whether there was evidence of greater assimilation and the adoption of British identities.

Platt found that, among minority ethnic groups, 99 per cent of the UK-born compared with 71 per cent of those born elsewhere claimed a British identity. Furthermore, among the non-UK-born, the longer they had lived in the UK the more likely they were to express a sense of British identity. This seemed to suggest strong support for assimilationist views. However, in all minority ethnic groups religious beliefs remained widespread, with over 90 per cent of Black Africans, Bangladeshis and Pakistanis saying that religion was important to them. When these findings were broken down into different ethnic groups, in all but one, religion was stronger among those born in the UK than those born overseas. The only exception was among Muslims, for whom there were contradictory indications with no clear evidence of a decline in religiosity.

Platt also looked at whether there was evidence that minority ethnic groups were placing more emphasis across generations on their *religious* identity as opposed to their *ethnic* identity. Again, she found no evidence for this among most ethnic groups, with the only exception being Indian Hindus. Both religious identity and ethnic identity remained important for all the groups.

Finally, Platt specifically tested the claim that perceptions of discrimination and racism encouraged a 'reactive ethnicity or religiosity' as a form of defence in a hostile environment.

Here there was some evidence that a sense of unfairness increased the extent to which members of minority ethnic groups identified with those from the same religious background. However, the effect was small and made little difference to the overall trend towards a gradual weakening of religiosity.

Overall, therefore, Platt argues that there is little evidence of religious revival among minority ethnic groups and more evidence that cultural defence is acting to slow down the gradual decline in religiosity from one generation to the next.

Activity

Muslims praying in Hyde Park, after protesting against Islamophobia and racial incitement, London, 2016.

Why does this image seem to contradict one of Platt's findings?

Contemporary issues: The Burnley project: Islam, radicalisation, ethnicity and age

Some commentators have argued that in recent years the religiosity of Muslims from minority ethnic groups has been increasing.

A 2005–07 research project involving a survey of 1000 teenagers in the northern English town of Burnley investigated changing attitudes and values in the Muslim community (Holden, 2009). The study involved five schools, one where all the pupils were Muslim. It found that even in the exclusively Muslim school, where you might expect religion to be particularly strong, the majority of pupils in this school were not very religious. For example, only around half of the pupils in this school said they prayed most days. Furthermore, 56 per cent said that they were less religious than their parents with only 10 per cent saying they were more religious.

There was little evidence, then, of Islamic beliefs strengthening. Paul Heelas (2015) argues that these results show that most young Muslims have been influenced by the widespread non-religious, secular beliefs in British society. Heelas suggests that is not surprising because most of the original Islamic immigrants who settled in Burnley and some other areas of the UK were from Mirpur in Kashmir where moderate Islam is practised. More conservative Muslims were unlikely to emigrate to a Western, liberal country such as the UK. For these reasons, Heelas does not believe that the relationship between ethnicity and religious belief will get stronger among Muslims in the UK nor that younger generations of British Muslims are generally more religious than their parents.

School children in Burnley.

Question

In view of the analysis above, discuss whether you think the next generation of children from Islamic backgrounds in the UK will be more or less religious than their parents. Provide a sociological justification for your answer.

Conclusion

Despite the evidence presented by Platt, religiosity remains significantly higher among minority ethnic groups in the UK and this seems likely to be the case for some time to come. Levels of religiosity may decline somewhat from generation to generation, but a number of factors are likely to produce greater resilience for religiosity in minority ethnic groups than the ethnic majority.

Key terms

Cultural defence The role of religion when it helps to reinforce and maintain ethnic identity and pride in areas where religious or ethnic communities are in conflict.

Cultural transition The role of religion when it helps a minority ethnic group to cope with social change and migration.

Apostasy Abandoning a set of religious beliefs in a hostile environment.

Accommodation Adapting religious beliefs in response to a changed environment.

Renewed vigour An increase in the intensity of religious feelings in response to perceived hostility.

Summary

1. The religion of Black and minority ethnic groups is closely connected with the ethnicity and countries of origin of first-generation immigrants.

2. Most Black and minority ethnic groups in the UK tend to be more religious than their White counterparts.

3. John Bird explained higher levels of religiosity for minority ethnic groups in terms of ethnic origins, religion acting as a basis for community solidarity, religion as a way of maintaining cultural identity, the maintenance of religion through socialisation, and religion as a way of coping with oppression.

4. Steve Bruce argues that the cultural role of minority ethnic religions explains their continued vitality because religions act as a form of cultural defence or a way of coping with transition to a new society.

5. Bruce believes that the influence of secularisation will lead to the decline of minority ethnic religions in the UK over time but Chryssides suggests that they can develop in three ways: apostasy, renewed vigour or accommodation.

6. Brierley has found evidence of increased attendance at church by minority ethnic groups but Platt has found evidence of a decline in religiosity for all minority ethnic groups apart from Muslims.

7. Evidence from The Burnley project suggests that most young British Muslims are less religious than their parents.

Unit 3.5.4 Age, generation and religiosity

There is clear evidence that older age groups tend to be more religious than younger age groups. This applies to both the UK and in many parts of the world. But how consistent is this difference and how can it be explained?

Statistical evidence on age and religiosity

The 2011 census (ONS, 2012) found that in England and Wales, 22 per cent of Christians were 65 and over but this group made up just 16 per cent of the population. Furthermore, younger people were more likely than older people to say they had 'no religion'. In 2011, 31 per cent of the population were under 25, but 39 per cent of those with no religion were in this age bracket. Similarly, 82 per cent of those saying they had no religion were under 50, but this group only made up 65 per cent of the population. The 2011 census data also showed that since 2001 the fastest fall in those claiming a religious identity was among males aged 35 to 39.

Research evidence shows that in Britain, and in most countries in the world, the young tend to be less religious than the old. For example, the World Values Study (discussed in Burkimsher, 2008) found that young people (classified as those who were under 30) were less likely to say they attended places of worship than older people (those who were 50 or over). This was the case in the vast majority of countries: in 76 out of 84 countries in 2004 the older age group were found to be more religious than the younger age group. The only exceptions were Georgia, Armenia, Bosnia Herzegovina, Uganda, Bulgaria, the Philippines, Zimbabwe and Nigeria. In Great Britain, 24.1 per cent of those aged 50 or over said they attended a place of worship regularly, compared to 12.1 per cent of the young – a ratio of almost 2:1.

The English Church Census (Brierley, 2006a) found that the average age of the church-goer had increased from 37 in 1979 to 45 in 2005. This relative lack of interest in the religious or spiritual by the young is also found in New Age beliefs, with Heelas *et al*. (2005) observing that most of those involved in the holistic milieu are middle-aged or older (see Unit 3.4.4).

Activity

Soul Survivor, a Christian summer event in the UK.

With reference to the image, discuss the view that religiosity among young people from Christian backgrounds will increase if churches and other organisations try to make religion more appealing to younger age groups.

Reasons for age differences in religiosity

David Voas and Alasdair Crockett (2005) note that there are three possible explanations for age differences in religiosity.

1. The differences could be the result of age. Many commentators have suggested that people tend to get more religious as they get older and therefore see themselves as coming closer to death. Religious belief might also be affected by life events such as having children. People may return to active involvement in religion because they think it is important for the socialisation of their children. From this perspective, substantial numbers of the young or middle-aged will return to religion as they get older.

2. The differences could be explained by a **period effect**. Perhaps society is becoming less religious because of forces or events that have an impact on everyone. Allowing shops to open on Sunday, for example, might reduce church attendance. Scandals that damage the reputation of clergy and senior religious leaders could reduce the authority of organised religion. Major innovations in communications (like the internet and social media) might affect beliefs in ways that are hard to predict.

3. Those born in a particular era (a cohort) might be particularly unlikely or likely to be religious because of specific events or social changes during the time they were growing up. An example of such a theory is put forward by Brierley, commenting on the rapid decline in church-going among the young in the 1990s. Brierley (2006a) says, 'Those in "Generation Y", defined by some as those born in the 1980s, have been found to have little spiritual interest, being rather focused on "happiness".' Such differences could bring about the progressive decline of religion, if each generation is less religious than the previous one. Supporters of this view generally favour the theory of secularisation or religious decline (see Part 6).

Evidence

Voas and Crockett examined data from the British Social Attitudes Survey to consider which of these theories was most plausible. The data allowed them to see whether a cohort was more or less religious than other cohorts and whether their attitude to religion changed as they aged.

Voas and Crockett found little evidence that people became markedly more religious with age or personally less religious over time. They say, 'Although many individual adults become more, or less religiously committed our investigation suggests that in the aggregate such age and period effects have little impact' (Voas and Crockett, 2005). Instead they concluded that in Britain 'change has occurred because each generation has entered adulthood less religious than its predecessors'. In part, they claimed, this was because each generation was less likely to socialise their children into religious beliefs than the previous generation.

The conclusions reached by Voas and Crockett may not apply to all types of religious and spiritual belief. Heelas *et al.* (2005) reach different conclusions with respect to spiritual beliefs of the holistic milieu. They claim that this type of belief is growing rapidly despite few young people being involved, because people do not usually start to engage with such spiritualities until middle age.

Taking an international perspective, Marion Burkimsher (2008) found similar patterns in many, but not all, countries. She examined statistical evidence from the European Values Surveys of 2002, 2004 and 2006 and the World Values Survey of 1995 and 2004. She found that evidence from 'stable developed countries' (including Western Europe) suggested that recent generations were less religious than earlier generations. In addition to this **cohort effect**, an **age effect** is also seen: there tends to be a trough in religious attendance as young people pass through their 20s, followed by a modest rebound as they enter stable partnerships and have children.

Looking at how the proportions of young people attending religious services have changed over time she saw some period effects. In some ex-communist countries in Eastern Europe (e.g. Georgia and Russia), the Balkans (ex-Yugoslavia) and some Latin American countries (e.g. Brazil), there is evidence of religiosity among the young having increased over recent years. The Catholic countries of Europe have seen the greatest declines in religious observance in recent years, although they started at a high level. By contrast, China, where religious attendance was very low because of state-imposed atheism, has seen growth in religious attendance in recent years.

Age and religion – conclusion

The conclusions of Voas and Crockett appear to provide support for the theory that religion is declining – the theory of secularisation. However, those of Burkimsher would support secularisation theory only in relation to some countries. Burkimsher, therefore, concludes that 'the global wave of secularisation – even if it exists – is not touching each country equally; churches, both locally or nationally, which respond to the needs of each new generation can stem or reverse the tide' (Burkimsher, 2008). Furthermore, it should not be assumed that the same process affects all religions and all ethnic groups in the same way or to the same extent. For example, the research by Platt (2014) discussed above suggests that Islamic groups are not experiencing a decline in religiosity across generations. As in other areas of social life, age cannot be considered in isolation from other social divisions, particularly those relating to ethnicity, gender and social class.

Key terms

Age effect The influence of being in a certain age group, e.g. young, middle-aged, elderly. This is associated with leaving home, being single/married, having children, being widowed, having life-limiting disabilities, etc.

Period effect A change in attitudes or behaviour that affects all ages at a certain time period.

Cohort effect The influence of belonging to a certain generation, e.g. the Baby Boom generation (those born mid-1940s to early 1960s) or the Millennial generation (born early 1980s to late 1990s).

Summary

1. Statistical evidence suggests that both in the UK and most countries of the world young people are less religious than older people. Church attendance statistics suggest an ageing of British congregations.

2. Voas and Crockett, and Burkimsher, show that secularisation can be due to either a period or cohort effect.

3. Data from the British Social Attitudes Survey suggest that in Britain, generational differences in religiosity are the main driver of secularisation.

4. Heelas claims that New Age beliefs are growing, being driven by the young age profile of participants.

5. Burkimsher, using the European Values Survey and the World Values Survey, found that secularisation was affecting most developed countries but that in Eastern Europe, the Balkans and China there was evidence of young people becoming more religious.

271

PART 6 THE SIGNIFICANCE OF RELIGIOSITY IN THE CONTEMPORARY WORLD – SECULARISATION AND RELIGIOUS REVIVALS

Contents

A few decades ago, most sociologists believed that the modern world of urban living, rational planning and progress in science and technology was resulting in the long-term decline of religion.

The theory of secularisation suggested that this decline was unlikely to be reversed, particularly in modern, Western societies. More recently, however, this view has been questioned. Some types of spirituality, for example those associated with the New Age, appear to be on the rise. In the USA, religion appears to be much more popular than in north-western Europe. In a global context, the theory of secularisation is, on the surface, less credible than it is in a European context. The growth of fundamentalist movements in a range of religions challenges the assumptions of secularisation theory. Furthermore, the process of globalisation itself provides opportunities for religious beliefs and religious organisations to spread their influence across and between continents. This part of the chapter examines theories, evidence and arguments which suggest that religion is declining and counterclaims that it is not, in British, American and global contexts. While some sociologists have sought a single answer to questions about whether religion is declining or not, the answer may depend upon how exactly you define and measure religiosity, and which parts of the world you are discussing.

Unit 3.6.1 Theories of secularisation and religious revival

The idea of secularisation has been closely linked with several major theories about the development of Western societies. Early theorists generally believed that secularisation would occur, but in recent decades some have come to the opposite conclusion claiming that religious revivals are happening or are likely in the future. This unit examines these competing claims and sets the scene for the remainder of the final part of the chapter.

Support for the theory of secularisation

In the 19th century it was widely believed that industrialisation and the growth of scientific knowledge would lead to **secularisation**, which was defined by Bryan Wilson, a leading British proponent of secularisation as, 'the process whereby religious thinking, practice and institutions lose social significance' (Wilson, 1966). But why have so many sociologists claimed that religion would decline in significance?

Classical theories of secularisation

Many of the founders of sociology thought that as societies developed, religion would either decline (for example Durkheim) or even disappear (Marx believed that this would happen after communism). Max Weber was perhaps the most influential classical theorist who shared this belief.

Weber argued that religion would decline in importance because of the development of modernity. Modern societies are seen to be incompatible with religion having a central role in society. Weber thought that in modern societies people would act less in terms of emotions and tradition, and more in terms of the rational pursuit of goals. **Rationalisation** would gradually erode religious influence as people turned to science for their understanding of the world and ceased to believe that prayer was a way to achieve their aims (Weber, 1958, 1963, first published 1904; Gerth and Mills, 1954). Weber's approach and that of other classical theorists of secularisation has been taken forward by a number of contemporary theorists, one of whom will now be discussed in detail.

Activity

The Trafford Centre, Manchester.

With some reference to the picture, discuss the view that secular pursuits such as shopping have replaced religious and spiritual beliefs in the UK.

Contemporary theories of secularisation

One of the most influential contemporary theories of secularisation has been put forward by the British sociologist Steve Bruce. Bruce's ideas are complex and will be explored in detail as this section develops, but the main features of his theory are illustrated in Figure 3.6.1 and summarised here.

Following Weber (see Unit 3.3.1), Bruce (2011) puts particular emphasis on Protestantism as beginning the changes in beliefs that promoted secularisation. However, according to Bruce, changes within religion were accompanied by important changes in the wider society, and together these changes created the conditions for secularisation.

Structural differentiation in modern societies led to the separation and specialisation of major institutions, including churches, which resulted in churches becoming less central to social life. They no longer had such a major role in politics, the education system, the legal system or the provision of welfare, and instead they concentrated on providing a belief system for individuals. At the same time, **social differentiation** took place. In feudal times, (roughly the 9th to the 15th centuries) in mainly agricultural societies, all social groups lived close together and saw themselves as part of a single universe (albeit a very unequal one). In modern urban societies, different social groups (e.g. social classes) became increasingly separated physically. Movement between social roles became increasingly common and this made it more difficult for people to accept the idea that they were part of a single moral universe with God at the pinnacle.

Individualism also developed, making people less strongly tied to collective institutions such as churches. The special status of the priesthood was undermined, as a more complex and flexible ranking system developed in society in which people were judged less in terms of the positions they held and more as individuals.

These processes were linked to **societalisation**, whereby 'close-knit, integrated communities gradually lost power and presence to large-scale industrial and commercial enterprises, to modern states, coordinated through massive, impersonal bureaucracies, and to cities' (Bruce, 2011).

Big business and central government exercised increasing influence over local people. According to Bruce, religion can best be sustained in

Figure 3.6.1 The secularisation paradigm of Steve Bruce

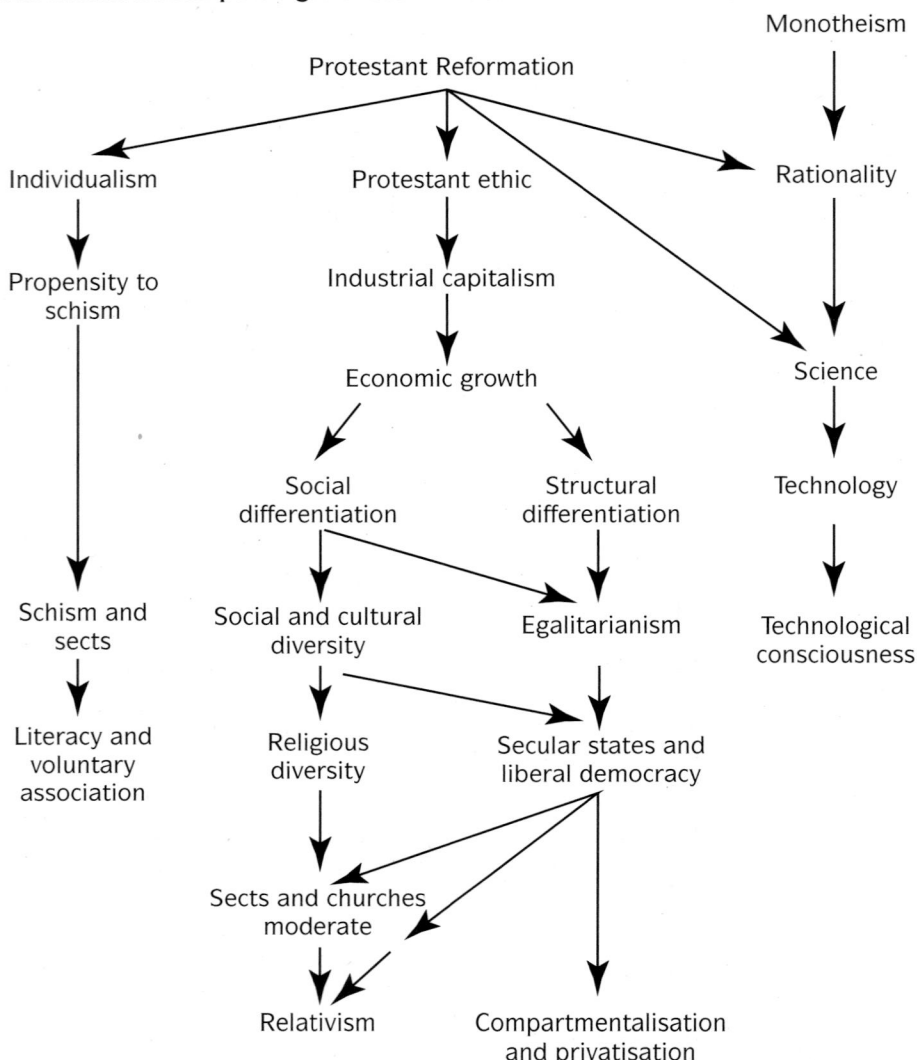

Source: Bruce, S. (2011), *Secularization,* Oxford University Press, Oxford, p. 27.

well-integrated local communities where everyone shares the same religious views and where as a result these views are taken for granted and never questioned. Societalisation undermined such communities and therefore undermined the social base that supported religion.

Schisms (splits) in established religion and increasing social and cultural diversity (e.g. as a result of immigration) exposed more people to diverse religious views, making the established religion less pervasive throughout society and less persuasive as a set of beliefs. This made it more difficult to automatically socialise children into unquestioningly accepting the same religion as their parents.

With greater religious variety or **pluralism,** it became more difficult for the state to suppress alternative religions or to allow a single church to dominate public life or policy making. This resulted in increased compartmentalisation, with religion becoming separated from the central working of society. Alongside this, privatisation developed, so that religion became a matter of private preference rather than public duty.

Bruce places less emphasis on scientific rationalism as a cause of secularisation than some people, but he does accept that the application of science through technology was important. As humans developed increasing mastery over nature, they became less reliant upon religious or supernatural explanations or remedies for problems. For example, medical science became more important for dealing with illness than prayer.

Ultimately people's worldviews became more open to alternative views and interpretations of the world, rather than believing one account to be the absolute truth. In these circumstances, people could still choose to believe in a religion, but the absolute truth of religion no longer went unquestioned by the majority of people.

Problems with the theory of secularisation

For a considerable time, the theory of secularisation was widely accepted by sociologists. However, there were always problems with a theory using such a vague concept as secularisation and in recent decades the evidence for secularisation, at least as a worldwide phenomenon, has become less compelling. So how has the theory been challenged?

The limits to secularisation

Supporters of the theory of secularisation do not necessarily believe that religion will disappear completely. They all argue that in one or more ways religion will decline in significance, but theorists have different views about how extensive they think secularisation is likely to be. Some think that secularisation will ultimately be a global process as the world westernises and modernises. Others, including Bruce (2011), see it as largely confined to Western societies. However, Bruce does believe that once it has progressed so far in societies such as Britain, it can never be reversed. Religious beliefs may remain, but the centrality of religion to society cannot be reinstated.

Problems in defining secularisation

A major problem with the concept of secularisation is that it is given different meanings by different sociologists. Problems, therefore, arise in evaluating the theory of secularisation because of the absence of a generally agreed definition. Because there are different definitions, there is also no agreed, single, way of measuring whether it is taking place.

José Casanova (2003) identifies a particularly significant division between two definitions of the term 'secularisation'. One way of using the term sees secularisation broadly as 'the secularization of societal structures or the diminution of the social significance of religion' (Casanova, 2003). In this definition, the main emphasis is on religious institutions and religious beliefs playing an ever-decreasing role in influencing public life so that religion becomes an essentially private matter. This definition of religion is one which is not easily measured statistically.

The other main way of using the term is narrower and refers to the 'decline of religious beliefs and practices among individuals' (Casanova, 2003). In this case, the emphasis is on such issues as how many people believe in God and how many attend churches or other places of worship and how many affiliate to a religion. (See Unit 3.6.6 for a more developed breakdown of definitions of secularisation by Casanova.)

Even in terms of religious beliefs and practices, there can be problems measuring religiosity. For example, Grace Davie (2007) believes that religion may have declined in terms of *belonging* (that is being an active member of religious organisations) but this may not be the case in terms of *believing* – for example, believing in God. Furthermore, the validity and reliability of much data on religiosity, for example church attendance figures and opinion poll statistics on religious beliefs, have been called into question (see Unit 3.6.2).

Another problem arises in terms of identifying what exactly is meant by the term 'religion'. As we saw in Unit 3.1.1, there are very different definitions of religion and religiosity, and more inclusive definitions can encompass a range of activities and beliefs that may not be traditionally be seen as religious. An important example is New Age beliefs, which may not take place in institutional settings and may not involve a belief in God. Should evidence of increased belief or participation in the New Age be seen as evidence against secularisation, or is it irrelevant because the beliefs are not religious?

Theories of religious resilience and revival

Some theorists have directly contradicted the theory of secularisation. Some have argued that religion has been resilient, resisting the forces of secularisation and maintaining its importance. Others have gone further and have argued that religion has increased in importance in religious revivals.

Revival as a response to modernisation and secularisation

Gilles Kepel (1994) claimed that any trend towards secularisation was reversed around 1975. Furthermore, the various religious revivals were very ambitious – they were aimed at 'recovering a sacred foundation for the organization of society – by changing society if necessary'.

Kepel used the examples of Christians in the USA and Europe, Jews in Israel and Muslims throughout the world to support his case. All of these revivals represent attempts to counter secularism. They are a reaction to the apparent failure of attempts to base the policies of nation states upon secular principles. He says, 'They regard the vainglorious emancipation of reason from faith as the prime cause of the ills of the twentieth century, the beginnings of a process leading straight to Nazi and Stalinist totalitarianism.' As such, they are very much a reaction against modernity. Kepel's ideas imply that modernity does encourage secularisation but that modern societies are so problematic that they will be rejected by a significant number of people. Kepel's views appear to account for the spread of fundamentalist ideas (see Unit 3.6.7).

Stark and Bainbridge – Religious Market Theory

Rodney Stark and William Sims Bainbridge (1985) argued that religion serves a universal human need: the desire to live forever (see Unit 3.2.4). In the absence of any scientific way of achieving this, people make do with the compensators offered by religion – that is the promise of eternal life as a reward for following a set of religious beliefs. As discussed in Unit 3.2.4, to Stark and Bainbridge this suggests that religion will never die out. Instead, if one type of religion disappears then it will be replaced by another. From their point of view, religion acts like a marketplace in which different sets of beliefs compete for market share. As one religion declines, another moves in to fill the vacuum. This theory of religious resilience and revival suggests that neither modernity nor any other type of society will cause long-term secularisation because religion will always be needed. Stark and Bainbridge's approach has been particularly applied to religion in the USA with some established mainstream religions declining but new denominations taking their place. It has also been applied to competition between Catholicism and Pentecostalism in Latin America.

Postmodernity

The postmodernist Jean-François Lyotard (1979) argued that postmodernity involved growing 'incredulity towards metanarratives', or a lack of faith in any big stories about society and human progress. Both religion and scientific rationalism can be seen as types of metanarratives that individuals are coming to reject. From this point of view, people do not feel that they should have to follow any single set of beliefs but rather they wish to find their own truth.

These ideas have been developed by David Lyon, author of the book *Jesus in Disneyland* (2000). According to Lyon, Western societies are becoming increasingly consumerist and consumerism is now affecting religion as well as other spheres of social life. As consumers, people do not wish to be told what religion to adopt (just as they do not wish to be told which products to buy) and instead they want to be able to make up their own minds. According to Lyon, religion is not therefore declining, it is simply relocating to the sphere of consumption. Religion has moved out of the traditional institutions and instead has become more commercial so that people can consume and celebrate religion in a variety of ways. Religion has become part of popular culture so a fall in attendance at churches and denominations does not indicate an overall decline in religious beliefs. From this point of view religion did decline in modernity, but societies have now moved beyond the modern era and religious/spiritual beliefs are enjoying a revival as a consequence. (For more details on religion and postmodernity see Unit 3.2.5.)

Key terms

Secularisation The decline in the social significance of religion. According to Wilson's definition 'the process whereby religious thinking, practice and institutions lose social significance' although exact definitions vary between sociologists.

Rationalisation The process by which actions are increasingly governed by trying to use the most efficient means to achieve your goals and not by, for example, tradition or emotion.

Structural differentiation The process by which institutions in society become separated and specialised.

Social differentiation The increasing physical and social separation of groups in society.

Societalisation The process by which close-knit local communities lose power to larger towns and cities or bureaucratic states.

Schisms Splits in religious organisations to form separate groups.

Pluralism The existence of numerous separate religious organisations and belief systems in a single society.

Summary

1. Bryan Wilson defined secularisation as 'the process whereby religious thinking, practice and institutions lose social significance'.

2. Most classical sociologists believed that the development of science and modern societies would lead to religion becoming less important.

3. Max Weber argued that rationalisation would erode the influence of religion.

4. Steve Bruce provides a contemporary theory of secularisation, which links it to the development of modernity and changes in the nature of social life.

5. Theorists differ over which parts of the world have been affected by secularisation and how they define secularisation.

6. Some sociologists, such as José Casanova, believe that religion is increasing in importance in the contemporary world and Rodney Stark and William Sims Bainbridge argue that new religions will develop to replace religions that are in decline.

7. The postmodernist David Lyon claims that religion is not declining but simply relocating to the sphere of culture.

Unit 3.6.2 Secularisation, believing, belonging and participation in the UK

The UK is often seen as one of the countries which has been most affected by the process of secularisation. Certainly, there is evidence that participation in mainstream religions has declined significantly in the UK and there are strong arguments that the role of religion in public life has become less significant. However, there are counterclaims that religious identities and religious beliefs have not declined as much as is widely assumed and that spiritual beliefs have taken the place of more traditional religions. This unit examines these competing arguments in relation to religious belief, belonging and participation in the UK.

Religious participation – church attendance in Britain

Some of the strongest evidence for the theory of secularisation as applied to Britain seems to come from church attendance statistics. The earliest available survey statistics on church attendance originate from the 1851 'Census of Religion'. This found just under 40 per cent of the adult population attending church. In England and Wales, the numbers had dropped to 35 per cent by the turn of the century and 20 per cent by 1950. Between 1980 and 2005, attendance fell from 11.1 per cent to 6.3 per cent (BRIN, 2018). Between 2010 and 2015, weekly attendance in England fell further from 5.8 per cent of the population to 5.4 per cent (Brierley Consultancy, 2018).

However, the reliability of these figures is open to question. Between 1979 and 2005, figures were based on an annual church census that took place on one Sunday each year. Figures for 2010 and 2015, however, are based upon a new methodology that involves churches themselves counting weekly attendance including midweek services. Typically, around 20 per cent of attendance takes place midweek, but the same people may attend more than once in a week, so the number of attendances is not the same as the number of individuals who attend. Over time, therefore, the figures are not strictly comparable.

As Figure 3.6.2 shows, according to the available statistics, there has been a fall in attendance in most churches between 1980 and 2015. However, there has been a rise in attendance at New churches, Orthodox churches and Pentecostal churches, though nothing like enough to offset the falls in other institutions.

Writing in 2006, Peter Brierley argues that between 1998 and 2005 church attendance was still falling,

277

Activity

Figure 3.6.2 English church attendance by denomination 1980–2015

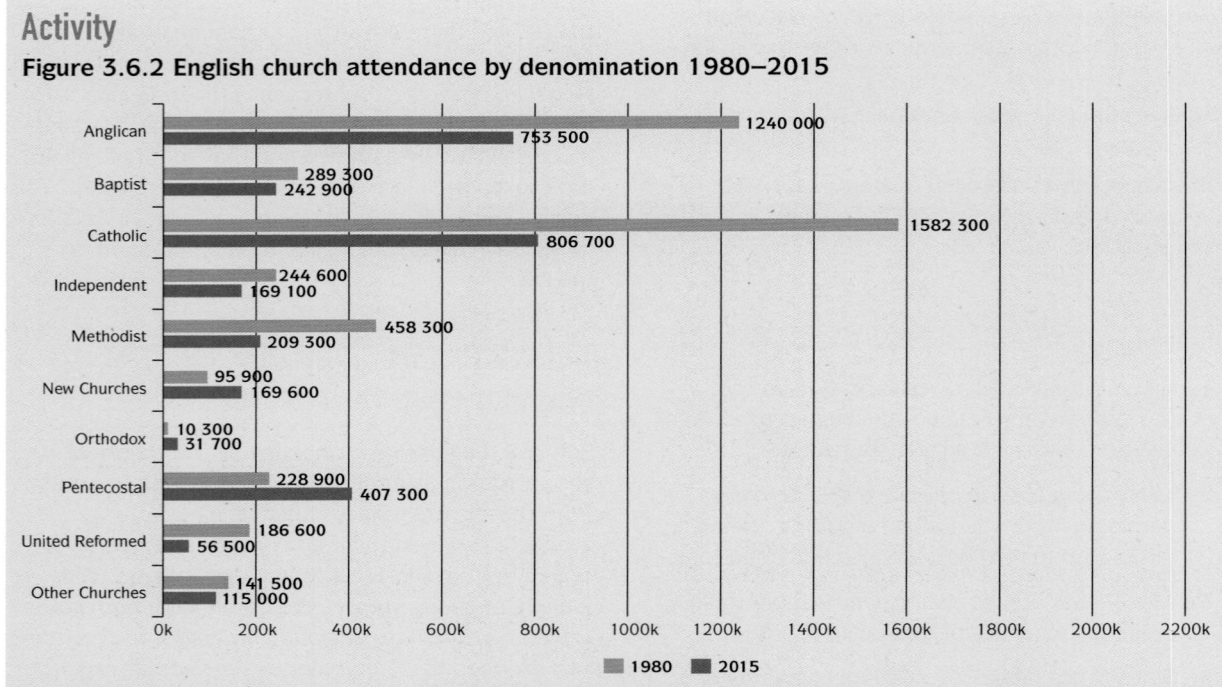

Source: *UK Church Statistics* No. 3, 2018, Peter Brierley (Table 13.2.1)

Does Figure 3.6.2 suggest that secularisation is taking place or instead that there has been a shift in the popularity of different denominations? Justify your answer.

but the rate at which it was falling was slowing down. This led him to be moderately optimistic about the future of English churches and he entitled his book *Pulling Out of the Nose Dive*. However, attendance has continued to fall since then and overall there is little reason to doubt that church attendance has fallen very significantly. Indeed, according to the figures on a typical Sunday, only 1.4 per cent of the population attended an Anglican service in England (Bingham, 2016).

Other forms of participation

Other types of participation in organised religion have also declined. In the 1920s and 1930s, over 90 per cent of babies were baptised, but by 2001 this was down to 45 per cent (Brierley, 2005) and by 2009 it had reduced to just over 20 per cent (Brierley, 2011). While the number of baptisms of babies has continued to decline, there has been some increase in baptisms of older children. However, it

has been claimed that this is partly explained by parents getting their children baptised in order to meet the criteria to get into religious secondary schools, particularly Roman Catholic ones (Paton and Turner, 2014).

There has also been a noticeable drop in the number of marriages conducted in church. According to Bruce, nearly 70 per cent of English couples were married in the Church of England at the start of the 20th century. By 1990, the number had fallen to 53 per cent. In 2012, only 30 per cent of marriages in England and Wales involved religious ceremonies (University of Oxford, 2015). However, Brierley points out that the decline was partly due to the expansion of 'approved premises' where weddings could take place outside churches or register offices.

Other indicators also show a general decline in religious ceremonies and participation. For example, BRIN (British Religion in Numbers) points out that the Church of England's figures show that between 2002 and 2009 the number of confirmations went down by 25 per cent and the number of religious funerals by 21 per cent (BRIN, 2011).

Activity

Alma de Cuba – a Cuban-themed bar and restaurant converted from the former St Peter's Roman Catholic Church known for its cocktails and entertainment from carnival dancers.

1. How can the evidence discussed above be used to explain the conversion of former churches for other purposes in the UK?

2. What does it suggest about attitudes to religion in the UK that some former church buildings are used for drinking and dancing?

Belonging — Membership of religious organisations

Table 3.6.1 shows the number of church members, and the number of denominations in the UK in 2012 and 2017 (Brierley, 2017). The data were collected by sending questionnaires to every denomination and asking them to estimate membership. As the Roman Catholic Church does not have to define believers as members, they were asked to use attendance at mass to produce estimates. The figures indicate that between 2012 and 2017 overall membership fell by 7 per cent although there was growth in some

Activity

Table 3.6.1 UK church membership 2012–2017

Denominations	2012 membership	2017 membership	Percentage of change 2012–2017
Roman Catholic	1 475 000	1 301 000	–12%
Anglican	1 424 000	1 167 000	–18%
Presbyterian	731 000	593 000	–19%
Orthodox	440 000	514 000	17%
Pentecostal	359 000	400 000	11%
Methodist	234 000	198 000	–15%
Independent	221 000	233 000	6%
Baptist	191 000	180 000	–6%
New churches	186 000	210 000	13%
Smaller denominations	177 000	193 000	9%
Fresh expressions	41 000	96 000	135%

Source UK Church Statistics 3: 2018 edition Peter Brierley. 2017 http://brierleyconsultancy.com/statistics.html

1. Describe the main trends in church membership shown in Table 3.6.1.

2. What do these trends suggest about secularisation theory?

denominations. Brierley notes that this is part of a long-term trend with data revealing steady falls in the membership of churches, the number of churches and the number of ministers. In 2010, 11.2 per cent of the population are estimated to have been church members in the UK, compared to 12.3 per cent in 2005. The projected figures predict a further fall to 9.4 per cent in 2020.

Changes in membership vary from church to church. As Table 3.6.1 shows, New churches, Pentecostal churches and Orthodox churches have grown in recent years. The Messy church (classified as one of the smaller denominations) has been the fastest growing organisation (though from a small base).

Recent figures on non-trinitarian churches and other smaller religious organisations are not available but statistics covering the period 1995–2005 suggested that membership of non-trinitarian religions was increasing, rising from 511 000 in 1995 to over 547 000 in 2005 (Brierley, 2001, 2005). Non-trinitarian churches include Jehovah's Witnesses, Mormons and Christadelphians. New religious movements, which take the form of sects or cults, involve small numbers. *Religious Trends 5* lists 34 such movements and estimated that their membership, along with that of other new religious movements, had increased from over 29 503 in 2000 to 37 412 in 2005. Other groups, which are defined as sects or cults, are listed in *Religious Trends 5* as non-trinitarian churches. According to the *Religious Trends* figures, between 1995 and 2000 membership of the Unification Church (Moonies) rose from 1000 to 1200, and the number of Scientologists increased from 144 400 to 165 400.

None of these figures includes membership of non-Christian world religions such as Hinduism and Islam, but other indicators suggest that such religions are growing in the UK (see below).

Affiliation with religion

Another way of measuring religiosity is to look at religious affiliation, that is, the number of people who identify themselves as belonging to a particular religion. Census figures provide this information and have the advantage of including all religious groups and not just Christians.

Activity

Table 3.6.2 Religious affiliation in the 2001 and 2011 Censuses (percentages)

	No religion	Christian	Muslim	Other	Not stated
2001	14.8	71.7	3	2.8	7.7
2011	25.1	59.3	4.8	3.6	7.2

Source: ONS (2012) Religion in England and Wales, 2011.

1. Describe the trends in religious affiliation shown in Table 3.6.2.

2. Compare these trends with those in relation to participation and membership.

Table 3.6.2 shows that, as well as a large rise in the proportion saying they had no religion, there has been a significant fall in the percentage claiming an affiliation with Christian religions and a substantial increase in the percentage of those saying they were Muslim or affiliated with other religions. The rise in the proportion of the population saying they were Muslim is associated with population change in the proportion of the population from minority ethnic groups (see Unit 3.5.3).

Data were also collected on religions that are not mentioned in this table. In 2011, around 1.5 per cent of the population identified as Hindu, 0.8 per cent as Sikh and 0.5 per cent as Jewish.

As well as choosing from a list of major religions, census respondents had an option to state their religion if it did not appear in the list. In 2011, 176 000 claimed to be Jedi Knights (down from over 390 000 in 2001), over 56 000 said they were Pagan and 36 000 Spiritualist (ONS, 2015).

Interpreting the evidence on participation, membership and affiliation

Most of the long-term evidence on membership and attendance in Britain seems to support the secularisation theory. Although recent years have seen a growth in smaller religious organisations, compared to the 19th century and early decades of the 20th, there is little doubt that fewer people attend a place of worship or belong to a religious organisation.

However, both the reliability and the validity of the statistics are open to question. The 19th-century church attendance figures for Britain pose special problems because the methods of data collection used do not meet today's standards of reliability. More recent British figures may be hard to trust as well. Some commentators argue that attendance and membership figures may be distorted by the ulterior motives of those who produce them. Some churches – for example, the Roman Catholic Church – may underestimate the numbers in their congregation in order to reduce the fees they have to pay to central church authorities. Others, particularly Anglican churches, may overestimate the figures to produce impressive totals, particularly where there may be a risk of a church with a small congregation being closed down.

Membership figures can be calculated in different ways, and various churches, denominations and other religious groups use different criteria. Members of the Church of England are normally taken to be those who have been both baptised and confirmed. The numbers may, therefore, include people who, although officially members, have taken no part in church life since their confirmation. In contrast, Membership of Roman Catholic Churches is based on attendance at mass.

Because of these variations, statistics on church membership may be unreliable, and the trends indicated by the figures may be misleading.

The validity of statistics on attendance as a measure of religiosity is also open to question. For example, David Martin (1969) claimed that in Victorian Britain church attendance was a sign of middle-class respectability to a greater extent than it is today. Many Victorians may have attended church to be seen, rather than to express deep religious convictions.

Census figures are based on the only voluntary question on the census, and around 7 per cent of people did not answer. The census statistics are based upon the simple question 'What is your religion?', but specifying a religion does not necessarily demonstrate genuine commitment to the religion, belief in its teachings or active participation in the religion. The number of people giving their religion as Jedi or Jedi Knight in both 2001 and 2011, following an internet campaign, suggests that not everyone took the question seriously.

Privatised religion – believing without belonging?

Despite the question marks over the validity of census statistics for measuring religiosity, they do suggest at least some minimal identification with religion for a large, but declining proportion of the population in the UK. This suggests that religion is more resilient than is indicated by church attendance figures. Some sociologists develop this idea, claiming that religion today may be expressed in different ways. Religion may have become increasingly **privatised**; people develop their own beliefs and relationship with God and see religious institutions as being less important. Grace Davie (1994, 2007) coined the term 'believing without belonging' to describe this situation. If religion is increasingly seen as a choice open to an individual, rather than a social obligation imposed by society, then people may increasingly hold religious beliefs in private without feeling the need to demonstrate them in public.

Belief and atheism

Opinion poll evidence is perhaps the simplest type of data relating to religious beliefs. There are a variety of questions that can and have been asked about religious beliefs, and the questions asked determine the impression given by the data. Opinion poll data generally finds that many more people retain religious beliefs than are members of religious organisations or regular attendees at places of worship. However, there are inevitably question marks over the validity of opinion poll data when complex beliefs are being measured using simple, fixed-choice questions. Furthermore, respondents may not give truthful answers and stated beliefs might not be reflected in behaviour. Nevertheless, survey data provide some indication of the extent to which beliefs have changed over time.

Table 3.6.3 is compiled from the results of British Social Attitudes Surveys and shows a decline in the total number believing in God in Great Britain, from 62 per cent in 1991 to 48 per cent in 2008. However, as Table 3.6.3 shows, if the number of people who have some sort of spiritual beliefs is included, the figures are higher. For example, in 2008, in addition to those who had some belief in God, a further 14 per cent said they believed in a 'higher power'.

Table 3.6.3 Beliefs about God reported in British Social Attitudes Surveys, carried out by the National Centre for Social Research, in response to the question 'Which statement comes closest to expressing what you believe about God?'

	1991	2008
Don't believe in God	10%	18%
Don't know if God exists, no way to find out	14%	19%
Higher power	13%	14%
Believe sometimes	13%	13%
Doubt, but believe	26%	18%
I know God really exists and that I have no doubts about it	23%	17%
Don't know	–	–
Not answered	2%	1%

Source: British Social Attitudes Information System. www.britsocat.com.

More recent figures using slightly different questions suggest that belief in God has declined further. A 2015 YouGov/Sunday Times Poll asked the following question:

'People have different beliefs about God, which of the following best applies to you?'

The responses were as follows:

I believe there is a God 32%

I do not believe in a God, but do believe there is some sort of spiritual greater power 20%

I do not believe in any sort of God or greater spiritual power 33%

Don't know 14%

The findings of all opinion polls of this type are open to different interpretations. They could be seen as indicating a shift from traditional belief in God towards a greater pluralism of belief involving a move towards greater spirituality as opposed to conventional religion. Because belief remains more widespread than participation, it could be seen as suggesting that religious belief remains resilient.

However, Steve Bruce (2001) argues that the opinion poll data show a progressive weakening of religious beliefs. Belief in a personal God has declined markedly, and vague beliefs about a 'spiritual power' have little cultural influence and hardly affect people's day-to-day behaviour. Increasing atheism also supports this view. Bruce (2011) therefore argues that all the different types of evidence consistently show religious decline.

This view is supported by David Voas and Alisdair Crockett (2005), who explicitly address Grace Davie's claim that there was a shift from religion within institutions to a more personal sort of religion outside organisations (Davie, 2007). (Davie calls this 'believing without belonging'). Voas and Crockett have found that church attendance, identification with a religion and religious belief have all declined at roughly the same rate. An increasing proportion of the British population is 'neither believing nor belonging'. Many people have shifted instead to a very vague belief that there is 'something out there'.

Activity

Taking account of Table 3.6.3 and the discussion which follows, what interpretation would you place on the trends shown in the data?

Contemporary issues: Between the religious and the secular – fuzzy fidelity

Over recent years, sociologists have begun to pay increasing attention to the large number of people who are neither atheists nor fully fledged followers of a religion. Although there is considerable evidence of quite rapid decline in religious participation and strong religious belief in the UK and some other parts of Europe, the number of self-proclaimed atheists has gone up much more slowly. Davis Voas (2009) was the first to highlight this issue and he identified those with only vague connections to religion as having **fuzzy fidelity**. They come from a Christian background, but their faith is vague, generalised and weak. This group has come to be referred to as the 'fuzzies' and they might, for example, support a religion because it represents their national identity or because they like aspects of religious tradition (for example carol services). Alternatively, they might have given up on Christianity altogether, but they find New Age beliefs appealing. They may believe that 'there is something out there' but little more than that. Voas argues that the 'fuzzies' are at a 'staging post' on a journey from being religious to being atheists. It takes some time for people to abandon their beliefs entirely but eventually even 'fuzzy fidelity' will fade away and most people from Christian backgrounds from Europe will become atheists.

A very different view is taken by Paul Heelas (2015). Basing his arguments largely on Britain, he claims that there is little evidence to suggest that most people will end up as atheists with no spiritual beliefs at all. A survey in 2013 (Theos, 2013 cited in Heelas, 2015) found that just 13 per cent of Britons agreed that 'humans are purely material beings with no spiritual element'. David Hay (Hay, 2012, cited in Heelas, 2015) refers to research which suggests that 75 per cent of people claimed there was a spiritual dimension to experience. To Heelas, the increasing popularity of the New Age and complementary and alternative medicines (such as acupuncture, Tai Chi and reflexology) suggests that most people still seek a sense of meaning beyond the scientific, rational and secular. Many feel let down by the purely secular. The endless quest for material success leaves people lacking a sense of meaning in their lives. Therefore, Heelas claims, the 'fuzzies' are not moving towards secularity but have opted for spirituality instead. They still seek meaning in their lives, but they look for a sense of purpose in a spiritual humanism, finding meaning inside themselves rather than in traditional religions.

Question

With some reference to the images below, discuss whether humanism is more likely to produce widespread atheism or increased spirituality.

A poster from and photograph of the British Humanist Association, a consciousness-raising group of the human potential movement in the 1960s.

Key terms

Privatised religion Religion of significance to the individual but which has relatively little connection to religious institutions and which has little or no importance in wider society.

Fuzzy fidelity A vague belief that there may be some sort of religious or spiritual force without any adherence to specific religious belief.

Summary

1. Statistical evidence suggests that church attendance and other types of participation in organised religion (such as church weddings) have fallen considerably in Britain.

2. Some churches, such as Pentecostal churches, have seen an increase in attendance.

3. Membership of most types of religious organisation in the UK has fallen although there have been increases in membership of some non-Christian religions and in some sects and denominations.

4. Census figures suggest that most people identify with a religion although the numbers doing so declined between 2001 and 2011.

5. There are problems in interpreting all figures on religious participation, membership and affiliation.

6. Grace Davie believes the general trend is towards 'believing without belonging'.

7. There is some evidence of a move away from traditional religious belief towards spiritual beliefs although the extent and significance of this change is disputed.

Unit 3.6.3 Secularisation and the institutional role of religion in the UK

Religious belief and participation may be the most obvious areas in which to look for evidence in favour of, or against, secularisation. However, some theorists argue that it is the changing role of religion in society which is more important. From this point of view, individual beliefs are less important than the declining social significance of religion in shaping other aspects of society.

Disengagement

Disengagement involves the withdrawal of the church from wider society as a result of its declining influence on other institutions, particularly politics and law. David Martin (1969) argued that, compared with the Middle Ages, the power, wealth and prestige of the established church in Britain has declined dramatically. Steve Bruce (1995) argued that the Church of England has lost power as it has become more distant from the British state. This distancing has given it freedom to be more critical of governments.

For example, Tony Blair, UK prime minister from 1997 to 2007, was known to have quite strong religious convictions, but he made little comment on these while in office. Indeed, when asked about religion in 2003, his 'spin doctor' (or director of communications and strategy), Alastair Campbell, intervened to prevent Blair answering, saying 'We don't do God' (Brown, 2003).

Another example of how little influence religion may have on wider social life is a High Court judgement in the UK in March 2011 in which a ruling to ban two Pentecostalists from being foster parents was upheld (Hough, 2011). The Pentecostalists believed that homosexuality was wrong because of their religion, but the High Court judges argued that the rights of homosexuals took precedence over religious conviction. The then prime minister, David Cameron, an avowed Christian, refused to intervene or comment in detail. A spokesman said that he was not going to take sides in the dispute.

Social differentiation

Another way in which religious institutions have been seen as losing social significance is in terms of social differentiation (Bruce, 1995, 2011). Steve Bruce sees social differentiation as the separation of institutions and individuals from one another. This has meant that religion increasingly confines itself to spiritual issues and loses its influence on non-religious spheres of social life. Indeed, to Bruce, social life becomes dominated by the logic of capitalist production, with its emphasis on calculability, efficiency and profit. Religious faith and morality become less and less significant in the culture and institutions of modern societies. Areas such as health, education, welfare and social control have largely passed out of church control. Where churches do still have some formal influence (for example in faith schools), Bruce believes that the influence is minimal, and that they are run very much in the same way as secular institutions.

Activity

Children taking part in school prayers.

1. Daily collective worship and Religious Education (RE) are still required by law in state schools, but parents can withdraw their children from assemblies and RE if they wish. Does this provide evidence against the theory of secularisation?

2. In your own experience, is state education strongly influenced by religion?

Societalisation

Bruce (1995, 2002, 2011) uses the term 'societalisation' (first used by Bryan Wilson) to refer to a process in which social life becomes fragmented and ceases to be locally based. Like social differentiation, he sees this as being a consequence of a general process of modernisation. Modern societies do not have close-knit communities. People's lives are increasingly dominated by large impersonal bureaucracies, and in suburbs people rarely know and mix with their immediate neighbours. People interact with one another at the level of society as a whole rather than within local communities.

According to Bruce, the decline of community undermines religion in three ways. First, without a strong sense of community, churches can no longer serve as the focal point for communities. For example, large proportions of the community will not turn out for a local wedding or funeral at the parish church because most people will not know the people getting married or the deceased.

Second, people's greater involvement with the broader society in which they live leads them to look far more widely than to religious institutions for support. Today, they are less likely to turn to the local priest or vicar for practical or emotional support than they were in the past.

Third, the cultural diversity of the society in which people live leads them to hold beliefs with less certainty. Bruce (1995) said, 'Beliefs are strongest when they are unexamined and naively accepted as the way things are.' In a society where we no longer get constant reinforcement of a particular religious view, religious belief becomes a matter of personal choice.

Evaluation

According to Bruce, then, fundamental changes in social life in modern societies lead to institutional religion losing its social base, many of its social roles and its main source of legitimation. However, Bruce may exaggerate the extent of change and the consequences for religion. For example, there has been a longstanding debate about whether, and to what extent, there has been a decline of community, with many commentators questioning the view that there has been a straightforward movement from strong to weak communities (see, for example, Slattery, 1985).

However, Bruce is certainly correct to point out that there has been a growth of religious diversity in many modern societies. The significance of this will now be considered.

Key term

Disengagement The withdrawal of churches from wider society because of their declining influence on other institutions, particularly politics and the legal system.

Summary

1. Disengagement involves the declining influence of the church on other institutions. There is evidence that in the UK the church has less influence over politics and the law than in the past.

2. Social differentiation involves the separation of individuals and institutions from one another and Steve Bruce believes that this has led to churches having less influence over areas such as health, education and welfare.

3. Societalisation involves the fragmentation of social life so that it is less locally based. Bruce believes that this has undermined the community base that helps to sustain religious beliefs.

4. Bruce may exaggerate the extent to which some of these changes have taken place.

Unit 3.6.4 Secularisation and religious pluralism in the UK

Some researchers imply that the truly religious society has one faith and one church. In Durkheim's (1961, first published 1912) view, religion is important because it creates social solidarity and it only does this when the community shares a single set of beliefs. Some theorists of secularisation follow Durkheim in this argument and claim that societies in which there are many different religions (or religious pluralism) are essentially less religious than societies in which one religion dominates. Unlike in medieval times when a single religion (Roman Catholicism) dominated, in the UK Christian religions have become more varied and non-Christian religions have grown, partly due to migration. However, why should this be seen as evidence of secularisation and are theorists right to see it in this way?

Pluralism – weak and strong religion

According to Bruce, (1992, 2011) modernisation and industrialisation brought with them the **social fragmentation** of society into a plurality of cultural and religious groups. Industrialisation reduced the contact between social classes and helped to create new, predominantly working-class versions of Christianity, such as Methodism.

Religious pluralism reminds individuals that their beliefs are a personal preference, a matter of choice, and no longer part and parcel of their membership of society (Bruce, 2011). As a consequence, **strong religion** (Bruce, 2002), which dominates people's lives and shapes how they live in profound ways, is no longer widespread in a fragmented society. It may survive in isolated pockets (such as in some sects) but, in order to continue, such communities must try to isolate themselves from the secular climate of the wider society.

Weak religion, which is more a matter of personal choice, has relatively limited impact on people's lives and does not claim to be the only legitimate religion, is more suited to fragmented societies. It accepts there may be more than one way to spiritual truth and does not seek to dominate individual lives to the same extent as strong religion. In this form, religion can be more widespread in modern secular societies such as the UK. However, because it is voluntary, a matter of choice, and does not govern how people live their lives, it has little social impact. Weak religion is typified by liberal Protestant churches, the New Age and some cults.

Evaluation

Contrary to Bruce's view, it could be argued that a truly religious society is simply one in which religious beliefs and institutions thrive. It is not necessary for everyone to share the same religious beliefs for religion to be important. Northern Ireland is a case in point. There the divisions between Catholics and Protestants are associated with higher rates of church membership and attendance than in other parts of the UK. Furthermore, in most parts of the UK, some denominations and sects have been growing. These include New churches and Pentecostal churches, which arguably promote what Bruce would regard as strong religion.

Religious pluralism and ethnicity

Much religious diversity in the UK is related to ethnicity, which in turn is linked to immigration. Immigration from Ireland from the 19th century onwards has contributed to the growth of the Roman Catholic population in Britain. Religious pluralism has also increased because of the growth of non-Christian world religion. Although some of this growth has been the result of conversion by people from Christian backgrounds (for example to Buddhism), most has been the result of immigration. Migration from the Caribbean, the Asian subcontinent and elsewhere has added to religious diversity. However, does this growth represent a revival of religion or does it just result in further fragmentation and a decline in the influence of religion in society?

Ethnicity and religious diversity – arguments for secularisation

Steve Bruce (1996) acknowledges that certain ethnic groups often retain strong religious beliefs. However, he does not see this as an argument against the theory of secularisation. This is because Bruce believes religion remains strong in such groups because of its *social* importance rather than because the members of the group have deep religious convictions as individuals.

Bruce (1996, 2011) claims that religion tends to serve one of two main purposes for minority ethnic groups: **cultural defence** or **cultural transition**.

1. Religions take on the role of cultural defence where:

    there are two (or more) communities in conflict and … the religious identity of each can call forth a new loyalty as religious identity becomes a way of asserting ethnic pride.   Bruce, 1996

From Bruce's point of view, it is their ethnic identity that is important, rather than religiosity. For example, he (Bruce, 2011) argues that the strong religious identification between Protestant Unionists (who strongly support the union of Northern Ireland within the UK) and Catholic Republicans (who seek a united Ireland) has as much to do with defending their communities from the hostility of the other group as it does to do with deep religious conviction. During the 'troubles', when there was considerable violence between the two groups, there were strong religious affiliations. However, since the Good Friday Agreement in 1998 brought relative peace, statistics suggest that religiosity has declined.

2. Cultural transition:

    involves religion acquiring an enhanced importance because of the assistance it can give in helping people cope with the shift from one world to another. It might be that the people in question have migrated; it might be that they remain in the same place while that place changes under their feet.   Bruce, 1996

Religion is used as a resource for dealing with situations where people have to change their identity to some extent. For example, Asian and African Caribbean migrants to Britain and their descendants can use mosques, temples and churches as centres for their communities, and their religion as a way of coping with the ambiguities of being Asian or Black and British.

However, Bruce believes that religion loses this role where a group becomes increasingly integrated into the host community. For example, Irish Catholics who migrated to England and Scotland were originally subject to considerable hostility and discrimination from the host population. Catholicism was very important to this group for several generations. However, as Irish Catholics have married outside their own ethnic group and have enjoyed increasing success, prosperity and acceptance by other members of the population, the importance of their religion as a focus for community identity has declined.

Bruce concludes: 'Cultural defence and cultural transition may keep religion relevant but they will not create a religious society out of a secular one.'

Arguments against secularisation

However, not everybody shares this interpretation. The historian Callum G. Brown (1992) argued that 'ethnic defence' has long been a key function of religion in the modern world and it is nothing new. There has always been some diversity in religious outlooks and there have always been some who were sceptical or hostile towards religion and groups that defended themselves through mutual support in religious communities. Brown denied that there was ever a 'Golden Age' in which religion provided a single, unifying worldview for all members of a society. However, Brown did accept that there has been some shift towards a greater fragmentation of religion over time, but that this has just meant that religion tends to draw more of its strength from individual communities (including ethnic communities) rather than from society as a whole. It does not mean that secularisation has taken place.

Certainly, there is plenty of evidence that religion can and often does remain strong among minority ethnic groups although there is also some evidence of religious commitment getting less strong across generations. (See Unit 3.5.3 further details.)

Sects, cults and secularisation

On the surface, the existence and apparent growth of sects and new religious movements seems to contradict the theory of secularisation and instead seems to show the vitality of religion. Nevertheless, some sociologists see the growth of sects as evidence of secularisation. Peter Berger (1970) was the first to argue that growth of sects is evidence in favour of secularisation. He argued that strong religious beliefs can only exist in Western societies where its followers cut themselves off from widespread scepticism about religion by isolating themselves in small, self-enclosed communities. Sects are therefore a symptom of secularisation.

Bryan Wilson (1982) claimed that sects are the last outpost of religion in societies where religious beliefs and values have little consequence. Wilson is particularly scathing in his dismissal of new religious movements such as Krishna Consciousness, which emerged during the 1960s. He regards them as 'almost irrelevant' to society as a whole, claiming 'They add nothing to any prospective reintegration of society, and contribute nothing towards the culture by which a society might live.' Their members live in their own enclosed, encapsulated little worlds.

Steve Bruce (2002, 2011) argues that new religious movements are too insignificant to undermine secularisation theory. They only recruit very small numbers compared to the massive decline in mainstream Christian religions. World-rejecting new religions have very few followers. World-affirming new religions have influenced a greater number of people, yet even in this case numbers are small.

Activity

Hare Krishna followers in London in 2016.

1. How much significance do new religious movements such as Hare Krishna have in the UK today?

2. In your view, are these movements numerous enough and important enough to undermine the theory of secularisation?

Bruce (2002) estimates that the active membership of Eastern-based spiritual groups such as Hare Krishna and TM 'is not likely to be much above 10 000 – fewer than the number lost to the Christian churches in a month'. He points out that in England and Wales only 1781 people described themselves as Scientologists in the 2001 census (Bruce, 2011).

Evaluation

According to Andrew Greeley (1972), writers such as Berger, Wilson and Bruce are wrong to see the growth of sects and new religious movements as evidence for secularisation. Greeley believed that the growth of new religious movements represents a process of **resacrilisation**: interest in, and belief in, the sacred is being revived. Societies such as Britain and the USA are, if anything, becoming less secular.

Similarly, Rodney Stark and William S. Bainbridge (1985) also denied that the growth of such movements shows that secularisation has taken place in Western societies. Some established churches may have lost part of their emphasis on the supernatural, but Stark and Bainbridge believed that secularisation never advances far because new religious groups with more emphasis on the supernatural constantly emerge to take their place. From their point of view, religion never declines because people retain a need for a belief in life after death. If conventional religion declines, other religions take their place.

Secularisation and the New Age

Another area that seems to challenge the theory of secularisation is the growth of New Age beliefs. Although it is debatable whether these beliefs can be seen as constituting a religion, they can be seen as having a basis in spiritual and non-rational beliefs. As such, they represent a challenge to at least some theories of secularisation, a number of which claim that modern societies lose faith in all non-rational beliefs.

Arguments for secularisation

Bruce has also commented on what he views as the lack of significance of the New Age. He puts forward a number of arguments which suggest that it has little importance and it therefore poses little or no threat to the validity of the theory of secularisation.

First, Bruce (2011) argues that the New Age has only a small number of followers who take it seriously and regard it as spiritual. He discusses a 2001 survey conducted in Scotland (Glendinning and Bruce, 2006, cited in Bruce, 2011). The survey revealed that 15 per cent of the sample described themselves as spiritual but not religious, and as many as 44 per cent had tried alternative medicine. However, many fewer, just 8 per cent, had tried an alternative practice, regarded it as spiritual and seen it as important.

Second, Bruce believes that, by its very nature, the New Age has less effect on society than more conventional religious beliefs. Although it affects more people than sects, it 'cannot aspire to promote radical and specific change because it does not have the cohesion and discipline of the sect' (Bruce, 1996).

The beliefs advocated by the New Age are diffuse (Bruce, 2002). **Diffuse religion** promotes individualism and tolerance – people can believe whatever they choose and need not follow a single set of teachings. According to the New Age, what works for you is your truth, while others can have different truths. This solves the problem of living in pluralistic societies such as Britain. It allows many different beliefs to exist side by side, but it produces only 'slight commitment and little agreement about detail'. People will not make sacrifices or change their lives in profound ways for diffuse religion. Without a community to constantly reiterate and reinforce a

set of beliefs, New Age beliefs are very weak and it is difficult to sustain serious commitment to them.

Third, Bruce (1996) claimed that the New Age is simply an extreme form of the individualism that is characteristic of modern societies. As such it has a role as 'symptom and as cause in the erosion of faith in orthodoxies and the authority of professional knowledge'.

Arguments against secularisation

It could be argued that Bruce underestimates the significance of the effects he identifies. If substantial numbers of people are willing to question scientific orthodoxy and place some trust in beliefs that require a degree of faith, this could be taken as evidence against the secularisation theory.

Paul Heelas (1996) certainly regarded the New Age as rather more significant than Bruce does. He quoted a 1993 Gallup opinion poll which found that in Britain 26 per cent of people believed in reincarnation, 40 per cent in some sort of spirit, 17 per cent in flying saucers and 21 per cent in horoscopes; while a 1989 Gallup poll found that no less than 72 per cent had 'an awareness of a sacred presence in nature'.

Contemporary issues: The Kendal project

Some indication of the vitality of the New Age is provided by a study conducted by Paul Heelas, Linda Woodhead and colleagues in the town of Kendal in Cumbria, in northern England (Kendal Project, 2001a, 2001b; Heelas et al., 2005). The study attempted to find every religious group and groups with a spiritual dimension in Kendal and within a five-mile radius.

The researchers identified 26 different churches, and on 26 November 2000 a total of 2315 people attended these churches. They also found 62 groups with a spiritual dimension, including yoga groups, healing groups, Tai Chi classes and Buddhist groups. All of these groups used a language of spiritual growth. They also found 90 people who practised alternative therapies, of whom 63 said their practice had a spiritual dimension. From their research, they were able to estimate that around 730 people were involved in spiritually inclined but non-Christian activities in a single week. This compared to 674

who worshipped in Anglican churches in a typical week.

These findings led Heelas et al. to suggest that both secularisation and sacralisation were occurring at the same time. These changes were seen as part of a **spiritual revolution** in which the nature of spirituality was changing.

Secularisation was defined as a decline in traditional theistic religions (based on a strong belief in God). The decline was evident in the falling numbers involved in the **congregational domain**, where members of congregations meet together to pray in places of worship.

On the other hand, sacralisation (an increased emphasis on the sacred) was taking place in the holistic milieu. The **holistic milieu** involves support for 'body–mind spirituality' and is evident in New Age beliefs and the beliefs of some religions. It exists in groups, therapy sessions, individual encounters and in shops selling products with spiritual connotations.

According to the Kendal Project, then, secularisation is only taking place in the narrow sense of a decline in traditional religion. From a broader perspective, beliefs are shifting away from traditional religion towards more individualist, spiritually inclined beliefs.

However, Bruce (2011) is sceptical of the conclusions reached on the basis of this research. He argues that much of the 'New Age' activity identified in the Kendal study does not necessarily have a spiritual element for participants. A lot of it can be seen as recreational (for example yoga and Tai Chi); other activities, such as massage, are a form of 'pampering'; and even much of the 'healing and complementary therapy', such as homoeopathy, can be seen as 'pseudo-scientific' rather than spiritual. Indeed, in the Kendal research itself only a quarter of the respondents involved in these various activities described 'spiritual growth' as the main reason for their involvement. On this basis, Bruce calculates that less than 1 per cent of the Kendal population were involved in New Age spirituality. The study found only three people aged under 30 directly involved in spiritual activities. Bruce concludes that there is little chance of significant growth of New Age spirituality in the future with its appeal largely confined to particular cohort of people who grew up during the 1960s and 1970s.

The Parish Church in Kendal, Cumbria.

Questions

1. Explain why a decline in attendance at this and other churches in Kendal does not necessarily show that secularisation is taking place.

2. How convincing do you find the arguments of Heelas *et al.* that sacralisation is occurring in Kendal with the growth of New Age spirituality?

Danièle Hervieu-Léger – religion and spiritual individualism

The arguments put forward in the Kendal Project about a spiritual revolution are broadly reflected in the work of the French sociologist Danièle Hervieu-Léger (2000, 2006).

Hervieu-Léger argues that religion is generally part of a **chain of memory** (Hervieu-Léger, 2000) – something that is passed down from generation to generation which, as Durkheim argues, helps to integrate society. Rather than God being experienced in a direct and personal way, churches have acted as intermediaries and religion has been learned more than directly experienced. However, in many European countries, this chain of memory has, to some extent, been broken. Secularisation has weakened the hold of the traditional churches so that collective memories about religion are no longer passed down from parents to children with the force that they once were. Furthermore, with the declining influence of tradition, individuals are unwilling to have religious beliefs imposed on them by those in authority.

As a result of this, individuals have been left to choose (or to reject) their own religious path. This has resulted in individuals engaging in **spiritual individualism** (Hervieu-Léger, 2006) in which people shop around for the religion that best suits them. They may try to experience a variety of religions and spiritual beliefs to see which suits them best. Some will become **converts**, deciding to adopt a set of beliefs long term, for example by joining a sect or cult. Others will remain **pilgrims**, continuing their quest for spiritual enlightenment by trying out a range of new beliefs and experiences, for example by trying different New Age practices.

Hervieu-Léger does not believe that the influence of Christian churches will disappear. Some individuals will choose them as a 'personal option'. Furthermore, many people will be nostalgic for church services and keen to maintain the fabric of beautiful church buildings. Churches, however, will become less and less important as a source of collective identity, individual beliefs and moral values.

Key terms

Social fragmentation The division of society into a variety of cultural and religious groups.

Strong religion Religion that dominates people's lives and shapes the way they live.

Weak religion Religion that is a matter of personal choice, does not dominate people's lives and does not claim to be the only legitimate religion.

Cultural defence The role of religion when it helps to reinforce ethnic identity in areas where religious or ethnic communities are in conflict.

Cultural transition The role of religion when it helps a minority ethnic group to cope with social change and migration.

Resacrilisation The process by which interest in and belief in the sacred is revived.

Diffuse religion Religion that accepts and promotes individualism and tolerance of different beliefs.

The spiritual revolution Radical change in the nature of spirituality moving from the congregational domain to the holistic milieu.

Congregational domain The site of conventional religious organisations where congregations meet together to pray in a consecrated place of religious worship.

Holistic milieu The varied settings in which New Age spirituality is promoted and practised, including groups and therapy sessions.

Chain of memory The way that memories (including religious beliefs) are passed down from one generation to the next.

Spiritual individualism Religion in which individuals follow their own spiritual path rather than following the teachings of a particular religious leader or religious institution.

Converts Those who have committed themselves to a particular set of religious beliefs.

Pilgrims Those who lack a commitment to one set of spiritual beliefs but who are still trying out different beliefs and practices seeking those which suit them best.

Summary

1. Durkheim believed that a truly religious society was one in which people share the same religion. From this viewpoint, religious pluralism suggests that secularisation is taking place.

2. Bruce believes that strong religion is associated with acceptance of a single religion in a particular society, whereas religious pluralism leads to weak religion.

3. Contrary to Bruce's view, some religiously divided societies have very strong religious beliefs.

4. Bruce believes that the apparent strength of some minority ethnic religions in the UK is linked to cultural defence and cultural transition rather than to the maintenance of religious beliefs as such.

5. The growth of sects and cults is seen by Burger, Wilson and Bruce as evidence of the wider weakness of religion in largely secular societies.

6. Greeley sees the growth of sects and cults as evidence of resacrilisation.

7. The significance of New Age beliefs is disputed with Bruce seeing it as a form of diffuse religion which has little influence but Paul Heelas seeing it as evidence of a spiritual revolution.

Unit 3.6.5 Secularisation, science and rationalisation in the UK

A number of sociologists have argued that the sacred has little or no place in contemporary Western society, that society has undergone a process of **desacralisation**. This means that supernatural forces are no longer seen as controlling the world, action is no longer directed by religious belief, and human consciousness has become secularised. But are these claims too sweeping? Has the magic really gone out of the modern world?

Weber – disenchantment and desacralisation

Weber's interpretation of modern society provides one of the earliest statements of the desacralisation thesis. He claimed that modern society is 'characterized by rationalization and intellectualization and, above all, by the "disenchantment of the world"' (Weber, quoted in Gerth and Mills, 1948). The world is no longer charged with mystery and magic; the supernatural has been banished from society. The meanings and motives that direct action are now rational.

Briefly, rational action involves a deliberate and precise calculation of the importance of alternative goals and the effectiveness of the various means of attaining chosen goals. For example, if an individual's goal is to make money, he or she will coldly and carefully calculate the necessary initial investment and the costs involved in producing and marketing a commodity in the most economical way possible. Their measurements will be objective: they will be based on factors that can be quantified and accurately measured. They will reject means to reach that goal that cannot be proven to be effective.

Rational action rejects the guidelines provided by emotion, by tradition or by religion. It is based on the cold, deliberate reason of the intellect, which demands that the rationale for action can only be based on proven results.

Science and reason

A number of sociologists have accepted Weber's interpretation of the basis for action in industrial society. In *Religion in a Secular Society* (1966), Bryan Wilson stated: 'Religious thinking is perhaps the area which evidences most conspicuous change. Men act less and less in response to religious motivation: they assess the world in empirical and rational terms.'

Wilson argued that the following factors encouraged the development of rational thinking and a rational worldview:

1. Protestantism encourages a more rational and pragmatic approach to the world than other religions.

2. The rational organisation of society in firms, educational institutions, government bureaucracies and so on.

3. A greater knowledge of the social and physical world, which results from the development of the physical, biological and social sciences. Wilson maintained that this knowledge was based on reason rather than faith.

4. The development of rational ideologies and organisations to solve social problems. Ideologies such as communism and organisations such as trade unions offer practical solutions to problems. By comparison, religious solutions, such as the promise of justice and reward in the afterlife, do not produce practical and observable results.

Wilson argues that a rational worldview is the enemy of religion. It is based on the testing of arguments and beliefs by rational procedures, on assessing truth by means of factors that can be quantified and objectively measured. Religion is based on faith and as such is non-rational. Its claim to truth cannot be tested by rational procedures.

Steve Bruce (2002, 2011) stresses the importance of rationalisation and the importance of technology, rather than science itself. He argues that science and religion can coexist quite easily. Religious faith, where it is backed up and supported by a strong religious community, is not susceptible to being disproved by science. This is because 'modern people are quite capable of believing nonsense and hence [...] the declining plausibility of any one body of ideas cannot be explained simply by the presence of some (to us) more plausible ones' (Bruce, 2011).

However, technology has been more important. Bruce points out that religion often claims to have practical uses, such as when 'Holy water cures ailments and prayers improve crop quality'. Technological advances reduce the number of times that people turn to religion to solve problems, and have given individuals a greater sense of control over the natural world. When technological solutions to problems prove more reliable than the power of prayer, faith in religion is undermined.

Bruce acknowledges that such events as the death of a loved one or an injustice suffered may lead people to turn to God. There are some things in the modern world that science and rationality cannot deal with. However, when people do turn to God, they do so as individuals. Furthermore, they tend to do so as a last resort after the rational, scientific alternatives have all been fully exhausted. Thus:

> *When we have tried every cure for cancer, we pray. When we have revised for our examinations, we pray. We do not pray instead of studying, and even committed believers suppose that a research programme is more likely than a mass prayer meeting to produce a cure for AIDS.*   Bruce, 1996

Activity

∝ Darwin Day ∝

February 12

A fish is often used as a symbol of Christianity. Supporters of Darwin's theory of evolution have added legs to this Christian symbol to show their rejection of creationism and in celebration of 'Darwin Day'.

1. Suggest why supporters of evolution have used the image above.

2. How can the theory of evolution be seen as a challenge to Christian teaching and a possible cause of secularisation?

3. Some people are both Christians and believers in Darwin's theory of evolution. What does this suggest about the relationship between science and religion?

Arguments against science and reason undermining religion

Although the argument that science and/or rationalism have triumphed over religion and superstition appears strong, not everybody finds it convincing. For example, the development of New Age beliefs seems to suggest that the non-rational has a place in contemporary societies. Furthermore, there is plenty of evidence that appears to point to a religious revival in a global context (see Unit 3.6.7).

The theory of postmodernism suggests that societies have begun to move beyond the scientific rationality of modernity, partly because they have started to mistrust science. People are increasingly aware of the failures of science and, more importantly, the negative side-effects that can be produced by science and technology. Examples might include global warming, air pollution, the death of coral reefs as the seas become more acidic and increasing cancer rates. In these circumstances, people may turn to religion of one sort or another as an alternative to science. (For discussion of the

relationship between religion and postmodernity, see Unit 3.2.5 and for a discussion of the relationship between science and religion see Unit 3.1.2).

Key term

Desacralisation The process by which supernatural forces are no longer seen as controlling the world.

Summary

1. According to Weber, the modern world involved disenchantment and desacralisation.

2. Bryan Wilson argued that a rational worldview and the development of scientific knowledge and technology would lead to a loss of faith in religion.

3. Bruce argues that technology reduces reliance upon religious faith.

4. The development of New Age beliefs seems to contradict claims of disenchantment and desacralisation.

5. Postmodernists believe that there has been a movement away from the belief in traditional religions and science back towards non-rational beliefs.

Unit 3.6.6 Secularisation and religious revival in the USA

So far, the discussion of secularisation has focused on the UK. In this context, there appears to be quite strong evidence to support the theory of secularisation. However, a number of theorists suggest that the UK in particular, and Europe in general, are not typical of other parts of the world. For example, Grace Davie, Linda Woodhead and Rebecca Catto (2016) argue that 'hard' versions of secularisation theory claim that modernisation makes secularisation inevitable. To justify this claim, they use the example of Europe and assume that similar changes are occurring elsewhere. On the other hand, 'soft' versions of the theory suggest that secularisation may occur but that it is contingent on a range of factors that mean it occurs to different extents in different places and, in some cases, does not occur at all. Europe may be the exception rather than the norm. Supporters of this position such as Grace Davie (2002, 2006,

293

2007) often use the USA as an example to support their arguments. Like Europe, the USA is a modern society with a population who are largely from Christian backgrounds. Therefore, if secularisation is not occurring there, then this appears to vindicate the argument that there is nothing inevitable about modernisation leading to secularisation. So, what is the evidence to support the argument against secularisation in the USA?

Participation, belief and belonging

A range of evidence suggests that religion is much stronger in the USA than in the UK.

In terms of participation, opinion poll evidence collected by Gallup suggests that about 40 per cent of Americans attend church weekly, and that this figure has been consistent over several decades (Shattuck, 2017). For example, Norris and Inglehart (2004) found no change in the percentage of Americans saying that they attended church between 1939 and 2003. A study conducted by the Pew Research Center (Cooperman, Smith and Cornibert, 2015) found in 2014 that 77 per cent of Americans claimed a religious affiliation. Of those claiming an affiliation, 97 per cent believed in God, 66 per cent said they prayed daily and 62 per cent said that they attended a religious service at least once a month. Most Americans, therefore, both believed in and belonged to a religion.

However, some have questioned the reliability and validity of statistics on church attendance in the USA. In the United States, attendance statistics have generally been based upon the responses to survey questions asking how often people attend church. Steve Bruce (2011) argues that these kind of data are very unreliable. Evidence to support his claim is provided in a study by Hadaway et al. (1993) questioning the reliability of data on attendance. They conducted a detailed study of church attendance in a part of Ohio by counting cars in car parks and by getting estimates from clergy. Their conclusion was that, overall, twice as many people claimed to attend church or a synagogue as actually did so.

Furthermore, there is some evidence that religious affiliation and belief are declining to some extent in the USA. The Pew Research Center found that between 2007 and 2014 the percentage of Americans claiming a religious affiliation had fallen by six percentage points from 83 per cent to 77 per cent, the overall percentage of those who prayed daily

had fallen from 58 per cent to 55 per cent, and the percentage who said religion was very important had fallen from 56 per cent to 53 per cent (Cooperman Smith and Cornibert, 2015).

Disengagement and differentiation – the New Christian Right

In US society and politics, religion appears to retain an important role with little obvious evidence of the disengagement of religion from politics and law, or of social differentiation leading to the withdrawal of religion from other spheres of social life.

Christians with strong religious beliefs are active in politics particularly the so-called New Christian Right (Johnstone, 2007). The New Christian Right emerged in the mid-1970s and encouraged Americans to vote for candidates who supported their policies. They consist of conservative and fundamentalist Christians who believe that what they see as moral decline in the USA should be opposed, and that some aspects of the Bible should be taken literally. They are opposed to the easy availability of pornography, abortion and the acceptance of homosexuality (for example through same-sex marriage). They first became influential in the mid-1970s and supported successful campaigns to elect Ronald Reagan as President in 1980 and 1984, and George W. Bush in 2000 and 2004. They have also supported numerous individual Senators and other politicians.

In the 2016 Presidential Election, the New Christian Right were more divided in their opinions of Donald Trump, but some influential religious leaders, such as Jerry Falwell Junior, advocated Christians voting for Trump despite allegations of sexual misconduct against him (Green, 2016). Jerry Falwell Junior is the son of Jerry Falwell Senior who was perhaps the most important founder of the New Christian Right. The latter founded the Moral Majority in 1978, which used its own radio and TV stations and publishing companies to further their campaigns. By 1980, the Moral Majority was able to claim 4 million members and 72 000 ministers.

The Moral Majority has campaigned against the secularisation of public life, for example by campaigning for compulsory prayer and Bible readings in state schools.

Activity

A megachurch in Dallas, Texas.

Evangelical Christian megachurches attract large congregations (they have to have more than 2000 worshippers per week to be classed as a megachurch) and some livestream their services via the internet. In 2018, there were over 1600 megachurches in the USA (Levin, 2018).

Based on the evidence and arguments discussed so far, suggest reasons why megachurches are found in the USA but not in the UK.

However, some have questioned the significance of the New Christian Right. For example, Steve Bruce (1988, 1996, 2011) argues that they have had very little impact. He points out that abortion has not been banned (as the New Christian Right would like), and, 'Far from making the lives of homosexuals more difficult, all the legislative and judicial decisions since the founding of the Moral Majority in 1978 have been in the liberal direction' (Bruce, 2011). More recently, this general trend continued when in June 2015 the Supreme Court ruled that same-sex marriage should be legal throughout the USA.

Bruce (1996) acknowledges that the USA is less secular than Britain, but he believes that the New Christian Right may have merely slowed down the process of secularisation within its own religious institutions, and that it has failed to do any more than that. Indeed, he believes the only reason the New Christian Right gets so much attention is that its members are unusual for holding strong religious convictions in a largely secular world.

Pluralism

The USA is a religiously pluralistic country. There is no established church and instead there are a range of different Christian denominations and sects as well as some non-Christian religions. Some sociologists see this as a reason why the United States appears to be more religious than many European countries that still have an established church. Stark and Bainbridge (1985) argued that pluralism has helped to make religion more successful in the USA than Europe because there is more choice for the consumers of religious ideas. From their point of view, healthy competition between organisations trying to attract believers and converts, the 'supply side' of religion, is thriving in the USA. Because there is such a range of denominations and sects, there is something for everyone.

Others have argued though that a diversity of religious organisations leads to an overall decline in religious commitment (Christiano, Swatos and Kivisto, 2008). However, the research on this issue is inconclusive. A review of 26 studies on the effects of diversity in the USA found about half suggested that greater diversity made people less likely to be actively involved in practising religion, while the other studies produced the opposite result (Chaves and Gorski, 2001, cited in Christiano, Swatos and Kivisto, 2008).

Religion in the USA: conclusion

Grace Davie, Linda Woodhead and Rebecca Catto (2016) are among those who believe that evidence suggests that secularisation, however it is defined, is not taking place in the USA. They point out that church attendance is much higher than in most European countries, and claim that religion has become more significant in public life rather than less. There is widespread agreement that religion remains more important in the USA than in, for example, the UK, but Bruce (2011) believes that there are particular reasons why religion has been relatively resilient in the USA. US politics has a more decentralised system for selecting candidates for the main political parties than most European countries, which provides more opportunity for minority religious parties to gain support, and the demographic base of the New Christian Right in the southern states of the USA has been expanding relative to the overall size of the population. However, Bruce concludes that there is, nevertheless, clear evidence of the declining influence of religion in the USA, albeit a slower decline than that in most European countries.

Hugh Mcleod (2017) broadly agrees with the views of Steve Bruce. McLeod claims that before the early 1970s secularisation was occurring in the USA as well as in Europe. Since then, several specific factors have led to the development of 'Two Americas'. One part of the US population has continued to become more secular, as in Europe, while the other part has reacted to a perceived moral decline following the Civil Rights movements and American defeat in the Vietnam War by becoming more religious. The latter group is particularly strong in the southern states and it has been very effective in using popular culture to gain support. McLeod, though, argues that it is uncertain whether the USA will continue to be more religious than Europe for the remainder of the 21st century.

Summary

1. In the USA, religion appears to play a much bigger role in society than it does in the UK.

2. Statistical evidence suggests that religious participation, religious belief and religious affiliation in the USA are all significantly higher than in the UK.

3. However, the statistical evidence has been questioned and there is some evidence of religious decline in all the above areas.

4. The New Christian Right has a much more active role in politics than religious groups in the UK, but Steve Bruce questions whether they have had much influence on US governments.

5. The USA is religiously pluralistic and Stark and Bainbridge believe that this has contributed to the resilience of religion in the USA, although others have seen it as evidence of the limited role of religion in society.

Unit 3.6.7 Secularisation and religious revival in a global context

So far, the discussion of secularisation has focused on two countries, the UK and the USA. As two advanced capitalist countries, they are exactly the type of country that most theoretical approaches to secularisation suggest will have seen the greatest decline in the importance of religion. But as we have seen, there are question marks over the extent to which secularisation has taken place in these countries, particularly the USA. So what does the evidence suggest about the significance of religion outside the UK in Europe and in the rest of the world?

The resilience of Christianity

Grace Davie (2002) suggests that Europe may be the 'exceptional case' – the only part of the world in which there is real evidence of secularisation. However, even within Europe there are some countries, such as Poland and the Republic of Ireland, where religious participation remains high. In most parts of Europe, participation has fallen but religion may still be important to the people of those countries. Although most people might not wish to be actively involved in religion, they are still broadly supportive of churches as institutions, they have no wish to see them disappear, and indeed welcome them as a resource they can draw on in times of need. Many people are happy in the knowledge that in times of personal or national crisis they can turn back to religion and religious leaders for guidance. Davie calls this **vicariousness** – people enjoy the benefits of religion without themselves taking an active role.

According to Davie (2002), in terms of Christian belief there is little evidence of religious decline in sub-Saharan Africa or Latin America. Indeed, according to Davie, in many parts of the world Christianity is thriving. Davie (2002) describes the vitality of religion in the USA, Africa, Latin America and the Far East (for example, in South Korea). She particularly draws attention to the success of Pentecostalist churches in Latin America and elsewhere. (See Unit 3.2.4 for a discussion of the growth of Pentecostalism in Latin America). Mark Faulkner (2016) describes the success of the African Pentecostalist Church, the Winner's Chapel. Founded in Lagos, Nigeria, where it has an auditorium which holds over 50 000 worshippers, this church has expanded into a number of other African countries.

Religious affiliation worldwide

The most comprehensive set of data on global religion has been produced by the Pew Research Center (2012). It is based on analysis of more than

2500 censuses and surveys conducted in different parts of the world. It measures self-identified religion. The study found that a big majority of the world's population identified with a religion. Overall around 5/6 people (84%) identified with a religion. As Figure 3.6.3 shows, Christians were the largest group, followed by Muslims and Hindus. Just under one in six of the world's population identified themselves as not having a religious affiliation. However, among this group, many said that they did have a belief in God or a spiritual force even if they did not identify with a particular religion. Furthermore, many of this group lived in China rather than in countries associated with a major world religion.

These figures provide little support for a general theory of secularisation that suggests religion will lose social significance in all societies. Rates of religious affiliation do, of course, vary between countries. However, the Pew Research Center study found only six countries in which the unaffiliated were the largest group in the population. These were Hong Kong, Estonia, Czech Republic, North Korea, China and Japan.

More recently, The Pew Research Center (2017) has analysed differences in the age profiles and fertility rates of different religious and non-religious groups in order to estimate the likely changes in religious affiliation in the world's population in the future. Because the unaffiliated tend to have lower than average birth rates, the research center predicts that by 2060 just 9 per cent of babies would be born to unaffiliated mothers but 36 per cent would be born to Muslim mothers and 35 per cent to Christian mothers. According to this analysis, differences in the age profile and birth rates of different groups will tend to *increase* the proportion of the world's population who are religious and not reduce it.

There are a number of problems with this research, suggesting that it should not be seen as definitive in estimating religiosity in the world.

First, it is based upon a wide range of research studies which used a variety of methods, samples and measures, raising questions about the comparability, reliability and validity of the statistics.

Second, religious affiliation does not necessarily indicate the strength of religious influence on individuals or on wider society. For example, religious affiliation in the UK census may indicate only a weak commitment to religion among many of those claiming to be Christian. Third, the projections are based on many assumptions about future birth rates and the extent to which beliefs will be passed on from one generation to the next.

Nevertheless, this research does suggest that in the world as a whole it is hard to make a case for either a general process of secularisation or an inevitable future decline in religiosity. As such, it seems to support the view that if it is occurring, secularisation is far more significant in some countries than others.

Activity

Figure 3.6.3 Size of major religious groups, 2010 (percentage of the global population)

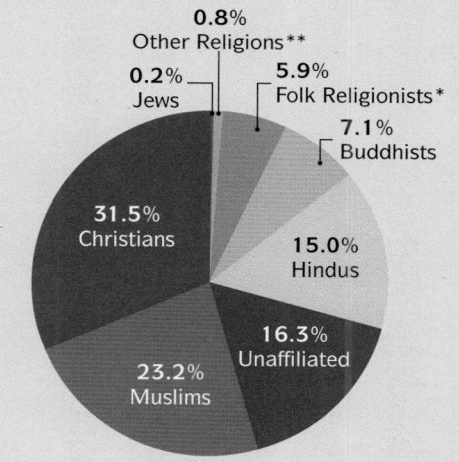

*Includes followers of African traditional religions, Chinese folk religions, Native American religions and Australian Aboriginal religions.

**Includes Bahai's, Jains, Sikhs, Shintoists, Taoists, followers of Tenrikyo, Wiccans, Zoroastrians and many other faiths.

Percentages may not add to 100 due to rounding.

Source: *Pew Research Center's Forum on Religion & Public Life, Global Religious Landscape, December 2012*

1. Compare the data in this figure with the data about the UK in Table 3.6.2 on p. 280.

2. In view of your answer to the previous question, why might it be misleading to base a discussion of secularisation on UK figures alone?

Pippa Norris and Ronald Inglehart – Existential security theory

Perhaps a better indication of religiosity than that provided by stated religious affiliation comes from survey data that examines a wider range of attitudes and values. The most comprehensive attempt to measure religiosity and secularisation worldwide using these types of survey was carried out between 1981 and 2001 using the World Values Survey and the European Values Survey. These surveys collected data from countries in which more than 85 per cent of the world's population live, ranging from countries with some of the lowest per capita income in the world to those with some of the highest. The data from these surveys were analysed by Pippa Norris and Ronald Inglehart (2004) in order to provide the first comprehensive test of secularisation theory.

Survey findings

Norris and Inglehart examined the findings in relation to different types of society. The 20 most affluent and developed states were categorised as post-industrial societies (where the service sector was dominant). A total of 58 countries with somewhat lower levels of development and income were classified as industrial societies. The remaining countries were defined as agrarian societies where agricultural production and the extraction of natural materials were the most important parts of the economy.

In terms of these broad categories, fairly consistent patterns were found, with agrarian societies being the most religious and post-industrial societies the least religious. As Table 3.6.4 shows, those in agrarian societies tended to participate more in religion than those in other societies; they were more likely to regard religion as being 'very important' and also more likely to hold a variety of religious beliefs.

Activity

Table 3.6.4 Religiosity by type of society (percentages)

	Agrarian	Industrial	Post-industrial
Religious participation			
Attend church at least weekly	44	25	20
Pray 'every day'	52	34	26
Religious values			
Religion 'very important'	64	34	20
Religious beliefs			
Believe in life after death	55	44	49
Believe that people have a soul	68	43	32
Believe in heaven	63	45	44
Believe in hell	59	36	26
Believe in God	78	72	69

Source: Norris, P. and Inglehart, R. *Sacred and Secular: Religion and Politics Worldwide*, Cambridge University Press, Cambridge, p. 57.

1. Summarise the differences in religiosity between different types of society.

2. Analyse the extent to which the data in Table 3.6.4 support existential security theory (see the explanation of the theory opposite).

Norris and Inglehart found no evidence that religion was likely to disappear in advanced post-industrial societies, although it was declining to some extent. However, although secularisation appeared to be occurring in more advanced societies, the proportion of the world's population living in such societies was falling, due to differences in fertility. As the size of agrarian societies grew, relative to the population of the world as a whole, the world was in fact becoming a somewhat more religious place.

Evidence of religious participation suggested that younger cohorts in post-industrial societies were much less likely to attend religious services than older cohorts. However, in agrarian societies this was not the case, with younger cohorts slightly more likely to attend services than older ones. This evidence suggested that a progressive decline in religious participation was characteristic only of advanced post-industrial societies rather than all societies.

Norris and Inglehart therefore provided evidence to support the claims of sociologists such as Steve Bruce (2002, 2011) who see secularisation as characteristic of Western societies alone.

Existential security

Norris and Inglehart (2004) go beyond measuring secularisation and provide a theory to explain the variations in religion suggested by the survey data. They argue that the strength of religion is closely related to the level of **existential security** in a country, such that the higher the sense of existential security the less strong religion is likely to be. A sense of existential security is defined as 'the feeling that survival is secure enough that it can be taken for granted'.

Post-industrial societies provide a strong sense of existential security because of 'their levels of economic and human development and socioeconomic equality'. For example, they generally have more developed welfare systems, good quality health care and little extreme poverty. However, this is not the case in agrarian societies, which have less well-developed welfare states and lower life expectancy.

Norris and Inglehart believe that the reason for this difference is that religion provides reassurance for those who feel vulnerable. Therefore, the demand for religion varies and tends to be greatest among those populations that feel most vulnerable. They argue that this theory explains why the USA has stronger religious views and higher levels of religious participation and belief than other post-industrial

societies. Compared to most of Western Europe, for example, the USA has higher inequality and a less comprehensive welfare state. US citizens therefore experience greater existential insecurity than citizens of other highly developed societies.

Evaluation

While impressive in its scope, and based upon detailed evidence, the work of Norris and Inglehart has not been without its critics. John von Heyking (2005) argues that a major flaw in their theory is the failure to make any direct attempt to measure a sense of existential security. Instead they infer this from other statistics, but this means that they fail to establish any direct link between people's subjective sense of insecurity and their religiosity.

Secularisation and public religion

The discussion of religion in a global context has so far concentrated on the religiosity of individuals, whether in terms of their religious participation or their beliefs. This section looks at the role of religion in public life and considers whether there is any evidence that religion has withdrawn from the public sphere to become something which is only of concern to private individuals. Some sociologists argue that, far from withdrawing from public life, religion worldwide is becoming more important in this sphere.

José Casanova – the revival of public religion

José Casanova (1994) distinguished three aspects of secularisation:

1. Secularisation as a decline of religious beliefs and practices: In this case, secularisation takes place when fewer individuals take part in religious activities or hold religious beliefs.

2. Secularisation as differentiation: In these terms, secularisation takes place when non-religious spheres of life (such as the state and the economy) become separate from and independent of religion.

3. Secularisation as privatisation: With this type of secularisation, religion stops playing any part in public life and does not even try to influence how politicians make decisions or individuals in society choose to live their lives.

Casanova believed that recent history shows that while there has been some decline in religious beliefs and practices in parts of Europe, this has not been the case in other parts of the world and in other senses there is little evidence of secularisation taking place. Differentiation has taken place in some parts of the world, but this does not mean that secularisation has taken place in other ways. For example, in the USA there is formal separation of the churches and the state, but religion is still very important in terms of individual beliefs and practices and in having a role in public life. However, Casanova's central argument is that in terms of privatisation (the third aspect of secularisation), religion is becoming stronger not weaker; 'public religions' are becoming more important in many countries and as a global force.

According to Casanova (1994), from the 1980s onwards, politicians, social scientists and the general public paid increasing attention to religion, and religious leaders were increasingly willing to enter public and political debate. Casanova says, 'During the entire decade of the 1980s it was hard to find any serious political conflict anywhere in the world that did not show behind it the not-so-hidden hand of religion.' Examples include the conflicts between Jews and Muslim Arabs in the Middle East, and between Muslims, Serbs and Croats in Bosnia. Religion played an important part in the revolts that led to the collapse of communism in Eastern Europe and the former USSR in the 1990s.

Casanova therefore believed that there has been a **deprivatisation** of religion. Before the 1980s, religion was becoming confined to the private sphere. It was considered a matter of personal conscience, and religious organisations were withdrawing from trying to influence public policies. From the 1980s, this was reversed, with religions again trying to exert an influence on public life.

Casanova therefore saw the privatisation of religion as a 'historical option', which has been followed in some societies at some times, but which is not an inevitable or irreversible aspect of modernity and which, since the 1980s, has become an increasingly unpopular option.

More recently, Casanova has reviewed his previous arguments to consider whether his claims about deprivatisation still hold good (Casanova, 2011). He finds that the arguments for deprivatisation have been 'amply confirmed by subsequent developments practically everywhere' (Casanova, 2011). Furthermore, religion has been deprivatised not just within nation states but to become a force in public affairs globally. Major religions now act to influence public affairs as **transnational religious regimes**,

that is, as movements which act independently of individual nations. For example, Catholicism has increased its global role with the Papacy intervening in global affairs and the Pope's visits to many countries around the world attracting huge crowds. The globalisation of migration has meant that followers of particular religions move between and live in many different countries. The electronic mass media has allowed transnational religious movements to thrive. Islam and Buddhism have always had transnational elements which are not tied to particular territories, but Islam has a crucial role in many nation states as well. Hinduism has a 'civilizational home' in 'mother India' but Hindus in different countries form an 'imagined community' that seeks to influence world affairs. Furthermore, there are some 'hybrid globalized religions' such as the Moonies and Hare Krishnas that have taken on public roles as well.

Activity – The Pope visits Cuba

Cuba gets ready for the visit of Pope Francis in 2015.

The Pope performed mass in Havana. After the communist revolution in 1959, religious people in Cuba were banned from being members of the Communist Party. In 2015, the leader of the country, Raúl Castro, relaxed this rule and accepted that you could be both religious and a party member.

Questions

1. Using your knowledge of Marxist theories of religion, explain why the Cuban Communist Party banned practising Catholics from membership of the party.

2. How can this example be used to support the arguments of Casanova?

Fundamentalism and secularisation

The theory of secularisation suggests a progressive decline in religion, but, as the previous unit indicates, there are many parts of the world where religion appears to be thriving or reviving. In a number of contexts, the term '**fundamentalism**' has been used to describe the nature of religion, particularly where it is undergoing an enthusiastic revival in strongly held beliefs.

In a major comparative study of *Strong Religion* (or fundamentalism), Gabriel Almond, R. Scott Appleby and Emmanuel Sivan (2003) identify fundamentalist movements among Jews in Israel; Muslims in Pakistan, Palestine, Egypt, and the Russian regions of Dagestan and Chechnya; Sikhs and Hindus in India; Christians in the USA and Ireland; and Buddhists in Sri Lanka. Islamic fundamentalism has perhaps been subject to more attention than other forms, particularly after the Islamic fundamentalist group Al Qaeda's 9/11 attacks in the USA and the rise and fall of Islamic State in Syria and bordering countries. However, fundamentalism is by no means confined to Islam. Furthermore, most Islamic people (like most Christians, Hindus and the followers of other religions) are not fundamentalists.

The nature of fundamentalism

According to Steve Bruce (2000), the term 'fundamentalism' was first used in the 1920s when conservative evangelical Protestants published a series of pamphlets in which they called for a return to 'The Fundamentals of the Faith'. These Protestants were 'anti-modernist' in that they objected to the way in which, as they saw it, their religion was becoming diluted in the modern world.

Bruce believes that fundamentalism involves 'movements that respond to problems created by modernization by advocating society-wide obedience to some authentic and inerrant text or tradition and by seeking the political power to impose the revitalized tradition' (Bruce, 2000). (An inerrant text is one that is believed by followers to be incapable of being wrong.)

Almond *et al*. (2003) define fundamentalism as 'a discernible pattern of religious militance by which self-styled "true believers" attempt to arrest the erosion of religious identity, fortify the borders of the religious community, and create viable alternatives to secular institutions and behaviors' (Almond *et al*., 2003).

Although fundamentalists claim to be reasserting the true meaning of a religion, it should be borne in mind that there is often much room for dispute over what the fundamentals of a religion actually are.

Steve Bruce – fundamentalism and secularisation

Steve Bruce (2000) sees fundamentalism as a reaction to **modernisation**. Modernisation involves societalisation (in which social life becomes increasingly fragmented) and differentiation (in which religious life is separated from other aspects of social life such as the economy). Modernisation also involves rationalisation, in which social life is planned to achieve certain goals, not based upon faith or prayer. A further feature of modernity is a tendency towards **egalitarianism**, in which all members of society share certain rights. For example, it involves increasingly egalitarian gender roles as women gain full citizenship rights. According to Bruce, all of these processes challenge the authority of religion, and in some circumstances groups with strongly held religious beliefs will try to defend their religion against the perceived threats.

In 'first world' countries such as the USA, modernisation has provided a local and immediate challenge to religious belief. Elsewhere – for example, in Islamic countries such as Iran and Turkey – a process of modernisation has been imposed upon society from outside by regimes friendly to the West. Examples include the regimes of the Shah (King) of Iran (1941–1979) and Kemal Ataturk, the President of Turkey 1923–1938.

In both sets of circumstances, Bruce believes that 'the main cause of fundamentalism is the belief of religious traditionalists that the world around them has changed so as to threaten their ability to reproduce themselves and their tradition' (2000). He sees fundamentalism as a 'rational response of traditionally religious peoples to social, political and economic changes that downgrade and constrain the role of religion in the public world' (Bruce, 2000). The response is rational, because Bruce believes that the threat to traditional religion from secularisation is real and very strong. He believes that the social changes which threaten religion are so strong that 'Fundamentalism in the West has no chance of winning' (Bruce, 2000).

Outside the West its prospects are better, and Islamic fundamentalism in particular has centuries-old roots which mean that it is unlikely to disappear any time soon. However, Bruce still believes that it faces an

301

uphill struggle. He quotes a study of Jordanians (Antoun, 1994, discussed in Bruce, 2000) who had worked or studied in the West before returning to their village. Although the Jordanians valued Islam and valued many of the traditional aspects of village life, they accepted the need to become more Western by accepting science, technology and rational bureaucracy. Ultimately, Bruce believes, these kinds of secular Western influence will undermine traditional religions throughout the world.

Gabriel Almond, R. Scott Appleby and Emmanuel Sivan (2003) – secularisation and other factors

Gabriel Almond, R. Scott Appleby and Emmanuel Sivan (2003) discuss the findings of a major comparative study of fundamentalist religions throughout the world. A total of 75 case studies were carried out by researchers over a 20-year period, and interviews were conducted in the Middle East, North Africa and the United States.

They follow Bruce in seeing fundamentalism as a reaction to the social changes associated with modernisation and secularisation. Without secularisation, there would be no need for a fundamentalist movement. Furthermore, the development of communications has led to globalisation, and with it the influence of Western secular rationalism has spread to non-Western countries. However, it has also provided opportunities for fundamentalists to organise and spread their message. Thus, the New Christian Right in the USA have made extensive use of the media, including starting their own TV stations. The internet has been important in spreading Islamic fundamentalism worldwide. It also allows the 'demonstration effect' or copy-cat behaviours such as some suicide bombings.

However, Almond et al. do not see modernisation and secularisation as the only important factors. They identify a number of structural causes – causes located in the structure of society. These are as follows:

> *Inequality and deprivation*. Almond et al. quote a study in the USA by Nancy Ammerman (1990, discussed in Almond et al., 2003), which found that Christian fundamentalism among Southern Baptists thrived among those from working-class backgrounds.

> Major *migration* movements. Where large numbers of people are displaced – for example, Palestinians after the creation of the Israeli state in 1948 – this can breed the resentment on which fundamentalism feeds. Recent migrants who form a minority in a country can also become fundamentalist if they feel that their religion and traditions are under threat.

> *Economic problems*. Unemployment, famine and inflation can all encourage the growth of fundamentalism. However, economic problems can make fundamentalist movements unpopular where they have gained political power, as has occurred at various times in Sudan, Turkey and Iran.

> *Western imperialism*. Fundamentalism is often tied up with nationalist movements against Western control and influence in colonies, former colonies and countries with pro-Western regimes. A prime example is the 1979 Iranian revolution against the Shah (king), who was supported by the USA and other Western powers. He was overthrown by popular protests that installed as ruler of the country the Ayatollah Khomeini, an Islamic leader who had been exiled in France by the Shah. Another example is the growth of fundamentalism among Palestinians after Israel seized land from them during the 1967 Arab–Israeli war.

In addition, Almond et al. believe that whether fundamentalist movements develop depends upon whether effective leaders emerge to further the movement. They also argue that chance plays a part. For example, the illness of the Shah in 1970s Iran played a part in the overthrow of his regime by Islamic leaders.

Contemporary issues: Islamic State

Perhaps the most notable fundamentalist movement of recent years is IS – or Islamic State (also known as ISIL, ISIS and Daesh). This group of Islamic fundamentalists started as a splinter group from the terrorist organisation Al-Quaeda (which carried out the 9/11 attacks). IS has claimed responsibility for, or has inspired, numerous terrorist attacks, including attacks in Tunisia, Egypt, Paris, Turkey,

Brussels, Nice and the 2017 Manchester Arena bombing, which killed 22 people at an Ariana Grande concert. Unlike most other terrorist groups, IS has tried to establish its own state, occupying a large area of territory in Iraq and Syria between 2013 and 2018. In June 2014, the leader of the group, Abu Bakr al-Baghdadi, declared a worldwide Islamic caliphate, claiming authority over Muslims throughout the world. The Caliphate in Iran and Iraq was characterised by the use of extreme violence in upholding Islamic Sharia law (BBC, 2015) but nevertheless it attracted a considerable number of recruits from Western countries. Social media has been used extensively and effectively to support the ideology of IS, meaning that it has attracted support in places where it lacks an organisational structure (Davies, 2016). IS was driven out of much of the territory it controlled in Iraq and Syria in 2017, but it continued to attract followers for its fundamentalist interpretation of Islam and its call for a *jihad* (violent struggle) against all its opponents (Davies, 2016). For example, the group Boko Haram, a violent jihadist group in Nigeria, has claimed affiliation to Islamic State.

Activity

Three young British women are recorded on CCTV as they journey to join ISIS in Syria in 2015.

1. Explain why the development of IS can be seen to contradict the theory of secularisation.

2. With reference to the image and the text, explain why IS can be seen as a transnational religious movement.

3. Based upon the sociological arguments in this chapter, suggest reasons for the appeal of IS to some people.

José Casanova – fundamentalism and multiple modernities

The approach developed by Almond *et al.* demonstrates that there is much more to the development of fundamentalism than simply a reaction to modernisation. However, some theorists go further and argue that it is misleading to see the growth of fundamentalism as a reaction to modernisation and secularisation at all. Instead, fundamentalism should be seen as a different *type* of modernity.

José Casanova (2011) argues that far from being a reaction against modernisation, fundamentalism can be seen as a product of modernisation. Casanova draws on the work of S.N. Eisenstadt (2000), who argues that there are **multiple modernities**. From this viewpoint, modernity does not abandon tradition but instead tries to transform tradition in a pragmatic way.

Western societies became modern before other parts of the world and they tended to base themselves around the ideological appeal of the nation state. Western modernisation did not reject the idea of tradition entirely, but instead encouraged loyalty to the nation state by emphasising the traditions associated with the nation. (For example, in Britain some of the traditions that encourage loyalty to the nation include the state opening of Parliament and Remembrance Sunday, when those who died fighting for their country in world wars are remembered.) If modernity involves the rational pursuit of overarching goals, in Western societies these tend to be framed in terms of the interests of the nation. In Western societies that emphasise the primacy of the nation-state, religion may be sidelined as a source of identity. However, it never completely disappears. For example, the Catholic Church still plays an important role in the national identity of some Southern European countries. Nevertheless, because the role of religion becomes more marginal, there is a tendency towards secularisation taking place.

However, according to Casanova, there are other versions of modernity in which religion plays a much bigger role. In some non-Western countries, religious beliefs are central to the traditions that are used to encourage loyalty to the nation. Religion and politics are fused together in many Islamic countries (for example Iran and Pakistan). Similarly, the Jewish religion is closely connected with politics in Israel, Hinduism with politics in India and Buddhism with politics in Sri Lanka. They have all embraced a version of modernity, but one that is different from secular modernity in Western countries such as the UK. Loyalty to the country is justified in terms of supporting aims that are seen to derive from religion rather than from secular nationalism.

Religion can also take on a transnational character. It exists not just within nations but also across nations. All world religions are forced to respond to the global expansion of modernity by 'reformulating their traditions in an attempt to fashion their own particular civilizational versions of modernity' (Casanova, 2011). For example, Islamic fundamentalism has become a political force in its own right.

Casanova's idea may be questionable to the extent that fundamentalist groups can be seen as a rejection of modernity rather than an alternative version of modernity. While Islamic State may have embraced the use of social media, in other respects it is very hostile to modern culture. For example, during the Caliphate women were prohibited from leaving their own homes without a male relative (Cockburn, 2015).

Secularisation – conclusion

If Casanova is right, then there is no inevitable association of religious decline with modernity and the idea of secularisation as an inevitable and universal process should be rejected. However, as the variety of views discussed in this section illustrate, the theory of secularisation has not been definitively proved or disproved. This is partly because sociologists have used the term 'secularisation' in many different ways. This has led to considerable confusion, as writers discussing the process of secularisation are often arguing about different things.

Grace Davie (2007) accepts that 'Secularization is a multi-dimensional concept; its dimensions, moreover, frequently operate independently of each other.' She goes on to say, 'Hence the need for conceptual clarity in order to ensure that like is being compared with like and that accurate inferences are drawn from the argument.' One way to achieve this is to clearly distinguish different types of secularisation.

The various conclusions reached by different sociologists reflect the different ways in which secularisation is defined and the different areas of the world that are studied. Those who adopt more exclusive definitions and define religion in terms of traditional churches and denominations tend to provide stronger evidence in favour of secularisation than those who adopt more inclusive definitions that encompass New Age beliefs and other forms of spirituality. Those who focus on Western European societies tend to provide more convincing arguments in favour of secularisation than those who include other societies in their discussion.

Without an agreed definition of secularisation, there is unlikely to be agreement about whether it is taking place. However, there is some agreement that religion is changing and that, at least in parts of Europe, traditional church-based religion is in decline. While most sociologists agree that there is increasing interest in New Age beliefs, some (such as Bruce) see this as insignificant, whereas others (such as Heelas *et al.*) see it as evidence of important cultural change.

Most theorists who either support or attack the theory of secularisation are now willing to admit that the theory cannot be unproblematically applied to all groups in all societies. It can, therefore, be argued that the national, regional, ethnic and social-class differences in the role of religion make it necessary to relate theories to specific countries and social groups.

Key terms

Vicariousness Enjoying the benefits of religion through the activities of others without taking an active role yourself.

Existential security The belief that your survival is not seriously threatened and can therefore be taken for granted.

Deprivatisation The process by which religion stops being a purely private matter and re-enters the public sphere.

Transnational religious regimes Religious movements that are independent of individual nation states.

Fundamentalist A set of religious beliefs that advocates returning to the 'fundamental' original teachings of a particular religion.

Modernisation The process by which modern societies which are characterised by the increasing importance of rationality and the declining importance of tradition and faith develop.

Egalitarianism A belief that all members of society should be treated equally.

Multiple modernities Different versions of modernity that draw upon different types of tradition.

Summary

1. Grace Davie suggests that there is little evidence of the declining influence of Christianity in most parts of the world and in some places, such as Latin America and Africa, there is evidence that it is thriving.

2. The Pew Research Center has estimated that 84 per cent of people in the world identify with a religion, and based on demographic trends they predict that this figure is likely to increase. However, the validity and reliability of this research can be questioned.

3. Norris and Inglehart put forward the existential security theory to suggest that religious beliefs are stronger where human life is more insecure, and vice versa.

4. Casanova believes that, in many parts of the world, religion is playing an increasingly important part in public life with some major religions acting as transnational religious regimes to influence global affairs.

5. Fundamentalist religions involve a return to traditional religious teachings and they have thrived in recent years in many parts of the world.

6. Bruce sees fundamentalism as a reaction to modernisation but he believes that ultimately it will not prevent the spread of secular influences.

7. Almond, Appleby and Sivan see fundamentalism as being caused by a variety of factors, including inequality and deprivation, and not just by modernisation and secularisation.

8. Casanova believes that fundamentalism is simply a different type of modernity and as such shows that secularisation is not inevitable in modern societies.

EXAM PRACTICE QUESTIONS

A-LEVEL PAPER 2
BELIEFS IN SOCIETY

| 1 | 3 | Outline and explain **two** features of religion as a belief system. **[10 marks]**

| 1 | 4 | Read **Item A** and answer the question that follows.

Item A

Gender inequality in religion can result in the subordination of women. It has been argued that in all the main world religions there are elements which are patriarchal. Feminists argue that religion does not serve the needs of all members in society; instead it serves the interests of certain social groups in society. Tracing the nature of religion and gender back in history, we can see that religion was not always a source of inequality as women were considered central to spirituality. However, feminists suggest that most religious organisations today continue to have gender inequality in relation to many beliefs and practices such as scriptures, dress and worship.

Applying the material from **Item A** and elsewhere, analyse **two** ways in which religious organisations can be linked to the exploitation of women. **[10 marks]**

| 1 | 5 | Read **Item B** and answer the question that follows.

Item B

Sociologists cannot agree whether religion is a source of stability or a force for social change. Because people are socialised into the dominant religion of their culture, it brings them a sense of cohesion. Sharing the same norms and values as others in a culture means social life can remain stable. However, religion can also be used to challenge a culture's dominant beliefs, including norms, values and social structure. Some sociologists argue this could promote social change.

Applying the material from **Item B** and your knowledge, evaluate the view that religion can be a force for social change. **[20 marks]**

4 EXAM PREPARATION AND PRACTICE

In this chapter you will find sample responses to
the exam questions included at the end of Chapters
1 to 3 of this book. Guidance on how to respond
effectively is provided for each question and the
sample responses are annotated with examiner
commentary to help you understand how to improve
your work.

The sociology skills pyramid

AQA Sociology requires you to demonstrate specified skills in order to be successful in the exam. These skills can be seen as being in a hierarchy, with some foundational skills that need to be demonstrated before you can go on to demonstrate the higher-level skills. Very often these skills are closely interconnected, and you demonstrate them simultaneously through the way you write about the subject.

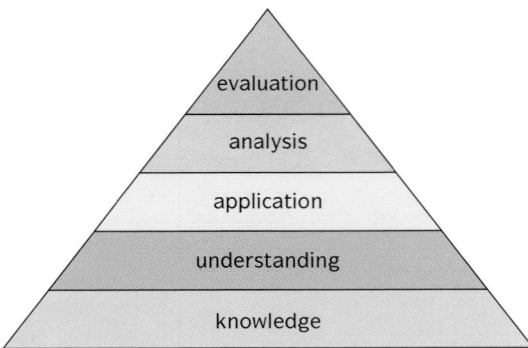

All five skills are examined in A-level sociology. They are grouped into the three Assessment Objectives (AOs) as shown in the table below.

Table 4.1 Assessment Objectives

Assessment Objective	What they say
AO1	Demonstrate knowledge and understanding of: • sociological theories, concepts and evidence • sociological research methods.
AO2	Apply sociological theories, concepts, evidence and research methods to a range of issues.
AO3	Analyse and evaluate sociological theories, concepts, evidence and research methods in order to: • present arguments • make judgements • draw conclusions.

Using this chapter

Practice exam-style questions for each of the topics covered in this book have been provided in this chapter to help you develop your writing skills and test your knowledge and understanding.

Read each question carefully, taking note of the Remember tips, which suggest how to respond effectively in the time available in the exam.

When you have written your own response to the question, read through the sample responses and commentaries and decide whether your answer could be improved.

Timing

As a rough guide, allow around 1.5 minutes for each mark allocated. For example, spend around 15 minutes answering a 10-mark question and about 45 minutes answering a 30-mark question. However, it is important to remember that these suggested timings include reading the questions (including the items, where relevant), so you will not have the full time for writing your response. For longer questions, you should also allocate some of the time for planning your response.

A-level Paper 2 Beliefs in Society exam practice questions

1 3 Outline and explain **two** features of religion as a belief system. **[10 marks]**

Remember

> This is worth 10 marks and must be written in continuous prose.

> The question asks you for two features. You must make these clearly distinct. Do not be afraid to use sentence starters such as 'One feature is… A second feature is…'.

> Spend around 15 minutes on this question.

> Out of the 10 marks awarded, you are not given 5 marks for your explanation of each feature. You will be awarded marks for the overall quality of your response. Sometimes, one of your explanations may be longer or you may remember more evidence for one feature, but there is no need to worry about that. Your response will be marked in a holistic manner.

> To get into the top mark bands, you need to include substantial analysis.

> You might want to state which feature has more significance, as this will help you to analyse.

> You should use examples to support your ideas.

C grade response

One way in which religion can be seen as a belief system is through the use of a set doctrine or text. Most religions have a guide such as the Bible for Christianity, the Torah for Judaism and the Qur'an for Islam. The scriptures provide explanations, for example in order to help us understand pain or death. The religious texts offer an explanation as to why these things occur and so people subscribe to that belief system.

Another way in which religion can be seen as a belief system is that it attempts to give a reason or explanation for everything: for example, the meaning of life can be explained by the need to serve God or death can be explained by the entrance into Heaven. Therefore, religion can be seen as a belief system as people can find answers to their questions within its texts.

The candidate could have developed this idea by giving more detailed examples from specific religious faiths. They could also have mentioned Durkheim on the sacred element of following a text or taking part in collective worship, or they could have discussed how fundamentalist religions tend to take sacred texts literally.

This point lacks clarity: functionalism could have been used to develop the idea that religion as a belief system reinforces norms and values and promotes cohesion.

Examiner's comments

This response displays accurate knowledge of two ways in which religion can be seen as a belief system. Both points lack depth and remain underdeveloped. The second point becomes repetitive towards the end.

Mark 6/10

A grade response

Religion can be defined as a belief system; the sociologist Polanyi notes that there are certain characteristics of religions that match the definition of what a belief system is.

A short introduction which displays awareness of relevant sociological evidence.

One of these features of religion is that there is a circularity of beliefs, meaning that the ideas within a particular religion are further explained in relation to other ideas. Christianity, for example, considers the power and influence of God in order to understand events that occur in life. Reasons for events such as miracles, illness and death can be linked back to the power of God. For many Christians the Bible acts as a source of comfort and a guide as there is always an answer to any philosophical question in that God has the ability to do anything as an omnipotent force. This means that the circularity of beliefs theory works by the ability to be able to link occurrences back to the one controlling and dominant force, that of God. Many people have questioned this as our belief in science has strengthened.

This shows a good depth of knowledge with relevant examples from specific faiths. There is analysis present at the end.

Another feature of religion is that any alternative belief systems are rejected. In Islam, for example, one of the pillars of the faith is to accept Allah as the only God and Mohammed as the one and final prophet. This means that Islam does not tolerate belief in other deities within their faith as this does not fit within the parameters of the faith as a belief system. Islam would reject the idea of religious pluralism or adopting practices from alternative faiths such as Christianity, Hinduism or Buddhism as this would be stepping outside the defined characteristics of the Islamic belief system. In this case, the faith is very clear that the Qur'an is the definitive word of God and therefore alternative explanations other than those cited in the text would be rejected.

Therefore, if we take Polanyi's definition of a belief system then religion certainly holds some of the relevant features and characteristics.

Clear knowledge and understanding displayed with specific examples from religious faiths. A short conclusion is presented.

Examiner's comments

This response clearly shows two very distinct and appropriate features of a belief system and within this demonstrates a good knowledge and understanding of religion which has depth. The response also benefits from applying the ideas to two different faiths in the form of Christianity and Islam. This again helps to make the two features distinct from each other.

Mark 10/10

1 4   Read **Item A** and answer the question that follows.

Item A

Gender inequality in religion can result in the subordination of women. It has been argued that in all the main world religions there are elements which are patriarchal. Feminists argue that religion does not serve the needs of all members in society; instead it serves the interests of certain social groups in society. Tracing the nature of religion and gender back in history, we can see that religion was not always a source of inequality as women were considered central to spirituality. However, feminists suggest that most religious organisations today continue to have gender inequality in relation to many beliefs and practices such as scriptures, dress and worship.

Applying the material from **Item A** and elsewhere, analyse **two** ways in which religious organisations can be linked to the exploitation of women.

[10 marks]

Remember

» This is worth 10 marks and must be written in continuous prose.

» The question asks you for two ways. You must make these clearly distinct. Do not be afraid to use sentence starters such as 'One way is…, A second way is…'.

» Spend around 15 minutes on this question.

» Out of the 10 marks awarded, you are not given 5 marks for each way. You will be awarded marks for the overall quality of your response. Sometimes, your analysis of one of the ways may be longer or you may remember more evidence to support your points, but there is no need to worry about that. Your response will be marked in a holistic manner.

» To get into the top mark bands, you need to include substantial analysis and evaluation.

» You might want to state which way is most significant, as this will help you to analyse.

» You should use examples to support your ideas.

» You must use the Item. It will help form the basis of your ideas, but you must develop its ideas and not simply repeat the points.

C grade response

One way in which religious organisations can be linked to the exploitation of women is through sexism in some of the scriptures. Feminists believe that religion often places men in higher positions of power than women: for example, in Christianity God is referred to as male and the representation of God on earth is through a male in the form of Jesus. Likewise, the Qur'an refers to male figures such as Allah as the one and only God and Mohammed as the prophet to spread the word of God. Feminists believe that this enforces the idea that men are more powerful than women and continues to legitimise the system of patriarchy.

A second way of religions exploiting women can be seen through ideas on dress, for example in the expectation that Muslim women should cover

This first point is stronger than the second and gives specific examples from two religious faiths. This could have been analysed by a comparison to Hinduism which has many female deities or to Judaism where women have an important role within the family.

their head or body. Feminists believe that this is unfair because Muslim men are not under the same strict guidelines as women and it seems to be a punishment to women for being sexually attractive to men rather than a punishment to men for looking at women as sexual objects.

As Item A states, many religions in the past were not as sexist or unequal as they are today as many religions actually held females as equal to men in terms of power.

> This point lacks depth and analysis. For example, there is a range of literature which suggests that some women find the veil liberating. There is also some debate as to whether wearing a veil is a religious inequality or a cultural practice.

Examiner's comments

This response uses the Item and displays basic development. The response includes ideas on feminism but does not reference the work of any specific sociologists or particular strands of feminism and is therefore a little generic. While some good knowledge is included, there is a lack of depth and analysis.

Mark 7/10

A grade response

Feminists believe that religion is one of the key agents of socialisation that enforces a system of patriarchy through its belief system and further reinforces gender inequality through some of its practices. Many feminist writers believe that this has not always been the case as many ancient religions placed women in more important positions in the hierarchical system.

The second wave feminist Simone de Beauvoir took a Marxist-Feminist look at religion. She saw religions such as Christianity as oppressive to women by stating that their place is in the home, taking on the expressive role. As noted in Item A, the scriptures defend this by suggesting that females will reach equality in the afterlife once they gain their place in heaven. De Beauvoir believed this was an example of exploiting females through religion as earlier faiths such as Hinduism regarded the role of women and goddesses as of key importance rather than seeing women's role as inferior to that of men. Of course, in many faiths today women are gaining more power, such as the acceptance of female clergy in some strains of Christianity.

> The item has been used and the candidate is able to expand on this giving examples from different religious faiths. Analysis is present.

Another way in which religion can be seen as exploiting women is through dress and practices. The Feminist writer El Saadawi has been critical of the Islamic faith due to the expectation that women have to cover up their bodies whilst less expectation of modesty is placed upon males. El Saadawi has also discussed extensively female genital mutilation and how women are often expected to not show their sexual attraction or feelings to others for fear of being classed as temptresses. Many female Muslims have rejected this claim, though, and say that the wearing of the hijab or burka is a personal choice rather than something enforced by religion.

> The second point is distinctly different and again makes use of the item and expands on it. Relevant sociological material is applied.

It does seem that although many religions are far from equal in terms of gender equality there are small steps being made towards equality with each generation and a move back to women having more power in religions as there was in some of the earliest faiths. However, it is clear to see that in some faiths there is a lack of progress, such as the Roman Catholic faith which still refuses to ordain women.

Analysis is displayed in a short conclusion showing awareness of the issues raised by the question.

Examiner's comments

This response shows good knowledge which has depth. Two very different points are made, each referencing relevant sociological evidence. The Item has been used and then developed. Knowledge is also displayed of different strands of feminism. Analysis is present.

Mark 10/10

1 5   Read **Item B** and answer the question that follows.

Item B

Sociologists cannot agree whether religion is a source of stability or a force for social change. Because people are socialised into the dominant religion of their culture, it brings them a sense of cohesion. Sharing the same norms and values as others in a culture means social life can remain stable. However, religion can also be used to challenge a culture's dominant beliefs, including norms, values and social structure. Some sociologists argue this could promote social change.

Applying the material from **Item B** and your knowledge, evaluate the view that religion can be a force for social change.

[20 marks]

Remember

» This question requires an essay-style answer and must be written in continuous prose with a short introduction and conclusion. You may find it helpful to make a short plan.

» This question carries the most marks.

» Spend around 30 minutes on this question.

» Each point you make must be developed with reference to some sociological theory, a sociological study or some evidence.

» To get into the top mark bands, you need to include substantial analysis and evaluation.

» Keep referring back to the question so your response stays relevant. Make sure that you meet the demands of the question by referring to the Item, applying your own knowledge and evaluating the view in the question.

» You must use the Item. It will help form the basis of your ideas, but you must develop the ideas and not simply repeat its points.

» A short conclusion is required. However, it must add some value rather than just summarising. In the conclusion, try to give a direct answer to the question based upon the arguments you have put forward.

C grade response

Many sociologists believe that religion can be a force for social change as it has the power to change a society, though other theorists believe that the point of religion is actually to maintain the norm and act as a conservative force.

The candidate misses an opportunity to link these ideas to sociological theory, for example Max Weber believes religion is a force for social change.

Weber studied Calvinists and their belief system. He identified that the believers followed a disciplined and ascetic life in the hope that they would be rewarded with money and success. In turn this success may indicate to them they had been selected by God to be one of the few to get into heaven. Weber believed that this was the start of capitalism in the western world; he said that you can trace the origins of capitalism back to the Calvinist religion and therefore this shows religion can be a force for social change.

This paragraph displays good knowledge but it fails to fully explain how change came about by linking the Protestant ethic to the development of capitalism. There is also no evaluation of Weber; some sociologists argue that he was mistaken about the historical origins of capitalism.

There are also other examples of how religion has had a huge impact on political changes. The US civil rights movement of the 1950s, for example, had strong connections to the Baptist church, and this movement broke down the barriers for black and white people to be able to live side by side. Likewise, the liberation movement in Latin America during the 1960s and 1970s caused a move against oppression and again religion was considered the driving force behind the movement.

This paragraph lacks detailed sociological evidence. The candidate could have included the work of Steve Bruce on how religion was of high importance in the civil rights movement. The candidate could have also included some evaluation of liberation theology in Latin America.

Religion can also cause social change through the fact that there are new religious groups being formed all the time such as new age movements and also the increase in new age practices. This shows that religion does not always stand still but has the ability to change through time.

However, traditional theories from functionalism, Marxism and feminism still maintain that religion actually acts as a conservative force rather than a force for social change; this means that it maintains traditions and keeps the norm. The functionalist Durkheim, for example, stated that religion maintains stability by bringing people together; it forms a state of consensus.

This point has not been explicitly linked to the question. Further discussion and examples of how new age movements are a force for social change would be required in order for this point to be fully developed and relevant to the question.

Marx too felt that religion was a conservative force but in a negative way. He believed that religion acted like a drug to justify the poor staying poor and the rich staying rich as religion gives people the hope of a better life once they are in heaven. Marx believed that religion actually held people in their place rather than giving them the power to change society.

This paragraph is list-like and lacks depth; the candidate could have explored one of the theories in more depth, for example the functionalist view point that religion is a force which aids stability.

There is no evaluation of Marx. For example, while religion may have been a conservative force in the past, secularisation may have limited the ability of religion to prevent change.

Feminists too believe that religion is a conservative force as it maintains patriarchy; Christianity for example justifies the man as the head of a household and the woman in the role of housewife and child bearer. Writers such as de Beauvoir have long stated that religion keeps people in their place rather than allowing them to change society.

> This point lacks development. Some evidence or examples could have been included such as the lack of women in religious roles and the scarcity of women in sacred texts.

In conclusion then there is evidence on both sides of the debate that religion can cause change as well as trying to act like a conservative force. It may be linked to where in the world the religion is.

> This is a summative conclusion; the candidate could have made an attempt to directly answer the question by weighing up the evidence.

Examiner's comments

This is an accurate discussion of religion as a force for change. Reasonable evidence is given for both sides of the argument though these explanations are brief and lack the development needed to gain a higher grade. There is also a lack of analysis and evaluation. The essay also tends to focus mainly on Christianity rather than looking at other faiths as well.

Mark 12/20

A grade response

For sociologists such as Weber, religion is a force for social change as it can influence the culture and beliefs of a particular society; there are various examples throughout history which demonstrate the impact of religion in changing a society. Other theorists such as functionalists and feminists, however, believe that religion acts as a conservative force through the maintaining of stability and tradition and that the aim of religion is actually to hold onto values and structure rather than to change it.

> This is a conceptually sound introduction which displays knowledge of opposing theories.

In his classic study 'The Protestant Ethic and the Spirit of Capitalism' Weber believed that the Calvinist religion was actually the catalyst for capitalism as those who followed the faith believed that a hard-working ethic could improve their chances of being selected to go to heaven. The Calvinists believed in predestination but felt that working a long day, leading an ascetic life and being financially rewarded for this could demonstrate their acceptance to heaven. Weber recognised this as the starting point of all western capitalism and if he was accurate then his theory certainly demonstrates the power of religion to cause mass social change. However, Tucker does not necessarily agree with Weber on how capitalism emerged from religion. He argues that the introduction of money and banks play a more important part in explaining why capitalism developed faster in the West than in other parts of the world.

> This is a well-developed point which is conceptually sound; analysis and evaluation are present. The candidate could have further evaluated Weber with other criticisms.

Functionalists such as Durkheim also disagree with the idea of religion contributing to social change. Durkheim believed that religion acts as a conservative force by providing a collective conscience for the people. By this he means a shared set of beliefs, values and norms that, as the Item states, brings a 'sense of cohesion'. Durkheim believed that without religion a society would become less integrated and regulated; he referred to this as a state of anomie. What religion offers for functionalists is a sense of security in that it does not change. In a world of confusion, instability or mixed messages, the religious texts such as the Bible and the Qur'an offer a consistent message that provides a sense of security for many of their followers.

> This point has an evaluative tone as it describes how religion is a conservative force rather than a force for change. An opportunity has been missed to evaluate the idea that religion is in decline and it is therefore less effective in promoting cohesion.

Another example of religion bringing social change can be seen in the 1950s civil rights movement in the US with preacher Martin Luther King Jnr. as one of the most iconic figures behind the campaign and Christianity playing an important part in this change. Bruce notes that the Christian ideology of treating all men as equal was pivotal in the civil rights movement because it forced many White clergymen to question their personal values. Bruce observed that Martin Luther King Jnr. referred frequently to Christianity in his speeches and concluded that religion can underpin huge social and political changes. Marxists, however, believe that in most cases religion actually keeps the disadvantaged in their place rather than acting as a form of liberation. Marx argued that 'religion is the opium of the people', it is the drug that justifies their place in society and therefore for Marxists religion acts as a negative conservative force rather than a mechanism for change.

As a counterargument to traditional Marxist views, though, there are millenarian movements: the aim of these religious groups is to cause a major transformation of society and, according to the sociologist Worsley, these movements often focus on poverty and the saving of people due to the belief in the second coming of Christ. Such movements could be found across Europe and the Western Pacific and they often influenced uprisings and the overthrowing of colonial governments.

> This is a comprehensive point with in-depth theoretical evaluation.

Likewise, the liberation movement took place in Latin America in the late 1960s. Its aim was to try and help those in poverty, and it fought against many of the dictatorships in place. In contrast to traditional Marxists, Neo-Marxists, therefore, recognise that religion can impact on development. The sociologist Maduro stated that this movement is a classic example of religion inspiring social change; previously, the Catholic church had adopted a conservative stance but liberation theology encouraged it to take a more left-wing approach to help those in need.

In Iran, there was also revolution in the late 1970s from Shia Muslims against the Shah advocating the introduction of Sharia law, which again showed the power of a religious and political movement.

> This displays good contemporary knowledge and a deeper understanding of the topic area.

Many feminists, however, debate the true extent of liberation in religion and also believe that religion acts as a conservative force especially in its views on gender and patriarchy. Theorists such as de Beauvoir feel that religion does not adapt and change as social attitudes change, therefore leaving religious attitudes seeming antiquated and out of touch with contemporary society. This may explain why followers of religion are decreasing at a rapid rate in many nations. However, some feminists argue that women can play an active part in resisting patriarchy and can therefore encourage change, for example in the successful recent campaigns for the acceptance of female priests and bishops.

> This whole paragraph has an evaluative tone.

Therefore, there is evidence that religion can cause social change but also act as a conservative force. In reality it seems that religion often acts as a mechanism to support a political or social change rather than engineering a huge change on its own. For many the whole point of religion is actually to maintain the traditions of the original scriptures and therefore any change actually goes against the fundamental belief systems of religion. Nevertheless, in some circumstances religious beliefs can be used by groups to help justify change.

> This answer reaches a fully supported critical conclusion.

Examiner's comments

This is a strong response both in range and depth. Relevant sociological material is accurately and sensitively applied to the question. Analysis and evaluation are present. The essay is also well structured and arrives at a sophisticated conclusion.

Mark 20/20

A-level Paper 3 Crime and Deviance exam practice questions

0 1 Outline **two** ways in which laws may benefit the ruling class. **[4 marks]**

Remember

> This is a short answer question; you should spend around six minutes on it.

> You will need to outline two ways. To make them clearly distinct, you could use sentence openers such as 'One way is… Another way is…'.

> Identify the reasons and briefly develop each one with further explanation or an example, ensuring that the two points do not overlap.

C grade response

Marxists believe that laws may benefit the ruling classes because laws themselves are made and enforced by those in power and therefore tend to benefit those at the top and go against those with less status.

Another way in which the laws benefit the ruling class is that many of those in government and power are of the ruling class and therefore make the laws to serve their own interests.

Examiner's comments

This response has made two points but essentially they both link to the same area of Marxist criminology – that laws are created by the ruling class to benefit themselves.

Mark 2/4

A grade response

Marxists believe that laws benefit the ruling classes and oppress the proletariat as the laws themselves are constructed by the people in positions of power and high status. One example of this can be seen in property. Laws about property serve to keep the poor away from housing and land ownership.

Another way in which laws may benefit the ruling class is through the old boys network. This refers to the contacts that many of the ruling classes have within the legal system to make sure that they are not punished to the same degree as the poor, with tax evasion being treated much less severely than benefit fraud, for example.

Examiner's comments

This response outlines two good examples which are distinct from each other. The candidate demonstrates good knowledge and understanding. It is also useful to look at different forms of crime, in this case property law in the first point and tax/benefit crime in the second point.

Mark 4/4

0 2   Outline **three** reasons why official crime statistics may not give a true representation of crime.   **[6 marks]**

Remember

> This is a short answer question; you should spend around nine minutes on it.

> You will need to outline three reasons. To make them clearly distinct, you could use sentence openers such as 'One reason is…'.

> Identify the reasons and briefly develop each one with further explanation or an example ensuring that the three points do not overlap.

C grade response

One reason for crime statistics being inaccurate is because certain crimes are not detected.

Likewise, not all crimes get reported.

Certain groups will not show up in crime statistics such as under 18s. This means the official statistics only show a picture of adult crime rather than a representative account of all crime.

Examiner's comments

The first two suggestions made by this response have only been awarded one mark out of the potential two marks. This is because, although accurate, they lack development. The candidate could have suggested why not all crimes are detected and reported, for example because a victim is unaware that a crime took place. The third point is accurate and fully developed so is awarded two marks.

Mark 4/6

A grade response

One reason may be due to the dark figure of crime, which refers to those crimes that are unreported to the police. This could be due to the fact that a crime in seen as insignificant or a petty theft and therefore the victim fails to report the incident.

Likewise, crimes that are only uncovered by the police because they are 'victimless' do not appear in the statistics unless the police go out looking for them. An example is selling drugs because neither the seller nor the buyer is likely to report themselves so the number of recorded crimes depends on whether the police actively go looking for drug dealers.

Finally, there are certain groups that will not show up in crime statistics such as under 18s. This therefore means the official statistics only show a picture of adult crime rather than a representative account of all crime.

Examiner's comments

This response shows three very clear and distinct reasons as to why crime statistics may not be valid, which are all fully developed. The variety of factors demonstrates good knowledge and understanding.

Mark 6/6

0 3 Read **Item A** and answer the question that follows.

Item A

Feminists have argued that women's involvement in crime has been ignored. Women have always offended, yet we know very little about the reasons why they offend. Much sociological crime literature has focused on the male offender, exploring the reasons for men's higher involvement in criminal and deviant behaviour. One argument for this is because official crime statistics show us that women do not participate in high levels of criminal behaviour and therefore explanations with regard to gender focus on the lack of criminal involvement of women. Different theorists have attempted to explain this by exploring both culture and control.

Applying material from **Item A**, analyse **two** reasons for the lesser involvement of women in criminal and deviant behaviour.

[10 marks]

Remember

» This question is worth 10 marks and your response must be written in continuous prose.

» The question asks you for two reasons. You must make these clearly distinct. Do not be afraid to use sentence starters such as 'One reason is…', 'A second reason is…'.

» Spend around 15 minutes on this question.

» Out of the 10 marks awarded, you are not given 5 marks for each reason. You will be awarded marks for the overall quality of your response. Sometimes your analysis of one of your reasons may be longer or you may remember more evidence for it, but there is no need to worry about that. Your response will be marked in a holistic manner.

» To get into the top mark bands, you need to include substantial analysis and evaluation.

» You might want to state which reason has more significance, as this will help you to analyse.

» You should use examples to support your ideas.

» You must use the Item. It will help form the basis of your ideas, but you must develop its points and not simply repeat them.

C grade response

One reason why women are less likely to be involved in crime and deviant activities is due to a lack of opportunities to do so because of other commitments. Feminists believe that the family is a patriarchal unit and in the traditional nuclear family the female has the role of a housewife. This means that a large part of her time is spent in the home carrying out cooking, cleaning, ironing and the general maintenance of the house. The majority of crimes occur outside of the home environment and therefore women may not be in a position to carry these out or have the time to actually carry out a crime.

The candidate misses an opportunity to analyse this point; for example, by exploring how the role of women has changed in society and they now have more opportunities.

Women are also more likely to have the task of childcare which again takes up both time and focus. Feminists such as Oakley note how women are still expected to carry out the majority of childcare duties such as taking the children to and from school, sorting out uniform and clothing for the children and making their appointments for the doctor or dentist. The role of primary child-carer is of course a demanding and time intensive role which would not allow much time to be involved in any criminal or deviant activities.

The second point essentially makes the same point as the first. Oakley could have been used to explain sex-role theory and how girls are socialised by the family into a more passive and law-abiding role.

Examiner's comments

This response shows good knowledge but it repeats the same idea. Sociological evidence is present and accurately applied to the question; however, there is a lack of analysis.

Mark 6/10

A grade response

Official statistics show that women are less likely to be involved in criminal and deviant behaviour and one reason for this, as mentioned in the Item, is that women have less opportunity to participate in such activities. Marsh notes that in a patriarchal society women are less likely to be in control of finances in the family and therefore less likely to steal to provide or be involved in a financial fraud compared to men. Likewise, Abbott and Wallace argue that women are given less freedom to be independent outside of the home and so this system of patriarchy means lots of female time is restricted to the home rather than in places which offer opportunities for crimes to be conducted. This of course is a changing trend as Adler refers to the liberation thesis in that society is becoming less patriarchal and as a result female crime rates are increasing.

This point is fully supported with relevant sociological evidence.

A further reason for lower female crime rates can be linked to cultural factors and primary socialisation. Heidensohn refers to this as sex role theory in that girls are more likely to be brought up as passive and conformist while boys are socialised into being tough and risk taking. Oakley also refers to canalisation within toys given to children whereby girls are given empathetic and caring toys such as dolls whereas boys receive toy guns and action figures, which shows that early socialisation can influence attitudes towards non-conformist behaviour. Carlen argues however that female crime is actually higher than statistics in some cultures suggest but the chivalry thesis means that many females are not punished due to their femininity and therefore fall into the dark figure of crime.

This is a sophisticated point and displays a good range of accurate sociological material.

Therefore, there are various reasons why female criminal activity may be lower than that of males but, as Westwood notes, gender identities are changing particularly in western societies and the gender-quake (women have made an impact on shaking up traditional roles) means that women are now more likely to adopt male characteristics and vice versa.

> The candidate is able to introduce a new concept and draw a conclusion which has an analytical tone.

Examiner's comments

This response shows two very distinct reasons for low female crime in terms of opportunities and then socialisation. These two points build on the Item and the response applies relevant sociological material. Analysis and evaluation are present at the end of each paragraph and at the end of the answer.

Mark 10/10

0 4   Read **Item B** and answer the question that follows.

Item B

Most sociological theories have assumed that crime and deviance are harmful to society. They have concentrated on explaining why crime and deviance occur and have assumed that something must have gone wrong in society to cause the criminality and deviance. They have therefore tended to advocate new policies to reduce deviance and offending.

However, other sociological theories have suggested that crime and deviancy can be functional for a society and help a society to evolve.

Applying the material from **Item B** and your own knowledge, evaluate the view that crime can be functional for a society.

[30 marks]

Remember

> This question requires an essay-style answer and must be written in continuous prose with a short introduction and conclusion. You may find it helpful to make a short plan.

> This question carries the most marks.

> Spend around 45 minutes on this question.

> Each point you make must be developed with some sociological theory, a sociological study or some evidence.

> To get into the top mark bands, you need to include substantial analysis and evaluation.

> Keep referring back to the question so your response stays relevant. Make sure that you meet the demands of the question by referring to the Item, applying your own knowledge and evaluating the view in the question.

> You must use the Item. It will help form the basis of your ideas, but you must develop its ideas and not simply repeat them.

> A short conclusion is required. However, it must add some value rather than just summarising. In the conclusion, try to give a direct answer to the question based upon the arguments you have put forward.

C grade response

Functionalists believe that crime can be positive for society and should not always be seen as a negative thing. They believe that crime 'can be functional for a society and help a society to evolve' (Item B).

Functionalists such as Durkheim believe that deviant behaviour is useful for society as it helps set the boundaries in society for what is and is not acceptable. In fact he says crime is necessary because people need to know where the boundaries of acceptable behaviour are. He believed that crime can actually be healthy for a society because it praises those that do not commit crimes and punishes those that do; the law therefore acts as a form of socialisation.

Albert Cohen also agreed with Durkheim by saying that criminal behaviour actually maintains social order and stability as it can act as a safety valve for letting off tension. For example acts such as visiting prostitutes and protests are examples of people using a criminal or deviant act to release tension and frustration. Without this outlet then people would feel even more restricted by what they can and cannot do in society.

Marxists, however, believe that crime is negative for society and the reason for crime is not functional but it is rather due to the unfair system of capitalism. Marxists believe that if there was more equality in society between the rich and the poor then the crime rate would fall. In other words they believe that communism would make people less greedy and would get rid of poverty and therefore crime rates would fall.

Functionalists also believe that crime can be used to assist the consensus of social control. By this they mean that people begin to have a clear idea of what is acceptable in society and what is not. This forms what are called norms: the expected forms of behaviour in any society. Likewise the fear of going to prison acts as a sanction and a mechanism to stop people offending.

Feminists, however, argue that crime is still a male dominated activity. It is estimated that 80% of all crime is conducted by men and therefore feminists would criticise the functionalist view as crime is clearly linked to male power and the system of patriarchy. Feminists would also be critical of the nature of male on female crime serving a function, for example rape or domestic violence could never be functional for a society, but functionalists ignore this.

Functionalism is also considered rather outdated now as much of it was written a long time ago and issues to do with crime, crime monitoring and policing have massively changed since the likes of Durkheim were writing. Functionalism is also considered to be too simplistic as it does not accept the negative impacts of crime on both the individual and wider society.

This is a basic introduction which is essentially recycled from the Item. The candidate could have explored an opposing theory such as Marxism. Marxists would not agree with the idea of crime being functional.

This is an accurate point but it lacks depth. More could have been added on the work of Durkheim such as a discussion on crime levels, anomie and the positive functions of deviancy. Relevant examples could have been added with some evaluation from a different sociological perspective.

This could have been evaluated with a feminist critique.

This point is valid yet it is not developed well. Marxist criminology suggests that crime could be functional for the ruling classes, as they make laws to suit and protect themselves while the actions of the working class are much more likely to be seen as criminal.

This point lacks evidence. Erikson on the publicity function of crime could be added, or Althusser on the ideological state apparatus.

This point is well developed with some sociological evidence; there is some basic evaluation also.

Although simple ideas are presented, this paragraph lacks development. Some evaluation is included. However, this evaluation could be more in-depth and could be based on more specific and contemporary examples and theory.

In conclusion, crime can be functional for society on a small scale by reminding people of appropriate boundaries of what is acceptable. However, it must also be considered that crime is a form of dysfunction and is the main problem for many societies even in very developed countries such as the USA.

A conclusion is present but it is summative and adds little to the response. The candidate could have reached a critical conclusion that answers the question: is crime functional or not?

Examiner's comments

This response shows a range of basic knowledge and understanding of the functionalist viewpoint. There is a lack of depth and analysis to the points made. Other sociological theory is presented yet it is not always made explicit to the question. Evaluation lacks range and depth.

Mark 18/30

A grade response

The view that crime can be both functional and necessary for society comes from the functionalist perspective which is known as a consensus theory and therefore says that crime is required in a society in order for society to remain stable and to develop and progress. Conflict theorists such as Marxists and feminists disagree, however, and focus on the negative aspects of crime and the necessity to both understand and reduce crime in order to improve the societies that we all live in.

This is a comprehensive introduction which displays clear knowledge of not only functionalism but also opposing theories.

Durkheim first developed the idea of crime being functional for society in the late 1800s by arguing that a society can only develop through deviance. By this he means that deviant acts become re-evaluated all the time by people and therefore acts that were once deviant may become non-deviant in the future. For Durkheim, it was healthy for a 'society to evolve' as stated in the Item. Durkheim notes that this assessment of behaviour meant that new boundaries could be set and that actually a society with no crime or deviance cannot progress. The interactionist Lemert is critical of Durkheim's ideas, however, as he stated that deviant behaviour is only labelled after it has occurred in what he calls secondary deviance. Therefore, Lemert felt that deviant behaviour is not always agreed upon by those in society as the same behaviour often gains differing reactions. This means deviance could only create progress if most people agreed an act was deviant and society needed to change.

This point is well developed, displays a range of sociological evidence and has theoretical evaluation.

Durkheim suggested that there were a range of positive functions of deviancy such as strengthening bonds and social cohesion, or producing changes in law. For example, when a heinous crime takes place it can shock a community, and they can be brought closer together through a support network reaffirming the commitment to the value consensus. Or if enough members feel strongly about a crime or about something which wasn't deviant but now is, they could make a change in society and potentially make society better.

This point displays sound knowledge of positive functions of deviancy; however, it lacks depth and sociological evidence. The candidate could have provided an example of how bonds are strengthened. Responses to terror attacks in recent years could have been used as one example. An example of a law change could have been provided such as the hunting act or the ban on smoking in public places. This point also lacks evaluation.

324

Merton, although a functionalist, believes that a high level of crime is dysfunctional and indicates that something has gone wrong with the structure and culture of society. He stated it is often a response to not achieving the goals of society; he refers to this as the strain theory. Merton uses the example of the American dream as being the path many would like to follow. For him crime is a reaction by those who do not reach that goal. When people place all their emphasis on success and not enough on sticking to society's norms, then anomie occurs and some people 'innovate' by turning to crime to get what they want. Merton, however, assumes that everybody has the same success goals (money and power) when some people may make a happy family life their priority. This raises the important point that if groups in society have different goals then it can be difficult to decide whether crime is functional for society or not, it might be good for some but bad for others.

> This a comprehensive point which is evaluated and developed to provide some thoughtful evaluation of whether it is possible to decide whether crime is functional or not.

Hirschi took a different approach to exploring the nature of crime and deviance. Instead of the focus being on why people commit crime, he focused on why most do not commit crime. He argued that bonds of attachment, such as how involved with society they are, prevent a person from committing crime. This means that those who are less bonded to society may commit crime. Therefore, Hirschi does not agree with Durkheim and does not think that crime is functional for society as it means too many lack the bonds of attachment.

> This point is sophisticated and links a different theoretical approach to the question. It has an analytical tone, yet it does lack depth and some examples of bonds of attachment could be given.

Taylor, Walton and Young disagree with this theory for assuming that the majority of people always aspire to be part of the mainstream legitimate culture and that people always desire wealth and status. It also ignores the fact that some people drift in and out of legitimate and illegitimate opportunity structures rather than following a linear path. Marxists also argue that the illegitimate structure is only apparent due to the capitalist system; Pearce refers to this as criminogenic, meaning that capitalism naturally leads to crime because it causes people to be greedy, jealous and desire more. Marxists argue that if society were more socialist and based on equality then the crime rates would naturally reduce anyway.

> This paragraph has a reflective analytical tone.

The social action approach is also critical of the functionalist view for failing to look at individual factors surrounding criminality. Becker, for example, notes that functionalists focus on the causes of crime rather than the labels and reactions to criminal behaviour. By this he means that functionalists look at the structures of institutions and agents in impacting crime rather than focusing on the individual idiosyncrasies that cause one person to be deviant or commit a crime. Furthermore, he believes that the labelling of crime leads to further deviance as labelling becomes a self-fulfilling prophecy and causes deviance amplification. Rather than benefiting society, this harms it as well as causing problems for the individuals who are labelled. For example, Jock Young, writing as a labelling theorist, showed how the labelling of marihuana smokers in Notting Hill led to more people turning to hard drugs.

This paragraph displays some in-depth application and evaluation skills.

Therefore, there is evidence that crime can provide a function for society because it reinforces boundaries and allows society to develop and change over a period of time. For functionalists, progression and development can only come about as a result of deviant behaviour. For conflict theorists, however, this is naïve as they believe that a society with fewer crimes and more equality would actually lead to more social and political progress.

Examiner's comments

This response has both range and depth and displays comprehensive knowledge and understanding. The candidate makes use of the Item and also presents a range of sociological material from their own knowledge. The use of theory and sociological evidence is sound and there is good range of analysis and evaluation.

Mark 26/30

A-level Paper 3 Theory and Methods exam practice questions

0 5 **(Example 1)** Outline and explain **two** advantages of using questionnaires in sociological research.

[10 marks]

Remember

> This is worth 10 marks and must be written in continuous prose.

> The question asks you for two advantages. You must make these clearly distinct. Do not be afraid to use sentence starters such as 'One advantage is...', 'A second advantage is...'.

> Spend around 15 minutes on this question.

> Out of the 10 marks awarded, you are not given 5 marks for each advantage. You will be awarded marks for the overall quality of your response. Sometimes your explanation of one of your advantages may be longer or you may remember more evidence for it, but there is no need to worry about that. Your response will be marked in a holistic manner.

> To get into the top mark bands, you need to include substantial analysis.

> You might want to state which advantage is more important, as this will help you to analyse.

> You should use examples to support your ideas.

C grade response

One advantage of using questionnaires in sociological research is that they tend to produce representative data; the reason for this is that questionnaires tend to be carried out on a large scale and therefore cover a big sample. The larger the sample then the more chance there is that a spread of people is covered within the sample group.

This is a valid and relevant point yet it lacks depth. The candidate could have discussed the positivist perspective of data collection. The point could have also been analysed by suggesting a weakness of using questionnaires, for example that a poor response rate could impact on representativeness.

A second advantage of questionnaires is that from a practical point of view they are fairly cheap and quick to produce compared to some other methods. Questionnaires can now be sent out online and therefore they can cost nothing to send out and often they can be completed and returned instantly. Many sociologists will use questionnaires as practically they are a fairly easy form of research to conduct if the researcher needs information quickly and efficiently.

This is another generally valid point but it also lacks some depth. To extend the discussion, the candidate could have pointed out that the time and expense involved in producing questionnaires can increase if they are tested in a pilot study.

Examiner's comments

This response presents two very clear points about questionnaires and while they are both accurate, they do lack depth. Analysis is simplistic.

Mark 6/10

A grade response

Questionnaires are a set of pre-set questions that tend to be conducted on a large scale and are more likely to be used by positivist researchers. One of the advantages of questionnaires is that they are likely to produce representative data. This means that because they tend to cover large samples of people the results are more likely to be reflective of a wider audience and it is therefore possible for the researcher to make generalisations. One such example of this is the national census which is a large scale questionnaire completed by each household every 10 years. The sample is representative of the population as it is completed by such large numbers, which therefore means generalisations can be made from the findings of this research.

This is a sophisticated point with relevant examples and analysis.

A second advantage of questionnaires is that they are considered to be reliable. This refers to the consistency of the data and the degree to which a questionnaire can give the same results each time that it is used. Questionnaires are reliable because they use pre-coded questions so that the same questions are given to different members of the sample. This consistency means that it becomes possible to look for patterns and correlations between the results. An example of this can be seen in La Pierre's famous questionnaire asking institutions if they would allow a Chinese customer to stay at their facility; La Pierre gained reliable results as he asked all the institutions exactly the same question.

The candidate could have commented on the possibility that questionnaires might lack validity depending on the topic being addressed and the type of question being included.

Therefore, questionnaires have the advantage of being both representative and reliable which are the attributes of research that positivist sociologists seek in order to match their top down, large scale form of research. They are criticised by interpretivists, however, for lacking validity, depth and detail.

The candidate reaches a conclusion which also displays analytical skills.

Examiner's comments

This response presents two very clear benefits of questionnaires and each is well described, explained and uses relevant sociological evidence such as census and the La Pierre study. Theory is used to support the points made and analysis is present.

Mark 9/10

0 5 **(Example 2)** Outline and explain **two** advantages of following ethical guidelines when conducting sociological research.

[10 marks]

C grade response

One advantage of following ethical guidelines is so that the sociologist does not cause harm to their sample group. This is a form of protection that needs to be followed. For example, if a sociologist carries out participant observation and becomes involved in the research then they run the risk of causing harm to the other participants; this would be particularly true were the sociologist looking at crime for example.

> The candidate could have suggested a way in which the participants may be harmed, such as having to discuss a personal or sensitive issue. An example of research could have been added.

Another advantage is so that the sociologist does not cause harm to themselves. A sociologist may put themselves in a vulnerable or dangerous position and therefore they may need to make sure they are protecting themselves. For example, in Venkatesh's study on drug gangs he put himself in a difficult and dangerous position and was held hostage by the group. He therefore did not follow best practice within ethical guidelines.

> This point is more developed but still lacks analysis.

Examiner's comments

This response provides two valid points but both lack some depth. The second point is stronger and provides relevant sociological evidence to support the point being made, though the analysis is a little simplistic.

Mark 7/10

A grade response

Sociological research should aim to meet ethical guidelines and good practice. These rules are set out by academic bodies such as the British Sociological Association (BSA) and the Social Research Association (SRA) and research may also need to be agreed by an ethics committee before it is published.

> This candidate displays excellent knowledge of ethical guidelines in sociological research.

One advantage of following these guidelines is due to the issue of informed consent and privacy; it is important that the sociologist accurately informs the sample group about the nature of their research and gains their consent to study them. Failure to do so may break privacy rules especially once the research has been made available for others to read. One such study that broke this code of practice was Humphreys' study of the tea room trade where he admitted to breaking privacy rules by recording the number plates of the sample group and following them. Breaking codes of ethical practice may result in the researcher not having their work published or even being stripped of their academic qualifications, plus it is always advantageous that informed consent is gained.

> This point is well made and uses relevant sociological material; analysis is present.

A second advantage of following ethical guidelines is there will be no harm or exploitation of the sample. Hammersley and Atkinson state that the researcher should avoid negative consequences for those being studied and should also not use respondents to gain information for little or nothing in return. The sociologist also needs to consider issues of harm to themselves such as in the research 'Gang Leader for a Day' whereby Venkatesh was held hostage for 24 hours by a drugs gang. Therefore, a key advantage of following ethical guidelines is for protection of the sample group and of the researcher themselves.

This point is also well made with relevant supporting studies and analysis. The candidate does miss an opportunity for further analysis. As the answer concludes, they could have suggested which advantage is most important, for example making sure that participants are not harmed in sociological research.

Examiner's comments

This is a strong response as it presents two clear examples of how following ethical guidelines is advantageous. Knowledge and understanding is well developed with both range and depth offered. Relevant sociological material is sensitively applied to the question, with some analysis.

Mark 9/10

| 0 | 6 | **(Example 1)** Read **Item C** and answer the question that follows.

> **Item C**
>
> Many sociological theories have based their ideas on the assumption that society has a structure. This means that human behaviour and identity can be explained by examining the structure of society, which is sometimes known as a 'top down' approach. However, other perspectives have challenged this idea. They see the individual as having a more active role to play in shaping their own behaviour and identity. Human beings are not always shaped by the structure of society but through their interaction with other individuals. This is sometimes described as a 'bottom up' approach. The focus of studying society should be to analyse the actions and interactions of social actors.

Applying material from **Item C** and your knowledge, evaluate the usefulness of social action approaches in understanding society.

[20 marks]

Remember

> This question carries the most marks.

> Spend around 30 minutes on this question.

> This question requires an essay-style answer and must be written in continuous prose with a short introduction and conclusion. You may find it helpful to make a short plan first.

> Each point you make must be developed with some sociological theory, a sociological study or some evidence.

> To get into the top mark bands, you need to include substantial analysis and evaluation.

> Keep referring back to the question so your response stays relevant. Make sure that you meet the demands of the question by referring to the Item, applying your own knowledge and evaluating the view in the question.

> You must use the Item. It will help form the basis of your ideas, but you must develop its points and not simply repeat them.

> A short conclusion is required. However, it must add some value rather than just summarising. In the conclusion try to give a direct answer to the question based upon the arguments you have put forward.

> Think about the different areas of sociology you have studied such as education or the family and apply examples from those as well.

C grade response

The social action approach to sociology adopts a small scale form of research and therefore tends to look at individual behaviours and studies small groups.

This is a short introduction; the candidate could have expanded on some of the key ideas from the social action perspective.

Social actionists or interactionist sociologists take a bottom up approach to understanding behaviour which means they look from the view of the individual. In order to understand individuals, social actionists will adopt small scale methods of research such as unstructured interviews, diaries and observations. The reason for this is that they are aiming to obtain detail, depth and the meanings behind why things happen. Sociologists such as Weber agree with this approach.

In order to make this paragraph stronger, the work of Max Weber could have been analysed.

An example of a social actionist form of research is Becker's research on teacher labelling in the classroom. This was an in-depth form of research that used observations to understand how teachers often categorise or label students based on attributes such as social class. Social actionists believe that small scale methods are more likely to provide valid and detailed information.

An opportunity is missed here to expand on labelling theory and to discuss how helpful it has been in the field of education. This would have displayed evaluative skills.

Small scale research also gives meaning and detail of individual behaviour. As mentioned in the item, 'they see the individual as having a more active role to play in shaping their own behaviour and identity' and therefore it makes sense to carry out small scale research rather than looking at large scale data on wider societies.

This point lacks depth: for example, which areas of sociology have benefited from this approach? The candidate could have included a discussion on a type of identity such as gender.

Positivists disagree with this approach however and believe that to understand society it is important to look at the structure of society and also the large institutions that hold a society together. Therefore, positivists believe that research should be carried out using large scale methods such as statistics, surveys and large scale questionnaires.

This paragraph displays some fair evaluative skills although the evaluation is a little superficial.

An example of Positivist research is Durkheim's study of suicide which analysed the statistics of several European countries. The aim of Positivist research is to gather representative data from large numbers, as this makes it appropriate to form generalisations.

This paragraph is accurate in terms of knowledge yet an opportunity has been missed for deeper evaluation, for example social action theory would criticise Durkheim's study of suicide.

331

Larger scale methods are also likely to be quantitative which means that it is possible to look for patterns and correlations as well being able to gain reliable data because the research can be repeated.

Therefore, social action theory is useful for small scale research to try to understand individual behaviour.

Sound evaluation here.

Although accurate, this is a summative conclusion that adds little value. The candidate could have compared a different approach and stated which approach has made more of a contribution to our understanding of society.

Examiner's comments

This is a generally accurate yet simplistic analysis of the social action approach that lacks both range and depth. There is some use of other sociological theory but its relevance is not always made explicit to the question. It relies too much on discussing methodology with a lack of theoretical content on, for example, Weber, interactionism, Marxism and functionalism. Analysis and evaluation remain underdeveloped.

Mark 12/20

A grade response

Within sociology there are two differing approaches known as structural and social action perspectives. An action based approach focuses on the behaviour of individuals to understand wider society. Functionalists and most Marxists however take a top down approach which means that the focus is on how society works in terms of structures within society.

This introduction shows good knowledge of the basics of sociological theory.

Early sociologists such as Durkheim and Comte adopted a structural approach to understanding society by looking at human behaviour using a model of society's structure to explain behaviour. They also adopted scientific methodologies similar to those used in the natural sciences to explain behaviour in terms of external stimuli rather than meaning and motives which are internal factors. Weber, however, suggested that if we want to understand human behaviour then we cannot take a scientific approach as humans have free will and consciousness. As the Item states, social action approaches see individuals taking an active role in shaping their own behaviour and Weber therefore thought it was important to adopt a different approach to research that aims to understand humans in an empathetic manner; Weber referred to this as verstehen.

Although the knowledge here is good, the candidate could have explained what Weber meant by the concept of *verstehen* and why it is important.

Weber developed the social action approach as he believed that to understand societies and behaviours we needed to look through the eyes of those being researched. He suggested therefore that ethnographic research was far more preferable to scientific research methods. This enabled you to understand the meanings behind behaviour. For example, he explained the actions of Calvinists in terms of a desire to be sure they had been chosen to go to heaven. Structural perspectives argue though that we can only understand individual behaviour by deconstructing the societal institutions that humans live within because, as the Item suggests, 'society has a structure'. Marxists, for example, note that you can only understand working class behaviours once you have analysed the capitalist system of oppression that the proletariat live under. For example, to understand crimes of the poor you first have to understand the unfair distribution of wealth in society that would drive a poor person into a possible life of crime. Therefore, the Marxist approach makes more of a contribution to our understanding of social class in comparison to the social action perspective, which only focuses on the meaning of belonging to different classes rather than why those meanings exist in the first place.

This is a comprehensive point which displays sound knowledge and understating. Relevant sociological material is applied and reference is made to the question.

The social action approach was further developed by sociologists such as Mead, who introduced the ideas of the 'I and the Me' and stated the importance of individual research because humans are such complex characters who portray a different persona on the outside (the me) compared to how they feel on the inside (the I), Mead believed that this can only be understood through small scale, in-depth research. Functionalists such as Durkheim and Parsons however believe that human behaviours are influenced by the agencies around them because all structures of a society are integrated and interlinked. Parsons used a systems approach and therefore believed that individuals must by definition be influenced by the agencies around them as we are all part of the same system. They acted to meet the basic needs or functional prerequisites of society.

Mead's research was also supported by the ideas of Goffman who developed the theory of 'the presentation of self' which argues that humans are like social actors who perform in front of others like actors on a stage. He therefore says that behaviours in relation to our gender for example are often due to expectations of how males and females believe they should behave and therefore they act accordingly. Feminists from both the liberal and radical perspectives however believe that our gender behaviours are enforced by the patriarchy within the system; Oakley for example states that women will often perform the housewife role because they are oppressed by men and had little chance of getting good jobs in the labour market.

The social actionist Cooley also identified the importance of detailed, small scale methods in his research on 'the looking glass self' in which he argues that human behaviour is developed through personal self-reflection. He notes that humans spend a long time thinking about and developing their character based on self-reflection of situations and experiences. Structural theorists would argue, however, that humans build their character based on the feedback from societies, for example people are likely to adopt the religion of their society or adopt the political opinions of their parents. Therefore, structural theorists believe that many behaviours are socialised into us rather than being based on individuals' decisions.

> This point has a reflective and evaluative tone.

Therefore, the importance of social action theory is key to understanding individual behaviours of humans and gaining an in depth, detailed understanding of society and the meanings behind individual actions. Structural theorists however would argue that you can only truly understand individual behaviour in the context of the wider society that an individual lives within. Interpretivism has taught us, however, that there is a way in which to study humans that does not have to adopt the scientific model of methodology but rather a more valid and rich form of data collection which allows you to get inside people's minds and understand their meanings and motives. Increasingly, sociologists are recognising that you need to understand both the structure of society and social action by individuals and groups. For example, Paul Willis in his study of the 'lads' in the education system showed how working class boys reacted to and dealt with their oppression in the social structure by rejecting school, having a 'laff' and forming their own subculture.

> The response reaches a sophisticated conclusion suggesting how the different approaches could be combined and illustrating it with an example of sociological research.

Examiner's comments

This is a strong response which shows an excellent range of knowledge and both social action theories and structural approaches are discussed. There is sound use of relevant sociological material applied sensitively to meet the demands of the question. There are also links to both theory and methods. Parts of the answer are a little simplified, but the answer provides a distinct and clear argument. Analysis and evaluation are present.

Mark 18/20

0 6 (Example 2) Read **Item C** and answer the question that follows.

> **Item C**
>
> Classic social theory was concerned with the changes in society produced through industrialisation and urbanisation, particularly in the 19th century. Many assumed that western societies had entered an era of modernity which would continue indefinitely. However, by the late 20th century important changes were taking place in UK society in science, technology and many areas of social life including education, the media and family life. These have meant there have been significant changes to UK society. There has also been increasing globalisation as countries became more interdependent and national boundaries became less important. Because of these changes, some sociologists argue we are now in the era of postmodernity and therefore classic sociological theories are out of date.

Applying material from **Item C** and your knowledge, evaluate the usefulness of postmodern approaches in understanding society.

[20 marks]

Remember

» This question requires an essay style answer and must be written in continuous prose with a short introduction and conclusion. You may find it helpful to make a short plan first.

» Spend around 30 minutes on this question.

» Each point you make must be developed with some sociological theory, a sociological study or some evidence.

» To get into the top mark bands, you need to include substantial analysis and evaluation.

» Keep referring back to the question so your response stays relevant. Make sure that you meet the demands of the question by referring to the Item, applying your own knowledge and evaluating the view in the question.

» You must use the Item. It will help form the basis of your ideas, but you must develop its points and not simply repeat them.

» A short conclusion is required. However, it must add some value rather than just summarising. In the conclusion, try to give a direct answer to the question based upon the arguments you have put forward.

C grade response

Postmodernists are sociologists who have developed ideas and theories based on the contemporary world in which we live in today; they believe that older sociological theories are now outdated and so new ideas need to be developed. Classic sociological theories such as functionalism and Marxism, however, disagree with the postmodernists as they believe that their theories are still relevant in the world today.

Postmodernists such as Bauman believe that the UK has changed significantly in terms of science, technology, education, media and family life as stated in the Item. One of the reasons for this is due to globalisation as scientific techniques and popular technology is available around the world such as Apple products from the USA and Sony products from Japan. However, it must be argued that globalisation and global products

> This introduction displays good knowledge of sociological theory. The candidate could have expanded on the key postmodern theme 'meta narrative' which is used to discuss how classic sociological theory is outdated.

are not available everywhere and some cultures and societies have not been impacted by globalisation to the same degree.

An opportunity is missed to add depth to the discussion of globalisation, perhaps using the work of Giddens.

Another Postmodernist idea is that a person could have a hybrid identity. This is the idea that because people are now more geographically mobile there are more people mixing with other cultures and living in new places, which means that cultures and behaviours are more shared rather than specific to a particular culture. Some criticise this belief, however, and state that what we are actually experiencing is Americanisation rather than multi-culturalism so cultures are being influenced by American television and fashion rather than mixing together.

An opportunity is missed to discuss the family and how modern families have become more multicultural and hybrid. The work of Stacey could be used to illustrate how families have changed.

Functionalist and Marxist sociologists believe in structural theories, which is the idea that the institutions and agents govern and control. For example, Marxists argue that society is formed of the bourgeoisie and the proletariat and it is the superstructure that holds this in place. Althusser for example says that the government and the law keep a clear divide between the rich and the poor. Postmodernists such as Lyotard however now think that there has been a breakdown of the meta-narratives, by this he means that no one believes in a blueprint for improving society any more and big structures no longer exist in the same way as they did in the past.

This is a good point but an opportunity has been missed to evaluate. For example, despite postmodernists arguing that social class is no longer relevant in the UK, there is plenty of evidence that social class does have an impact on an individual life.

Postmodernists such as Baudrillard also argue that people in society today have more freedom, choice and diversity and so attitudes towards issues such as gender and sexuality are far more liberal than perhaps they once were. For example, attitudes towards male and female dress, behaviours and roles are more equal than they were in modern times. Feminists, however, disagree with this and believe that a system of patriarchy still exists; radical feminists in particular believe that men still oppress women and that women continue to have less freedom than men.

This paragraph makes some good points which are supported with relevant material and it displays some evaluation.

In conclusion, postmodern ideas are interesting in order to understand the contemporary western world and some of the changes that have taken place in society; however, it is also important to consider that many of the ideas of structuralist theories are still also important in order to understand society today.

Examiner's comments

This response demonstrates some knowledge and understanding but lacks depth and range. Use of the Item is present with some expansion in places. There is limited analysis and evaluation.

Mark 12/20

A grade response

The postmodern perspective emerged within sociology because it was felt by researchers such as Bauman and Lyotard that the world had developed and progressed to the point that classic theories such as functionalism, Marxism and feminism had become outdated, and therefore a new approach should be developed that would represent the contemporary world. However, supporters of many classic perspectives within sociology feel that the issues they focus on and discuss are still just as relevant in the world today as they have ever been.

This introduction displays sound knowledge of sociological theory.

Bauman argues that key changes in society are a result of 'technology and globalisation' as mentioned in the Item, which is the belief that there is an increasing inter-connectivity between countries and more multi-culturalism that was not as apparent in the modern world. Bauman says that this is important as cultural traditions are mixing or fusing with other cultures to form hybrid identities or even become homogenised and therefore issues such as social class are more difficult to define compared to the two tier system Marxists discuss. Neo-Marxists, however, believe that social class and inequality are actually still very important in the world today and that the gap between the rich and poor is significantly widening causing a super-rich elite group and a growing underclass. Postmodernists therefore possibly overestimate the true extent of hybrid identities.

A fully supported point with relevant sociological evidence and evaluation.

Postmodernists also discuss the idea of hybrid identities in relation to gender as they believe that the impacts of the gender-quake have caused men to pick up more feminine characteristics and vice versa, which results in what is called gender fluidity where the social norms and expectations of each gender become broken down. Examples of this include the increasing numbers of new men, househusbands, alpha females and ladettes. Third wave feminists however believe that the suggested march of progress towards gender equality is overstated and the reality is that the system of patriarchy is still very much alive and well; El Saadawi in particular notes that the move towards gender equality is still alien in parts of the world such as the Middle East and Africa.

This point is sophisticated and uses different strands of feminism to evaluate.

Postmodernists such as Lyotard go even further in dismissing functionalist and Marxist theories through what they call the 'breakdown of the meta-narratives'. This means that postmodernists do not believe that the big scale theories of how society works are accurate any more and that there is no longer a definitive monopoly on the truth but rather we are in a state of what Baudrillard calls hyper-reality, whereby it is now impossible to tell what is real from what is not. The Marxist theorist Harvey argues that this is a rather simple view and capitalism still shapes the world. Consumers have more choice now, but this just helps to maintain the profits made by capitalist companies. It is also hypocritical because postmodernists themselves are forming their own new meta-narratives.

Lyons claims that another feature of the postmodern era is the change in religion so that it is being revived as a type of consumer product ('Jesus in Disneyland') and people can pick and choose their religion as a form of 'spiritual shopping'. This is unlike the modern era when the process of secularisation was taking place. Similarly, New Age beliefs are growing. So, while there is no single metanarrative of religion, the decline in religion in response to the growth of science is being reversed. However, Steve Bruce denies this and argues that religion is still in decline as it was in the modern era and therefore we are not becoming postmodern.

A final element to postmodernism is the view that humans now have more freedom, choice and diversity especially in the areas of science, technology, education, media and family life as mentioned in the Item. For example, in education there is a wider choice of courses and degrees to study compared to any other point in history and in terms of technology we have become media saturated with the amount of choice we have at all times causing us to become obsessed with consumerism. On this note, neo-Marxists actually agree and believe that we are indeed becoming more materialistic and they reference terms such as pester power whereby children continually ask parents for new toys and games. However, they think that the ability to consume is very much shaped by class differences in wealth and therefore doesn't produce freedom to create whatever identity you choose.

The points made show excellent knowledge and understanding. Analysis and evaluation is present throughout.

Therefore it is difficult to judge the usefulness of postmodern theory. Postmodernists have obviously introduced the sociological world to some new and interesting theories but it seems rather naive of them to dismiss the modernist theories and some of the classic theories completely as they are obviously still relevant to the world today. It seems that *postmodernism only concerns itself with the developed western world rather than considering a wider range of nationalities and cultures.*

Perhaps what we are realistically experiencing in the world today is what Giddens calls late modernity or high modernity, which is the idea that we are actually in a period that is a continuation of modernity rather than a clear break from it. In this respect postmodern theory would perhaps benefit more from building on and developing the ideas of classical sociology rather than simply dismissing them as outdated.

The essay reaches a conclusion which adds value and states a clear position which avoids over-simplification.

Examiner's comments

This is a strong and detailed essay which demonstrates excellent knowledge and understanding throughout. Key sociological terms are used and relevant sociological material is applied to the question. There is good application of theory here from both postmodernists but also classical sociology. Analysis and evaluation has both range and depth. The candidate makes good use of the Item and is able to reach a conclusion.

Mark 18/20

GLOSSARY OF KEY TERMS

2-step flow model A theory of media effects that claims that the effects are mediated through people's relationships with informal 'opinion leaders'.

Absolute poverty The inability to meet basic needs such as adequate food and shelter.

Accommodation Adapting religious beliefs in response to a changed environment.

Accommodating masculinity One that does not challenge the power differential between teachers and pupils.

Adaptation The need for society to set goals for its members.

Adventist sect A sect that emphasises that the end of the world is approaching and that there are a limited number of places in heaven for true believers.

Affective or emotional action Action directed by emotion, often regardless of the consequences.

Age effect The influence of being in a certain age group, e.g. young, middle-aged, elderly. This is associated with leaving home, being single/married, having children, being widowed, having life-limiting disabilities, etc.

Alienation The cutting off of people from their work, the things they produce, from others and from their true selves.

Anomie A situation where social norms are unclear, conflicting or unintegrated.

Anthropocentric An outlook that places the concerns and interests of human beings above those of all other creatures.

Anti-colonial struggles against British Imperialism The resistance to the colonial rule of one country by another, in this case the British Empire. Many of the post-World War II immigrants to Britain came from countries such as those in southern Asia and the Caribbean that had once been colonies of the British Empire.

Anti-Semitic Characterised by hostility or prejudice against Jews.

Anti-social personality disorder A personality disorder is a type of psychiatric disorder in which people habitually display abnormal patterns of thoughts, feelings and behaviour. People with APSD lack empathy and are generally callous, manipulative, impulsive and irresponsible.

Apostasy Abandoning a set of religious beliefs in a hostile environment.

Artefacts Things produced by the research process (resulting from, for example, a technical glitch or error) that do not exist in the phenomenon being studied.

Atheist A person who does not believe in the existence of a god or gods.

Audience cults Cults that involve little commitment by followers and little face-to-face interaction by them.

Austerity A policy based on reducing government spending as a solution to economic and social problems.

Authoritarian regime A type of state in which elections are absent or merely serve a cosmetic function (i.e. take place merely to make the regime *appear* to be democratic) and in which political power is concentrated in an authority not responsible to the people.

Bedroom tax The 'bedroom tax' is the colloquial name for a reform contained in the Welfare Reform Act 2012, which means that people receive less in housing benefit if they live in a housing association or council property that is deemed to have one or more spare bedrooms.

Beliefs Ideas or convictions that individuals or groups hold to be true even when they are not based on evidence.

Black Power A social movement that developed out of the Black Civil Rights movement in the USA in the 1960s dedicated to Black empowerment.

Blue collar An alternative label for the working class based on the typical colour of the shirts worn by people doing manual work in the past (ditto, white collar).

Bodily capital Aspects of people's bodies that can be used to generate an income.

Breaching experiments Experiments that goes outside social norms to see how people will react.

Bulimic society Bulimia is a medical condition in which the sufferer binges on food and then induces vomiting to expel it. Young is using the term metaphorically to describe a society that both draws people in culturally (to consumerism) and at the same time expels them economically through increasingly poorly paid and insecure employment.

Capitalist patriarchy The form that patriarchy takes in capitalist society.

Capitalist societies Industrial societies based on private ownership of the means of production and a market economy.

CCTV   Closed-circuit television.

Centrifugal and centripetal
Centrifugal forces draw people in; centripetal forces push them out.

Chain of memory   The way that memories (including religious beliefs) are passed down from one generation to the next.

Church   The dominant religious organisation in a society, which usually claims a monopoly of the religious truth.

Civil religion   A belief system such as nationalism that provides a functional alternative to conventional religions by fulfilling the same functions, for example by providing shared values and promoting social cohesion.

Client cults   Cults that offer services (courses or rituals) to their followers but that require little commitment.

Clientelism   A political or social system based on the relation of a client to a patron with the client giving political or financial support to a patron (e.g. in the form of votes) in exchange for some special privilege or benefits.

Closed belief system   A set of ideas that is not open to testing or criticism so its beliefs tend not to change. Religion and magic are seen as examples of closed belief systems. Religion, for instance, is based on faith rather than on the testing of evidence.

Closed system   A system in which all the variables can be controlled.

Cohort effect   The influence of belonging to a certain generation, e.g. the Baby Boom generation (those born mid-1940s to early 1960s) or the Millennial generation (born early 1980s to late 1990s).

Collective conscience   The shared morality of members of society.

Common-sense knowledge   The shared knowledge constructed to make sense of the social world.

Compensators   Beliefs that rewards can be obtained at some point in the future.

Conflict theory   Sociological theory, suggested by Marx, which views society as consisting of groups with conflicting interests vying for dominance. This can be contrasted with consensus theories such as functionalism, which see societies as essentially harmonious.

Confluent love   Intimacy, emotional communication and mutual disclosure.

Congregational domain   The site of conventional religious organisations where people meet together to pray in a consecrated place of religious worship.

Consensus theory   A theory that sees consensus – agreement – about values as essential for the welfare of society.

Conservative force   A factor such as religion or the mass media that inhibits rather than promotes social, economic or political change.

Consumerism   An ideology that encourages the acquisition of more and more consumer goods and services.

Contested concept   A concept or key idea such as religion for which there is no agreement on its meaning: it means different things to different theorists.

Contingent   Dependent on something else, accidental or arbitrary.

Control theory   A theory of delinquency developed by Travis Hirschi (1969) that explains non-delinquency in terms of the existence of a bond between the individual and society based on four elements: attachment, commitment, involvement and belief.

Conversionist sect   A sect that tries to convert as many people as possible to its beliefs.

Converts   Those who have committed themselves to a particular set of religious beliefs.

Correctional criminology   A label applied by critics to criminological approaches which take for granted that the purpose of criminology is to find out what's wrong with criminals so that they can be reformed.

Correlation   A statistical link between data.

Counter culture   A subculture opposed to a society's dominant culture.

Criminalisation   Making an act or omission against the criminal law.

Criminogenic   Generating crime.

Crisis of legitimacy   A situation where people start to question the government's right to govern.

Culpable negligence   A failure to do something that is legally required, for example, protecting employees from health hazards.

Cult movements   Cults that involve followers/believers fully and act as full religious organisations.

Cultural defence   The role of religion when it helps to reinforce and maintain ethnic identity and pride in areas where religious or ethnic communities are in conflict.

Cultural imperialism   The practice of imposing a culture, viewpoint or civilisation on people in another, less powerful country.

Cultural transition   The role of religion when it helps a minority ethnic group to cope with social change and migration.

Cybercrime and online fraud   Cybercrime refers to crime involving computer networks and online fraud is fraud facilitated by the internet.

Deductive approach   Starting with a theory and using evidence to test that theory.

Defamiliarisation   Looking at the familiar in new and novel ways.

Defence mechanisms In psychoanalysis, defence mechanisms are unconscious mental processes initiated to avoid experiencing psychic conflict or anxiety.

Degradational Designed to reduce an individual's social status.

Denomination A religious organisation that has broken away from the main religious organisation in a society and that accepts the legitimacy of other religious organisations.

Deprivatisation The process by which religion stops being a purely private matter and re-enters the public sphere.

Desacralisation The process by which supernatural forces are no longer seen as controlling the world.

Determinism The idea that all actions, decisions and events are determined by previously existing causes. In particular, the idea that behaviour is shaped by causes that are external to human beings, who are like puppets with society pulling the strings.

De-traditionalisation The rejection of traditional sources of claims about the truth, for example scientists and church leaders.

Deviance Actions that are seen to depart from standard and accepted ways of behaving.

Deviance disavowal To 'disavow' something is to claim that it is untrue, so deviance disavowal involves the rejection of a deviant label.

Deviancy amplification A social process in which actions intended to reduce deviance have the opposite effect. A deviancy amplification spiral can occur when attempts to control deviance feed back on themselves, producing increased deviance.

Deviant career A life-path based on pursuing socially disapproved activities.

Differential socialisation The contrasting ways in which males and females are brought up within and outside the family.

Diffuse religion Religion that accepts and promotes individualism and tolerance of different beliefs.

Disciplinary power Power that seeks to get people to follow social rules by threatening them with sanctions if they do not and by encouraging the development of self-discipline.

Disenchantment To Weber, the removal of religion, 'magic', warmth and humanity in an increasingly rational society.

Disengagement The withdrawal of churches from wider society because of their declining influence on other institutions, particularly politics and the legal system.

Disintegrative shaming Penal policies based on the idea that the way to reform offenders is to publicly shame them.

Documentary method The method that people use to give the social world an appearance of sense and order.

Dominant ideology In Marxist terms, this refers to the ideological power of the ruling class in society. In capitalist societies, for example, the ideas of the bourgeoisie are the ruling ideas.

Dramatisation Turning mundane events and situations into something dramatic.

Dramaturgical analogy A comparison of human actions with a theatrical performance.

Dual consciousness The idea that the subject class have two views of society, one based on ruling class hegemony, the other a true picture.

Duet theory The theory that it is the interaction between the victim and offender that produces the offence.

Dysfunctionalism Parts of society that are harmful to society as a whole.

Economic crisis In the 1970s the UK economy was under pressure from falling profits, faltering economic growth, rising prices and growing unemployment.

Economic determinism The idea that economic factors determine and shape human behaviour and the structure of society.

Ecosystem A community of interdependent animals, plants and micro-organisms, together with the habitat where they live.

Egalitarianism A belief that all members of society should be treated equally.

Egoistic Self-centred individualism.

Elect The people chosen by God to be saved and destined to go to heaven.

Embezzlement Theft or misappropriation of funds placed in one's trust or belonging to one's employer.

Emergent ideologies The ideologies of new groups that are outside the ruling class.

Enlightenment The period from the 17th century in Europe that emphasised reason, was sceptical about religious belief systems and put its faith in natural science and progress.

Entrepreneurship The taking of risks in order to set up a business. Both Thatcher and Reagan sought to encourage an 'enterprise culture'.

Ethnic cleansing The UN defines ethnic cleansing as 'rendering an area ethnically homogeneous by using force or intimidation to remove from a given area persons of another ethnic or religious group'.

Ethnomethodology   The study of the methods that people use to make sense of the social world.

Evangelicalism   A movement within Protestant Christianity that is seen as conservative in its support of traditional values.

Evidence Champion   A position in the Department for Education to ensure that policy decisions are based on evidence.

Exclusive definitions (of religion) Narrow definitions that include traditional religions but exclude other belief systems.

Existential security   The belief that your survival is not seriously threatened and can therefore be taken for granted.

False class consciousness   A false picture of the class system that conceals the exploitation on which it is based.

Falsification   Looking for evidence to disprove a theory.

Fantasy crime wave   An imaginary increase in crime.

Feminist methodology   A methodology designed to reflect feminist ideals and values.

Feminist sociology   A viewpoint which states that society is gendered, that women are oppressed and that society mirrors male dominance in the wider society.

Folk devils   Groups seen by the public as irredeemably evil.

Forces of production   The materials and technology used in the production of goods and services.

Fordist/post-Fordist production In the first part of the 20th century, manufacturing industry was based on high-volume, assembly line production such as that pioneered by the Ford Motor Company. Towards the end of the century, manufacturing turned to more flexible methods of production aided by advances in automation and ICT.

Function   The contribution made by the parts of society to the maintenance of society as a whole.

Functional definitions (of religion) Definitions that focus on the functions or roles of religion, or what religion does rather than what it is.

Functional prerequisites   The requirements that must be met if society is to operate effectively.

Fundamentalism   A form of religion whose adherents want to return to what they see as the core doctrines of the faith as set out in sacred texts such as the Bible or the Qur'an. Christian fundamentalists, for example, adopt a literal interpretation of Biblical accounts of miracles and the Creation.

Fuzzy fidelity   A vague belief that there may be some sort of religious or spiritual force without any adherence to specific religious belief.

Gender mainstreaming Embedding feminist projects in the institutions of society and the agendas of governments.

Geneva Conventions International rules – dating initially from 1864 – that apply only in times of armed conflict and seek to protect people who are not, or are no longer, taking part in hostilities.

Globalisation   An increasing interconnection between various parts of the world.

Glocal   A word formed by combining 'global' and 'local', drawing attention to the two-way relationship between the local and the global.

Goal attainment   Shared goals in society that direct behaviour.

Goddess religion   Religion that honours the Divine Feminine, the female side of the divine.

Greenhouse gases   Greenhouse gases are a group of compounds that are able to trap heat (longwave radiation) in the atmosphere, keeping the Earth's surface warmer than it would be if they were not present. The main one is carbon dioxide, which is released when fossil fuels such as coal and gas are burned.

Grounded theory   Starting from the systematic collection of 'concrete data' and building upwards to theory.

Hacking   Gaining unauthorised access to data in a system or computer.

Hegemony   The means by which the ruling class maintain their dominance and control over the subject class.

Holistic milieu   The networks of one-to-one encounters, small-group activities and commercial activities in which New Age spirituality is promoted and practised.

Hyperreality   The blurring of reality and illusion.

Hypodermic syringe model   A theory of media effects that likens the impact of the media to that of an injection of a drug into a vein.

Ideal victim   Someone who fits the ideal type (or stereotype) of a victim (not 'ideal' in the sense of preferable).

Ideological State Apparatus (ISA)   Mechanisms that transmit ruling class ideology, which enforces the submission of the subject class. They include the educational system, religion and the family.

Ideology   A set of dominant ideas in a society that distort reality and serve the interests of a particular group such as men or the ruling class.

Illegitimate opportunity structures   Illegal routes to financial success.

Impression management   The process by which people try to influence the impressions others form of them by regulating or controlling information in social interaction.

Inclusive definitions (of religion)   Broad definitions that could include traditional religions and other belief systems such as nationalism, communism and humanism.

Indexicality   Deriving sense of an object or activity by seeing it in terms of its context.

Indispensability   Institutions or social arrangements that are seen as essential for the operation of society.

Individualisation   A growing emphasis on the individual rather than the group.

Inductive approach   Starting with evidence and developing a theory from that evidence.

Industrialisation   The process involving the introduction of mechanised methods of mass production in, for example, the manufacture of goods in factories and the use of machines in agriculture to increase productivity.

Infrastructure   The economic base of society made up of the forces and relations of production.

Insider trading (or dealing)   Making use of confidential information to buy or sell stocks and shares illegally.

Insuperable   Too great to overcome.

Integration   The need for order and stability in society.

Inter-class truce   A situation where class conflict is limited because both sides are prepared to make concessions.

Interpretative frameworks/ frames   Ways in which the media represent the topics they cover to their audience.

Interpretivist and qualitative methodologies   Approaches which state that understanding human action involves seeing the world through the eyes of those being studied.

Iron Curtain   The Iron Curtain was the name coined by Winston Churchill for the boundary dividing Europe into two separate areas from the end of World War II in 1945 until the end of the Cold War in 1991. The term symbolised the efforts by the Soviet Union to block off itself and its satellite states from open contact with the West and non-Soviet controlled areas.

Islamic fundamentalism   Individuals or groups who favour a literal interpretation of the Qur'an and who see their religious duty as the establishment of a caliphate (a territory ruled by a person seen as a successor to Muhammad).

Knowledge claims   Information or statements (such as claims about what the world is like) that a particular individual, group or belief system believes to be true but are nonetheless open to debate.

Labelling theory   A theory of deviance drawing upon symbolic interactionism and pluralism.

Late modernity   The term used by Anthony Giddens for what he sees as a late phase of modernity.

Latent functions   Functions that are not intended and recognised by members of society.

Left   Those on the left are in favour of greater equality and see the state as having an important role intervening in the operation of capitalist economies (e.g. by providing unemployment benefit) or believe in replacing capitalism with socialism.

Left and right   Shorthand terms used to describe two opposed political outlooks.

Liberal democracies   Countries such as those in Western Europe and North America with political systems based on representative democracy in which individual rights and freedoms are officially recognised and protected.

Liberation theology   A movement of radical Roman Catholic priests in Latin America dating back to the 1960s, who promote political change, fight oppression and support the poor.

Life crises   Situations such as birth, puberty, marriage and death that could produce anxiety and stress.

Lifeworld   The world people live in on a daily basis.

Liquid modernity   Zygmunt Bauman's term for his view of the latest phase of modernity.

Longitudinal survey   A research method that involves following the same sample of people over an extended time period.

Lumpenproleteriat   Literally, the 'proletariat of rags' (from the German *lumpen* meaning rag), Marx's disparaging term for a class of people living on the margins of society and not in regular employment.

Malestream   A term involving a play on words ('mainstream') coined by feminist sociologists to draw attention to the way in which sociology had marginalised and ignored women's lives. Malestream sociology is characterised by its focus on exclusively men's issues and men's concerns.

Manifest functions   Functions that are intended and recognised as such by members of society.

Marginality Being outside the mainstream of social life.

Marketisation The process of subjecting the supply of goods and services to the forces of demand and supply.

Master status A social status that overwhelms all the other statuses that a person has.

Materialism The belief that money and possessions are the most important things in life.

Materialist A term to describe someone who believes that material forces (such as economic and technological factors) shape society, including people's beliefs and ideas.

Mechanism of social control A means by which individuals are persuaded to conform to the rules in society.

Metamorphosis A radical transformation from one thing to another.

Metanarratives Grand stories that claim to explain things.

Mixed methods Using different methods for the same research project, often mixing qualitative and quantitative methods.

Mode of production Marx used this term to refer to the prevailing system under which people produce the things they need to subsist. Examples include feudalism and capitalism.

Modernisation The process by which modern societies which are characterised by the increasing importance of rationality and the declining importance of tradition and faith develop.

Modernity A term often used to describe the period from the Industrial Revolution to the present.

Money laundering The crime of moving money that has been obtained illegally through banks and other businesses to make it seem as if the money has been obtained legally.

Monopolisation practices A monopoly exists where one company dominates the market for a particular good or service.

Monotheism The belief in one god rather than in many gods. Islam and Christianity are examples of monotheistic religions.

Moral crusade The campaign waged by moral entrepreneurs in order to get the law changed.

Moral entrepreneurs Individuals or groups who make moral judgements and seek to bring about social change in line with these judgements.

Moral panic Widespread public anxiety about a particular kind of crime or deviance.

Multiple aetiology Aetiology is the study of the cause or causes of sickness or disease, so the term is being used metaphorically to refer to the many causes of social ills or social problems.

Multiple interpretations Seeing the social world from different vantage points and in terms of different perspectives.

Multiple modernities Different versions of modernity that draw upon different types of tradition.

National Crime Agency (NCA) The NCA was established in 2013 to tackle serious organised crime in the UK. It replaced SOCA (the Serious Organised Crime Agency).

Nation-state An independent state where the majority of people are from one national group and share the same language, history and traditions.

Negative globalisation A negative experience of globalisation.

New Age A term for a wide range of broadly spiritual beliefs and practices involving non-scientific beliefs that emphasise the discovery of spirituality within individuals more than in external reality. People seek spiritual experiences, inner peace or growth through, for example, meditation, crystal healing and/or aromatherapy.

New Christian Right A term originating in the USA to describe Christian groups with links to the right-wing Republican Party. They have conservative views on social issues and want religious culture to be central in public life.

Non-functional Parts of society that have no effect on the rest of society.

Non-utilitarian crime Crime that appears to serve no useful purpose, and has no monetary gain, for example joyriding or vandalism.

Normal science Science that operates within an established paradigm.

Objectivity A value-free, impartial, unbiased view.

Objective/value free Research findings that are free from the values of the researcher.

Open belief system A set of ideas that makes knowledge claims based on the testing of evidence. As a result, its beliefs develop over time. Science is seen as an open belief system that tests evidence through observation and experimentation.

Open system A system in which it is not possible to control all the variables.

Outsiders People who are seen as living outside the boundary of respectable society.

Pacifism The belief that violence, including war, can never be justified and that conflict should be resolved through peaceful means.

Paradigm   A framework of concepts and theories that states how the natural world operates.

Patriarchy   Male domination and oppression of women.

Pattern maintenance   The need for value consensus.

Period effect   A change in attitudes or behaviour that affects all ages at a certain time period.

Phenomenology   The theory that sees the social world as comprising sets of social meanings that constitute reality for the members of society. Phenomenological sociologists reject the idea that there is an objective social reality underlying or hidden behind this subjective social reality.

Phishing   The sending of emails from supposedly reputable companies asking the recipients to reveal personal details such as passwords.

Pilgrims   Those who lack a commitment to one set of spiritual beliefs but who are still trying out different beliefs and practices seeking those which suit them best.

Pluralism   A theory of political power in liberal democracies which argues that power is spread out among numerous different interest groups and that the state mediates between these interests in the national interest.

Polarisation   The growing gap between the two classes in terms of income and wealth as intermediate groups sink down into the subject class.

Political correctness   A term coined by those on the political right to undermine efforts by oppressed minority groups to challenge their oppression by painting supporters of such efforts as overzealous and humourless do-gooders.

Popular culture   Cultural products such as popular music, reality television, blockbuster films and sport that are accessible to everyone.

Popular punitivism   The idea that the general public want politicians to be tough on criminals and will vote for those who promise to be so.

Positivism   According to Comte, a method of study based on directly observable facts, which can be objectively measured and quantified, and from which it is possible to identify cause and effect relationships.

Postmodernity   A term used by some sociologists for what they see as a new period following modernity.

Predestination   The belief that God has predetermined whether people will be saved or damned after they die.

Primary institutions   Institutions or social arrangements that are seen as essential for the operation of society.

Private sphere   The social world inside families and involving personal relationships.

Privatised religion   Religion of significance to the individual but which has relatively little connection to religious institutions and which has little or no importance in wider society.

Problematising   Identifying something as in need of examination rather than as something to be taken at face value.

Proletarian revolution   A period of radical change in society during which the proletariat overthrows capitalism, and replaces it with communism.

Proto-revolutionaries   People at the earliest stage of developing a revolutionary consciousness.

Psychoanalysis   A branch of psychology associated with Sigmund Freud.

Public sphere   The social world outside the family and personal life.

Pure relationships   Relationships based on confluent love.

Quantitative methodology   An approach to research which states that human behaviour should be quantified, i.e. put in the form of numbers.

Quasi-religious movements Movements concerned with spiritual issues such as ultimate meaning but which are not overtly religious. Examples include astrology, Transcendental Meditation and New Age spiritualism.

Rational action   Action directed by reason with a clearly defined goal and a selection of the most appropriate means to do so.

Rationalisation   The process by which actions are increasingly governed by trying to use the most efficient means to achieve given goals and not by, for example, tradition or emotion.

Realist approach   Assumes that events in both the natural and social worlds are produced by underlying structures and mechanisms.

Reflexivity   In the context of research, reflecting on yourself, looking back at your research, and examining how your values and background might have influenced your feelings.

Regimes of truth   Descriptions of the world that claim the status of being true and, by doing so, serve the interests of the state.

Reintegrative shaming   Treating offenders in a way that allows them to remain a part of society while making clear that they have done something morally wrong.

Relations of production   The relationships people enter into in order to produce goods and services.

Relative deprivation   Deprivation or disadvantage felt when people compare their situation with that of others.

Relative poverty   An inability to afford a reasonable standard of living according to the standards of the day.

Relativism   The idea that all knowledge is relative to time, place, culture and the individual, and that no one set of ideas reveals the whole truth.

Reliable   Data are reliable when different researchers using the same methods obtain the same results. Data can be reliable without being valid.

Religion   Often defined narrowly as a belief system related to supernatural beings or divine forces. However, there are several ways of defining religion including substantive, functional and social constructionist approaches.

Religiosity   The quality of being religious.

Renewed vigour   An increase in the intensity of religious feelings in response to perceived hostility.

Representative or liberal democracies   Types of states in which the government is made up of people elected by citizens to represent them in a parliament and in which citizens, in principle, enjoy a wide range of rights and freedoms.

Repressive State Apparatus (RSA)   Social institutions, such as the government, police and army, that control the population by the use or threat of force.

Resacrilisation   The process by which interest in and belief in the sacred is revived.

Residual ideologies   Ideologies of a social class that, although still important, is declining.

Response rate   The percentage of the sample that participates in the research.

Right   Those on the right emphasise freedom over equality and see a 'big state' as a threat to such freedom. They also favour private enterprise over state-provided goods and services.

Risk   The possibility of danger. As used by Ulrich Beck, 'the anticipation of catastrophe'.

Rituals   Religious practices or ceremonies comprising a set of actions that are carried out in an established order.

Role-taking   Placing yourself in the position of others.

Routinisation of charisma   The process by which the leadership of a charismatic leader is gradually replaced by leadership through bureaucratic organisation.

Ruling class   The class who own the forces of production.

Ruling class ideology   A set of beliefs that present a false picture of society and justify the position of the ruling class.

Scientific revolution   The overthrow of an established paradigm by a new paradigm.

Secondary institutions   Institutions associated with caring for others, such as the family and religion.

Sect   A relatively small religious organisation which is in conflict with other belief systems in a society. To Stark and Bainbridge, they are also offshoots of an existing religion.

Secular   Not having any connection with religious institutions, beliefs and practices.

Secularisation   The decline in the social significance of religion. According to Wilson's definition 'the process whereby religious thinking, practice and institutions lose social significance' although exact definitions vary between sociologists.

Selective exposure   People select which media messages they will consume.

Selective interpretation   People interpret media messages in light of their pre-existing knowledge, values and predispositions.

Self   A person's individuality and essence as seen by themselves and others.

Self-fulfilling prophecy   A prediction that comes true because it provokes people to act in ways that produce the predicted outcome.

Self-spirituality   The practice of searching for spirituality inside yourself.

Shell companies   Companies set up purely for purposes such as tax avoidance or evasion.

Simulacrum   A simulation. (The plural is simulacra.)

Situational crime prevention strategies   Strategies designed to reduce the vulnerability of crime targets or increase the likelihood of being caught.

Social action   To Weber, action that takes account of the actions of others.

Social action theories   Theories that see the meanings people construct as directing their action.

Social cohesion   The idea that members of society should share a set of values that unite them into a body of citizens.

Social construct   Something which has the appearance of being a straightforward and inevitable feature of human existence, but is actually a product of social processes.

Social constructionist approach (to defining religion) Rather than trying to provide a single definition that all sociologists would accept, this approach focuses on how religion is used in daily life.

Social differentiation The increasing physical and social separation of groups in society.

Social equilibrium The parts of society in balance.

Social exclusion Exclusion from mainstream society.

Social facts The institutions, norms and values of society that are external to individuals and that shape their behaviour.

Social fragmentation The division of society into a variety of cultural and religious groups.

Social mores Shared ideas of morally proper conduct.

Social order A society that runs smoothly without disruption and conflict.

Social policy Government policy on social issues such as poverty, education and health.

Social problems According to Worsley, 'social behaviour that causes public friction and/or private misery and calls for collective action to solve it'.

Social solidarity Social unity.

Socialisation The passing on of society's norms and values.

Sociological problems According to Worsley, 'any pattern of relationships that calls for explanations'.

Spiritual individualism Religion in which individuals follow their own spiritual path rather than following the teachings of a particular religious leader or religious institution.

Spiritual revolution A move away from traditional religions which are practised through attendance at churches or denominations towards spiritual beliefs in the holistic milieu of New Age small-group encounters, commercial products and services, and one-to-one therapies.

Standpoint theory The view that a researcher's position in society, their background and experience, can provide valuable insights.

State-socialist societies Societies with a centrally planned economy organised by the state, known as 'communist' societies because power was monopolised by a single party – the Communist Party.

Status frustration Feelings of annoyance and distress generated by the inability to acquire social respect.

Stigma Characteristics that are seen as socially discrediting.

Strong religion Religion that dominates people's lives and shapes the way they live.

Structural differentiation The process by which institutions in society become separated and specialised.

Structural location The position of different social groups within the social structure, for example the greater involvement of men in paid employment than women.

Structural theories Theories that see the structure of society as directing behaviour.

Structuration A theory that attempts to combine structure and action.

Subject class The class who are subject to the rule of the ruling class and who are oppressed and exploited by them.

Subjective turn/subjective life Concerned with an increasing emphasis on discovering your inner feelings and your 'true self' rather than meeting social obligations by performing social roles.

Subjectivity A personal view based on an individual's values and beliefs.

Substantive definitions (of religion) Definitions that focus on the substance or content of religion, or what religion is rather than what it does.

Summary offences Offences in England and Wales are divided into three categories: summary, triable either way and indictable. Indictable offences are seen as the most serious and must be tried in a Crown Court rather than a Magistrates' Court. Summary offences are seen as the least serious.

Superstructure The rest of society that is largely shaped by the infrastructure.

Surveillance society A society where surveillance technology is widely used to monitor people's everyday activities.

Symbol Something that stands for and gives meaning to an object or event.

Techniques of neutralisation A term coined by Matza and Sykes (1957) to describe a number of ways in which delinquents sought to deny that they had done anything wrong by reframing their behaviour in ways that made it seem reasonable or legitimate.

Teleology Explaining the cause of something by its effects.

The individual sphere The sphere of social life concerned with individual identity.

The middle ground New religious movements which developed after the 1960s and which have a mixture of characteristics that are typical of different types of new religious movement.

The Network Society Manuel Castell's term for his view of the latest phase of modernity.

The Reinvention Society Anthony Elliott's term for his view of the latest phase of modernity.

The sacred and the profane The distinction that Durkheim made between things that are set apart and inspire reverential attitudes among followers (the sacred) and ordinary, everyday things (the profane).

The Second Modernity/World Risk Society The terms used by Ulrich Beck for what he sees as a late phase of modernity.

The shadow economy Economic activity that is both unregulated and out of sight of the tax authorities where work is done for cash in hand.

The spiritual revolution Radical change in the nature of spirituality moving from the congregational domain to the holistic milieu.

The Third Way A new direction in Labour Party policy based in part on the ideas of the sociologist Anthony Giddens.

Theodicy of disprivilege A set of religious views that provides hope and/or explanations for the position of those who are disadvantaged.

Theodicy of good fortune A religious explanation for suffering that claims that wealth and worldly success are indicators of virtue.

Theodicy of misfortune A religious explanation for suffering that claims that wealth and worldly success are indicators of evil.

Total institutions Places where people are confined, usually under strict supervision, for 24 hours a day.

Totalitarian A type of state in which every aspect of citizens' lives is monitored and regulated by the government and there is an absence of citizenship rights and freedoms.

Totemism A form of religion practised by the Australian Aboriginal peoples in which a totem (usually a plant or animal) symbolises the clan and is sacred.

Traditional action Action directed by custom.

Trafficking Either the transportation and dealing of illegal products or the transportation and dealing of legal products illegally acquired.

Transnational religious regimes Religious movements that are independent of individual nation states.

Truth claims Statements or ideas that particular individuals, groups or belief systems (such as religions or science) hold to be true.

Typifications Common-sense ideas about the nature of individuals or groups which see them as sharing particular sets of characteristics.

Typology A classification of different types of something (e.g. religious organisations) that identifies the distinct characteristics of each type.

Unconscious Below the level of a person's awareness.

Underdogs Individuals or groups who are treated as inferior by society.

Universal Applying to everyone/ everywhere.

Universal functionalism The view that all parts of the social system make positive contributions to society as a whole.

Utilitarian Utilitarianism is the philosophical doctrine that an action is right in so far as it promotes happiness, and that the greatest happiness of the greatest number should be the guiding principle of conduct.

Utopian Imagining that a perfect (in this case, crime free) society is possible.

Valid Data are valid if they represent a true and accurate description or measurement.

Value consensus An agreement about the values of society.

Verstehen As used by Weber, a method for interpreting the meanings and motives that direct behaviour.

Vicariousness Enjoying the benefits of religion through the activities of others without taking an active role yourself.

Victimless crimes Crimes where there is no apparent victim because the act is consensual or because the perpetrator and 'victim' are one and the same person.

Weak religion Religion that is a matter of personal choice, does not dominate people's lives and does not claim to be the only legitimate religion.

World-accommodating new religious movements Religious movements that developed after the 1960s and that are positive about mainstream society and in which the religious practices tend to encourage or facilitate social and economic success.

World-rejecting new religious movements Religious movements that developed after the 1960s and that are hostile to the social world outside the movement.

Zemiology The study of harm.

Zero tolerance policing A policing strategy that involves treating even minor infringements of the law harshly.

REFERENCES

Abbott, P., Wallace, C. and Tyler, M. (2005) *An Introduction to Sociology: Feminist Perspectives*, 3rd edn, Routledge, Abingdon.

Abel-Smith, B. and Townsend, P. (1965) *The Poor and the Poorest*, G. Bell & Sons, London.

Adel, E. (2016) 'Understanding and explaining corruption: A case study of Afghanistan', Södertörns University, Department of Social Science.

Adler, S. (1975) *Sisters in Crime: The Rise of the New Female Criminal*, McGraw Hill, New York.

Akbarzadeh, S. (2012) 'The paradox of political Islam', in S. Akbarzadeh (ed.) *Routledge Handbook of Political Islam*, Routledge, London.

Aldridge, A. (2000) *Religion in the Contemporary World: A Sociological Introduction*, 1st edn, Polity Press, Cambridge.

(2007) *Religion in the Contemporary World: A Sociological Introduction*, 2nd edn, Polity Press, Cambridge.

(2013) *Religion in the Contemporary World: A Sociological Introduction*, 3rd edn, Polity Press, Cambridge.

Allison, D.B. *et al.* (2008) 'Obesity as a disease: A white paper on evidence and arguments'. Commissioned by the Council of The Obesity Society. *Obesity*. vol. 16. no. 6, pp. 1161–1177. June 2008. Authors: The Council of The Obesity Society. Available at: http://onlinelibrary.wiley.com/doi/10.1038/oby.2008.231/full

Almond, G.A., Appleby, R.S. and Sivan, E. (2003) *Strong Religion: The Rise of Fundamentalism Around the World*, University of Chicago Press, Chicago.

Althusser, L. (1972) 'Ideology and ideological state apparatus: notes towards an investigation' in B.R. Cosin (ed.) *Education, Structure and Society*, Penguin, Harmondsworth.

Amir, M. (1968) 'Victim precipitated forcible rape', *Journal of Criminal Law and Criminology*, vol. 58, no. 4.

Anderson, A.H. (2014) *An Introduction to Pentecostalism*, 2nd edn, Cambridge University Press, Cambridge.

Archer, M.S. (1982) 'Morphogenesis versus structure and action', *British Journal of Sociology*, vol. 33, no. 4.

Armstrong, K. (1993) *The End of Silence: Women and the Priesthood*, Fourth Estate, London.

(2001) 'September apocalypse: who, why and what next?', *The Guardian*, 13 October.

(2014) *Fields of Blood: Religion and the History of Violence*, The Bodley Head, London.

Atkinson, J.M. (1978) *Discovering Suicide*, Macmillan, London.

Babiak, P. and Hare, R.D. (2006) *Snakes in Suits*, HarperCollins, New York.

Badawi, L. (1994) 'Islam', in J. Holm and J. Bowker (eds) *Women in Religion*, Pinter, London.

Bainbridge, W.S. (2009) 'Science and Religion', in P.B. Clarke (ed.) *The Oxford Handbook of the Sociology of Religion*, Oxford University Press, Oxford. pp. 303–318.

Bandura, A., Ross, D. and Ross, S.A. (1963). 'Imitation of film-mediated aggressive models', *Journal of Abnormal and Social Psychology*, vol. 66, no. 1.

Barr, B., Taylor-Robinson, D., Stuckler, D., Loopsta, R., Reeves, A. and Whitehead, M. (2016) '"First do no harm": are disability assessments associated with adverse trends in mental health?', *Journal of Epidemiology and Community Health*, vol. 70, no. 4.

Barrett, M. (1988) *Women's Oppression Today: Problems in Marxist Feminist Analysis*, Verso, London.

Baudrillard, J. (1983) *Simulations*, Semiotext, New York.

Bauman, Z. (1992) *Intimations of Postmodernity*. Routledge, London.

(2003) *Liquid Love*, Polity Press, Cambridge.

(2007) *Liquid Times*, Polity Press, Cambridge.

(2012) *Liquid Modernity*, 2nd edn, Polity Press, Cambridge.

Baumberg, B., Bell, K. and Gaffney, D. (2012) 'Scroungers, fraudsters and parasites: how media coverage affects our view of benefit claimants', *New Statesman*, 20 November.

BBC (2004) 'Iraq war illegal, says Annan', 16 September, available at http://news.bbc.co.uk/1/hi/world/middle_east/3661134.stm Accessed 02/03/2018.

BBC (2015) 'Is Islamic State Caliphate here to Stay?' [online] Available at http://www.bbc.co.uk/news/world-middle-east-33291429 Accessed 15/02/2018.

Beck, U. (1992) *Risk Society: Towards a New Modernity*, Sage, London.

(2009) *World at Risk*, Polity Press, Cambridge.

(2016) *The Metamorphosis of the World*, Polity Press, Cambridge.

Becker, H.S. (1963) *Outsiders: Studies in the Sociology of Deviance*, Free Press, New York.

(1970) *Sociological Work*, Transaction Books, New Brunswick.

(1974) 'Labelling theory reconsidered' in P. Rock and M. McIntosh (eds) *Deviance and Social Control*, Tavistock, London.

Beckford, J.A. (1985) *Cult Controversies*, Tavistock, London.

(1996) 'Postmodernity, high modernity and new modernity: three concepts in search of religion', in K. Flanagan and P. Jupp (eds) *Postmodernity, Sociology and Religion*, Macmillan, Basingstoke.

(2003) *Social Theory and Religion*, Cambridge University Press, Cambridge.

Beirne, P. and South, N. (eds) (2007) *Issues in Green Criminology: Confronting Harms Against Environments, Humanity and Other Animals*, Cullompton, Willan.

Bell, C. and Newby, H. (1983) *The Problem of Sociology*, Routledge, London.

Bellah, R.N. (1967) 'Civil religion in America', *Journal of the American Academy of Arts and Sciences*, vol. 96, no. 1, pp. 1–21.

Berger, P. (1970) *A Rumour of Angels: Modern Society and the Rediscovery of the Supernatural*, Allen Lane, London.

Bhaskar, R. (1978) *A Realist Theory of Science*, (2nd edn), Harvester, Hassocks.

Bingham, J. (2016) 'Church of England attendance plunges to record low', *The Telegraph*, 12.01.2016 [online] Available at http://www.telegraph.co.uk/news/religion/12095251/Church-of-England-attendance-plunges-to-record-low.html Accessed 15/02/2018.

Bird, J. (1999) *Investigating Religion*, Collins Educational, London.

Blumer, H. (1962) 'Society as symbolic interaction', in A.M. Rose (ed.) *Human Behaviour and Social Processes*, Routledge, London.

(1969) *Symbolic Interactionism: Perspective on Method*, Prentice Hall: Englewood Cliffs, NJ.

Bonger, W.A. (1916, orig. 1905) *Criminality and Economic Conditions*, Little Brown, Boston.

Bottomore, T.B. and Rubel, M. (eds) (1963) *Karl Marx: Selected Writings in Sociology and Social Philosophy*, Penguin, Harmondsworth.

Bowling, B. and Phillips, C. (2012) 'Ethnicities, racism, crime and criminal justice' in M. Maguire, R. Morgan and R. Reiner (eds) *The Oxford Handbook of Criminology*, 5th edn, Oxford University Press, Oxford.

Braithwaite, J. (1989) *Crime, Shame and Reintegration*, Cambridge University Press, Cambridge.

Braun, V. and Clarke, V. (2013) *Successful Qualitative Research: A Practical Guide for Beginners*, Sage, London.

Brierley, P. (2001) *Religious Trends 3, 2002/2003*, Christian Research, London.

(2005) *UK Christian Handbook: Religious Trends 5*, Christian Research, London.

(2006a) *Pulling Out of the Nose Dive: A Contemporary Picture of Churchgoing*, Christian Research, London.

(2017) 'UK Church Statistics 2: 2018' [online] Available at http://brierleyconsultancy.com/statistics Accessed 23/12/2017.

Brierley Consultancy (2018) 'Strengthening Christian Leadership' [online] Available at http://www.brierleyconsultancy.com/ Accessed 23/12/2017.

BRIN (2011) 'Church of England statistics for Mission 2009' [online] Available at http:// www.brin.ac.uk/news/?tag = baptisms Accessed 21/10/2017.

(2017) 'The 2008 British Social Attitudes Survey' [online] Available at http://www.brin.ac.uk/figures/the-2008-british-social-attitudes-survey/ Accessed 23/12/2017.

(2018) 'Church Attendance in Britain, 1980–2015' [online] Available at http://www.brin.ac.uk/figures/church-attendance-in-britain-1980-2015/ Accessed 24/02/2018.

Brittain-Catlin, W. (2005) Offshore: The Dark Side of the Global Economy, Farrar, Straus and Giroux, New York.

Bromley, D. (2009) 'New religions as a specialist field of study', in Clarke, P. (ed.) The Oxford Handbook of the Sociology of Religion, Oxford University Press, Oxford.

Bromley, D.G. and Melton, J.G. (2012) 'Reconceptualizing types of religious organization. Dominant, sectarian, alternative, and emergent tradition groups', Nova Religio: The Journal of Alternative and Emergent Religions, 1 February 2012, vol. 15, no. 3, pp. 4–28.

Brown, C. (2003) 'Campbell interrupted Blair as he spoke of his faith', Daily Telegraph, 4 May. http://www.telegraph.co.uk/news/ uknews/1429109/Campbell-interrupted-Blair-as-he-spoke-of-hisfaith-We-dont-do-God.html Accessed 31/10/2011.

Brown, C.G. (1992) 'A revisionist approach to religious change', in Bruce (ed.) (1992).

Bruce, A.S. and Becker, P.J. (2007) 'State corporate crime and the Paducah Gaseous Diffusion Plant', Western Criminology Review, vol. 8, no. 2.

Bruce, S. (1988) Rise and Fall of the New Christian Right in America, Clarendon Press, Oxford.

(1992) 'Religion in the modern world', in M. Haralambos (ed.) Developments in Sociology, vol. 8, Causeway Press, Ormskirk.

(ed.) (1992) Religion and Modernization: Sociologists and Historians Debate the Secularization Thesis, Clarendon Press, Oxford.

(1995) Religion in Modern Britain, Oxford University Press, Oxford.

(1996) Religion in the Modern World: From Cathedrals to Cults, Oxford University Press, Oxford.

(2000) Fundamentalism, Polity Press, Cambridge.

(2002) God is Dead, Blackwell, Oxford.

(2011) Secularization, Oxford University Press, Oxford.

Burke, J. (2017) 'Rise and fall of Isis: its dream of a caliphate is over, so what now?', The Guardian. 21.10.2017. Available at: https://www.theguardian.com/world/2017/oct/21/isis-caliphate-islamic-state-raqqa-iraq-islamist.html Accessed 08/14/2018.

Burkimsher, M. (2008) 'Young people: are they less religious than older people and are they less religious than they used to be?', conference paper delivered at the 5th International Researchers Conference, Melbourne. http://drmarionb.free.fr/YoungPeopleReligiosity.pdf Accessed 04/10/2011.

Carlen, P. (1988) Women, Crime and Poverty, Open University Press, Milton Keynes.

Casanova, J. (1994) Public Religions in the Modern World, University of Chicago Press, Chicago.

(2003) 'Beyond European and American exceptionalisms', in G. Davie, L. Woodhead and P. Heelas, P. (eds) (2003) Predicting Religion: Christian Secular and Alternative Futures, Ashgate, Aldershot.

(2011) 'Cosmopolitanism, the class of civilizations and multiple modernities', Current Sociology, March.

Cassidy, J. (1997) 'The next big thinker', The Independent on Sunday, 7 December.

Castells, M. (2000) The End of the Millennium: The Information Age, Blackwell, Cambridge, MA.

(2009) The Rise of the Network Society, (2nd edn), Blackwell, Oxford.

(2012) Networks of Outrage and Hope: Social Movements in the Internet Age, Polity Press, Cambridge.

Chaiken, J. M. et al. (1974). The Impact of Police Activity on Crime: Robberies on the New York City Subway System. New York City Rand Inst., New York, NY.

Chambers, C. (2013) 'Feminism', in M. Freeden, L. Tower Sargent and M. Stears (eds) The Oxford Handbook of Political Ideologies, Oxford University Press, Oxford. pp. 562–582.

Chambliss, W.J. (1976) 'Functional and conflict theories of crime' and 'The state and criminal law' and 'Vice, corruption, bureaucracy and power', in W.J. Chambliss and M. Mankoff (eds) Whose law? What order?: A conflict approach to criminology, Wiley, New York.

Chambliss, W.J. and Mankoff, M. (eds) (1976) Whose law? What order?: A conflict approach to criminology, Wiley, New York.

Charlton, T., Gunter, B. and Hannan, A. (2000) Broadcast Television Effects in a Remote Community, Lawrence Earlbaum, Hillsdale, NJ.

Christiano, K.J., Swatos, W.H. and Kiviston, P. (2008) Sociology of Religion: Contemporary Developments, 2nd edn, Rowman and Littlefield Publishers Inc, Lanham, Maryland.

Christie, N. (1986) 'The Ideal Victim', in E. Fattah (ed.) From Crime Policy to Victim Policy: Reorienting the Justice System, Macmillan, London.

Chryssides, G. (1994) 'Britain's changing faiths: adaptation in a new environment', in G. Parsons (ed.) The Growth of Religious Diversity in Britain, Routledge, London.

Church of England (2016) Ministry statistics 2012–2015 [online] Available at https://churchofengland.org/media/2521560/ministry_statistics_2012_to_2015.pdf

Church of England (2016) 'Statistics for Mission' Church of England, Research and Statistics, London [online] Available at https://www.churchofengland.org/media/3331683/2015statisticsformission.pdf Accessed 17/10/2017.

Cicourel, A.V. (1968) The Social Organization of Juvenile Justice, Heinemann, London.

Clancy, A. et al. (2001) Crime, Policing and Justice: The Experience of Ethnic Minorities. Findings from the 2000 British Crime Survey. Home Office Research Study 223, Home Office, London.

Clarke, R.V. (1983) 'Situational crime prevention: Its theoretical basis and practical scope', Crime and Justice 4.

Clarke, R.V. (1998) 'The theory and practice of situational crime prevention', www.badlandsmm.files.wordpress.com

Clegg, S.R. (1992) 'Modern and postmodern organisations', Sociology Review, vol. 1, no. 4.

Cloward, R.A. and Ohlin, L.E. (1961) Delinquency and Opportunity, Free Press, Glencoe.

Cockburn, P. (2015) 'Life under Isis: The everyday reality of living in the Islamic "Caliphate" with its 7th century laws, very modern methods and merciless violence', Independent, 15 March [online] Available at http://www.independent.co.uk/news/world/middle-east/life-under-isis-the-everyday-reality-of-living-in-the-islamic-caliphate-with-its-7th-century-laws-10109655.html Accessed 16/01/2018.

Cohen, A.K. (1955) Delinquent Boys, Free Press, Glencoe.

Cohen, L.E. and Felson, M. (1979) 'Social change and crime rate trends: a routine activities approach', American Sociological Review, vol. 44, no. 4, pp. 588–608.

Cohen, S. (1972) Folk Devils and Moral Panics, Paladin, London.

(2001) States of Denial: Knowing about Atrocities and Suffering, Polity Press, Cambridge.

Collier, R. (1998) Masculinities, Crime and Criminology, Sage, London.

Collins, P.H. (2000) Black Feminist Thought: Knowledge, Consciousness and the Politics of Empowerment, Routledge, New York.

Comte, A. (1986) The Positive Philosophy, Bell & Sons, London.

Connell, R.W. (1995) Masculinities, Polity Press, Cambridge.

Cooper, V. and McCulloch, D. (2017) 'Britain's dark history of criminalising homeless people in public spaces', The Conversation, 10 March.

Cooperman, A., Smith, G.A. & Cornibert, S.S. (2015) 'US Public Becomes Less Religious', Pew Research Center [online] Available at https://assets.pewresearch.org/wp-content/uploads/sites/11/2015/11/201.11.03_RLS_II_full_report.pdf Accessed 15/02/2018.

Corston, J. (2007) The Corston Report: Building a Safe, Just and Tolerant Society, Home Office, London.

Crawford, A. et al. (1991) The second Islington Crime Survey 1990, Middlesex Polytechnic, London: Centre for Criminology.

Critchfiend, R. (1978) Look to Suffering, Look to Joy, American Universities Field Staff, Hanover, NH.

Croall, H. (2011) Crime and Society in Britain, 2nd edn, Pearson, Harlow.

Cumberbatch, G. (2004) Video Violence: Villain or Victim? Report for the Video Standards Council.

REFERENCES

Cumberbatch, G., Woods, S. and Maguire, A. (1995) *Crime in the News*, Aston University Communications Research Group, Birmingham.

Daly, M. (1973) *Beyond God the Father*, Beacon Press, Boston.

Davie, G. (1994) *Religion in Britain Since 1945: Believing Without Belonging*, Blackwell, Oxford.

   (2002) *Europe: The Exceptional Case*, Darton, Longman and Todd, London.

   (2006) 'The future of religion and its implication for social sciences', in A. Droogers, P.B. Clarke, G. Davie, S.M. Greenfield and P. Versteeg (eds) (2006) *Playful Religion: Challenges for the Study of Religion*, Eburon, Delft.

   (2007) *The Sociology of Religion*, Sage, London.

Davie, G., Woodhead, L. and Catto, R. (2016) 'Secularism and secularization' in L. Woodhead, C. Partridge and H. Kawanami (eds) *Religions in the Modern World: Traditions and Transformations*, 3rd edn, Routledge, London.

Davies, T. (2016) 'Understanding the radicalisation of young British Muslims', *Sociology Review*, vol. 26, no. 2, November.

Davis, M. (1990) *City of Quartz: Excavating the Future in Los Angeles*, Verso, London.

Dawkins, R. (2006) *The God Delusion*, Bantam Press, London.

Dawson, A. (2011) *Sociology of Religion*, SCM Press, London.

Day, D. (1991) *The Eco-Wars*, Paladin, London.

Dean, J. (2017) *Doing Reflexivity: An Introduction*, Policy Press, Bristol.

de Beauvoir, S. (1953, first published 1949) *The Second Sex*, Jonathan Cape, London.

Delamont, S. (2003) *Feminist Sociology*, Sage, London.

Dill, B.T. and Zambrana, R. (eds) (2009) *Emerging Intersections: Race, Class and Gender in Theory, Policy and Practice*, Rutgers University Press, New Brunswick, NJ.

Ditton, J., Bannister, J., Gilchrist, E. and Farrall, S. (1999) 'Afraid or Angry? Recalibrating the "Fear" of Crime', *International Review of Victimology*, vol. 6, no. 2, pp. 83–99.

Dobash, R. and Dobash, R. (1979) *Violence Against Wives*, Open Books, London.

Donnison, D. (2001) 'The changing face of poverty', in M. May *et al.* (eds) *Understanding Social Problems: Issues in Social Policy*, Blackwell, Oxford.

Douglas, J.D. (1967) *The Social Meanings of Suicide*, Princeton University Press, NJ.

Downes, D. and Rock, P. (1988) *Understanding Deviance*, 2nd edn, Clarendon Press, Oxford.

Drane, J. (1999) *What is the New Age Still Saying to the Church?* Marshal Pickering, London.

Dunlop, S. and Ward, P. (2014). 'Narrated photography: Visual representations of the sacred among young Polish migrants in England'. *Fieldwork in Religion*, vol. 9, no.1, pp. 30–52.

Durkheim, É. (1938, orig. 1895) *The Rules of Sociological Method*, Free Press, New York.

   (1947, orig. 1883) *The Division of Labour in Society*, Free Press, New York.

   (1961 [1912]) *The Elementary Forms of the Religious Life*, Collier Books, New York.

   (1970) *Suicide: A Study in Sociology*, Routledge, London.

Edwards, R. and Holland, J. (2013) *What is Qualitative Interviewing?* Bloomsbury, London.

Eisenstadt, S.N. (2000) 'Multiple Modernities', *Daedalus*, vol. 129, no. 1 (Winter), pp. 1–29.

Elliott, A. (2009) *Contemporary Social Theory: An Introduction*, Routledge, Abingdon.

   (2013) *Reinvention*, Routledge, Abington.

El Saadawi, N. (1980) *The Hidden Face of Eve: Women in the Arab World*, Zed Books, London.

Engels, F. (1957) 'On the history of early Christianity', in K. Marx and F. Engels (1957) *On Religion*, Progress Publishers, Moscow.

Eschholz, S., Chiricos, E. and Gertz, M. (1997) 'Crime, news and fear of crime: Toward an identification of audience effects', *Social Problems*, vol. 44, no. 3, pp. 342–357.

Esposito, J.L. and El-Din Shahin, E. (2013) 'Introduction', in J.L. Esposito and E. El-Din Shahin (eds) *The Oxford Handbook of Islam and Politics*, Oxford University Press, Oxford.

Faith Survey (2015) 'Christianity in the UK' [online] Available at https://faithsurvey.co.uk/uk-christianity.html Accessed 23/10/2017.

   (2017) 'UK Religion Survey, 2017' [online] Available at https://faithsurvey.co.uk/uk-religion-survey.html Accessed 14/02/2018.

Farrington, D.P., Coid, J.W., Harnett, L.M., Jolliffe, D., Soteriou, N., Turner, R.E. and West, D.J. (2006) *Criminal Careers up to Age 50 and Life Success up to Age 48: new findings from the Cambridge Study in Delinquent Development*, Home Office Research Study, 299.

Faulkner, M. (2016) 'Religion in Africa' in L. Woodhead, C. Partridge and H. Kawanami (eds) *Religions in the Modern World: Traditions and Transformations*, 3rd edn, Routledge, London.

Fausto-Sterling, A. (2000) *Sexing the Body: Gender Politics and the Construction of Sexuality*, Basic Books, New York.

Ferguson C. and Hussey, D. (2010) *2008–09 Citizenship Survey: Race, Religion and Equalities Topic Report*, Office for National Statistics, London.

Firestone, S. (1974) *The Dialectic of Sex: The Case for Feminist Revolution*, Morrow, New York.

Foucault, M. (1977) *Discipline and Punish: The Birth of the Prison*, Pantheon Books, New York.

Galtung, J. and Ruge, M. (1970) 'The structure of foreign news', in J. Tunstall (ed.) *Media Sociology: a Reader*, Constable, London.

Garfinkel, H. (1967) *Studies in Ethnomethodology*, Prentice Hall, Englewood Cliffs, NJ.

Garland, D. (1986) 'Foucault's Discipline and Punish: An exposition and critique', *Law and Social Inquiry*, vol. 11, no. 4.

   (1991) 'Sociological perspectives on punishment', *Crime and Justice*, vol. 14.

   (2001) *The Culture of Control: crime and social order in contemporary society*, University of Chicago Press, Chicago.

Garside, R. (2015) 'Crime is down. Crime is up. What's going on?' Centre for Crime and Justice Studies, 24 April.

Gauntlett, D. (1998) 'Ten things wrong with the "effects model"', in R. Dickinson, R. Harindranath and O. Linné (eds) *Approaches to Audiences – A Reader*, Arnold, London.

Gautney, H. (2011) 'What is Occupy Wall Street? The history of leaderless movements', *The Washington Post*, 10 October.

Geertz, C. (1973) *The Interpretation of Cultures*, Basic Books, New York.

Gerbner, G. and Gross, L. (1976) 'Living with television: The violence profile', *Journal of Communication*, vol. 26, no. 2, pp. 173–199.

Gerth, H.H. and Mills, C.W. (eds) (1948) *From Max Weber, Essays in Sociology*, Routledge & Kegan Paul, London.

Giddens, A. (1984) *The Constitution of Society*, Polity Press, Cambridge.

   (1991) *Modernity and Self-Identity: Self and Society in the Late Modern Age*, Polity Press, Cambridge.

   (1998) *The Third Way: The Renewal of Social Democracy*, Polity Press, Cambridge.

   (2000) *Runaway World: How Globalisation is shaping our lives*, Routledge, New York.

   (2009) *Sociology*, 6th edn, Polity Press, Cambridge.

Giddens, A. and Sutton, P.W. (2013) *Sociology*, 7th edn, Polity Press, Cambridge.

Gill, A.J. (1998) *Rendering Unto Caesar: The Catholic Church and the State in Latin America*, University of Chicago Press, Chicago.

Gilliat-Ray, S. (2010) *Muslims in Britain: An Introduction*, Cambridge University Press, Cambridge.

Gilroy, P. (1983) '"Police and thieves" in Centre for Contemporary Cultural Studies', *The Empire Strikes Back*, Hutchinson, London,

Goffman, A. (2014) *On the Run: Fugitive Life in an American City*, University of Chicago Press, Chicago.

Goffman, E. (1959) *The Presentation of Self in Everyday Life*, Doubleday Anchor, New York.

   (1963) *Stigma: Notes on the Management of Spoiled Identity*, Penguin, Harmondsworth.

   (1968) *Asylums*, Penguin, Harmondsworth.

Goldthorpe, J.H. (1973) 'A revolution in sociology', *Sociology*, vol. 7, no. 3.

Gomm, R. (1982) 'Science and values', in R. Gomm and P. McNeill, *Handbook for Sociology Teachers*, Heinemann, London.

Goode, E. and Ben-Yehuda, N. (1994) *Moral Panics: The Social Construction of Deviance*, Blackwell, Oxford.

Gordon, D.M. (1976) 'Class and the economics of crime', in W.J. Chambliss and M. Mankoff (op. cit).

Gouldner, A.W. (1971) *The Coming Crisis of Western Sociology*, Heinemann, London.

(1975) *For Sociology*, Penguin, Harmondsworth.

Gramsci, A. (1971) *Selections from the Prison Notebooks: Notebooks of Antonio Gramsci*, Lawrence & Wishart, London.

Greeley, A. (1972) *Unsecular Man: The Persistence of Religion*, Shocken Books, New York.

Green, E. (2016) 'The Evangelical Reckoning Over Donald Trump', *The Atlantic*, 10.11.2016 [online] Available at https://www.theatlantic.com/politics/archive/2016/11/the-evangelical-reckoning-on-trump/507161/ Accessed 15/02/2018.

Green, P. and Ward, T. (2012) 'State crime: a dialectical view', in M. Maguire, R. Morgan and R. Reiner (eds) *The Oxford Handbook of Criminology*, 5th edn, Oxford University Press, Oxford.

Hadaway, C.K., Marler, P.L. and Chaves, M. (1993) 'What the polls don't show: a closer look at US church attendance', *American Sociological Review*, vol. 58, no. 6.

Hall, S. (1973) *Encoding and Decoding in the Television Discourse*, University of Birmingham, Centre for Contemporary Cultural Studies.

Hall, S., Critcher, C., Jefferson, T., Clarke, J. and Roberts, B. (1979) *Policing the Crisis*, Macmillan, London.

(2009) 'Rational choice theory', in P. Clarke (ed.) *The Oxford Handbook of the Sociology of Religion*, Oxford University Press, Oxford.

(2013) *Policing the Crisis: Mugging, the State and Law and Order*, 35th anniversary edn, Palgrave Macmillan, Basingstoke.

Hamilton, M. (2001) *The Sociology of Religion*, 2nd edn, Routledge, London.

Hammersley, M. (2011) *Methodology: Who Needs It?* Sage, London.

(2013) *What is Qualitative Research?* Bloomsbury, London.

Hannon, L. and Defronzo, J. (1998) 'The truly disadvantaged: public assistance and crime', *Social Problems*, vol. 45, no. 3.

Hartmann, H. (1981) 'The unhappy marriage of Marxism and feminism: towards a more progressive union', in L. Sargent, *Women and Revolution: a Discussion of the Unhappy Marriage of Marxism and Feminism*, South End Press, Boston, Massachusetts.

Harvey, D. (1974) *The Sociology of Housework*, Martin Robertson, Oxford.

(2010) *The Enigma of Capital and the Crises of Capitalism*, Profile Books, London.

(2011) 'The party of Wall Street meets its Nemesis', SocialistWorker.org blog 29.10.2011.

(2014) *Seventeen Contradictions and the End of Capitalism*, Profile Books, London.

Hedderman, C. (2010) 'Government policy on women offenders: Labour's legacy and the Coalition's challenge', *Punishment and Society*, vol. 12, no. 4.

Heelas, P. (1996) 'De-traditionalisation of religion and self: The New Age and postmodernity' in

K. Flanagan and P. Jupp (eds) *Postmodernity, Sociology and Religion*, Macmillan, Basingstoke.

(1996) *The New Age Movement*, Blackwell, Oxford.

(2015) 'Religion and sources of significance' in Holborn, M. (ed.) *Contemporary Sociology* Polity Press, Oxford.

Heelas, P., Woodhead, L., Seel, B., Tusting, K. and Szerszynski, B. (2005) *The Spiritual Revolution: Why Religion is Giving Way to Spirituality*, Blackwell, Oxford.

Heidensohn, F. (1985) *Women and Crime*, Macmillan, London.

(2002) 'Gender and crime', in Maguire *et al.* (eds) (2002) *The Oxford Handbook of Criminology*, 3rd edn, Oxford University Press, Oxford.

Heidensohn, F. and Silvestri, M. (2012) 'Gender and crime', in M. Maguire, R. Morgan and R. Reiner (eds) *The Oxford Handbook of Criminology*, 5th edn, Oxford University Press, Oxford.

Heilman, B., Barker, G., and Harrison, A. (2017). *The Man Box: A Study on Being a Young Man in the US, UK, and Mexico*. Promundo-US and Unilever, Washington, DC and London.

Hervieu-Léger, D. (2000) *Religion as a Chain of Memory*, Polity Press, Cambridge.

(2006) 'The role of religion in establishing social cohesion', *Eurozine*, 17/08/2016.

Hesseling, R. (1994) 'Displacement: A review of the empirical literature', in *Crime Prevention Studies*, vol. 3, edited by Ronald V. Clarke. Criminal Justice Press, Monsey, NY.

Hillyard, P., Pantazis, C., Tombs, S. and Gordon, D. (eds) (2004) *Beyond Criminology: Taking Harm Seriously*, Pluto Press, London.

Hindelang, M.J., Gottfredson, M.R. and Garofalo, J. (1978) *Victims of Personal Crime: An Empirical Foundation for a Theory of Personal Victimization*, Ballinger, Cambridge, MA.

Hinnels, J. (1997) *The New Handbook of Living Religions*, Blackwell, London.

Hirschi T. (1969) *Causes of Delinquency*, University of California Press, Berkeley, CA.

Hobbs, D. and Dunningham, C. (1998) 'Glocal organised crime: context and pretext', in Ruggiero *et al.* (eds) *The New European Criminology: Crime and Social Order in Europe*, Routledge, London.

Holden, A. (2009) *Religious Cohesion in Times of Conflict*, Continuum, London and New York.

Hollis, M.E. (2014) 'Assessing the experiences of female and minority police officers: Observations from an ethnographic researcher', in K. Lumsden and A. Winter (eds) *Reflexivity in Criminological Research*, Palgrave Macmillan, Basingstoke.

Holm, J. (1994) 'Introduction: raising the issues', in J. Holm and J. Bowker (eds) *Women in Religion*, Pinter, London.

Home Affairs Committee: Evidence, 24.03.2009. Witness Professor Kevin Browne, Nottingham University gave evidence, p.80 of House of Commons Home Affairs Committee 'Knife Crime', Seventh Report of Session 2008–2009, Volume II.

Home Affairs Select Committee (2009) *Knife Crime*, Available from www.parliament.uk.

Hope, T. (2005) 'Things can only get better', *Criminal Justice Matters*, vol. 62, pp. 4–39.

(2015) 'We need a different crime survey', Centre for Crime and Justice Studies, 21 May.

Hopkins Burke, R. (2009) *An Introduction to Criminological Theory*, 3rd edn, Willan Publishing, Cullompton.

Horton, R. (1993) *Patterns of Thought in Africa and the West: Essays on Magic, Religion and Science*, Cambridge University Press, Cambridge.

Hough, A. (2011) 'David Cameron defends ban on anti-gay foster parents', *The Daily Telegraph* [online] Available at http://www.telegraph.co.uk/news/religion/8370280/David-Cameron-defends-ban-on-anti-gay-foster-parents.html Accessed 14/02/2018.

Hough, M. and Mayhew, P. (2006) 'What is happening to crime?', *Sociology Review*, vol. 15, no. 6.

Hughes, G. (1991) 'Taking crime seriously? A critical analysis of New Left realism', *Sociology Review*, vol. 1, no. 2.

Hunt, S. (2004) *Religion and Everyday Life*, Routledge, Oxford.

Huntington, S.P. (1993) 'The clash of civilizations', *Foreign Affairs*, Summer.

Hutton, W. (1996) 'The 30/30/40 society: the economic and fiscal implications', *RSA Journal*, vol. 144, no. 5467 (March).

Iganski, P. (2008) *'Hate Crime' and the City*, Polity Press, Cambridge.

Jewkes, Y. (2015) *Media and Crime*, Sage, London.

Johnstone, R.L. (2007) *Religion in Society: A Sociology of Religion*, 8th edn, Pearson/Prentice Hall, New York.

Jones, J. (2015) 'Church attendance dominated by middle class' [online] Available at https://www.premier.org.uk/News/UK/Church-attendance-dominated-by-middle-class Accessed 09/11/2017.

Jones, P., Bradbury, L. and Le Boutillier, S. (2011) *Introducing Social Theory*, 2nd edn, Polity Press, Cambridge.

Jones, S. (2009) *Criminology*, 4th edn, Oxford, Oxford University Press.

Juergensmeyer, M. (2009) 'Religious violence', in P. Clarke (ed.) *The Oxford Handbook of the Sociology of Religion*, Oxford University Press, Oxford.

Kaluzynska, E. (1980) 'Wiping the floor with theory: a survey of writings on housework', *Feminist Review*, vol. 6, pp. 27–54.

Kaplan, A. (1964) *The Conduct of Inquiry*, Chandler Publishing, New York.

Kaspersen, L.B. (2000) *Anthony Giddens*, Blackwell, Oxford.

Katz, E. and Lazarsfeld, P. (1965) *Personal Influence*, Free Press, New York.

Kautsky, K. (1953) *Foundations of Christianity*, Russell, New York.

Keizer, K., Lindenberg, S. and Steg, L. (2008) 'The spreading of disorder', *Science*, vol. 322, no. 5908.

Kelly, E. (2001) *Routes to (In)justice: a research review on the reporting, investigation and* prosecution of rape cases, The Child and Woman Abuse Studies Unit (CWASU), London.

Kelman, H.C. and Hamilton, L. (1989) Crimes of Obedience: Toward a Social Psychology of Authority and Responsibility, Yale University Press, New Haven.

Kendal Project (2001a) Newsletter no. 1, [online] Available at http.www.kendalproject.org.uk/. Accessed 13/07/2002.

(2001b) Newsletter no. 2, [online] Available at http.www.kendalproject.org.uk/. Accessed 13/07/2002.

Kepel, G. (1994) The Revenge of God: The Resurgence of Islam, Christianity and Judaism in the Modern World, Polity Press, Cambridge.

Kitch, M.J. (1967) Capitalism and the Reformation, Longmans, London.

Knorr Cetina, K. (2005) 'Science, Technology and their Implications', in C. Calhoun, C. Rojek and B. Turner (eds) The SAGE Handbook of Sociology, Sage Publications Ltd, London, pp. 546–560.

Kramer R. and Michalowski, R. (1990). 'State-Corporate Crime', paper presented at the Annual Meeting of the American Society of Criminology. November: 7–12.

Kramer, R.C. (1992) 'The space shuttle Challenger explosion', in K. Schlegel and D. Weisburd (eds) White Collar Crime Reconsidered, North East University Press, Boston.

Kramer, R.C. and Michalowski, R.J. (1991) 'State-corporate crime', prepared for American Society of Criminology Meeting, Baltimore, Maryland, 7–12 November 1990, revised: September 1991.

Kramer, R.C., Michalowski, R.J. and Kauzlarich, D. (2002) 'The origins and development of the concept and theory of state-corporate crime', Crime & Delinquency, vol. 48, no. 2, pp. 263–282.

Kuhn, T.S. (1962) The Structure of Scientific Revolutions, University of Chicago Press, Chicago and London.

Lakatos, I. (1970) 'Falsification and the methodology of scientific research programmes', in I. Lakatos and A. Musgrave (eds) Criticism and the Growth of Knowledge, Cambridge University Press, Cambridge.

Lammy, D. (2017) The Lammy Review: An independent review into the treatment of, and outcomes for, Black, Asian and Minority Ethnic individuals in the Criminal Justice System, HMSO.

Lampkin, J.A. (2016) 'Green criminology and fracking in the UK: An application of utilitarian ethics', Papers from the British Criminology Conference. 2016.

Latour, B. and Woolgar, S. (1986) Laboratory Life: The Construction of Scientific Facts, Princetown University Press, Princetown.

Lea, J. and Young, J. (1984) What is to be Done about Law and Order? Penguin, Harmondsworth.

Lemert, E.M. (1951) Human Deviance, Social Problems, and Social Control, Prentice-Hall, Englewood Cliffs, NJ.

(1952) 'Stuttering among the North Pacific Coastal Indians,' Southwestern Journal of Anthropology, vol. 8, no. 4, pp. 429–441.

Levin, M. (2018) 'Here are Texas' biggest megachurches' Chron, 05.02.2018 [online] Available at http://www.chron.com/life/houston-belief/article/Here-are-Texas-biggest-megachurches-6071667.php Accessed 15/02/2018.

Lewis, O. (1951) Life in a Mexican Village: Tepoztlan Restudied, University of Illinois Press, Urbana, IL.

live from thessalonica (2009) 'Class and religion in the UK' [online] Available at https://demas.wordpress.com/2009/10/06/class-and-religion-in-the-uk/ Accessed 09/11/2017.

Loopstra, R. and Lalor, D. (2017) Financial Insecurity, Food Insecurity and Disability, The Trussell Trust.

Lynch, M. (1983) Art and Artefact in Laboratory Science, Routledge & Kegan Paul, London.

Lyon, D. (2000) Jesus in Disneyland: Religion in Postmodern Times, Polity Press, Cambridge.

(2015) Surveillance after Snowden, Polity Press, Cambridge.

Lyotard, J.F. (1984) The Postmodern Condition, Manchester University Press, Manchester.

MacGregor, S. (2001) 'The problematic community', in M. May et al. (eds) Understanding Social Problems: Issues in Social Policy, Blackwell, Oxford.

McGuire, M.B. (2002) Religion: The Social Context. 5th edn, Wadsworth, Belmont, CA.

McLellan, D. (1971) The Thought of Karl Marx. An Introduction, The Macmillan Press Ltd, London.

(1987) Marxism and Religion, Harper & Row, New York.

McLeod, D. (2017) 'Religious America secular Europe', in Hempton, D. and McLeod H. (eds) Secularization and Religious Innovation in The North Atlantic World, Oxford University Press, Oxford.

Macmillan, L. (2011) 'Measuring the intergenerational correlation of worklessness', CMPO Working Paper No 11/278, University of Bristol, Bristol.

Macpherson, Sir W. (1999) The Stephen Lawrence Inquiry, Stationery Office, London.

Maduro, O. (1982) Religion and Social Conflicts, Orbis Books, New York.

Maguire, M., Morgan, R. and Reiner, R. (2002) The Oxford Handbook of Criminology, 2nd edn, Clarendon Press, Oxford.

Malinowski, B. (1954) Magic, Science and Religion and Other Essays, Anchor Books, New York.

Mankoff, M. (1976) 'Introduction to perspectives on the problem of crime', in Chambliss, W.J. and Mankoff, M. (op. cit.).

Mannheim, H. (1965) Comparative Criminology, Routledge and Kegan Paul, London.

Marhia, N. (2008) Just Representation? Press reporting and the reality of rape, The Lilith Project, Eaves, London.

Marshall, G. (1982) In Search of the Spirit of Capitalism: Max Weber and the Protestant Ethic Thesis, Hutchinson, London.

Martin, D. (1969) The Religious and the Secular, Routledge & Kegan Paul, London.

(2013) 'Pentecostalism: An alternative form of modernity and modernization?', in R.W. Hefner

(ed.) Global Pentecostalism in the 21st Century, Indiana University Press, Indiana.

Marx, K. (1844) 'A contribution to the critique of Hegel's philosophy of right' Deutsch-Französische Jahrbücher, 7 & 10 February, Paris.

(1859) 'Population, crime and pauperism', New York Daily Tribune, 16 September.

(1964) Selected Writings in Sociology and Social Philosophy (translated by T.B. Bottomore), McGraw-Hill: London.

Marx, K. and Engels, F. (1957) On Religion, Progress Publishers, Moscow.

Mayer, J.P. (1943) Max Weber and German Politics, Faber & Faber: London.

Matthews, R. (2005) 'The myth of punitiveness', Theoretical Criminology, vol. 9, no. 2.

Matza, D. (1964) Delinquency and Drift, John Wiley & Sons, New York.

Maynard, M. (1989) Sociological Theory, Longman, Harlow.

McCabe, B.A. and Martin, G.M. (2005) School Violence, the Media and Criminal Justice Responses, Peter Lang, New York.

McLaughlin, E. (2001) 'States of fear', in J. Muncie and E. McLaughlin (eds), The Problem of Crime, Sage, London.

McRobbie, A. and Thornton, S. (1995) 'Rethinking "moral panic" for multi-mediated social worlds', British Journal of Sociology, vol. 6, no. 4, pp. 559–574.

Mead, G.H. (1967) Mind, Self and Society, Chicago University Press, Chicago.

Merton, R.K. (1949) Social Theory and Social Structure, The Free Press, New York.

(1968, orig. 1938) Social Theory and Social Structure, enlarged edn, Free Press, New York.

(1973) The Sociology of Science, The University of Chicago Press, Chicago.

Messerschmidt, J.M. (1993) Masculinities and Crime: Critique and Reconceptualization of Theory, Rowman & Littlefield, Lanham, MD.

Miers, D. (1989) 'Positivist victimology: a critique', International Review of Victimology, vol. 1, no. 1.

Mies, M. (1993) 'Towards a methodology for feminist research', in M. Hammersley (ed.) Social Research: Philosophy, Politics and Practice, Sage, London.

Milgram, S. (1974), Obedience to Authority: An Experimental View, Tavistock Publications, London.

Miller, A.S. and Hoffmann, J.P. (1995) 'Risk and religion: an explanation of gender differences in religion', Journal for the Scientific Study of Religion, vol. 34, no. 1.

Miller, W.B. (1962) 'Lower class culture as a generating milieu of gang delinquency' in M.E. Wolfgang et al. (eds) The Sociology of Crime and Delinquency, John Wiley & Sons, New York.

Miner, H. (1956) 'Body ritual among the Nacirema', American Anthropologist, vol. 58, no. 3.

Mirza, H. (1992) Young, Female and Black, Routledge, London.

Murphy, D. (2013) 'Money laundering and the drug trade: The role of the banks' Global Research, 13 May.

Murray, C. (1989) 'Underclass: A disaster in the making', *The Sunday Times Magazine*, 26 November.

Nelson, G.K. (1986) 'Religion', in M. Haralambos (ed.) *Developments in Sociology*, vol. 2, Causeway Press, Ormskirk.

Newburn, T. (2007) *Criminology*, Willan Publishing, Cullompton.

Newson, E. (1994) *Video Violence and the Protection of Children*, Report of the Home Affairs Committee, HMSO, London.

Niebuhr, H.R. (1929) *The Social Sources of Denominationalism*, Shoe String Press, Connecticut.

Norris, P. and Inglehart, R. (2004) *Sacred and Secular: Religion and Politics Worldwide*, Cambridge University Press, Cambridge.

Oakley, A. (1981) 'Interviewing women: A contradiction in terms', in H. Roberts (ed.) *Doing Feminist Research*, Routledge, London.

(2014) *Father and Daughter: Patriarchy, Gender and Social Science*, Policy Press, Bristol.

Office for National Statistics (2005) *The National Statistics Socio-economic Classification: User Manual*, Palgrave Macmillan, Basingstoke.

(2011) *Social Trends 41*, Office for National Statistics, London, p. 28.

(2012) 'Religion in England and Wales', 2011 [online] Available at https://www.ons.gov.uk/peoplepopulationandcommunity/culturalidentity/religion/articles/religioninenglandandwales2011/2012-12-11 Accessed 14/02/2018.

(2015) 'How Religion has Changed In England and Wales' [online] Available at https://visual.ons.gov.uk/2011-census-religion/ Accessed 15/02/2018.

O'Toole, R. (1984) *Religion: Classic Sociological Approaches*, McGraw Hill, Toronto.

Paden, W.E. (2009) 'Reappraising Durkheim for the study and teaching of religion', in P. Clarke (ed.) *The Oxford Handbook of the Sociology of Religion* Oxford University Press, Oxford.

Page, R. (2001) 'The exploration of social problems in the field of social policy', in M. May *et al.* (eds) *Understanding Social Problems: Issues in Social Policy*, Blackwell, Oxford.

Parsons, T. (1937) *The Structure of Social Action*, McGraw-Hill, New York.

(1951) *The Social System*, Free Press, New York.

(1955) 'The American family: its relations to personality and social structure' in T. Parsons and R. Bales (eds) *Family, Socialization and Interaction Process*, Free Press, New York.

(1964) *Essays in Sociological Theory*, Free Press, New York.

(1965) 'Religious perspectives in sociology and social psychology', in W.A. Lessa and E.Z. Vogt (eds) *Reader in Comparative Religion: An Anthropological Approach*, 2nd edn, Harper & Row, New York.

Paton, G. and Turner, C. (2014) 'Surge in late baptisms to get into top Catholic schools', *The Telegraph 3* Jan [online] Available at http://www.telegraph.co.uk/education/educationnews/10549532/Surge-in-late-baptisms-to-get-into-top-Catholic-schools.html Accessed 15/02/2018.

Pawson, R. (1992) 'Feminist methodology', in M. Haralambos (ed.) *Developments in Sociology*, vol. 8, Causeway Press, Ormskirk.

Pearce, F. (1976) *Crimes of the Powerful*, Pluto Press, London.

Pearce, F. and Tombs, S. (1998) *Toxic Capitalism: Corporate Crime and the Chemical Industry*, Dartmouth, London.

Pearce, F. and Woodiwiss, M. (1993) *Global Crime Connections*, Macmillan, Basingstoke.

Pearson, G. (1983) *Hooligan: A History of Respectable Fears*, Macmillan, London.

Pew Research Center (2012) 'The Global Religious Landscape' [online] Available at http://www.pewforum.org/2012/12/18/global-religious-landscape-exec/ Accessed 15/04/2018.

(2016) 'The Gender Gap in Religion around the World' [online] Available at http://www.pewforum.org/2016/03/22/the-gender-gap-in-religion-around-the-world/ Accessed 11/09/2017.

(2017) 'The Changing Global Religious Landscape' [online] Available at http://www.pewforum.org/2017/04/05/the-changing-global-religious-landscape/ Accessed 15/02/2018.

Phillips, C. and Bowling, B. (2007) 'Racism, ethnicity, crime and criminal justice', *The Oxford Handbook of Criminology*, 4th edn, Oxford University Press, Oxford.

Philo, G. and Miller, D. (2002) 'Circuits of communication and power: Recent developments in media sociology', in M. Holborn (ed.) *Developments in Sociology*, vol. 18, Causeway Press, Ormskirk.

Platt, L. (2014) 'Is there assimilation in minority groups' national, ethnic and religious identity?', *Race and Ethnic Studies* vol. 37, no. 1.

Pollak, O. (1950) *The Criminality of Women*, University of Philadelphia Press, Philadelphia.

Popper, K.R. (1959) *The Logic of Scientific Discovery*, Hutchinson, London.

(1979) *Objective Knowledge: An Evolutionary Approach*, The Clarendon Press, Oxford.

(2002) *The Logic of Scientific Discovery*, Routledge, London.

Posner, E. (2014) 'The case against human rights', *The Guardian*, 4 December.

Pryce, K. (1979) *Endless Pressure*, Penguin Publishing, Harmondsworth.

Ransome, P. (2010) *Social Theory for Beginners*, Policy Press, Bristol.

Redfield, R. (1930) *Tepoztian: A Mexican Village*, University of Chicago Press, Chicago.

Reiman, J. and Leighton, P. (2009) *The Rich Get Richer and the Poor Get Prison*, Routledge, Abingdon.

Reiner, R. (1984) 'Crime, law and deviance: the Durkheim legacy', in S. Fenton, with R. Reiner and I. Hamnett, *Durkheim and Modern Sociology*, Cambridge University Press, Cambridge.

(2007) *Law and Order: An Honest Citizen's Guide to Crime Control*, Polity Press, Cambridge.

(2010) 'Media made criminality: the representation of crime in the mass media', in M. Maguire, R. Morgan and R. Reiner (eds) *The Oxford Handbook of Criminology*, 5th edn, Oxford University Press, Oxford.

Rinaldo, R. (2010) 'Women and piety movements' in B.S. Turner (ed.) *The New Blackwell Companion to the Sociology of Religion*, John Wiley and Sons, Chichester.

Ritzer, G. (1996) *The McDonaldization of Society*, Pine Forge Press, Thousand Oaks, CA.

Ritzer, G. and Stepnisky, J. (2017) *Classical Sociological Theory*, 7th edn, SAGE, London.

Rhodes, R. (2000) 'The media violence myth', *New York Times*, 17 September.

Roe, S. and Ashe, J. (2008) 'Young people and crime: Findings from the 2006 Offending, Crime and Justice Survey', Home Office Statistical Bulletin 0908 [online] Home Office, London.

Rose, S. and Rose, H. (2005) 'Why we should give up on race', *The Guardian*, 4 March.

Rossetti, P., Dinisman, T. and Moroz, A. (2016) *An Easy Target? Risk factors affecting victimisation rates for violent crime and theft*, Victim Support, London.

Roy, D. (2004) 'Feminist theory in science: working towards a practical transformation', *Hypatia*, vol. 19, no. 1.

Ruggiero, V. (1996) *Organised and Corporate Crime in Europe: Offers that Cannot be Refused*, Dartmouth, Aldershot.

Rusche, G. and Kirchheimer, O. (1939) *Punishment and Social Structure*, Columbia University Press, New York.

Savelsberg, J.J. (1995) 'Crime, inequality and justice in Eastern Europe', in J. Hagan and R.D. Peterson (eds) *Crime and Inequality*, Stanford University Press, Stanford, CA.

Sayer, A. (1992) *Method in Social Science: A Realist Approach*, Routledge, London.

Schweinhart, L.J., Montie, J., Zongping, X., Barnett, W.S., Belfield, C.R. and Nores, M. (2005) *Lifetime Effects: The High/Scope Perry Preschool Study Through Age 40*, High/Scope Press, Ypsilanti, Michigan.

Schwendinger, H. and Schwendinger, J. (1975) 'Guardians of order or defenders of human rights?', in I. Taylor, P. Walton and J. Young (eds) *Critical Criminology*, Routledge & Kegan Paul, London.

Scott, A. (2000) 'Risk society or angst society? Two views of risk, consciousness and community', in *The Risk Society and Beyond: Critical Issues for Social Theory*, B. Adam *et al.* (eds), Sage, London.

Scottish Government (2014) *What Works to Reduce Crime?: A Summary of the Evidence*, www.gov.scot Accessed 09/10/2017.

Scraton, P. (2016) 'Researching "truth", delivering "justice" on Hillsborough', *Times Higher Education*, 01.12.2016.

Sharp, C. and Budd, T. (2005) *Minority Ethnic Groups and Crime: Findings from the Offending,*

Crime and Justice Survey 2003, 2nd edn, Home Office, London.

Sharpe, G. and Gelsthorpe, L. (2009) 'Gendering the youth justice agenda: introduction to a special issue on girls and young women', *Youth Justice*, vol. 9, no. 3.

Shattuck, T. (2017) https://churchleaders.com/pastors/pastor-articles/139575-7-startling-facts-an-up-close-look-at-church-attendance-in-america.html Accessed 10/01/2018.

Shih, Fang-Long (2010) 'Women, religions, and feminisms', in B.S. Turner (ed.) *The New Blackwell Companion to the Sociology of Religion*, John Wiley and Sons, Chichester.

Silverman, D. (2010) *Doing Qualitative Research*, 3rd edn, Sage, London.

   (2015) *Interpreting Qualitative Data*, 5th edn, Sage, London.

Slapper, G. and Tombs, S. (1999) *Corporate Crime*, Longman, London.

Slattery, M. (1985) *Urban Sociology*, Causeway Press, Ormskirk.

Smart, C. (1989) *Feminism and the Power of Law*, London, Routledge.

Smith, N. (2004) *A Few Kind Words and a Loaded Gun: the autobiography of a career criminal*, Viking, London.

Snider, L. (1993) 'The politics of corporate crime control', in Pearce and Woodiwiss (1993).

Sombart, W. (1907) *Luxury and Capitalism*, University of Michigan Press, Ann Arbor.

Soothill, K. and Walby, S. (1991) *Sex Crime in the News*, Routledge, London.

South, N. (1997) 'Drugs: use, crime and control', in M. Maguire *et al.* (eds) *The Oxford Handbook of Criminology*, 2nd edn, Oxford University Press, Oxford.

   (1998) 'A green field for Criminology? A proposal for a perspective', *Theoretical Criminology*, vol. 2, no. 2, pp. 211–34.

Spencer, D. and Walklate, S. (eds) (2016) *Reconceptualizing Critical Victimology: Interventions and possibilities*, Lexington Books, London.

Stanko, E. (1985) *Intimate Intrusions: Women's Experience of Male Violence*, Routledge, London.

Stark, R. and Bainbridge, W.A. (1985) *The Future of Religion*, University of California Press, Berkeley, CA.

   (1987) *A Theory of Religion*, Lang, New York.

Steward, K. (2006) 'Gender considerations in remand decision making', in F. Heidensohn (ed.) *Gender and Justice: New Concepts and Approaches*, Willan, Cullompton.

Straus, S. (2006) *The Order of Genocide: Race, Power, and War in Rwanda*, Cornell University Press, Ithaca.

Sutherland, H., Sefton, T. and Piachaud, D. (2003) *Progress on Poverty, 1997 to 2003/4*, Joseph Rowntree Foundation.

Swedberg, R. (2011) 'Theorising in sociology and social science: Turning to the context of discovery', *Springer Science + Business Media*, 12 November.

Syal, R. (2016) 'HMRC admits to winding up inquiry into HSBC tax evasion claims', *The Guardian*, 13 January.

Sykes, G.M. and Matza, D. (1957) 'Techniques of neutralization: a theory of delinquency,' *American Sociological Review*, vol. 22, no. 6, pp. 664–670.

Taylor, I. (1999) *Crime in Context: A Critical Criminology of Market Societies,* Wiley, London.

Taylor, I. Walton, P. and Young, J. (1973) *The New Criminology*, Routledge & Kegan Paul, London.

Taylor, L. (1971) *Deviance and Society*, Michael Joseph, London.

Teti, A. and Mura, A. (2009) 'Islam and Islamism', in J. Haynes (ed.) *Routledge Handbook of Religion and Politics*, Routledge, London.

The Religious Literacy Project. 'Pentecostalism in Brazil'. Harvard Divinity School. Available at: https://rlp.hds.harvard.edu/faq/pentecostalism-brazil

Thwaites, C.J. (2013) *Increasing the Effectiveness and Impact of Community Safety Partnerships in Two London Boroughs: Practitioners' Perspectives*, Portsmouth Research Portal, University of Portsmouth, Portsmouth.

Tombs, S. (2013) 'Corporate crime', in C. Hale, K. Hayward, A. Wahidin, and E. Wincup. (eds), *Criminology*, 3rd edn, Oxford University Press, Oxford, pp. 227–246.

Tombs, S. (2016) 'Better regulation: Better for whom?', Centre for Crime and Justice Studies, 1 May.

Tombs, S. and Whyte, D. (2013) 'The myths and realities of deterrence in workplace safety regulation', *The British Journal of Criminology*, vol. 53, no. 5, pp. 746–763.

Tonry, M. and Farrington, D.P. (1995) 'Strategic Approaches to Crime Prevention', *Crime & Justice*, vol. 19.

Toor, S. (2009) 'British Asian girls: crime and youth justice', *Youth Justice,* vol. 9, no. 3.

Townsend, P. (1979) *Poverty in the United Kingdom*, Penguin, Harmondsworth.

Troeltsch, E. (1981) (first published 1931) *The Social Teachings of the Christian Churches*, vols. 1 and 2, University of Chicago Press, Chicago.

Trzebiatowska, M. and Bruce, S. (2012) *Why are Women More Religious than Men?*, Oxford University Press, Oxford.

Tunnell, K.D. (1996) 'Choosing crime: Close your eyes and take your chances', in B.W. Hancock and P.M. Sharp (eds), *Criminal Justice in America*, Prentice-Hall, Englewood Cliffs, NJ.

Turner, B. (2005) 'The Sociology of Religion', in C. Calhoun; C. Rojek and B. Turner (eds) *The SAGE Handbook of Sociology*, Sage Publications Ltd, London. pp. 546–560.

University of Oxford (2015) 'Just one in three marriages in England and Wales has a religious ceremony' 21 July [online] Available at http://www.ox.ac.uk/news/2015-07-21-just-one-three-weddings-england-and-wales-has-religious-ceremony Accessed 15/02/2018.

Venkatesh, S. (2009) *Gang Leader for a Day*, Penguin, London.

Voas, D. (2009) 'The rise and fall of fuzzy fidelity in Europe', *European Sociological Review*, vol. 25, no. 2.

Voas, D. and Crockett, A. (2005) 'Religion in Britain: neither believing nor belonging', *Sociology*, vol. 39, no. 1.

von Hentig, H. (1948) *The Criminal and His Victim*, Yale University Press, New Haven.

von Heyking, J. (2005) 'Secularization: not dead but never what it seemed', *International Studies Review*, vol. 7, no. 2.

Walby, S. (2011) *The Future of Feminism*, Polity Press, Cambridge.

Walklate, S. (2004) *Gender, Crime and Criminal Justice*, 2nd edn, Willan, Cullompton.

Wall, S. and Christyakova, Y. (2015) 'How organised crime in the UK has evolved beyond the mafia model', *The Conversation,* 18 May.

Wallis, R. (1977) *The Road to Total Freedom: A Sociological Analysis of Scientology*, Columbia University Press, New York.

   (1984) *The Elementary Forms of the New Religious Life*, Routledge & Kegan Paul, London.

Walsh, A. and Bolen, J.D. (2016) *The Neurobiology of Criminal Behaviour: gene-brain-culture interaction*, Ashgate Publishing, Farnham.

Warner, R.S. (1993) 'Work in progress toward a new paradigm for the sociological study of religion in the United States', *American Journal of Sociology*, vol. 98, no. 5.

Watson, H. (1994) 'Women and the veil: personal responses to global process', in A. Ahmed and H. Donnan (eds) *Islam, Globalization and Postmodernity*, Routledge, London.

Weber, M. (1958) *The Protestant Ethic and the Spirit of Capitalism*, The Free Press, New York.

   (1963) *The Sociology of Religion*, Beacon Press, Boston, MA.

   (1964) *The Theory of Social and Economic Organisations*, The Free Press, New York.

Welsh, B.C. and Farrington, D.P. (2007) 'Save children from a life of crime', *Criminology and Public Policy*, vol. 6, no. 4.

   (2009) 'Public area CCTV and crime prevention: An updated systematic review and meta-analysis', *Justice Quarterly*, vol. 26, no. 4.

   (2012) *The Oxford Handbook of Crime Prevention*. Oxford University Press; New York.

White, R. (2008) *Crimes Against Nature: Environmental Criminology and Ecological Justice*, Willan Publishing, Cullompton.

Whyte, D. (2007) 'Victims of corporate crime', in S. Walklate (ed.) *A Handbook of Victimology*, Willan/Routledge, Cullompton.

Wilkins, L. (1967) *Social Deviance*, Tavistock, London.

Williams, P. and Dickinson, J. (1993) 'Fear of crime: read all about it?', *British Journal of Criminology*, vol. 33, no. 1.

Williams, R. (1978) 'Forms of English fiction in 1848', in F. Barker *et al. 1848: The Sociology of Literature, proceedings of the Essex Conference* on the Sociology of Literature, University of Essex, Colchester.

Wilson, B. (1970) Religious Sects, Weidenfeld & Nicolson, London.

(1982) Religion in Sociological Perspective, Oxford University Press, Oxford.

(2003) 'Absolutes and relatives: Two problems for new religious movements', in J.A. Beckford and J. T. Richardson (eds) Challenging Religion: Essays in Honour of Eileen Barker, Routledge, London.

Wilson, B.R. (1966) Religion in a Secular Society, C.A. Watts, London.

Wilson, J.Q. (1975) Thinking about Crime, Basic Books, New York.

Wilson, J.Q. and Hernstein, R. (1985) Crime and Human Nature, Simon & Schuster, New York.

Wilson, J.Q. and Kelling, G. (1982) 'Broken windows', Atlantic Monthly, vol. 249, no. 3, pp. 29–38.

Winlow, S. (2001) Badfellas: Crime, Tradition and New Masculinities, Berg, Oxford.

Woodhead, L. (2001) 'The impact of feminism on the sociology of religion: from gender-blindness to gendered difference', in R.K. Fenn (ed.) The

Blackwell Companion to the Study of Religion, Blackwell, Oxford, pp. 67–84.

(2005) 'Gendering secularisation theory', Kvinder, Køn og Forskning (Women, Gender and Research; Denmark), vol. 1, pp. 24–35.

(2007) 'Gender differences in religious practice and significance', in J.A. Beckford and N.J. Demerath (eds) The SAGE Handbook of the Sociology of Religion, SAGE Publications Ltd, London, pp. 284–301.

(2007a) 'Why so many women in holistic spirituality? A puzzle revisited', in K. Flanagan and P.C. Jupp (eds) A Sociology of Spirituality, Ashgate, Aldershot.

Woolgar, S. (1988) Science: The Very Idea, Tavistock, London.

Worsley, P. et al. (1977) Introducing Sociology, Penguin, Harmondsworth.

Wright, A. (1994) 'Judaism', in J. Holm and J. Bowker (eds) Women in Religion, Pinter, London.

Yinger, J.M. (1970) The Scientific Study of Religion, Routledge, London.

YouGov (2015) https://d25d2506sfb94s.cloudfront. net/cumulus_uploads/document/6v34wr1cpg/

TimesResults_150209_atheism_Website.pdf Accessed 12/01/2018.

(2015) https://yougov.co.uk/news/2015/02/12/ third-british-adults-dont-believe-higher-power/ Accessed 23/11/2017.

Young, J. (1971) The Drug Takers: The Social Meaning of Drug Use, Paladin, London.

(1992) 'Ten points of realism', in J. Young and R. Matthews (eds) (1992) Issues in Realist Criminology, Sage, London.

(1997) 'Left realist criminology: radical in its analysis, realist in its policy', in M. Maguire et al. (eds) The Oxford Handbook of Criminology, 2nd edn, Oxford, Oxford University Press.

(1999) The Exclusive Society, Sage, London.

(2007) The Vertigo of Late Modernity, Sage, London.

Young, T. (2009) 'Girls and gangs: "shemale" gangsters in the UK?' Youth Justice, vol. 9, no. 3.

Zimmerman D.H. and Wieder D.L. (1971) 'Ethnomethodology and the problem of order', in J.D. Douglas (ed.) Understanding Everyday Life, Routledge, London.

INDEX

PERMISSIONS ACKNOWLEDGEMENTS

The publishers gratefully acknowledge the permission granted to reproduce the copyright material in this book. Every effort has been made to trace copyright holders and to obtain their permission for the use of copyright material. The publishers will gladly receive any information enabling them to rectify any error or omission at the first opportunity.

Images: (l = left, r = right, t = top, b = bottom)

Cover weedezign/Shutterstock, p.1 David Crockett/Shutterstock.com; p.3 Matt Timson; p.5 Lebrecht Music and Arts Photo Library/Alamy Stock Photo; pp.8–9 Matt Timson; p.11 Emmanuel Dunand/AFP/Getty Images; p.16 Mahathir Mohd Yasin/Shutterstock.com; pp.18–23 Matt Timson; p.28 Paul Davey/Alamy Stock Photo; p.29 Matt Timson; p.32 travelview/Shutterstock.com; p.34 Matt Timson; p.35 Francois Mori/AP/REX/Shutterstock; p.37 Marwan Naamani/AFP/Getty Images; p.41 Matt Timson; p.43 Everett Collection Historical/Alamy Stock Photo; pp.45–46 Matt Timson; p.47l Matt Timson, r © Ricardo Barros; p.53 Astrakan Images/Alamy Stock Photo; p.59 Drevs/Shutterstock.com; p.61 Historic Collection/Alamy Stock Photo; p.62 67photo/Alamy Stock Photo; p.65 Wichaiwish/Shutterstock.com; p.66 © World Productions; p.70 David J. Green/Alamy Stock Photo; p.75 Popperfoto/Getty Images; p.76 Pressmaster/Shutterstock.com; p.80t & b Open Gov. licence; p.82 leolintang/Shutterstock.com; p.85 Fran/CartoonStock.com; p.87 Source: United Nations Office on Drugs and Crime (UNODC), The Globalization of Crime: A Transnational Organized Crime Threat Assessment, Vienna, 2010, p.2, courtesy UNODC; p.88 Courtesy OCCRP; p.91 Lindsay Foyle/CartoonStock.com; p.92 akturer/Shutterstock.com; p.93 Granger/REX/Shutterstock.com; p.94 Everett Historical/Shutterstock.com; p.95 Pete Maclaine/Alamy Stock Photo; p.98 Ashley Cooper pics/Alamy Stock Photo; p.101 Pieter Bruegel the Elder – Peasant Wedding; p.102 Alessia Pierdomenico/Shutterstock.com; p.103 karen roach/Shutterstock.com; p.106 Hervé de Gueltzl/Getty Images; p.108 Charlie Hamilton/PA Archive/PA Images; p.110 Champion studio/Shutterstock.com; p.112 Patrick Eagar/Popperfoto/Getty Images; p.113t Kyle Hightower/AP/REX/Shutterstock, b © Mark Pinder; p.119 Courtesy the Bonger Institute, Amsterdam; p.120t Roy Nixon/CartoonStock.com, b photobyphm/Shutterstock.com; p.122 Jeremy Selwyn/Evening Standard/REX/Shutterstock; p.125 Ken McKay/REX/Shutterstock; p.127 Yabresse/Shutterstock.com; p.130 Daniel Christian/Getty Images; p.132 Courtesy Crown Prosecution Service; p.133 Photofusion/REX/Shutterstock; p.135 Nigel Wallace/Shutterstock.com; p.136 Michael J P/Shutterstock.com; p.139 Stocksolutions/Alamy Stock Photo; p.140 Paul Daniels/Shutterstock.com; p.141 ZUMA/REX/Shutterstock.com; p.144 Snap2Art/Shutterstock.com; p.145 Raigo Pajula/AFP/Getty Images; p.149 By Ian Miles-Flashpoint Pictures/Alamy Stock Photo; p.151 Stone Age peoples, 1999 (w/c on paper), Wood, Rob (b.1946) / Private Collection / Wood Ronsaville Harlin, Inc. USA / Bridgeman Images; p.153 PYMCA/Contributor/Getty Images; p.155 Andrew Aitchison/Contributor/Getty Images; p.157 Photofusion/REX/Shutterstock; p.160 David Sandison/The Independent/REX/Shutterstock; p.163 Dinodia Photos/Alamy Stock Photo; p.165 Alisdair Macdonald/REX/Shutterstock; p.167 Gideon Mendel/Contributor/Getty Images; p.170 Enigma/Alamy Stock Photo; p.172 Reproduced courtesy of gratefulgardens.net; p.175 Matt Cardy/Stringer/Getty Images; p.178 Wikimedia Commons; p.179 Wilbur-Dawbarn-/CartoonStock.com; p.183 WENN Ltd/Alamy Stock Photo; p.185 Martin Harvey/Alamy Stock Photo; p.187 fstockfoto/Shutterstock.com; p.191 Mark Christopher Cooper/Shutterstock.com; p.193 Alexander Raths/Shutterstock.com; p.194 kurhan/Shutterstock.com; p.195 Derek Meijer/Alamy Stock Photo; p.197 Matt Timson; p.199 Pontino/Alamy Stock Photo; p.201 Pressmaster/Shutterstock.com; p.203 left Golden Shrimp/Shutterstock.com; p.203 r Penny Tweedie/Alamy Stock Photo; p.204 Tanya Lapidus/Shutterstock.com; p.207 Dutourdumonde Photography/Shutterstock.com; p.210 Mary Evans Picture Library; p.213 F.Vorobyov/Shutterstock.com; p.214 Courtesy Goddess Temple, Glastonbury; p.216 meunierd/Shutterstock.com; p.218 Baloncici/Shutterstock.com; p.221 Marcio Jose Bastos; Silva/Shutterstock.com; p.223 Ken Wolter/Shutterstock.com; p.225 The Editorialist/Alamy Stock Photo; p.227 Pictorial Press Ltd/Alamy Stock Photo; p.229 Alf Ribeiro/Shutterstock.com; p.230 Mohamed Elsayyed/Shutterstock.com; p.231 vectorx2263/Shutterstock.com; p.233 Tomas Davidov/Shutterstock.com; p.235 Everett Historical/Shutterstock.com; p.237tl Pawel Kowalczyk/Shutterstock.com, tr Kevin Foy/Alamy Stock Photo, bl Robert Clay/Alamy Stock Photo,